TRASH OR Treasure

How to Find the Best Buyers of Antiques, Collectibles and other Undiscovered Treasures

Tony Hyman

Nationally known authority
on buying and selling
collectibles by mail.
Host of the twice-weekly
Trash or Treasure Show
heard on radio stations
across America.

Treasure Hunt Publications
Shell Beach, California 93448

Hyman's Where To Sell Directories
are published by
Treasure Hunt Publications
PO Box 3028
Shell Beach, CA 93448

Book design by Steve Gussman, North Hollywood
Cover photos of collectibles courtesy of various listees
Printed in the United States of America

3 4 5 6 7 8 9 10

ISBN: 0-937111-03-1

Dear Reader:

Thousands of people just like you say "if you do what this book advises, you will be smarter and richer."

I'm going to try and explain as simply as I can how *Trash or Treasure* can help you.

This book is for people of all ages who

- ✔ Want information about an antique or collectible
- ✔ Want to sell a single item...or sell an entire estate
- ✔ Want to be treated fairly and honestly

This book is not for antique dealers. It was written for you. Many of the nation's most successful dealers use *Trash or Treasure* every day, but it was designed to help the average home owner and make it possible for everyone to get fair treatment.

You are holding a valuable book in your hand. I've packed this book full of information and valuable tips to help you find a collector/buyer who will buy your "treasures."

I've been involved with antiques and collectibles since 1952, buying and selling in every state and province. Besides writing nine books and countless articles on collectibles, I now write a monthly column on antiques, host a radio show to help people sell collectibles, advise museums and historical societies, and have the best collection in the world in my own field (the history of cigars). Also my professional public service career has given me the opportunity to work with libraries and public television stations, run a publishing company and teach college.

I have a lot of good hands-on practical experience. **This experience taught me two things I want to share with you:**

(1) It always pays to deal with people who know what they're doing. No exceptions. Good intentions don't count when it's your money at risk. When you want something done fast and right, always deal with the very best people available.

(2) Honest people still exist. Yes, there are a lot of greedy people in the world, but there are also lots of decent people who will treat you fairly. Honest people (like us) are happiest when they can trust people they are dealing with.

These lessons are particularly important when dealing with antiques and collectibles because comparatively little accurate information is written down in many fields of collectibles. The most reliable up-to-date information is in experts' heads.

If you want accurate information and fair prices, you should always deal with honest experts. I've learned that experts will give me more accurate information 100% of the time, and higher prices 90% of the time. If you deal with the right people, you'll get that same treatment. **This book makes that possible.**

TRASH OR TREASURE HELPS YOU WITH ANTIQUES AND COLLECTIBLES THREE WAYS

❶ Teaches you my F.A.S.T. and easy way to get:
- ✔ accurate information and expert opinion;
- ✔ fair prices;
- ✔ honest treatment;
- ✔ safety and privacy.

The F.A.S.T. way has proved successful for 15 years. Everyone from teenagers to octogenarians can do it.

❷ Gives you a comprehensive list of items sought by collectors. More than 2,500 categories represent millions of items you might own right now! Whether you're selling your own items or buying and selling for profit, you'll know what to look for.

❸ Introduces you to 1,200 of the nations's most active and important experts who can do one or all of the following for you:
- ✔ buy one or more things from you;
- ✔ advise about antiques and collectibles;
- ✔ preserve family history, pictures, and records.

Some buyers will also:
- ✔ appraise your items, either free or for a fee;
- ✔ sell something on consignment;
- ✔ auction things for you in a specialty market;
- ✔ sell you a book, club membership or newsletter;
- ✔ help you find something you're looking for.

TRASH OR TREASURE
IS A GUIDE TO GETTING THE BEST PRICES

This book is not a "price guide." It is a "guide to getting the best prices." That's an important difference.

One reader was disappointed *Trash or Treasure* didn't list and picture everything she owned and give its value! Let me make it clear, there is no such book. A book that lists and pictures every known item would be miles high with millions of pages.

Another reader understood the concept behind my books and wrote, "***Trash or Treasure* is better than a price guide** because it tells me what to do and how to do it. I've made a small fortune. No price guide ever did that for me."

PRICE GUIDE LIMITATIONS

"Price guides" are lists of numbers that may or may not be accurate. Two kinds are sold, general and specific. General guides like *Kovel's, Antique Trader*, and *Warman's* cover about 60,000 items (out of a possible 1,000,000,000). They are widely available in bookstores, but your chances of finding your item included are slim.

Hundreds of specialty guides have been printed, some good, some not. They cover from 5% to 10% or common collectibles, and can be very difficult to find as most are printed in small quantities and they go out of print and out of date quickly. All you can do with a price guide is read them, hoping the author is qualified (some aren't) and that your item is listed. If your item happens to be listed, you must determine whether the quoted price is a retail price, wholesale price, an auction price, a guess by the author, or a computer generated combination of the above.

If you are seeking only the comfort of attaching "value" to your item, and accuracy isn't a concern, a price guide may be useful to you.

However, if you wish to sell or give away your item, it is important you know an item's actual market value. **Price guides don't tell you that.**

Amateurs (that's you, probably) must be very careful as price guides can be misleading, sometimes deliberately. One notorious fishing tackle "guide" pictures the author's collection with prices at two or three times what items usually sell for. He put those high prices to increase the value of his collection, preparing for future sale. When you read in his guide that something is "worth" $75, you have no way of knowing it regularly retails for $30 and you can expect to be paid around $15 to $20. The author of another similar book wants to keep fishing tackle prices low, so that same "$75" item (that you may sell for $20) is listed in *his* book at $4.

Don't assume that the price for one item has meaning for a similar unlisted item. Tiny variations can be small fortunes. Two extra letters printed on a baseball card listed in guides at $15 turned it into a $10,000 treasure for an alert seller. One popular general guide listed a glass vase in six different colors at $40. Readers weren't told there was a seventh color, yellow, worth $800. Beware! Wrong information can be costly to you.

Turn to *Trash or Treasure* for accuracy, reliability, real prices and cash in your pocket.

GETTING THE BEST PRICES THE F.A.S.T. WAY

When you join me using the F.A.S.T. way to sell antiques and collectibles you'll be joining tens of thousands of other readers who've made a fortune by following a few simple steps.

The biggest single sale I know was of a $200,000 meteorite. 1993's top F.A.S.T. seller got $176,000 for a 1923 uniform. Great reports are already pouring in from 1994, including a man who got $4,800 for a stoneware crock the F.A.S.T. way...after his local antique dealer offered "$50 or $60." I could fill a book with all the letters and calls I get saying things like:

> "I bought an adding device at a yard sale for $3. It was a plain piece of brass with some wheels and numbers made by a NY firm in 1910. A TOT buyer gave me $1,000 for it. I make a great living selling things the F.A.S.T. way." R.S.., Florida

> "A large camera store in Ft. Wayne told me my projector had no value. Someone in TOT paid me $175. I've sold other things as well, and paid for the book many times over." M.J.P., Indiana

You too can make money when you think F.A.S.T.

F = find something you own.
A = ask TOT for an expert in that area.
S = send a Sell-A-Gram.
T = take the offer (or not).

F.A.S.T. STEP ONE

Find something you own and would like to sell or know the value of so you can consider selling. You probably had some item or items in mind before you started reading. *Trash or Treasure* will show you how **you can make money with thousands of other things...** items you didn't realize were valuable.

Turn to page 538 and skim read all the way through to page 561. There are two thousand five hundred *categories* of things with value to collectors. Some of those categories contain tens of thousands of items you might own now.

More than 2/3 of the people in America own collectible things worth money. You probably do too. If in doubt whether something is trash or treasure, check it out. It's easy when you use the F.A.S.T. system.

F.A.S.T. STEP TWO

Ask an expert. *Trash or Treasure* gives you access to authors, editors, experts...people who have studied what you have, know what it is, and what it actually sells for. *Trash or Treasure* tells you who they are and how to reach them: addresses, phone numbers, fax numbers...all at your fingertips.

You don't call a stonemason to spay your cat or a dentist to fix your toilet. Ridiculous? Of course. You go to the experts in other parts of your life. Why not antiques experts as well? For example, I'm the world's authority on cigar boxes. When you ask me about a cigar box, my answer is backed by 42 years experience handling 120,000 boxes. Do you think you can get a better evaluation of your boxes by asking a local antique dealer?

When I want to sell I use the F.A.S.T. method. I contact experts and ask them to make an offer. About 90% of the time I accept their offer. I've come to expect fair treatment and reasonable offers. Sometimes the offers are the highest price I could get anywhere. Sometimes not. But I'm confident that I will always get fair treatment quickly, easily, and discreetly.

HOW DO YOU FIND AN EXPERT?

You'll have F.A.S.T. success by using the "Index of Things You Can Sell." Look on pages 538-561. The Index is a list of 2,500 categories of things that have value to collectors. You will find collectible items in many different forms:

- ✔ Things (purse, book, baseball card);
- ✔ The companies that made those things (*Planter's, Pepsi*);
- ✔ What it is shaped like (cat, taxi, cartoon character);
- ✔ What is depicted (hunting, smoking, firemen);
- ✔ What it is made of (glass, china, plastic, wicker);
- ✔ Where it was made or used (Alaska, Puerto Rico, Montana);
- ✔ The artist who painted it (Walt Kelly, Norman Rockwell);
- ✔ Who used it (Lincoln, Charles Lindberg, Adolph Hitler).

As a rule of thumb, when looking for a buyer, start with the most specific description of your item, then go to the general. Look up your items in the order they're listed above.

I took a phone call from someone yesterday who said he had Trash or Treasure but "couldn't find a buyer for a Humphrey Bogart autograph." I asked him if he had looked in the index under Bogart? Under autographs? Under movies? He hadn't. If he had, he would have found buyers in all three categories.

The index is your key to a world of information that can put money in your pocket. The index will give you a page (or pages) where a buyer will be found. When you turn to the pages listed, you will see I have grouped buyers of similar items. This means you can sometimes find more buyers by reading the pages before and after those suggested in the index.

F.A.S.T. STEP THREE

Send a Sell-A-Gram. Sell-A-Grams are easy-to-use form letters that help you sell F.A.S.T. because all you do is fill in the blanks. The purpose of a Sell-A-Gram is to give an expert enough information so that he or she can make you a fair and accurate offer for what you have.

Sell-A-Grams contain blanks for all the information you need to tell a buyer. Most of it is self explanatory. In any correspondence, follow the Sell-A-Gram for by giving your name, address, a description of the item and its condition. Indicate what service you would like from the expert to whom you are writing.

What information you include on your Sell-A-Gram depends upon what you are selling. Different buyers want different info. **You will find easy-to-follow instructions as to what to tell a buyer at the beginning of each chapter.** See the Table of Contents for the exact pages to find the information you need.

Many experts will ask you to include specific information about your item, such as what kind of lid it has, the shape of the handle, whether or not it has feet, etc. A few expert buyers want to know an item's history. When buyers have special requests, you will find them in the buyer's entry. Describing an item to a possible buyer usually involves telling

- ✔ what it is,
- ✔ its size and color,
- ✔ all names, numbers, trademarks, etc.,
- ✔ its condition.

Describing condition is very important, as it is the single greatest determiner of value. You should note all tears. stains, spots, dents, scratches, chips, cracks and other damage. It is a good idea to include a photo or a Xerox© copy of what you have but is not necessary in all cases. See the information at the beginning of each chapter for information specific to dolls, toys, comic books, china, etc.

Many of you got a pad of Sell-A-Grams along with your book. A Sell-A-Gram has been reduced in size so I could include a copy on the next page. If you did not get a pad of Sell-A-Grams, or if you used them all, you may duplicate up to 50 copies of this handy copyrighted form. Ask your copy center to enlarge one to full size, then use that as a master for making copies. Print the form on yellow paper like the original Sell-A-Grams since buyers give special attention to this comprehensive yellow form.

> **In addition to** the detailed assistance given you at the beginning of each chapter, brief helpful hints are scattered throughout this book. These tips will give you more ideas how to best profit the F.A.S.T. way.

TO:

FROM:

Phone: ( )

I have the following item:

Remember to include the (1) shape, (2) colors, (3) dimensions, and (4) all names, dates, and marks.

It's condition is:

List all scratches, dents, cracks, creases, chips, rips, tears, holes, stains, fading, and foxing. Note any missing pages, parts, or paint. Describe any repairs that have been done.

C H E C K   O N E

☐ The item is for sale for $_____ plus shipping.

☐ The item is for sale. I am an amateur seller and would like you to make an offer.

☐ The item may be for sale if the price is sufficient. Would you like to make an offer?

☐ The item is not for sale, but I am willing to pay a fee to learn its value.

To assist you to evaluate the item, I am enclosing a:

☐ Sample ☐ Photocopy ☐ Photo ☐ Tracing ☐ Sketch ☐ Rubbing ☐ Nothing

This is to certify that, to the best of my knowledge, the item is genuine and as described. Buyer has a 5 day examination period during which the item may be returned for any reason.

Signature: _____   Date: _____

☐ Answer Requested (SASE enclosed).   ☐ No answer needed.

BUYER'S RESPONSE:

F.A.S.T. STEP FOUR

Take the offer...or not.

Most readers buying this book want to know what one or more items are worth. Their decision whether or not to sell their item often depends upon how much cash they will be paid. When an expert responds to a Sell-A-Gram, you will find out the cash value of what you have.

These offers are at the heart of Hyman's F.A.S.T. system of selling antiques and collectibles. By requesting top experts to make an offer you are assured of accurate information and a proper assessment of the cash value of what you have. Everyone hopes for a million dollars, but realistically, you can't expect it. You will get a variety of responses from these expert buyers.

In some cases you will be told your item has no collector value. You are then free to give it away or sell it cheaply at a yard sale without worry that you might be losing a fortune.

In other cases the value will be less than you hoped. That gives you a set of choices:
- ✔ You can accept less than you hoped;
- ✔ You can contact other buyers, hoping someone else will pay more;
- ✔ You can decide not to sell at this time. If you are considering this choice, please do remember that things do not always go up in value.

The best response you can hope for is a cash offer bigger than you hoped. Once again, you must decide whether to sell or not.

Buyers do not like to be placed in "bidding wars" and that shopping your item to lots of buyers in hopes of a few additional dollars may cause the entire deal to collapse. This is particularly true in art, where the more people that see your item, the more likely the price will drop. A recent seller was offered $500,000 for a painting, got greedy, shopped it all over the U.S. and Europe. Now, two years later, the highest offer he has is $35,000. Always deal first with the most likely buyer who is expert in the field you have to sell.

The people listed in Trash or Treasure have made a personal commitment to making reasonable offers to amateur sellers. They have the expertise to <u>know</u> (not guess) what your item is, what the market interest is, and how much cash it will bring. They share that expertise in the expectation you will sell.

I have tried hard for fifteen years to bring you buyers you can trust to make fair and reasonable offers. Personally, when I get a good offer, I take it. I have faith in my buyers. I'm sure you will also have many years of happy and rewarding selling to them.

WHO ARE THE BUYERS?

Buyers are all sorts of people. Collectors, dealers, museums and libraries, part time dealers, retirees. For the most part they are very active busy people. They give time to you to in exchange for the opportunity to buy things. One buyer told me he buys 80% of what's offered to him. Another buys about 5%. But all collectors and dealers welcome the opportunity to obtain "fresh merchandise," that hasn't been picked over. Most buyers pay premium prices for fresh goods.

They are important people. Use them wisely. Treat them well by following their instructions and you will end up with everyone winning, everyone getting what they want.

That's what I want for you and for all my friends I'm introducing you to in **Trash or Treasure**. I'm trying to make it so you're happy, they're happy, and some thing or piece of information gets preserved by getting into a collector's hands.

WHAT DO BUYERS WANT FROM YOU?

Buyers expect you to treat them the way you want them to treat you. Honestly and fairly. Here's some guidelines:

[1] **Be honest about whether or not the item is for sale.** If an item isn't for sale, don't pretend that it is. Go find a "price guide" and accept whatever figure it tells you.

(2) **Don't obtain an offer from someone I recommend** and then sell your item for that price to someone else. That's like asking Bill to mow your lawn and paying Sam. It's not fair.

[3] **Be honest about the item's condition.** More merchandise gets returned because of poor condition than any other reason. Save your time and the buyer's by accurately describing condition.

[4] **Read the buyer's entry carefully and offer things they want**, not other items. Each entry tells you what the person is expert in and what he or she wants to buy. In many cases, it will also tell you what they don't want to buy. If it says "No tribbles," don't offer a tribble. It's not a good use of their time or yours.

As a courtesy, include a Self-Addressed Stamped Envelope. Put your name, address and a 1st class stamp on a long #10 envelope, fold it in thirds, and include it with your Sell-A-Gram.

In the unlikely event you have a misunderstanding with one of these folks, I want to hear about it. In some cases, I may inquire and see what can be done to ease the situation. Obviously I can't guarantee the transactions of hundreds of thousands of readers. That would be unrealistic. But you're dealing with some important, interesting, knowledgeable, informative, usually friendly, often generous, folks who should give you a fair shake with what you have. Trouble is very rare.

In nearly all cases, you will do better dealing with people in **Trash or Treasure** than you will selling locally or dealing with other people you don't know. Don't let shipping things be a barrier to dealing by mail. It is not hard. Ask for help and many buyers will provide simple instructions.

Some readers are suspicious. They want to know why I can trust the people in my book. "What's to keep people from cheating me," I am asked occasionally.

"Honesty," I answer. Ethics. Perspective. Integrity. The same thing that keeps the other people with whom you deal from cheating you. I personally believe in treating people fairly. I've tried to do that all my life. I believe I'm introducing you to lots of other folks who think likewise. You're getting the best recommendations I can give you. In the past 14 years, I've learned it is more likely that a seller will cheat one of my buyers than the other way around.

Other readers just like you have used the F.A.S.T. way to pocket $100,000,000 thanks to buyers listed in Trash or Treasure. That's a lot of money. That's a lot of people helped.

Why do I recommend these people and not others? If a favorite dealer of yours isn't listed, there may be a number of reasons:
(1) I've never met them, so can't evaluate them;
(2) They were invited, but they did not want the publicity and large amounts of mail and calls generated by being in my books and dealing with amateurs;
(3) They were omitted for cause.

YOU DON'T HAVE TO BE A SELLER TO USE TRASH OR TREASURE.

DO YOU WANT AN APPRAISAL? Many of these experts do appraisals. Many do it for free. Don't let "for a fee" scare you. Jim Supica charges $1 to appraise your handgun. If in doubt, don't be afraid to ask. If you use Sell-A-Grams, most will do it for free.

DO YOU WANT TO BUY SOMETHING? "You should call it a buy and sell book," enthused one reader. The experts, many of whom are dealers, knew where to find the things he wanted. Buyers are often well connected with other collectors. Need something? Ask. They may be able to help.

DO YOU HAVE FAMILY PICTURES OR HISTORY YOU WANT PRESERVED? People are discovering that their children and grandchildren have little interest or ability to take care of family history and artifacts. Medals, Civil War letters, diaries, company records, photos...they're all items which deserve to be preserved along with the stories behind them. Only historians can do that.

Whatever use you have for *Trash or Treasure*, you have my best wishes for a rewarding experience.

Tony Hyman

TABLE OF CONTENTS

TABLE OF CONTENTS

TABLE OF CONTENTS

YOU CAN SELL FURNITURE, RUGS, AND LAMPS BY MAIL.

If you own "furniture store" bedroom or dining room suites made after 1920 they probably have little if any collector value. Sell factory furniture from this period through classified ads in your local newspaper. Read the next few pages to see what you can sell. Many pieces have been reproduced or copied, so a good clear photo is essential.

Some ordinary looking furniture can have value. Be especially careful with hand carved items, mission oak, and designer furniture from the 1930-1960 period. Before contacting a possible buyer, examine the legs and underside looking for signatures, maker's marks, or labels. They can make a big difference in selling price.

Damaged rugs lose value, but very old Oriental rugs should be evaluated by an expert, no matter what their condition. The finest Oriental rugs are not thickly piled, but are rather thin so don't think your carpet has no value just because the threads aren't long and lush. One reader found a $2,000 carpet (3'x5') used as a mud rug outside a mountain cabin. All you need to avoid expensive mistakes is a good photo and the buyers in **Trash or Treasure**.

If sending a photo is not possible, you may wish to phone the buyer and discuss your item. Always call with the item in front of you. Be prepared to answer questions about colors, dimensions, type of wood, labels, etc. It is very difficult to sell a rugs, lamps, or furniture without a photo, however.

Make certain when selling large or heavy items that you and the buyer agree who has responsibility for packing and shipping. This cost is normally born by the buyer, but sellers make the arrangements. If this will be difficult for you, ask the buyer to help. Generally, you should request the buyer to have large items picked up as part of the sale. This is particularly important if you are elderly, have difficulty getting around, or if you live outside a big city.

FURNITURE

☆ **Entire estates which include furniture and accessories from the American colonial period,** art, or important collections of toys, dolls, guns, decoys, miniature lamps, art glass, advertising, or other specialties. Your estate or collection must have a value in excess of $50,000 to be handled by this important firm. No interest in minor collectibles, limited edition plates, or common items.

> James D. Julia Auctioneers
> PO Box 80
> Fairfield, ME 04937
>   (207) 453-7904   Fax: (207) 453-2502

☆ **Heavily carved or decorated American furniture made between 1820-80** including fancy Empire, Gothic revival, rococo, American Renaissance, etc., especially furniture made by *Belter, Roux,* or *Meeks.* Also **gas chandeliers and** *Argand Astral* **lamps**. This prestigious dealer does not make offers so research is in order since many of these pieces can be very valuable. Send her a photo of the furniture plus a copy of every label or maker's mark you can find. She will help an amateur seller if you're really *selling* and not fishing for free appraisals.

> Joan Bogart
> PO Box 265
> Rockville Centre, NY 11571
>   (516) 764-0529 voice and fax

☆ **Furniture and accessories from the Arts and Crafts or "Mission" period.** Buys oak furniture, light fixtures, and metalwork by *L. & J.G. Stickley, Gustav Stickley, Roycroft, Limberts, Lifetime, Charles Stickley, Rohlfs, Stickley Brothers,* and *Dirk Van Erp,* especially unusual pieces, custom made pieces, and items inlaid with silver, pewter or copper. Also textiles, various publications, and catalogs from these firms. "If you have any doubts, please call. I will be glad to help."

> Robert Berman
> Le Poulaille
> 441 South Jackson Street
> Media, PA 19063
>   (610) 566-1516

Do not even think about refinishing oak furniture that you plan to resell. Collectors want that dark original finish found on most Mission pieces. An original finish is worth more than what you or your local refinisher will do.

☆ **Arts & Crafts or "Mission" style furniture** but only signed pieces by *Gustav Stickley, L. & J.G. Stickley, Roycroft, Limbert* and other important makers. "I don't want furniture by generic makers." A *Gustav Stickley* inlaid armchair with rush seat and in its original black finish can bring as much as $10,000. Send a photo and include the dimensions, and a drawing of the mark. Marks on furniture can be on legs, underneath, on the back, and elsewhere so look carefully for labels or woodburned names. This well known expert in the Arts & Crafts period has agreed to make offers to amateur sellers who learn about him through this book if they are serious about selling what they own, but states clearly that he "does not wish readers to price fish or to involve him in bidding wars with other buyers." If you need an appraisal for estate or insurance purposes, the fee is $10 per item.

> David Rago
> 9 South Main Street
> Lambertville, NJ 08530
>   (609) 397-9374   Fax: (609) 397-9377

☆ **Furniture and accessories from the Arts & Crafts or "Mission" period.** Buys oak furniture, lamps, light fixtures, and hammered copper metalwork by *L. & J.G. Stickley, Gustav Stickley, Roycroft, Limberts, Lifetime, Charles Stickley, Rohlfs, Stickley Brothers, Jarvie, Albert Berry, Onondaga Metal Shop, Karl Kipp, Harry Dixon* and *Dirk Van Erp*, especially Morris chairs, case pieces (like dressers), bedroom and living room furniture, and benches. Smaller items include desk sets, bookends, lamps, vases, trays, and candle holders. Prices can be high, as a *Van Erp* lamp brings $2,500 and up, *Stickley* Morris chairs bring $3,000 and up, and *Jarvie* candlesticks start at $600. Photo is helpful as part of your description. Note the maker and any repairs or damage. Note whether the original finish is still there. "I expect sellers to give me a minimum acceptable price. If their item is worth a great deal more, I'll let them know." Bruce wrote *The America Arts & Crafts Movement in Western NY, 1900-1920*, available for $16 postpaid.

> Bruce Austin
> RIT College of Liberal Arts
> Rochester, NY 14623
>   (716) 475-2879   (716) 223-0711 eves

☆ **Furniture that is square in appearance,** made of oak, and characterized by square spindles, cut out designs, and/or inset tiles. Wants chairs with adjustable backs, benches, beds, couches, dressers, desks, library tables, book stands, cabinets, sideboards, etc. Examine the piece carefully for woodburned maker's marks or paper labels. A photo is strongly suggested. Does not want refinished pieces. Call if in doubt.

> Gary Struncius
> PO Box 1374
> Lakewood, NJ 08701
>   (800) 272-2529

☆ *Roycroft* **furniture and accessories.** Buys and sells lamps, waste baskets, clocks, frames, art, pottery, china, glassware, and all books and paper ephemera associated with the *Roycroft* company or its founder, Elbert Hubbard. When you write, make certain to state honestly whether the item is for sale or whether you are seeking identification and appraisal. Please give the source of the item for sale and include any stories or history you know about the piece(s).

> Tom and Rosaline Knopke, House of Roycroft
> 1430 East Brookdale Place
> Fullerton, CA 92631
> (714) 526-1749

☆ **Wicker furniture and luggage.** "I'll consider any good condition old wicker, but am most interested in Bar Harbor Victorian characterized by curled arms and an open weave that you can see through. Pieces can be in any color, but natural is usually best. **Wicker luggage** can have either leather or brass trim, but should be in fine condition, inside and out, suitable for resale. Give the dimensions, status and color of the lining, condition of the wicker, hardware, and the leather trim."

> Joan Brady
> 834 Central Ave.
> Pawtucket, RI 02861
> (401) 725-5753

☆ **Designer furniture from the 1940's through the present** by Herman Miller, Knoll, Eames, Nelson, Gilbert Rohde, Frank Lloyd Wright, Heywood Wakefield, Noguchi, Thonet, and other national and international designers. Also interested in unusual plastic and fiberglass designer furniture. Most pieces are signed on the bottom. Primarily interested in bent plywood chairs, tables, couches, desks, and dressers as well as chrome furniture by Frank Lloyd Wright.

> Frank and Jay Novak
> 7366 Beverly Boulevard
> Los Angeles, CA 90036
> (213) 933-0383   Fax: (213) 683-1312

☆ **Blond furniture by Heywood Wakefield** from the 1930's through 1960's. Please send a photo and information about any markings or labels. Describe condition accurately. Also interested in buying catalogs of Wakefield furniture.

> Don Colclough
> Cadillac Jack
> 6911 Melrose
> Los Angeles, CA 90038
> (800) 775-5078   Fax: (213) 931-6372

☆ **Adirondack and other rustic furniture.** "I'll buy rustic furniture made of roots, twigs, antlers, willow, or birch bark, and hickory furniture from the *Old Hickory Company*. Dealers must price their goods but I will help amateur sellers set a price, as long as their letter includes a photo and a complete description, including all damage."

> Barry Friedman
> 22725 Garzota Drive
> Valencia, CA 91355
>   (805) 296-2318

☆ **Twig furniture.** "I'm interested in any type of rustic or Adirondack furniture. This includes pieces by *Old Hickory* and *Twig Furniture*. The wilder the style, the more I will want it. As always the better the condition, the more I will pay. If you have any doubts, call."

> Robert Berman, Le Poulaille
> 441 South Jackson Street
> Media, PA 19063
>   (610) 566-1516

☆ **Unusual furniture** made of twigs (Adirondack), horn, horse shoes, found objects and other "wild, eccentric, and unusual stuff" like small **folk art chairs and tables** in original paint. A photo is essential because of the nature of these items.

> Matt Lippa and Elizabeth Schaaf
> Artisans
> 599 Cutler Avenue
> Mentone, AL 35984
>   (205) 634-4037

☆ **Furniture made with or decorated with steer horns** is sought by this long time scholar of the genre. "I'll buy chairs, tables, hat racks, etc., made from cattle or buffalo horn. I prefer pieces that have the appearance of being artfully or creatively constructed with as many horns as possible, and made between 1880 and 1920. I have no interest in contemporary horn furniture. The fabric on most horn furniture is in poor condition, so we are mostly concerned with the condition of the horns themselves so make sure you check for cracks and bug damage. These pieces can be fairly valuable, so it is worth your time to take pictures from the front, back and sides. Give the dimensions of the furniture you have. I also want furniture which is decorated with inlaid horn, particularly fine examples of which can be worth in the multiple thousands of dollars."

> Alan Rogers
> 1012 Shady Drive
> Kansas City, MO 64118
>   (816) 436-9008

☆ **Folding chairs.** Interested in everything dealing with folding chairs including photos of chairs in use in lodges, churches, picnics or other events. Send a photo or photocopy of items offered. Especially wants chairs with advertising on the back.

>Richard Bueschel
>414 North Prospect Manor Ave.
>Mt. Prospect, IL 60056

RUGS

☆ **High quality rugs and tapestries.** Oriental, Chinese, European, American Indian, and large hooked rugs are of interest if of sufficient quality and condition. Buys Art Deco, Art Nouveau, and Arts & Crafts rugs and textiles as well. Worldwide interest in fine tapestries, textiles, embroideries, and weavings as well as paisley and Kashmir shawls. A good clear color photograph is important. Make certain to mention wear or stains. Appraisals and offers are made *only* after actually seeing your rug. Gallery open by appointment only.

>Renate Halpern Galleries
>325 East 79th Street
>New York, NY 10021
>(212) 988-9316

☆ **Oriental rugs.** Claims "highest prices paid" for Oriental rugs of all types: "antique, used, or just old."

>David Tiftickjian, Jr.
>260 Delaware Ave.
>Buffalo, NY 14202
>(716) 852-0556   (716) 634-8835

☆ **Oriental rugs** made by hand before 1950 in any size or condition. A good sharp photo plus the dimensions is essential for this dealer/appraiser with 24 years experience to make an offer. Aaron's buys, sells, cleans and repairs antique Oriental rugs.

>Robert Anderson
>Aaron's Oriental Rug Gallery
>1217 Broadway
>Fort Wayne, IN 46802
>(219) 422-5184

☆ **Rugs with advertising logos, cartoons or images** such as Buster Brown, *Coca-Cola*, etc.

>Charles Martignette
>PO Box 293
>Hallandale, FL 33009
>(305) 454-3474

☆ **Grenfell hooked mats and rugs.** "I'll buy any tightly hooked mat, rug, or purse labeled GRENFELL LABRADOR INDUSTRIES as long as it is in excellent condition. These always depict Northern scenes like polar bears, hunters, Eskimos, etc. Please send dimensions and a photo with your first letter. Dealers are expected to price their goods, but amateurs may request an offer."

> Barry Friedman
> 22725 Garzota Drive
> Valencia, CA 91355
> (805) 296-2318

LAMPS

☆ **Lamps and lamp parts of all types from all periods.** Buys a wide range of wall, floor, and table lamps from the Betty lamps of the 1700's right through to the 1950's. Will buy kerosene, whale oil, electric, *Aladdin*, organ, marriage, student, desk, and other lamps. Also interested in *Tiffany* and other high quality leaded and painted lamps. This major Western dealer can be very helpful to amateurs with just about any type of lamp to sell. **Especially wants *Aladdin* lamps and parts** including galleries, chimney cleaners, bug screens, flame spreaders, wick cleaners, wick raisers, finials, and anything else made by *Aladdin*. Also buys parts from other lamp makers. If you have lamps or parts for sale, please note whether they are brass or nickel plated and give all numbers and wording. A photo is very helpful if asking for an offer.

> Richard Melcher
> PO Box 1812
> Wenatchee, WA 98807
> (509) 662-0386

☆ **Lamps and light fixtures from the early 1800's to the early 1940's** are wanted by this veteran lighting restoration dealer. He buys old iron, brass, or tin electric or gas fixtures, wall sconces, chandeliers, colored glass shades from fixtures, and damaged fixtures suitable for scavenging parts. He will buy inside or **outside lighting fixtures** (including street lights) and has particular interest in those from commercial buildings as well as homes. He notes that large fixtures can be disassembled and shipped at his expense. Note all cracks or chips in glass. He is not interested in reproduction shades or in any fluorescent fixtures. He is, however, strongly interested in **catalogs from manufacturers** or retailers which depict large numbers of lighting fixtures from before 1920.

> Robert Daly's Historic Lighting Restoration Sales & Service
> 10341 Jewell Lake Court
> Fenton, MI 48430
> (313) 629-4934

Lamp collectors want to know if your lamp is original and complete, and if there is anything wrong with it. You should mention if it shows any signs of repair or of being a marriage of parts from different lamps. Describe the quality of the finish on the base and whether the glass shows any cracks or chips. A signature on the base or shade usually makes a lamp worth more. Look carefully, as signatures can be hard to locate on some valuable lamps.

☆ **Reverse painted, leaded glass, or art glass lamps** including table lamps, boudoir lamps, and floor lamps. "I am interested in buying **shades, bases or parts** for lamps of these types. I have a special interest in *Moe-Bridges*, *Classique Studios*, or *Phoenix Light Co.* I am also interested in catalogs from lamp and lighting fixture manufacturers (not retailers) before 1935." Does not want oil lamps, hurricane lamps, Gone With the Wind lamps, etc. No lamps after 1920's. Give all names and numbers found anywhere on the lamp or shade, and all dimensions. Please set the price you want for your lamp and include a photo.
   Merlin Merline
   PO Box 16265
   Milwaukee, WI 53216
      (414) 871-6261

Many leaded lamps have been reproduced. These reproductions sell new for around $250 and are worth only $20 to $100 in local markets. If you have original leaded or painted lamps from before 1930, however, the value can top a thousand dollars, so don't be hesitant to ask an expert for assistance.

☆ *Tiffany* **and other high quality glass lamps.** "I believe we are the only auction firm in North America that conducts specialty auctions for rare lamps only." Collections, large or small, of *Tiffany, Handel, Jefferson, Pairpoint,* and other quality lamps, lamp bases, and lamp shades from both **large and small oil and electric lamps** will be considered by this record setting auctioneer. Photos are a must. Telephone if you have a large group of lamps to sell.
   James D. Julia Auctioneers
   PO Box 80
   Fairfield, ME 04937
      (207) 453-7904   Fax: (207) 453-2502

☆ *Tiffany* **lamps, chandeliers, and other high quality glass lighting fixtures.** Please include photos and your phone number.

Carl Heck
PO Box 8416
Aspen, CO 81612
   (303) 925-8011

☆ **Student lamps,** lamp shades, and lamp burners, 1870-1890, are wanted, especially lamps made by *Griffin*. A double *Griffin* can be worth $1,500 in fine condition and a single up to $450. "Make certain your lamp has an oil or kerosene tank that lifts out of the lamp, as many reproductions do not." Note if your lamp has been electrified, as well as any other damage which may have occurred.

Jerry and Martha Ritch
8357 Bridlewood Drive
East Amherst, NY 14051
   (716) 741-9580

Broken lamps and lamp parts before 1930 almost always can be worth some cash to you.

☆ **Lamps and light fixtures from the "Mission" or Arts & Crafts period.** Anything signed by *L. & J.G. Stickley, Gustav Stickley, Roycroft, Limberts, Lifetime, Charles Stickley, Rohlfs, Stickley Brothers,* and *Dirk Van Erp*, especially unusual pieces, custom made pieces, and items inlaid with silver, pewter or copper. Also **catalogs from these firms**. "If you have any doubts, please call. I will be glad to help."

Robert Berman, Le Poulaille
441 South Jackson Street
Media, PA 19063
   (610) 566-1516

☆ *Emeralite* **and** *Bellova* **lamps,** 1909 to 1940's, wall, desk, table, and floor models. Buys green-shaded, acid etched or reverse painted models. These are found with brass or with other metal bases. Prefers signed pieces. Unsigned pieces must be heavily decorated to be of interest. A photo "is essential."

Bruce Bleier
73 Riverdale Road
Valley Stream, NY 11581
   (516) 791-4353

☆ **Miniature oil lamps** made of metal, art glass, or milk glass. Give the size, and indicate all names and numbers you can find on the lamp. A photo is appreciated.
　　Carl Cotting
　　1441 Crowell Road
　　Vienna, VA 22182
　　　　(703) 759-5646

☆ **Revolving radio and TV lamps** from the 1930's, 40's, and 50's that are driven by the heat of the light bulb. These were made by *Econolite Corp, Scene In Action,* and *Rev-O-Lite* among others. "I will pay $350 for the scene in a fish bowl, and other substantial amounts for mermaids, motorcycles, snow skiers, sailing ships, water skiers, Santa Claus, and many others. Please call if you have one for sale." The Montgomerys wrote *Animated Motion Lamps Price Guide,* available from them for the bargain price of only $13 postpaid.
　　Bill and Linda Montgomery
　　PO Box 68572
　　Portland, OR 97268
　　　　(503) 652-2992

If you shop at yard sales to make money, revolving lamps are good to watch for. They are often found for $5 or so. Don't buy a lamp with broken glass or plastic parts if you want to resell it.

☆ **Lamp shades of cloth or beaded silk** from 1890 to the 1930's that are in near perfect condition. He'd like you to send a photo, the dimensions, and your asking price.
　　Charles Martignette
　　PO Box 293
　　Hallandale, FL 33009
　　　　(305) 454-3474

☆ **Catalogs from lamp and lighting** fixture companies published before 1935, especially catalogs which show lamps with leaded or scenic glass shades. Especially interested in catalogs from one of the many companies based in Milwaukee. Does not want department store catalogs with lighting sections. Xerox© the cover and send a page count and an indication of how many color illustrations are included.
　　Merlin Merline
　　PO Box 16265
　　Milwaukee, WI 53216
　　　　(414) 871-6261

CLOCKS

☆ **Old wall and shelf clocks.** This family business describes itself as "a clock adoption agency, looking for nice items in need of a good new home." They buy a wide range of 18th and 19th century shelf and wall clocks, but are especially interested in the following:

- **Victorian shelf and wall clocks.** Wants ornate ones, with busts, hanging teardrops, busts, cherubs or side mirrors;
- **Reverse painting on glass pillar and scroll clocks** about 36" high with free standing wooden pillars and curved scroll ("swan's neck") tops;
- **Steeple or beehive shelf clocks,** but *only* if the veneer is perfect, or nearly so. "These are plentiful with poor veneer. I want those in beautiful condition;"
- **Any American carved clocks.** "I'm a pushover for clocks with carved columns or splats, eagles or fruit baskets;"
- *Eli Terry* clocks or those by any of his sons;
- *Seth Thomas* clocks;
- **French, German** and **English clocks** from the 18th and 19th century. "Some excellent 20th century German clocks were made in Mission style, but no matter how good the clock we don't buy 20th century," he cautions, so don't ask.
- **Cuckoo clocks** if very old, very heavily carved, and in perfect condition. "I'm afraid I'll open a floodgate if I mention I'll buy cuckoos, because there are so many junk ones around. I only want those that are very early and very ornate." No souvenir clocks. Photo a must.
- **Black Forest trumpeter clocks.** These are chiming clocks, like cuckoos, but instead of a bird have a man who plays a tune on a trumpet. "These are valuable, and we'll travel to pick yours up if it's a nice one."

"We buy clocks with walnut or cherry cases. We buy spring driven clocks but especially like to find older weight driven clocks. We buy clocks with wooden works only if in running condition," they say, "but there are a few exceptions, so it's worth inquiring. We don't buy any 20th century clocks, oak gingerbread kitchen clocks, electric clocks, or Mission (Arts and Crafts) clocks. Nor do we buy *Lux* or *Keebler* novelty clocks with rolling eyes or swinging tails. We also do not buy plain ogee clocks (rectangular veneered clocks with fronts that look like picture frames). We almost never buy clocks that have undergone restoration or modification. We don't want to spend lots of time with the clocks. We prefer to buy them in nearly perfect condition."

> Old Timers
> PO Box 392
> Camp Hill, PA 17001
> (717) 761-1908   Fax: (717) 761-7446

*To describe a clock, answer as many
of the following as you can:*

What name is on the dial?
What name is on the movement?
How tall and wide is the case?
What is the case made of?
Is the case decorated?
Is there a label inside the case?
Is there a serial number?
Is there anything unusual about its looks?
How is it wound or activated?
Do you have the key and weights?
Is it presently running?

☆ **American wall and mantle clocks** from the 1700's through the
Arts & Crafts movement of the early 20th century. "I'll buy, sell, or
trade a wide range of clocks, but my specialties are weight driven calendar and regulator clocks that hang on a wall. I also buy interesting,
unusual, and better grades of shelf (mantle) and other wall clocks of the
1800's. Especially like clocks with multiple dials or faces in either
plain or fancy cases." Some of the many names to look for include
*Simon-Willard, E.N. Welch, Howard, Ithaca, Waterbury, Seth Thomas,
New Haven*, and other early Connecticut makers. Bruce is well versed
in clocks of all types so can be helpful to the amateur seller. "If I'm offered something I can't use, I try to refer folks to someone who might
like to buy it. Early electric clocks don't interest me much, but I may
be able to give readers some help in identifying or evaluating them."
Bruce says, "For my own collection, I like to find ones that are a little
out of the ordinary." Some interest in **European clocks with porcelain dials, or with fine cases with gilt, inlay, or marble.**

Bruce Austin
RIT College of Liberal Arts
Rochester, NY 14623
(716) 223-0711 eves

☆ **Grandfather clocks.** "I prefer tall floor clocks made in the United
States, especially in Pennsylvania, but will also consider fine grade European and English clocks. I generally don't buy them myself, but I
screen clocks for one of the world's expert buyers of good clocks. If
you have something good in the way of an old tall case clock, we will
put you in touch with the buyer."

Mark Kenley
Old Timers
PO Box 392
Camp Hill, PA 17001-0392
(717) 761-1908   Fax: (717) 761-7446

☆ *Howard Miller* **clocks** from the 1950's and 60's. These are usually metal or metal and wood and marked on the back (and sometimes the front). A photograph or sketch is helpful.

> Frank and Jay Novak
> 7366 Beverly Blvd.
> Los Angeles, CA 90036
>   (213) 933 0383   Fax: (213) 683-1312

☆ **Winking eye clocks.** "I'll buy any good specimens of these 19th century figural cast iron clocks which wink their eyes as the hands go around. Made in Connecticut during the 3rd quarter of the 19th century by *Bradley and Hubbard*, figures include dogs, owls, lions, elves, Topsy, a man on a barrel, and others. They bring $1,000 up in fine condition and paint, but I'll buy them in any condition, including broken, missing paint, or incomplete. Take photos from more than one angle or phone me with the item in front of you."

> Gregory "Dr. Z" Zemenick
> 1350 Kirts #160
> Troy, MI 48084
>   (810) 642-8129   (810) 244-9426

☆ **Electric clocks covered with colored mirrors.** Wants 1930's clock brands like *GE, Telechron,* and *Seth Thomas* covered with blue, peach, or green mirrors as long as the mirrors are not cracked or damaged. It's OK if the clock doesn't work. Give the brand, model, dimensions, and the color of the glass.

> David Escoe
> 1025 Palo Verde Avenue #32
> Long Beach, CA 90815

When you ask someone for information or an offer, include a long business size #10 envelope, address it to yourself, and put a stamp in the corner. This is a Self-Addressed Stamped Envelope (SASE). Use a long envelope because many buyers will send you information which won't fit into smaller envelopes. If you do not include an SASE, you are telling buyers not to bother answering your letter if they are not interested in what you have to sell. "If my help isn't worth an envelope and stamp to the seller," said one expert, "it's not worth my time and money either."

☆ **Advertising clocks** made by *Baird.*
Jerry Phelps
6013 Innes Trace Road
Louisville, KY 40222
(502) 425-4765

In most cases, buyers will want to inspect your timepiece before making a final offer. Always discuss exact shipping procedures with the buyer.

☆ **Wall clocks that are battery driven** made by *Bangor, Monarch, Sempire, Automatic Electric, Eureka, Warren* and a host of other makers. Does not want clocks with metal or plastic cases. Identify the maker and type of wood (as best you can). He wants you to tell whether it runs and to note repairs or modifications, but he does buy these even when incomplete. Emphasizes, "I don't want anything that plugs in." Dealers, price your goods.
Steve Cunningham
3200 Ashland Drive
Bedford, TX 76021
(817) 267-9851   Fax: (817) 267-0387

☆ **Alarm clocks**, 1880-1910. These battery driven "tin can" clocks usually have a bell on top, but he's looking for unusual varieties that strike the hour, have calendars, play music, or are in unusual shapes. *Parker* and *Kroeber* are two important early brands. He does not want anything that plugs in, or any modern wind-up clocks like *Big Ben* and *Ingersoll.* Give the brand name and any other info you can find on the clock. Dealers must price their goods. Amateurs may request offers.
Steve Cunningham
3200 Ashland Drive
Bedford, TX 76021
(817) 267-9851   Fax: (817) 267-0387

POTTERY AND GLASS CAN BE WORTH YOUR TIME!

Pottery, porcelain, china, bisque, parian, and stoneware are names which confuse amateur sellers. Fortunately, to sell the **Trash or Treasure** *way, you need to know only the simplest basics about pottery.*

All these names describe ceramics or earthenware made from one form or another of clay. The different names signify the quality and colors of the raw materials and the processes by which they are fired and decorated. You don't need to know too much more than that, because I'm going to steer you to people who care about those distinctions and can make them for you. If you want to explore the topic, head for your local public library.

Pottery ranges in value from a few pennies to thousands of dollars. *Collectors often pay well for items once thought ordinary, so take caution when disposing of pottery items of all types. Valuable pottery is not always easy for the untrained eye (that's you) to detect.*

The output of a few 20th century factories such as Rookwood, Roseville, Cowan, Fulper, and Weller are popular, *while the work of other makers is ignored by collectors. Some one-person operations, like that of eccentric George "The Mad Potter of Biloxi" Ohr, created unusual pottery in great demand today.*

Stoneware crocks were made in unimaginative shapes, but their folksy decorations (usually in blue on a grey crock) make them desirable. Prices can reach $20,000 or more, although most sell for less than $300 A reader reports being told by his local antique dealer his crock was worth about $50. He turned to a previous edition of **Trash or Treasure** *and found crock expert Dick Hume who paid $4,800 for the same crock. You'll meet Dick in a few pages.*

Determining the value of earthenware is not easy. The quality of the clay and the delicacy of the painting do not guarantee collector interest and high prices. Popularity and scarcity do.

The same is true of glass. The work of some companies and periods is hotly sought after, while other older and more rare glass goes relatively ignored.

Glass, like clay, is manufactured into many forms and colors, some worth tens of thousands of dollars, *others only worth recycling! Advice in selling glass is essential since it is difficult for the amateur to tell the good from the bad, the common from that worth $100 or more.*

Because color has so much to do with value of both glass and earthenware, a photo is almost essential *to sell anything. An otherwise identical piece of glass or pottery can be worth fifty times as much in one color as in another. If you can't send a photo, "at the very least," advises Majolica buyer Denise Sater, "accurately describe the color, give the dimensions, patterns, and marks, along with a statement of condition."*

When purchasing earthenware or glass, buyers seldom want chipped, stained, or damaged items, *although a few very large and/or rare "bruised" pieces may find a market at a small percent of the price of a perfect one.*

Always inspect glass and pottery carefully for damage. *Look along all rims, including the base, lid and inside lip. Check the top and bottom for cracks. The best way to do this is to run your fingernail along the top and other edges. Your fingernail will find cracks your eye will miss.*

Pottery and glass can be shipped safely. *Buyers will give you specific instructions telling you how they want their newly purchased items packed. If you double box your breakables you'll usually be safe.*

A number of the buyers you'll meet in the next few pages have written books, price guides, and catalogs. Others edit newsletters or are officers in clubs.

They are all valuable sources of information capable of putting money in your pocket. *I recommend them.*

POTTERY, CERAMICS (earthenware)

☆ **American art pottery of all types.** Buys pottery from *Fulper, Paul Revere, Rookwood, Grueby, Dedham, TECO, Tiffany, Clewell, Marblehead, Saturday Evening Girls, Newcomb College, George Ohr, Van Briggle, Cowan, Grand Feu, Losanti, New Orleans Art Pottery, Robineau,* and other quality American art pottery. Also buys good **quality European pottery** such as *Martin Bros, Moorcroft,* and others. Especially likes large and unusual pieces, and has been known to consider damaged pieces if they are important. "If you have any doubts, phone me and I will be glad to be of assistance."

> Robert Berman, Le Poulaille
> 441 South Jackson Street
> Media, PA 19063
> (610) 566-1516

☆ *Rookwood* **and other art pottery** is wanted by the world's largest dealer in *Rookwood,* who also buys other American and European art pottery, both production and artist-signed pieces. Brand names they will buy include *Grueby, Teco, Van Briggle, Newcomb, Marblehead, Weller, UND, Roseville, Fulper, Overbeck,* and *Cowan* among American companies. European pottery makers of interest include *Moorcroft, Massier, Amphora, Gustavsberg, Bock, Freres, Deck, Lachenal, Haviland, Robj, Longwy, Delaherche, Picasso, Zsolnay, Lauger, Rorstrand, Clarice Cliff* and *Ruskin.* Pieces made between 1890 and 1950 are generally the most desirable. Quality *Rookwood* pieces will be considered even if damaged, although value is reduced. "If you have any questions about the value of your art pottery, *Rookwood* or other, please write or call for information at no charge." When writing, include a photo and describe all markings found on the bottom. Please give the dimensions of each piece, and mention any damage no matter how tiny. This well-known dealer has bought, sold, and auctioned high quality pottery for more than twenty years, and offers beautiful illustrated catalogs of past and future auctions at prices ranging from $20 to $50.

> Riley Humler
> Cincinnati Art Galleries
> 635 Main Street
> Cincinnati, OH 45202
> (513) 381-2128

Because color has so much to do with value of both glass and earthenware, a photo is almost essential to sell anything other than a stock item from a well-known factory

☆ **Hand decorated art pottery**, American or European, is sought, but David emphasizes that his interest as a dealer is exclusively in "hand decorated" pottery, such as that by *Newcomb College, Grueby, George Ohr, Robineau, Overbeck,* and *Marblehead.* Artist signed *Rookwood* is also of interest, but "we are not looking to buy factory production *Rookwood* or *Roseville.*" He needs to know the maker, condition, size, shape, decoration, and markings on the bottom, so including a photo is a good idea. This well known expert in the Arts & Crafts period has agreed to make offers to amateur sellers who learn about him through this book if they are serious about selling what they own, but states clearly that he "does not wish readers to price fish or to involve him in bidding wars with other buyers." If you need an appraisal for estate or insurance purposes, the fee is $10/ item. Dave writes a monthly column on pottery, and publishes *Arts and Crafts Quarterly*, an attractive and informative magazine available by subscription for $25/year. His book on Fulper may be purchased from him for $35. Other books, catalogs, and materials on art pottery are available. SASE for more information.

David Rago
9 South Main Street
Lambertville, NJ 08530
(609) 397-9374 Fax: (609) 397-9377

☆ *Van Briggle* **and other American art pottery.** A variety of fine pottery will be considered, including *Rookwood* that is artist signed, *North Dakota School of Mines* pottery "with good color contrast," *Hylong, Newcomb,* decorated *Marblehead,* and the like. But his primary interest is in pre-1913 *Van Briggle* pottery, the man who created it, and the company that produced it. Wants company records and catalogs, as well as paintings and pots signed by Van Briggle. Will even accept damaged pre-1913 pieces "if priced accordingly." Is not interested in undated *Van Briggle* or in *ND School of Mines* that is plain. Describe the size, shape, colors, glaze quality, bottom markings, and condition. Scott is a former president of the American Art Pottery Association and author of *The Collector's Guide to Van Briggle*, available from him for $35 and a *Van Briggle Price Guide* for $6.50. He does appraisals for a fee, and expects you to price your own goods.

Scott Nelson
PO Box 6081
Santa Fe, NM 87502
(505) 986-1176

☆ **John Bell pottery** made in the 19th century in Waynesboro, especially fancy pieces which can bring $1,000 or more.

Ken Broyles
PO Box 42
Waynesboro, PA 17268
(717) 762-3068

☆ *Stangl* **pottery.** "We especially want *Stangl* toby mugs with ashtray hats, *Stangl* birds and animals, flower pots, and flower ashtrays. We want "rainbow ware," and drippy blue, green, orange, and yellow art ware. Also the following dinnerware patterns: Fruit, Fruit and Flowers, Country Gardens, Country Life, Blueberry, Garden Flower, Thistle, Town and Country, Chicory, Yellow and Blue Tulip, Wild Rose, and all Christmas patterns. We don't want brown stains, chips, or cracks, but minor flaws are acceptable."

    Bob and Nancy Perzel, Popkorn Antiques
    PO Box 1057
    Flemington, NJ 08822
        (908) 782-9631

☆ *TECO, Weller* **and other American art pottery.** "*TECO* pottery is my favorite. I'll buy geometric and organic vases with square or built in handles. Sculptural leaves and plant forms, usually in matte finish with green tones, but also brown, yellow, gray, etc. This is often highlighted in a black/gray gunmetal color. I am also a strong buyer of *Weller* vases with raised figures, lizards, snakes, nudes, etc. *Weller* also comes in strong geometrics. Colors are rose, pink, blue, gray, yellow, brown and matte green, often mixed, often veined with gunmetal. Normally signed. I buy a great deal of *Weller*, including many of their other lines." He also buys a wide range of other art pottery including *Grueby, Saturday Evening Girls, Newcomb College, University of North Dakota, Jervis, American Art Clay, Fulper, George Ohr, Arequipa, California Faience, Chelsea Keramic, Clewell, Clifton* (large vases only) and many more. Strongly advise you take a picture since the form and color of pottery determines value. When you send your photo, write down carefully all the marks on the bottom.

    Gary Struncius
    PO Box 1374
    Lakewood, NJ 08701
        (800) 272-2529

☆ **Art pottery of Eastern Europe**, especially pottery made in Art Nouveau or Secession style by *Zsolnay* in Pecs (Hungary), *Fischer* in Budapest, *E. Whaliss* in Vienna and *Amphora* in Turn Teplitz (Czechoslovakia) between 1890 and 1920. The names of these makers are typically incised into the bottom of the items, the values of which can range from $50 to more than $1,000. "Though we do buy rare examples that are damaged, the value is diminished." They do not buy *Zsolnay* made after 1940. Please send a photo, the size, and markings on the bottom.

    Federico Santi
    The Zsolnay Store
    152 Spring Street
    Newport, RI 02840
        (401) 841-5060

☆ **Quimper** ("kam-pair"), a form of antique French peasant pottery, is sought, especially older large examples such as candlesticks, chargers, jardinieres, and figures. New pieces are not wanted. Send a clear photo, the dimensions, and a statement of condition. It is important to describe the markings on the bottom (most pieces are marked), including the color. Among other books, the Bagdades wrote *English and Continental Pottery and Porcelain: An Illustrated Price Guide* and a similar guide to American pottery and porcelain, each available for $22.95. Send an SASE for more information about books written by these popular columnists.

> Susan and Al Bagdade
> The Country Peasants
> 3136 Elder Court
> Northbrook, IL 60062
> (708) 498-1468

☆ **Shawnee pottery**, 1937 - 1961, especially figural cookie jars and water pitchers such as Chanticleer the rooster, Smiley Pig, Winnie Pig, Puss 'n Boots, etc. Also salt and pepper shakers, planters, and any item that has been decorated with gold trim and/or decals. Has a special interest in Valencia dinnerware and kitchenware in good condition (look for bright yellow, cobalt, green, tangerine and maroon). "All Shawnee items for sale that are brought to my attention could end up in good homes eventually as I have a national network of collectors, and will often refer sellers to potential buyers if I am not interested in the item offered. I am not interested in the more common planters and shakers, but any gold trimmed products will be considered and larger items will be referred on to a good home." Your descriptions must note chips and hairline cracks. Include your phone number along with the color and marks on the bottom. Dealers must price your goods. If you are really an amateur seller, you may request an offer, "but I'd like an idea of what you think its value is." People with large collections for sale are encouraged to join the club for $25 and advertise in their folksy, illustrated and very informative *Exclusively Shawnee* newsletter for free.

> Pamela Curran, Shawnee Pottery Collectors Club
> PO Box 713
> New Smyrna Beach, FL 32170
> (904) 345-0150

☆ **Children's dishes.** "Any china used by children to eat or drink" is sought, "but I prefer American items, and I prefer those made by *Roseville* (both unmarked and those marked R on the bottom), *S.E.G., Paul Revere* or *Dedham*. No damaged pieces.

> Steve Kelley
> PO Box 695
> Desert Hot Springs, CA 92240
> (619) 329-3206

☆ *Roseville* **pottery** in many patterns in both their Rosane and production lines. Does not want "brown florals." Photo urged.
> Gary Struncius
> PO Box 1374
> Lakewood, NJ 08701
>> (800) 272-2529

☆ *Roseville* **pottery,** especially in Sunflower, Pinecone and Jonquil patterns. No cracks or chips. Please send photo and dimensions plus any markings you find on the bottom.
> Leda Andrews
> 2110 Staples Avenue
> Key West, FL 33040
>> (305) 296-4195

☆ *Cowan* **pottery** flower vases and frogs decorated with women (especially in colors other than white), bookends ($250+), vases (up to $500 depending on the artist, design and skill of execution). Black sculptures trimmed in gold can go even higher. Pieces are usually marked but COWAN can be hard to read under the glaze, so he advises you to look closely. Many *Cowan* artists including Thelma Frazier Winter, Waylande Gregory, and Viktor Schreckengest continued to make pottery and ceramic sculpture on their own after *Cowan* closed in 1931. These are also wanted by this *Cowan* researcher who notes, "bowls and candlesticks are of little interest unless they have an unusual design, such as those shaped like women." He requests you give the height of your piece along with a photo. The color of the glaze is so important in valuation, it's impossible to give values without a clear sharp photo. Examine the piece carefully for chips, repairs, or hairline cracks as well as worn patches or scratches in the finish.
> Mark Bassett
> PO Box 771233
> Lakewood, OH 44107
>> Moving. Call (216) information after 8/94

☆ **Ceramic flower frogs and candelabra** depicting ladies dancing or posing in the Art Deco style. "I'm especially interested in those made by the Ohio pottery company called *Cowan*, but will buy European makers as well." He especially seeks *Cowan* frogs number 708, 717, 803, 804, 805, 812, and 853 as well as the figural dancing candelabra #752. These can bring from $150 to $600, depending on the figure, colors, and condition, so are definitely worth your time. To sell your frog, note all the markings you can find.
> William Sommer
> 9 West 10th Street
> New York, NY 10011
>> (212) 260-0999

☆ **Stoneware crocks and jugs with blue decorations.** Especially likes pottery with clear markings from NY, NJ, OH, PA, and New England. "I'll pay top dollar for unusual forms decorated with people, animals, ships, trees, houses, strong blue florals, etc. Dated pieces are particularly desirable. I pay from $100 to as much as $10,000 for the right items." He emphasizes that he is interested only in stoneware that is blue decorated, not brown or white. Also buys inkwells, flasks, and unusual small items made of blue decorated stoneware. Needs to know the size of the piece in quarts or gallons if marked, in inches if not. Take a photo or make a good sketch of the decoration because the more unusual the decoration, the more he pays. Mention the darkness of the blue. He will help amateur sellers determine what they have. "If you are interested in forming a stoneware collectors club, call me."

    Richard Hume
    1300 North Stream Parkway
    Point Pleasant, NJ 08742
      (908) 899-8707 eves

☆ **Spongeware, stoneware, and redware pottery and crockery.** Note all markings on the sides and bottoms, please, if you'd like this important dealer to evaluate what you have. These are often incised with the name of the maker or user, and their city and town, as well as the size of the container. Minor damage and cracks are acceptable in very rare pieces, but you must note all damage, no matter how small. The decoration is the key to value, so photos are essential.

    Louis Picek
    Main Street Antiques and Art
    PO Box 340
    West Branch, IA 52358

☆ **Stoneware pottery.** "I'll buy pre-1900 stoneware pottery crocks, jugs, pitchers, flasks, churns, and bottles with cobalt blue decoration, especially those depicting birds, animals, people, flowers, buildings, flags, or dates. I also buy pottery marked ROBINSON CLAY PRODUCTS, OLD SLEEPY EYE, or with elongated (stretched out) numbers on the bottom. I do not buy *Red Wing* pottery." Please send a photo, dimensions, and list of any defects. Dealers are expected to price their goods, but he will help amateur sellers. "Nobody answers faster."

    Barry Friedman
    22725 Garzota Drive
    Valencia, CA 91355
      (805) 296-2318

☆ **Redware plates, bowls, and other pieces.** When describing, mention all marks on the bottom and take a photo or make a sketch of the pattern, indicating what part of the pattern is yellow or green. Make certain you note if there are any cracks or chips.

> Richard Hume
> 1300 North Stream Parkway
> Point Pleasant, NJ 08742
> (908) 899-8707 eves

☆ **Buffalo Pottery.** "I'll buy almost any marked piece."

> Seymour "Si" Altman
> 8970 Main Street
> Clarence, NY 14031
> (716) 634-4488

☆ **Italian pottery (Majolica)** of all types: flower pots, vases, dinnerware, bottles, lamps, tiles, dishes, figurines, pockets, etc. "The pieces are all hand-painted in bright colors, often on a white background. There are hundreds of types of decoration: fruit, flowers, people, mythical and religious themes, architecture, etc, but always in bright reds, blues, yellows, greens, and rose (usually all of the above!). Many are reproductions of pieces created during the Renaissance, others are more modern and look like souvenirs. I am interested in all types marked MADE IN ITALY on the bottom. Sometimes the markings also identify the region where they were made, such as GUBBIO, DERUTA, ASSISI, etc." A photo is "very helpful," but at the very least, give the dimensions, patterns, colors, and marks, along with a statement of condition. The price you'd like is "helpful" but not required.

> Denise Sater
> 871 Holly Tree Road
> Manheim, PA 17545
> (717) 665-2229

☆ **Majolica pottery.** Interested in Majolica pieces of all types, primarily those from England and the U.S. Look for brightly colored utilitarian pottery, cheese covers, salts, creamers, humidors, etc. Popular patterns include dragonflies and seashells, but this folksy pottery comes in a wide variety of forms. Some significant names and marks to look for include JOSIAH WEDGWOOD, ETRUSCAN, GEORGE JONES, and MINTON (makes of high grade pottery). Claims to pay top dollar for this brightly colored pottery. Asks you to send a photo. Majolica was often made and painted in factories by children, so the quality and appeal varies.

> Rick Kranz
> 702 West Olive
> Stillwater, MN 55082
> (612) 430-3016

GLASS

☆ **Antique and 20th century art glass.** This well known auctioneer conducts cataloged auctions of art glass, so can handle collections and fine individual pieces of *Daum Nancy, Steuben, Galle, Tiffany* and other art glass, as well as collections and fine pieces of *Wedgwood* and other fine porcelain.

> James D. Julia Auctioneers
> PO Box 80
> Fairfield, ME 04937
> (207) 453-7904   Fax: (207) 453-2502

☆ **Antique Bohemian glass goblets, beakers,** and other drinking vessels. "I'll buy colored or clear glass with wheel engraved landscape scenes, portraits, animals, spa scenes, religious themes, etc. In addition to wheel engraved items, I'm seeking pieces decorated with transparent or opaque enamels, overlays, gilt work, cutting, paintings, etc. Cameos are particularly desirable." Not interested in any other glass. He notes, "There are many, many reproductions of this glass. It takes a trained eye to tell the difference." Common and not desirable pieces include deer and castle, deer and pine trees, and bird and castle. Later pieces are simple and the engraving lacks detail in the animals. You must send a close-up photo of this potentially valuable glass and note every chip, flake, or crack. Dealers are expected to price their goods, but he will make offers to amateur sellers. You must include an SASE if you wish your photos back.

> Tom Bradshaw
> 325 Carol Drive
> Ventura, CA 93003

When a listee says he or she is not interested in a particular item, please do not waste his or her time and yours by offering what they do not want.

☆ **Black amethyst glass** (looks black until you hold it to the light and find it's really purple). This advanced collector will buy only the odd and rare, especially dinner plates with silver or gold overlay, large bowls, water and juice glasses, lamp bases, candlesticks with three or more candles, and figurines. She will answer all mail that includes a photo, dimensions, and SASE. As with all glass, condition is crucial.

> Judy Polk Harding
> 2713 Friendship Street
> Iowa City, IA 52245
> (319) 354-2379

☆ **Antique glass paperweights and other items** including art glass, glass pens, canes, and whimsies. "I'm looking for the old and rare." Make certain to note all damage, no matter how small.

> Stanley Block
> PO Box 51
> Trumbull, CT 06611
>   (203) 261-3223

☆ **Antique glass paperweights,** 1845-1900. "I will buy fine French (*Baccarat, Clichy, St. Louis*), American (*New England Glass Company, Sandwich*), English, and Bohemian paperweights. I am looking for millefiori, flowers, sulfides, fruit and animals." Among the most valuable are large 19th century French paperweights by *Pantin* which contain a lizard on rocky ground with flowers and plants around it. These can be worth as much as $50,000 but have been widely copied and the copies are worth as little as $50. It takes an expert to tell the difference. Other paperweights have also been copied, often including fake dates and wear. "I don't want china paperweights, Italian copies, plain glass, weights with photos, mottoes, or advertising, and no weights with air bubbles as part of the design." A close up color photo of your weight is important and should be accompanied by a good description. "I don't mind surface wear and nicks, but cracks in the glass are not acceptable." Include an SASE if you want photos returned. "I will make offers to amateur sellers, but dealers are expected to price their goods."

> Tom Bradshaw
> 325 Carol Drive
> Ventura, CA 93003

☆ **Antique glass paperweights,** 1845-1900. "I will buy fine French (*Pantin, Baccarat, Clichy, St. Louis*), American (*Boston Glass Co., Sandwich Glass Co., New England Glass Co., Gillinoer, Mt. Washington*), English (*Bacchus, Whitefriars*), Russian and Bohemian paperweights. I am especially looking for *Pantin* paperweights from the late 1870's for which I will pay from $2,000 to $35,000. I also seek early *Clichy* bouquet on a moss background which can be worth as much as $40,000. I don't want paperweights with blobs of colored glass or with large bubbles in the design." A close up color photo of your weight is important and should be accompanied by a good description, including the diameter. This well known author and collector does not send out a wants list because, he explains, "I will purchase all top quality weights." Paul's book *The Jokelson Collection of Antique Cameo Incrustation* is available with price guide for $60.

> Paul Dunlop, The Dunlop Collection
> PO Box 6269
> Statesville, NC 28687
>   (800) 227-1996

☆ **Many kinds of glassware and china** are sought by one of the country's larger auction firms specializing in post-Victorian glass. He buys outright or accepts on consignment for auction:

- **Carnival glass,** especially pitcher sets, tumblers, whimsies, opalescent pieces, and common items in rare patterns and colors. He encourages you to contact him with one item or a giant collection since there are many valuable pieces that only an expert will recognize;
- **Victorian pattern glass;**
- **Cameo glass vases,** plates,urns, and other glass items made by the *Phoenix Glass Co.;*
- **RS Prussia china** with scenes, portraits, or pearlized florals;
- *Noritake* **china** with geometric designs;
- **Nippon china humidors** and large high relief "blown out" vases depicting birds, animals, or figures;
- **Mandarin red glassware** by *Fenton Glass Company.*

Include your phone number if the piece is for sale. Tom has a reputation for being slow to respond, but helpful with amateur sellers. Phone him midweek if you think you have something good.

> Tom Burns
> Burns Auction Service
> 109 East Steuben Street
> Bath, NY 14810
> (607) 776 7942

☆ **Carnival glass** is wanted "in any amount and any color." Prefers dealers to price, but warns that some of the standard price guides are highly overpriced. This 25 year veteran collector is willing to help amateurs "who are actually selling, not just calling everyone fishing for free appraisals and the highest price."

> Dick Hatscher
> 142 Walnut Hill Road
> Bethel, CT 06801
> (203) 743-1468

☆ **Carnival glass.** "I'll buy one piece or a collection, in any colors." Prefers you to set the price.

> W. J. Warren
> 38 Mosher Drive
> Tonawanda, NY 14150
> (716) 692-2886

Don't take chances with carnival glass.
Differences in color or pattern can
result in dramatic differences in value.
Do not trust what you read in a price guide.

☆ **Victorian glassware.** "We pay cash for collections, estates, or single pieces of the following:
- Decorated glass;
- **Cobalt blue** glass;
- **Ruby-stained** glass;
- **Cranberry** glass;
- **Brown opalescent** glass;
- Fancy art glass.

Buys all types of Victorian glass including pitchers and tumblers, salt shakers and sugar shakers, syrup jugs, and **milk glass vases** in silverplated holders. He does *not buy* depression glass, bottles, clear glass (without color), or anything that is chipped, cracked or damaged. Please give a detailed description and tell how you came to own it. A picture is important. Dealers should price their goods; amateurs ready to sell may ask for offers."

> Scott Roland
> Glimmer Glass Antiques
> PO Box 262
> Schenevus, NY 12155

When looking for something to sell, do not overlook the colored glass dinnerware of 1910-1940, called "depression glass." A few pieces are surprisingly valuable. Covered butter dishes, for example, usually bring you $100 - $400 each. Candy dishes and water pitchers also bring better than average prices. Expert advice is essential, because pieces with little value in one color or pattern can be worth $100 in another.

Be careful setting a price on carnival glass, which ranges from $10 to $10,000. Work with the buyer when it comes to pricing, as rarities are very hard for anyone but an expert to recognize. A North Carolina woman sold a carnival glass plate for $1. The picker who bought it resold it by phone for $10,000 to Tom Burns, a buyer listed in this book. Tom paid $10,000 for a pitcher owned by someone who called in to my radio talk show.

☆ **Depression glass** in various colors and patterns. A Xerox© copy is very helpful if you don't know the pattern. Do not count pieces that have chips. A photo helps if your item is colored. "I'll pay fair prices for any depression glass I can resell in my shop."

> Nadine Pankow
> 5 Cliffside Circle
> Willow Springs, IL 60480
>   (708) 839-5231

Color is so important in the value of glass that it is almost essential to send a photo. Condition is also critical. Buyers seldom want glass that is chipped or cracked.

☆ *Fostoria* **glass and memorabilia** are wanted by the founder of the *Fostoria* Glass Society in Southern California. "I'll buy dealer signs, dealer catalogs from before 1940, postcards, displays, trade cards, calendars, magazine ads (1924 to 1931 only), and any other *Fostoria* Glass Company memorabilia that's in mint condition." His glass wants are more restricted as he only buys frosted or clear **Victoria** (pattern #183) and rare pieces of pattern #2412 called **Colony**. He is not interested in common Colony glassware or other *Fostoria* patterns, but finding a Victoria oil lamp is high on his list. "All items must be in mint condition or don't bother."

> Gary Schneider
> 7301 Topanga Canyon Blvd. #202
> Canoga Park, CA 91303
>   (818) 998-4588   (818) 702-9967

☆ **Glass toothpick holders** in mint condition. She seeks numerous patterns. Make a photocopy or photo of your holder if you don't know the name of its pattern, and describe the color as best you can. There are many reproduction holders, so she'll have to examine yours before making a final offer. Will also consider interesting holders made of metal or china. Judy is founder of the National Toothpick Holder Collectors Society and has published their newsletter for 20 years.

> Judy Knauer
> 1224 Spring Valley Lane
> West Chester, PA 19380
>   (610) 431-3477

☆ **Early American glass in Willow Oak pattern** in amber, blue, or Vaseline colors.

> Audrey Buffington
> 2 Old Farm Road
> Wayland, MA 01778
>   (508) 358-2644

☆ **Fine crystal.** Buys crystal for resale, and repairs glass, crystal, porcelain, bisque, and figurines. He also buys damaged and undamaged figurines and *Hummels* for resale.

> David Jasper
> 46508 267th Street
> Sioux Falls, SD 57106
>   (605) 361-7524   Fax: (605) 361-7216

ACCESSORIES

 *Accessories is a word used to describe many of those useful things we have around our homes. It can include lamps, vases, clocks, boxes, bookends, desk sets, frogs, cigarette boxes, even some ashtrays. Collectors seek accessories because of what they are made of, who made them, or the style in which they were made.*

__It is always important to check for marks__, as signed pieces are often of better quality and more likely to be collected. You should look for quality of workmanship, fine materials, and good design. Deciding what is good design is difficult, especially when artistic judgment comes into play. I'm sure you've seen valuable things you thought were ugly. I know I have. Many of these items may not appeal to you personally, but that shouldn't keep you from profiting when you find them. Good luck!

☆ **Arts & Crafts period lamps and accessories** made by *Van Erp, Roycroft, Limberts, Stickley*, and others. Lamps are often copper and colored glass, as are **cigarette boxes, bookends, ashtrays, humidors, desk sets**, and other items. Better pieces are often inlaid with silver. This active Arts & Crafts expert also buys **furniture** by these makers, whose work tends to be massive square oak furniture, often with dark finishes, visible pegs and hinges, and simple unornamented lines. Many people call it "mission oak." Send a photo or call if you think you have one of these pieces, as some can be quite valuable.

    David Rago
    17 South Main Street
    Lambertville, NJ 08530
       (609) 397-9374   Fax: (609) 397-9377

☆ **Accessories from the Mission or Arts & Crafts period** including light fixtures and metalwork by *L. & J.G. Stickley, Gustav Stickley, Roycroft, Limberts, Lifetime, Charles Stickley, Rohlfs,* and *Dirk Van Erp*, especially unusual pieces, custom made pieces, and items inlaid with silver, pewter or copper. He is also interested in catalogs from these firms. "If you have any doubts about what you have, please call. I will be glad to help."

    Robert Berman
    Le Poulaille
    441 South Jackson Street
    Media, PA 19063
       (610) 566-1516

☆ **Hammered copper** and other Arts and Crafts period items such as:
- Lamps with mica or glass shades;
- Vases and candlesticks by *Roycroft*, *Van Erp*, *Jarvie* and
  others working in the Arts & Crafts style;
- Silver by *Kalo*;
- Metal with applied or cut-out squares by *Roycroft*;
- Arts & Crafts jewelry.

Descriptions are difficult without a photo. Since some of these pieces are fairly valuable, it could be worth your time. Describe all maker's markings, damage, and give dimensions.

> Gary Struncius
> PO Box 1374
> Lakewood, NJ 08701
> (800) 272-2529

☆ *Roycroft* **accessories** such as bookends and other small items. A photo or Xerox™ is a good idea if requesting an offer.

> Richard Blacher
> 209 Plymouth Colony/Alps Road
> Branford, CT 06405

☆ **Art Deco accessories.** "I'll buy Deco items to compliment my radio collection." Ed wants a wide range of distinctive Deco items, so give him a try for items like clocks, **picture frames**, and **lamps**. If you are the original owner, he'd appreciate the item's history. He prefers you to set your price but will make offers to amateurs intending to sell.

> Ed Sage
> PO Box 13025
> Albuquerque, NM 87192
> (505) 298-0840

☆ **Small wicker items** such as lamps, picture frames, foot stools, planters, end tables, etc. Not interested in big couches and chairs but does want **child sized furniture**. The general guideline is "Can it be mailed?" Wants early pre-WWII items, not modern Asian stuff. Describe color, condition, and dimensions. "A photo would be helpful."

> Leda Andrews
> 2110 Staples Ave.
> Key West, FL 33040
> (305) 296-4195

☆ **Standing picture frames** made of wood, brass, silver plate, celluloid, copper, ivory and bronze, usually from 3" to 15" high. "Larger OK, smaller even better. Missing glass OK, too, but the frame itself must be in fine condition and made before 1950, preferably with the easel in back. Best frames are marked *Gorham, Tiffany, Germany* or *Aspreys*. Porcelain or ivory pictures in the frame add greatly to value, but ordinary portraits do not. Photocopies and good description will bring a cash offer.

> Carol Payne
> Carol's Gallery
> 14455 Big Basin Way
> Saratoga, CA 95070
> (408) 867-7055

☆ **Wooden picture frames** that are early, unusual, and in perfect condition. A photograph is very helpful. Give a call if you're nearby.

> Craig Dinner
> PO Box 4399
> Sunnyside, NY 11104
> (718) 729-3850

☆ **Bookends** made before 1940 that are three dimensional figures of men, women, or animals that are at least 7" high. Metal are preferred, but glass, wood and plaster will be considered, as will metal bookends with interesting designs that are not necessarily figural. Do not offer small bookends, singles, or newer items. Picture preferred, along with dimensions. Point out any cracks, flaws, or wear. "This is a new hobby for me, so you must price what you have so I can decide whether it appeals to me at your price. Don't contact me with things not for sale."

> Susan Mast
> 849 Almar Avenue #C-270
> Santa Cruz, CA 95060
> (408) 423-9786 eves   Fax: (408) 423-7001

☆ **Victorian era boxes** which held collars, cuffs, gloves, brush and mirror sets, shaving sets, neckties, etc. "The items we collect have lithographs on the front or top of the piece. Our favorite lithos are of women and children, and we do not buy those picturing French or Colonial attired folks. Boxes are usually covered with celluloid. Nothing will be considered that isn't in top condition, that has cracked celluloid, split seams, or missing hardware." Interior condition is not as critical. Color photo needed. Note all damage. Pays finder's fees.

> Mike and Sherry Miller
> 303 Holiday Ave.
> Tuscola, IL 61953
> (217) 253-4991

☆ **Photo and autograph albums.** "The items we collect have lithographs usually affixed to the front or top of the piece. Our favorite lithos are of women and children, and we do not buy those picturing French or Colonial folks. The albums are usually covered with celluloid, but may also be velvet, or printed paper. Musical albums are particularly desirable; we pay from $100 to $250 for nice ones. Nothing will be considered that isn't in top condition, that has cracked celluloid, split seams, or missing hardware. Interior condition is not as critical." Color photo needed. Note all damage.

> Mike and Sherry Miller
> 303 Holiday Ave.
> Tuscola, IL 61953
> (217) 253-4991

☆ **Gold bearing quartz items.** Masculine items made from or decorated with quartz containing gold flakes and nuggets are sought. Items include **matchsafes, cane handles, watch fobs, watches, desk sets, money clips**, etc. Sandra doesn't have much interest in jewelry, "unless it's exceptional." A Xerox™ or photo is the best way to sell.

> Sandra Whitson
> PO Box 272
> Lititz, PA 17543
> (717) 626-4978

☆ **Items made of banded agate.** Will purchase **pens, button hooks, snuff boxes**, and **small decorative items** made entirely or mostly of banded agate. If you want to sell, give dimensions and condition.

> Stanley Block
> PO Box 51
> Trumbull, CT 06611
> (203) 261-0057 eves

☆ **Indian motif sterling silver** items made for men by *Unger Bros*. Items she seeks include **desk sets, clothes brushes, matchsafes**, etc. Has only limited interest in women's items and jewelry by *Unger*, but will buy some items.

> Sandra Whitson
> PO Box 272
> Lititz, PA 17543
> (717) 626-4978

CHINA MAY OR MAY NOT BE TREASURE.

You'll find out when you go to sell it. First, ask yourself, "Would I want to buy this and use it?"

No one wants chipped, stained, or damaged items. Dishes less than 150 years old must be in perfect condition to find a buyer. Don't waste your time and theirs by offering items with chips and/or cracks, crazing, heavy knife scratches and pattern wear. Pay particular attention to gold trim. If the gold is worn to where you can see the china underneath, you must mention that fact. Don't be surprised if the value of your china drops by 60% to 80% if gold is worn.

Your set does not have to be complete to sell. That's the big advantage to selling to matching services. Since their goal is to fill in someone else's china, your set doesn't have to be complete to have some value.

Serving pieces and items with lids are worth the most. Serving pieces, especially large pieces and those with lids (like soup tureens) are harder to find and as a result worth more than ordinary table settings. The more unusual the piece, the more likely it is to have a market. Cups and saucers are the most common pieces.

You can sell your china with a few simple steps. Begin by listing the pieces, and how many of each you have. Do not list damaged pieces. If you don't know the pattern name, don't despair. It is easy to tell buyers what you have, even when you don't know yourself.

A photocopy (Xerox™) machine is a seller's best friend. Send a photocopy of the front and back of a small plate andindicate the colors in your pattern and the color of the maker's mark on the back (as some companies use color codes). Photocopies usually give excellent detail, hence give an expert an accurate look at what you have. Many china companieshave similar names. There are many Wedgwood and Haviland companies. The marks on the bottom tell experts what you have and the photocopy machine can capture them accurately.

If possible, take a close up 35mm photograph. If you are able to take sharp, close-up 35mm photographs, include a photo which shows the shape of a cup handle. If you can't take photos, a sketch which shows the shape of the handle and base of the cup compared to the bowl can be very useful.

Keep your expectations of value reasonable. Don't expect to be paid a fortune for old china just because it belonged to great granny. China patterns and companies fall in and out of favor. Recent trends toward informality mean you can't assume people are waiting to purchase your old china, silver, or glassware, no matter how lovely. If your set is reasonably complete, or not a popular pattern, consider consider giving it to a friend or relative who has admired it and would use it.

Packing china is not difficult as long as two pieces never touch. The buyer will provide packing instructions. If packed properly, china can be shipped around the world safely as two pieces of china don't touch while packed. Padding such as bubble pack, styrofoam sheets, or similar material must separate every packed piece. Lids will chip or break if they are left on sugar bowls or other covered dishes while they are being shipped.

Remember these simple steps:

List how many of each type item (plates, saucers, cups, and other items) you have;

Include a color photograph or a b/w photocopy which indicates the colors and patterns;

Include a drawing or Xerox™ of all marks on the bottom of the china, remembering to indicate the color of the marks.

CHINA

☆ **China, crystal, and flatware** is sought for resale. More than 48,000 different patterns from 1,200 American, European, and Japanese manufacturers will be purchased if in fine condition. Chips, cracks, stains, or serious knife marks are not acceptable. Pieces with some pattern or gold wear may be purchased if the pattern is rare or in high demand. Provide the maker's name, pattern name and/or number, and an accurate count of what and how many pieces are available. If you do not know the pattern or the manufacturer, make a Xerox™ of a small plate and describe the colors, or make a copy of a place setting of silverware along with any serving pieces you have, and include whatever is written on the back of your silver. A good sharp photo is always helpful, particularly with stemware. They have 1,600,000 pieces in stock and will try to fill your china, crystal, or silverware needs.

> Robert Page
> Replacements, Ltd.
> 1089 Knox Road or PO Box 26029
> Greensboro, NC 27420
> (800) 562-4462   Fax: (910) 697-3100

☆ **Wedgwood, Adams, Coalport, and Midwinter dinnerware** in discontinued patterns is wanted by one of the leading experts on discontinued *Wedgwood* dinnerware in the United States. All pieces must be in mint condition, with no chips, cracks, crazing (age lines), stains, or severe scratches. Please list the mint condition pieces only, and how many of each type. Give the dimensions of plates and bowls. Note the maker and the pattern, if you can. If you do not know the maker or the name of the pattern, please send a photocopy or photo of one of the plates, front and back. She does not want *Johnson Brothers* or *Franciscan* dinnerware (two other companies owned by *Wedgwood)* nor does she want *Waterford* crystal. Note that *Enoch Wedgwood* and *Wedgwood, Ltd.* are not the same as *Wedgwood* and ARE NOT WANTED.

> Gloria Voss Beyer
> 740 North Honey Creek Parkway
> Milwaukee, WI 53213
> (414) 259-1025

☆ *Wedgwood, Royal Doulton* and *Lenox* **china**. Also wants *Spode, Castleton, Coalport, Franciscan, Gorham, Pickard, Royal Worcester, Minton,* and *Flintridge* china. No giftware. Ives offers the free pamphlet *On Caring for your China* if you send her a business size SASE.

> Jacquelynn Ives
> China Match
> 219 North Milwaukee Street
> Milwaukee, WI 53202
> (414) 272-8880

☆ **Sets and pieces of obsolete dinner china.** Primarily interested in English china, but buys American, European and Japanese patterns. Buys *Adams, Aynsley, Coalport, Minton, Paragon, Rosenthal, Spode, Royal Albert, Royal Crown Derby, Royal Doulton, Royal Worcester, Shelley, Wedgwood* and others. European chinas wanted are *Bernardaud & Co, Elite, M. Redon, MZ, Schumann, T&V* and *Vignaud. Oxford, Castleton, Theodore Haviland, Haviland & Company, Franciscan, Syracuse, Pickard, Flintridge-Gorham, Lenox* and some crystal is also of interest. They do business worldwide and will make offers for items they can use. Items *must* be in excellent condition. If you wish china or stemware appraised, there is a fee, which is refundable if and when they buy your dishes. Send a Xerox™ of the pattern and the markings on the underneath. Note the colors of the markings and all pattern elements. They do not buy giftware, figurines, or floral arrangements. Remember, no SASE to foreign countries.

> Old China Patterns Limited
> 1560 Brimley Road
> Scarborough, Ontario
> M1P 3G9, CANADA
> (416) 299-8880   Fax: (416) 299-4721

☆ **Discontinued English and American china patterns** in perfect condition, produced by *Castleton, Franciscan, French Haviland, Lenox, Spode, Minton, Pickard, Royal Doulton, Royal Worcester, Syracuse, Wedgwood,* etc. "We buy sets or incomplete sets consisting of ten pieces or more. For patterns in demand we buy outright; others are listed in our computer system and customers notified as to availability and prices." They do not want to buy Japanese china or *anything* imperfect. Prefers you to set the selling price, but will make offers.

> J. Warren Roundhill
> Patterns Unlimited TOT
> PO Box 15238
> Seattle, WA 98115
> Fax: (206) 524-1252

☆ *Wedgwood, Adams, Coalport* and *Midwinter* **china in discontinued patterns** in mint condition. Especially likes to find Patrician, Wellesley, and Quince patterns. Please state how many of each type piece you have, the manufacturer, and the name of the pattern. If you don't know the pattern, Xerox™ both sides of a small plate. This *Wedgwood* expert does not buy *Johnson Brothers, Franciscan, Enoch Wedgwood* or *Wedgwood, Ltd.*, and is not interested in glassware.

> Gloria Voss Beyer
> A Wedgwood China Cupboard
> 740 Honey Creek Parkway
> Milwaukee, WI 53213
> (414) 259-1025

☆ *Wedgwood* **commemorative ware transfer print china.** Earthenware or bone china plates, hollow ware, trivets, tiles, etc., that contain American scenes, views of historic places, children's topics, or scenes from literature. "We mainly want items of American interest, but will also buy some Canadian and Australian scenes." These pieces bear backstamps marked JOSIAH WEDGWOOD & SONS, WEDGWOOD ETRURIA or ETRURIA & BARLASTON. Calendar tiles are from 1879 to 1929. Those before 1890 are worth in excess of $200. Jugs such as the Washington Light Infantry depicting the Civil War are worth in excess of $400 each. "It's hard to tell what we don't want. People are better off to inquire by giving a good description or sending a photo or Xerox™ of the item and its marks. Some items will have to be seen before we can make an offer."

    Benton and Beverly Rosen
    Mansion House
    9 Kenilworth Way
    Pawtucket, RI 02860
        (401) 722-2927 winter   (508) 759-4303 summer

☆ *Haviland* **china for resale.** Buys sets or single unusual pieces. Especially wants jardiniers, claret jugs, unusual tea or toast sets, free form salads, syrup jugs, spoon trays, tea caddies, lemonade sets, and other unusual pieces. No individual saucers. If your Limoge china isn't marked *Haviland*, she doesn't want it. Pieces must be in mint condition with no wear or scratches. To sell your dishes, give the pattern name on the back-stamp, a photocopy of the pattern, and note the colors. Eleanor has 22,000 pieces in stock and has a computerized search service to help customers find other dishes.

    Eleanor Thomas
    Auld Lang Syne
    7600 Highway 120
    Jamestown, CA 95327
        (209) 984-DISH

☆ **French, American, or English china and stemware,** especially pieces by *Haviland, Castleton, Franciscan, Oxford, Royal Doulton, Lenox, Spode, Syracuse,* and *Wedgwood.* Wants **stemware** by *Cambridge, Duncan, Fostoria, Heisey, Imperial, Lenox, Rock Sharp,* and *Tiffin.* List only the perfect pieces, and give the measurements of all serving pieces. She does not buy German or Japanese china. Medley has been a dealer for 20+ years.

    Laura Medley
    Laura's China & Crystal
    2625 West Britton Road
    Oklahoma City, OK 73120
        (405) 755-0582

☆ *Royal Doulton, Royal Worcester,* and *Fitz and Floyd* **fine china and crystal by** *Fostoria, Gorham, Lenox, Royal Doulton* and selected patterns of *Mikasa* **and** *Noritake* are purchased for stock. Buys whole or partial sets. Some *Spode, Wedgwood* and *Willeroy and Boch* will be "purchased if I have a ready customer." She cannot use worn, damaged, or repaired pieces. "If an item is in fine condition, but I do not wish to buy it, I will try to refer the seller to someone else who may." Give the maker and pattern name and number. Send a Xerox™ if convenient for you. Connie has inherited the family business from her mom, Freda Bell, a lady whom we have recommended for years.

> Connie Stolz
> China Match & Crystal Match
> 9 Elmford Road
> Rochester, NY 14606
> (716) 338-3781

☆ **Grandmother's Ware - Chelsea - Applied Sprigware**... Whatever you call it, this mid 1800's English china, ironstone, stoneware and porcelain is sought by this veteran collector-dealer who is currently writing a book on this white ware with applied blue/lavender sprigs (grape, thistles, etc) accompanied by other design elements. She wants mugs, tureens, toilet sets, vases, and more. "I do not buy items with chips on rims, major cracks, or bad stains. Hairline cracks make any item worth less than $10." She does not want common cups and saucers with simple sprigs. Tell her the type of item, size, pattern, and maker's mark. Photo if possible. Xerox™ copy of the pattern is a good idea.

> Stephanie Schnatz
> 17 Tallow Court
> Baltimore, MD 21244
> (410) 955-5910 days   (410) 944-0819 eves

☆ **Dishes with dark blue decoration** made in England or the U.S. before the turn of the century. Many different makers, especially those pieces with impressed marks such as CLEWS, ADAMS, or HALL. Teapots, sugars, creamers, cups and saucers are particularly wanted, Staffordshire, flow blue, *Spode, Wedgwood* and historical patterns are all desirable, although items marked E.WEDGWOOD are not *the* Wedgwood and are a lot less valuable. Xerox™ flat pieces, photograph others. Send photo, description of condition and accurate drawing of marks found on the bottom if you'd like her to make an offer.

> Carol Payne
> Carol's Gallery
> 14455 Big Basin Way
> Saratoga, CA 95070
> (408) 867-7055

☆ **Crystal stemware**. Buys English, American, Japanese and European manufacturers, but is only interested in named and numbered patterns. Indicate the maker and pattern, and how many of each item you have. Do not count anything damaged.

>
> Old China Patterns Limited
> 1560 Brimley Road
> Scarborough, Ontario
> M1P 3G9, CANADA
>   (416) 299-8880   Fax: (416) 299-4721

☆ **Autumn Leaf (*Jewel Tea*) china** and other items marked with *Jewel Tea's* distinctive red, orange, and brown leaf pattern. He points out there are 300+ different pieces of Autumn Leaf china and that it takes an expert to tell the difference between a $10 piece of china and a $100 piece. Common cups, saucers, plates, and mixing bowls are only a dollar or two, but items like candle holders, teapots, bud vases, and butter dishes can bring $40 to $500 each, with a few worth more than $1,500. Silverplated and stainless steel *Jewel Tea* tableware is also highly collectible, bringing in excess of $10/$15 per item, with some as much as $100. Other Autumn Leaf products, including canisters, bean pots, and linens are also worth an inquiry. "If your item is in good condition, but it's not something I want to buy, I've got a dozen friends who I can route you to." Send a Stamped Self-Addressed Envelope with any requests. Dimensions are always a good idea. Annual membership in the National Autumn Leaf Collector's Club includes a 40+ page newsletter and is only $20.

>
> Tom Whipple
> National Autumn Leaf Collector's Club
> Route 16 Box 275
> Tulsa, OK 74131
>   (918) 227-0184

☆ ***Buffalo Pottery* or *Buffalo* china.** "I'll buy almost any marked piece made in that factory," he says.

>
> Seymour Altman
> 8970 Main Street
> Clarence, NY 14031
>   (716) 634-4488

☆ ***Deldare Ware*** made by the *Buffalo Pottery Company*. No damaged pieces, please.

>
> Jerome Puma
> 78 Brinton Street
> Buffalo, NY 14214
>   (716) 838-5674

☆ **Nippon and** *Noritake* **china**. "We're seeking large vases, urns, portrait pieces, dolls, chocolate and tea sets, jugs, wall plaques, smoke sets, humidors, and anything else that's quality and perfect. We'll buy *Coralene, Moriage*, blown-outs, rectangulars, pieces with silver overlay, you name it! We're also in the market for *Noritake* with Art Deco decorations of men and women. Call or write if you have any."

> Mark Griffin and Earl Smith
> 1417 Steele Street
> Fort Myers, FL 33901
> (813) 334-0083

☆ *Noritake* **dinnerware** in full or partial sets of either fine china or stoneware. Also buys selected pieces of **crystal stemware including** *Fostoria, Cambridge, Heisey, Morgantown, Tiffin* (both etched and colored), and *Imperial Candlewick*. This replacement service does not want *Fostoria* American, *Noritake* Azalea or individual art pieces and figurines of *Noritake*. Give her a list of pieces along with the pattern name if you know it. If you don't, send a photo or good drawing.

> Michelle Fredrickson
> Miki's Crystal & China
> 100 Bridge Avenue
> Delano, MN 55328
> (612) 972-6885 Fax: (612) 972-6865

☆ *Noritake* **china in Azalea pattern.** Also *Noritake's* scenic Tree in the Meadow pattern and all raised gold patterns by *Noritake*. No chips, cracks, or worn gold or paint. Provide all info on back of pieces.

> Ken Kipp
> Box 116
> Allenwood, PA 17810
> (717) 538-1440

☆ *Noritake* **china in "Azalea" or "Tree in the Meadow"** patterns in any quantity from single pieces to entire sets, as long are there are no chips, cracks, or worn gold or paint. Azalea pieces are backstamped "#19322." Tree in the Meadow pieces must have blue water in the foreground and a tree in the rear of the house. Serving pieces, children's sets, and salesmen's samples are the most desirable and will bring from $100 to $1,000. Does not want "Azalea" pattern with a blue backstamp that reads NIPPON. Include the dimensions of your pieces.

> Gloria Munsell
> Box 116
> Allenwood, PA 17810
> (717) 538-1440 Fax: (610) 965-2872

☆ **Sets or pieces of German, Bavarian, Czechoslovakian, and Austrian china** in fine condition. Companies stocked include *Johann Haviland, Bavarian, Heinrich, Fronconia, Meissen, Rosenthal Thomas, Royal Heidelberg, Krautheim,* and many more. China need not be old, just discontinued. They also purchase **a few French patterns**, but do not want French *Haviland,* Japanese china, or English china. "We buy no china with cracks, crazing, chips, or with the color in a pattern worn off, although we will accept pieces with a slight amount of gold wear. We ask that anyone wishing to sell would send us a colored photocopy of a 6" or 8" plate. Copy the front for the design and the back so we can see the hallmark. We also need a good color photo of a plate and a cup. The cup should be photographed in silhouette so we can see the shape of the handle and if the cup is footed or flat. We will quote a fair purchase price for any items we can use. If we cannot use what you have, we will try to tell you how you can sell it in your locality."

> Joan Nackman
> 56 Meadowbrook
> Ballwin, MO 63011
> (314) 227-3444

☆ *Clarus Ware* **plates, bowls, vases and other china.** "We also buy old pieces of *Pope Gosser China Ware* and want any vase, bowl, plate, or other china signed AST VAN HISE."

> C.W. and Hilda Roderick
> 27858 TR 31
> Warsaw, OH 43844
> (614) 824-3083

☆ **Phoenix bird china,** both English and Japanese made is wanted. As an advanced collector, she is interested only in serving pieces and unusual shapes in the pattern. She does not want cups, saucers, small sauce dishes, bread & butter plates, or 7 1/4" salad plates. Please give condition, noting if any hairline cracks exist. Give the diameter of plates or bowls, and describe any markings on the bottom. Please tell her what you think the item is worth. She also edits an infrequent newsletter on this striking blue/white china for $8 a year. Her four books on Phoenix are available at $16 each postpaid.

> Joan Oates
> 685 South Washington
> Constantine, MI 49042
> (616) 435-8353

☆ **Flying phoenix china.**

> Carl Cotting
> 1441 Crowell Road
> Vienna, VA 22182
> (703) 759-5646

☆ **Series Ware** by *Royal Doulton* includes hundreds of shapes and patterns of pitchers, mugs, plates, and other useful but highly decorated items. This popular transfer ware with a hand-painted look includes a wide variety of themes such as motoring, golfing, fishing, and coaching. Value is dependent on the rarity and desirability of the form and the image. There have been four books written on *Doulton* Series Ware, so you can get information at your local public library. If your item is for sale, call Ed, who lectures frequently in the U.S. and England, and has edited price guides to *Royal Doulton*. Also buys ***Royal Doulton* figurines, figural bottles and red animals** (see his listings in this book under Animals, Whiskey, and Figurines for more information). He is not interested in buying dinnerware, and does not do pattern matching.

> Ed Pascoe, Pascoe & Co.
> 101 Almeria Avenue
> Coral Gables, FL 33134
>   (800) 872-0195   Fax: (305) 445-3305

☆ *Clarice Cliff Bizarre Ware.* This English hand painted pottery is decorated with fanciful, geometric, and floral themes. Most pieces are marked, often with the name of the artist, but usually CLARICE CLIFF or BIZARRE. Does not want transfer patterns, only painted ones such as Crocus, Fantasque, Delecia, Caprice, Ravel, and many others. A photo or photocopy is very important as the company made so many patterns, it's almost impossible to know which you have without seeing it.

> Darryl Rehr
> 2591 Military Ave.
> Los Angeles, CA 90064
>   (310) 477-5229

☆ *Coors* **pottery and porcelain**, including lines of dinnerware, art pottery, older ashtrays, Colorado State Fair memorabilia, spittoons, malted milk containers, advertising (including paper), etc. "I also buy other *Coors* Malted Milk and dairy items such as labels, boxes, back bar containers, milk bottles, and all advertising related to them." Does not want small vases, common mugs with lions on them, newer bar ashtrays, *Coors Beer* ads, or anything newer than 1950. "You may call my toll free number, workdays 9-5 MST, to get an estimate or offer on *Coors* pottery. I cannot answer questions about brewery items, but if you have something very old, I may be able to recommend a buyer."

> Jo Ellen Winther
> 8449 West 75th Way
> Arvada, CO 80005
>   (800) 872-2345 days   (303) 421-2371 eves

☆ **Oyster plates.** Nothing damaged, please.
　　　Sheldon Katz
　　　211 Roanoke Ave.
　　　Riverhead, NY 11901
　　　　　(516) 369-1100

☆ **Eggcups.** If you have a fine eggcup to sell, the *Eggcup Collectors Corner* may be your best source of information. Sample copies of this club newsletter cost only $5 and will give you insights into cups and their prices, plus a bibliography. When you order your sample, tell Joan why you want one and she'll pick an appropriate issue. Eggcup Collectors' Club members share information about buying and selling.
　　　Joan George, editor, *Eggcup Collectors Corner*
　　　67 Stevens Ave.
　　　Old Bridge, NJ 08857
　　　　　(908) 679-8924

☆ *Warwick* **china, especially portrait items.** Include a photo with your complete description, and he'll return it. Promises to answer every letter regarding the work of this fine American china maker. Prefers you to set the price wanted, but "amateurs should still write."
　　　Jeff Mauck
　　　1900 Warwood Avenue
　　　Wheeling WV 26003
　　　　　(304) 277-2356

☆ **Roseville Juvenile china** designed for children not dolls.
　　　Bill and Linda Montgomery
　　　12111 SE River Road
　　　Milwaukee, OR 97222
　　　　　(503) 652-2992

☆ **Children's dishes.** "Any china used by children to eat or drink" is sought, "but I prefer American items, and I prefer those made by *Roseville* (both unmarked and those marked R on the bottom), *S.E.G., Paul Revere* or *Dedham*. No damaged pieces.
　　　Steve Kelley
　　　PO Box 695
　　　Desert Hot Springs, CA 92240
　　　　　(619) 329-3206

Packing china for shipment is not as hard as you think, but does require some care. Never allow two pieces to touch. Ask your buyer for specific packing instructions.

☆ **Pictorial souvenir china** with views of towns, streets, and places of interest. Especially interested in pictorial china with New England views, but all are considered. Indicate what the scene is, where the item was made, and whether there are any cracks or chips. Gary publishes *Antique Souvenir Collectors News,* the magazine marketplace for antique souvenir plates, mugs, and other items.

  Gary Leveille
  PO Box 562
  Great Barrington, MA 01230
    (413) 528-5490

☆ **College plates** depicting scenes or seals of universities and colleges. Prefers those made by *Wedgwood, Spode* and *Lamberton.* Items must be in perfect condition without cracks or chips, even if they have been professionally restored. He prefers you to set the price you want, but will make offers.

  Pat Klein
  PO Box 262
  East Berlin, CT 06023
    (203) 828-3973 eves

☆ **Presidential and patriotic English urns, vases and mugs** with American historical motifs, pictures of political figures, battles, or famous events. May be any type of china by any maker. A delft teapot advocating NO STAMP ACT would bring around $8,000.

  Rex Stark
  49 Wethersfield Road
  Bellingham, MA 02019
    (508) 966-0994

☆ **Advertising china made by** *Royal Doulton.* All types including ashtrays, jugs, mugs, bottles, ginger beers, display signs. Old and rare pieces do not have to be in perfect condition to be considered for purchase, but you must indicate any flaws in your description. Make sure to mention the item, the product being advertised, size, color, condition, and any markings.

  Diane Alexander
  20834 San Simeon Way #70-C
  North Miami Beach, FL 33179
    (305) 770-4422

TABLE ITEMS

☆ **Sterling flatware and serving pieces** are wanted by the nation's largest buyer and seller of second hand sterling tableware. "If a customer sends a SASE and the name of their pattern and its maker, we will send a written offer." If you do not know the name of the pattern, make a picture on a copy machine and list how many pieces you have. "Most sterling is standard, so if you know the name of the pattern, we know exactly what you have. As a result, we do not need to see what you have before buying. Please note, we do not make offers on non-standard items. We don't offer on coin silver, souvenir items, old unmarked tea sets, and the like, although we will consider them for purchase if you send a photograph or photocopy and set the price you want. We only make offers on standard items." If an item is damaged, worn, or monogrammed, be certain to note that fact. MidweSterling also repairs and restores flatware.

> Thomas Ridley, Head Buyer, MidweSterling
> 4311 NE Vivion Road, Dept HY
> Kansas City, MO 64119
>   (816) 454 1990   Fax: (816) 454-1605

☆ **Sterling and silver plated flatware,** especially made by *Holmes & Edwards, 1847 Rogers,* and *Community.* Also all old grape patterns. Send the information on the back of your silver, and a photocopy if you don't know the name of the pattern. An SASE will get you a pattern guide. Particularly interested in more unusual pieces such as pie forks, punch ladles, ice tongs, sardine forks, etc. "We do not want monogrammed, damaged or worn silver except large serving pieces or very rare patterns." A 30 year veteran of buying through the mail.

> L.C. Fisher, Silver Exchange
> Route 8 Box 554 (Hwy 190 East)
> Huntsville, TX 77340
>   (409) 295-7661

☆ **Sterling silver flatware and serving pieces** as well as novelty items such as goblets, mint julep cups, and trays, especially in elaborate antique patterns. You should take photos of larger pieces, and make photocopies of flatware. Everything must be in fine condition, cautions this 25 year veteran dealer. **Will also buy unusual old silver plated serving pieces** such as tea services, large trays, and elaborate multi-branched center-pieces which held dishes, trays, or candles but she is not interested in silver plated knives, forks and spoons, ordinary small silver plated items, or in silver coins.

> Helen Cox, As You Like It Silver Shop
> 3025 Magazine Street
> New Orleans, LA 70117
>   (800) 828-2311   Fax: (504) 895-4149

☆ **European sterling silver and silverplate** from companies like *Christophle, Buccellatti, Puiforcat*, etc. Buys and sells.
>Russ Burkett
>PO Box 4231
>Mission Viejo, CA 92690
>   (714) 364-3844

☆ **Pickle castors** and other castor sets for the Victorian table. Sets must be complete and in fine condition, with no missing or broken parts. A photo is suggested.
>Betty Bird
>Antiques, Etc.
>107 Ida Street
>Mt. Shasta, CA 96067

☆ **Unusual condiment sets.** Combination salt, pepper, and mustard sets are wanted if they are unusual and figural. Wants pieces without chips or repairs, but will consider slightly damaged goods if the piece is extremely unusual. Especially likes German sets, and those with designs related to water. A picture is important.
>Sylvia Tompkins
>25-C Center Drive
>Lancaster, PA 17601
>   (717) 569-9788

☆ **Victorian figural silverplate napkin rings.** Wants small figural napkin rings. Describe your rings to her well, including all markings, and "I'll probably know what you have."
>Sandra Whitson
>PO Box 272
>Lititz, PA 17543
>   (717) 626-4978

☆ **Napkin rings and other small silver objects** such as **children's rattles**, which are made of silver in the shape of animals, people or other objects. Must be in fine condition. A photo is suggested, Make sure to list all names, numbers and other marks.
>Betty Bird
>Antiques, Etc.
>107 Ida Street
>Mt. Shasta, CA 96067

☆ **Open salt cellars.** Salt cellars are small open bowls, often with a tiny spoon, that were used instead of salt shakers at the table. They can be almost any material or shape, including humans, animals, and other figures. "I am especially looking for art glass, colored glass, pressed pattern glass and silver with colored glass liners, and pay from a few dollars to hundreds, depending on the quality and rarity. I do not want plain clear glass (except in sets), but I will buy individual salt spoons. To sell to me, you need to provide a clear photo, dimensions and a description of any markings you find on the piece. Condition is vital. Any chips, cracks, flakes, or nicks may drop the value by 70% or more. Every major glass company, china manufacturer and potter, as well as many silversmiths, made these so there are plenty out there somewhere." Buys collections or individual cellars. Will also buy **condiment sets and salt and pepper sets which contain open salt cellars.**

Betty Bird, Antiques, Etc.
107 Ida Street
Mt. Shasta, CA 96067

☆ **Gold or sterling silver open salt dishes,** American or European, in any size, with or without glass liners, as long as they are in fine condition. Describe well, and include your asking price if you are a dealer. Amateur sellers may request help from this veteran appraiser.

Monica Murphy, Savannah's Antiques
9337 Lenel Place
Dallas, TX 75220
(214) 352-4137

☆ **Toast racks** (silver or ceramic frames, usually footed, with 6-8 wire racks to hold toast upright at the table). Values from $25 to $175 depending on fanciness and rarity. Fine condition only. Please draw any maker's marks and give measurements.

Carol Payne, Carol's Gallery
14455 Big Basin Way
Saratoga, CA 95070
(408) 867-7055

☆ **Tea caddies** (3" to 6" high boxes for holding loose tea at the table). Wants square or round, hinged or lift-off lids, especially in silverplate although wood/silver combination will be considered. Values vary from $50 to $300 depending on rarity. Photos are helpful. Describe size, shape, decoration, and condition. Xerox™ the bottom to show marks if you can't draw accurately.

Carol Payne
14455 Big Basin Way
Saratoga, CA 95070
(408) 867-7055

SPOONS

☆ **Sterling silver souvenir spoons**, U.S. or foreign, particularly those made between 1890 and 1920. "Almost any spoon which is a turn-of-the-century quality souvenir will be considered for purchase or accepted on consignment for my auctions." Of most interest are spoons with:
- Enameled bowls, especially *Gorham;*
- Figural handles;
- Special topics like Negroes, Indians, military, coins, music, historic sites, etc.;
- Famous persons, especially on European spoons;
- World's Fair themes before 1920.

"I only want old, pre-WWI souvenir spoons, not modern spoons which are typically sold in airports and tourist shops." Values range from a few dollars for some, $20-$30 for most, to more than $300 for top items like the *Gorham* spoon with their factory depicted in the bowl. Please make a photocopy of your spoon(s) and make a drawing or copy of the markings on the back. If you don't Xerox™ the spoon, please give the total length.

> Chris McGlothlin
> "The Original Spoon Auctioneer"
> 780 Rock Springs Road
> Kingsport, TN 37664
> (615) 239-6776

☆ **Sterling spoons with "cute" Negro figures.** Will pay up to $150 for enameled teaspoons and $100 for enameled demitasse spoons.

> Elijah Singley
> 2301 Noble Ave.
> Springfield, IL 62704
> (217) 546-5143 eves

☆ **Silver spoons with advertising** on them. Either sterling or plate.

> W.T. Atkinson
> 1217 Bayside Circle West
> Wilmington, NC 28405

CAST IRON COOKWARE

☆ **Cast iron muffin pans,** gem pans, popover pans, and maple sugar molds in unusual patterns and shapes. Also interested in old catalogs, etc., which list multi-sectioned baking or muffin pans. Buys *any* cast iron item marked *Griswold*. Will pay $500+ for *Griswold* #13, 50, and 2800 pans. If you're a dealer, send for his wants list. Publishes a bimonthly 8 page newsletter, *Kettles 'n Cookware*, for $20.

> David "The Pan Man" Smith
> PO Box B
> Perrysburg, NY 14129
> (716) 532-5154

☆ **Early kitchen items made of cast iron** or of wood which has been folk carved or decorated are wanted by this important dealer.

> Louis Picek
> PO Box 340
> West Branch, IA 52358
> (319) 643-2065

☆ **Iron pans and broilers in odd or decorative shapes,** including pans for muffins, popovers, rolls, and maple sugar molds. Roll pans shaped like hearts bring $100 and up, while those shaped like fruits and vegetables are worth $150. Pans made by *GF Filley* start at $75. Cast iron broilers look like strange frying pans with grid work, slots, and holes. Not interested in reproductions (they have rough surface and grind marks) or in tin pans of any type. Trace your pans or photocopy.

> David Smith
> PO Box B
> Perrysburg, NY 14129
> (716) 532-5154

☆ **Griswold cast iron.** This veteran collector is interested only in less common forms in excellent condition.

> Alan Stone
> PO Box 500 or 5170 County Road 33
> Honeoye, NY 14471
> (716) 229-2700

KITCHEN TOOLS

☆ **Apple parers**, but only specific ones. He will pay from $200 to $500 for the following brands only: *Bergner, Browne's Nonpareil, Buchi, Champion, Climax by Brokaw, Dandy, Eagle, Electric, Empire State, Excelsion, GEM, Jersey, Little Giant, Mammoth, Maxam, Monarch, Nonpareil, Oriole, Oscillator, Parker, Peerless, Returnable, Rices, SS Hersey, Selick's, Star (Foster & Cotton), Standard, Thompson, Tripp Bros., Victor, Wiggins,* and *Yankee.* He does not buy other brands or rusted or broken parers. Give the name and date, if marked, the material from which it's made, and the number of gears.

    John Lambert
    117 East High
    Mount Vernon, OH 43050
       (614) 393-2508

☆ **Butter molds** that are hand carved of wood, ivory or clay. Will consider all sizes and forms, especially those with carvings of people, animals, or things rather than abstract patterns. Does not want machine carved items or anything new. Give the shape and size, material, and make a Xerox™ of the design.

    Carl Cotting
    1441 Crowell Road
    Vienna, VA 22182
       (703) 759-5646

☆ **Hand can openers.**
    Craig Dinner
    PO Box 4399
    Sunnyside, NY 11104
       (718) 729-3850

☆ **Tin can openers.** Will consider wall, counter, or hand operated kinds, but he wants old ones (1810-1940), not modern openers. There are more than 1,200 patents for can openers! Give all information that is stamped on the opener.

    Joe Young
    PO Box 587
    Elgin, IL 60123
       (708) 695-0108

☆ **Fancy or unusual nutcrackers,** big or small, made of iron, brass, wood, or any other material. A sketch or photocopy is suggested. Include dimensions, colors, and all writing or marks.

    C. J. Davis
    East 4400 English Point Road
    Hayden Lake, ID 83835

☆ **Toasters.** "I buy early electric toasters with unusual mechanisms and/or design, especially those made of porcelain in whole or in part and those with buttons or cranks that flip the toast. I do not want toasters in poor condition, or most pop-up types." Please give the make, model, color, and condition. Dealers, price your goods; amateurs may ask for offer. Will pay $600-$750 for a *Pan-Electric* porcelain toaster.

　　Dan Lunzmann
　　PO Box 482
　　Auburn, NE 68305
　　　　(402) 274-4555　or　(402) 274-4931

☆ **Toasters.** "I'll buy old or unusual electric toasters in good, non-corroded condition, as long as there are no pieces missing. I am especially interested in very old or very unusual toasters, porcelain models and ones with toast racks. Prices vary greatly, according to rarity. Mint condition examples and ones with original boxes bring the best prices, but toasters do not have to work to be desirable. I am not interested in pop-up toasters unless they are very unusual. Please call or write if you have specific questions." Give the maker's name and model number. A sketch is helpful, but a photo is best. An accurate description of condition is essential. Toasters bring $10 and up, with rare ones bringing you $100 or more.

　　Joe Lukach
　　7111 Deframe Court
　　Arvada, CO 80004
　　　　(303) 422-8970　　(303) 623-2262

☆ **Hand operated egg beaters, cream whips, and glass bottomed mixers** are wanted, if they are American made and before 1920. Buys either rotary or dasher (up and down) type, wall or table style. Cast iron beaters are particularly desirable, especially those with "Flat fold" beaters. There are a great many beaters he'll buy, and quite a few he won't. No beaters with plastic handles or stainless steel dashes. No *A&J* hand held rotary egg beaters, no *Ladd* hand beaters, no *Ekco* or *Maynard* brand beaters, no butter churns (except *Dazey* models 10, 20, or 30). "No electric beaters," he says, but is willing to make exception for pre-1920 electric beaters in excellent condition. Nearly all had dates and maker's marks to help you describe them. A photo is requested, but "even a pencil sketch or outline will help." Include all dates and everything printed. Describe condition accurately, including the glass jar. "I pay a premium for original labels, containers or pamphlets accompanying desirable mixers. The more nearly perfect, the higher its value."

　　Reid Cooper
　　5639 Amaya Drive #293
　　La Mesa, CA 91942
　　　　(619) 286-1563　eves

☆ **Egg beaters.** "I'll buy pre-1910 cast iron rotary crank egg beaters, the older the better, the more unusual the better." Also buys rotary cranks that came with jars, especially looking for the *E-A-S-Y* and *Family* brands. Does not want any beaters after 1910. Descriptions should include the height and any markings. He is author of *Beat This: The Eggbeater Chronicles* and editor of the Kitchen Collectibles newsletter, available for $24/year.

> Don Thornton
> 1345 Poplar Avenue
> Sunnyvale, CA 94087

☆ **Tunbridge Ware** is attractive woodware with geometric or mosaic designs, or with embedded pictures created with cut woods of different colors. She buys boxes, candlestick holders, tea caddies, etc. made in Tunbridge. These pieces are rarely marked. If in doubt, send a good photo or a photocopy of the patterned portion of the item.

> Lucille Malitz, Lucid Antiques
> PO Box KH
> Scarsdale, NY 10583
> (914) 636-7825

☆ **Twentieth century plastic items.** This veteran collector buys:
- **Dishes**, singles or sets, especially serving pieces; look for *Branchell, Color-Flyte, Arrowhead, Russel Wright Ideal Ware*, others;
- **Salt and peppers**, especially boxed figurals or geometrics;
- **Character mugs** of people or animals, especially *Dennis the Menace* by *F&F; Soaky* **Bubble Bath** and other figurals;
- **Cookie jar** figurals in plastic; *Funny Face, Big Pitcher, Tony the Tiger* and other characters.

Give the dimensions, colors, and maker (if you can), as well as a piece count and statement of condition.

> Mary Anne Enriquez
> 1741 West Albion Street
> Chicago, IL 60626
> (312) 243-3425

☆ **Russian samovars** from before 1930. Please send picture with descriptive information and a statement of condition. He needs to know the size, shape, type of metal, markings, condition, and whether there are any additional matching pieces. He prefers you to price what you have. Wants written material on samovars, especially catalogs.

> Jerome Marks
> 120 Corporate Woods #260
> Rochester, NY 14623
> (716) 475-0220   Fax: (716) 475-0208

KITCHEN CERAMICS & GLASS

☆ **Figural cookie jars.** "I'll buy amusing, colorful jars in the shape of various people and animals dating before 1950. Especially want those depicting fairy tales, nursery rhyme and cartoon characters." Also buys **teapots and pitchers from the Art Deco era.** "I'll buy solid color Deco era teapots and pitchers that exemplify the streamlined, geometric designs of the late Art Deco/moderne period." Makers to look for are *Fiesta, Riviera, Harlequin,* and others. Especially interested in *Hall* teapots. No items with gold trim or other decoration. "I do not buy jars if they have any damage at all." Wants a photo or good description.

    Kier Linn
    2591 Military Avenue
    Los Angeles, CA 90064
      (310) 477-5229

☆ **Cookie Jars,** old and new, are wanted, but only those which advertise a product or are three-dimensional representations of comic or other characters. Especially wants Disney's standing Alice in Wonderland, for which she will pay $1,000. Fine condition is vital. No free appraisals, but will make offers if your item is really for sale.

    Mona Cook
    3288 White Cloud Drive
    Hacienda Heights, CA 91745
      (818) 333-7107 after 6 p.m.

☆ **Figural cookie jars** are wanted by Chicago's only shop devoted exclusively to kitchen counter novelties. Wants figural ceramic jars and jar tops, but nothing cracked or repaired. Jars that aren't figural aren't of interest. She also buys **figural salt and pepper shakers.** She declares a photo to be essential, plus wants you to describe all markings on the bottoms of jars or salt sets. Make certain to mention every chip! Prefers you to price what you want to sell. She charges $10 per jar to make appraisals for insurance or estate purposes.

    Mercedes DiRenzo, Jazz'e Junque
    3831 North Lincoln Avenue
    Chicago, IL 60613
      (312) 472-1500

☆ **Figural cookie jars**, especially featuring Disney, comic characters, advertising, Negroes, unique animals, etc. Brands to look for include *Poppytrail, Metlox, Brayton Laguna, USA, Abbingdon, McCoy,* others. Prefers no damage, but will consider some restoration. Please include a good description and sketch or photo for this major jar dealer.

    Loretta Hamburg
    PO Box 1305
    Woodland Hills, CA 91365
      (818) 346-9884   Fax: (818) 346-0215

☆ **Jadite green (a milky light green) or delphite blue (a similar blue) kitchen ware.** Wants bowls, reamers, canisters, **salt and peppers** and "anything else." A wide range of items, often in a variety of shapes, were made. Green pieces start at $4, with rare pieces reaching $100, whereas the blue is much more scarce with most pieces starting around $75. Tell what piece you have, its size, whether it is marked on the bottom (most weren't), and the condition, indicating any flakes or chips in the rim and base, and the condition of the painted decoration on canisters, salts, etc. There are other similar glass makers, and very little is marked, so it's best if Steve looks at a photo of what you have. "I feel badly for your readers," he says, "because most of what I'm offered isn't what I'm looking for, but I urge them to keep trying."

> Steve Kelley
> PO Box 695
> Desert Hot Springs, CA 92240
> (619) 329-3206

☆ **Older fruit (canning) jars with unusual closures or in unusual colors** other than aqua or clear. Colors wanted include amber, brown, deep green, and shades of cobalt blue. Is willing to pay up to $400 for a pint sized embossed cadiz jar with a glass screw top. Also wants pre-1960 **advertising**, promotional brochures, letterheads, signs and paperweights from jar and bottle manufacturers, including **wooden canning jar boxes** or box ends, which generally bring $10-$30. Give the size and color, and report *exactly* what is embossed on the jar. Note all cracks, chips, dings, or unwashable stains.

> Tom and Deena Caniff
> 1223 Oak Grove Avenue
> Steubenville, OH 43952
> (614) 282-8918

☆ **Glass knives** are wanted, especially those colored amber, emerald green, opal, and cobalt blue, as well as those with ribbed handles or combinations of clear blades with colored handles. "I would really love to find a 6.5" *Westmoreland* with a certain type of thumb guard. I'd also love to find a 'glass pig,' the blob of glass with two or three knives attached, before they were broken off." Buys printed material, catalogs, photos, etc. on all aspects of 1920 to 1940's glass knives. Brands include *Kitchen Gadget Company, Kitchen Novelty Company, Buffalo Knife, ES Pease, John Didio*, and a number of others. Please describe the size, colors, pattern on the handle and the condition. You must price your knife.

> Michele Rosewitz
> PO Box 3843
> San Bernardino, CA 92413
> (909) 862-8534

☆ **Glass knives** are wanted in most configurations and colors. Values run from $8 to $200 or more. It's worth having her check out your knife because it's difficult for amateurs to tell the rare from the common. Send a photocopy and describe color. She edits a quarterly newsletter about glass knives. If you want a reply, send an SASE.

Adrienne Escoe
PO Box 342
Los Alamitos, CA 90720
(310) 430-6479 eves

☆ **Salt and pepper shakers.** "I buy figural shakers made of pottery, porcelain, china or plastic. I pay most for Black Americana, Disney and other comic characters, advertising, and figural nodders. I especially value old comic character sets such as German porcelain Mickey Mouse, Kewpies, and Felix the Cat. Shakers that are part of a condiment set (on a tray with mustard jar, etc.) are also wanted, especially those with comic characters, baseball, nursery rhyme, dinosaurs, and outer space themes. Anthropomorphic sets (animals or inanimate objects dressed as people) are of particular interest. Topic and form are more important in determining value than age or country of origin. When you contact me with shakers for sale, please tell me the size, color, and condition. You must note any chips, cracks, or other defects. Photos are helpful. Send a long SASE for my illustrated wants list. I am an active buyer and welcome all offers except I do not buy wooden or glass shakers."

Judy Posner
Route 1   Box 273
Effort, PA 18330
(717) 629-6583   Fax: (717) 629-0521

☆ **Salt and pepper shakers.** "After 35 years, I'm looking only for fine condition novelty shakers, especially those featuring Negro stereotypes, but I also buy animals, people, and other types of objects. I'll buy your collection, no matter how large or small. Also want German-made **condiment sets with mustard jars**. About the only thing I don't want is reproductions or shakers made of wood. Please send a photo or video of your collection. I would like the seller to tell me the price they'd like for their collection." Larry is president of the Novelty Salt and Pepper Shakers Club ($20/year) and co-author of *Salt and Pepper Shakers: Over 1001 Shakers,* available from him for $22.

Larry "The Salt & Pepper Man" Carey
PO Box 329
Mechanicsburg, PA 17055
(717) 766-0868

COOKBOOKS

☆ **Hard and soft covered cookbooks,** especially soft cover advertising recipe books published by various food companies, such as *Jell-O, Rumford* baking powder, etc., especially fine condition ones from before 1900. Will pay $50 each for the 1930's *Jell-o* cookbooks based on the OZ books by Frank Baum. The founder of the Cook Book Collectors Club, and editor of its newsletter, does not want appliance company recipe books, diet books, or other modern health cookbooks such as heart and cholesterol related cookbooks. As with all books for sale, sellers should give complete bibliographic information. Sellers must price the books they offer.

    Col. Bob Allen
    Cookbook Collectors Club of America
    PO Box 56
    St. James, MO 65559
       (314) 265-8296 anytime

☆ **Spiral bound church, community, charity, fund raiser, ethnic and other privately published cookbooks** with limited distribution.

    Bob Roberts
    PO Box 152
    Guilderland, NY 12084

☆ **Spiral bound church, community or other privately published cookbooks.** Will buy singles, collections or multiple copies of the same title. Please indicate the sponsoring organization and the number of recipes. Mention the quantity you have, the original retail price, and the price you want for them all wholesale. Helen publishes cookbooks and a newsletter for recipe collectors.

    Helen Jump
    PO Box 171
    Zionsville, IN 46077

☆ **Cookbooks and related pamphlets** from before 1950. State condition and price or just ship for immediate offer.

    Alan Levine
    PO Box 1577
    Bloomfield, NJ 07003

MISCELLANEOUS HOUSEHOLD ITEMS

☆ **Desk, ceiling, or pedestal fans** that are antique or unusual, especially mechanical fans not powered by electricity. Wants brands like *G.E., Westinghouse, Emerson, Peerless, Diehl* and others, but especially those made before 1920 or with unusual mechanisms. These early fans are usually cast iron and brass. Also wants literature, catalogs, ads and other information about fans and the companies that made them. He has no interest in steel fans made after 1940. If you want to sell your fan, include the brand, nameplate information, dimensions of the blades, number of blades, and what the various parts are made of, if you can. When describing condition, indicate whether your fan operates. Michael is president of the American Fan Collectors Association and editor of its quarterly newsletter.
> Michael Breedlove, Antique Fans of Indiana
> 15633 Cold Spring Court
> Granger, IN 46530
> (800) 858-3267

☆ **Fans** with brass blades and cages. Also wants loose brass blades and cages, name tags, motors, oscillating mechanisms, advertising for fans as well as fan and motor catalogs. Also wants ceiling fans "made by companies you never heard of before" but will also buy *Western Electric* and G.E. if they are very ornate. Does not want fans with steel cages or steel blades, but will buy parts of non-working old fans. Give the size of the blade and cage, the information on the motor tag, and the condition. Dealers, price your goods. Amateurs may request offers.
> Steve Cunningham
> 3200 Ashland Drive
> Bedford, TX 76021
> (817) 267-9851   Fax: (817) 267-0387

☆ **Early and unusual floor and desk fans.** Buys electric fans from before 1915 (check your patent dates). Very interested in fans not propelled by electricity, such as wind-up, heat engine, water powered, battery powered, etc. Has some interest in ceiling fans, but does not want fans by *G.E.* or fans made in the 1920's or later.
> Kevin Shail
> 30 Old Middle Road
> Brookfield, CT 06804
> (203) 775-7015

☆ **Wall model match safes made of cast iron.** No others, no matter how early or how lovely.
> George Fougere
> 67 East Street
> North Grafton, MA 01536

☆ *Glascock* **stoves and other ephemera.** "We want cook stoves, heaters, ranges and other items (whether complete or not) produced by G.T. Glascock & Son[s] or Glascock Stove & Mfg. Co. of Greensboro, NC. Also want all advertising, catalogs, and other items related to Glascock. I'd even like a photo of your stove if it's still in use!" There were many models, and stoves were produced under many names, such as *Carolina, Charter, Carbon Banner, Blue Ridge, Victor, Tar Heel* and many more. This company historian is interested in everything you have. Do not try to repair or repaint anything, please. Please send a photo, and anything you know about the piece's history and use.

> Nollie Neill, Jr.
> PO Box 38
> Ennice, NC 28623
> (910) 657-8152   Fax: (910) 282-8132

☆ **Washing machines.** "I buy old and unusual washing machines from 1935, usually wooden, galvanized, or copper tubs with wringers, although some hand-operated varieties did not have wringers. What may look worse than junk may be quite restorable and indeed an exciting machine so you are encouraged to inquire. I usually do not buy machines with porcelain tubs. If you have something I want, I'll pick it up so send a good sharp photo and list any information on the nameplate."

> Lee Maxwell
> 35901 WCR 31
> Eaton, CO 80615
> (303) 454-3856

☆ **Pressing irons**. "I'll buy unusual pressing irons of all types including goffering irons, crimping irons, fluters, charcoal heated irons, slug irons, *Pyrex* glass irons, miniature irons of any material, irons with animals or other figures for handles, ruffle irons, hat irons, and flower irons used in making artificial flowers." He also buys advertising for irons by various companies and some smoothing boards. If you have an **unusual electric iron**, especially if it's in its original box, he encourages you to inquire. He does not want common cast iron sad irons or ordinary electrics. Dave is author of *Irons by Irons*, available for $44 postpaid, and *Pressing Iron Patents,* available for $23 postpaid.

> Dave Irons
> 223 Covered Bridge Road
> Northampton, PA 18067
> (610) 262-9335

☆ **Miniature sad (flat) irons.** Wants irons smaller than 4 inches only. No electric irons, no matter how early.

> George Fougere
> 67 East Street
> North Grafton, MA 01536

☆ **Vacuum cleaners** that are hand powered. "I pay well for information leading to the location of unusual and scarce items, and am prepared to travel anywhere. I buy single items or entire collections, and for the right items, I pay in cash immediately without fuss or bother."

>Peter Frei
>26 Marquista Road
>Worcester, MA 01606
>(800) 942-8968

☆ **American sewing machines from before 1875,** especially rare early treadle machines with low serial numbers for which he will pay from $1,000-$10,000. Small hand operated machines in the shape of animals are of particular interest. Also photographs of sewing machines in use before 1890. Tell him the maker and the serial number as well as the condition. If there is no name, send a photograph. Carter does not buy *Singer, White, Wheeler & Wilson, Willcox & Gibbs*, or other machines with brand names you recognize, nor does he buy treadle machines in oak cases, or any sewing machine with a chrome or nickel plated flywheel. "High serial numbers on your machine mean it's a common one and of no collector interest." His beautiful new *Encyclopedia of Early American Sewing Machines* is available for $49.

>Carter Bays
>143 Springlake Road
>Columbia, SC 29206
>(800) 332-2297

☆ **Light bulbs** (1878-1905) with ball or other tips on the end of the glass bulb. Also wants screw in plugs, and socket adaptors that look like upsidedown mushrooms. Also wants **all types of pre 1900 electrical items:** ammeters, switches, and especially bipolar motors by *Crocker-Wheeler, Holtzer-Cabot, C&C* and others.

>Steve Cunningham
>3200 Ashland Drive
>Bedford, TX 76021
>(817) 267-9851   Fax: (817) 267-0387

☆ **Figural light bulbs and neon glow lights** are wanted by this long time collector. Christmas figurals are preferred, but all types of novelty light bulbs, such as *Playboy* bunny, Abraham Lincoln and the Statue of Liberty will be considered. Also buys all types of advertising and display materials for figural bulbs. Send a description with a photo. Cindy wrote *Neon Glow Lights* and runs a bimonthly auction of Christmas collectibles.

>Cindy Chipps
>4027 Brooks Hill Road
>Brooks, KY 40109
>(502) 955-9238   Fax: (502) 957-5027

☆ **Victorian celluloid household items**. Wants pictorially decorated celluloid **photo albums, autograph albums, shaving mirrors, and boxes** that held collars, cuffs, jewelry, brush sets, neckties, etc in the Victorian era. Large boxes in very fine condition can bring $500. She does not want pins, buttons, jewelry, toys, brush and comb sets, or celluloid items other than those requested above. Nothing made of hard plastic. Send a photo along with dimensions. Note condition carefully. Dealers must price their goods. Amateurs may request an offer.

> Judith Rubin
> This Time Around
> 8515 Troutman Court
> Manassas, VA 22110

☆ **Thermometers,** pre-1920, especially ornate Victorian desk or mantle types. "I buy just about every *non advertising* one I can locate," but outdoor and decorative models are particularly prized, as are those from Russia and Eastern Europe. "I have the largest antique thermometer collection in the world but am always looking for more." Not wanted: commercial, industrial, clinical, advertising or "cutesy" thermometers. No barometers or souvenir key chain thermometers. Send a photo, accompanied by information regarding the maker, any dates or numbers, condition and whether mercury or red liquid is in the bulb. "Many of the items go to the American Thermometer Museum in Baker, CA." Thermometer catalogs and other ephemera are sought.

> Warren Harris
> 6130 Rampart Drive
> Carmichael, CA 95608
> (916) 654-2097 days   Fax: (916) 966-7140

☆ **Small hand painted American boxes.**

> Louis Picek
> Main Street Antiques
> PO Box 340,
> West Branch, IA 52358
> (319) 643-2065

☆ **Lightning rods** made of copper, brass, or steel. Also wants decorative glass balls, especially in red colors and odd shapes. The least desirable color is white. No chipped or damaged pieces are accepted. Photos are helpful.

> Craig Donges
> 6724 Glenwood Avenue
> Youngstown, OH 44512
> (216) 726-1830   Fax: (216) 726-4740

☆ **Gadgets.** "I'll buy interesting old small mechanical devices such as:
- **Pocket typewriters or sewing machines**;
- Pocket size **calculators**;
- Miniature cameras;
- Small optical devices, like **sundials** and instruments;
- Trick, tool, gadget or **special purpose knives**;
- Lighters, compacts, and other pocket items combined
    with other tools;
- Things that fold, hide-away or look like things they aren't;
- **Personal check protectors** and other small business devices;
- Scientific instruments;
- Combination pen-pencil-rulers;
- Adding machines.

I'm interested in everything that whirs, buzzes, clanks, or just looks interesting." Darryl is particularly fond of typewriters and adders, paying $1,500 for important pocket typewriters. A photo is generally a good idea, and your description should include a detailed statement of condition. Will respond promptly to all offers.

> Darryl Rehr
> 2591 Military Ave.
> Los Angeles, CA 90064
> (310) 477-5229

☆ **Strap type watch fobs picturing machinery or advertising products.** No lodge, American Legion, VFW or similar fobs. He'd like you to tell him how much wear it shows and the name of the stamper, usually found at the bottom. No fakes or modern fobs.

> Albert Goetz
> 1763 Poplar Ave.
> South Milwaukee, WI 53172
> (414) 762-4111

☆ **Sewing items** such as old tape measures, sewing birds, thimbles and thimble cases and other items from a 19th century sewing box. Fine condition only. "I don't want anything common or easily found, anything made after 1960, or any reproduction." Making a Xerox™ is the best way to describe what you have.

> Betty Bird
> Antiques, Etc.
> 107 Ida Street
> Mt. Shasta, CA 96067

☆ **Flashlights.** Old flashlights, advertising, and catalogs are wanted, especially anything early marked *Eveready*.

> Bill Utley
> PO Box 4095
> Tustin, CA 92680
> (714) 730-1252

CAST IRON

☆ **All useful items made from cast iron** in the shape of figures. "I'll buy doorstops, bottle openers, lawn sprinklers, paperweights, pencil holders, match holders, string holders, windmill weights, horse weights, shooting gallery targets, and firemarks. I have no interest in buying modern reproductions and castings." Include your phone number.

> Craig Dinner
> PO Box 4399
> Sunnyside, NY 11104
>   (718) 729-3850

Remember when you write to buyers to always include an SASE. If you don't receive an answer right away have patience. Many of our top buyers are very busy people and travel frequently.

☆ **Cast iron doorstops and windmill weights** are sought by this prominent dealer. No reproductions or modern pieces.

> Louis Picek, Main Street Antiques
> PO Box 340
> West Branch, IA 52358
>   (319) 643-2065

☆ **Cast iron lawn sprinklers, doorstops, windmill weights, shooting gallery targets** and other figural cast iron. Does not want reproductions, damaged and repaired items, or items with new paint. He is also not interested in "small shooting gallery targets such as ducks and birds." Please include color photo, phone number, and price range you'd like.

> Richard Tucker, Argyle Antiques
> PO Box 262
> Argyle, TX 76226
>   (817) 464-3752   Fax: (817) 464-7293

☆ **Cast iron outdoor items** including yard sprinklers shaped like tractors, yard jockeys, hitching posts, flower urns, etc. Also wants patterns and molds used to produce these items. Describe condition, and give the casting number and other names and numbers you find on the items.

> Craig Donges
> 6724 Glenwood Avenue
> Youngstown, OH 44512
>   (216) 726-1830   Fax: (216) 726-4740

EYEGLASSES & CANES

☆ **Eyeglasses,** but *only* old, rare, and unusual ones. Not interested in any common eyeglasses or in buying them for their gold content. "I only want pre-1850 glasses with unusual lenses, frames, or history." Describe all writing on frames. Also wants any eye-related ephemera, display advertising, eyeglass trade signs, and "eye quackery."
W.H. Marshall
PO Box 1023
Melrose, FL 32666
(904) 475-5990

☆ **Antique eyeglasses and spectacles** are sought. Also would like to purchase early catalogs and trade cards featuring eyeglasses, unusual reading glasses, antique ophthalmoscopes, and any material from the *McAllister Optical Co.* He has some interest in textbooks on ophthalmology from before 1890. Please describe the condition thoroughly.
Charles Letocha
444 Rathton Road
York, PA 17403
(717) 846-0428

A photocopy machine will take a good picture of most eyeglasses or cane tops. Remember to give standard bibliographic information for books

☆ **Canes.** Especially likes dual purpose, container, weapon, gadget, and fancy carved canes made with ivory, gold, or silver. "Any cane or walking stick that does something, or has something enclosed or attached to the shaft for purposes other than support, is of interest, as are well executed hand-carved canes." Describe the tip of the cane and indicate whether it gives any evidence of having been shortened. Is there a hole in the shaft? What materials?
Arnold Scher
1637 Market Street
San Francisco, CA 94103
(415) 863-4344

☆ **Letter seals** for stamping your initials in wax on letters and documents. Please make a rubbing of the initial you have for sale. Unless made of precious metal, these are not high value items, she advises.
Monica Murphy
9337 Lenel Place
Dallas, TX 75220
(214) 352-4137

PENS & PENCILS

Pen collectors want to know the brand name.
Less than 12 brands are considered premium
but a great many others are also collected.

Pen collectors want any and all numbers
you find anywhere on your pen. Check the
end of the barrel, the clip, etc.

Pen collectors want to know the color.
Color is very important in determining value.
The earliest pens are black, red, or swirly red and black.

The size of your pen is important. Men's pens sell for more than
smaller ladies' pens. Measure the length with the cap on. Pens
longer than 5" are generally worth more than pens less than 5".

Pen points are best if wide and gold. Points that say WARRANTED or
WARRANTED 14K are cheap. Write down what it says on the point.

Condition is important to collectors of pens. Take off the cap and
run your fingernail around the rim, feeling for hairline cracks. More
than 50% of the value is gone if you find one. Inspect the two
halves looking for fading. Make sure the clip, fill lever, and any
gold banding is still there. Roll the barrel of the pen on a flat surface to see if it is warped.

Is it worth your time to do all this for a fountain pen? Someone
who didn't do all this...someone who didn't contact one of our
recommended buyers...donated a $15,000 pen to a rummage
sale in Hartford. The rummage sale folks sold it for $55.
Don't let that happen to you.

☆ **Unusual quality fountain pens,** pre-1940, by makers such as
*Eversharp, Waterman, Swan, Dunn, MacKinnon, Laughlin, Shaeffer,
Chilton, Wahl, Moore, Camel* and many others. Some of these can be
worth several hundred dollars. She also buys old **quill cutters, stylus
pens,** and **glass pens. Advertising related to pens** is also wanted, including signs, trade catalogs, repair manuals, and spare parts. Also
wants packaged powdered ink. To sell your pen, tell her the maker's
name, model, color, and length of your pen. Describe the pen point and
all decorations on the pen. Best to make a photocopy. Pens will have
to be inspected before final price offered. No unbranded pens,
Wearever, Esterbrook, ball point pens, or magazine ads. She will send a
guide to help you describe pens.
    Mrs. Ky
    PO Box 957
    Port Jefferson Station, NY 11776
      (516) 584-4246 voice or fax

☆ **Fountain pens, quill pens, desk sets and inkwells.** "I want better quality items in excellent condition only." Does not want pencils or ball point pens. Please send a Xerox™ of what you have, along with a description of color, any markings, and condition. Glen is publisher of *Pen World* magazine, available for $42/year and author of *Collectible Fountain Pens*, available for $25. He has other publications as well.

> Glen Bowen
> 2240 North Park Drive
> Kingwood, TX 77339
> (713) 359-4363   Fax: (713) 359-4468

☆ **Fountain pens** in fine condition are sought by the head of the Pen Collectors of America ($25/year to join), who provided the info on the previous page. Check condition carefully and don't forget an SASE.

> Boris Rice
> 11319 Wickersham Lane
> Houston, TX 77077
> (713) 496-2290 voice or fax

☆ **Inkwells,** either U.S. or foreign, figural or traveling, whether made of pottery, glass, or wood. Especially would like one made by *Tiffany*. He does not buy desk sets or fountain pens.

> Eli Hecht
> 19 Evelyn Lane
> Syosset, NY 11791

☆ **Ball point pens and pencils that are out of the ordinary.** Wants:
- Oddly shaped pens or pencils, especially that look like something else (sports shapes are a real favorite);
- Pens with multi-color mechanisms;
- Souvenirs from amusement parks, carnivals, and gift shops;
- Scented pens;
- Pens or pencils encased in other things, like thermometers.

She does not want fountain pens, calligraphy pens, feather pens, or any pen or pencil with missing parts or otherwise in non-working order. Give its size, shape, condition, and the color of the ink or lead. These are generally inexpensive items, but she's glad to get them.

> Selena Kyte
> PO Box 1022
> St. Ann, MO 63074

☆ **Ball point pens,** but only those made of solid gold or sterling silver. Brands include *Tiffany, Parker, Wahl-Eversharp, Waterman* and others.

> David Wilcox
> Box 11203
> Indianapolis, IN 46201
> (317) 488-8728

☆ **Mechanical pencils with advertising on them** are wanted. Most advertising mechanical pencils are modestly priced 50¢ to $3, with some national ads worth $10, and a few as much as $20. Some non-advertising pencils are wanted including brands like *Parker, Conklin, Shaeffer, Wahl, Eversharp, Swan* and others. Prices on these can range as high as $200 for rare, high quality pencils. He enjoys finding dual-purpose pencils, such as those combined with knives, magnifying glasses, etc. "I will consider **all items related to pencils, pre-1960,** such as catalogs, brochures, display cases, salesman's samples, sample cases, or signs that relate to mechanical pencils, but no magazine ads, please. I do not want new mechanical pencils or those with Bible verses. I am **not** interested in wood pencils, ink pens or fountain pens unless they are part of a set that includes a mechanical pencil. I will accept shipments up to 50 pencils for immediate response and payment. Please phone first if you have more than 50." He cautions "do not clean dirty or frozen pencils as you are more likely to destroy their value than to help it." He will make offers on collections of mechanical pencils, but only after inspecting them in person.

Tom Basore
715 West 20th Street
Hutchinson, KS 67502
(316) 665-3613 eves

☆ **Pencil sharpeners.** Wants small hand-held figural pencil sharpeners made of metal, celluloid or *Bakelite*. She is only looking for those made in Germany or Japan during the 1930's and 40's. Don't offer her the small bronze colored sharpeners from Hong Kong made in the shape of various antiques. To sell your sharpener, give the shape, condition, country of origin, size, condition of the blade, and price.

Martha Crouse
4516 Brandon Lane
Beltsville, MD 20705

☆ **Pencil sharpeners,** but *only* figural hand-held sharpeners from the 1920's, 30's and 40's. Most of the desirable ones are metal or celluloid made in Germany and Japan, although the Disney sharpeners made of Bakelite are U.S. made. "I do not want plastic sharpeners made in the last 30 years or the common die-cast fake antiqued sharpeners found at every flea market. Detailed description of condition is most important. Dealers must set your price wanted. Genuine amateurs may request offers. I will gladly share my knowledge with beginning collectors."

Bernice Kraker
9800 McMillan Avenue
Silver Spring, MD 20910
(301) 589-2544

RAZORS & ACCESSORIES

☆ **Straight razors with fancy handles** made of gold or sterling silver. Also razors with figural handles, multiple blades, fancy etching on the blade, or with fraternal emblems or advertising on the handle. Handles may be made of horn, mother-of-pearl, or multi-colored celluloid. Rare razors will be considered even if they are slightly damaged. Also **razor and cutlery advertising** and memorabilia, catalogs, trade cards, etc., including oversize displays.

> William Campesi
> PO Box 140
> Merrick, NY 11566
> (516) 546-9630

☆ **Straight razors with handles of sterling, rough bone, mother-of-pearl, or aluminum.** Celluloid or pressed horn razors with several characters are also wanted. Good razors generally bring from $50-$75, with some higher, some less. Please provide all information found on the blade or handle. He does not want plain handled razors from Solingen, Germany. Make photocopies with the blade(s) open. Indicate the material from which the handle is made.

> Charles Stapp
> 7037 Haynes Road
> Georgetown, IN 47122
> (812) 923-3483

☆ **Safety razors and accessories.** This 20 year veteran collector wants to buy odd safety razors and advertising for razors including posters, magazine ads, and signs. He'd love to find oversize store display razors or oversize shaving mugs or brushes. Give all colors and metals and note "all writing on the items. A good clear photo is best," he says, but photocopies will suffice.

> Cary Basse
> 6927 Forbes Ave.
> Van Nuys, CA 91406
> (818) 781-4856

☆ **Razor blades and blade sharpeners.** "I'll buy U.S. or foreign blades, in singles, packages, or on cards as well as interesting advertising signs, posters, and displays related to razor blades." Describe your sharpener carefully, pointing out all damage, and noting any words or numbers on it.

> Cary Basse
> 6927 Forbes Ave.
> Van Nuys, CA 91406
> (818) 781-4856

☆ **Safety razors,** stropping machines, **packs of blades**, blade banks, and other early or unique shaving items, "with highest prices paid for safety razors with unusual or oddly shaped blades." Phil wrote *The Complete Gillette Collector's Handbook* available from him for $24.

> Phillip Krumholz
> PO Box 4050
> Bartonville, IL 61607
>   (309) 697-1120

☆ **Safety razor shaving memorabilia,** 1880-1930, including safety razors, mechanical blade sharpeners, razor blade banks, advertising signs and buttons, counter and window displays, giveaways, catalogs, and miscellaneous paper associated with any of the above. Also wants figural shaving mugs in the shape of animals, people, or birds and shaving brushes with figural handles. Shaving mugs and barber bottles which appear to be covered with imitation bark are also of interest. The following brands of safety razor are NOT WANTED: *Rolls, Durham, Valey* or *Gillette* (if the serial number is higher than 500,000). Blade sharpeners that are too common to have value are *Kriss Kross* and *Twinplex*. Blade banks given away by *Listerine* are also very common. Please provide as much detail as possible, including all names, letters, dates, colors, etc. A drawing is helpful.

> Lester Dequaine
> 155 Brewster Street
> Bridgeport, CT 06605
>   (203) 335-6833

The value of straight razors lays almost all in the handle. When buyers ask for unusual handles, they really mean it!

Ordinary black handled straight razors have little if any value. Save your time and theirs by not asking.

PERFUME

☆ **Perfume bottles**. Wants high quality commercial, miniature and other perfume bottles from 1700 to 1950. Especially wants elaborate 18th and 19th century scent bottles and 20th century bottles made by famous glassmakers like Lalique and Baccarat. She does not want anything made by *Avon*. Please indicate the size in inches, color of the glass and stopper, whether or not the original label and box are present, and if the bottle is signed (look very closely at both bottle and stopper with a magnifying glass as signatures and markings can be very small). If the stopper does not seem to match the base, it may be OK as many valuable bottles have unusual stoppers which seem mismatched. Photos or Xerox© copies of your bottle are helpful. Ms. Parris is a founding member of the Perfume & Scent Bottle Association and their membership chairperson. Please contact her only if your bottle is old, in perfect condition, and for sale, or if you would like to join the club. SASE.

    Jeane Parris
    Sugarplums, etc.
    2022 East Charleston Boulevard
    Las Vegas, NV 89104
        (702) 385-6059 days

Collectors seek many perfume bottles from the 1920's, 30's, and 40's. Since these bottles were designed and made by top European art glass companies, they are frequently worth $100 and up. Record prices of over $10,000 have been paid, so advice is essential.
Look for pretty shapes, silver trim, atomizers, glass stoppers, and anything unusual, figural, or particularly decorative.

Avon perfume and toiletry bottles have no resale value at this time. They are widely offered at $1 and $2 each retail.

☆ **Perfume bottles, decanters, and vases with silver overlay.** Describe all markings and give dimensions and colors.

    Arnold Reamer
    Timepiece Antiques
    PO Box 26416
    Baltimore, MD 21207
        (410) 944-6414 or (410) 486-8412

☆ **Perfume bottles made of blown or cut art glass,** singles or matching sets. Wants fine beautiful bottles including those with atomizers. Some important makers include *DeVilbis, Daum Nancy, Galle, Baccarat, Webb, Moser, Czechoslovakian, Lalique,* and *Steuben.* Also English scents, bottles with sterling overlay, and figural perfume bottles. The proprietor of this unusual shop for women does not make offers, nor does she buy *Avon* bottles.

> Madeleine France
> Past Pleasures for the 20th Century Woman
> 3 North Federal Highway
> Dania, FL 33004
>   (305) 584-0009 days   Fax: (305) 584-0014

☆ *DeVilbis* **atomizers,** with or without original bulb, tube, and cord. Describe the size, colors, and condition. A detailed sketch or close up photo is essential. "If you have items to sell me, I prefer you to write rather than phone."

> Bruce Bleier
> 73 Riverdale Road
> Valley Stream, NY 11581

☆ **Perfume bottles** with glass stoppers. Wants art glass bottles, large department store display bottles, and samples. Give the brand of perfume and make a Xerox™ of the bottle. No *Avon.*

> Annette Chaussee
> PO Box 150
> Calhan, CO 80808
>   (719) 347-2780

☆ *California Perfume Company* **(CPC) products made between 1886 and 1929,** especially *Natoma Rose* fragrances. He also wants CPC products marketed as *Goetting and Company, Savoi Et Cie, Gertrude Recordon, Marvel Electric Silver Cleaner,* and the *Easy Day Automatic Clothes Washer.* Please give a complete description of the item you have for sale, including its condition and whether or not it has its original box. Is there a label and/or a neck band? Are there cracks or chips? Photocopy is helpful. Dick's collection is open to the public by advance appointment. Be prepared to leave a message stating exactly what you have, its condition and the price you'd like for it. Dealers price your goods. Genuine amateurs may request help in setting prices. Dick does not want anything with AVON or PERFECTION on the label, although he will answer specific questions about *Avon* if you include a Self-Addressed Stamped Envelope.

> Dick Pardini
> 3107 North El Dorado Street, Apt T-H
> Stockton, CA 95204
>   (209) 466-5550 7am to 11pm

COMPACTS & MAKEUP

☆ **Women's sterling silver dresser sets, hair brushes, mirrors and other boudoir items.** The proprietor of this unusual shop for women does not make offers, so you'll have to price what you have.

> Madeleine France
> Past Pleasures for the 20th Century Woman
> 3 North Federal Highway
> Dania, FL 33004
>   (305) 584-0009

☆ **Women's powder compacts,** from before 1950. All types of good looking, fine condition compacts are wanted, as long as the compact is complete. Unusual, Art Deco and precious metals are preferred.

> Bird In the Cage
> 110 King Street
> Alexandria, VA 22314
>   (703) 549-5114

☆ **Compacts.** Wants unusual compacts:
* Shaped like phone dials, pistols, hot air balloons, suitcases, hands, drums, guitars, lady bugs, flying saucers, etc.;
* Enameled Art Deco designs;
* Jeweled vanities;
* Molded plastic Bakelite vanities;
* Mesh and beaded purses with compact tops;
* Canes or hat pins concealing compacts.

"I don't buy 1940's and 50's carryalls (usually 3"x5" or 4"x6"), nor am I interested in plain brass, sterling, or silver plate without color." No compacts with damaged enamel. Photo helpful.

> Lori Landgrebe
> 2331 East Main
> Decatur, IL 62521
>   (217) 423-2254

Avon bottles are everywhere, and I have not been able to locate a buyer for collections of Avon items. You may wish to subscribe to Avon Times, a monthly newsletter with 6 pages of "Buy and sell" ads for $19 (PO Box 9868, Kansas City, MO 64134). A sample newsletter is $3. A price guide to Avon is advertised as being available from them for $18.

In my experience it's difficult to find buyers for most items. They generally sell one at a time, for $1 or $2 at flea markets.

COSTUME JEWELRY CAN BE TREASURE TOO.

You must get all jewelry into the hands of someone trained and experienced in old jewelry. If you try to evaluate it yourself, you could make costly mistakes. Diamonds and other precious and semi-precious stones are often mistaken for glass in old jewelry. You cannot rely upon local jewelers and diamond merchants for accurate appraisals of antique jewelry.

A certified gemologist and costume jewelry expert said, "Few dealers know who the important makers of costume jewelry are. If they sell good pieces at junk prices, that means they paid junk prices for them. The original owner lost money. Sellers should always go to jewelry experts."

19th century gemstones were cut differently than is popular today. *A reader showed me a two and a half carat diamond ring he bought at a yard sale for a quarter. I hope he wasn't shopping at your house!*

Jewelry buyers want to know:

(1) *The basic material from which your item is made, such as silver, gold, brass, plastic, etc.*
(2) *All names, numbers, and markings. The right mark can put hundreds of dollars in your pocket.*
(3) *Shape, color, and number of any stones.*
(4) *Dimensions are helpful; values can be influenced by size. Photocopying is a good way to describe hatpins, brooches, bracelets and other jewelry.*

Be prepared to ship your jewelry with a five day return privilege. *Buyers want to inspect jewelry before commiting to buy. If they do pay first, you must give the money back if the buyer isn't happy for any reason with what you send.*

When mailing items worth more than $500, send them Registered Mail. *It costs between $5-$10 to mail safely throughout the U.S. with insurance as high as $25,000. All recipients must sign for Registered Mail. Ask your post office because some minor restrictions apply.*

JEWELRY

☆ **Old and antique jewelry,** especially:
- **Karat gold pieces**, particularly signed pieces with Art Nouveau and Art Deco designs;
- **Sterling silver items** signed by *Unger Brothers* or *Kerr*, mostly Art Nouveau brooches featuring female faces;
- **Designer costume jewelry** signed by *Trifari, Mariam Haskell, Hattie Carnegie, Coro* or *Eisenberg Original;*
- *Georg Jensen* **jewelry**;
- **Silver puffed heart fancy charms**.

Describe your items completely, or make a photocopy. If you know the item's ownership history, please give it. Note all markings.

    Arnold Reamer, Timepiece Antiques
    PO Box 26416
    Baltimore, MD 21207
       (410) 944-6414 or (410) 486-8412

☆ **Antique jewelry** of 8K to 22K gold with or without stones, made pre-1900. Especially wants **earrings**, but also complete sets. Also:
- **Cameos** (shell or stone) and tiaras;
- **Seed pearls**;
- **Miniature ivory portraits**;
- **Tortoise shell** jewelry;
- **Jewelry made of hair**, including mourning jewelry;
- Fine quality **hair combs**;
- **Victorian aluminum** and early cut steel with riveted studs.

"I buy jewelry worn from head to toe." She requests photo or description with your asking price. Monica conducts seminars on jewelry.

    Monica Murphy, Savannah's Antiques
    9337 Lenel Place
    Dallas, TX 75220
       (214) 352-4137

☆ **Costume jewelry** is sought, but only particular kinds:
- All signed designer pieces by **B.David** and/or **Schreiner** of NY.
- **Rhinestone jewelry** with red or purple stones in any size or style;
- Czech jewelry (especially bracelets, brooches and necklaces with drop pendants); pieces tend to be large, intensely colored, and have brass filigree often marked CZECH or CZECHOSLOVAKIA.

Judy buys broken pieces of good jewelry as she repairs jewelry and needs stones and some other parts. "I'll buy one piece or a showcase full," she says. Xerox™ recommended.

    Judy Polk Harding
    2713 Friendship Street
    Iowa City, IA 52245
       (319) 354-2379

☆ **Hatpins and hatpin holders** and related objects such as pincushion dolls from before 1930. "Especially interested in plique-a-jour hatpins for which I'll pay up to $350 or more if artist signed. I also like sterling hatpins marked "C.H." and will pay $45-$110. Always interested in vanity or figural hatpins such as compacts, pin-holders, perfume tops, thimble with needle, etc., especially if art nouveau design atop 12" pin stems. My special want is a hatpin hinged on the top ornament which opens to reveal a teeny nude baby and I would pay up to $500 for a perfect one on a long pin. I also want to buy **figural hatpin holders** by *Royal Beyreuth, RS Prussia* (red mark only), *Oriental, Schafer & Vater* (S&V), others." Mrs. Baker has written books on jewelry and an encyclopedia of hatpins available from her for $79 postpaid. Give the history of your hatpin, and whether it has any flaws. Will make offers to amateurs only after inspection. She founded the International Club for Hatpin Collectors. An SASE brings information about the club and six of her currently available books on hatpins, plastic jewelry, and costume jewelry of the last 150 years.

    Lillian Baker, The Hatpin Lady
    15237 Chanera Ave.
    Gardena, CA 90249
    (310) 329-2619

☆ **Tassie cameos** made of marble dust with gold paper wrapped around or made of wax with a gold rim. These are most often of mythological characters or classical themes. Also want the molds in which the cameos were made. Very rare and hard to find, Tassie cameos are named after James Tassie who, in the 1700's, invented glass cameo molds used by *Wedgwood* to make decorations on their pottery. Tassie cameos are most often hung in picture frames. Pledges to pay premium prices for these rarities. Send a photo and/or description.

    Monica Murphy, Savannah's Antiques
    9337 Lenel Place
    Dallas, TX 75220
    (214) 352-4137

☆ **Old jewelry before 1930,** garnets, black jets, cameos, rings, **lockets, charms,** filigree beads, glass beads, and glass buttons. Craftsmanship and detail ("ornate and unusual") is more important than whether it's made of gold or not. **Lockets, hearts,** stars, flowers and other keepsake jewelry is wanted in gold or silver. "I look for all unusual items of clothing, jewelry, and accessories." Photocopy is suggested. Jewelry may be broken and need repair.

    Linda Gibbs
    10380 Miranda Ave.
    Buena Park, CA 90620
    (714) 827-6488

☆ **Plastic or metal *Hummel* jewelry** from 1940's in shapes similar to their figurines. She buys both painted and unpainted jewelry.
    Sharon Vohs-Mohammed
    PO Box 7233
    Villa Park, IL 60181
       (708) 268-0210

☆ **Woodburned glove and jewelry boxes** are purchased for resale, as are **jewelry boxes made of cast iron,** particularly those that are silk lined. Please give a thorough description.
    Linda Gibbs
    10380 Miranda Ave.
    Buena Park, CA 90620
       (714) 827-6488

☆ **Gold scrap.** "I buy all marked and unmarked gold and silver rings, wedding bands, and scrap," says this giant dealer in coins, medals, and tokens. Hartzog says you may ship whatever you have for his offer.
    Rich Hartzog
    PO Box 4143 BFT
    Rockford, IL 61110
       (815) 226-0771

Jewelry buyers want to know:

(1) The basic material from which your item is made, such as silver, gold, brass, plastic or material you don't recognize.

(2) All names, numbers, and markings. Try to record these accurately. A magnifying glass may help.

(3) Shape, color, and number of any stones.

(4) Size, as it too can affect value.

IS YOUR WATCH TRASH OR TREASURE?

Watches have been made by the hundreds of millions for a century!

A great variety of watches exist and a great variety of collectors seek them. Values can range from a dollar or two to prices over $100,000.

Whenever a great deal of money is at stake, it is smart to get expert advice.

Be cautious about selling watches locally. Your local jeweler is probably not qualified to evaluate and price old watches even though he sells new ones. You may put five or ten times as much money in your pocket when you deal with watch buyers who keep up with the international used watch market.

If you wish to sell your watch, answer the following:

> *What is the case made of?*
> *What is the size of the case?*
> *Is the case decorated or engraved?*
> *What name is on the dial?*
> *What name is on the movement?*
> *Does it say how many jewels?*
> *Is there a serial number?*
> *How is it wound? Do you have the key?*
> *Is it running?*
> *Is there anything unusual about the case or watch?*

Watch buyers will want to inspect your timepiece before making a final offer. Send watches via Registered US Mail, insured. This is usually a safe way to ship, and requires the recipient to sign for the package.

Always discuss exact shipping procedures with the buyer.

WATCHES

☆ **High quality and collectible watches** by *Patek Phillipe, Rolex, Cartier, Tiffany, Audemars* and types of watches like chronographs, repeaters, alarm, doctor's watches, two time zone, and rectangular faces made between 1870 and 1960. **Also advertising items relating to watches.** Irv deals in watches from rare to common. Buys parts, cases, boxes, movements, dials, and bands from all *Rolex, Patek* or *Cartier* watches. If you are thinking of auction, Irv says, "We will buy any piece that interests us at 95% of anticipated net sellers hammer proceeds." Irv promises: "Fair prices, next day payment, postage refunded, and free appraisals," adding "I will come to you if what you have is very valuable or if you have many good pieces." Describe metal, shape, details, all names and numbers, as indicated on previous page. Irv offers a priced wants list.

    Irv Temes, American International Watch Exchange
    113 North Charles Street
    Baltimore, MD 21201
        (410) 882-0580

☆ **Wrist and pocket watches,** both men's and women's, in gold, silver, or gold fill. Pocket watches may be in other metals if they date before 1940. Doesn't matter whether running or not. Describe all markings and give dimensions.

    Arnold Reamer, Timepiece Antiques
    PO Box 26416
    Baltimore, MD 21207
        (410) 944-6414 or (410) 486-8412

☆ **Antique pocket watches and specific wristwatches.** "I buy any American made railroad pocket watch marked on the inside as being 21 or more jewels. If your watch is not marked as 21 or more jewels, please send me a Xerox™ showing the face (dial) and include all names, serial numbers, etc., you find inside or outside. Please do not call unless your watch is marked 21 jewels or more. If your pocket watch is marked *Patek Philippe, Cartier, Vacheron & Constantin, Audemars Piguet, Lange & Sohn* or *Frodsham* you may call. We buy men's wristwatches by the following makers ONLY: *Rolex, Patek Philippe, Cartier, Audemars Piguet, Vacheron & Constantin.* We do not buy ANY other wristwatches. I buy no women's watches, nor do I do repairs or insurance appraisals. Please call us only if you have one of the watches listed above, running or not. If you cannot figure out what you have, write me, describing your watch according to instructions given on page 78."

    Maundy International
    PO Box 13028 TH
    Shawnee Mission, KS 66282
        (800) 235-2866 if you have one of the above only

☆ **Racing stopwatches, pocket watches, dashboard clocks, and schoolhouse clocks with the name of a horse,** horse race, carriage company, or automobile manufacturer on the face. Also sterling silver clock cases, with or without clocks. Also leather cases for car clocks that clip over the dashboard of a carriage. "When in doubt, please write and inquire. Send your watch on approval for an immediate response."

    Donald Sawyer
    40 Bachelor Street
    West Newbury, MA 01985
       (508) 346-4724 days   Fax: (508) 346-4841

☆ **Watches and clocks with cartoon characters or products on the face.** Any items mint in their original box are particularly desirable. Tell whether face is round or rectangular, any wording on the face or back, defects (including scratches), the condition of the box (if any), and whether it is working. Don't overwind! Free appraisals for amateur sellers. Maggie both buys and sells these pop-culture watches.

    Maggie Kenyon
    One Christopher Street #14G
    New York, NY 10014
       (212) 675-3213

☆ *Hamilton* **wristwatches,** especially "electric" watches and mechanical watches with unusual case styles. An electric watch repairman, he also wants dealer's stock, parts, movements, **advertising materials, catalogs**, and anything else related to the *Hamilton Watch Co.* No *Hamilton Electronic* watches. Only American made pre-1970 watches. Rene's comprehensive book on *Hamilton* electric watches is $30.

    Rene Rondeau
    120 Harbor Drive
    Corte Madera, CA 94925
       (415) 924-6534

☆ **Pocket watches,** better quality wristwatches, and clocks are wanted.

    Robert Kolbe's Clock Repair
    1301 South Duluth
    Sioux Falls, SD 57105
       (605) 332-9662

☆ **LED watches** from the early 70's. These lit up, usually in red, when you pressed a button. He most wants a *Hewlett-Packard* HP-01 combination watch/calculator in gold or stainless steel, especially if complete with original stylus. List make and model and indicate if it works. Please indicate type and condition of strap. Xerox© if possible.

    Guy Ball
    14561 Livingston Street
    Tustin, CA 92680
       Fax: (714) 730-6140

CLOTHING & ACCESSORIES

☆ **Vintage clothing and hats.** "I buy and sell mint condition men's, women's, children's and fancy baby clothing dating from the 1890's through the 1940's, especially flapper dresses, stylish women's suits and jackets, 1940's rayon dresses, evening suits and dresses. Both day wear and evening wear are desirable.
- **Stylish hats** from the early 1930's or before with full lining;
- **Old draperies**, and old bolts of material;
- Early **bridal clothing** and headpieces;
- Accessories such as **shoes, hats, belts,** etc.;
- Jewelry, compacts, etc.;
- **Handbags and parasols**;
- **Lace**.

Individual prices run from $10 to $75, with only "absolutely incredible" items bringing more. "I do *not* want things that are ripped, faded, have underarm stains, too small for today's wearers (with tiny neck or arm holes), worn out, or that have poor craftsmanship. Nor do I want anything from the 1950's or 60's except designer clothes. I do not buy fur. If you want to sell clothing, you must tell me the period, give the size and color, indicate whether it has a zipper or buttons, identify the material if possible, and list any defects." Note whether hats have lining. Amateur sellers may request an offer, which will be made after seeing the item. Dealers must price their goods. Photo a good idea. Call her about shipping on approval to make it easy on everyone.

> Pahaka September
> 19 Fox Hill
> Upper Saddle River, NJ 07458
> (201) 327-1467 eves

Stained or torn clothing is not wanted. Always describe the style, color, material, size, and label. Clothes with designer labels are very desirable, but Levis may have value.

☆ **Vintage clothes made before 1950** such as beaded sweaters and **beaded purses and bags**, evening gowns, prom dresses, men's tuxedos and hats, etc. Also buys **parasols** and **piano shawls**. No damaged or stained items as items are purchased for resale in her 2,000 sq.ft. shop. Price your goods when possible.

> Bird In the Cage
> 110 King Street
> Alexandria, VA 22314
> (703) 549-5114

☆ *Levis, Lee,* **and** *Wrangler* **jeans and jackets** for resale. "I'll buy all pre-1970 *Levi Strauss* jeans and jackets and some older *Wrangler* and *Lee* jeans and jackets." The *Levis* he wants all have a small red tag on the front pocket (jackets left, pants right) which spells out LEvis. That capital "E" makes these called "Big E" jeans, and they are a hot fad item in some places today. Jackets from 1920-1949 bring $500 to $1,500; if heavily worn, still $100 to $300. Other jackets, with two front pockets, bring from $25 to $500. Does not want *Levis* with tags of any color other than red. Pants with waists larger than 34" are not of interest either. If you have a red Big E *Levis* tag in one of your front pockets, and want an immediate cash offer, describe condition carefully noting stains, holes, wear, the condition of the leather ID tag. The serial number on the back pocket leather ID tag would be helpful. Also buys advertising signs or figures from these same companies.

> David Bailey, Bailey's Antiques & Aloha Shirts
> 517 Kapahulu Avenue
> Honolulu, HI 96816
>   (808) 734-7628

☆ **Vintage Hawaiian shirts, 1930-1955.** The label, size, coloration, and pattern are important, as is the material, so include all that when you write. Shirts can be made of cotton, rayon, or silk. A silk shirt with a fish pattern (his personal favorite) could bring as high as $500. Most are considerably less, but well worth your time. "I'm willing to answer questions and provide information to people who are not sure if their shirts are old enough." A photograph or photocopy is helpful.

> Evan Olins, Hula Heaven
> 75-5744 Alii Drive
> Kailau-Kona, HI 96740
>   (808) 329-4122

☆ **Hawaiian shirts made before 1960.**

> David Bailey
> 517 Kapahulu Avenue
> Honolulu, HI 96816
>   (808) 734-7628

☆ **Men's and women's clothing and accessories,** 1900-1940. Wants average sizes in good condition. Very interested in old warehouse stock and in **rayon yardage**.

> The Way We Wore
> 1094 Revere Ave #A-29
> San Francisco, CA 94124
>   (415) 822-1800 10 a.m. to 5 p.m.

☆ **Women's figural compacts.** "We buy compacts that are in the shape of something else, like a hat, suitcase, stuffed animal, etc. We'll buy them in any material, but they must be in very fine condition, with no damage. It is best if the original rouge, powder and mirror are present, but the more unusual the compact, the more forgiving we are. We do not collect conventional round or square compacts even if they have an embossed, engraved or applied figure on the lid. Plush animal compacts are worth from $225 to $500 each." A clear close-up photo is needed, or a good Xerox™ if possible. Your description should indicate the condition of the mirror, the puff, and the contents. "Small markings stamped into the metal on the inside are critical to mention."

> Mike and Sherry Miller
> 303 Holiday Ave.
> Tuscola, IL 61953
>   (217) 253-4991

☆ **Purses** from before 1930. Primarily seeking:
- Enameled mesh purses in bright colors, scenic designs, etc.
  from the late 1920's, especially with jeweled frames;
- **Beaded purses**, particularly large ones with scenic or figural
  designs, Persian carpet or Egyptian motifs;
- *Bakelite* purses;
- **Plastic compacts** which are actually small purses;
- Trinity plate very small purses made of brass with
  complex filigree work and stones, often with tassels.

Good purses must be without wear in mint to near mint condition and will bring prices from $50 to $300. She does not want purses from the 1930's or later, nor does she want common bags. "I'm looking for the out of the ordinary." Your description should include the style, design, and color. A photo or Xerox™ is a good idea. Dealers should price their goods. Amateurs may request an offer from this veteran collector.

> Leslie Holms
> PO Box 596
> Los Gatos, CA 95031
>   (408) 354-1626   Fax: (408) 395-0803

☆ **Metal mesh purses** with designs painted into the mesh. Prefers mint condition items but will consider some in poor condition for parts. Also wants ads, photos, catalogs, and other items showing mesh bags. Will buy some **beaded bags**, but only the older purses with very small beads (18-22 beads to the inch) strung into a scene, a figure, or into the design of an Oriental rug. Must be in mint or nearly mint condition. A Xerox™ copy is a good way to describe your purse.

> Mike and Sherry Miller
> 303 Holiday Ave.
> Tuscola, IL 61953
>   (217) 253-4991

☆ **Alligator and crocodile handbags and luggage.** In addition to fancy leather bags, she wants **designer luggage by** *Hermes, Chanel,* **and** *Vuitton.* Send measurements and sketch or photo. Describe condition inside and out including handles and hardware. Give the color of the bag and lining, and any special features. She also buys some **unusual vintage purses.** Everything must be in resale condition.

> Joy Horvath
> 12 Belair Road
> Norwalk, CT 06850
> (203) 847-9035

☆ *Louis Vuitton* **trunks and hard case luggage**, the older the better, especially in early cloth designs other than the typical *LV* pattern. "We'd pay $4,000 for a mint condition steamer trunk, but we do not want things in less than fine condition and we do not buy any soft sided luggage." Send a photo, dimensions and history of the item, if possible.

> Duane and Eunice Bietz
> Les Meilleurs
> 6461 SE Thorburn
> Portland, OR 97215
> Fax: (503) 233-1602

☆ **Handpainted neckties.** "Most are 1940's vintage wide ties in silk or rayon blend with various scenes or abstracts. Especially wants nudes, lusty women, and hula dancers (worth up to $100 each), but also prizes cowboy and fishing themes (which can bring to $75). Does not want narrow ties. Please give the name of the maker and send a Xerox™. Condition is critical.

> Don Colclough
> Cadillac Jack
> 6911 Melrose
> Los Angeles, CA 90038
> (800) 775-5078   Fax: (213) 931-6372

☆ **Neckties by Dali.** Also wants men's extra large **grey felt spats** and men's crocodile or **alligator wallets** big enough to accommodate the large pre-1930 bills. *Playboy* **blazer buttons** in silver or 14k gold. Still looking for a diamond studded **belt buckle given away by Al Capone** (they are inscribed on the back).

> David Wilcox
> Box 11203
> Indianapolis, IN 46201
> (317) 488-8728

☆ **Women's spiked or high heeled shoes** in excellent condition from the 20's through the 60's. Please send photos, shoe size, and the height of the heels. Particularly interested in sexy 5" and 6" heels.

> Charles Martignette
> PO Box 293
> Hallandale, FL 33009
> (305) 454-3474

☆ **Ladies' hand fans** from 1600 to 1900 are wanted in ivory, mother-of-pearl, tortoise shell, horn, or wooden sticks with painting or decor on silk, lace, paper, or chicken skin. All origins are sought: French, German, English, American, Chinese, Viennese, and Spanish, but only in good to mint condition. Send a photocopy. Monica is available for appraisals and lectures in jewelry and fine antiques.

> Monica Murphy, Savannah's Antiques
> 9337 Lenel Place
> Dallas, TX 75220
> (214) 352-4137

☆ **Antique fancy buttons.** Wants those with metal pictures, Oriental, pearl, *Bakelite*, etc. The way to tell whether she wants your buttons is to ask two questions before contacting her:

> (1) Does the button have holes through it? If yes, she is not
>   interested in your button. If no, ask question #2.
> (2) Is it fancy or unusual? If yes, she wants it. If not, she doesn't.

She does not want shirt buttons or ordinary plastic buttons with visible sewing holes. Almost all the buttons she buys are shank type. Please price your buttons for resale. Photocopies or approvals are suggested.

> Barbara Bronzoulis, Barbara's Button Bracelets
> 1931 Laurel Hill
> Kingwood, TX 77339
> (713) 358-1518   Fax: (713) 358-3750

☆ **Buttons,** especially U.S. military, Confederate, military school, and uniform buttons with state seals.   He also buys "high quality clothing buttons of porcelain, satsuma, or with pictures." He does not want WWI or WWII buttons or "simple clothing buttons made of plastic or bone." Please describe the design, and note anything stamped on the back. This director of the National Button Society prefers that you ship for inspection prior to final offer.

> Warren Tice
> PO Box 8491
> Essex, VT 05451
> (802) 878-3835 voice and fax

SEWING & TEXTILES

☆ **Handmade lace** from 1500-1900. "Unless you are a lace scholar or have access to important reference books on lace, the best thing is to photocopy as much of the piece as possible. From a photocopy I can often tell whether a full appraisal is warranted or if it is a piece I might like to buy. Even small pieces are worth your attention." She does not want lace known to be machine made or ordinary crochet and tatting. She prefers sellers to set the price, but will assist genuine amateurs to identify what they have "if it's for sale." Produces an interesting newsletter for lace fanciers for $20 a year.

> Elizabeth Kurella
> Lace Merchant
> PO Box 222
> Plainwell, MI 49080
> (616) 685-9792

A great deal of valuable lace is lost each year because people don't take time to inquire. Small pieces of high-quality lace can bring up to $100 and large pieces a great deal more.

☆ **Lace, linens, and stichery** including:
- **Table linens** especially with large napkins, lace, or handiwork;
- **Lace curtains, panels** and **hankies**, if fine quality;
- **Embroidered pictures** and **samplers**;
- **Metallic** embroideries;
- **Lace collars** and **lace yardage** from before 1940;
- **Pillow cases** and **sheets** with hand stitchery or lace before 1925;
- **Embroideries** and **printed fabrics** of the Arts and Crafts period;
- **Embroidered** religious articles;
- **Unusual weaving, textiles and stitchery** from before 1930;
- **Heavy textiles, weavings, wall hangings**..."big clunky stuff."

No hand towels, plain linen, Damask, damaged goods, or items made after 1960 are wanted. If Paul is interested in buying your items, he will request you ship on approval. Photographs or Xerox's are useful.

> Paul Freeman
> 1847 5th Street
> Manhattan Beach, CA 90266
> (310) 379-0207

☆ **Lace, trimmings, embroidery** and **stitchery.** Wants assortments of pre-1920 rosettes, fabric or ribbon trims for clothing or hats, tatted items that are more than 5" in size (including doilies), white on white stitchery, red stitchery on white, **beaded clothing and accessories,** and clothing (including pantaloons, skirts, and dresses) with decorative handiwork. Also buys quilt tops, crazy quilts, and other handmade cloth items. Send a good photograph or photocopy of what you wish to sell. "Items can be partially damaged if I use them to make other things. Please, no hankies or crochet items." Include SASE for response.

> Linda Gibbs, Heirloom Keepsakes
> 10380 Miranda
> Buena Park, CA 90620
> (714) 827-6488

☆ **Quilting and patchwork patterns, books** and **tools** from before 1950. Also wants vintage fabric, cloth scraps, patterned flour and feed sacks, and other material useful for old style quilting.

> Judy Speezak
> Box 2528 Rockefeller Center Station
> New York, NY 10185

☆ **Blankets with Indian or cowboy patterns** made by *Beacon, Buell, Candelario, Capps, Esmond, Hamilton, Oregon City, Pendleton,* and *Racine (Badger State).* "I'm writing a book on these blankets and am buying blankets, catalogs, and advertising pieces, especially swatch books. I prefer all material to be priced, but will make offers to people who are not dealers. I answer calls and letters promptly." A photograph or photocopy is a must, and you are requested to list all flaws, holes, etc., in your first letter. Because blankets are often washed improperly, and therefore undesirable, dimensions are a must. Also buys **similar bedspreads.**

> Barry Friedman
> 22725 Garzota Drive
> Valencia, CA 91355
> (805) 296-2318

☆ **Mexican weavings,** including serapes, saltillos, rugs, and other pre-1940 items. Excellent condition only. Photo and dimensions essential.

> Barry Friedman
> 22725 Garzota Drive
> Valencia, CA 91355
> (805) 296-2318

Buyers of quilts and samplers are found in the chapter on folk art. Use the index or table of contents.

TOYS AND GAMES ARE OFTEN TREASURES.

Games and toys are usually treasures, especially if they are colorful, in their original box, and in excellent condition. There is a market for lesser items, but **prices drop to nothing for anything shabby.** *It seems as if nearly every toy is collected by someone, and you'll find the very best buyers in the following pages.*

If you carefully read sections in **Trash or Treasure** *about Toys, Dolls, Games, and Pop Culture, you will see a wide range of small and seemingly insignificant items sought by collectors. Games based on movies and TV usually find ready buyers in the $20 to $100 range (see pp111-126). You will also find a buyer for nearly all toy vehicles made from tin, steel or cast iron. The market is not good for plastic vehicles, though some other plastic toys, especially comic characters will sell. Baby boomer toys of the 1960's and 70's are particularly popular right now.*

Common games with names you recognize are seldom collectible, *unless they are prototypes or hand made.*

To sell something, you should provide the potential buyer with a complete description, including the following information:

(1) What you have, including its size, color, and the material from which it is made;

(2) Names, dates, and numbers printed, embossed, stamped, or labeled on the item;

(3) Condition, including mention of any missing parts, pieces, or paint, or damage to what remains;

(4) Whether it has the box and/or instructions, especially important when selling games.

Wooden, tin, and iron toys were usually painted. **The amount of paint that still remains is vital information** *to a collector, as is any evidence that the toy might have been repainted. You should estimate what percent of original paint remains.*

Don't forget your Self-Addressed Stamped Envelope.

19th century toys with moving parts regularly bring more than $2,500 and top the $500 mark often.

At least one Trash or Treasure find resulted in an $18,000 sale last year. You should be very careful how you dispose of any 100 year old toy in fine condition.

Here's some folks I think you'll enjoy doing business with.

EARLY TOYS

☆ **Fine old kaleidoscopes** made of wood and/or brass especially elaborate inlaid or complex instruments from the mid 19th century. No cardboard toys.

> Lucille Malitz, Lucid Antiques
> PO Box KH
> Scarsdale, NY 10583
>   (914) 636-7825

☆ **High quality kaleidoscopes** from the 1800's, made of wood and/or brass by makers such as *Bush, Brewster, Carpenter,* or *Leach.* Prefer perfect original condition brass instruments in wooden cases with the Royal seal, but will consider less. He does not buy cardboard or other inexpensive kaleidoscopes. Nothing made in the 1900's. Include your phone number and time you're home so he can phone.

> Martin Roenigk, Mechantiques
> 26 Barton Hill
> East Hampton, CT 06424
>   (203) 267-8682   Fax: (203) 267-1120

☆ **Polyramapanoptiques and megalethescopes.**   The former are early 19th century cardboard or wooden boxes with flaps for slides, which permit viewing of hand painted or pin-pricked scenes. Megalethescopes, invented in 1860, are large wooden cabinets, often heavily carved, also devices for slides, usually seen as day and night views of the same scene in 3D. Lucile buys and sells slides for these early optical toys.

> Lucille Malitz, Lucid Antiques
> PO Box KH
> Scarsdale, NY 10583
>   (914) 636-7825

☆ **Collections of fine tin and iron toys** are sought for cataloged specialty auctions by this well known New England auctioneer. No junk, reproductions or items made after 1940.

> James D. Julia Auctioneers
> PO Box 80
> Fairfield, ME 04937
>   (207) 453-7904   Fax: (207) 453-2502

☆ **Antique toys** of many different types:
- **Mechanical banks,** pre-1920, made of tin or iron;
- Cast iron **bell toys**, circa 1890;
- **Figural clockwork toys**, in tin or iron, from the 1870's;
- **Political campaign toys** and banks;
- European **tin toys** and large boats;
- Colorful **paper on wood boats and trains** from the 1890's;
- Colorful **Victorian children's games** and **block sets**;
- **Hand painted tin wind-up toys**.

Not interested in anything after 1940, nor does he want banks marked BOOK OF KNOWLEDGE, repainted items or things that have been dug up. Broken mechanical banks or toys that are incomplete may be of minor interest. Give the size, condition of the metal, and the condition of the paint including fading. List all repairs and note if the item has been lacquered or refinished. This 17 year veteran insists you set the price you want for your items.

> Mark Suozzi
> PO Box 102
> Ashfield, MA 01330
>   (413) 628-3241

☆ **Antique toys** in excellent condition, including cars, carousels, and character and comic wind-ups. German and American tin toys, penny toys, nested blocks, and pop-up books are all sought. Has no interest in dolls or trains. List manufacturer, size, and condition. Photo desirable.

> James Conley
> 2758 Coventry Lane NW
> Canton, OH 44708
>   (216) 477-7725   (216) 499-9283

☆ **Cast iron bell toys,** working or not. He will consider incomplete specimens of these early toys which move and ring a bell when pulled on a string. Send clear photos taken from more than one angle, or phone with the item in hand.

> Gregory "Dr. Z" Zemenick
> 1350 Kirts #160
> Troy, MI 48084
>   (810) 642-8129   (810) 244-9426

☆ **Sets of early wooden 9 pins or 10 pins bowling games.**
Craig Dinner
PO Box 4399
Sunnyside, NY 11104
(718) 729-3850

☆ **Victorian toys:** Jack-in-the-boxes, animals on rolling platforms, nine pins bowling games, and other traditional toys, especially those with nursery rhyme tie-ins. He does not want anything made after 1920. This 25 year veteran requests a photo or photocopy of what you'd like to sell. Prefers to find toys in like-new condition, because they are frequently used as part of Christmas theme displays.
Dolph "Father Christmas" Gotelli
PO Box 8009
Sacramento, CA 95818
(916) 456-9734

☆ **Clockwork (wind-up) toys** from before 1910, made of tin or iron, working or not, complete or not. "I want wind-up cars, boats, horses and buggies, people, and what have you, with particular interest in large ocean boats and steamships." Send a good clear sharp photo of both sides of the toy and include your telephone number.
Greg "Dr. Z" Zemenick
13560 Kirts #160
Troy, MI 48084
(810) 642-8129   (810) 244-9426

☆ *Schoenhut* **circus animals, games and dolls.** "I'll pay $150+ for each glass-eyed animal in original or near original condition. Also want circus wagons, tents, and comic characters, but no pianos."
Harry McKeon, Jr.
18 Rose Lane
Flourtown, PA 19031
(215) 233-4094

You should give the following information:

    (1) What you have, including its size, color, and the material from which it is made;
    (2) Names, dates, and numbers printed, embossed, stamped, or labeled on the item;
    (3) Condition, including mention of any missing parts, pieces, or paint, or damage to what remains;
    (4) Whether it has the box and/or instructions.

Don't forget your Self-Addressed Stamped Envelope.

20th CENTURY TOYS

☆ **Old one of a kind kites from before 1940** especially those made by important inventors. Names on desirable kites include *Hargrave, Lecornu, Saconney, Conyne, Perkins, Bell,* and many others including *Barrage Kite, Target Kite,* and the *U.S. Weather Bureau.* Also wants prototype models of production kites. Also traditional kites of Europe, the Orient, Malaysia, or South America. If it's old, interesting, or unusual, she'd like to hear about it. As publisher of *Kite Lines,* Valerie says she can act as a contact person to help you sell your kite if it's something she doesn't want. Rare and important kites are scarce but the market is small. They bring from $100 to $500. Give the history of your kite if you can.

> Valerie Govig, Kite Lines
> PO Box 446
> Randallstown, MD 21133
> (410) 922-1212   Fax: (410) 922-4262

☆ **Any sand-operated self contained toys,** including the "not very old" enclosed boxes with figures set in motion by flipping over the box. Also **small toy scales** made of tin.

> Donald Gorlick
> PO Box 24541
> Seattle, WA 98124
> (206) 824-0508

☆ *Fisher-Price* **toys** and **Raggedy Ann dolls.**

> Patricia Wagner
> 10585 Knight Ave.
> Waconia, MN 55387
> (612) 442-4036

☆ **Yo-Yo items** including displays, boxes, pins, awards and patches.

> John Fawcett
> Rural Route 2, 720 Middle Turnpike
> Storrs, CT 06268
> (203) 429-9228

☆ *Erector* **sets** by *A.C. Gilbert.* Will buy complete sets, partial sets, manuals, signs, and sales catalogs. Give model numbers and dates whenever it's possible.

> Elmer Wagner
> 256 South Pitt Street
> Carlisle, PA 17013
> (717) 243-3539

TOY BANKS

☆ **Cast iron mechanical banks**, 1870-1920, and **Japanese tin battery operated banks,** 1946-1960. Include a bottom tracing. Indicate whether it works or not and if you still have the original box. Battery banks *must* be in near mint condition. No plastic banks.
>Rick Mihlheim
>PO Box 128
>Allegan, MI 49010
>(616) 673-4509

*Tin and iron toys were usually painted.
The amount of paint that still remains is vital
information to a collector. So is evidence
that the toy might have been repainted.
You should estimate the percentage (%) of paint remaining.*

*Toy banks are desirable, particularly 19th century originals.
These were sold in boxes, which can add hundreds of dollars to
the value. Banks marked BOOK OF KNOWLEDGE on the bottom are
not of interest. Advertising cards which depict banks sell for $200
to $1,000 each!*

Here's a couple pages of people who pay that!

☆ **Mechanical and still banks made of cast iron, tin, or wood.** Especially any mechanical bank with its original box, packing, and receipt. Also buys painted and stenciled cast iron or tin still banks shaped like buildings. Will consider incomplete, broken and non-working specimens, if old and genuine. No banks made after 1930, especially those which say BOOK OF KNOWLEDGE on the bottom. Also buys trade cards, catalogs, empty packing boxes, advertising depicting mechanical banks and photos of children with banks. Send sharp photos of the bank from different angles, or phone with it in front of you. Greg is the former president of a club for bank collectors.
>Gregory "Dr. Z" Zemenick
>1350 Kirts #160
>Troy, MI 48084
>(810) 642-8129   (810) 244-9426

☆ **Cast iron or tin banks, still or mechanical.** Also buys original boxes and color trade cards for mechanical banks. No banks after 1950. Indicate any repairs, repaints, and give the dimensions. Prefers you to set the price you want.

> Virginia Jensen
> 22410 Wilson
> Dearborn, MI 48126

☆ **Still banks made of cast iron or metal** with special emphasis on unusual or rare examples in excellent to near-mint condition. Letters should include an accurate description including an estimate of how much of the original paint is still there. Carefully measure the length, width, and height. Photos are appreciated. Private collector answers all letters which include SASE.

> Ralph Berman
> 3524 Largo Lane
> Annandale, VA 22003
> (703) 560-5439

☆ **Banks, both still and mechanical** made of cast iron, tin, or zinc alloy before 1935. Also wants bank related items such as the wood boxes used to package banks by the manufacturer, ads, **trade cards**, and flyers depicting mechanical banks. Also photos of children with mechanical banks. Does not want reproductions or rusted items. Tell him the condition and exact size of the bank as well as how you got it. He notes that it is impossible to make a firm offer without actually seeing your bank in person. Sy writes a monthly column on banks for *Antique Toy World*. Dealers must price their goods. "Amateurs? I want some idea of how much they would like for the bank. I do not want shoppers who call me, then call a dozen other collectors trying to get the best price for their bank. Leave me out, please."

> Sy Schreckinger
> PO Box 104
> East Rockaway, NY 11518
> (516) 536-4154

GAMES & PUZZLES

☆ **American boxed games** of all types (board games, card games, skill and action games) made before 1970 and some **jigsaw puzzles**, **mechanical puzzles**, and miscellaneous playthings. "I specialize in games whose theme reflect American culture (pop culture, leisure, pastimes, fads, history, etc.). I look for games that show the name or logo of the manufacturer. I am always interested in unusual games or games that have very good illustrations of the box or gameboard. I also collect game parts and pieces, gameboards, and any advertising or ephemera related to American games or game companies. Game collectors want games made by McLoughlin Brothers, 19th century games by Parker Brothers, Singer, Bliss, Ives, and others. I look for games with exceptional lithography on the box, boards or cards. I also seek games representing certain themes or depicting historical events or achievements such as the Civil War, Brooklyn bridge, comic characters, World's Fairs, mysteries, sports heroes or teams, transportation, military, Western themes, radio, movies before 1950, TV shows before 1970, commercial products, fictional characters, etc. *I do not want* games that don't indicate the manufacturer, or common games such as *Authors, Beano, Bingo, Bridge, Checkers, Chess, Doctor Busby, Fish Pond, Flinch, Jack Straws, Keno, Lost Heir, Lotto, Monopoly, Old Main, Parcheesi, Pick-Up-Sticks, Pit Rook, Snap, Tiddly Winks,* or *Touring*. Games made recently, like *Charlie's Angels* or *Kojak* are not of interest. Please don't offer games that are not complete and in near mint condition unless they are before 1900." Give the title, maker, box size, the contents and material from which the pieces are made, and make a Xerox™ of the cover of the box and board. Dealers price your goods. Amateurs may request offers. Bruce wrote *American Boxed Games and Their Makers, 1822-1992* which you can order for $22.

> Bruce Whitehill
> The Big Game Hunter
> 620 Park Avenue #202
> Rochester, NY 14607
> (716) 442-8998 days

☆ **Card and board games.** A wide range of adult and children's games are wanted, especially games that are hand made, patriotic, or have unusual themes. The following will be considered *only if in some way unusual*: Strategy games, domino sets, backgammon sets, cribbage boards, pre-1935 *Monopoly* games, **Mah Jongg sets**, anagrams, and playing card decks. Pre-1970 items preferred. Best if complete with rules, all pieces, and original box. No *Authors, Flinch, Rook, Touring* and other common games are wanted except prototypes.

> Dave Galt
> 302 West 78th Street
> New York, NY 10024
> (212) 769-2514

☆ **Games.** Buys children's and adult games in colorful pictorial boxes copyrighted before 1960 including:
- Victorian games before 1900;
- Comic character games;
- Television games from the 1950's and 60's;
- Sports games with famous players named on the box;
- Space and science fiction games before 1950;
- Games based on children's book series;
- Lesser known games with colorful names or pictures.

Does not want generic games, any common game, or "baby boomer games" from the 1960's and 70's. Condition of games is very important as he is buying for resale. Give the name of the game, the maker, copyright (©) date, and list all missing pieces, if any.

      Paul Fink's Fun & Games
      PO Box 488
      Kent, CT 067547
        (203) 927-4001

☆ **Antique and collectible board and card games** made in the U.S. from 1840-1960's. Any game before 1860 is wanted, especially those made by *Ives, Crosby, Magnus,* or *Adams*, for which they will pay $500 and up. Other items of particular interest are baseball games before WWI and games about TV shows, cartoon characters, space exploration and pop culture (including movies) of the 1930's-1970's. They also buy **wooden jigsaw puzzles, blocks**, and **paper toys**. No chess, checkers, *Pit, Lotto, Rook, Flinch, Autobridge, Parcheesi, Touring,* variants of *Bingo*, TV "game show" games, or "kiddie" games like *Chutes and Ladders*. Give name, condition, size, maker, copyright date, and the degree of completeness.

      Dave Oglesby and Sue Stock
      57 Lakeshore Drive
      Marlborough, MA 01752
        (508) 481-1087

☆ **Almost any complete playable game,** especially out-of-print titles by *Avalon Hill, 3M, SPI,* pre-1964 *Parker Bros.*, war games, sports games, political games, and TV related games. Include the name of the manufacturer and copyright date. Please thoroughly check the contents and note if anything, no matter how small, is missing. Describe how much wear shows on the box and pieces. Also buys **gaming magazines** such as *The General, Wargamer, The Dragon,* and *Games & Puzzles*. Please, no checkers, chess or common children's games like *Authors*.

      H.M. Levy
      PO Box 197-TH
      East Meadow, NY 11554
        (516) 485-0877

☆ **Chess sets.** "I'll buy rare and unusual chess sets of all sorts, but primarily those with *themes* such as Disney, Watergate, etc. I like historical, literary, fictional, and mythological." If it's out of the ordinary in theme, design, material, or whatever, give him a call. He would especially like to find the 3-D chess set from *Star Trek* in the late 1960's. No plastic or "typical wooden sets," he warns. "I'm looking for works of art or imagination." Describe the board if one accompanies your set. Provide whatever background you can about the history of the board and pieces. Describe condition of both. Photo or photocopy, please.

> Dennis Horwitz
> PO BOX 301
> Topanga, CA 90290
> (310) 455-4002

☆ **Chess sets, as well as books and art related to chess.**
- "I'll buy figural or very ornate sets" made of ivory, bone, amber, wood, silver, metal, glass, or porcelain. Sets from before 1900 are preferred. Artist signed sets are of particular interest as are ivory sets from 19th century Europe or Russia. Standard looking sets are not wanted.
- Art sought includes paintings, prints, figurines, and anything else with a chess related theme.
- Books related to playing chess, chess pieces, or chess history. "Will consider any book related to chess" including those on other topics with chess sections.
- Ephemera such as photos, autographs, postcards, score cards of well known players, medals, souvenirs from chess Olympiads, and what have you.

Nothing made of plastic is wanted. Books should be complete, but early and rare items will be considered even if damaged. A photo or Xerox™ is helpful. When offering a set for sale, note the material from which it is made and measure the height of a pawn and the king. Note whether pieces are boxed or loose. Dealers, price your goods. Amateurs may request an offer.

> Jeffrey Litwin
> PO Box 5865
> Trenton, NJ 08638
> (609) 275-0996

☆ **Checkers ephemera,** primarily books about checkers or draughts, but also early handmade boards or anything unusual related to checkers. Give standard bibliographic information, and Don would like you to send a photocopy of any advertising in the book.

> Don Deweber, Checker Book World
> 3520 Hillcrest #4
> Dubuque, IA 52002
> (319) 556-1944

☆ **Mechanical and dexterity puzzles.** Wants all types of mechanical and dexterity puzzles. Not interested in jigsaw or paper and pencil puzzles. Please send a photocopy, sketch, or clear photo of your puzzle.

    Cary Basse
    6927 Forbes Ave.
    Van Nuys, CA 91406
    (818) 781-4856

☆ **Mechanical puzzles of all types** including **trick locks** and matchsafes "and all others." Also expresses some interest in advertising for trick locks and puzzles. A photocopy, photograph, or good sketch is appreciated. Dealers should price their goods, but he will help amateurs to determine the value of what they have.

    "Mr. Slocum"
    PO Box 1635
    Beverly Hills, CA 90213
    (310) 273-2270   Fax: (310) 274-3644

☆ **Jigsaw puzzles and board games with a space theme** are bought. Only wants items from before 1966 in excellent condition. Puzzles may be jigsaw or frame type. Will pay $50 for *Lost in Space* puzzle. Pop culture, not real life space themes are wanted. Also buys greeting cards and phono record sleeves with space theme. Does not want items made after 1966 or puzzles or games related to the real moon landing.

    Don Sheldon
    PO Box 3313
    Trenton, NJ 08619
    (609) 588-5403

☆ **Games and jigsaw puzzles with sentimental or sexy themes** dating from 1920-1959, such as pin-ups, children and animals, parents and children, patriotism, etc. Must be in the original box.

    Charles Martignette
    PO Box 293
    Hallandale, FL 33009
    (305) 454-3474

Pencil and paper puzzles like rebuses and crosswords are sought by a different type of collector. You will find this type of puzzle in the section on paper. Look in the index under "crossword puzzles" and you'll be steered to pages 460, 506 and 517.

MARBLES

☆ **Marbles and marble-related toys.** Wants old marbles including clay, china and porcelain marbles decorated with flowers, people, animals or geometric designs. He also buys Indian swirls, German swirls, clam broth, sulfides and machine made marbles if before 1940. "I'll pay up to $2,000 for colored sulfide marbles with unusual objects or people in them and up to $1,000 for porcelain or china marbles decorated with flowers, ships, birds, or people and animals." He also wants, and will pay well for, early boxed sets of marbles made by *Christensen Agate Co., Peltier Marble Co.,* or *Akro Agate.* Toys related to marbles are also often of interest. He does not want *Chinese Checker* marbles and boards or any cat's-eye marbles. If you know your marble's history, tell him. Otherwise a good description should include what is on or in the marble and its diameter.
>   Edwin Snyder
>   PO Box 156
>   Lancaster, KY 40444
>   (606) 792-4816 eves

☆ **Marbles and marble-related items.** "I'll buy marbles with pontil marks (from where they were hand-blown), toys or games using marbles, marble bags, tournament pins and medals, and boxes of marbles. Also pictures, magazine ads, and postcards which depict marble games." He does not buy "beat up" or chipped marbles, machine made marbles, homemade games, or *Chinese Checkers*. When selling marbles, it is important to give the diameter as part of your description.
>   Larry Svacina
>   2822 Tennyson
>   Denver, CO 80212
>   (303) 477-9203

☆ **Better quality marbles.** Stan is the publisher of *Marble Mania Quarterly* and will make offers on marbles if you describe them well.
>   Stanley Block
>   PO Box 51
>   Trumbull, CT 06611
>   (203) 261-0057

☆ **Marbles and marble related ephemera.** Will buy postcards, magazine covers, ads, trade cards, stories, calendars, or "anything depicting or written about kids playing marbles."
>   William Nielsen
>   1379 Main Street
>   PO Box 1379
>   Brewster, MA 02631
>   (508) 896-7389

ELECTRIC TRAINS

☆ **Toy trains and accessories, U.S. or foreign, made between 1900 and 1970.** Will buy any maker and gauge except HO gauge trains. Items do not have to be in perfect condition to be considered. **Also buys train catalogs and literature**. A wind-up *American Flyer* train with cars marked *Coca-Cola* is worth $350 in mint condition. This 40 year veteran will make offers **only if you're serious about selling**. Lazarus is past president of the Toy Train Operating Society and publisher of its attractive monthly newsletter. He will accept donations for the Society's exhibit at the California State Railroad Museum in Sacramento. Make certain to include a stamped envelope for a replay.

    Hillel Don Lazarus
    14547 Titus Street #207
    Panorama City, CA 91402
    (818) 762-3652 eves

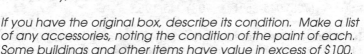

When describing electric trains, give the brand name, any model numbers found on the engine, and a list of the cars. It's worth your time to indicate the color of each car, its purpose, and RR line name, since minor variations can affect value. If the car has been repainted or otherwise modified by someone other than the factory, make certain to note that fact.

If you have the original box, describe its condition. Make a list of any accessories, noting the condition of the paint of each. Some buildings and other items have value in excess of $100.

☆ **All makes of old toy trains except HO gauge and hand made scale models.** Buys *Lionel, American Flyer, Ives, Marx* and all foreign trains larger than HO. "I'll buy engines, cars, accessories, signals, and incomplete sets that are new, like new, used, and even incomplete but useful for parts, but no layouts, transformers, track, rusty junk, or other toys." This 37 year veteran hobby shop operator offers a very large price guide to trains for only $6.

    Allison Cox
    18025 8th Avenue N.W.
    Seattle, WA 98177
    (206) 546-0114

☆ *Marklin* **and other European toy trains and metal toys.** "I'll buy trains powered by clockwork, electricity, or live steam. Other *Marklin* toys such as airplanes, boats, circus toys, and many others will also be considered for purchase. *Marklin* toys are generally marked with the company name, but others are marked with an entwined GM. "I want anything by *Marklin* before 1950 in decent condition." Also want *Bing, Schuco, Carlyle & Finch, Carette,* and *Bassett-Lowke* trains and metal toys in very good or better condition. "I will buy common items in excellent condition, but don't want repros, fakes, or toys with pieces missing. I'm a collector so prefer people not contact me unless they actually want to sell or trade what they have. I pay fair prices and am willing to travel to inspect collections." *Marklin* trains from the 1930's are worth from $500 to as much as $10,000 to Ron so check carefully.

Ron Wiener
Packard Bldg #1200
111 South 15th Street
Philadelphia, PA 19102
(215) 977-2266   Fax: (215) 977-2334

☆ **Toy trains in all gauges and types** are wanted, including electric, wind-up, floor type, etc. "Age is not the main consideration, but I do want items from before World War II. I like to buy large collections, but will buy smaller units, and consider properly priced junkers, but no reproductions." Wants to know the train's gauge, maker, condition, the number of pieces and the markings on each, and how many of the original boxes you have.

Jay "The Chicago Kid" Robinson
PO Box 529
Deerfield, IL 60015
(708) 945-8691   (708) 945-1965

☆ **HO trains and accessories,** preferably in running order, but they don't have to be old. He also buys **HO railroad books and magazines**.

Cliff Robnett
7804 NW 27th
Bethany, OK 73008
(405) 787-6703

☆ **Trains and other vehicles.** Will make an offer on trains in any gauge, especially HO, Standard, and O. He is also in the market for any fine old toys, but especially **steam engines, tin plate toys, and airplanes.** A color photo must accompany your description if you wish to sell to this long time dealer.

Heinz Mueller, Continental Hobby
PO Box 193
Sheboygan, WI 53082
(414) 693-3371   Fax: (414) 693-8211

☆ **Electric trains by** *Marx* with metal or plastic cars that have eight wheels. Especially wants complete sets in original boxes. "I'll pay $100 for *Marx* Pennsylvania RR car #53941. I also buy *American Flyer* Standard (large) gauge freight cars, and prewar *American Flyer* three-rail trains and sets (1938-1942). Not interested in plastic engines numbered #400 or #490 or cars with only four wheels." When writing, give him all numbers you find on boxes or cars.

> Robert Owen
> PO Box 204
> Fairborn, OH 45324

If toy trains interest you, consider joining the Toy Train Operating Society. Their Bulletin is one of the truly fine club publications. For information write to the Society at 25 West Walnut Street, Room 408, Pasadena, CA 91103. They'll send complete information and a sample copy.

TOY MOTORS & ENGINES

☆ **Toy outboard motors,** either battery or wind-up, alone or mounted on toy boats. "I'll buy motors by *K&O Fleetline* made between 1952 and 1962 with names of popular manufacturers of real outboard motors." Will pay $75-$400 for your toy depending on the model. Describe both the decals and the color.

> Jack Browning
> 214 16th Street NW
> Roanoke, VA 24017
> (703) 982-1253   (703) 342-1283

☆ **Toys run by live steam or hot air** wanted, as are accessories and catalogs related to steam and hot air toys. "I'll pay $100 to several thousand dollars for steam engines or for boats, trucks, cars, trains or tractors, American, English or German made. Makers include *Weeden, Buckman, Union, Bing, Marklin, Carette* and others. I don't want modern steam toys made by *Wilesco, Mamod,* or *Jansen.*" Give dimensions and markings. Some *Marklin* power plants were 4' tall and can be worth up to $10,000. "I usually require a photo before I buy, since most people do not understand the technical aspects of steam toys."

> Lowell Wagner
> 10585 Knight Ave.
> Waconia, MN 55387
> (612) 442-4036

☆ **Model engines run by gas or steam**, running or not. "These can be either factory built or built in the home shop. I would consider buying engines that are not completed, engines still in kit form, engine plans, or books on model engines. Also want **any scale model equipment** run by gas or steam engines." Please include make, model, dimensions, power rating if available, condition, and degree of completeness. Photos are helpful.

 Craig Donges
 6724 Glenwood Avenue
 Youngstown, OH 44512
  (216) 726-1830 Fax: (216) 726-4740

☆ **Toy electric battery driven motors** for kids, 1910 to 1930, made by *Ajax, Lil Hustler, Porter, Kent, Edison, Leavitt* and others. These range in size from lemons to large apples and had a variety of applications. Dealers please price.

 Steve Cunningham
 3200 Ashland Drive
 Bedford, TX 76021
  (817) 267-9851 Fax: (817) 267-0387

☆ **Early miniature outboard marine motors** used on model boats. Wants fuel type motors only. No electric motors or boats. Condition should be described carefully.

 Sven Stau
 PO Box 437
 Buffalo, NY 14212
  (716) 825-5448 (716) 822-3120

PLASTIC MODEL KITS

☆ **Plastic model kits** especially from the 1950's made by *Monogram, Hawk, Aurora, Bachman, Comet, ITC, Frog, Allyn, Monogram, Revell, Strombecker*, and others. Models can be autos, airliners, commercial ships, spacecraft, TV and movie subjects, and science fiction and other figures. Also manufacturers catalogs and store display models. Kits must be complete and unbuilt, with minimal damage to the box. Sealed unopened kits are best. He offers to send a copy of the grading system used by kit collectors for an SASE. He'll pay $100 for a perfect condition *Athearn* **gas-powered flying model** of the *Convair XFY-1 Pogo*. Bob publishes *Vintage Plastic*, the journal for kit collectors.

 Bob Keller's Starline Hobbies
 PO Box 38
 Stanton, CA 90680
  (714) 826-5218 days

☆ **Plastic model kits** of airplanes, tanks, ships, figures, cars, buildings, or what have you *if complete, unbuilt, and in original box.* Include the manufacturer and kit number. John publishes *Kit Collector's Clearinghouse*, a bimonthly newsletter for kit collectors and is the author of *Value Guide for Scale Model Plastic Kits,* available for $30, and other model books.

> John Burns
> 3213 Hardy Drive
> Edmond, OK 73013
> (405) 341-4640

☆ **Plastic model car kits depicting antique cars.** Unbuilt kits from before 1970 only, please.

> Henry Winningham
> 3205 South Morgan Street
> Chicago, IL 60608
> (312) 847-1672

☆ **Plastic 1/25th scale model car kits,** built or not. Also buys dealer promotional materials, model car books and magazines, if issued before 1975. Does not want anything currently available. Give the name of the maker and the model number on the box. If you have **dealer promotional models**, give the color, condition, and note whether the original box is present.

> Rick Hanson
> PO Box 161
> Newark, IL 60541
> (815) 695-5135

☆ **Model car kits & dealer promotional cars** from the 1950's, 60's and 70's. "I will consider kits in any condition, including those that have been started, completed kits, or boxes of junk parts." He points out that dealer promotional models "have a tendency to warp," which does affect value, but he will consider them in any condition. No interest in foreign items, reissues, aircraft, or items made after 1980.

> Paul Madsen
> PO Box 1380
> Burbank, CA 91507
> (818) 563-2527

TOY VEHICLES

☆ **Metal vehicles and toys,** pre-1959, including cars, trucks, boats, airplanes, trains and construction equipment:
- **Large steel toys** by *Buddy-L, Sturditoy, Turner, Kingsbury, Sonny, Keystone*, and *Structo*;
- *Tootsietoys* with white rubber tires or all metal wheels;
- **Old tin toy boats,** the larger the better;
- **Children's pedal cars** and trucks made before 1940;
- *Smith-Miller* or *M-I-C* **trucks** made of steel in California between 1945 and 1957;
- **Tin windup automotive, aviation, or comic toys,** U.S. or European, working or not. Will pay $2,500 for an 8" truck with "Aunt Eppie Hogg" in perfect condition;
- *Dinky* **toys**, pre-1964, from England or France;
- **Any metal motorcycle** 8" or longer, especially *Hubley Indian* delivery cycle, worth $1,500 in original condition;
- **Japanese scale models of U.S. cars;**
- **Cast iron toys** by *Hubley, Arcade, Kilgore*, and *Williams*.

Plastic, rubber, or wooden vehicles are not wanted. Describe the condition carefully, paying particular attention to the quality of the paint and whether or not all the parts and pieces are present. Describe the condition of the wheels and tires. Dimensions are helpful.

> Larry Bruch
> PO Box 121
> Mountaintop, PA 18707
> (717) 474-9202 eves

☆ **Cars, trucks and race cars** made of metal before 1960 are wanted.
- Toy cars by *Hubley, Dinky, Arcade, Kilgore, Williams, Tootsietoy, Sun Rubber*, and *Auburn Rubber* are wanted;
- Race cars, with or without engines, are wanted made by *Cox, Thimbledrome, Ohlson and Rice, Rodzy*, and others;
- Trucks by *Smith-Miller, MIC, Tonka, Marx* and others are sought.

Please send a photo and good description. "Prompt response assured."

> Bill Hamburg
> PO Box 1305
> Woodland Hills, CA 91365
> (818) 346-1269   Fax: (818) 346-0215

☆ *Tonka, Doepke,* **and** *Smith-Miller* **toy trucks** and catalogs, ads and photos depicting them. He does not want *Tonka's* "Mighty" or "Mini" series trucks or anything repainted. Photos of both sides are necessary.

> Nollie Neill, Jr.
> PO Box 38
> Ennice, NC 28623
> (910) 657-8152 Fax: (910) 282-8132

☆ **Larger pressed steel toy cars and trucks** are wanted by this 10 year veteran collector-dealer. "I'll buy *Smith Miller, Doepke, Tonka, Buddy-L, Keystone, Arcade* and other makes of toy vehicles including construction types, boats, airplanes, and farm tractors." To sell your vehicles, tell him [1] the maker if you can, [2] what it looks like, including what type of vehicle it is, [3] how many you have, and [4] the condition of each. Make an estimate of what percentage of the original paint is left. "I prefer not to buy rusty or damaged vehicles, but this policy is not written in stone."

> Jay "The Chicago Kid" Robinson
> PO Box 529
> Deerfield, IL 60015
>   (708) 945-8691   (708) 945-1965

☆ **Pedal cars.** "I'll buy any pre-WWII pedal car, pedal plane or pedal truck, and will consider some from the mid-1950's. I'm a most generous buyer, as I buy to keep not to resell. Condition is not a problem. I'll even buy half a vehicle if that's all you have. Please send photos." Will also purchase large (bigger than 12") metal cars, trucks, and planes made by *Keystone, Buddy-L, Dayton,* etc. No interest in *Tonka.*

> Sandy Weltman
> 39 Branford Road
> Rochester, NY 14618
>   (716) 442-8810

☆ **Pedal cars.** "I'll buy pedal cars made after WWII in excellent original condition, and pedal cars made before the war in any condition. I will pay over $1,000 for the better examples." This relatively new collector also will buy any pedal car advertising, sales catalogs, and the like as well as photos of kids with their pedal cars. He does not want pedal cars with plastic wheel covers and/or plastic steering wheels, as they are considered too new by collectors. The *one* exception to that rule is the *Ford Mustang* pedal car which he does want. Give the name of the manufacturer and the length of the vehicle. "I will not purchase or make offers without a good clear color photo of both sides."

> Frank Martin
> 7669 Winterberry Drive
> Youngstown, OH 44512
>   (216) 758-4470

☆ **Toy garbage trucks** in any size or condition. Please give the maker, size, and condition of tires and paint.

> A.J. Perez
> 5408 North Diversey
> Whitefish Bay, WI 53217
>   (414) 964-5399

☆ **Hard rubber toys,** especially **vehicles,** motorcycles, trains, airplanes, ships, **animals, soldiers, football and baseball players,** especially by *Rainbow Rubber Co.* Hard rubber toys only. No vinyl. Hard rubber is painted. Vinyl is made in the color of the toy and is the same color throughout. Give the maker, size, colors, condition, and description of features. Also buys **all toy vehicles of all sizes, from** *Dinky* **to pedal cars** made before 1950. "Photos are best."

    Steve Kelley
    PO Box 695
    Desert Hot Springs, CA 92240
       (619) 329-3206

☆ *Dinky* **toys** of all types except army vehicles. Also wants to buy all types of **toy motorcycles.**

    Don Schneider
    PO Box 1570
    Merritt, BC
    V0K 2B0 CANADA
       (604) 378-6421

☆ *Hot Wheels* are hot. With more than 700 basic body styles, 5,000 different color combinations, and 10,000 minor variations it's important to get expert advice before disposing of these toys. Values begin at a few dollars, but some can be worth more than $1,000 each! If you want to sell your cars, give the name of the car, the color, and the condition, including an estimate of the percent of original paint remaining. If all you want is an estimate of value, Mike wrote *Price Guide to Hot Wheels,* available from him for $30. He edits *Hot Wheels Newsletter,* available for only $20. "I give honest evaluations and pay fair prices," says this 20 year veteran collector/dealer, "but condition is important in the value of cars, and sellers really don't know how to properly evaluate condition, so I will never send money without seeing the cars first."

    Mike Strauss
    26 Madera Avenue
    San Carlos, CA 94070
       (415) 591-6482

☆ **Toy farm tractors and equipment** from 1970 or older. "I'll buy the ones with real farm equipment company names like *John Deere, Farmall, Oliver, Ford, Allis-Chalmers* and the like, in plastic or metal, and pay over $100 for some tractors." Also buys other scale model toys, like outboard motors, with tractor company names, and is interested in all scale *Caterpillar* **tractor and heavy equipment toys.** Does not want repros or anything made after 1980. Give the color, size, brand, model, condition, and the status of the original box, if available.

> Dave Nolt
> PO Box 553
> Gap, PA 17527
> (717) 768-3554

☆ **Toy firetrucks and fire related toys.** This veteran collector/dealer wants U.S. made fire toys built prior to 1960. Buys all types, all sizes, all styles as long as they are in good condition. Is particularly interested in finding *Ahrens Fox* and *Bulldog Macks* and other large steel firetruck toys, some of which can be worth $700 or more. Buys toy fire stations, firemen, and other toys and **games that are fire related.** Requests color photos, the price you'd like, and a statement of condition. Include your phone number. Will assist amateurs to set price. No Japanese tin toys or anything made after 1965.

> Luke Casbar, Toys for Boys
> 22 Garden Street
> Lodi, NJ 07644
> (201) 478-5535

☆ *Aurora* and *AFX* **electric race cars,** track, accessories after 1968.

> T. Pat Jacobsen
> 437 Minton Court
> Pleasant Hill, CA 94523
> (510) 930-8531

☆ *Atlas* and *Aurora* **electric race cars.** "No limit," he says, but prefers to buy entire collections. He particularly wants items in complete sets and original boxes or store displays and stock, but "will consider any *Atlas* and *Aurora* electric race cars you have." Photos are requested, but if you have a large collection for sale, you are encouraged to phone him. "I also collect colorful **hockey related games**, preferably complete in original box, but will consider incomplete sets if the boxes are good."

> Joe Bodnarchuk
> 62 McKinley Ave.
> Kenmore, NY 14217
> (716) 873-0264 voice or fax

TOY SOLDIERS

☆ **Toy soldiers of all types** including:
- Boxed sets of fine British soldiers;
- Dime store soldiers, 1930-50, made in the USA of painted lead;
- German composition soldiers of WWII.

Make photocopies of your soldiers if you'd like a free appraisal.

> Larry Bruch
> PO Box 121
> Mountain Top, PA 18707
>   (717) 474-9202

☆ **Toy soldiers.**

> Lt. Col. Wilfred Baumann
> PO Box 319
> Esperance, NY 12066
>   (518) 875-6753

☆ **Reparable lead soldiers.** "I'll buy them if you have the broken pieces and you set the price wanted."

> Ken Cross
> 6003 Putnam Ave.
> Ridgewood, NY 11385
>   (718) 456-0798

BB GUNS

☆ **BB Guns.** Wants American made spring-air BB guns in excellent condition. Numerous brands are wanted, although *Daisy* guns are preferred from the Plymouth, MI, factory. Does not want recently made guns, or those that are damaged, broken or otherwise in less than very good condition. You must list everything that is broken or missing. Is the stock, forestock, or grip broken, cracked or worn? Describe the finish on all metal and wooden parts. Include all names, numbers and addresses found on the gun. Indicate if it works or not.

> James Buskirk, Toy Gun Collectors of America
> 175 Cornell Street
> Windsor, CA 95492
>   (707) 837-9949

☆ *Quackenbush* **air guns.** Send a complete description, including a sketch or photo. Will make offers, but appraisals are for a fee.

> Charles Best
> 11523 Pinevalley Drive
> Franktown, CO 80116
>   (303) 660-2318

CAP PISTOLS

☆ **Cap pistols.** Especially interested in cast iron guns by *Kilgore, Stevens, Hubley* and *Kenton*. Premium paid for character guns such as the*Kilgore Long Tom, Big Horn, Roy Rogers, Lone Ranger*or*American*, the *Kenton Lawmaker*, the *Stevens Cowboy King,* or any of the many different models of *Gene Autry* guns made by *Kenton*. Also interested in the 1950's and 60's die cast guns. Buys any guns marked *Gene Autry, Roy Rogers, Dale Evans, Trigger, Lone Ranger, Tonto, Paladin, Alan Ladd, Hopalong Cassidy, Hoppy*, or *Shane*. Particularly seeks character guns made in Los Angeles by the *Schmidt Company* or by *LATCO*. Must give all identifying marks, numbers, etc., found on the guns and a complete accounting of damage or wear to the gun, finish, or handles (grips). Buys only guns in fine condition. Publishes the *Toy Toy Gun Collectors Newsletter*, available with club membership for the bargain price of $15/year.

    James Buskirk, Toy Gun Collectors of America
    175 Cornell Street
    Windsor, CA 95492
       (707) 837-9949

☆ **Cap pistols made of cast iron,** especially animated guns from the 1800's or guns featuring movie cowboys and other Pop Culture heroes before 1940. A magnet *must* stick to your gun or he's not interested.

    George Fougere
    67 East Street
    North Grafton, MA 01536
       (508) 839-2701

☆ **Cap pistols.** "I'll buy Western style cap guns made before 1965 by *Kilgore, Hubley, Stevens, Leslie-Henry, Chas. Schmidt, Nichols, Mattel,* and others. Especially looking for *Kilgore* "disc cap" guns such as the American, Big Horn, Long Tom and Roy Rogers models. Also seeking any cap gun or holster sets association with cowboy movie and TV actors like Gene, Hoppy, Paladin, the Lone Ranger, etc. Condition is important. Guns must be complete, working, and have little wear. Top prices paid for guns or holster sets in their original box. Photo if possible. Xerox™ your gun if you don't know what it is.

    Bill Hamburg
    PO Box 1305
    Woodland Hills, CA 91365
       (818) 346-1269   Fax: (818) 346-0215

Minor differences in castings, handles, or decoration can put extra money in your pocket. Accurate descriptions are important.

DOLLS AND TEDDY BEARS ARE WORTH YOUR ATTENTION

Doll collecting is the second largest hobby in the United States. Doll lovers spend one-half billion dollars annually. Collectors want all types from the high priced 19th century mechanicals and French fashion dolls which cost many thousands of dollars to modern plastic dolls worth a fraction as much. Because you are more likely to have the more modern dolls, a greater emphasis has been placed on them in this book.

Buyers of most dolls want the following information:

(1) Length of the doll, important because some dolls made in multiple sizes have different values;

(2) How big around the head is, important on old dolls; use a seamstress's tape or string to measure;

(3) Material from which the head, hair, hands, feet and body are made (may be from different materials);

(4) Type (painted, button, glass) and color of eyes and whether or not they move;

(5) Whether the mouth is open and whether teeth (molded, painted, or attached) show;

(6) Marks incised into the scalp, neck, shoulders, or back of the doll;

(7) How the doll is dressed and whether the clothes seem to be original;

(8) Any chips, cracks, repainting, or other repairs.

When offering a doll for sale, a photo can be helpful, but you can often get better results faster, easier, and cheaper with a photocopy machine. Photocopies are particularly useful for showing how a doll is dressed.

The original box for your doll may add as much as 50% to the doll's value. When describing modern dolls such as Barbie whose accessories are frequently marketed in plastic bubble packs mention packages that are unopencd and unfaded as they are worth two or three times the value of loose items.

ANTIQUE DOLLS

☆ **Dolls, antique and modern.** Buys dolls of bisque, china, wood, cloth, papier-maché, composition and hard plastic from the beginning of time to the 1960's. Will buy Kewpies, bears, and other animals, too. Also wants doll accessories like shoes, clothing, wigs, purses, opera glasses, combs, etc., and small props like buggies, furniture, tea sets, and the like. "I prefer things priced, but will make offers."
>
> Madalaine Selfridge
> Hidden Magic Doll Museum
> 33710 Almond Street
> Lake Elsinore, CA 92530
> (909) 674-9221

☆ **Collections of antique dolls** are sought for cataloged specialty auctions by this well known New England auctioneer. No junk, reproductions, or dolls made after 1940 will be considered.
>
> James D. Julia Auctioneers
> PO Box 80
> Fairfield, ME 04937
> (207) 453-7904   Fax: (207) 453-2502

☆ **Dolls.** Buys a variety of character dolls:
- **Barbie dolls** from 1964 and before, especially the Color-Magic and "American Girl" models. Also buys factory-made *Barbie* clothes, but not home-made ones;
- **Raggedy Ann and Andy** and related items, including **Beloved Belindy.** She emphasizes a willingness to pay top prices for very early high quality dolls;
- **Howdy Doody** dolls and marionettes. Also interested in dolls of all other characters on the show: , Clara Belle, Mr. Bluster, Princess, Flubba Dub, and Dilly Dally;
- **Black (Negro) dolls** of any size, type, and design, whether factory or home made;
- **Little Lulu & Tubby** dolls and related items in all sizes;
- **Red Riding Hood** and related items;
- **Cinderella** and related items.

Follow the basic rules for describing what you have to sell, including dimensions and an accurate statement of condition. "I don't want reproductions, common items, or junk."
>
> Gwen Daniel
> 18 Belleau Lake Court
> O'Fallon, MO 63366
> (314) 281-3190 anytime

☆ **Dolls.** This 30 year veteran doll dealer wants large collections or single antique dolls from France, Germany or the U.S. made from bisque, wood, china, composition or other material. Also
- **Shirley Temple dolls;**
- 1950's and 60's dolls such as *Ginny, Terri Lee, Buddy Lee,* etc.;
- *Barbie* **dolls** and accessories before 1970 and all limited eds.;
- **Kewpie** dolls;
- Doll **buggies, furniture and dishes**.

"I pay especially well for these dolls in their original packages." Prices vary widely depending on the individual doll, its rarity and its condition. "I do not want any dolls that are still available in stores or any new reproduction porcelain or artist dolls. In most cases, I need you to tell me the size, any marks or identifications, and what you know of its history. Dealers, price your goods; amateurs may request an offer."

Donna Purkey
Old Chicago
PO Box 2871
Anaheim, CA 92804
(714) 828-5909

☆ **Old dolls and their parts.** "I buy, both as a collector and as a dealer, a large variety of old dolls and their parts.
- Old **German dolls** (a particular favorite);
- **Cloth comic characters** such as Lulu, Tubby, Nancy, or Sluggo;
- **Raggedy Ann or Andy** dolls, but only old ones;
- Bisque **snow babies;**
- Wooden jointed creche-type dolls for display at Christmas;
- **Damaged dolls** if priced reasonably;
- **Accessories for old dolls,** such as shoes, clothing, wigs, purses;
- **Doll carriages** and quality furniture;
- **Buster Brown china dishes**.

I have no interest at all in Japanese bisque or currently made dolls. Send a Xerox™ or photo of what you have."

Patricia Snyder
My Dear Dolly
PO Box 303
Sparta, NJ 07871
(201) 729-8087

☆ **Dolls, doll parts, and doll clothes.** Buys old bisque and china heads even if the body or other parts are missing. Also wants to buy baby gowns, slips, bonnets, etc. "I do not make offers or bid against other collectors. You must price what you have."

Annie Nalewak, Shop 4 Trading Fair II
5515 South Loop, East Crestmont Exit
Houston, TX 77033
(409) 935-8029

☆ **Dolls of all types.** This active dealer will consider a wide range of good looking fine condition dolls made of papier-maché, wood, china, or bisque, including:
- Expensive **French fashion dolls**, character dolls, etc.;
- Early **cloth dolls**;
- **Teddy bears**;
- **Steiff character and animal dolls**;
- **Vogue Ginny** dolls;
- Kathe Kruse, Chase, Madame Alexanders, or Izannah Walker;
- **Doll houses.**

Follow guidelines on page 110 for describing dolls correctly.

> Valerie Makseyn
> 61 6th Street
> Cambridge, MA 02141
> (617) 576-0796

☆ **Teddy bears that are fully jointed with glass or shoebutton eyes.** Wants pre-1920 *Steiff* bears in any condition and will pay $1,000+ for those larger than 20" long. Not interested in any non-jointed bears or bears made after 1940. Also teddy bear books, postcards, photos, trays, etc. Polly also buys **stuffed animal toys on cast iron wheels**.

> Polly Zarneski
> 5803 North Fleming
> Spokane, WA 99205
> (509) 327-7622

☆ **Teddy bears**, but only mohair fully jointed bears with glass or shoe-button eyes. "I'll pay the best prices for early German bears in very fine condition." Follow basic rules for describing.

> Gwen Daniel
> 18 Belleau Lake Court
> O'Fallon, MO 63366
> (314) 281-3190 anytime

☆ **Mohair teddy bears with long arms and big feet** made between 1903 and 1915 are wanted in all sizes as long as they are fully jointed. Also wants perfume and compact bears in various colors and any unusual mohair teddy or teddy related items. Also looking for early *Steiff* **cats and dogs** with printed ear buttons. Also wants **Billy Possum stuffed dolls with shoebutton eyes** and all Billy Possum items including doll dishes and silverware, banks and postcards. Mimi wants you to know your dolls are going to a "loving home, not a dealer."

> Mimi Hiscox
> 12291 St. Mark
> Garden Grove, CA 92645
> (310) 598-5450

MODERN DOLLS

☆ *Barbie* **dolls.** Wants to buy all *Barbie* dolls, fashions and accessories, 1959-1972. "Anything *Barbie* related," she says, especially prototypes, gift sets, licensed Mattel products, watches, ponytails, color magic, bendable leg *Barbies*, and the rest of *Barbie's* family, especially Francie, introduced in 1966. Will pay $1,000 for a mint in box airplane and $500 for a MIB *Barbie* boat. She does buy Bob Mackie *Barbies*, porcelain, holiday, Xmas, and FAO Schwartz *Barbies* too. It's worth your time to look for early dolls, especially for the clothes and accessories in their original boxes, because some were made for a very short time or sold in very limited markets. Some inside tips:

The first *Barbie* sleep eyes were introduced in 1964.

If the knees bend, the doll was made after 1965.

Rooted eyelashes came into use in 1966.

Talking *Barbie* family arrived in 1968.

Black Barbies Julia and Christie arrived the same year.

Dolls that are easy to pose, and those with growing hair, are both products of the 1970's and too late to interest most *Barbie* collectors. To describe a *Barbie*, you must give the name of the doll, hair color, lip color and condition. "Please," she asks, "do not send or write about *Barbies* because they say 1966 on their back. Today's dolls still say 1966 on them." Marl offers an important clue about how to tell if your *Barbie* is old. "If it does not say JAPAN on the buttocks, I don't want it." Marl buys dolls for her personal collection and for resale.

Marl Davidson, WS7
5707 39th Street Circle East
Bradenton, FL 34203
(813) 751-6275

The first Barbie *wore a black and white swimsuit and had copper tubes set in holes in the bottom of her feet. Barbie stood on a round black plastic disk. Her white irises and black eyeliner looked Oriental.*

The second Barbie was like the first except the stand holes were gone. Barbies three through six had blue eyes.

The first (ponytail) Barbie from the late 1950's and early 60's had MCM LVIII embossed on her behind. This remains until 1962. For 20 years, beginning in 1966, Barbie was tush marked "1966."

Barbie was made worldwide, and tush marked accordingly. Only those marked JAPAN *are sought by most collectors.*

☆ *Barbie* **dolls and accessories from 1958 through 1966** are wanted, especially items still in their original box. "I'll also buy other members of the *Mattel* family of dolls from that era, and clothing for them all. HINT: *Barbie's* clothing is numbered. The earliest clothing is in the 900 series, but I also want the 1600 series outfits sold in the early 1960's. Call even if your outfit isn't all there, because you may have just the parts I need to complete a set. Of all the *Barbie* items, the one I'd like to find the most is the case of 30 or 31 Barbies that was carried by salesmen in 1958 in an effort to sell the doll to toy stores. It contains #1 *Barbies* wearing the old outfits that were going to be available. If you have one of these in perfect condition it could be worth as much as $100,000. Pink display box dolls that retailers used in the early 60's containing dressed *Barbies* are also sought, and can put from $3,000 to $5,000 in your pocket if in fine condition. In 1964 when *Mattel* introduced the bendable *Barbies*, they tried a variety of hair styles, so *Barbie* came with bubble cuts, pony tails, and page boys. The American girl dolls with side-parts in their hair are among the rarest of the *Barbie* dolls, and can be worth $2,000 to $4,000 or more if in their original boxes." She is not buying *Barbies* from the 1970's and 80's, or earlier dolls with serious flaws such as damaged toes or missing limbs or fingers. Describe your *Barbie* and accessories thoroughly, paying particular attention to condition. Describe the condition of the box as well. You may set the price wanted or request an offer if your doll is for sale.

Linda Brundage
2717 West Olive Avenue #200
Burbank, CA 91505
(818) 843-8616

☆ **Modern collectible fashion dolls.** Buys a range of scarce collectible modern dolls:
- *Nancy Ann Storybook Dolls,* particularly black or brown dolls in either bisque or plastic. Wants others too, but notes most *Nancy Anns* need to be unused to be of interest to her;
- *Miss Revlons* modern woman of the 50's;
- *Ideal* **fashion dolls** from the 1950's, such as *Miss Clairol, Toni* and *Bonnie Braids*. Dolls usually marked on their heads.
- *Hollywood* **dolls**, in either bisque or hard plastic. "The costume's the thing." Often, but not always, marked HOLLYWOOD on the back. Look for boxes covered with Hollywood stars.

If you have a perfect condition doll, especially one with its original box, give length, description, and tell whether clothes are original. Photocopy is helpful.

Sharon Vohs-Mohammed
PO Box 2891
Glen Ellyn, IL 60138
(708) 858-1852

Most amateurs trying to research dolls are limited by what is available in their local public library. If you have 20th century dolls, books by Pat Smith may be of help. Ask the reference librarian to obtain these and other doll books through interloan if you can't find what you need in your local branch.

Researching dolls on your own can be frustrating. A specialty book like Barbie Rarities *by Florence Theriault is excellent, but at $45 is for the serious collector. For most other types of dolls, there is no single book certain to help you.*

☆ **Cabbage Patch Kids are wanted.** A variety of CPK's exist:
- Xavier Roberts' soft sculptured originals (1978 on);
- Mass market dolls by *Coleco* and *Hasbro* with vinyl heads and yarn or nylon hair (1983-present);
- Porcelain dolls by *Applause* or *Shader* (1985-86);
- Porcelain figurines by *Extra Special* (1984-85);
- Vinyl figurines and "numerous accessories."

Many of these sell for below issue price, but some originals bring $200-$300 and rare models by *Coleco* bring $150 and up. If you want to sell your doll, determining its value requires expertise and a lot of information. If your doll is still in its original box, open it from the bottom and untwist the wire holding the CPK in place. Then give the following:
- Head mold number impressed on the back of the neck;
- Hair style and color;
- Eye color and whether there are freckles or not;
- Description of the clothing (look for a tag and CPK logo);
- Color of the Xavier Roberts signature found on the left butt;
- If the CPK's butt has a date, please give it as well;
- Whether the box and birth papers are present;
- And lastly, the the name of the manufacturer and the factory ID letters in the circle on the body tag found under the diaper on the left side. Letters should be J, P, IC, KT, OK, PMI or UT.

A color photo is helpful. An SASE is a must. For her own collection Ann wants 1983 *Colecos* (black signature) with freckles, boy dolls with fuzzy or shag hair, dolls from molds 4, 6, 19 or 30. She also wants UT tags, dolls sold in foreign countries, mint clothing accessories, and some porcelains. Ann wrote a dictionary that identifies CPK details (it's only $7) and publishes a monthly newsletter for $22. Although not a dealer, Ann may be able to assist you to find a buyer for better dolls.

Ann Wilhite
The Cabbage Connection
610 West 17th
Fremont, NE 68025
(402) 721-0954

☆ *Nancy Ann Storybook Dolls* were created in the mid 1930's. These early dolls were bisque (unglazed china) made in Japan, and usually marked with a sticker reading NANCY ANN DRESSED DOLL. After 1942, dolls were "frozen legged." *Nancy Anns* were the number one selling girls' toy in the 1940's. In 1947 they introduced plastic arms, then all plastic bodies. In 1949, eyes opened and shut. Many different series were created including Sports, Masquerade, and Famous pairs like Hansel and Gretel (all desirable). You may also find:

- Nursery rhymes, days of the week, and months of the year (the most common of her dolls);
- *Margie Ann* is same doll but dressed as a little girl in a suit;
- *Audrey Ann* in an organdy dress and white boots is hard to find;
- *Geraldine Ann* with eight outfits and a "movie set" with a director's chair, lights, etc., is fragile and very desirable;
- *Judy Ann*/USA dolls, which are very scarce;
- *Muffie* and *Debbie*, 8" and 10" hard plastic dolls, were the tops of the line, and came with many matching outfits.

Nancy Ann made a great many dolls, so values range from $20 to $175 with a few over $500. Dolls must be individually evaluated, however, because there are so many different costumes. In general, the frozen leg and plastic dolls are less valuable, but boy (male) dolls are rare and desirable in any form as is some furniture. *McCalls* pattern #811 for making cardboard furniture at home is $50+ to you! All Nancy Ann dolls have a hat or ribbon in their hair. A missing hat reduces the value of a doll by more than half, and "you can't put just any old ribbon in the hair." To sell a *Nancy Ann*, you must tell whether it's plastic or bisque, has moving or frozen legs, has eyes that move or not (and their color), and the height. Make a photocopy of the doll which shows the dress. If you have the original box, copy that too, since some boxes are more valuable than others.

Elaine M. Pardee
PO Box 6108
Santa Rosa, CA 95406
(707) 538-3655 Fax: (707) 537-0604

Many readers do not want to sell their dolls, but are looking for info about their heirloom. Information seekers usually want the reassurance their emotional treasure has financial value as well. If you're not selling, make that clear up-front when you contact someone in Trash or Treasure.

☆ *Annalee Dolls.* Wants 1950's, 60's and 70's versions of these felt dolls with painted faces, most of which have internal wires for positioning arms and legs. All types considered, including human, animal, and holiday, especially those with embroidered (woven) tags. Tags, more than copyright dates, are indicators of when a doll was made, although early dolls didn't always have tags, and doll owners often cut them off. Dating dolls by their tags is a job for experts, and never foolproof, as many different tags appear on the oldest dolls. Some *Annalee Dolls* were custom made, some limited production, and others factory made in fairly large quantities, so Sue will often need to talk to you or inspect the doll before giving an offer. Dolls tend to be worth $20 to $150 with a very few worth more. "I'll analyze your doll and will always give you a fair price." Pictures are helpful, but "if you can't send a photo, you must tell me what the doll is (human or animal) and what it's doing and how it's dressed. I also need to know the height of the doll, as they come in many different sizes. Condition is important in determining price. If you have an *Annalee Doll*, I want you to call with the doll in front of you. Before you call, please make a careful inspection for moth and silverfish damage in the form of holes, pock-marks, etc., and for any signs of fading in the doll or clothing." Sue is willing to train pickers who regularly shop at yard sales and flea markets if you send a Stamped Self-Addressed Envelope. Please include your phone number.

> Sue Coffee
> 10 Saunders Hollow Road
> Old Lyme, CT 06371
> (203) 434-5641

☆ *Horsman* **composition or plastic dolls.** Only wants pre-1970 dolls labeled on the back of their head "EIH" or HORSMAN. Older dolls are not dated. Excellent condition required. Photo is a must.

> Sandra Stone
> PO Box 500 or 5170 County Road 33
> Honeoye, NY 14471
> (716) 229-2700

☆ *Renwall* **plastic dolls and furniture.** *Renwall* made hard plastic jointed dolls ranging in height from a few inches to a foot. They are embossed "Renwall USA" and with a number. In addition to *Renwall* dolls, she is also interested in other kinds of **hard plastic dolls and furniture that were made by** *Ideal* **and** *Acme.* Especially wants a 35" tall doll by *Ideal.* No foreign plastic furniture or anything with broken or missing parts or clothing. Prefers communication by fax or mail.

> Judaline McNece
> 122 Camino Rio
> Santa Fe, NM 87501
> (800) 855-2881 Ask relay operator for (505) 982-7033
> Fax: (505) 982-7033 Fax: (505) 827-6911

☆ *Madame Alexander* **dolls of the 1950's.** Mid 1920's dolls were cloth, then composition. The 1950's Alexanders were made of hard plastic jointed at neck, shoulders and hips, and often knees, elbows, and even ankles! In the early 1960's, these hard plastic dolls gave way to squeezable vinyl dolls with rooted hair. "I want **good condition hard plastic dolls with glued wigs and original clothes."** Wants all sizes, from 8" to 21", but they must be in good condition with original clothes. The same doll might have 80 or more different costumes, and a variety of hair. "Some that don't look too exciting may actually be rare and valuable because they didn't sell and were only offered for a short time." The 1950's dolls she seeks were generally tagged and marked. To sell your doll, give her the information on the clothing tag, a description of the costume, and a statement of condition. Note whether you have the original box. Have the doll in hand if you call. Lia says, "I will consider older composition or cloth *Alexander* dolls, but only if in mint perfect condition. They don't have to be in the original box, but must be like new."

    Lia Sargent
    74 The Oaks
    Roslyn Estates, NY 11576
       (800) 421-9912   Fax: (516) 621-7517

☆ **Betsy McCall dolls and clothing**, especially packaged and/or boxed dolls and outfits for 8" and 14" *American Character* dolls. The 8" Designer Studio, A Day at the Ranch and Day with Betsy McCall are particularly sought. Also buys fine to mint 14" Betsy McCall dolls by *Ideal* and 20" and 22" sizes of the *American Character* Betsy. Describe condition carefully for this veteran collector dealer.

    Marci Van Ausdall
    PO Box 1233
    Westwood, CA 96137

☆ **Doll houses and furniture circa 1900**, but *only* wooden houses covered with colorfully lithographed paper, especially made by *Bliss*.

    Jerry Phelps
    6013 Innes Trace Road
    Louisville, KY 40222

☆ **Doll houses and miniatures,** especially *Schoenhut* and *Bliss* houses for which they pay $500-$1,500. "We are one of the oldest and most experienced companies in the doll house and miniatures industry," Bob says, "and we will consider buying anything in miniatures that is old and in good condition." Their catalog of new doll house parts is fascinating, and well worth the $5.50 charge.

    Robert Dankanics, The Dollhouse Factory
    PO Box 456
    Lebanon, NJ 08833
       (908) 236-6404

ETHNIC DOLLS

☆ **Realistic ethnic costume dolls from India, Indonesia, Bali and Java,** 6"-14" tall, with nicely sculpted realistic adult faces made of clay, porcelain or wax. Dolls should represent peasants, dancers, musicians, and theatrical characters. Whether old or new, high quality sculpture is a must. No Chinese or Japanese dolls, baby dolls, home-made dolls, or dolls from the United States, Western Europe, tropical Africa, or South America. If you wish to sell to her, a photograph is essential. Dealers must price their goods. She pays from $50 to $200.

Karen Kuykendall
PO Box 10845
Casa Grande, AZ 85230
(602) 836-2066

☆ **Chinese Door of Hope dolls** sold by Christian missionaries to raise funds between 1909 and 1947. Also **china or bisque headed dolls** less than 12" high made before 1925. Will buy **doll parts**, bodies, heads, and old clothes, but will make no offers. Everyone price your goods.

Marjorie Gewalt
94 East Parkfield Court
Racine, WI 53402
(414) 639-2346

☆ *Skookum* **Indian dolls.** If you own an Indian doll wearing a colorful Indian pattern blanket, chances are it's a *Skookum*, and he buys perfect examples from the smallest sizes up to those five feet tall. Some dolls marked SKOOKUM and/or BULLY GOOD on the underside of the feet. He does not want *Skookums* with plastic parts. Please send a photo for offer.

Barry Friedman
22725 Garzota Drive
Valencia, CA 91355
(805) 296-2318

POP CULTURE: TRASH THAT CAN BE A TREASURE

Pop Culture is called "the fun stuff in life."
When folks talk about *Pop Culture,* they mean
radio, television, music, magic, celebrities,
personalities, cartoons and comic characters.
*Pop Culture is Little Lulu, Donald Duck and
Superman. Pop Culture is Tom Mix, G.I. Joe,
and Star Wars. It's Elvis, P.T. Barnum, and Batman.
It's Frankenstein! And Gilligan.*

Advertising has become part of pop culture. More 7
year olds recognize Mr. Clean *than Santa Claus.* Aunt
Jemima, Speedy Alka-Seltzer, *The* Campbell's Soup *kids,
and* Reddy Kilowatt *are among advertising icons that have
become collector favorites,*

Lots of this stuff is only worth $10 or $20, but someone
paid $1,000 for a cardboard cereal box and $2,000 for a
plastic model less than 30 years old. Prices for Pop Culture
reflect the law of supply and demand perfectly. Desirability (demand), not rarity, drives the market place.

**Pop Culture collectors want rare, brightly colored items
in original boxes and mint condition.** *Sometimes, but not
always, they will settle for less. Depends on how highly
sought after the item is. That's the advantage of dealing
with the people I'm suggesting. They know what you have
and what it is worth; they know what the market is, and
they're committed to paying you fair prices for good items.*

Whether you already own this stuff, or whether you want
to make money by finding it at other people's yard sales,
**the best way for you to cash in is to read all the Pop Culture
entries** *as well as those in the closely related Entertainment
and Advertising sections to see what's hot. By selling to
buyers in* **Trash or Treasure** *you can cash in.*

Good close-up photos or Xerox© copies are important
since many vehicles, dolls, robots, and other Pop Culture
toys and games are worth $100+ and a surprising number
bring $1,000 or more. Buyers want to see exactly what you
are offering, as the condition affects value greatly.

To sell Pop Culture items, you should give the buyer the following information:

(1) What it is, its size, color, and the material from which it is made;

(2) Names, dates, and numbers found on the item;

(3) Accurate statement of condition, noting missing parts, pieces, or paint and all other damage;

(4) Description of all repairs or repainting;

(5) Whether the original box, packaging and paper work are included and in good condition.

It's not hard, and a Xerox™ machine can be a big help.

POP CULTURE

☆ **Americana and Pop Culture of all sorts** is wanted by Ted Hake, the longest established mail dealer and auctioneer of pop collectibles. The wide range of items Ted buys includes:
- **Political and other pin back buttons**;
- **Premiums from radio, TV or cereal**;
- **Disney** characters from before 1970;
- **Animation art** from Disney and other cartoons;
- **Battery or wind up toys,** especially comic and movie characters;
- **Television related toys**, games, lunchboxes, etc., 1950's to 60's;
- **Singing cowboys** and other western film heroes' guns, etc.;
- **Robots and space toys**;
- **U.S. Space Program** items;
- **Elvis Presley** pre-death items;
- *Beatles* and other famous rock and roll personalities;
- **Movie posters**, lobby cards, etc.;
- **Toys of the 1960's** like *GI Joe, Capt. Action, Batman,* etc.

"I'll buy or auction just about any item related to a famous character or personality." Ted wants to know the material your item is made from, its size, any dates you can provide, and general condition. Firm offers are made only after inspection of your item. Hake has written four books on pin back buttons which are the basic reference works in the field. No reproductions are wanted, nor are political items after 1968.

Ted Hake
Hake's Americana
PO Box 1444
York, PA 17405
(717) 848-1333 days

☆ **Radio premiums** associated with superheroes, fictional detectives, movie heroes and villains are sought by this well known mail order dealer of high quality collectibles. Rex DOES NOT BUY things made after 1960. No exceptions.

- **Maps** from radio shows: Sherlock Holmes' map of London, *Gang Busters, Flash Gordon Macy's Commandos* map, and others from *Mickey Mouse, Sea Hound, Tarzan,* etc.;
- **Rings** with lightning bolts, skulls, scarabs, spiders, and similar images, including **rare decoders** like *Red Ryder, Buck Rogers* and *Don Winslow.* "No common *Ophan Annie* or *Captain Midnight* decoders, please."
- **Guns** from the *Jr. G-Men* in the original mailer, *Crusade Against Crime Gang Busters* submachine gun in its original box and condition, *Dick Tracy* rapid fire tommy gun in its box;
- **Pins:** Ellery Queen, *Chandu, Ace Drummond, Sky King, The Shadow, Flash Gordon Movie Club, Tarzan, Fu Manchu* and others, but no *Pep* pins;
- **Store displays** involving heroes or comic characters.

"I do not want *Hopalong Cassidy* and other 1950's cowboys, nor do I buy lunchboxes, movie *Batman* or *Dick Tracy,* beat up lobby cards, coverless comics, or junk...just fine condition items, please. I pay more than anyone for the top range items, but if you want to sell to me it has to be on my terms. You must write first, providing a full description of the item and its condition." If Rex is interested he will request that you ship for inspection. Rex pays postage both ways on items he does not buy. "I have bought and sold this way for 20 years," he adds, pointing out numerous awards he has won for dealer integrity. Do not contact him with anything except perfect items. If you have something really good, "call between 10 and 10."

Rex Miller
Route 1 Box 457-D
East Prairie, MO 63845
(314) 649-5048

☆ **Comic character toys and collectibles from the 1930's and 40's,** made of any material from cardboard to cast iron, especially **Disneyana**, radio premiums, and all **children's play suits** from western heroes to sailor suits. No Halloween costumes. There are also many pieces of **comic character related sheet music** Ralph is seeking.

Ralph Eodice
Nevermore
161 Valley Road
Clifton, NJ 07013
(201) 742-8278

☆ **Pop culture items**, including:
  • **Radio premiums from children's adventure programs** such as
    *The Lone Ranger, Jack Armstrong, Tom Mix, Sky King, The
    Shadow, Doc Savage, Buck Rogers, Dick Tracy,* etc.;
  • **Cereal boxes offering premiums** from the 30's through the 60's;
  • **Superhero action figures,**
  • **Space adventure items;**
  • **Disney.** "I'll buy anything that isn't pictured in one of the price
    guides to Disney that I wrote."
  • *Mickey Mouse* **from the 1930's** ONLY (the "rat" Mickey) in all
    materials and forms: wind-up, dolls, figurines, etc.;
  • **Any odd Pop Culture item** in its original box.
Prefers items to be priced, but will make an offer only after seeing the
item in person. Write first, with complete details and photo.
  Tom Tumbusch
  3300 Encrete Lane
  Dayton, OH 45439
       (513) 294-2250   Fax: (513) 294-1024

To sell Pop Culture items,
    you should give the buyer
    the following information:

(1) What it is, its size, color, and the
    material from which it is made;
(2) Names, dates, numbers found
    anywhere on the item;
(3) Accurate statement of condition, noting missing
    parts, pieces, or paint. Mention scratches, dents,
    dings, tears, stains, etc.
(4) Be certain to describe all repairs or repainting;
(5) Mention if the original box, packaging and paper
    work are included and in good condition.

It's not hard, and a Xerox™ machine can be a big help.

☆ **Comic character pin back buttons,** 1896-1966, from the earliest
Yellow Kid to all comic strip and comic book characters since then.
This *Star Trek* actor (Chekov) pays up to $500 for rare buttons like the
Flash Gordon Movie Club or *Washington Herald Mickey Mouse.* Ask
and he'll send an illustrated wants list.   Include your phone number.
  Walter Koenig
  PO Box 4395
  North Hollywood, CA 91607

☆ **Pop Culture toys** related to radio, television or movie characters and superheroes including :
- **Western movie & TV toys**, watches and premiums from riders of the range like: Roy Rogers, Gene Autry, Hopalong Cassidy, *The Lone Ranger, Red Ryder* and Tom Mix;
- **Western style cap guns** made of metal;
- **Disney and other comic character toys**;
- **Doll houses** of tin in fine condition and *Renwall* plastic doll houses and accessories;
- **Toy vehicles** by *Smith Miller, Tonka, Doepke, Dinky, Renwall* (plastic), *Auburn* (rubber), *Arcade, Marx*, and *Wyandotte*;
- *G.I. Joe* **dolls**, accessories, pre-1970, in the 12" size;
- **Toys which advertise** nationally known products.

Condition is critical and only excellent condition items are wanted. Items in original box always preferred. Descriptions should include dimensions. Photo helpful. "Generous prices paid, but all offers not final until I've seen the item in person." Will answer all inquiries that have an SASE. Calls welcome.

William Hamburg
PO Box 1305
Woodland Hills, CA 91365
(818) 346-1269   Fax: (818) 346-0215

☆ **Pop Culture treasures,** especially made of paper, including:
- **Comic books**, 1890's-1980's, but only hero comics after 1963;
- **Sunday comics** from the 1890's to 1959;
- **Original comic strip art**;
- **Walt Disney** books and anything else before 1960;
- *Big Little Books*, 1933-1950;
- **Movie magazines,** 1920-1945;
- **Television collectibles,** 1948-1970;
- **Radio and cereal premiums** and giveaways pre-1960;
- **Song magazines**, 1929-1959, like *Hit Parader* and *400 Songs;*
- **Popular music magazines** 1920-1959 like *Downbeat*, *Billboard*;
- **Pulp magazines**, 1930-49, except love, Westerns, and crime.

Wants nothing in poor condition. Ken has been in business 25 years. He pays Americans in U.S. dollars and drafts for quick payment.

Ken Mitchell
710 Conacher Drive
Willowdale, Ontario   M2M 3N6 CANADA
(416) 222-5808

Pop rings worth 2¢ and rings worth $1,500 can look quite similar to the inexperienced. Don't take chances. Deal with my buyers.

☆ **Comic, cartoon, and other Pop Culture items** such as:
- **Advertising product figures** Mr. Clean, Speedy Alka-Seltzer, and others, worth up to $500 or more;
- **Original animation and comic strip art** from before 1970;
- **Watches and clocks** but only if pre-1978 and in original box;
- **Empty boxes** for toys, watches, and models;
- **Cereal, gum, candy and food wrappers and boxes**, some of which, like the *Kix* atom bomb box, are worth $500+;
- **PEZ candy dispensers**, premiums, and store displays;
- **Premiums from radio and TV shows, comic books or cereal**, 1920-70's; pays $5,000+ for *Superman of America* member rings or *Superman* secret compartment rings, and $1,000+ for *Superman* and *Captain Marvel* wooden statues;
- **Monster toys and masks**, especially masks made by Don Post;
- **1960's TV characters** such as *Munsters, Addams Family, Jetsons, Flintstones, Lost in Space, Batman* and the like;
- **Children's books** (coloring, sticker, paper doll, cut-out, pop-up) if in near mint condition only. $2,500+ for *Mickey Mouse* or *Wizard of Oz* Waddle Books;
- **Celluloid, battery, wind-up or friction toys,** especially Disney and *Popeye*; pays $10,000+ for German *Mickey* and *Minnie* on a motorcycle or celluloid *Horace Horsecollar* pulling *Mickey* in a cart;
- *Captain Action* and *G.I. Joe* **dolls** with painted hair, their accessories and vehicles, but **only if in their original boxes.**

Condition is crucial. Make certain to note all damage and if there are missing parts. Make certain to mention if item is in its original box or wrapper since they can be "worth more than the item they held." Photos are "very helpful." Does not buy reproductions.

David Welch
PO Box 714
Murphysboro, IL 62966
(618) 687-2282 Fax: (618) 684-2243

☆ **Robots and space toys** made of tin before 1965, either wind-up or battery operated, are wanted. "I'll pay $2,000 for *Mr. Atomic* and $750 for the *Robby Space Patrol* vehicle. Condition is important with these toys, so I'll pay an extra 10% for any toy in its original box." Also buys tin wind-up **comic character toys** made in the USA or Europe, whether working or not, and any **Disney toys,** especially celluloid toys from the 1930's. **Santa Claus toys** are also of interest.

Larry Bruch
PO Box 121
Mountaintop, PA 18707
(717) 474-9202 eves

*The cheaters of the world have built
so many fakes that most dealers
will not make final payment until
they have actually held the item.
This is not unreasonable.*

☆ **Disneyana from before 1946,** especially:
- *Mickey* or *Donald* painted **plaster lamps**;
- **Waddle Books** from the 1930's;
- **Animation cels** from before 1960;
- *Mickey, Minnie,* and *Donald* **costume dolls**;
- *Vernon Kilns* **ceramic statues**;
- **Tin or celluloid plain or wind up toys** of Disney characters;
- **Wood or porcelain figurines**;
- **Original art** for WWII combat insignia.

Art from the 1950's is of interest, but nothing newer. Include dimensions, color, maker's markings, condition (mention all damage or missing parts). Dennis will make offers for items "only when I'm holding it in my hand," preferring you to set the price. Include your phone number when you write.

> Dennis Books, Comic Characters
> PO Box 99142
> Seattle, WA 98199
> (206) 283-0532

☆ **Pop Culture toys**, including
- Older **comic books**;
- **Marilyn Monroe** memorabilia;
- **Elvis** memorabilia from before 1977;
- **Disney** paper collectibles;
- **Non-sports cards**;
- **B-movie cowboy colletibles**.

This well known magazine collector/dealer has expanded into the above related ephemera. Please describe what you have fully. Items are purchased for resale.

> Stan Gold
> 7042 Dartbrook
> Dallas, TX 75240
> (214) 239-8621

*Experienced dealers make their livings
buying and selling. They can't and don't
stay in business long if dishonest. The world
of collecting is very small. Word gets around fast.*

TRASH OR TREASURE

☆ **Wind-up and battery operated toys** made in Germany, Japan, or the U.S., including comic characters, carnival items like merry-go-rounds, airplanes (no jets), and **space toys**. "I'll pay over $1,000 for a *Mr. Atomic* robot or *Mickey the Magician*, two battery toys." He does not want common items like the Charlie Weaver bartender toy, plastic toys, wind-up dogs, toy trains, dolls, items with missing parts, or toys made in the third world. Tell this toy consultant and restorer the condition of the item and box, and about any restoration or repainting.

> Don Hultzman
> 5026 Sleepy Hollow Road
> Medina, OH 44256
>   (216) 225-2668

To sell Pop Culture items, you should give the buyer the following information:

(1) What it is, its size, color, and the material from which it is made;

(2) Names, dates, numbers found anywhere on the item;

(3) Accurate statement of condition, noting missing parts, pieces, or paint. Mention scratches, dents, dings, tears, stains, etc.

(4) Description of all repairs or repainting;

(5) Whether the original box, packaging and paper work are included and in good condition.

It's not hard, and a Xerox™ machine can be a big help.

☆ *Marx* **playsets and plastic figures** from the 1950's to early 1970's. These toys came with metal buildings and loads of plastic people and accessories. Particularly desirable are boxed sets of *Gunsmoke, Wells Fargo, The Civil War, Disneyland, The Untouchables, Alaska, Ben Hur, Johnny Ringo,* and the *Revolutionary War*. Some of these, if clean and complete in the original box, can be worth several hundred dollars. Rare individual parts can sometimes be worth that much. Condition is extremely important. Figures from one inch to six inches tall that were not sold in boxed sets are are also wanted.

> David Welch
> PO Box 714
> Murphysboro, IL 62966
>   (618) 687-2282   Fax: (618) 684-2243

☆ *G.I. Joe* **action figures.** "I'll buy figures, uniforms, vehicles and accessories." Prefers items from the 1964-69 era, but "will consider anything in good condition whether boxed, carded or loose." Especially seeks store displays and stock, dolls, novelties, puzzles, games, vehicles, and carded stock but will buy nearly anything. He notes that painted headed dolls are more valuable than fuzzy headed ones, and that a 1967 nurse doll, mint in her box, could bring $2,000. Purchases both for his personal collection and for resale.

   Joe Bodnarchuk
   62 McKinley Avenue
   Kenmore, NY 14217
      (716) 873-0264   phone and fax

☆ **Action figures** by *Marx*, 1965 to 1976. These 8" and 12" fully jointed figures had solid color plastic bodies and soft flesh colored heads and hands. They were made as cowboys, Vikings, and knights and came with soft plastic accessories. "I will buy large or small lots of these figures in any condition, whole or in parts, if they are reasonaly priced. Horses must be complete. I am particularly interested in finding the *Noble Knight and Horse* in black armor." Also buys some *Star Warss* **action figures,** in or out of their original package, as long as they are complete. When describing your item, tell the color of the plastic. "Price sought is helpful," but not necessary.

   Arnie Starkey, Starkey Art
   11054 Otsego Street   #5
   North Hollywood, CA 91601

☆ **Pop culture characters** especially *Captain Action* and *Mego Superheroes*. "I buy, sell, and trade most any character collectibles including superheroes, cartoon characters, and action figures like *G.I. Joe* and *Barbie*. I specialize in premiums, rings, and superhero items from the 1940's through 1960's such as Superman, Batman, etc." The 1940's buttons have been reproduced. "If the colors are bright, they're fake!" He does not want decks of cards unless on the original blister card, nor does he buy books of any kind. He requests you call with what you have. If it sounds good, you will be required to ship it for inspection and an offer. Do not send things unannounced. "For large collections, I'll come to you."

   Michael Herz
   PO Box 300546
   Fern Park, FL 32730
      (407) 260-8869   Fax: (407) 260-2289

Experienced dealers make their livings buying and selling. They can't and don't stay in business long if dishonest. The world of collecting is very small. Word gets around fast.

☆ **Toy robots and** *Erector* **sets** are sometimes purchased by this specialist in toy vehicles.
>   Jay "The Chicago Kid" Robinson
>   PO Box 529
>   Deerfield, IL 60015
>   (708) 945-8691 or (708) 945-1965

☆ **Space toys and ray guns** from the 1930's through the 1950's, particularly *Buck Rogers, Flash Gordon, Tom Corbett, Capt. Video,* and *Space Patrol.* Fine condition toys of all types are wanted, even rocket shaped pedal cars. He does not want *Star Wars, Star Trek,* the new *TV Buck Rogers* and other characters from after 1960. Leslie is author of the award-winning *Zap! Ray Gun Classics* available for $16 postpaid.
>   Leslie Singer
>   103 West Capitol #1104
>   Little Rock, AR 72201
>   (501) 275-1860 days   Fax: (501) 375-1860

To sell Pop Culture items, you should
give the buyer the following information:

MEMO

(1) What it is, its size, color, and the
     material from which it is made;
(2) Names, dates, numbers found
     anywhere on the item;
(3) Accurate statement of condition, noting missing
     parts, pieces, or paint. Mention scratches, dents,
     dings, tears, stains, etc.
(4) Description of all repairs or repainting;
(5) Whether the original box, packaging and paper work
     are included and in good condition.

It's not hard, and a Xerox™ machine can be a big help.

☆ **Monster items** of all types including:
- **Gum cards, display boxes and wrappers** such as *Mars Attack, Outer Limits, Terror Tales, Spook Stories,* etc.;
- **Plastic model kits** of Frankenstein's monster, wolfman, mummy, *King Kong, Rodan, The Munsters,* and so on, built or unbuilt. Will even purchase some broken models for parts, and pay up to $50 for some empty boxes;
- **Toys and games**, puzzles, novelties, and the like that feature any movie, TV, or comic book monsters or creatures. Will pay $75 for the board game, *Outer Limits;*
- **Halloween masks** of monsters, especially masks by Don Post;
- **Comic books** by *Zenith, E.C.* and other 10¢ monster titles;
- **Magazines and record albums**, especially *Famous Monsters, Castle of Frankenstein, World Famous Creatures, Monster Parade* and similar titles.

"I welcome any calls or letters, and am always happy to talk with anyone who has monster items." If you write, include where you got the item. Don't forget your phone number.

> Joe Warchol's Small World
> 5345 North Canfield
> Chicago, IL 60656
>   (708) 843-2442 days   (312) 774-1628 eves

☆ **Model kits of human, monster, comic, or science fiction characters** are sought. Kits were produced by *Aurora, Hawk, Revell, MPC, Multiple,* and *Lindbergh.* Any kit containing figures (not cars and boats) may be of interest as long as it is unbuilt in its original box. Will also buy empty boxes, factory promos, store displays and advertising and manufacturer's catalogs. A few items like *Godzilla's Go-Cart* or *King Kong's Thronester* can bring $1,000+.

> David Welch
> PO Box 714
> Murphysboro, IL 62966
>   (618) 687-2282   Fax: (618) 684-2243

☆ **Cartoon and comic character books** such as *Big Little Books*, *Pop-Up Books, Fast Actions, Fawcett Dime Action Books, Cupples and Leon*, and other early **comic reprint books** from 1910's, 20's and 30's. Also **coloring books**, *Whitman* hard cover children's books with dust jackets, *Whitman Penny Books, Nickel Books, Buddy Books*, and any similar books published by *Salsfield, Mclaughlin, Lynn Publications, Engel Van Wiseman*, etc. "Let me know what you have and what you want for it, or ship for my immediate offer."

> Alan Levine
> PO Box 1577
> Bloomfield, NJ 07003
>   (201) 743-5288

☆ **Plastic advertising and comic characters** by *F and F Mold and Die Works*. This Dayton company was responsible for an enormous number of Pop characters including *Aunt Jemima, Uncle Mose, Keebler Elf, Dennis the Menace, Yogi Bear, Bugs Bunny* and the like. They made cups, bowls, cookie jars, salt and pepper shakers and other items. Pieces are marked, usually on the bottom or lower back, and the mark can sometimes be hard to see. "I do not want broken items or those with excessive paint chipping (though some chipping is to be expected). *Aunt Jemima* has been reproduced, but without the *F and F* logo. I am not interested in repros. I pay from $5 to $30 for items and have paid as much as $400 for rare cookie jars. Pictures are helpful or phone with the item right in front of you."

Tom Basore
715 West 20th Street
Hutchinson, KS 67502
(316) 665-3613 eves

☆ **Children's lunch boxes and/or** *Thermos©* **bottles**, metal or vinyl, in excellent condition, especially radio, TV and space characters from the 1950's and 60's. "Call about any fine condition item as I am always glad to talk to anyone any time about lunch boxes, and will be happy to give a reasonably accurate assessment of the value of your old character lunchbox." Joe has prepared guidelines for describing the condition of your box and information on cleaning which he will send if you include a long SASE with your inquiry. If you telephone, first inspect your box carefully for a date.

Mark "Joe Lunchbucket" Blondy
PO 865
Royal Oak, MI 48068
(313) 646-8215

☆ **Comic character children's lunch boxes,** both metal and vinyl, from 1970 or before. Must have pictures depicting space, cartoon, TV, sports, western, or other kid-related themes. Condition is very important. Boxes and bottles should look as if they were only slightly used, with no rust, bad rubbing, dents, serious scratches, or names written on the outside of the box. The most sought after boxes bring over $100.

David Welch
PO Box 714
Murphysboro, IL 62966
(618) 687-2282   Fax: (618) 684-2243

☆ **Cartoon and character glasses** issued by restaurants, fast food chains, TV shows, and others. Peter buys outright, aand also accepts items on consignment from pickers, dealers and private parties for his twice a year auctions of glasses, **mugs, steins** and related items. Some cartoon characters bring as much as $50. He does not want foreign glasses, anything issued in the last 10 years, or anything not in mint condition. He suggests you send a picture whenever possible. His 60+ page auction catalogs are $9 each and come with prices realized for nearly 2,000 auctioned items. Back issues are available.

>   Peter Kroll
>   Glasses, Mugs & Steins Auction
>   PO Box 207
>   Sun Prairie, WI 53590
>   (608) 837-4818 days

If you have a PEZ dispenser that does not have feet on the character, it is likely to be worth at least $10, perhaps a lot more.

☆ *PEZ* **candy dispensers**, premiums and store displays. Pays up to $1,000 for *Make-A-Face* dispenser if the package is unopened. Author of THE book on *Pez* dispensers, available from him for $22.

>   David Welch
>   PO Box 714
>   Murphysboro, IL 62966
>   (618) 687-2282

☆ *PEZ* **dispensers**, advertising, and other items, especially old or European. Prices can go as high as $500, but nothing new or still available is wanted. Fine condition a must.

>   Craig Robbins
>   PO Box 5249
>   Chatsworth, CA 91313
>   (818) 882-5090

☆ **Cereal boxes with advertisements for giveaways** or the premiums themselves, if before 1970. Jerry also buys **radio, TV, and movie cowboy** and space premiums and pre-1960 *CrackerJack* boxes, **premiums, and signs.** Send for his wants list of other Pop Culture ephemera. No *Orphan Annie* decoders or manuals. Does not make offers.

>   Jerry Doxey
>   HCR#1, Box 343
>   Sciota, PA 18354
>   (717) 992-7477

☆ **Cereal boxes depicting comic characters or giveaways.** Wants 1930-1959 boxes and the premiums they offered. A series of 1940's *Cheerios* boxes featuring Disney characters is particularly desirable as is the 1946 atom bomb ring box of *Kix*.

    John Fawcett
    Route 2, 720 Middle Turnpike
    Storrs, CT 06268
        (203) 429-9228

The following people are specialists in particular characters, TV shows, and the like. They generally pay very well for items they need, but already own all the common items. General line pop culture dealers (pp122-127) may also be a market for these items.

☆ **Tom Mix collectibles** including *Shredded Ralston* cereal boxes from the 1930's and 40's with Tom Mix markings, arcade and gum cards, postcards, unusual photos, feature films, short subjects, various radio premiums, and the 1930's Tom Mix *Ingersoll* pocket watch. This 40 year veteran is author of *The Tom Mix Book*, available from him for $24.95. Note that he does not want lobby cards, movie posters, newly made items, common photos, *Big Little Books,* clothing, video tapes or any material that is not in good condition. He insists that sellers price what they have.

    Merle "Bud" Norris
    1324 North Hague Ave.
    Columbus, OH 43204
        (614) 274-4646

☆ *Hopalong Cassidy* **collectibles.** Offer any in good condition.
    Ron Pieczkowski
    1707 Orange Hill Drive
    Brandon, FL 33510

☆ *Lone Ranger* **items.** Wants a wide range of 1930-59 items including cereal boxes, dolls, games, posters, premiums, gun sets, carnival plaster figures, books with dust jackets, autographs, and other items.
    John Fawcett
    Route 2, 720 Middle Turnpike
    Storrs, CT 06268
        (203) 429-9228

☆ *Superman* **items.** Buys all rare or unusual *Superman* items, particularly dating from 1938 to 1966, but "I purchase interesting items from all years." Seeks toys, figurines, puzzles, watches, games, buttons, advertising, etc. "Please write me about any good *Superman* item because I buy duplicates and quantity." No comic books, except free premiums. No homemade items. Give a complete description, including *every* defect, and include its color, manufacturer, copyright date and country of origin. Photo or photocopy is appreciated. Danny has collected *Superman* for 30 years and is co-author of *The Adventures of Superman Collecting.*

> Danny Fuchs
> 209-80 18th Ave.
> Bayside, NY 11360
> (718) 225-9030   Fax: (718) 225-9030

☆ *Captain Marvel, Captain Marvel Jr.,* **and** *Mary Marvel* **memorabilia** including toys, buttons, posters, comic books, mechanical items, and statues produced between 1940-1953. Also items related to similar *Fawcett Comics* characters.

> Michael Gronsky
> 10328 Royal Woods Court
> Gaithersburg, MD 20879
> (301) 445-9088

☆ *Dick Tracy, Sparkle Plenty* **and** *Bonny Braids* **collectibles.** "I'm buying premiums, toys, books, paper, figures...anything!"

> Larry Doucet
> 2351 Sultana Drive
> Yorktown Heights, NY 10598

☆ *James Bond 007* **and Ian Fleming memorabilia** including first edition hard and soft cover books, magazines with articles about Bond, movie posters, record albums, toys, dolls, plastic model kits, beer cans, clothing, games, comic books, and much more. Especially wants books autographed by Fleming, the British 1st edition of *Casino Royale,* and one of the signed and numbered limited editions of *On Her Majesty's Secret Service.* Give standard bibliographic information on any books, paying attention to the condition of the dust jacket (or the covers on paperbacks). On other items, indicate whether you have the original packaging for the item or not, and if you do, describe its condition as well as that of the item itself. He does not want *Saturday Evening Post, Life* or *Look* magazines. Neither does he want *Signet* paperbacks after 1961 or U.S. Book Club editions.

> Gary Pimenta
> 64 Lakeside Drive
> Tiverton, RI 02878

☆ **Green Hornet.** "I have one of the world's largest collections, but I buy for resale and for my collection. A mint Green Hornet Captain Action suit in a mint box could be worth as much as $3,500, and some posters will bring as much as $500 to $1000."

Michael Herz
PO Box 300546
Fern Park, FL 32730
(407) 260-8869   Fax: (407) 260-2289

☆ *Tarzan* **and Edgar Rice Burroughs memorabilia** including books, magazines, and collectibles. This enormous library collection still seeks items, such as the 1915 edition of *Return of Tarzan* with a dust jacket for which they'll pay over $1,000. Also seeking early *Tarzan* movies, foreign editions, Armed Services Editions and many smaller items associated with Burroughs or any of his characters. George advises, "Don't waste your time if your items aren't in fine to mint condition, including dust jackets. Please describe what you have carefully, give a guarantee, and tell us in what form you'd like payment."

George McWhorter
Burroughs Memorial Collection
University of Louisville
Louisville, KY 40292
(502) 588-8729

☆ *Tarzan* **books, comics and memorabilia.**

Jim Gerlach
2206 Greenbrier
Irving, TX 75060
(214) 790-0922

☆ **Comic character items from the 1920's and 30's** are wanted, especially Disney but also *Betty Boop, KoKo the Clown,* **Felix the Cat,** *Maggie and Jiggs, Mutt & Jeff, Krazy Kat and Ignatz, Little Nemo, Barney Google,* and more. Wants figurines, masks, toys, premiums, posters, dolls, pins, original art, lamps, radios, store displays, etc.

John Fawcett
Route 2, 720 Middle Turnpike
Storrs, CT 06268
(203) 429-9228

☆ *Yellow Kid* **character items.** Wants tins, buttons, dolls, paper items, "anything."

Craig Koste
1329 Route 22-B
Morrisonville, NY 12962
(518) 643-8173

☆ *Yellow Kid* **memorabilia.** Wants tins, toys, buttons, postcards, advertisements, "and anything else with the Kid on it."

> William Nielsen
> PO Box 1379
> Brewster, MA 02631
> (508) 896-7389

☆ *Peanuts* **cartoon character toys and memorabilia** of all types and characters including advertising, music boxes, ceramics, jewelry, etc., as long as it is marked UNITED FEATURES SYNDICATE and in fine condition. Especially wants a musical ice bucket and the *Ansi* and *Schmidt* music boxes made of wood. Not interested in *Avon*, squeak toys, or other common items, though. A picture is appreciated. This top collector is author of the price guide to *Peanuts* collectibles; send her $12 if you want one. She reminds you not to assume the © date is the date the item was produced. "It's not," she says.

> Andrea Podley
> Peanuts Collector Club
> 539 Sudden Valley
> Bellingham, WA 98226

☆ *Snoopy* **and** *Peanuts* **toys and memorabilia** such as ceramics, music boxes, advertising, pins, buttons, books, magazines, toys. Especially wants a *Snoopy Says See and Say* game, *Charlie Brown's Talking Book*, and wooden *Snoopy* music boxes, pianos, etc. Boxes are needed for many of his toys, so don't throw one away. All items *must* be marked UNITED FEATURES SYNDICATE or UFS. Freddi co-authored the price guide to *Peanuts* collectibles, and says about *Peanuts* items, "If I don't have it, I want it."

> Freddi Margolin
> 12 Lawrence Lane
> Bay Shore, NY 11706
>   (516) 666-6861   (516) 665-7986

☆ *MAD* **magazine collectibles**, dolls, busts, straight jackets, bookends, jewelry, and all collectible items related to Alfred E. Newman. Wants only first printings of softcover books and hardcover books only if complete with dust jacket and all inserts. Does not want anything in poor condition. Also wants original art by any of the *MAD* artists. Promises to answer all letters accompanied by an SASE.

> Dr. Gary Kritzberg
> 1217 Game Farm Road
> Yorkville, IL 60560
>   (708) 553-7653 eves

☆ *MAD* **magazine collectibles:** dolls, jewelry, hand puppets, busts, straight jackets, bound volumes, and other EC comic items. Also wants any and all pictorial representations of Alfred E Neuman's face from pre-*MAD* days. Nothing made after 1974 or in poor condition.

> Grant Geisman
> Box 56773
> Sherman Oaks, CA 91413
>   (818) 501-0884   Fax: (818) 501-0886

☆ **Walt Kelly and Pogo** items. This dedicated collector/historian seeks items produced by and associated with Kelly and his work, not only on Pogo, but as an illustrator for Disney, Peter Wheat, advertising, and various children's books. Of interest are first edition books, comics, records, plastic and porcelain figures, pin-back buttons, magazines, newspaper strips, original artwork, and what have you. Prices can be high for items like the 1968 button set, porcelain figures, plastic figures, records, and other scarce items. Books other than first editions are not wanted unless they are signed by Kelly. Photocopies are helpful. Complete bibliographic information should be provided for all books. Give specific information about all flaws. Steve publishes a wide variety of Kelly originals and reprints, including a bimonthly newsletter (membership is $20/year) and the *Walt Kelly Collector's Guide* (with prices) available for $16.50 postpaid.

> Steve Thompson
> 6908 Wentworth Avenue South
> Richfield, MN 55423
>   (612) 869-6320

☆ **Smurfs**, especially those produced in Europe before 1979.

> Smurf Collectors' Club
> 24 Cabot Road W.
> Massapequa, NY 11758

☆ *Uncle Wiggily* **items** including books, toys, Sunday comics, puzzles, mugs, dishes, games, and "all other memorabilia." Especially wants *Uncle Wiggily's* paint books, drums, *Put-Together* puzzles, candy tins, *Animal Crackers* boxes, kid's tea sets, and wind-up toys.

> Martin McCaw
> 1124 School Avenue
> Walla Walla, WA 99362
>   (509) 525-6257

☆ *Uncle Wiggily* **items** including toys, paper dolls, 1st edition books, comics, dishes, etc.

> Audrey Buffington
> 2 Old Farm Road
> Wayland, MA 01778

☆ **Radio show giveaways,** membership cards, pins, photos, games, rings, toys, etc. from *Lone Ranger,* Tom Mix, *Sky King, Capt. Midnight, Charlie McCarthy*, Gene Autry, etc.

> John Fawcett
> Route 2 720 Middle Turnpike
> Storrs, CT 06268
> (203) 429-9228

☆ **Radio show giveaways** such as rings, badges, decoders, etc. Wants *Captain Midnight, Superman, Little Orphan Annie, Buck Rogers, Howdy Doody, The Shadow, Sgt. Preston, Doc Savage, Sky King*, and other characters. Also buys the manuals from old radio, TV and cereal advertising campaigns. "Please advise what you have and what you want for it, or ship for offer."

> Alan Levine
> 292 Glenwood Ave. or PO Box 1577
> Bloomfield, NJ 07003
> (201) 743-5288

☆ **Jimmie Allen radio show giveaways** from the 1930's. "I will pay $100 each for certain Jimmie Allen wings and premium prices for other items." Since dozens of different types of wings, membership cards, and certificates were given away, it is important to make a photocopy and indicate which sponsor's name is printed on the item. Manuals, model kits, I.D. bracelets, and "other rare and/or unusual Jimmie Allen premiums" are sought. Include your phone number when you write.

> Jack Deveny
> 6805 Cheyenne Trail
> Edina, MN 55439
> (612) 941-2457

☆ **TV related memorabilia.** "I'll buy toys, puzzles, games, lunchboxes, etc., but specialize in all types of records and fan magazines associated with television." Wants records in all speeds, adult and children's, serious or funny, as long as it is related to television. Also TV fan type magazines like *TV-Radio Mirror, TV Fan, TV Carnival, TV Western* and the like as well as paperback books spun off from TV series. Items from before 1970 only, please. Examine your fan magazines carefully and note if they have had pictures clipped. **No movie fan mags.** When describing, give the date, volume and issue number and condition of magazines. Record info should include title, label, condition, and whether or not it has a sleeve.

> Ross Hartsough
> 98 Bryn Mawr Road
> Winnipeg, MB R3T 3P5 CANADA
> (204) 269-1022

☆ *Star Trek, Star Trek: the Next Generation* **and** *Deep Space Nine* **collectibles** are sought, especially action figures, toys, model kits, trading cards, books and authentic props. Of particular interest are 8" high action figures of aliens which, on their original card, will bring $500. Will send a news letter for Trekkies and collectors for $12.

> Kevin Stevens
> 1324 Palms Blvd
> Los Angeles, CA 90291
>   (310) 836-9232 voice and fax

☆ **Television private detective and spy memorabilia.** Wants to buy games, puzzles, toys, books, photos, gum cards, wrappers, dolls, model kits, autographs, comic books, and just about everything else you can think of from shows like *77 Sunset Strip, Dragnet, Surfside 6, Peter Gunn, I Spy, The Man from U.N.C.L.E., The Wild Wild West, Secret Agent, Hawaiian Eye, Adventures in Paradise, The Untouchables* and others. This relatively new collector/dealer says he's interested in everything in good condition. Include photocopy or good description as condition is very important. Describe the package if you still have it.

> Gary Pimenta
> 64 Lakeside Drive
> Tiverton, RI 02878

☆ *Bewitched* TV series scripts, games, puzzles, comics, dolls, autographed photos, press releases, *TV Guide* covers and stories, taped episodes with commercials intact, tapes of show promos, gum cards, and much more. "If it's Bewitched, I'd like it, but I don't want anything dealing with the actors or actresses before or after the show." Cels from the opening credit animation could bring $500 or more and a Samantha doll in its original box, $250. Describe condition and completeness carefully. SASE.

> Carol Ann Osman
> PO Box 16383
> Pittsburgh, PA 15220
> (412) 922-0117

☆ *Charlie's Angels* **and** **Farrah Fawcett memorabilia** including cups, puzzles, walkie-talkies, pillows, Halloween costumes, radios, store displays for dolls, etc. Also wants original photos, magazines, posters, displays, videos, etc. Does not want lunchboxes, dolls, doll outfits, games, models or bubble gum cards. He prefers items in absolute mint condition, never used or played with, with no bends, crushes, or tears. Wants list available.

> Jack Condon
> PO Box 57468
> Sherman Oaks, CA 91403
>   (818) 789-0862   Fax: (818) 501-1004

☆ *I Dream of Jeannie* items, especially board games, comic books, scripts, photos, or original film. Wants the *Libby* Majorette doll but none by *Remco*. Send a photo or Xerox™ and include your phone number. He's working on a *Jeannie* history.

> Richard Barnes
> 1520 West 800 North
> Salt Lake City, UT 84116
>   (801) 521-4400

☆ *Gilligan's Island* **collectibles.** "I'll buy or trade for all *Gilligan's Island* TV show items, including cast photos and videos of episodes." Especially interested in the 1965 *Gilligan's Island* bubblegum cards and the box they came in. Will also pay for video recordings of the cartoons *The New Adventures of Gilligan* or *Gilligan's Planet*. His club also produces a newsletter with classified ads for people who want to buy, sell, or trade *Gilligan* ephemera.

> Bob Rankin
> Gilligan's Island Fan Club
> PO Box 25311
> Salt Lake City, UT 84125
>   (801) 272-5729

☆ **Pee Wee Herman items** such as props from his TV show, movie promotional items, souvenirs, ads, fan club newsletters, giveaways and other toys. Also any size clothing put out by *JC Penny Stores* with the Pee Wee Herman label and designs. Especially large displays! He does not want small dolls, including the ventriloquist one. Xerox™.

> Everen T. Brown
> PO Box 296
> Salt Lake City, UT 84110
>   Fax: (801) 364-2646

☆ *Howdy Doody* **memorabilia** is wanted, including all items related to any character on the show. Especially seeks items in original boxes. Runs *Howdy* auctions, "so will buy anything in fine condition."

> John Andrea
> 51122 Mill Run
> Grander, IN 46530
>   (219) 272-2337   Fax: (219) 271-1146

☆ **Big Daddy Roth Rat Fink and Weird-oh** type collectibles including **model kits**, in store paint rack and paints, advertising displays, posters, factory built models, flyers, catalogs, decals, puzzles, masks and costumes, hats, rings...anything!
>   Paul Madsen
>   PO Box 1380
>   Burbank, CA 91507
>   (818) 563-2527

☆ *Smokey the Bear* **ephemera.**
>   Thomas McKinnon
>   PO Box 86
>   Wagram, NC 28396
>   (910) 369-2367

☆ **Red Riding Hood toys**, books, and other items.
>   Wes Johnson, Sr.
>   106 Bauer Avenue
>   Louisville, KY 40207
>   (502) 899-3030 extension 228 days only

☆ *Alice In Wonderland* **books and memorabilia** including films, figurines, tins, toys, games, puzzles, posters, greeting cards, dolls, etc. Especially wants a *Beswick* china figurine of the Cheshire Cat, but encourages all inquiries. Also wants other Lewis Carroll items, including **books, letters, and personal articles associated with Carroll**. No books published by *Whitman* or illustrated by John Tenniel but would love the Alice published by *Appleton* in 1866, worth at least $1,000!
>   Joel Birenbaum
>   2486 Brunswick Circle #A1
>   Woodridge, IL 60517
>   (708) 968-0664

☆ *Alice In Wonderland* **memorabilia** including dolls, figurines, tins, cookie jars, coffee mugs, and "anything else" is wanted, especially editions of **books in obscure languages**, or editions with lesser known illustrators like Allen, Adams, Appleton, McEune, Norfield, or Sinclair. Alice encourages you to "quote all Alice items."
>   Alice Berkey
>   127 Alleyne Drive
>   Pittsburgh, PA 15215
>   (412) 782-2686

COMICS AND COMIC ART ARE TREASURES.

Comic strips and books have been around since the turn of the century. Approximately 17,000 comic titles have been published, but only 300± of these have serious collector interest. Age has little to do with the value of comic books, and almost all comics, 1930's and 40's included, sell for $10 or less.

The popularity of the artist who drew the comic has more to do with value than any other characteristic. Other things that go into determining how much money you get are the popularity of the character, the popularity of the publisher, the historical significance of the series or specific issue, the condition and the current demand.

Comic collectors are fussy folks. Every tiny crease, tear, wrinkle, misprint, and off-center or rusty staple affects the value. Collectors tend to follow the grading standards suggested in Overstreet's *The Comic Book Price Guide*, the reference used by most folks as it contains values for nearly every American comic book. It is available at bookstores, public libraries, and by mail order.

Expect **buyers to pay you from 30% to 70% of prices quoted in Overstreet.** As a general rule, the more valuable the comic you are selling, the higher the percentage of the value listed in Overstreet's guide. Dealers don't want to buy lots of inexpensive comic books. They know top items move quickly. Low priced items don't sell. Badly worn comics, even rare titles and issues, are nearly impossible for you or for dealers to sell.

Buyers will usually ask you to send comics for inspection prior to payment since the value of comics is linked to condition. Ask your post office for "return receipt requested" which costs about one dollar. Always include a list of what you are sending and keep a copy of the list for yourself. Cautious sellers photocopy the covers of what they send, since the creases on the cover are like a finger-print and can identify your comic should it become necessary.

COMIC BOOKS

☆ **Comic books,** 1935-1970, especially superhero, Western, science-fiction, humor and funny animal, and movie or TV related. Particularly looking for comics published by the following companies: *E.C., Dell, Marvel*), *DC, Fawcett, Fiction House, Quality,* and *Harvey.* Also buys **Classics Illustrated comic books**, both originals and reprints. The comics most wanted are by *Timely Titles* including *Captain America, Marvel Mystery, Mystic, All Winners, Human Torch, Sub-Mariner, USA,* and *Young Allies.* He will pay up to $1,000 for early issues of *Marvel Mystery.* He does not want any comics newer than 1970 or any comics without covers, no matter how old or rare they may be. When writing or calling, give the title, publisher, and issue number (usually found on the cover, inside front cover, or first page). Describe condition including cover gloss, creases, stains, tears, tape, and damage to the spine. Note loose or missing pages, bends, and folds, as well as browning of the pages. A photocopy of the covers is very helpful. This 16 year veteran promises to answer all inquiries if you include a Self-Addressed Stamped Envelope.

> Joe Hill
> Phoenix Toy House
> 223 Fairview Road
> Erin, NY 14838
> (607) 796-2547

☆ **All 10¢ comic books**, for which he claims to have "unlimited funds" to pay 50% to 100% of price guide figures. Send a list of titles and issue numbers with a brief description of condition. No comics which sold for more than a dime originally. Also **comic strip original art** for daily or Sunday strips. This chain of comic book stores has six Illinois outlets.

> Gary Colabuono
> Moondog's
> 1201 Oakton Street #1
> Elk Grove Village, IL 60007
> (708) 806-6060   (800) 344-6060

☆ **Comic books** with 10¢ or 12¢ cover price. You may ship comics on approval. "I will send a check within 72 hours. If you return the check I will return your merchandise at my expense. If you cash the check, we got a deal."

> Myron Ross
> Heroes & Legends
> 5879 Kanan Road
> Agoura Hills, CA 91301
> (818) 991-5979   Fax: (818) 889-8972

☆ **Comic books** from the 1940's, 50's and 60's, especially crime, horror, romance and science fiction comics. Most interested in the work of the "E.C. gang" of Johnny Craig, Reed Crandall, Jack Davis, Wally Wood, George Evans, Al Feldstein, Frank Frazetta, Basil Wolverton, Graham Ingels, Bernie Krigstein, Harvey Kurtzman and a bunch of others like Matt Baker, Steve Ditko, Will Eisner, Lou Fine, Bob Powell, Alex Raymond and Alex Schomburg. "I'll buy in fair+ or better condition." Geoff offers to pay you cash or, if your prefer, to trade movie memorabilia for your comics. Geoff deals in movie memorabilia. Send $2 each for his three long catalogs of **inexpensive movie items for sale** in the Bad Girl, Western, and Science Fiction/ Horror genres.
> Geoffrey Mahfuz
> PO Box 171
> Dracut, MA 01826
> (508) 452-2768

☆ **All comic books in fine condition 1900 to 1969** are wanted by this active Canadian dealer. He also buys *Big Little Books* and *Better Little Books* from 1932 to 1950. He has no interest in anything brittle or damaged. Pays in U.S. dollars and bank drafts.
> Ken Mitchell
> 710 Conacher Drive
> Willowdale, Ontario
> M2M 3N6 CANADA
> (416) 222-5808

☆ **Comic books** from before 1968 are wanted, as are *Better Little Books* and *Big Little Books*. Hugh has been buying and selling comic books for twenty years.
> Hugh O'Kennon
> 2204 Haviland Drive
> Richmond, VA 23229
> (804) 270-2465

☆ **Flip books** from any period, in any style or size. These are small booklets whose pictures seem to move when the pages are flipped. Will pay $200 for *Santa Claus Play Pictures* and *Mother Goose Play Pictures*, which had pages to be cut out and assembled into flip books. He does not want *Big Little Books* with flip illustrations in the upper corner, nor does he want the recent reproductions by *Merrimack* or *Shackman & Co*. Photocopy the cover and give a brief description of the action. Give the dimensions, whether illustrations are color or b/w and whether cartoons or photos. Describe condition.
> Jeff Jurich
> 175 South Jersey Street
> Denver, CO 80224
> (303) 393-7210

SUNDAY COMIC PAGES

☆ **Sunday comic sections,** 1930-60. Prefers to purchase runs of several years. "A few odd sections are not needed." He especially wants the color comics from the Saturday issues of the Chicago or the NY *Journal American*, from 1934 to 1964.
>   Claude Held
>   PO Box 515
>   Buffalo, NY 14225

☆ **Sunday and daily adventure comic strips, 1930-60** such as *Tarzan, Prince Valiant, Flash Gordon, Terry and the Pirates, Steve Canyon, Casey Ruggles, Captain Easy,* and *Dick Tracy.* No single daily panels, humor strips or torn items. He is particularly interested in long complete runs of these adventure strips.
>   Carl Horak
>   1319 108th Ave.
>   SW Calgary, Alberta
>   T2W 0C6 CANADA

☆ **All Sunday comic sections in fine condition** from 1929 to 1959 *but nothing brittle or damaged.* Pays in U.S. dollars and bank drafts.
>   Ken Mitchell
>   710 Conacher Drive
>   Willowdale, Ontario
>   M2M 3N6 CANADA
>   (416) 222-5808

☆ **Full color comic sections from Sunday newspapers,** 1900-1940 in good or better condition. Value depends on what comics you have, the completeness of the run, the newspaper, and the condition. Write or phone giving the city, newspaper, date, number of pages, and list the major comics included. Free appraisals.
>   Al Felden
>   8945 Fairfield Street
>   Philadelphia, PA 19152
>   (215) 677-0657

Selling comic pages and original comic art is no different than selling other paper goods. Make a clear photocopy of what you have and send it to one of the potential buyers along with your Self-Addressed Stamped Envelope.

ORIGINAL COMIC ART

☆ **Original artwork for comic strips and cartoons**, 1920-1950, especially animation cels from Disney and Warner Brothers, for which this 25 year veteran has paid as much as $12,000. Jerry also buys original art from comic strips and magazine cartoons. Information he wants includes title, artist, description, the year, and any documentation you might have. In your description of condition, note any yellowing, folds, tears, cracked or missing paint, paste overs, etc. He does not want reproductions from newspapers or magazines, nor does he buy posters or prints of any type. Museum Graphics publishes a bimonthly newsletter and price list, available for $2 a year.

    Jerry Muller, Museum Graphics
    PO Box 10743
    Costa Mesa, CA 92627
      (714) 540-0808

Most comic art sells for $50 to $2,000, but some Disney pieces have sold for more than $50,000. Value depends upon age, artist, subject matter, and condition. Carl Barks at Disney is particularly popular as is Walt Kelly and a few other artists who bring premium prices.

☆ **Comic strip art by any noted cartoonist.** Dennis issues an illustrated annual catalog which you may write for.

    Dennis Books, Comic Character Shop
    PO Box 99142
    Seattle, WA 98199
      (206) 283-0532 eves

☆ **Orignal art used in creating comic books and strips.** Please make a photocopy of what you have.

    Charles Martignette
    PO Box 293
    Hallandale, FL 33009
      (305) 454-3474

☆ **Original comic book or comic strip art**. This well-known Canadian Pop Culture dealer pays in U.S. dollars or drafts.

    Ken Mitchell
    710 Conacher Drive
    Willowdale, Ontario
    M2M 3N6 CANADA
      (416) 222-5808

MOVIE AND ENTERTAINMENT ITEMS SHOULD BE CHECKED OUT.

Nearly everything associated with entertainment is Treasure to someone. Movie related items are the most popular entertainment collectible, but entertainment includes anything done on a stage, Disneyland, World's Fair souvenirs, and the like. Distinctions between entertainment, music, toys, advertising, sports and Pop Culture are arbitrary, so when selling an entertainment collectible, also try looking in these sections of **Trash or Treasure** *whenever appropriate.*

Stars like James Dean and Marilyn Monroe are hot and genuine autographed photos can be worth $1,000 or more, but most star photos and production stills from films bring a few dollars at most. Many movie star autographs and photos are signed by secretaries or machines. Real signatures on hand-written letters and on scripts are of much more interest to collectors.

Posters from popular stars and important or cult films can bring hundreds, even thousands, of dollars. Contact more movie poster buyers in the section on Posters.

Items sought by more than one type of collector are called "cross-over collectibles." A signed photograph of Marilyn Monroe would find buyers in movie, photo, and autograph categories. Cross-over items are often priced very differently by the different types of collectors.

Radio and television sets are popular with a different breed of collector than the "Entertainment" collector. Set collectors will often collect decorative "go-withs" to display with their sets. Go-withs are photos, catalogs, signs, and advertising related to a collector's main specialty. A photo of the interior of a radio store in 1923 would be a fine go-with for a radio collector. That some photo would also be of interest to a collector of photos of store interiors, or to a collector of something else pictured in the store. Many entertainment collectibles make attractive go-withs, so consider all possibilities when looking for a buyer.

MOVIE MEMORABILIA

☆ **Kinetoscopes and peep machines from old arcades and amusement parks.** He does not buy a great many machines, but is instead selectively looking for a few fine examples with historical or intrinsic value. "Amateurs can't tell one machine from another. An expert should look at all old arcade machines." Pays $7,500 for an Edison Kinetoscope from 1894. He suggests you shoot a roll of high speed 35mm film, covering all aspects of whatever machine you wish to sell. Send him the roll and he'll process it and reimburse you for your film. That's a good deal so it's not fair to waste his time with junk or late model machines. "It is very important for me to know where you got your machine." Richard is author of numerous books on slot machines, trade stimulators, pinball and arcade machines and is the historical editor of *The Coin Slot*, the quarterly magazine for people who collect coin operated machines.

> Richard Bueschel
> 414 North Prospect Manor Ave.
> Mt. Prospect, IL 60056
>   (708) 253-0791

☆ **Magic lanterns** (early glass slide projectors) from all countries in all sizes and shapes, colors and makes. Also wants all related materials such as glass slides, accessories, books, catalogs, handbills, and broadsides. "The older the better," with prices varying from $10 to more than $1,000." Does not want reproductions or small black magic lanterns with "EP" on them. Send a photo and indicate all markings found on the lantern. Dealers must price their goods; amateurs only may request an offer.

> Jack Judson
> Magic Lantern Castle Museum
> 1419 Austin Highway
> San Antonio, TX 78209
>   (210) 824-9995   Fax: (210) 822-1226

☆ **Magic lantern slides.** Glass slides, especially those that were individually hand painted. "I'm looking for fun, entertaining slides, especially those that tell a story as I'm going to actually use them as part of a children's lecture series." Sets are obviously preferred, as are the fancier wooden-framed slides with moving parts, kaleidoscopic images, etc. He is not particularly interested in the photographic slides. "I would be grateful if you could state the price you want."

> Lindsay Lambert
> 341 Bellwood Avenue
> Ottawa, ON
> K1S 1S6, CANADA

☆ **Silent movie memorabilia** including coming attraction slides, posters, lobby cards, figurines, sheet music, pin back buttons, paper dolls, and spoons by *Athens* or *Rogers Bros.* (but not *Oneida*). Has a specific interest in *Our Gang* handkerchiefs, Artamo needlework, star garment hangers, and the standee for *Robin Hood* shoes. Nothing from the talkies or from later stars. No autographs or photographs from any period are wanted.

> Richard Davis
> 9500 Old Georgetown Road
> Bethesda, MD 20814
> (301) 530-5904   Fax: (301) 530-8532

☆ **Professional motion picture cameras from the silent era,** 1900-1927, especially with wooden bodies and hand cranks, although some desirable cameras have metal bodies and electric motors. They range in size from small hand held to as large as suitcases. When describing, pay particular attention to the size, finish, and whether the film magazine is square or round, inside or outside the camera. There are a number of cameras that are worth more than $1,000 to him, including the *Bell & Howell #2709* and machines by *Mitchell* or *Gaumont*. He does not want home movie or 16mm cameras, nor does he want motion picture projectors. Wes is a member of numerous clubs devoted to film, and is publisher of *Sixteen Frames*, a quarterly bulletin for collectors of early cine equipment.

> Wes Lambert
> 1568 Dapple Ave.
> Camarillo, CA 93010
> (805) 482-5331

☆ **Movie ephemera** including posters, lobby cards, **souvenir booklets** and standees, both American and European. "I guarantee a fast decision and faster check."

> George Theofilis
> Miscellaneous Man
> PO Box 1776
> New Freedom, PA 17349
> (717) 235-4766 days   Fax: (717) 235-2853

☆ **Movie memorabilia,** including lobby cards (especially from B movies 1930-1960), theater souvenirs, tickets, programs, **photos of theaters**, and materials sent by studios to theater owners. Also wants **magazines** such as *Motion Picture Herald, Box Office, The Exhibitor*, and others aimed at theater owners and will buy them in any condition. This 20 year veteran collector does not buy items made after 1960.

> Chris Smith
> 26 Ridge Ave.
> Aston, PA 19014
> (610) 485-0814

☆ **Movie posters,** foreign or domestic, from 1900 to the present, in any size and any condition. "I want both original and rerelease posters, but not reproductions." Give the title of the movie, size, description of the image, year of release, and the condition of the poster. Joel markets *Warren's Movie Poster Price Guide* at $22.50 and *Collecting Hollywood* magazine at $5 an issue.

   Joel Bouchard
   American Collectors Exchange
   2401 Broad Street
   Chattanooga, TN 37408
      (615) 265-5515   Fax: (615) 265-5506

☆ **Movie posters** of all sizes, with particular interest in collections of pre-1940 posters. All posters printed in color will be considered. Give the film title, general description of the image and the *exact* dimensions of the poster.

   Dwight Cleveland
   PO Box 10922
   Chicago, IL 60610
      (312) 525-9152

☆ **Movie posters** from before 1940 with interesting graphics. "I do not necessarily want major film titles, just good images." Will buy posters for **movie cartoons** of the 1940's too.

   Tom Horvitz
   21520 Burbank Boulevard #315
   Woodland Hills, CA 91367
      (8180 716-8664   Fax: (818) 347-2357

☆ **Cartoon posters from silent movies.** "I buy posters featuring cartoon characters like *Felix the Cat*, *Out of the Inkwell*, and other silent films, but will consider other silent movie posters as well."

   Richard Davis
   9500 Old Georgetown Road
   Bethesda, MD 20814
      (301) 530-5904   Fax: (301) 530-8532

☆ **Paper movie ephemera,** 1925-1950, including movie heralds, posters, sheet music, photographs, and studio disks of film music. Wants **studio disks** (78rpm records for studio use only). Interested in **movie magazines**, 1930-1944, and in **trade journals sent to theater owners**.

   Buddy McDaniel
   2802 West 18th Street
   Wichita, KS 67203
      (316) 942-3561

☆ **Original studio production movie scripts** with original binders or covers when possible. "I am not interested in photocopies, TV scripts, or unproduced scripts unless the latter are by very important writers." Indicate author's name, whether script has its cover, what draft (or the date), whether all pages are present, and whether there are notations.

> Grayson Cook
> 367 West Avenue 42
> Los Angeles, CA 90065
> (213) 227-8899

☆ **Comedy movie posters (and a few others).** Dennis wants original posters from movies by the Marx Brothers, W.C. Fields, the Three Stooges, Laurel and Hardy, Buster Keaton, Charlie Chaplin, and Woody Allen. He also wants movie material from specific films: *Psycho, Bedtime for Bonzo, 2001: A Space Odyssey, Some Like It Hot, Midnight Cowboy, Clockwork Orange,* and *The Kid From Cleveland.* Prefers American posters but will consider foreign editions. When describing posters, mention folds, tears, and stains, whether rolled or linen backed, and if it is an original release poster. Photo is desirable.

> Dennis Horwitz
> PO Box 301
> Topanga, CA 90290

☆ **Movie memorabilia** including autographs of stars, promotional stills, lobby cards, and posters. This dealer wants bulk rather than single items from private parties, unless the single item's unusually good. Everything is purchased for resale.

> Ralph Bowman's Paper Gallery
> 5349 Wheaton Street
> La Mesa, CA 91942
> (619) 462-6268

☆ **Movie memorabilia** 1920-59, including **posters** of all sizes, inserts, and lobby cards. Also wants movie **autographs** and **magazines**. Stars of particular interest include Jean Harlow, Marlene Dietrich, Bette Davis, Errol Flynn, James Cagney, Humphrey Bogart, James Dean, and Marilyn Monroe. Condition is important. Include your phone number.

> Gary Vaughn
> PO Box 954
> Clarksville, TN 37041
> (615) 552-7852 eves

☆ **Movie memorabilia.** Buys posters, lobby cards, pressbooks, heralds, fan photos and other memorabilia from 1898 to 1970. Also movie **magazines** before 1950. "Please let me know what you have and what you want for it, or just ship for my immediate offer."

> Alan Levine
> 292 Glenwood Avenue or PO Box 1577
> Bloomfield, NJ 07003
>   (201) 743-5288

☆ **Autographs of film, TV, and Rock and Roll stars, make up artists, song and script writers,** including both minor and major figures. "I do not want Country & Western performers or current sports figures. Photocopies are recommended. Tell me where you got the item and set the price wanted as I do not bid on items. I will make offers to amateur sellers on very rare signatures only." SASE. Jim sells inexpensive books containing current addresses of movie, music and sex celebrities.

> Jim Weaver
> 405 Dunbar Drive
> Pittsburgh, PA 15235

☆ **B Western cowboy star memorabilia** from Hopalong Cassidy, Tom Mix, Ken Maynard, Roy Rogers, Tex Ritter and especially Gene Autry. "I'll buy buttons, photos, games, toy guns, radio giveaways, autographs, and most anything else that has to do with these stars." He is interested only in B westerns, not the epics. Has only minor interest in paper items, and does not buy "damaged or overpriced goods."

> Dennis Schulte
> 8th Avenue NW
> Waukon, IA 52172
>   (319) 568-3628 before 10 pm

☆ *Wizard of Oz* **items** from 1900 to the present whether associated with the books, the movie or various stage productions including posters, lobby cards, pressbooks, toys, games, magazine and newspaper features and original movie merchandise marked LOEW'S INC. The only exception: "No 50th anniversary movie merchandise unless it is foreign or a prototype." Your description should include all defects. Give the history you know. Dealers, price your goods; amateurs may request offers. *The Wizard of Oz Collector's Treasury* is available for $63.

> Jay Scarfone and William Stillman
> PO Box 167
> Hummelstown, PA 17036
>   (717) 566-5538

Don't forget to include an SASE with every letter you send.

GONE WITH THE WIND

☆ *Gone With the Wind* ephemera associated with the book, movie, stage play, or its author Margaret Mitchell, including items from her newspaper career, as well as various editions of her novel and promotional material for the book over the years. Will buy catalogs, pressbooks, lobby cards, programs, record albums, candy boxes, scarves, jewelry, neckties, games, bookends, buttons, clothing, hats, and many other items. He'd love to find an admittance card to Mitchell's 1949 funeral, but *does not want* anything made after 1980 such as plates, figurines, music boxes, dolls, reproduction posters, etc. Please give the dimensions and an "honest description" of its condition. Edits the *Gone With the Wind Collector's Newsletter*, available for $12/year.

> John Wiley, Jr.
> 1347 Greenmoss Drive
> Richmond, VA 23225
>   (804) 771-3561 days   (804) 330-5484 eves

☆ *Gone With the Wind* items associated with the film or the book such as tickets, posters, autographed books, magazines, scarfs, buttons, handkerchiefs, candy boxes, dress patterns, hair nets, bow ties, lockets and you name it. "I'd love to find a ticket to the premier," he says. He expects you to price what you have. NO OFFERS.

> Robert Buchanan
> 277 West 22nd Street #2B
> New York, NY 10011
>   (212) 989-3917

☆ *Gone With the Wind* memorabilia from 1939 only including jewelry, games, posters, music, paper dolls, press books, and the like. No reproductions, story books, fakes, copies, or junk. NO OFFERS.

> Frank Garcia
> 13701 SW 66th Street #B-301
> Miami, FL 33183
>   (305) 383-9006

☆ *Gone With the Wind* items associated with the film, the book, or its author. Wants book and Mitchell related items 1936-1965, foreign language editions of the book, movie scripts, movie posters, banners, props from the film, and all the promotional items such as dolls, games, scarfs, book ends, figurines, jewelry, nail polish, paint books, paper dolls, and more. Nothing printed after 1965. Herb no longer does free appraisals or make offers.

> Herb Bridges
> PO Box 192
> Sharpsburg, GA 30277
>   (404) 253-4934

☆ **Shirley Temple** items are always wanted by this specialty collector.
Rita Dubas
8811 Colonial Road
Brooklyn, NY 11209
(718) 745-7532

☆ **Shirley Temple memorabilia** especially sheet music and "unusual
stuff" including paper dolls and jewelry.
Frank Garcia
13701 SW 66th Street #B-301
Miami, FL 33183
(305) 383-9006

☆ **Humphrey Bogart and Woody Allen memorabilia.** "I want any-
thing of interest about these two personalities." Among special wants,
he lists film or video copies of early Bogart films: *Broadway's Like
That, A Devil with Women, Body and Soul, Bad Sister, A Holy Terror*
and *Women of all Nations.*
Dennis Horwitz
PO Box 301
Topanga, CA 90290

☆ **James Dean memorabilia** including magazines, photos, records,
sheet music, lobby cards, scrapbooks, plates and novelties. Description
should include size, year, and condition.
David Loehr
PO Box 55
Fairmount, IN 46928

☆ **Three Stooges memorabilia** of all types, especially related to their
tour of England in 1939. Buys items associated with any Stooge except
Joe Besser and Joe Derita, including toys, contracts, posters, tickets, autographs, checks, personal items, coloring books, records, puppets, etc.,
and will pay as high as $3,000 for some rare items. He does not want
comic books, gum cards, or things made after 1968, but has strong interest in animation cels from cartoons in which they appeared.
Neil Teixeira
PO Box 20812
Oakland, CA 94620
(510) 658-9938

☆ **Three Stooges and other comedy team memorabilia.** Frank buys
and sells items associated with all the classic teams.
Frank Reighter
10220 Calera Road
Philadelphia, PA 19114
(215) 637-5744

☆ **Marilyn Monroe and other sex symbol movie star memorabilia.**
He not only wants Marilyn, but also will buy ephemera related to Jayne
Mansfield, Mamie Van Doren, Diana Dors, Anita Ekberg, and Brigitte
Bardot. He asks that you quote prices for any pre-1962 items, inclu-
ding U.S. and foreign magazine covers, in excellent condition.

John Van Doren
60 Wagner Road
Stockton, NJ 08559
(609) 397-4803   Fax: (609) 397-2407

☆ **Marilyn Monroe.** Wants "anything and everything" U.S. and foreign including lobby cards, press books, sound track albums, collector
plates, dolls, and the like. Will buy magazines with Marilyn on the
cover if they are in uncut condition. He does not want scrapbooks, new
posters, or new pictures. Photocopies are helpful.

Clark Kidder
3219 East County Road N.
Milton, WI 53563
(608) 868-4185   (608) 868-6808

☆ **8"x10" studio glosses of sexy starlets** and actresses, 1920-1990.

Charles Martignette
PO Box 293
Hallandale, FL 33009

☆ **Stereoviews of Hollywood**, old movie theaters, movie stars, and
anything else that is movie industry related.

Chris Perry
306 Logenita Drive
Palm Springs, CA 92264
(619) 325-4530

☆ *Castle* **newsreels** from 1937 to 1975, sound or silent, 16mm or
8mm, as long as they are complete. No shortened 50' or 100' versions
are wanted. Will also buy selected titles of *Castle* space and moon
flight films. Private party requests you list the film number if possible.

Art Natale
Newsreels
PO Box 295-WT
Prospect Park, NJ 07010

OTHER AMUSEMENTS

☆ **Wild West show items** including posters, handbills, letterhead, photos, and cowboy and cowgirl outfits. Will buy anything in fine condition that can be tied to a show or one of its famous performers like **Annie Oakley or Buffalo Bill** including belt buckles, watch fobs, holsters, etc., except he does not want saddles, and specifies that he is not interested in rodeo items. You must send a photo or Xerox™ of what you wish to sell. Dealers price your goods. Amateurs may request offer.

> Emory Cantey, Jr.
> Our Turn Antiques
> 1405 Ems Road East
> Fort Worth, TX 76116
> (817) 737-0430 voice and fax

☆ **Circus ephemera.** "I'll buy anything directly related to circuses, especially Barnum & Bailey, but other tented shows as well. I want posters, programs, photos, route books, etc."

> Al Mordas
> 66 Surrey Drive
> Bristol, CT 06010

☆ **Emmett Kelly and Emmett Kelly Jr. items** related to their "Weary Willie the Clown" character including **porcelain figurines**, dolls, souvenirs, advertising, books, photos, posters, programs, and what have you. Does not want Emmett Kelly Senior items currently being made by Staton Arts, or Dave Grossman. A photograph "makes sure we are all talking about the same item." No other clowns.

> Nollie Neill, Jr.
> PO Box 38
> Ennice, NC 28623
> (910) 657-8152 Fax: (910) 282-8132

☆ **Chalk carnival prizes**. Wants Popeye and Disney characters, other cartoon favorites, Superman, Mae West, hula girls, fan dancers or jointed figures with original dress. Seeks figures marked *Jenkins, Rainwater, Portland Statuary, Venice Dolls*, or *Gittins*. No animals. When describing what you have, mention whether or not is has glitter highlights. His two illustrated volumes of *The Carnival Chalk Prize* are available for $15 each.

> Thomas Morris
> PO Box 8307
> Medford, OR 97504
> (503) 779-3164

☆ **Amusement park memorabilia:** catalogs, brochures, photos, tickets, stationery, sheet music, letterheads, pennants, tokens, advertisements, books, postcards, and anything else.

> Jim Abbate
> 1005 Hyde Park Lane
> Naperville, IL 60565

☆ **Roller coaster and amusement park memorabilia** including official or amateur photos, prints, blueprints, postcards, souvenirs, home movies, and *anything* else, no matter how small or odd, that is remotely related to roller coasters or amusement parks. This long time collector has ridden 230 different roller coasters, once for 9 hours!

> Thomas Keefe
> PO Box 464
> Tinley Park, IL 60477
>   Fax: (708) 349-0722

☆ **Ferris Wheel memorabilia** related to the **Columbian Expo** (1893) and the **St. Louis World's Fair** (1904), including folders, guide books, photos of the wheel (even in the background), sheet music, drawings, newspaper or diary accounts of first time riders. He will pay $1,500 for blueprints of the wheel.

> Richard Bueschel
> 414 North Prospect Manor Ave.
> Mt. Prospect, IL 60056

☆ **Mardi Gras souvenirs, tokens, and other ephemera** are wanted, especially pre-1900 ball invitations and colorful Carnival Bulletins originally printed in local newspapers. Hardy and his wife are always looking for photographs, postcards, early magazine articles, and other items from New Orleans before 1940 which they can reproduce in their annual *Mardi Gras Guide*. Please inquire about all illustrated items and this prominent New Orleans collector will help you with pricing.

> Arthur Hardy
> PO Box 19500
> New Orleans, LA 70179
>   (504) 838-6111   Fax: (504) 838-0100

☆ **Mardi Gras.** Relatively new collector is seeking a wide variety of Mardi Gras items from New Orleans and other cities. She is not interested in the coins or beads tossed by floats or in any costumes (but will buy scepters and the like which can be assoicated with a particular float). Give standard information along with SASE.

> Marilyn Bordelon, Enoch's Gallery
> 1750 St. Charles Avenue #303
> New Orleans, LA 70130
>   (504) 899-6686

☆ **Disneyland souvenirs.** Dean will buy all types including ceramic figurines, guidebooks, maps, buttons, pins, coins, postcards, employee materials, etc. All items should be marked DISNEYLAND. Also will buy *Disneykins,* tiny one to two inch high plastic figurines of Disney characters sold by *Marx* in the 1950's and 60's. Also will buy anything related to *Tinker Belle.* Special wants include Disneyland items from 1955-59, a *Tinker Belle* glow-in-the-dark wand, and Walt Disney's autograph. Everything must be in mint to near mint condition. Items may be sent on approval or described in writing if you want an offer.

> Dean Mancina
> PO Box 2274
> Seal Beach, CA 90740
> (310) 431-5671

☆ **Disneyland souvenirs and memorabilia** "from the California park" before 1980. Wants maps, guidebooks, tickets, food wrappers, brochures, parking tickets, special event programs, posters, passes, postcards, and what have you. Especially wants a *Marx Playset* of Disneyland. Linda has been to Disneyland more than once a month for thirty years! Nothing from Florida's Disney World is wanted.

> Linda Cervon
> 10074 Ashland Street
> Ventura, CA 93004
> (805) 659-4405

☆ **National Orange Show, San Bernardino, CA,** 1911-1920, souvenirs and paper ephemera.

> Gary Crabtree
> PO Box 3843
> San Bernardino, CA 92413
> (909) 862-8534

☆ **Carnegie Hall memorabilia.** Seeking relics of its own past, the Carnegie Hall Corporation wants especially to find programs and stagebills from 1892-98, 1929-31 and 1944-45. Also photos of the building in construction, or any interior shots of performers or speakers on stage. Also recordings, films and posters of events as well as any historical records. Interested in ephemera from any type of performance.

> Gino Francesconi, Archivist
> Carnegie Hall Corporation
> 881 Seventh Ave.
> New York, NY 10019
> (212) 903-9629

MAGIC APPARATUS & EPHEMERA

☆ **Magic apparatus of all sorts** including all paraphernalia and props, escape devices, tokens, programs, books, and other ephemera. Has a particular interest in pre-1900 posters, original photos of **Houdini**, and a complete set of Houdini letters, one on each of his twelve letterheads (worth $5,000 if you have it). A complete set of *Thayer Manufacturing's* wooden turned devices (1910-20) is worth $12,000 to some lucky seller. No items after 1950, newspaper clippings, radio premiums, or pulp books issued by *Wehman Bros.* An illustrated catalog of magic books and devices is available for $5 from this veteran collector dealer.

> Mario Carrandi, Jr.
> 122 Monroe Ave.
> Belle Mead, NJ 08502
>   (908) 874-0630   Fax: (908) 874-4892

☆ **Magic posters and memorabilia** including posters, books, lithographs, autographed photos and letters, and **children's magic sets**, particularly *Mysto*. Ken buys items from the famous and not so famous, including Kellar, Thurston, Blackstone, Nicola, Raymond, Germain, and especially Houdini. Prices offered will depend on the rarity and condition of what you have, so it is often necessary to inspect your item before a final offer can be made. Ken promises prompt response to any item you offer that is of interest.

> Ken Trombly
> 1825 "K" Street NW #901
> Washington, DC 20006
>   (800) 673-8158   (301) 320-2360   Fax: (202) 457-0343

☆ **Magic and magicians.** "I'm looking for everything related to magic and magicians, especially apparatus, pre-1940 books, posters, programs, advertising, newspaper and magazine articles, toy magic sets (particularly *A.C. Gilbert's Mysto Magic* sets), battery or windup toys with a magic theme, radio premiums with magic theme, and paintings and prints about magic." Will buy items associated with **mind readers, escape artists, ventriloquists, and Punch & Judy shows**, as well. Please send a photo of your item, along with notation about condition. He does not buy foreign language books, current magazine articles, or books that are severely damaged. Be certain to describe books using proper bibliographic information. Dealers, price your goods. Amateurs may request offers.

> Frank Herman
> 710 Anchor Way
> Carlsbad, CA 92008
>   (619) 434-2254

☆ **Magic posters, memorabilia**, tricks, and books printed before 1940. Describe condition and include a photo or Xerox™. If you are a dealer, price your goods. Amateurs may request an offer.

> Marvin Yagoda, Marvin's Marvelous Mechanical Museum
> 28585 South Harwich Drive
> Farmington Hills, MI 48018
> (810) 851-8158   Fax: (810) 851-8159

☆ **Harry Houdini memorabilia** including book, magazine and news-paper articles, photos, handbills, pamphlets, autographs, posters, personal apparatus and personal belongings. Anything relating to Houdini will probably be of interest. He especially wants to find a voice recording of Houdini or copies of any of his silent movies (including home movies) except *The Man From Beyond*. If you are offering personal apparatus or effects you must explain why you know it is from Houdini. You may price or he will make offer. Provide standard bibliographic information when offering books. Art is a 15 year veteran collector and happy to provide free appraisals and make offers.

> Arthur Moses
> 3512 Wosley
> Ft. Worth, TX 76133
> (817) 294-2494   Fax: (817) 732-3339

☆ **Harry Houdini memorabilia** of all types, including apparatus, posters, letters and books.

> Joe and Pamela Tanner, Tanner Escapes
> 3024 East 35th Street
> Spokane, WA 99223
> (509) 448-8457 voice and fax

STAGE & THEATER MEMORABILIA

☆ **Minstrel memorabilia of all sorts.** "I'll buy playbills, autographs, letters written by minstrels, news clippings, postcards, posters, radio and TV programs, rare book and magazine articles, recordings, and miscellaneous artifacts. I'm particularly interested in Bert Williams, **Al Jolson, Eddie Cantor, Sophie Tucker, and Jimmy Durante**." He can send you a lengthy multi-part wants list which details books, TV shows, movies, phonograph records and other items he seeks. If you have *anything* related to minstrels or minstrel shows, give Norm a call. Norm recreates minstrel shows and is a serious historian of this entertainment profession.

> Norman Conrad
> PO Box 184
> East Walpole, MA 02032
> (508) 668-6926 eves

☆ **Ventriloquist's dummies,** ephemera, photos and other items related to early ventriloquism.
> Vent Haven Museum
> 33 West Maple Ave.
> Ft. Mitchell, KY 41011
> (606) 341-0461

☆ **Theater programs.** Please send a Xerox™ of the cover and indicate the dates if known and not shown on the cover.
> Harvey Dolin
> 5 Beekman Street #406
> New York, NY 10038

☆ **Theater playbills** from before 1950. Give the name of the show, where it was playing, and the date if known.
> Jay Brand
> PO Box 871
> Reynoldsburg, OH 43068
> (614) 868-8655

☆ **Theater programs and souvenirs** especially items related to an anniversary such as 50th performance, 100th performance, etc. Wants pre- 1920 items mostly.
> Drew Eliot
> 400 West 43rd Street #25-T
> New York, NY 10036
> (212) 563-5444

☆ **Theatrical lighting from the gaslight era.** "I'll buy anything relating to 19th century gas, oil or candle stage lighting. This includes actual lamps and parts, prints showing them in use, catalogs with pictures of lighting or other theatrical equipment, lighting manuals, flash and fire effects torches, advertising for gas or lime light, etc. Anything electrical from the 20th century is too new for me, except for lighting equipment catalogs which I'll buy through the 1930's. I am especially interested in limelight spotlights (often called calcium lights). I also buy limelight burners from projectors. Please send a photo or good sketch. I am gathering these for educational purposes and would be grateful if people set the price they want." Lindsay would pay as much as $400 for a perfect condition complete spotlight from the mid 1800's.
> Lindsay Lambert
> 341 Bellwood Avenue
> Ottawa, ON
> K1S 1S6, CANADA

WORLD'S FAIR EPHEMERA

☆ **1851 Crystal Palace memorabilia** including books, engravings, stereo cards, photos, newspapers, tickets, guidebooks, awards, and various artifacts made of paper, glass, porcelain, metal, or something else. Ron wants **all material on the building's history (1851-1937)**, but is especially interested in the early years.

Ronald Lowden, Jr.
314 Chestnut Ave.
Narberth, PA 19072
(610) 667-0257

☆ **International expositions and fairs, 1851-1940.** The library buys print and photographic materials including reports from various governmental and official bodies relating to the construction, exhibits, awards, and demolition of expositions. Also interested in letters, sheet music, tickets, passes, award medals, maps, and photos (both commercial and non-commercial). The library does not collect exposition artifacts or souvenirs. "Purchase offers are made based on the value to the collection rather than on any other consideration."

Ron Mahoney, Head of Special Collections
Madden Library
Calif. State University
Fresno, CA 93740
(209) 294-2595

☆ **World's Fair ephemera from before 1935.** "I'll buy tickets, official and unofficial stationery, postcard sets, badges, pin back buttons, tokens, medals, elongated coins, toys, and souvenirs. Please write or ship for offer." Hartzog does not buy single items after 1935 except unusual items. Newer pieces are wanted only in large collections. Rich runs numerous auctions and invites your consignments.

Rich Hartzog
PO Box 4143 BFT
Rockford, IL 61110
(815) 226-0771

☆ **1876 Centennial** collectibles such as tokens, books, textiles, trade cards, tickets, posters, broadsides, pamphlets, medals, plates, and all other souvenirs of the exposition. Describe fully, noting all damage. Will make offers only on items he requests you send on approval.

Russell Mascieri
6 Florence Ave.
Marlton, NJ 08053
(609) 985-7711   Fax: (609) 985-8513

☆ **1895 Atlanta Cotton States Exposition** memorabilia, especially medals, tokens, and postcards. Also seeks **agriculture medals from Georgia state fairs**.

> R.W. Colbert
> 4156 Livsey Road
> Tucker, GA 30084
> (404) 938-2596

☆ **Tennessee Centennial and Exposition of 1897.** "I'll buy postcards, china plates, paperweights, booklets, tokens, medals, and just about any other item you can name, if it was a souvenir of the fair. I will pay $50 for the *Guide to the Tennessee Centennial* which depicts the buildings and describes the exhibits." A typical complete description will be enough: size, material, colors, marks, and condition.

> Paul Jarrett
> 111 West End Drive
> Waverly, TN 37185
> (615) 296-3151

☆ **Tennessee Centennial Expo of 1897.** This major token collector asks that you describe your item well, including its condition.

> Joe Copeland
> PO Box 4221
> Oak Ridge, TN 37831
> (615) 482-4215

☆ **1904 World's Fair in St. Louis** and other U.S. expositions from 1876 to 1940. Especially wants *Ingersoll* souvenir watches, clocks, banks, lamps, steins, lithopanes, hold-to-light postcards, china and ceramic souvenirs picturing fair scenes, ribbons and badges from judges and officials, full sets of stereo cards, photographs, complete decks of playing cards, and more. "I have less interest in fairs after 1940."

> Doug Woollard, Jr.
> 11614 Old St. Charles Road
> Bridgeton, MO 63044
> (314) 739-4662

☆ **World's Fair ephemera from 1904 or before** including china, wood, metal, textiles, paper, souvenirs, and glass. "Any and all items from a fair from 1851 to 1904 will be considered," although he has a particular interest in 1851, 1876, 1893, 1901, and 1904 fairs. A photo is requested, especially of any possibly expensive items. He requests you indicate the price you'd like for your item, although he will make offers on "things genuinely for sale."

> Andy Rudoff
> PO Box 111
> Oceanport, NJ 07757
> (908) 542-3712

☆ **1907 Jamestown Exposition memorabilia** of all types is sought, except "no postcards, please."
> W.T. Atkinson, Jr.
> 1217 Bayside Circle West
> Wilmington, NC 28405

☆ **1909 Alaska-Yukon-Pacific Exposition** in Seattle. "Postcards and memorabilia."
> W. E. Nick Nickell
> 102 People's Wharf
> Juneau, AK 99801
> (907) 586-1733

☆ **Trylon and perisphere at the 1939-40 NY World's Fair** pictured on paper items is sought by this major NY stamp dealer, in business for 50 years. Send a photocopy of what you have.
> Harvey Dolin
> 5 Beekman Street #406
> New York, NY 10038

☆ **1964 New York World's Fair.** Especially wants fabrics, jewelry, toys, and unusual items.
> Dave Oglesby
> 57 Lakeshore Drive
> Marlborough, MA 01752

☆ **Atlanta Cotton States Exposition memorabilia,** including paper such as postcards and envelopes.
> Gordon McHenry
> PO Box 1117
> Osprey, FL 34229
> Fax: (813) 966-4568

☆ **World's Fair memorabilia suitable for resale or auction.** All fairs before 1940 are wanted, especially very early ones. Rex is one of the larger mail order dealer/auctioneers in the country. He offers a large quarterly auction catalog, and constantly needs new quality items. No items valued under $20 are wanted, but "the very rare always is!"
> Rex Stark, Americana
> 49 Wethersfield Road
> Bellingham, MA 02019
> (508) 966-0994

RADIOS AND TV SETS CAN BE TREASURES.

Valuable radios and television sets are difficult for the typical person to recognize. Radios worth thousands of dollars are thrown away by people who keep other radios worth only $10 because they "look valuable."

The folks who buy old radios and televisions like to know the brand name, model name and number and cosmetic condition (what does the radio look like?). Describe whether it is scratched, faded, dented, chipped, cracked, or the paint or veneer is peeling. Examine the chassis carefully for missing parts or damage. If the chassis has blank spots where a component or tube might have originally been, tell the potential buyer.

Radios and TV sets are among those few collectible items that do not have to be in perfect condition to find a buyer. Certainly, the better the condition, thebetter the price, but scarce radios and television sets will sell in almost any condition, because parts are always in demand by people who enjoy rebuilding them.

Plastic table model radios can bring from $50 to $1,000 and even transistor radios can top $100. The most valuable radios are those covered with blue or other colorof glass. Large radios are $10,000 or more.

Do not test old electric equipment. Plugging it in may cause damage because insulation around wires deteriorates, resulting in short circuits or fire.

Buyers will arrange for packing and shipping of these bulky yet fragile items.

Look for TV sets that have channel one, or that have no channels higher than seven. The very earliest sets (1923-1939)are hard to identify as they don't look much like TV's. You are most likely to find early TV's in those cities where TV began: Los Angeles, New York, Chicago, Philadelphia, and Schenectady. We're a mobile society and they could turn up anywhere, however.

RADIOS

☆ **Radios of many types** including crystal sets, battery operated sets of the 1920's, wireless sets and parts, WWI military radios, unusual cathedral radios by *Grebe* or *Ozarka*, grandfather clock style, odd shapes, and all luxury models like *Zenith* Stratosphere (pays $6,000+). Other names and models to watch for are *Marconi, De Forest, Leutz, Wireless Specialty, EICO, Norden Hauck, E.H. Scott, Grebe*, and *RCA Radiolas VI* and *VII*. Also novelty radios like *Snow White, Peter Pan,* or *Mickey Mouse*. In addition, he likes radio dealer indoor and outdoor **advertising signs,** point of purchase displays, brochures, instruction books, and service manuals. Not interested in plastic radios of any kind. Don is former editor of *Radio Age* magazine. Don is a collector rather than a dealer but will consider buying large collections.

> Donald Patterson
> 636 Cambridge Road
> Augusta, GA 30909
> (706) 738-7227

☆ **Radios of many types 1905-40,** including crystal sets, wireless receivers and transmitters, battery operated radios 1914-1928, and small electric table models 1928-35. Buys radios in wood, metal, or plastic cabinets. Especially interested in large collections of usable speakers, **tubes and parts** for radios from this period. No large console models of the 30's except those with chrome plated interiors. Also radio **magazines, catalogs, service manuals, sales literature, and advertising**, pre-1935, including novelties, radio dealer **promotional items, and anything shaped like or depicting a radio** such as banks, toys, pin back buttons, games, postcards, and dealer promotional items. Gary formerly published *Antique Radio Classified*.

> Gary Schneider
> 14310 Ordner Drive
> Strongsville, OH 44136
> (216) 582-3094

☆ **Antique radios.** Wants horn speakers, crystal sets, *Atwater Kent* breadboards, *Radiola, Kennedy, Federal*, the older and the more primitive the better, working or not. Also buys **art deco and novelty radios of the 1930's** and **WWI wireless communications equipment** from ships, planes, and ground forces, either complete or for parts (worth from $200-$3,000 and up). Especially looking for old U.S. Navy equipment with CN prefixes. Also **pre-World War II television sets** and sports transmitting equipment. No floor model radios.

> Mel Rosenthal
> 5 The Strand
> New Castle, DE 19720
> (302) 322-8944   (302) 322-3030

☆ **Wireless, crystal sets, and battery radios** from before 1930 such as *Atwater Kent, Crosley, Amrad, Deforest, Federal, Grebe, Kennedy, Firth, Paragon, Marconi, R.C.A.*, and *Zenith*. Also early vacuum tubes with brass or *Bakelite* base. Also *Jenkins* **scanning disc television**. Also all wireless and radio books and magazines printed before 1930. Also radio advertising, parts, relays, earphones, horn speakers, amplifiers, batteries, meters, etc. Will pay $500 for a *Marconi CA294*, $600 for a *Marconi 106*, $800+ for a *Pacific Wireless Specialty* audio receiver, and some others to $2,000. "I do not want anything made after 1940, floor model radios, or transistor radios."

> David Shanks
> 115 Baldwin Street
> Bloomfield, NJ 07003
> (201) 748-8820

☆ **Unusual radios from the 1930's and 40's,** "the more odd looking the better." Look for sets shaped like baseballs, bottles, ships, horses, *Mickey Mouse* or *Charlie McCarthy*. Mirrored radios in blue, peach or silver can be worth from $1,000 to $15,000 (for a floor model *Sparton Nocturne*, model 1186). *RCA* radios made in black painted wood with chrome trim are worth between $500 and $5,000. Table top radios made of celluloid, *Catalin*, or colored *Bakelite* are $200 to $10,000. Look for *Air King, Fada, Garod, Emerson, Motorola, Kadette*, and more. Will buy floor model radios only if they are unusually shaped or colored. Will also buy **novelty transistor radios** shaped like hands, bottles, animals, or advertising items. "If you send a photo and an SASE, we'll try to help you sell your radio if we don't want it!"

> Harry Poster
> PO Box 1883
> South Hackensack, NJ 07606
> (201) 794-9606 weekdays before 7 p.m.

☆ **Mirrored glass radios.** "I'm especially fond of green mirrored glass radios and forever trying to acquire *Sparton* floor model mirrored glass radios (model 1186). I pay through the nose if I have to." That translates to as much as $35,000 for a perfect condition peach colored glass and up to $30,000 for a perfect blue glass radio. Glass covered radios do not have to work and the glass may be cracked as "I don't turn down mirrored glass radios offered to me." He claims to outbid anybody, and points out that he will either come pick up any radio or have it professionally moved so you don't have to worry about shipping. He also buys **colorful plastic radios** of the 1930's and 40's. He prefers you to price but will make offers if you seriously intend to sell.

> Ed Sage
> PO Box 13025
> Albuquerque, NM 87192
> (505) 298-0840

☆ **Old radios, tubes, test equipment, open frame motors, generators** and other electrical apparatus, switch board meters, knife switches, **neon signs, fans,** Tesla coils, **quack medical devices,** and **electric trains** and accessories, as well as early books on radio and electrical theory and practice. Give info from the item's ID plate. Include a sketch or photo.

> Hank Andreoni
> 504 West 6th Street
> Beaumont, CA 92223
> (909) 849-7539

☆ **Radios with wood cabinets.** Give make and model number, condition, and price. Does not make offers.

> Alvin Heckard
> Route 1 Box 88
> Lewistown, PA 17044
> (717) 248-7071

☆ *Antique Radio Classified* **magazine** may be helpful if you want to collect, learn about, or sell old radios. Send $3 for a sample copy.

> John Terrey
> Post Office Box 2
> Carlisle, MA 01741

☆ **Radio manuals, handbooks, and sales literature** pre-1940.

> Alan C. King
> PO Box 86
> Radnor, OH 43066

☆ **Microphones** used in radio studios, 1920's through 1960's that have their original station plates.

> Don Colclough, Cadillac Jack
> 6911 Melrose
> Los Angeles, CA 90038
> (800) 775-5078 Fax: (213) 931-6372

☆ **Microphones,** 1940-1960, but only the short stand-up desk type mics used by broadcasters and radio stations. Especially wants to find microphones with the station or network letters still attached.

> Charles Martignette
> PO Box 293
> Hallandale, FL 33009
> (305) 454-3474

HI-FI EQUIPMENT

☆ **Early tube high fidelity equipment** 1947-1960 especially monaural but also some early stereo from companies such as *Dynaco, Marantz, Fisher, McIntosh, Scott, Eico, Altec Lansing, JBL*, etc. Most makes and models are wanted, working or not, complete or for parts, as well as tubes, loudspeakers, schematics, manuals and **hi-fi magazines**. Of special interest are all **early *McIntosh* amps**. Nothing after 1970, "but I'll buy a wide range of things relating to early audio, from broadcast equipment to home systems."
> Jack Smith
> 288 Winter Street
> North Andover, MA 01845
> (508) 686-7250

☆ **Early tube-type stereo and hi-fi equipment** made by *McIntosh, Marantz, Dynaco, H.H. Scott, Heath, Leak, Harman Kardon, Eico, Polot, Grommes, Acrosound, Altec-Lansing*. Also any manuals or literature for this equipment. Also want large audio transformers by *Acrosound* like their model TO-300. **Old microphones** from the 1930's to 50's by *RCA, Shure, Western Electric, Astatic, Turner,* and *Electrovoice*. No stereos, phonographs, or clock radios.
> Jeff Viola
> 784 Eltone Road
> Jackson, NJ 08527
> (908) 928-0666 or (201) 902-3313

☆ **Radios and audio amplifiers** are sought, including:
- **Tube type audio amplifiers,** including *Western Electric, Marantz, Altec, Brook, Dynaco* and *McIntosh;*
- **Breadboard (open works) radios**, especially *Atwater-Kent*;
- **Battery powered radios**, pre-1930, especially early sets by *Crosley, Deforest, RCA,* and *Western Electric;*
- **Crystal radios** of any type.

Please give the maker, model number, the number of tubes remaining in the radio, and an estimate of condition. Don't plug it in to test. His sales catalog is yours for SASE and two stamps.
> Jim Cross
> 2817 Parklawn Drive
> Dayton, OH 45440
> (513) 298-5827 Fax: (513) 738-8273

☆ **Early tube high fidelity equipment** including stereo and mono amplifiers, pre-amps, tuners (especially *McIntosh, Marantz, Western Electric* and *Quad*), large old speakers (especially *Altec, JBL, Tannoy, Western Electric,* and *Jensen*). Also radios before 1920, vacuum tubes, homemade amplifiers and kits by *UTC, Dynaco,* and *Heath,* movie theater sound equipment (including amps, speakers, and microphones), **antique electrical, electronic, telephonic, and telegraphic items**. Also wants old **hi-fi magazines**, books, and other literature. Does not want "department store console stereos" from *Sears, Silvertone, Wards,* etc., television tubes, or any TV's made after 1940. Give the maker's name, model number, cosmetic condition (what it looks like in terms of scratches, dents, etc.), and whether the original literature is included.

> Vernon Vogt
> 330 SW 43rd Street #247
> Renton, WA 98055
> (206) 382-5571

☆ **Tube-type hi-fi amplifiers,** pre-amps, and tuners are wanted as are "some old guitars and guitar amps. There isn't anything special I'm looking for, as I like it all, but the more unusual the better. I love talking about this old stuff, so welcome calls, as long as they are ready with the name of the manufacturer and the model number." He also buys homemade hi-fi equipment.

> Steve Sebra
> 6839 Amigo Avenue
> Reseda, CA 91335
> (818) 708-9612

☆ **Electronic tubes** of all types: transmitting, receiving and special purpose, especially antique tubes, those of colored glass or those with brass bases. *Western Electric* tubes are of particular interest. No TV or CRT tubes are wanted. List any code numbers on the tubes and indicate whether they are new or used. His sales catalog is available for an SASE with two stamps.

> Jim Cross
> 2817 Parklawn Drive
> Dayton, OH 45440
> (513) 298-5827   Fax: (513) 738-8273

TRANSISTOR RADIOS

☆ **Pocket-size radios, 5" x 7" or smaller.** "If they fit in a shirt or coat pocket, I'm interested, whether they are tube, transistor, or crystal radios. I want the old ones made in the USA or Japan between 1954 and 1964. I collect for appearance and for history. I like cute colorful radios with interesting shapes on the front such as boomerangs, arrows, etc. Historical pocket radios are usually made in the USA and are often plain looking and made in dull colors. If a radio does not identify where it is made, it is probably American. I do not care if your radio works and will buy useful ones in any condition, but prefer they be complete and without chips or cracks. Radios with their original boxes and papers especially appeal to me." The most valuable radios are the *Regency TR-1*, a 1954 radio from Indianapolis, and the earliest *Sony* transistors, such as the *TR-55, TR-52, TR-2K, TR-33, TR-6,* and *TR-66*. A perfect condition *Sony TR-55* would bring $750 and you'd make $250 for a *Regency*. Note that most other radios are worth a great deal less. To sell your radio, give the brand name, model number, color, and country of origin. If your radio has no model number, Xerox™ the front. Important: he does not want radios made in Hong Kong, Taiwan or Korea or radios that claim to have 10 or more transistors.

> Eric Wrobbel
> 7210 Jordan #B-3
> Canoga Park, CA 91303
> (818) 884-2282

☆ **Pocket transistor radios.** Has a particular interest in the *Hoffman Trans-Solar*, offering to pay $250 each for fine specimens in various colors. "I don't want anything not in good cosmetic condition, but it doesn't matter whether they work or not. Give the make and model number (which you will probably have to open the case to get) or make a Xerox™ of the front of the radio and describe the color.

> Mike Brooks
> 7335 Skyline
> Oakland, CA 94611
> (510) 339-1751   Fax: (510) 444-4010

☆ **Novelty transistor radios** especially Japanese radios shaped like commercial products. Also wants radios shaped like, or related to, robots, rockets, household or personal items, media stars and heroes, TV and comic characters, food and drink, travel and transportation. He is *not* interested in radios shaped like animals, Sesame Street characters, or anything related to war or weapons. When describing a radio tell whether it has its battery cover and original box. Describe its condition carefully, noting scratches.

> Bob Roberts
> PO Box 152
> Guilderland, NY 12084

TELEVISION SETS

☆ **Early television items.** "If it's from before 1950 and it's related to television, let me know what you have."
Gary Schneider
14310 Ordner Drive
Strongsville, OH 44136
(216) 582-3094

☆ **Television sets** with a reflective mirror in the lid and other small screen television sets such as the *RCA TRK-9* or *TRK-12* ($2,000+ each), and the *GE HM 171* (worth $750). Don is only interested in TV sets dating from before 1940.
Donald Patterson
636 Cambridge Road
Augusta, GA 30909
(706) 738-7227

☆ **Early television sets.** "I'll buy old or unusual TV's, and will pay more than $2,000 for any TV sold before 1942, including mechanical scanners such as *Baird, Western, Empire, Pilot, ICA* and others. "Mechanical TV's are often mistaken for early electronic junk," he cautions, "so look for 12" metal disks containing tiny holes that spin in front of a neon glow lamp. These early TV's drew their sound from radio sets, and most had no cabinets. Also interested in mirror-in-lid sets by *Pilot, Andrea, Philco, RCA, GE, Garod,* and *Zenith.* I also buy *Fada* and *Meissner* 5" kit televisions. An *RCA TRK-5, TRK-9,* or *TT-5* will bring $3,000+ each. I pay $50 to $500 for unusual 1940's TV's with 3", 7", and 10" picture tubes." He will also buy selected sets made from 1941-1948 which can be recognized by having a Channel 1. Also buys early 1950 color TV's with 16" or smaller picture tubes, and color wheels, and color adapters. Will also buy **unusually shaped transistor TV's** such as the *Sony 8-301W, Panasonic TR-005* (flying saucer), *JVC Video-sphere* (ball). "I am willing to buy an entire TV shop, attic, or estate to get one TV I want." Harry is willing to travel.
Harry Poster
PO Box 1883
South Hackensack, NJ 07606
(201) 794-9606 weekdays before 7 pm

☆ **Television literature,** including books, catalogs, and company pamphlets (either internal or intended for the public) from before 1940.
Harold Layer
San Francisco State University-AV
1600 Holloway Ave.
San Francisco, CA 94132

MUSIC CAN BE TRASH OR TREASURE.

Music collectibles fall into five categories, each type sought by different collectors.

(1) **Musical instruments** *can be valuable, especially quality guitars and violins. To sell any instrument, you need to state the maker and the model, and describe the type and quality of finish. Mention all cracks, dents, and the like. If you have a piano or organ to sell, no national market exists so it is best to offer it for sale in a local classified ad.*

(2) **Mechanical music** *refers to phonographs, record players, player pianos, music boxes, and other devices which play music by mechanical means. Describing what you have is usually a matter of taking a good photograph, listing all the information on the maker's ID plate, and describing the condition. Buyers of juke boxes, a form of mechanical music, are considered part of the "Coin-Op" world and are listed in Trash or Treasure on pages 196-200.*

(3) **Sheet music** *collectors are more concerned with the picture on the cover than with the musical content, so, classical music and school scores are not of interest. Music must be in exceptionally fine condition, free of significant tears, writing, or other damage.*

(4) **Phonograph records** *are seldom exceptionally valuable, with most records still selling for $5 to $10 retail. Don't let the fact your records are worth only a dollar or two discourage you. Records come in piles, and can add up! Record buyers want to know the title, artist, record label, and catalog number (there's one on every record). Note the condition of the record, the record jacket, and the paper sleeve. Records in mint condition are preferred by collectors, but a few early 78's have never been found in perfect condition. If it lists for more than $15 in Les Docks' American Premium Record Guide, collectors may want it even if it looks a little beat up.*

(5) **Memorabilia** *of music, musicians and singers is like other Pop Culture items. Rare, colorful, and in fine condition describes what collectors want.*

STRINGED MUSICAL INSTRUMENTS

☆ **Fretted stringed musical instruments** such as banjos, guitars, mandolins, ukuleles, and the like. "A *Martin D-45* guitar made prior to 1942 could be worth as much as $20,000," so instruments are worth selling properly. Also **related memorabilia** such as manufacturer's catalogs, old photos of guitar shops and players, accessories, etc. State the preservation of your instrument. Examine carefully for repairs. Look for any signs that it might not be original. Mention the type and condition of the instrument's case. Offers a monthly 8 page catalog of new and used instruments for $4 per year.

> Stan Werbin
> Elderly Instruments
> PO Box 14210
> Lansing, MI 48901
>   (517) 372-7890 days

☆ **Most string, wood, and brass musical instruments** are of interest for trade or resale. "I'll buy **any museum quality instrument**." For his own collection he wants instruments that are rare, very old, pretty, unique, or hand crafted. He especially wants **trumpets or cornets** that have extra keys, fewer keys, or keys that are in unusual positions or shapes. Also **instruments of other cultures** including African, Asian, Pacific, etc., but no pianos or organs. A photo should go with a complete description, including all labels or markings.

> Sid Glickman
> 42 Butterwood Lane East
> Irvington, NY 10533
>   (914) 591-5371 voice and fax

To sell any instrument, you need to

(1) State the maker and the model;
(2) Describe the type and quality
*   of the finish;*
(3) Give an indication of its condition.
*   Include mention of all cracks,*
*   dents, and the like.*

If some thing seems unusual to you, make a sketch or include a photo. If you have a piano or organ to sell, unless it's a concert grade Steinway, there is no national market and it is usually best to offer it for sale in a local classified ad.

☆ **American guitars, banjos, and mandolins** made by the following: *C.F. Martin, Gibson, Fender* (older models only), *Dobro, National, D'Angelico, B&D (Bacon & Day), Epiphone* (older), *Paramount, Vega, Fairbanks, SS Stewart, Washburn, Lyon & Healy, Stromberg, Gretsch,* and *Rickenbacker.* "If you have fine condition instruments for sale by these makers *only* you may call us collect for an offer. Have your instrument in your hand. Be prepared to answer specific questions about condition, originality, serial number, color, and the type of case it has. Without this information, we cannot provide meaningful evaluation. *Serious sellers only may call collect.* All others are welcome to call for advice or information." Among instruments Jay would most like to find are the *Martin* D-45 with abalone inlay, the electric *Gibson* Les Paul Standard made in 1958-59, and *Gibson* Mastertone banjos made during the late 1930's. Dates and models are very important. "Another model made at the same time might be worth only 1/20 as much. Original condition matters a lot." Offers an interesting catalog of high quality new and used instruments. Wants list available.

> Stan Jay
> Mandolin Bros.
> 629 Forest Ave.
> Staten Island, NY 10310
>   (718) 981-8585 (718) 981-3226 Fax: (718) 816-4416

☆ **Stringed musical instruments** including electric and acoustic guitars, banjos, mandolins and ukeleles. No ukelins or mandolin-harps, please. He buys the following brands of guitar: *D'Angelico, Gibson Les Paul, Martin, Stromberg National, Epiphone, Fender, Gretsch,* and *Rickenbacker.* Many guitars purchased for $100-$300 in the 1950's are worth five to ten times as much today, and a *Martin D-45* would bring from $20,000 to $50,000. Buys gold plated four-string banjos and fancy five string banjos by *Fairbanks, Vega, Epiphone, Gibson, Weymann, Slingerland, Bacon & Day, Studio King, Recording King, Paramount,* and others. Mandolins by *Gibson, Martin* and *Washburn* are wanted, as are ukeleles by *Martin* and *Gibson.* Photos of the front and back of your instrument are requested. Pays all shipping costs. Appraisal services are available.

> Steve Senerchia
> The Music Man
> 91 Tillinghast Avenue
> Warwick, RI 02886
>   (401) 821-2865   Fax: (401) 823-1612

☆ **French and Italian violins, violas, and cellos.** "I'll pay high prices for quality instruments, both commercial and handmade from anywhere in the world, but especially France and Italy. I don't want children's or school violins nor any imitations of Stradivarius, Guarnerius, or other masters." Describe the label inside the instrument. Appraisal services are available.

> Robert Portukalian's Violin Shop
> 1279 North Main Street
> Providence, RI 02904
> (401) 521-5145

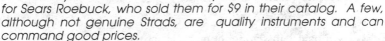

Many readers own violins with labels proclaiming them to be made by Stradivarius in the 1700's. These are usually cottage industry pieces made in Germany at the turn of the century for Sears Roebuck, who sold them for $9 in their catalog. A few, although not genuine Strads, are quality instruments and can command good prices.

☆ **High quality Italian violins and some of their imitators** are the prime interest of this 18 year veteran West coast dealer. Cremona school violins, 1650-1750, can be worth from $2,500 to $100,000 or more, but many copies exist. Jones will consider better French instruments and your fake "Stradivarius" violins. Most of the fake "Strads" sell for $100 or less, but a few more valuable "fake Strads" were made by fine craftsmen who affixed the Stradivarius label in an effort to sell the instrument. Others were high quality reproductions of the master's work, deliberately copied in homage to his craftsmanship. Many other **guitars, banjos, basses, violas, and mandolins** can be fairly valuable to Jones if you have one of better quality. It takes years of handling violins to be able to recognize originals or instruments of value. For this reason "it is difficult to buy through the mail, but not impossible." The reputation of the maker and the condition of the instrument are crucial in determining value. To sell a stringed instrument, you must describe all damage, the type and quality of finish, the bow, and give every word on the label. In many cases, he will request seeing the instrument before making a final offer. No Oriental instruments are wanted.

> David N. Jones' Violin Shop
> 3411 Ray Street
> San Diego, CA 92104
> (619) 584-1505

BRASS MUSICAL INSTRUMENTS

☆ **Brass musical instruments,** especially the unusual and obsolete. He wants "to know about all your old brass instruments since they all look the same to the untrained." Among other instruments, he especially wants a B-flat cornet with the bell pointing over the shoulder and a Schreiber horn with a straight up bell. He is attempting to assemble a representative collection of the hundreds of different brass instruments. Also interested in **band related memorabilia** such as photos of bands or individual musicians holding instruments, band programs, **catalogs** of instruments, mouthpieces, decorative or unusual **wooden music stands,** and old-style **conducting batons**. Also interested in your coffin shaped wooden instrument cases. If you regularly sell musical instruments, get his informative illustrated wants list.

> Jonathan Korzun
> 1201 Williamson Road
> North Brunswick, NJ 08902
> (201) 297-0308 eves

☆ **Brass musical instruments** made in the United States during the 19th century, especially keyed bugles and instruments which hang over the shoulder, worth $600 and up. He does *not* want saxophones or modern brass instruments. Give the maker's name, the number of valves, the shape of the instrument and whether it is made of brass or silver. You should include a photo or drawing of the shape of the instrument. He also wants photos of bands and bandsmen as well as old instrument catalogs.

> Mark Jones
> 2686 Green Street
> Eden, NY 14057
> (716) 992-2074 voice and fax

☆ **Saxophones made by** *Selmer*, especially in the early 1930's in Paris, but also other models as late as 1980. Serial numbers are found on the neck and on the back bottom, and must match. Look for serial numbers 60,000 through 89,000 on tenor saxes and numbers 50,000 through 120,000 on alto saxes, as they are the most desirable. Other serial numbers will be considered, however. Original finish, even if worn, is preferable to refinished instruments. Large dents and heavy scratches will take away some value. "Write or call collect if you want to sell an instrument described above." Other brands of sax considered by this nationally known specialist.

> Ed Hakal
> 10126 Signal Butte Circle
> Sun City, AZ 85373
> (602) 972-3091 evenings

OTHER MUSICAL INSTRUMENTS

☆ **Rare and unusual musical instruments** including harps, bagpipes, hurdy-gurdies, wooden flutes, concertinas, ethnic instruments, and all manner of **brass and woodwinds**, stringed instruments, dulcimers, autoharps, and others. No keyboards except a folding "preacher's organ." Mickie repairs instruments and will purchase good ones in "any restorable condition." Can make arrangements for consignment selling of instruments he doesn't wish to buy. This 20 year veteran conducts annual seminars on musical instrument history and performance. He charges reasonable rates for insurance appraisals, and will make offers. An extensive illustrated catalog may be ordered for $3. **Has no interest in accordions, pianos, pump or electric organs, or ukelins.**

> Mickie Zekley
> Lark in the Morning
> PO Box 1176
> Mendocino, CA 95460
>   (707) 964-5569

☆ **Drums and drum catalogs** from the early 1900's to 1970. Buys sets or single tom toms, bass drums, or snare drums, and buys uncracked **cymbals marked K.ZILDJIAN** but not those made by A.ZILDJIAN. "To save everyone effort, a thorough and complete inspection of your instrument should be done before contacting us. Check and note modifications and/or damage of any kind including scratches, cracks, peeling, bulging, holes drilled, rim warp, rust, pitting, stains, or discoloration." Information needed to evaluate your drum(s): the brand name, shape and color of the ID emblem, the diameter of the head(s), the depth of each drum's shell (not including the rims), and the color and type of finish of the drum(s) on both the outside and inside. Does not buy drums or drum catalogs produced after 1970, exotic or ethnic drums, or parade basses. He requests "serious inquiries only, please. Kindly keep in mind that we do not offer appraisals or estimates by mail or phone. If you have no idea of the value of your item(s), I'll give you a retail price range that your item sells for in the vintage drum market and then request you quote me your wholesale asking price. I'm willing to educate sellers so they can make an informed decision and determine a fair price, keeping in mind that we must recondition items, resell them, and make a profit. If you're just fishing for a price so you can sell your drums to someone else, please don't call us." One of the world's largest dealers in collectible drums, Vintage Drum Center publishes a quarterly catalog, available free to drum buyers.

> Ned Ingberman, Vintage Drum Center
> Route 1 Box 129
> Libertyville, IA 52567
>   (800) 729-3111 ext 5 (buy or sell)   Fax: (515) 693-3101

☆ **Harmonicas** and related items. Seeking unusual ones other than the standard 10 hole 4" long instrument: harmonicas with attached horns, bells, or whistles, those joined together with other harmonicas, those mounted in brass resonators, and instruments that are smaller than 2" long or larger than 12" long. He also wants:
- Toy instruments with harmonicas built inside;
- Canes with built-in harmonicas;
- Blow accordions (clarinet-like instruments with keys
  which when depressed make a harmonica note or chord;
- Advertising, display cases, posters, magazines;
- Catalogs with pages of harmonicas pictured;
- Records (old), sheet music, lapel pins, and what have you.

No Marine Band harmonicas or instruments in poor playing condition. Wants the maker, model, number of holes, length, width, number of rows of holes, whether it is double sided, whether all notes play, physical condition and whether the box is included. Dealers must price your goods. Amateurs who are actually selling may inquire as to value before shipment.

Alan Bates
495 Dogwood Drive
Hockessin, DE 19707
(302) 239-4296

☆ **Jew's harps** (also called jaw harps, juice harps), especially those that are hand-forged or made of ivory, bone, silver, or gold. They must be in good condition, complete with the tongue ("twanger"). "I'll buy Jew's harp cases in any material and want literature, instruction books, etc., and would love to find instruments composed of several harps joined together."

Leonard Fox
2965 Marlin Road, Box 729
Bryn Athyn, PA 19009
(215) 938-1840

☆ **Cigar box musical instruments.** Any type musical instrument made from a cigar box is wanted. When describing your item, please include any of the instrument's history you know. Mention whether strings, pegs, bow and carry bag are present, and describe any applied or painted decorations. Photo is helpful. Also buys toys and other items made from boxes, especially items which retain their basic "boxness" rather than items made from cut up pieces of boxes.

Tony Hyman
PO Box 3028
Pismo Beach, CA 93448
(805) 773-6777   Fax: (805) 773-8436

MECHANICAL MUSIC

☆ **Any pre-1930 device that plays music mechanically** including disk and cylinder music boxes, clocks and watches that play tunes, disk players, automata dolls, player organs, monkey organs, nickelodeons, horn phonographs in any condition from perfect to incomplete. Especially a barrel operated monkey organ with pipes ($2,000-$4,000), large disc music boxes that play more than one disc at a time ($10-$12,000), and cylinder music boxes with more than 175 teeth, and early musical watches. **No player pianos are wanted,** but most other mechanical devices bring $300 up. Give measurements of any disk or cylinder. Please include your phone number with correspondence.

> Martin Roenigk, Mechantiques
> 26 Barton Hill
> East Hampton, CT 06424
> (203) 267-8682   Fax: (203) 267-1120

☆ **Anything that makes music automatically or mechanically** such as phonographs, music boxes, **player pianos**, nickelodeons, organettes, and others. Also the records, discs, rolls, cobs, and anything else that plays on these instruments. Also any catalog, magazine, bulletin, book, literature or advertising pertaining to these items.

> Violet and Seymour Altman, Vi & Si's
> 8970 Main Street
> Clarence, NY 14031
> (716) 634-4488

☆ **Musical instruments that "play themselves"** by motor, springs, pneumatics or other means: **music boxes**, roller organs, cylinder music boxes, musical bird cages, nickelodeons, and organettes. Will buy rough condition items for parts or repair. Also musical disks, cylinders, piano rolls, old photos, postcards or paper ephemera depicting anything in mechanical music. Doug does not make offers.

> Doug Negus, Phonograph Phunatic
> 215 Mason Street
> Sutherland, IA 51058
> (712) 446-2270   (712) 446-3746

☆ **Horn phonographs in any condition.** Will buy parts from any machine made by the following companies: *Berliner Gramophone, National Gramophone, Universal Talking Machine*, or *Zonophone*.

> Charlie Stewart
> 900 Grandview Ave.
> Reno, NV 89503
> (702) 747-1439 days

☆ **Phonographs, music boxes, and related ephemera.** Would like to hear from you regarding all disc and cylinder phonographs with outside horns, especially those with wooden horns. Also floor model wind-up phonographs in deluxe or fancy cabinets. Also antique disc or cylinder music boxes, especially those that sit on the floor. Will pay from $200 to $10,000, depending on type, style, and condition. "I am also interested in purchasing old record catalogs, posters, metal signs, *Victor* dogs, needle tins, and the like. Phonograph related paper items before 1910 are especially desirable, particularly **items associated with Thomas Edison.**" Send descriptions and photocopies.

> Kurt Nauck, Vintage Records
> 6323 Inway
> Spring, TX 77389
>   (713) 370 7899   Fax: (713) 251-7023

☆ **Antique music boxes and phonographs.** Wants all types, 1850-1920, including cylinder, disc, paper roll, and cob organs. Brands like *Regina, Mira, Stella, Symphonian,* and *Kalliope* are sought. Especially interested in a *Regina Changer,* a 15 1/2 inch upright music box which changes automatically. He'd pay $12,000 for a nice one. He wants to know the brand, model, size, and condition. Pictures are most helpful. Is not interested in "late miniature music boxes."

> Chet Ramsay
> 3618 Strasburg Road
> Coatesville, PA 19320
>   (610) 384-0514

☆ **Music cylinders.** The following cylinders (early phonograph recordings) are wanted by a well known music auctioneer:
- Cylinders colored brown, pink, purple, white or orange;
- Cylinders 6" long or 5" in diameter;
- Blue cylinders numbered 5000 to 5750;
- Cylinders with historical content;
- Operatic cylinders.

It is a plus if the cylinders are in their original boxes, but not necessary. Cylinders can bring from $5 to $200 each, depending on the size, color, and condition. List the title, artist, catalog number, color, length and diameter, and note whether you have the box. If your collection is very large, so listing is impractical, phone him to make other arrangements. "Cylinders break or scratch easily. Avoid touching the surface. Do not play them, even if you think you have the right equipment."

> Kurt Nauck
> Vintage Records
> 6323 Inway
> Spring, TX 77389
>   (713) 370 7899   Fax: (713) 251-7023

☆ **Phonographs and related memorabilia** from before 1930 including cylinder and disc records, catalogs, needle tins, postcards, stereoviews depicting phonographs, toy phonographs, signs and other advertising except magazine ads. Also buys cylinder records of speeches by Taft, Teddy Roosevelt, and other famous people, for which he pays $10-$50. Also all **material related to Thomas Edison**. List make, model, and condition. Include label, artist, and title of records. SASE for offer.

> Steven Ramm
> 420 Fitzwater Street
> Philadelphia, PA 19147
> (215) 922-7050

☆ **Phonographs with outside horns,** complete or for parts. No Victrolas. Alvin doesn't want to be bothered unless you're serious about selling. Does not make offers.

> Alvin Heckard
> Rural route 1 Box 88
> Lewistown, PA 17044
> (717) 248-7071

☆ *RCA* or *Capehart* **radio-phonographs that automatically flip records over** to play the other side. Pays $500-$700 for these large complicated machines from the 1930's. "If your machine weighs less than 75 pounds, I'm probably not interested." Take a photo of the record changing mechanism or give him a call.

> Joseph Weber
> 604 Centre Street
> Ashland, PA 17921
> (717) 875-4401 from 3 to 5 p.m.

☆ **Catalogs, repair manuals, and advertising for phonograph records and piano rolls** published by record and piano roll companies, 1890 to 1960. Prefers to buy collections or very early pieces. No records, magazine ads, or damaged items. Tim is past president of the Association for Recorded Sound Collections, a national club for recording historians.

> Tim Brooks
> Box 41 Glenville Station
> Greenwich, CT 0683

☆ **Phonograph needle clippers and sharpeners.**

> Don Gorlick
> PO Box 24541
> Seattle, WA 98124

SHEET MUSIC

☆ **Old popular sheet music** from 1820-1970, with pictorial covers, especially music or songs from movies, shows, WWI or WWII. Wants ragtime, blues, Negro, ethnic music, and particularly likes covers with baseball, cartoons, fire, aviation, and automobile songs especially with illustrations by Homer or Nathaniel Currier. No classical or religious. **Also buys *Downbeat, Metronome, Billboard* and movie magazines.**

> Beverly Hamer
> PO Box 75
> East Derry, NH 03041
> (603) 432-3528

☆ **Sheet music** in small or large collections or accumulations. Primary interest is in popular music of the 20th century (1890-1970). Movie and show tunes are of primary interest, but "also any music that falls into any of the main collectible categories, like presidential, political, patriotic, war, transportation, cartoon, baseball, *Coca-Cola*, advertising, historical, Black related, and anything else that has interesting cover art." Particularly likes to find music published by the *ET Paull Music Company*, and will pay between $10 and $300, depending upon the title and condition. **Does not want to buy classical music or sheet music designed for teaching.** "If the person wants to sell the music as a lot, I need to know quantity, condition, and the rough percentage of movie, show, and pop tunes. I also want to know the percentage of large format (11" x 14") and small format (9" x 12") music."

> *"Please don't describe sheet music as 'good for its age.' That means fair or poor condition. 'Excellent' and 'mint' are terms reserved for music that has almost never seen the light of day, music store stock, or publisher's remainder."*

> Wayland Bunnell
> Clean Sheets
> 199 Tarrytown Road
> Manchester, NH 03103
> (603) 668-5466

*Sheet music collectors are very fussy about condition. **Don't waste their time and yours by offering items in poor condition.** They won't buy them! When trying to sell a few pieces of sheet music, a photocopy is the best strategy, but with large quantities, follow Wayland Bunnell's suggestions, giving quantity, general condition, number of songs in each of the two sheet music sizes, and the percentage of the pile that are movie, show, and pop tunes.*

☆ **Sheet music.** "I am a general sheet music collector who buys music in 500+ categories, so I look for whatever I don't have that interests me. What I don't need is the most popular songs of any era. I don't have much interest in "nice" music like love songs, moon songs, waltzes, etc. I'm more apt to buy music in major categories with strong illustrated covers such as movies, politics, cartoons, transportation, sports, or racism." To offer her your music, list the title, date, composer, name of the movie or show, condition, and what is on the cover.

"Don't expect to get rich on piles of old sheet music. Few pieces of sheet music have significant value...and those must be in outstanding condition. Some sheet are worth $100 or more, so it is important to check."

     Sandy Marrone
     113 Oakwood Drive
     Cinnaminson, NJ 08077
     (609) 829-6104

☆ **Bound volumes of sheet music from before 1900.** Pays $1 or more per title for illustrated ones, but rare publishers bring more. Prefers bound books with no titles removed. Also **songbooks with oddly shaped notes.** "I'll pay $25+ for singing school books with notes that are oblong, triangular, rectangular or oddly shaped, especially those in good condition published before 1860. Authors of popular versions of these books include Funk, Carden, Davisson, Swan, and others."
     Jim Presgraves, Bookworm & Silverfish
     PO Box 639
     Wytheville, VA 24382

☆ **Sheet music about WWI and WWII** in fine to mint condition. Also wants sheet music with pictures of Frank Sinatra or Presidents of the U.S. Also buys **music by Charles K. Harris and Irving Berlin.**
     Herman Rush
     10773 Ojai-Santa Paula Road
     Ojai, CA 93023

☆ **Song books and sheet music** are sought **as donations.** If you can't find a buyer, but hate to see those musical treasures go to waste, consider donating to a public library specializing in music. They'll take any usable sheet music or song books, any language, up to the present. They don't need "how to" books. Donations must be unrestricted. No need to contact them; just ship and request a receipt for tax purposes.
     May Anstee, Helen Plumb Library
     110 West Maple
     Lombard, IL 60148
     (708) 627-0316

To sell Hymnals, see Religion section, pp288-290.

PHONOGRAPH RECORDS

☆ **Rare 78 rpm records and phonograph cylinders.** Among his particular wants are:
- Jazz, blues, cajun and country 1925-1935;
- Rock and roll, 1948-1960;
- Records before 1903 (often 7" diameter with no paper labels);
- Speeches by historical figures;
- **Picture records** (transparent records w/ pictures under grooves);
- Advertising, promotional, and special purpose records, some of which are made of thin cardboard (*don't play them!*);
- Unusual sizes and shapes of records;
- Classical and operatic records made before 1908, especially disks smaller than 10";
- **Long play 78's** marked "longer playing," "five minute record," or some such;
- Puzzle, or multi-track, records;
- Rare labels, of which he can supply you a long list, including *Black Patti, KKK, Sunshine, Marconi, Vitaphone,* and more.

He urges you to read Les Docks' *The American Premium Record Guide* and to list any records you have that catalog for more than $15 in that publication. Include the label, number, artist, and any noticeable defects. "If you have a large collection so that making a list is impractical, call me and we can discuss the possibility of evaluating your collection in person." Send a long SASE and $2 for his wants list. He does not want big bands, Hawaiian, popular songs, religious music, album sets, country music after WWII, home recordings, or later opera and classical, nor does he want 45's or LP records of any type. "Just the early cylinders and 78's," says this well known auctioneer.

> Kurt Nauck
> Vintage Records
> 6323 Inway
> Spring, TX 77389
> (713) 370-7899 Fax: (713) 251-7023

☆ **Phonograph records, tapes, music videos, sheet music, books and magazines related to music,** 1900 to the present. Items must be in fine condition as they are purchased for resale. Buys in bulk, so indicate the type of record (78, 45, 33), the type of music (rock, country, classical, jazz, easy listening, spoken, soundtrack, etc.), and the number you have of each. SASE is a must. Produces *Record Finder,* a 56 page monthly for $12/year.

> W.H. Smith
> Memory Lane Records
> PO Box 1047
> Glen Allen, VA 23060
> (804) 266-1154 Fax: (804) 264-9660

☆ **78 rpm recordings, 1900-1940,** including popular, dance orchestra, vocal, military band, classical, jazz, country & western, instrumental, spoken word, personality, humor, and recordings in foreign languages. Also seeks picture records. Highest prices are paid for records in good condition with no cracks or chips into the grooves. Values range from $1 to $1,000 with 80% of them under $5 each (but a pile of them adds up). When listing your records, include the label, artist and catalog (index) number. Song titles are not necessary. A Stamped Self-Addressed Envelope should be included if you wish records evaluated. David will buy a wider range of items than most record buyers. He is especially interested in entire collections and will travel anywhere in the East. Catalogs of record companies before 1930 are also sought.

> David Alan Reiss
> 3920 Eve Drive
> Seaford, NY 11783
> (516) 785-8336

When describing phonograph records the most important pieces of information are the record label and catalog number. Record experts like buyers recommended in Trash or Treasure *will know what you have without your even listing the artist and title. Condition is not as important, but still should be mentioned. Some rare 78rpm records will be purchased in any condition.*

If your record is of a very popular song, there are many copies available, so it doesn't have much value.

☆ **American 78 rpm pop records, 1888-1949,** especially in quantity. Pays 10¢ to $1 apiece, less if records are not in fine condition. Buys disks, cylinders, and sapphire ball recordings at higher prices. Likes to find pre-1960 versions of *Froggy Went a Courtin'*, especially the *Victor* black label version from 1926, worth $100 in fine condition. Some interest in **sheet music for pop music and songs** from 1890-1925.

> Ron Graham
> 8167 Park Ave.
> Forestville, CA 95436
> (707) 887-2856

☆ **Jazz, blues, big band, hillbilly, rock and roll, rhythm and blues, rockabilly, and celebrity records** in 78rpm, 45rpm and LP's.
- Jazz and dance bands from the 1920's and 30's;
- Jug and washboard bands;
- Radio transcription disks;
- Anything recorded on *Autograph, Black Patti,* and 50 other labels (send for a list);
- Records marked "Fox Trot," "Stomp," or "For Dancing."

He buys many rare, obscure, and unpopular records, but does not want easy listening, hit records, or pop singing stars like Al Jolson and Bing Crosby. If you have 78's to sell, send $2 for the *Shellac Shack's Wants List,* a 72 page book listing the prices they pay for thousands of records. Les is author of *American Premium Record Guide,* the basic reference book on phonograph records, available for $26 postpaid from him.

> Les Docks, The Shellac Shack
> PO Box 691035
> San Antonio, TX 78269
> (210) 492-6021   Fax: (210) 492-6489

☆ **78 rpm *Columbia* Grand Opera Series** 10" one-sided records. Also buys *Mercury* **"Living Presence Series" LP's** in stereo. Does not want damaged items or reissues. Include the label and catalog number when you write.

> John Widmar
> 1610 27th Street Upper
> Kenosha, WI 53140
> (414) 654-6802

— ☆ *Vogue* **78 rpm picture records.** Will pay $500 for *Rum and Coca Cola.* Records must be clean and in excellent condition. Long SASE brings a list of other records John wants to buy.

> John Widmar
> 1610 27th Street Upper
> Kenosha, WI 53140
> (414) 654-6802

☆ **Children's 78rpm records,** 1900's-1960's, in all sizes on all labels. Children's records that do not have their original jackets or sleeves are usually not of interest unless they are picture records (with pictures right in the vinyl as these are usually not found in sleeves). Most items are $1-$10 but a handful can bring $100 each. The condition of the record and the sleeve should be described, along with the label name and catalog number. He's compiling a discography of 78rpm children's records, so welcomes all information you have.

> Peter Muldavin
> 173 West 78th Street, #5F
> New York, NY 10024
> (212) 362-9606

33 rpm LONG PLAYING ALBUMS

☆ **LP (long playing 33rpm) records** in the following categories may be of interest if they are in fine condition:
- **Modern jazz**, preferably from the 1950's (no Dixieland!);
- **Soul, doo-wop, blues, and rhythm & blues** from the 1950's and 60's; original albums only, not rereleases;
- *Bluenote* and *Prestige* jazz recordings in mono, not stereo;
- **Obscure Broadway original cast albums**, like *Clown Around;*
- **Soundtracks to obscure or unpopular movies**, or any **spoken soundtracks** such as *The Caine Mutiny* (especially desirable);
- **Classical stereo recordings** on *RCA Living Stereo, Mercury Living Presence Stereo, Decca FFSS* and *London* from the early days of stereo in the 1950's and 60's;
- **Classical recordings of solo performers** on piano, violin, cello, etc., especially of lesser known performers;
- **Oddities, including test pressings**, items never released, etc.;
- Some rare 1950's and 60's 45's;
- **Depression era 78's**, especially jazz, blues, and dance bands.

Many of these items are only a few dollars, but some are worth many hundreds, and a handful can bring $1,000 or more. There are some records which have no value and can be considered "yard sale" fare, including all easy listening, rock and roll recorded after 1960 (unless unusual in some way), and any LP's with no sleeves. If you want to offer records for sale, list the label, the catalog number, the title, artist, and condition to this 40 year veteran expert dealer.

    Rod Baum, Rare Records
    1432 Queen Anne Road
    Teaneck, NJ 07666
        (201) 833-4883 (10am to 6pm)   Fax: (201) 833-4874

☆ **Country music albums** by major artists such as Merle Haggard, Bonnie Owens, Loretta Lynn, Kitty Wells, etc. Albums are bought for resale and must be in original factory shrink wrap or in like new condition, with no scratches, major cover wear or split seams. "We do not buy items recorded after 1980. We also don't buy items which have been rewrapped or had a corner cut off to conceal cover damage. We will not buy any item which even looks like a rewrap." Give the name of the artist, title of the album, catalog number, the condition of the cover and, if the album has been opened, the color of the label. They make offers, but require you to ship the records for inspection prior to payment. They also buy country music 45's in like-new condition, but only in bulk lots as "it's too time consuming to buy single items."

    Jack Lawrence, Jr., Granny's Turntable
    PO Box 1585
    Hendersonville, TN 37077
        (615) 822-8675 days

☆ **Jazz LP's from the 1950's and 60's.** Also buys "all kinds of **jazz literature and magazines**, any years, and some other materials associated with jazz." No 45's or 78's. No music other than jazz. No records with poor condition covers. Please include your phone number.

> Gary Alderman
> PO Box 9164
> Madison, WI 53715
> (608) 274-3527   Fax: (608) 277-1999

☆ **Jazz records.** Wants 33rpm jazz records from before 1970. No 78's, big band, or Dixieland, please. Give the artist, label, catalog number, and the condition of both the jacket and record.

> Chuck Moore
> PO Box 280
> Gladstone, OR 97027
> (503) 654-9994

☆ **Jazz, soul and doo-wop 10" LP's** in very good condition. Also wants **pop Hawaiian LP's**, especially Martin Denny and Arthur Lyman LP's in stereo. "I don't want classical records or reissues of any kind." Give artist, title, label, catalog number, and condition of both the disc and the cover.

> Joe Flynn
> PO Box 1473
> Greenwood Lake, NY 10925
> (914) 477-9373

When describing 33rpm phonograph records the most important pieces of information are the artist, title, record label and catalog number. Since many albums went through editions, mention the color of the label, too. It is also important to note whether it is a mono or stereo recording, as some records are common in one form and rare in the other.

Condition of 33's is very important. Buyers care about the condition of the cover as well as the record. Make certain to mention writing (like owner's names), banged corners, split seams, and missing inside sleeves. Poor condition 33's that look like licorice pizza will not find a buyer.

It is very difficult for you to know which albums have value, because of surprises like the Caine Mutiny soundtrack worth more than $1,000, or the Bob Dylan album with the "missing song."

45 rpm RECORDS

☆ **Odd 45's from the 1950's and 60's.** "I want little known performers on little known labels. I have no interest in Elvis and other popular artists or in labels like *Columbia, RCA, Capitol* and the like. I don't buy 78's, classical music or other instrumentals. Be specific in your descriptions, including label and catalog number."

Otti Schmitt
Finders-Keepers Collectibles
7724 Hayfield Road
Alexandria, VA 22310
(703) 550-1454

☆ **Rhythm and Blues or Rock and Roll 45's from the 1950's.** Wants original recordings of groups like the *Flamingos, Robins, Wrens, Penguins,* etc. Will buy any 45's from race labels such as *Chance, Red Robin, Blue Lake, Harlem, Grand, Rockin, After Hours, Aladdin, Parrot, Flip, Allen, Rhythm, Club 51,* and *Swingtime.* No records that are reissues, bootlegged, or damaged. When writing, give the label, catalog number and condition.

John Widmar
1610 27th Street Upper
Kenosha, WI 53140
(414) 654-6802

☆ **Rock and roll, rhythm and blues, and country music records.** Wants 45 and 33 rpm, especially:
• 45's with picture sleeves;
• Odd ball items;
• Disc jockey radio promos;
• **Rock, blues, or country sheet music and magazines.**
Nothing having to do with classical, big band, opera, or polka music is wanted at all, no matter how old or interesting.

Cliff Robnett
7804 NW 27th
Bethany, OK 73008
(405) 787-6703

☆ **45 rpm records in quantity** in unplayed or nearly unused condition. Looking for store stock or radio station collections, but will also buy small collections if they contain desirable records. Nothing worn or scratched. "Phone if you think you have what I'm looking for."

Ken Clee
PO Box 11412
Philadelphia, PA 19111
(215) 722-1979

MUSIC, MUSICIANS & SINGERS

☆ **Songbooks and song broadsides:**
  • **Songsters (books)** from between 1700 and 1900, either British or
    American, in paper, leather, or hard covers, including political
    candidate songbooks, temperance song collections, medicine
    company advertising songbooks, and vaudeville performer
    songsters, as well as circus promotional songsters;
  • **Song broadsides and ballad sheets**, 1500-1900, U.S. or British;
  • **Hillbilly or Country and Western song folios** before 1946;
  • **Songbooks of occupational groups**, miners, sailors,
        lumberjacks, etc;
  • **Regional American folk song collections** from any period;
  • **British and Irish folk song collections** from before 1900.
This is a fairly restrictive list of books of collected songs. Ken is a
prominent authority, author, and producer in the world of folk music
and has no interest in common items or things not on this list. Full bib-
liographic information is required. **Please do not inquire about
collections of sheet music or religious songbooks**.
> Kenneth Goldstein
> 4840 Cedar Ave.
> Philadelphia, PA 19143
> (215) 476-5857

Always give Standard Bibliographic Information:
  Title as on the title page, not the spine;
  Author, editor, or compiler;
  Publisher and place of publication;
  Date of copyright and of publication (list all);
  Number of pages and illustrations;
  The condition of the binding, spine, pages, and the dust
    jacket. Note bookplates, writing, and other damage.
A photocopy of the title page will save you lots of writing.

☆ **Paper ephemera associated with the history of pianos** including
advertising signs, posters, catalogs, photos of factory and store interiors, models of pianos and mechanisms, tools used by piano tuners and
builders, and piano trade publications. He is not interested in magazine
ads. Your description should include size and condition as well as noting the materials from which your item is made. Photo or photocopy
helpful. "The history of pianos and of their manufacture fascinates me."
He does not want to buy your piano. No exceptions!
> Phillip Jamison III
> 17 Sharon Alley
> West Chester, PA 19382
> (610) 696-8449

☆ **Eubie Blake or Sissle and Blake memorabilia** and records, especially a 10" recording called *Jammin' at Rudi's.*
>Steven Ramm
>420 Fitzwater Street
>Philadelphia, PA 19147

☆ **Gilbert and Sullivan memorabilia** and ephemera, including art, prints, sculpture, porcelain, glass, candy boxes, fans, and what have you. "Please advise what items related to Gilbert and Sullivan you have available for sale." No sheet music, please, unless autographed.
>Philip Harris
>54 Margaret Avenue
>Lawrence, NY 11559
>(516) 371-1225

☆ **Music related photos, concert programs, and autographs related to opera and classical music.** Please give the title, date, and other information. Photocopies are very helpful.
>Steve Jabloner
>7380 Adrian Drive #23
>Rohnert Park, CA 94928
>(707) 795-3081

☆ **John Philip Sousa and Patrick Sarsfield Gilmore** items, including programs, posters, photos, real photo postcards, stereoviews, letterheads, uniform items, sheet music, correspondence, diaries, and autographed copies of Sousa's books. Condition of sheet music is important: corners and edges should not be trimmed or taped. *Does not* collect 78rpm or cylinder recordings, or anything published after Sousa's death in 1932. Please send a good description or Xerox™ copy.
>Barry Furrer
>491 Valley Road
>Gillette, NJ 07933

☆ **Big Band memorabilia from the 1930's and 40's** especially of Glenn Miller or Bunny Berigan. John buys phonograph records, home recordings, tapes of concerts or radio performances, transcription disks, autographs, photographs, newspaper articles, magazine articles, movie short subjects, home movies, posters, and sheet music if it has to do with big bands. This 30 year collector will negotiate an item's value.
>John Mickolas
>172 Liberty Street
>Trenton, NJ 08611
>(609) 599-9672   (609) 647-6618 days

☆ **Frank Sinatra memorabilia** including records, sheet music with his picture, radio items, stuff from TV shows, scrap books, and what have you. Please send Xerox™ copies or good description.
> Herman Rush
> 10773 Ojai-Santa Paula Road
> Ojai, CA 93023

☆ **Elvis Presley memorabilia** dating from before his death, including all marked E.P. ENT 1956, such as lipsticks, skirts, perfume, gloves, and anything else out of the ordinary. He also buys posters and promo-tional items from Elvis movies, records, and appearances. He'd especially like to find a plastic guitar with pictures on it, and issues of 1950's magazines such as *Dig* and *Teen Stories* with all Elvis features. Autographs are always wanted. No records except promotional copies.
> Robert "Nostalgia Bob" Urmanic
> 199 Brookvalley Drive
> Elyria, OH 44035
> (216) 365-3550

☆ **Elvis Presley collectibles.** After 30 years of avid collecting, Robin still buys Elvis items, especially:
* Autographed photos, records, and other items;
* 45rpm records in their original sleeve, 1950-1960;
* Personal items, including clothing;
* Tour books from 1955-1977;
* E.P. ENT (Elvis Presley Enterprises) items from the 1950's;
* Movie posters and lobby cards from Elvis films;
* Store displays and promotions for Elvis products.

Prices vary according to the item, condition, authentication and rarity. Not interested in shot glasses, ash trays, postcards, or anything made after Elvis's death. Give the condition, and describe how you got the item. Robin's collection is featured in *All the Kings Things* available from her for $18 postpaid.
> Robin Rosaaen
> The Elvis Special
> 101 Glen Eyrie Ave. #202
> San Jose, CA 95125
> (408) 297-0861   (408) 554-7715

☆ **Rock and roll memorabilia** is wanted, including the **Beatles, Kiss, The Monkees and other headliners**. Autographs of rock singers and musicians are especially desired. He does not purchase rock and roll records unless you have studio dubs or tapes or radio station promotional copies. No other exceptions.
> Robert "Nostalgia Bob" Urmanic
> 199 Brookvalley Drive
> Elyria, OH 44035

☆ **Beatles memorabilia** of all sorts including toys, dolls, games, tickets, cartoon kits, model kits, *Yellow Submarine*, Halloween costumes, wallpaper, talcum powder, shampoo, ice cream wrappers, blankets, jewelry, china, toy musical instruments, fan club items, etc., especially items sealed in their original factory cartons. Rick is also looking for hard-to-find Beatles albums such as *Beatles vs the 4 Seasons* or *Yesterday and Today* with the butcher block cover. "I'll pay $800 for a Beatles record player in mint condition, and up to $500 for an unopened bottle of pomade, and $250 for a *Kaboodle Kit* in new condition." Rick also buys **The Monkees ephemera** of all types. Co-author of *The Beatles Memorabilia Price Guide* available for $28.

> Rick Rann
> PO Box 877
> Oak Park, IL 60303
>   (708) 442-7907

☆ **Beatles memorabilia** from before their 1970 breakup. Everything is wanted, including games, toys, dolls, posters, movie related items, candid photos, concert posters and programs, tickets, and ads for merchandise or concerts. Would love any Beatles toy musical instruments picturing the group, and will pay from $200-$500 for Beatles bongos or banjos. Buys common items as long as they are old and original. Wants to know where you got your item, and requests your phone number. Co-author of *The Beatles Memorabilia Price Guide*.

> Jeff Augsburger
> 507 Normal Ave.
> Normal, IL 61761
>   (309) 452-9376

☆ **Michael Jackson** memorabilia, including magazines with him on the cover, licensed toys, comics, video memorabilia, books, autographs, etc. Her special interest is in magazines with cover stories about Michael or the Jackson 5. "I want only official merchandise and have no interest in fakes, repros, or autopen signatures. Describe condition and tell where you got the item."

> Carolyn Jamison
> PO Box 111752
> Nashville, TN 37222
>   (615) 252-4083

☆ **Bobby Breen phonograph records and song sheets** dating from the late 1930's.

> Ralph Eodice
> 161 Valley Road
> Clifton, NJ 07013

COIN-OPERATED MACHINES

"Coin-ops" is what collectors call slot machines, jukeboxes, arcade games, trade stimulators (games you play for product prizes), and other machines put into play by dropping a coin into a slot.

If you give the make, model, and serial number, most dealers will know what machine you have. A photo of older items is advisable, especially of vending machines and trade stimulators since unfamiliar ones turn up.

When writing about a coin-op, indicate whether it works and whether parts are missing or broken. Coin-ops do not need to be in perfect condition to sell. Most collectors and dealers restore them.

When describing pinball machines note how much paint is peeling off the back board illustration. If the illustration is not in perfect condition you must include a photo as the condition of the backboard is very important. When taking photos of pinball machines, include the play field in one photo and back glass (vertical pictorial area) in another.

Because the machines are large, heavy, and valuable, buyers will usually make shipping arrangements.

☆ **Coin-op machines** including jukeboxes, nickelodeons, arcade devices such as diggers and claws, view machines, coin-op fans and radios, and **vending machines** for gum, condoms, etc. Has particular interest in **slot machines** and **gambling devices that pay cash** rewards. These have a minimum value of $500 with the more unusual machines bringing considerably more. Pre-1910 gambling machines made on the west coast are very desirable. Also **paper ephemera** about coin-op machines including catalogs, brochures, advertising, and anything historical. No pinball, video, or service machines like washers.

> Fred Ryan, Slot Closet
> PO Box 83135
> Portland, OR 97203
>   (503) 286-3597

☆ **Coin-op machines,** especially early wood cabinet and cast iron machines 1885-1912, very rare pinball machines, kinetoscopes, and 1888-1905 peep machines. Offers $20,000 for the *Fey* 1906 Liberty Bell slot machine but has only minor interest in most other slots. Pays $7,500 for an *Edison* Kinetoscope from 1894. Particularly interested in paper ephemera about coin-ops including catalogs, advertising, letterheads, and anything else historical. Also photos of store or saloon interiors which depict machines. Also *The Coin Machine Journal, Automatic Age, Automatic World, Spinning Reels, The Billboard* (pre-1932), and other trade magazines devoted to coin-op machines. Bueschel is an editor of the quarterly *The Coin Slot* and responsible for dozens of guides to coin-ops. Since thousands of dollars are involved, he wants you to shoot a roll of 35mm film of details of your coin-op and ship the undeveloped roll to him. He'll reimburse. You *must* tell him where you got your machines.

Richard Bueschel
414 North Prospect Manor Ave.
Mt. Prospect, IL 60056
    (708) 253-0791

☆ *Gottlieb* **pinball machines,** 1948-58. Machines before 1948 don't have flippers and are not of interest. He explains that most of the games from before 1956 have wooden cabinets, trim, and legs; after 1956, they're metal. Will buy *Gottlieb* machines in any mechanical condition, but the back glass must be present and in good condition with little or no chipping, cracking, or paint flaking. Normal wear on the playing surface is expected, but severely damaged play fields make a game uncollectible. Damaged machines have some value for parts, but it's a fraction of what games in fine condition command. Pays $500 for *Gin Rummy* or *Mystic Marvel* games by *Gottlieb*. "I will consider games by other manufacturers, but only if they are in very good condition. No games which have revolving reels to record scores or that have metal cabinets. If you are in doubt, call and I will try my best to identify your game. When you describe your machine, pay attention to cosmetics, missing bumper caps, light shields missing, cracks, etc." He prefers amateurs to set the price wanted, but he will make offers, but only if you are serious about selling.

Gordon Hasse, Jr.
PO Box 1543 Grand Central Station
New York, NY 10163
    (212) 996-3825 eves

☆ **Coin-op machines,** especially pre-1940 slots and jukeboxes. No solid state pinball machines. Ted publishes the monthly *Coin Machine Trader* devoted to ads and information about coin-ops.

> Ted Salveson
> PO Box 602
> Huron, SD 57350
>   (605) 352-3870

☆ **Coin-op machines** including 78 rpm *Wurlitzer* jukeboxes from 1938-48, **penny arcade machines** from before 1920, **vending machines** from before 1910, and all **slot machines**.

> Martin Roenigk, Mechantiques
> 26 Barton Hill
> East Hampton, CT 06424
>   (203) 267-8682   Fax: (203) 267-1120

☆ **Jukeboxes,** jukebox speakers, wall boxes, remote equipment, literature and brochures are all wanted by this dedicated collector who also buys magazines associated with the coin-op world including: *Automatic Age* (1925-46), *Automatic World* (1927-57), *Cash Box Coin Machine Journal, National Coin Machine News,* and many others. His interest extends to all brands of jukeboxes, especially those made before 1946, and will consider them in any condition. Not particularly interested in those made after 1962. Only wants items he doesn't already have, but pledges to help you find a buyer if he doesn't want your item. When you write, include the brand name, the model number, and a photo or video. Wayne is author of the *Jukebox Speaker and Wallbox Guide*, available from the author for $30, and plans to open a jukebox museum. He can send you a list of specific items he is seeking.

> Wayne Kline
> 20750 Ventura Boulevard #160
> Woodland Hills, CA 91364
>   (818) 840-2296   Fax: (818) 840-2249

☆ **Table model jukeboxes.** He will buy *all* pre-1960 jukeboxes if you live close enough for him to pick them up. Also jukebox literature, advertising and parts. If you live far enough away that your machine must be shipped, he only wants the small ones. He doesn't want to ship the larger machines.

> Alvin Heckard
> Route 1   Box 88
> Lewistown, PA 17044
>   (717) 248-7071

☆ *Wurlitzer* and *Rock Ola* **jukeboxes,** working or not, especially *Wurlitzer* model 42 (worth up to $1,800) and model numbers 500 or above (which begin at $450 for a #500 and can go to nearly $12,000 for a nice condition model #950). Also **all slot machines, in any condition**, complete or not, working or not. All but the most common working machines will bring $500, many over $1,000. He advertises widely that $50,000 is waiting for the finder of a working *Fey* Liberty Bell slot machine. Will pick up machines anywhere in the U.S.

> Frank Zygmunt
> Antique Slot Machine Co.
> PO Box 542
> Westmont, IL 60559
> (708) 985-2742   Fax: (708) 985-5151

☆ *Wurlitzer* **jukeboxes** with model numbers lower than 500. These 1930's machines predate the "plastic-and-bright-lights era" favored by most collectors. Also *Capehart* **radio-phonographs** and **jukeboxes from the 1930's that flip records over.** Pays $500-$700 for *Wurlitzer 416* or *Capehart C20-30*. He'll buy these in any condition, but condition does affect value. Will pick up anything east of the Mississippi and arrange for shipments in the West.

> Joseph Weber
> 604 Centre Street
> Ashland, PA 17921
> (717) 875-4401 between 3 and 5 p.m.

☆ *Wurlitzer* **jukeboxes** from the 1940's. Also **paper ephemera, service manuals, and advertising related to jukeboxes** of all types. Rick publishes the monthly *Jukebox Collector Newsletter* and is author of three books about jukeboxes, including *A Complete Identification Guide to the Wurlitzer Jukebox* available from him for $15.

> Rick Botts
> 2545 SE 60th Court
> Des Moines, IA 50317
> (515) 265-8324

☆ **All types of coin-operated machines,** including slot machines, **pinball machines**, pre-electronic **arcade games** made of oak and/or iron, and **trade stimulators**. The more unusual, the better. "Tell me what it is, its condition, and whether it works. Please send a photo." Dealers should price your goods, but amateurs may request offers.

> Marvin Yagoda
> Marvin's Marvelous Mechanical Museum
> 28585 South Harwich Drive
> Farmington Hills, MI 48018
> (810) 851-8158   Fax: (810) 851-8159

☆ **Coin-ops**, including "light up" jukeboxes, *Coke* machines, fortune tellers, arcade games, *Poperette* popcorn machines, and ornate gumball and peanut machines. "If your item is old or unusual and takes coins, I'll probably want it." Your description should include a photo, the model number, and information about how you came to own the item.

> Kim Gutzke
> 7134 15th Avenue S
> Minneapolis, MN 55423
> (612) 866-6183

☆ **Countertop coin-operated machines** including arcade machines, trade stimulators, and vending machines from the 1920's through the 1950's. You must send a photo and the price wanted.

> Ken Durham
> 909 26th Street NW
> Washington, DC 20037
> (202) 338-1342

☆ **Penny arcade games** such as grip tests, target games, kicker and catcher, Pike's Peak, and the like. Prefers penny machines.

> James Conley
> 2758 Coventry Lane NW
> Canton, OH 44708
> (216) 477-7725

☆ **Pinball machines and coin-op kiddie ride animals** pre-1965.

> Don Olson
> PO Box 245
> Humboldt, IA 50548

☆ **Gumball and peanut vending machines** made of cast iron or porcelain before 1930, with glass globes that are faceted, shaped like light bulbs or otherwise unusual. Especially wants machines with original paint and pin striping. He does *not* want machines with square globes from the 1940's to the present. List the make of machine, shape of the globe, material from which it is made, any decals, condition of the paint, and whether or not it is working. Dealers must price your goods, but amateur sellers may request offers.

> Don Reedy
> 13 South Carroll Street
> Frederick, MD 21701
> (301) 662-5503 eves   Fax: (301) 663-3

SPORTS SOUVENIRS CAN BE BIG TREASURE!

This chapter is particularly important because of the large number of items you own or can find that have some value. I urge all readers to go through this chapter thoroughly. These are important people, good buyers...and mean profit for you.

Balls, gloves, bats, uniforms, programs, championship belts, trophies, photos... anything sports is collectible. *Professional championship rings, belts, and trophies brings top prices (within each category). Amateur sports, except The Olympics, generate little dollar interest.*

It is possible to cash in very large. *A Detroit listener followed my instructions and turned a baseball uniform into $176,000. Readers and listeners just like you have uncovered 14 Babe Ruth balls and thousands of other uniforms, bats, programs and other baseball items have turned up.*

In terms of dollar volume ,baseball leads all sports. Don't let baseball's high prices mislead you. **Items you are likely to find in other sports categories may bring as little as 10% of the value of a comparable baseball item.**

Thousand dollar prices are not unknown in other sports, but prices of $20 to $500 are a lot more common. Fishing tackle brings the most money to **Trash or Treasure** *readers and listeners. Find one good tackle box, and you could be thousands richer. Buyer Rick Edmisten reports spending $100,000 a year with Trash or Treasure readers and listeners. Small plugs (wooden and metal baits) purchased in the 1920's and 30's for pennies sell for hundreds of dollars today. Some boxes they originally came in are worth $50! Don't let them gather dust. Rick or other fishing tackle buyer will give them a good home...and give you a fatter purse or wallet.*

Keep alert for strings of old decoys *laying unused in barns, basements and boat houses. These regularly bring over $1,000 each and once sold for more than $300,000. Millions of dollars worth of decoys are sitting around in New England alone.*

Baseball collectibles bring high prices because there are so many collectors. Competition is not as great in other sports (including minor league baseball) so prices remain generally reasonable.

For example, the top price for a baseball card is over $100,000 while top value basketball and football cards sell for only $300. Expert advice is essential in sports cards. Prices are down substantially from their over-inflated days, but really rare cards still can bring you $100 or more each. I personally don't like the long range prospects of cards, so would sell now and put the money to better use.

The importance of condition depends upon the item you have to sell. Card collectors require near perfection while collectors of other baseball items like wear because it shows proof of use during a game.

When offering items for sale, provide the following:

(1) What it is, its size, color and the material from which it is made;
(2) All names, dates and numbers embossed, incised, labeled or decaled on the item;
(3) An accurate statement of condition, noting missing parts, pieces, or paint;
(4) Mention whether the original box, packaging and instructions are included and in good condition.

Since many sports collectibles are paper, remember that a photocopy (a Xerox™) machine is your best friend!

Pop culture dealers found on pages 122-127 also buy sports memorabilia of all types.

THE OLYMPICS

☆ **Olympic memorabilia** including all pins, badges, medals, torches, mascots, posters, and everything else Olympic. "Naturally, I'd rather collect items from before 1972, but when you come down to it, I like it all." Particularly interested in purchasing anything from 1904 St. Louis Games and winner's medals from any year. He warns that many items from the 1936 Berlin Olympics have been reproduced. When writing, tell what you know of the item's history.

> Jay Hammerman
> Shied Iron Works
> 15630 Softwood Road
> Elbert, Colorado 80106
> (719) 495-8938 eves

☆ **Olympic items** from any year they were played.

> Otti Schmitt
> Finders Keepers
> 7724 Hayfield Road
> Alexandria, VA 22310
> (703) 550-1454

☆ **Olympic memorabilia** of all sorts, from 1896 to the present. "I'll buy winner's medals, official's badges, reports, participation medals, official posters, torches, flags, banners, daily programs, patches, pins, uniforms, tickets, diplomas, post cards, stamps, etc. I'm particularly interested in items before 1980 but will review all years." He does not want pins from Moscow 1980 or Los Angeles 1984; nor does he want pins from the 1936 Olympics in Germany unless they have been in your family since then as these have been widely reproduced. The cigarette card album from Germany 1936 is not wanted, either. Please send a color photo of your item if possible. Include an SASE. Dealers should price their goods. Amateurs may request offers.

> Geoffrey Johnson
> Go for the Gold
> 3039 Bolling Way #100-B
> Atlanta, GA 30305
> (404) 261-5065   Fax: (404) 261-4134

☆ **Olympic memorabilia from the 1932 games** held in Los Angeles, including tickets, programs, postcards, photographs, literature, patches, and souvenirs. The more colorful and unusual, the better. Please send a photocopy.

> Reed Fitzpatrick
> PO Box 369
> Vashon, WA 98070
> (206) 463-3900 8am to 4pm

SPORTS EQUIPMENT & EPHEMERA

☆ **Sports memorabilia of all types, especially from baseball**, but also **football, boxing, hockey,** and others. Bill buys and sells:
- Professional **uniforms and shoes**;
- **Baseball bats and autographed balls**;
- Paper ephemera such as programs, contracts, scorecards, **tickets**, photographs, postcards, sheet music, and the like;
- Pin back **buttons, films, books, and advertising** featuring sports;
- **Gum cards.**

"I'll buy just about anything related to professional sports." Kenrich Co., one of the country's largest mail order sports dealers, has 23 years' experience buying and selling sports ephemera by mail.

Bill Colby, Kenrich Co.
9418-T Las Tunas Drive
Temple City, CA 91780
(818) 286-3888   Fax: (818) 286-6035

☆ **Baseball, football, and boxing memorabilia** especially autographs of dead Hall-of-Famers and other important players. Wants yearbooks of New York sports teams and programs from championship events in all three sports. Will buy tickets, pins, and advertising items which mention players or teams, but **not interested in sports cards.** "Sellers should be willing to send the item to me for inspection. In many cases a good photo or photocopy will do."

Richard Simon Sports, Inc. TH
215 East 80th Street
New York, NY 10021
(212) 988-1349

☆ **Baseball, football, basketball, and Olympic memorabilia** is wanted including items such as:
- **Uniforms, trophies**, and medals from famous athletes;
- Baseball gum cards pre-1920;
- Sports **photographs**, but only cabinet size;
- Posters and **advertising** pieces related to sports, pre-1930;
- World Series (1903-11), all star game programs and press pins;
- Black baseball bats;
- Autographed material from important dead players;
- Song sheets, games, and toys related to sports pre-1920.

"Unique and unusual" sports equipment and other material especially related to Hall of Fame baseball players from the 1920's and 1930's is sought. All items must be old, rare, and original. The gallery is now open to the public to see and to purchase rare sports collectibles.

Joel Platt, Sports Immortals Museum and Gallery
6830 North Federal Highway
Boca Raton, FL 33487
(407) 997-2575

☆ **Baseball, football, and boxing memorabilia,** with particular emphasis on the Victorian era, including:
- **Baseball equipment** from before 1920, especially early fingerless gloves;
- **Paper ephemera**: books from before 1920, display posters, baseball scorecards pre-1900, baseball guides pre-1920, World Series programs, and early ads featuring baseball;
- **Uniforms** from any sport before 1960;
- Football guides and equipment, pre-1930;
- **Trophies** for any 19th century sports;
- **Gum and tobacco cards.**

"Premium prices paid for 19th century baseball items." This 30 year veteran collector offers from $1,000 to $10,000 for posters depicting 1890's baseball cards, equipment, or sports figures. He does not want or buy *anything* after 1970. A clear photo is helpful.

John Buonaguidi
Monterey Bay Sports Museum
540 Reeside Ave.
Monterey, CA 93940
(408) 375-7345

☆ **Baseball memorabilia,** especially from before 1948. Wants gum and tobacco cards and silks picturing baseball players, postcards, photos, games, programs, yearbooks, guides, advertising, fans, sheet music and autographs from dead Hall-of-Fame players. This 25 year advanced collector-dealer does not buy anything after 1960. Be as accurate as possible with descriptions and include your phone number with your letter. Photocopies are helpful.

William Mastro
12410 Ridge Road
Palos Park, IL 60464
(708) 361-2117

☆ **Professional baseball and football equipment**, especially game worn jerseys, bats, and equipment. Does not want foreign items, other sports, paper ephemera, or cards. Each item must be evaluated individually as to value. For an offer, describe your item thoroughly, including age, condition, and history. David's *Vintage Baseball Glove Price Guide* is available for $17 postpaid and an abbreviated updated pocket version is only $6. A pocket guide t *Spalding* bats is also available.

David Bushing
Vintage Sports
342 North Third
Libertyville, IL 60048
(708) 816-6847   (708) 816-6861 eves

☆ **Early sports memorabilia.** "I'll buy sports ephemera, 1860-1970. I'm mainly interested in early baseball items such as pins, postcards, silks, leathers, advertising, and autographs, but will also buy paper and other ephemera from **boxing and football**." Describe the condition and indicate the price you have in mind.

    Steve Applebaum
    10636 Wilshire Blvd. #204
    Los Angeles, CA 90024
        (310) 475-3861

☆ **Canadian sports memorabilia.** "I'll buy all items associated with **Canadian hockey** teams and players before 1960, **Canadian lacrosse** teams and players, and **Canadian basketball** teams and players. I'm particularly looking for game schedules and calendars, programs, autographed photos, gum cards, etc. If practical, a clear photocopy is best. Small items can be sent on approval as I will always refund postage."

    Michael Rice
    PO Box 286
    Saanichton, BC
    V8M 2C5 CANADA
        (604) 652-9047 eves

☆ **Babe Ruth material.** Send Xerox© to this major ephemera dealer.

    Harvey Dolin & Company
    5 Beekman Street #406
    New York, NY 10038
        (212) 267-0216

☆ **Philadelphia Phillies memorabilia,** especially pre-1920 programs.

    Gary Gatanis
    3283-B Cardiff Court
    Toledo, OH 43606
        (419) 475-3192

☆ **Baseball memorabilia from the Pacific Coast League** and selected other minor leagues. Most items wanted date from the 1940's and early 50's and include programs, selected team and League year books, *P.C.L. Baseball News*, postcards of ball parks, 1947 *Signal Oil* cards, and team photos. No cards from *Mothers Cookies*, *Union Oil*, *Remar*, or 1948 *Signal Gasoline*. Also buys programs and other ephemera associated with the **non-baseball use of Gilmore Field, Gilmore Stadium and Pan Pacific auditorium.**

    Jerry Mezerow
    442 Via Porto Ave.
    Anaheim, CA 92806
        (714) 630-6198

☆ **Baseball gloves** and other items including bats, autographed balls, cut autographs, programs, ticket stubs, scorecards, and uniforms. Does not buy items after 1970 or any baseball cards.

>Gary Alderman
>PO Box 9164
>Madison, WI 53715
>   (608) 274-3527   Fax: (608) 277-1999

☆ **Old sports equipment** suitable for restaurant, theme, model home, and other decorative purposes, including:

- **Balls** from various sports including pre-1950 leather footballs, baseballs, soccer balls, and basketballs. Seeks moderately priced old leather balls from before 1940 for decorator use. Not interested in balls autographed by famous persons.
- **Wooden skis and bamboo poles**. Brand name doesn't matter, and neither do bindings, as long as they are all wood and in reasonably good condition;
- **Leather football helmets;**
- **Lacrosse equipment** such as sticks, balls, and leather knee pads;
- **Snow shoes,** which are preferred intact with original gut, but empty frames in fine condition will be considered;
- **Croquet mallets** or complete boxed sets if old and if the paint is in good condition;
- **Cricket bats** and balls;
- **Riding equipment** including tall boots, leather whips, velveteen riding hats, English style ladies' side saddles;
- **Wicker creels** and inexpensive bamboo fishing poles, nets, etc.

All items should be pre-1940 and be fairly well cared for. Please give a general description of what you have, or telephone with the item in hand. "I am seeking low-end items suitable for decorating theme restaurants, not fine expensive antiques. If what you have is very valuable, take it somewhere else. If you find that it isn't valuable, but you want it preserved, offer it to me."

>Joan Brady
>834 Central Ave.
>Pawtucket, RI   02861
>   (401) 725-5753

☆ **Rugby and soccer memorabilia** wanted for resale. Can be either U.S. or foreign. Wants prints, cigarette cards, stamps, postcards, and paper ephemera. Also buys large items like coin operated games and strength machines with soccer or rugby themes.

>Matt Godek
>PO Box 565
>Merrifield, VA 22116
>   (703) 280-5540

☆ **Soccer memorabilia** wanted for museum display. Especially interested in U.S. soccer, but will also consider World Cup relics. Wants uniforms, rule books, posters, photos, prints, home movies, etc. Particularly likes to find items from soccer played in places other than the Northeastern U.S. Also interested in games and coin machines with soccer themes that might be suitable for play in their museum. Describe what you have. It's helpful if you set the price you'd like.

> Al Colone, National Soccer Hall of Fame
> 5-11 Ford Ave.
> Oneonta, NY 13820
> (607) 432-3351

☆ **Pro football ephemera** including autographed balls, programs and yearbooks from before 1990, and other items. No trading cards.

> Gary Alderman
> PO Box 9164
> Madison, WI 53715
> (608) 274-3527 Fax: (608) 277-1999

☆ **Super Bowl memorabilia** including tickets, ticket stubs, programs, banners, press passes, and what have you. Greater interest in earlier Bowls, especially II through V.

> Marty Novak
> 1150 Cushing Circle #334
> St. Paul, MN 55108
> (612)-646-5567

☆ **Miami Dolphin memorabilia.**

> Joe Copeland
> PO Box 4221
> Oak Ridge, TN 37831
> (615) 482-4215

☆ **Notre Dame football programs and other memorabilia** from pre-1960, especially Knute Rockne and George Gipp autographs and other items. Other Notre Dame sports items will be considered.

> Michael Tiltges
> 2040 185th Street
> Lansing, IL 60438
> (708) 895-3222

☆ **College football programs** are a new interest for Charles, and not something that is widely collected, so prices remain modest. If your program is old or for a "big game" he'll probably want to buy it.

> Charles Reuter
> 6 Joy Avenue
> Mount Joy, PA 17552

☆ **Pro basketball ephemera** especially autographed team balls, All-Star balls, programs, yearbooks and older cards. Anything before 1990.
    Gary Alderman
    PO Box 9164
    Madison, WI 53715
        (608) 274-3527   Fax: (608) 277-1999

☆ **Pro hockey memorabilia**, especially autographed pucks, programs, and unusual items like the 1969 Rangers' paperweight/bottle opener.
    Gary Alderman
    PO Box 9164
    Madison, WI 53715
        (608) 274-3527   Fax: (608) 277-1999

☆ **Roller Derby memorabilia**, including programs, posters, uniforms, flyers, autographs and "anything collectible from any era." Please send a photocopy whenever practical, plus any information about where the item originally came from. He requests that you set the price wanted whenever possible, but says, "I will entertain all offers."
    Royal Duncan
    7600 North Galena Road
    Peoria, IL 61615
        (309) 691-2772

☆ **Running memorabilia.** "I'll buy medals, ribbons, trophies, cards, annuals, magazines, programs, and books related to running, track & field, road races and **the Olympics**." Not interested in items since 1960, but will consider reproductions of some posters and other printed material. Tell what you have and its condition. Ed is president of the Motor City Striders, has been director of numerous races, and writes for various running magazines.
    Ed Kozloff
    10144 Lincoln
    Huntington Woods, MI 48070
        (313) 544-9099

☆ **Self defense** magazines, photos, books, courses, equipment, posters, trophies, etc., printed before 1975. Doesn't want anything currently published. Please send an SASE with inquiries.
    William Moore
    PO Box 732
    Tuscaloosa, AL 35402

☆ **Diving** related items especially hard hat diving gear, old two-hose SCUBA regulators, manufacturer's catalogs and brochures depicting underwater gear, and all magazines (especially foreign) about any aspect of sport diving. Will also buy comic books such as *Sea Hunt* and *Primus* which focus on diving. No hardcover books, please.

> Thomas Szymanski
> 5 Stoneybrook Lane
> Exeter, NH 03833
> (603) 772-6372

☆ **Surfboards and surfing related items,** from before 1970, such as magazines, posters, stickers, patches, etc. Wants round nosed pre-1970 longboards over 9' long, but will consider "transitional" boards from 1967-1971, if unusual in some way. Wants to know the make and size of the board, shape, material, age, condition, and by whom it was used. Make certain to describe the fin. If you have a foam board, note the number, material, and thickness of the stringers. Would love to find a board ridden and signed by the legendary Duke Kahanamoku.

> Wayne Babcock
> 4846 Carpenteria Avenue
> Carpenteria, CA 93013
> (805) 684-8148

☆ **Surfboards** from the 1960's and before, for which he says he'll pay $500 to $1,000 for the right boards in fine condition. Also wants wood board era posters, decals, and other graphics with surfing as the major subject. Give the name of the board, size, and condition. Photo appreciated. No paddle boards.

> Dan Pincetich
> 318 Cutty Court
> Pacifica, CA 94044
> (415) 355-5264

☆ **Croquet ephemera.** Will buy distinctive full size mallets, pegs, wickets, table or parlor sets, books, pamphlets, catalogs, photos of people playing croquet, jewelry, and other items related to the game. Please send photocopies or photos, along with your description of condition. Prefers that you price what you have if possible.

> Allen Scheuch
> 356 West 20th Street
> New York, NY 10011
> (212) 929-2299 days voice and fax

☆ **Recreational and competitive horseback riding.** Wants books and paper ephemera related to Morgan horses, Arabians, saddlebred horses, polo ponies, sidesaddles, and Lippizzaners. She would especially like to find books by or illustrated by Paul Brown and George Ford Morris. Books and paper only!

> Barbara Cole, October Farm
> 2609 Branch Road
> Raleigh, NC 27610
>   (919) 772-0482   Fax: (919) 779-6265

☆ *Flexible Flyer* **sledding.** Wants "anything" having to do with *Flexible Flyer* sleds, including membership cards, models, pins, advertising, company literature, and rare sleds. Thorough description, with a photocopy or photograph, is helpful.

> Joan Palicia
> 15 Canton Road
> Wayne, NJ 07470
>   (201) 831-0527

☆ **Dog fighting.** Wants to buy prints, paintings, and statuary, especially as related to bull terriers. Books on dog fighting also wanted. Provide standard bibliographic information.

> Ron Lieberman
> RD #1   Box 42
> Glen Rock, PA 17327
>   (717) 235-2134   Fax: (717) 235-8042

☆ **Loving cup trophies** from before 1950. May be awarded for sports, beauty, service, heroism, or anything else as long as they have handles on each side and are 8" high or taller. No other style of trophy is wanted, nor is anything dating after 1950.

> Joan Brady
> 834 Central Ave.
> Pawtucket, RI 02861
>   (401) 725-5753

☆ **Pennants** of all types, sports, events, tourist spots, universities, etc. Particularly interested in larger quantities of older ones. Depending on quantity, condition, size, age and rarity he pays from $1-$5 each. Doesn't want tears, moth holes, fading, cracked or missing lettering, and has no interest in pennants "made of a stiff felt-like material." Usually not interested in pennants that are printed in neon or fluorescent colors, as they are newer. Please send a photo or photocopy.

> Curtis Sharp
> One Bank Street   #3-0
> New York City, NY 10014

BASEBALL & OTHER GUM CARDS

☆ **Baseball and all other sports and non-sports cards** from gum, tobacco, dairy, candy and other sources. This major sports card dealer especially wants baseball cards pre-1930. Also buys **wrappers** from pre-1970 sports and non-sports gum packs.
> Bill Colby, Kenrich Co.
> 9418-T Las Tunas Drive
> Temple City, CA 91780
> (818) 286-3888

☆ **Baseball and other sports cards** from gum, cigarettes, or candy. Also buys all yearbooks, programs, press pins, ticket stubs, autographs. "To a lesser degree" he also buys **basketball, football, and hockey items,** especially cards 1930-1959. Give condition details.
> Robert Sevchuk
> 70 Jerusalem Avenue
> Hicksville, NY 11801
> (516) 822-4089

☆ **Non-sports gum cards** from candy, tobacco, and other sources from before 1975. Wants *Horrors of War, Dark Shadows, Hogans Heroes, Lost in Space, Mars Attack,* etc. Also seeks unopened boxes, wrappers, original artwork, and advertising, especially for test issues of *Hee Haw, The Waltons, Green Acres* etc. "I'll pay $1,000 for the set of *Horrors of War.*" Items must be in excellent to mint condition with no creases and fairly sharp corners. Roxanne offers a catalog of cards for sale and produces *Non-Sport Update* magazine, a slick informative bi-monthly with a pull-out Price Guide, available for $21 a year.
> Roxanne Toser
> 4019 Green Street
> Harrisburg, PA 17110
> (717) 238-1936

☆ **Non-sports gum cards from 1930-49.** This *Star Trek* star wants only cards featuring pirates, WWII, Indians, cowboys, and comic strip characters. Cards must be in fine condition.
> Walter Koenig
> PO Box 4395
> North Hollywood, CA 91607

Sports and non-sports cards have been packed in tobacco, candy, gum, etc., for 100 years. Thousands of non-sports card sets depicting every imaginable topic from animals to zeppelins exist. Expect to get from 10¢ to $10 for most cards. 19th century cards occasionally bring more.

BOBBING HEAD DOLLS

☆ **Bobbing head sports and non-sports dolls of all types,** especially composition/papier-maché dolls from the 1960's. Wants all types of dolls from all sports, but especially miniature bobbing heads about 4" tall and real player dolls. When you write, give the color of the base.

    Dale Jerkins
    1647 Elbur Ave.
    Lakewood, OH 44107
      (216) 226-7349

Bobbing head dolls are in the Sports chapter because the most valuable nodders are baseball and football figures. Rising prices led to increased attention for all these kitschy collectibles, now considered among Pop Culture icons. When you describe a nodder for sale, give the height of the figure and the colors of the clothing, hat (helmet) and base.

☆ **Bobbing head sports and non-sports dolls,** Japanese ceramic or composition models only, no plastic dolls or dolls made in Taiwan or Korea. Indicate team or character portrayed. Also give the size, color, and shape of the base. Will pay $150 for any Blackface bobbing baseball doll in perfect condition and $600 for a perfect Roberto Clemente. Also wants **sports and non-sports plastic statues by Hartland.** Will pay between $100 and $700 for excellent and complete statues, depending on the character.

    Chip Norris
    PO Box 235
    Leonardtown, MD 20650
      (301) 475-2951

☆ **Bobbing head and nodder dolls.** Prefers people or famous characters. Special wants include the *Pillsbury Doughboy, Elsie* the *Borden's* cow, *Popeye*, Presidents Eisenhower and Kennedy, *Maynard Krebs*, *Minnie Mouse, Porky Pig*, and *Elmer Fudd*. Also wants double nodder salt and pepper shakers, nodder ashtrays and other unusual nodders.

    Roxanne Toser
    4019 Green Street
    Harrisburg, PA 17110
      (717) 238-1936

GOLF EQUIPMENT & EPHEMERA

☆ **Golf memorabilia** of all sorts, including:
- Wooden shaft clubs and early golf balls;
- Books, magazines and catalogs related to pre-1940 golf;
- Paintings, prints and photos with a golf motif;
- Golf trophies;
- Paper ephemera, scorecards and programs, catalogs, etc.;
- Miscellany, such as statues and ashtrays.

"If it has a golf motif, I'm interested, and will pay premium prices for premium pieces." Does appraisals for a fee. Accepts select high quality items on consignment for sale or auction.

     Richard Regan
     3 Highview Terrace
     Bridgewater, MA 02324
         (508) 826-3537   (508) 279-1296 eves

☆ **Golf memorabilia** from before 1930, especially:
- Wooden shaft golf clubs that are in some way unusual;
- Books, magazines, and catalogs related to pre-1930 golf;
- China and pottery with a golf motif by *Royal Doulton, Lenox,* and other fine makers;
- Golf balls and golf ball molds from before 1900;
- Miscellaneous items related to "the knickers era."

This 35 year veteran collector does not want common wooden shaft clubs or common golf bags, nor does he buy trinkets, ashtrays, petty jewelry or reproductions. Frank prefers you set the price you want, but will make offers on rare items.

     Frank Zadra
     Route 2   Box 2136
     Spooner, WI 54801
         (715) 635-2791

☆ **Golf antiques** and memorabilia. Wants *unusual* wooden shafted clubs with patent numbers and *unusual* golf balls, such as the pre 1850 ball stuffed with feathers for which he will pay $5,000. "I also buy golf pottery, items of silver, golf medals, pre-1920 golf books, and original art featuring golfers. I do not want clubs with simulated wood grain shafts or anything made after 1920. I'm really interested only in the very old and rare." You should follow standard rules for describing, including condition.

     Art DiProspero
     Highlands Golf
     PO Box 308
     Watertown, CT 06795
         (203) 274-8471

☆ **Old golf books, magazines, and ephemera.** No paperback reprints or magazines published after 1950.

> George Lewis
> Golfiana
> PO Box 291
> Mamaroneck, NY 10543
>   (914) 698-4579

☆ **Golf award medals from before WWII** and other pre-1930 golf ephemera. "If it's early and in good condition, ship it insured for my top offer." Items are purchased outright or, if you prefer, taken on consignment for his international auctions.

> Rich Hartzog
> PO Box 4143 (W7)
> Rockford, IL 61110
>   (815) 226-0771   Fax: (815) 397-7662

☆ **Golf ball markers**, especially markers advertising products or tournaments, those used by famous players, male or female, or markers used in major championships. Markers are worth from $1 to $5, depending on their text, picture, and association. Does not want large quantities of a single type, nor does he want those that do not have advertising of some sort. Other golf items such as postcards and medals will be considered.

> Norm Boughton
> PO Box 93262
> Rochester, NY 14692
>   (800) 581-2665   Fax: (800) 901-6676

BOXING MEMORABILIA

☆ **Boxing memorabilia of all types.** "I'm the world's largest dealer in boxing memorabilia. I sell to boxing collectors all over the United States and Canada. As a result, I need to continually replenish stock, which means I am always willing to buy, sell, or trade." Please send a photograph or photocopy of what you have.
> Jerome Shochet
> 6144 Oakland Mills Road
> Sykesville, MD 21784
> (410) 795-5879

☆ **Boxing photos and autographs** from before 1920. Please photo-copy what you have.
> Johnny Spellman
> 10806 North Lamar
> Austin, TX 78753
> (512) 836-2889 days   (512) 258-6910

☆ **Boxing memorabilia of all types.** Private collector who operates a gym seeks posters, programs, tickets, films, photographs, books and magazines about boxing, boxing awards, medals, belts and trophies from any level, Golden Glove to World Championship. "If you have single items or a large collection, whether it's from the earliest days or the present champs, I'd like to hear about it."
> Fred Ryan's Boxing
> 7217 North Jersey
> PO Box 83135
> Portland, OR 97203
> (503) 286-3597

☆ **Championship boxing belts** and robes, plus **song sheets, games, and toys** related to boxing from before 1920. This giant sports muse-um buys only quality unusual items that are old, rare, and original.
> Joel Platt
> Sports Immortals Museum
> 6830 North Federal Highway
> Boca Raton, FL 33487
> (407) 997-2575

☆ **Boxing ephemera of all types** dealing with James J. Corbett, Jim Jeffries or John L. Sullivan. A clear photo or photocopy is helpful.
> John Buonaguidi
> Monterey Bay Sports Museum
> 540 Reeside Ave.
> Monterey, CA 93940
> (408) 375-7345

TENNIS MEMORABILIA

☆ **Tennis memorabilia** such as trophies, figurines, art, postcards, cartoons, tableware, trade cards, lighters, first day covers, and all sorts of other little tennis-related knickknacks from before 1940. He does *not* want to buy rackets, photos, newspaper clippings, books, autographs, or programs, but "I'll buy any quantity of other reasonably priced items if they send a photo or photocopy and price what they have."
>Sheldon Katz
>211 Roanoke Ave.
>Riverhead, NY 11901
>>(516) 369-1100

☆ **Tennis rackets**. "My primary interest is in rackets produced in the 1940's through the 1960's, but earlier ones are considered. Most desirable are frames that were high quality in their day, and that are in excellent condition. Prices range from $1 to about $25 each depending on the age and scarcity." Identify the maker, model, decals, signature, length, any warpage, and the condition of the grip and strings. Also interested in catalogs and other literature picturing or describing rackets.
>Donald Jones
>24 Marvalingrove
>Savannah, GA 31406
>>(912) 354-2133

☆ **Tennis rackets and ball cans.** "I buy wooden 'bentwood' tennis rackets, with a preference for those made before 1940 but will consider those up to 1950. I consider any maker, foreign or domestic, but prefer strings to be intact. I also want metal tennis ball cans from anywhere in the world, especially third world, Pacific rim, and Soviet bloc countries. Anything made before 1970 with key type opener will be considered. I'm not interested in any metal or synthetic rackets or any plastic ball cans or sleeves." Give the name on the items and its condition.
>Rusty McInroy
>1331 West Chapala Court
>Tucson, AZ 85704
>>(602) 797-2030

☆ **Tennis items**, especially ball cans with metal lids, ball boxes, and 12 ball cans, for which he will pay as much as $300 if mint and unopened. "If it had tennis balls in it and it's old, I'm interested." Also buys pre-1940 rackets, lawn tennis sets, tennis trophies, "plus much more." Describe condition carefully.
>Michael Murphy, J&J Coins
>47 East Downer Place
>Aurora, IL 60505
>>(708) 896-9439 eves   Fax: (708) 892-7044

AUTO RACING EPHEMERA

☆ **Auto racing memorabilia.** If it's related to auto racing, and in good condition, George will probably want it. He'll buy one piece or a large collection: awards, arm bands, dash plaques, entry forms, flags, goggles, helmets, magazines, models (built or unbuilt), movies, photographs, paintings, passes, postcards, posters, rule books, toys, board games, trophies, uniforms, and "anything else auto racing related." If you know any history of the item, let him know when describing what you have and its condition. This ex-race driver has been collecting 25 years and will travel "a reasonable distance" to buy collections.

> George Koyt
> 8 Lenora Avenue
> Morrisville, PA 19067

☆ **Indianapolis 500** pit badges from before 1952 are wanted, as are race tickets from before 1950, racing programs from before 1941, and all rings or trophies, any year. Jerry will pay $300 for a 1946 pit badge.

> Jerry Butak
> 242 West Adams
> Villa Park, IL 60181
> (708) 834-6913

☆ **Auto racing ephemera,** including books, programs, posters, and what have you are purchased by this giant dealer in automobile parts, manuals, advertising, and ephemera.

> Walter Miller
> 6710 Brooklawn Parkway
> Syracuse, NY 13211
> (315) 432-8282   Fax: (315) 432-8256

☆ **Auto racing before 1916,** especially items associated with the Vanderbilt Cup races or with the Long Island Motor Parkway.

> George Spruce
> 33 Washington Street
> Sayville, NY 11782
> (516) 563-4211

☆ **Drag racing and hot rodding** from the 1940's through the 60's is wanted including: posters, programs, trophies, jackets, racing apparel, speed equipment advertising, car club plaques, hot rod movie posters, hot rod and custom car magazines and hot rod papers. Hot rod club jackets are especially wanted. "The older the better!"

> Michael Goyda, Car Crazy
> PO Box 192
> East Petersburg, PA 17520
> (717) 569-7149   Fax: (717) 569-0909

HORSE RACING MEMORABILIA

☆ **Thoroughbred racing** memorabilia including:
- Trophies;
- Paintings, prints and photographs;
- Paper ephemera including racing and breeding books, programs, posters, tobacco cards, postcards, games and "the unusual";
- Kentucky Derby programs, glasses and anything unusual.
- Phar Lap memorabilia, especially from his 1932 race at Caliente.

All material from all racing thoroughbreds will be considered. Not interested in anything having to do with harness horses or harness racing.

> Gary Medeiros
> 1319 Sayre Street
> San Leandro, CA 94579
> (800) 227-6049

☆ **Horse racing collectibles** including programs, glasses, books, magazines, posters, photos, postcards, art prints, decanters, parimutuel tickets, lapel pins, buttons, admission items, etc. "I do not want Kentucky Derby glasses after 1974, paper items in poor condition or newspapers except the *Daily Racing Form.*" Give the year, condition, and description. He conducts auctions of horse racing items every year.

> James Settembre
> 5115 Woodstone Circle East
> Lake Worth, FL 33463
> (407) 964-8230

☆ **Dan Patch memorabilia,** especially Dan Patch mechanical postcards. Also wants pre-1950 **Kentucky Derby programs** and **drinking glasses** featuring horse racing. He will consider other **horse racing programs** from the turn of the century.

> Gary Gatanis
> 3283-B Cardiff Court
> Toledo, OH 43606
> (419) 475-3192

☆ **Trotters, pacers, and harness horse memorabilia.** This former horse trainer wants advertising signs, county fair posters, tins, buttons, and other ephemera depicting famous trotters and pacers. He generally wants depictions of horses in harness or with their record winning time. The item he'd most like to find? A *Dan Patch* coffee container. Please describe thoroughly what you have, including an accurate description of condition. A photocopy is appreciated.

> Donald Ackerman
> 33 Kossuth Street
> Wallington, NJ 07057
> (201) 779-8785   Fax: (201) 746-7871

WRESTLING & STRENGTH

☆ **Pro wrestling autographs and other items** from 1800's to date are sought, especially signatures of Frank Gotch, Joe Stecher, Dan McLeod, Charley Cutler, Earl Caddock and Wayne Munn. Please copy what you have. No wrestling magazines except first 5 issues of any title. He requests you price what you have when possible. He wrote *Wrestling Title Histories*, available from him for $40.

> Royal Duncan
> 7600 North Galena Road
> Peoria, IL 61615
> (309) 691-2772

☆ **Women's pro or amateur wrestling.** Wants posters, magazines, film, trophies, autographs and what have you... good items from any era, but especially videos of any match after 1940. "I want real wrestling between women skilled at applying holds, executing aerial maneuvers, etc., not mud wrestling, nude wrestling and other degrading exhibitions." Selena wants information on more than 75 women pros.

> Selena Kyte
> PO Box 1022
> St. Ann, MO 63074

☆ **Ephemera related to Frank Gotch,** a turn of the century wrestling champion. He wants posters, postcards, books, photographs, etc.

> Don Olson
> PO Box 245
> Humboldt, IA 50548

☆ **Bodybuilding ephemera.** "I'll buy anything before 1975 related to strength, body building, physical culture, weight lifting, strongmen or women, etc. I buy books, magazines, training courses, photos, catalogs, posters, letters, trophies, medals, certificates and videos. I want (1) Weider magazines like *Your Physique,* etc., (2) anything *Milo Barbell Company*, and (3) anything by or about George Jowett or Eugen Sandow. No magazines after 1970, and nothing currently in print." Describe what you have, give date and condition. Send an SASE for info about collector's clubs and newsletter.

> William Moore
> PO Box 732
> Tuscaloosa, AL 35402

☆ **Strongmen, weightlifters, and bodybuilders.** "I'll buy magazines, photos, books, posters, sculpture, and equipment from these fields."

> David Chapman
> 656 32nd Ave. East
> Seattle, WA 98112
> (206) 329-7573

POOL & BILLIARDS

☆ **Pool tables** (fancier the better), cue sticks and racks, ball racks, antique advertising, catalogs and other items related to pool or billiard playing before 1940. Send a photo and dimensions.
> Ken Hash
> Classic Billiards
> 4302 Chapel Road
> Perry Hall, MD 21128
> (410) 882-7665 days

☆ **Pool and billiard tables and related items.** Wants:
- **Pool tables** with inlaid designs on the legs or bodies, or with ornate carved or cast iron legs; will also consider tables with round legs and tables in any condition;
- Cue racks with mirrors or in generally Victorian style;
- Cue racks that lock or revolve;
- Ivory balls, with or without numbers;
- Ball boxes that are old or unusual;
- Cues that are ornate and 30+ years old;
- Billiard lights, either gas or kerosene;
- **Benches and chairs** from billiard parlors;
- **Prints, paintings, posters**, and other art featuring billiards, especially by Currier & Ives;
- **Books on pool**, snooker, or billiards before 1940;
- **Magazines** and newsletters before 1940;
- **Catalogs** before 1900, especially for *Brunswick & Balke* or *Brunswick Balke Collender*;
- **Newspapers** containing prints or articles on billiards before 1900.

He does not want "bar type" pool tables, tables made after 1940, or plain square legged tables with no inlay. Send a photo of your item and give complete bibliographic information on books.
> Tim Lawrence
> 2489 Bexford Place
> Columbus, OH 43209
> (614) 235-9472 eves

☆ **Pool and billiard memorabilia.** Wants interesting and unusual items associated with pool such as light fixtures, cue sticks and racks. Also buys catalogs, advertising, prints and other related items.
> Dilworth Billiards
> 300 East Tremont
> Charlotte, NC 28203
> (704) 333-3021   (704) 377-9069

HUNTING & FISHING ITEMS

☆ **Fishing tackle from before 1945** including:
- **Lures** (especially wood with glass eyes or made of hollow metal). Easiest way to describe these is to make a Xerox™ and pencil in the colors of the lures. If made of wood or metal, most lures are $2 and up...and some are way up!
- **Reels**: quality-made fly, bait-casting, and ocean reels that have serial numbers or people's names engraved. Brass or very large reels, especially wanted. There are too many quality reels to list, so ask about all reels except *South Bend, Pflueger, True Temper Shakespeare,* or *Penn.* Dozens of makers have value, some in excess of $1,000. Reels with no names or serial numbers are junk.
- **Bamboo rods** in three or four pieces, stored in cases made of wood, aluminum or cardboard, often packed in a carry bag. Give the name of the maker or owner, usually found in ink or engraved on a metal fitting near where the reel attaches. Does not want "no name" rods or rods made in Japan, no matter how pretty. Other common rods not of interest include *Shakespeare, Montague* and *South Bend.*
- **Tackle boxes**: "If you have a tackle box that contains items from the 1930's or before, you may ship it for my free inspection, evaluation, and offer."
- **Catalogs** of fishing tackle before 1925.

Give names, model, patent dates and numbers, and serial numbers on all equipment. If you have a great many items, you may call collect. Don't overlook empty lure and reel boxes, as some of them can be worth $50 or more. CAUTION: don't clean or polish fishing gear you'd like to sell. Leave the cleaning to me."

"Most people can't tell good stuff from bad. I'll check it all for you."

"You're likely to damage it.

> Rick Edmisten
> PO Box 686
> North Hollywood, CA 91603
> (818) 763-9406

☆ **Old fishing lures,** especially *Heddon 7500* vamps, *Heddon 100* and *150* minnows, and all frog shaped lures. Also **odd fish scalers**. When writing, include a photocopy of your lures, and indicate their color. Please include your phone number if you'd like a quick response.

> Thomas McKinnon
> PO Box 86
> Wagram, NC 28396
> (910) 369-2367

☆ **Antique fishing tackle** including bait and fly reels, bamboo fly and bait casting rods, willow creels, wooden nets, fishing lures (especially those with glass eyes), and early tackle boxes made of leather. Wants to find brass *Snyder* bait casting reels from early 1800's. Also buys **fishing equipment catalogs and books**. Not interested in anything made in the last 25 years.

> Robert Whitaker
> 2810 East Desert Cove Ave.
> Phoenix, AZ 85028
>   (602) 992-7304   (602) 493-5598

☆ **Antique and classic fishing tackle** and ephemera from before 1940. Among items wanted are:
- Old wood or metal **lures** in good condition. Metal lures must be marked with the name of the maker or patent information, but wooden lures need not be marked. They do not want plastic lures or lures in poor condition;
- **Reels** of all types, especially higher quality or with unusual features; some broken or damaged reels will be considered. They do not want reels by *Penn, Ocean City, True Temper*, or *Lawrence* nor do they want spinning reels or spin casting reels unless very unusual;
- **Bamboo rods**. They do not want metal rods, fiberglass rods, or any rods in poor condition;
- Fishing paraphernalia, creels, tackle boxes and tools. Does not want lead sinkers;
- Early **fishing licenses**;
- **Paintings and prints** related to fishing, including calendars, advertising, and cigarette cards, but no damaged artwork.

"We will deal with experts or with novice sellers. We make offers when necessary, but prefer folks to set their own prices. You may call, *not collect*, between 9am and 10pm. When writing, include a photocopy or photograph. Please always include your phone number. Do not ship anything without our permission first." They do not want anything made in the Orient or made after 1940.

> Ed and Carolyn Corwin
> All-Safe Storage
> 200 State Road 206 East
> St. Augustine, FL 32086
>   (904) 797-6464 days   (904) 692-2037 eves

☆ **Antique and modern fishing tackle** is wanted by an "avid fisherman" who buys lures, rods, wooden tackle boxes, fly reels, large ocean reels, catalogs of hunting and fishing equipment, hardcover books on fishing, old calendars with fishing motif and early advertising items with fishing graphics. Fair value offers made. Make certain to include an SASE for reply.

> Lee Pattison
> 6 Christview Drive
> Cuba, NY 14727
> (716) 968-2458

☆ **Hunting and fishing ephemera** including catalogs, posters, calendars, pin back buttons, trade cards, and **envelopes** decorated with advertising from before 1940. He is also interested in possibly buying any fishing and hunting images from before 1900, including prints, original art, and illustrated books. He will make offers, but only after personally inspecting what you have for sale.

> Russell Mascieri
> 6 Florence Ave.
> Marlton, NJ 08053
> (609) 985-7711   Fax: (609) 985-8513

☆ **Hunting, fishing, and trapping licenses** and tags from all states up to the present. Also interested in entry and use permits for state and national parks. "Photocopies are very helpful."

> Bill Smiley
> PO Box 361
> Portage, WI 53901
> (608) 742-3714 eves

☆ **Gun, trap, and ammunition company items** such as posters and calendars (worth to $400), catalogs (up to $1,000), empty cardboard shotshell boxes (up to $5,000), pinback buttons (to $500), glass target balls and traps (up to $5,000), gunpowder cans (up to $1,000) and anything decorative or informative from before 1940. Does not want paper items that have been trimmed. No NRA items. "I am fair and honest," he says, exhorting, "Try me!"

> Ron Willoughby
> 1072 Route 171
> Woodstock, CT 06281
> (203) 974-1226

TRAPS

☆ **Traps of all types and sizes from fly to grizzly bear.** Wants fine examples of fly, mouse, rat, mole, and gopher traps, glass minnow traps and spring operated fish traps. Will purchase anything unusual in any material including plastic, wood, wire, cast iron, glass, cardboard, and tin. Is especially fond of old and unusual mouse traps. He also buys patent models, books, catalogs, and advertising (pre-1940) related to traps. Does not want rusty or broken traps unless they are odd 19th century items. Send a picture or drawing, a good description, and an SASE and he promises to answer.

    Boyd Nedry
    728 Buth Drive NE
    Comstock Park, MI 49321
       (616) 784-1513

☆ **Animal traps.** Has a special interest in oddly shaped and unusual traps. Will buy all sizes and pay up to $2,500 for unusually large ones. Will also buy pre-1940 trap and fur company catalogs, calendars, advertising items and scent and lure containers. All inquiries will be answered and everyone will be treated fairly and honestly."

    Ron Willoughby
    1072 Route 171
    Woodstock, CT 06281
       (203) 974-1226

☆ **Glass flytraps or flycatchers,** especially early or unusual ones. Will consider interesting traps in other materials. Also advertising and paper ephemera related to early flytraps.

    Maris Zuika
    PO Box 175
    Kalamazoo, MI 49004
       (616) 344-7473

☆ **Mouse traps** made of wood, metal or glass, as long as they are unusual. Also buy fly traps and very large bear traps.

    Steve Kelley
    PO Box 695
    Desert Hot Springs, CA 92240
       (619) 329-3206

DUCK & OTHER DECOYS

☆ **Wooden decoys and calls** for ducks, geese, crows, and fish. Buys ice fishing decoys, wooden plugs, and early reels made by *Meek, Talbot, Milan*, or *KY Bluegrass* (for which he will pay $100 up). Joe quotes prices of $200+ paid for better duck calls. Also buys various signs that are related to hunting or fishing. He suggests you send photos, but may require you to send the item for inspection before he purchases it.

> Joe Tonelli
> PO Box 130
> Spring Valley, IL 61362
>   (815) 664-4580   (605) 337-2301

☆ **Wooden decoys of all types** including duck, swan, goose, crow, owl, shorebird and fish. Only old wooden items are wanted, but will consider items in any condition. You must include photos of your decoy with your inquiry.

> Art Pietraszewski, Jr.
> 60 Grant Street
> Depew, NY 14043
>   (716) 681-2339

☆ **Old duck, crow, and goose calls and decoys.** "I'll buy wooden decoys and calls in any quantity." Send a note or call with the description and the price you'd like.

> Jack Morris
> 821 Sandy Ridge
> Doylestown, PA 18901
>   (215) 348-9561

Don't forget to include a stamped envelope when you write to someone and want them to answer. No stamped envelope means "don't reply unless interested in buying."

ALCOHOL, TOBACCO, SEX, AND GAMBLING.

If that title doesn't get your attention I don't know what will. You should give your attention, because this is another chapter crammed with great buyers of an incredible array of items...lots of things you have or can find relatively easily.

In tobacco and liquor collecting, top prices are paid for 19th century items with attractive pictorials, but **there are lots of items less than 50 years old that you can profit from.**

If making money is your goal, it's important for you to learn about tobacco and beer cans, both of which can put hundreds of dollars in your pocket in a single sale. Someone who wanted to make money would learn about lighters ($5 to $2,000), cigar boxes and labels ($5 to $1,000), and mugs, glasses, and steins given away by 20th century breweries and soda companies ª$5 to 250.

Briar pipes can be bought for pennies at yard sales and second hand stores. To make money, look for *Dunhill, Barling and Caminetto.* Worth $25 to $100 to collectors.

Thirty pages full of buyers are waiting to hear from you. Nice people, committed to helping you get a fair price and a quick, easy and private sale.

To sell, you should provide the following information:

  (1) What is advertised and what is depicted;
  (2) Size, color, and the material from which it is made;
  (3) Names, dates, and numbers on the item;
  (4) Statement of condition, noting missing chips, cracks, and missing parts, pieces, or paint.

When you offer paper goods, photocopy what you offer.

GAMBLING & CARD PLAYING

☆ **Gambling items** including **slot machines**, poker chips, playing cards, and other early casino items and advertising. Says he seeks "any fine condition advertising or ephemera on gambling, including books and catalogs on poker, playing cards, and gambling that were produced before 1960." He requests you tell where you got the item, and include a photo. Sellers must set the price they want.

> Larry Lubliner
> Re-Finders
> PO Box 1501
> Highland Park, IL 60035
>   (708) 831-1102

☆ **Clay, ivory, or mother-of-pearl gambling chips** and selected other memorabilia. No plain, paper, or interlocking chips. Send a sample, rubbing or photocopy. Tell how many chips of each color. Dale wrote *Antique Gambling Chips*, available with a price guide for $20.

> Dale Seymour, Past Pleasures
> PO Box 50863
> Palo Alto, CA 94303

☆ **Casino chips, plaques, and poker chips** from around the world, old or new, as long as they are marked with the name of the casino or club, or the initials of the person for who they were custom marked. His favorites include chips from Cuba and closed Atlantic City casinos. No plastic toy store chips, plain clay chips, or items currently in use in the U.S. Give the casino name, denomination, color, and how you came to own the piece.

> John Benedict
> PO Drawer 1423
> Loxahatchee, FL 33470
>   (407) 798-2520 voice and fax

Gambling collectors want items from the 19th century and pay well for them. Vale of newer items is relatively low.

See also the sections on coin-operated machines and saloons for related items. People who buy gambling items frequently also buy bottles, advertising signs, pipes, guns, and Old West type things.

PLAYING CARDS

☆ **Antique decks of playing cards** are wanted, complete with joker and box or wrapper. Wants decks before 1930, identifiable because they are 2 1/2" wide with no box and 2 5/8" wide if boxed. Robert is the founder of a club for antique playing card collectors, and wants new complete decks with those dimensions, but "might be interested" in open decks. Make a photocopy of the back of one card and the face of the Joker and the Ace of spades.

> Robert Harrison
> 582 Woodlawn Avenue
> Glencoe, IL 60022
>   (708) 835-0842   (708) 291-0880

☆ **Playing cards** and related ephemera. "I want complete decks of pre-1920 American cards in excellent to mint condition," she says, but indicates a willingness to consider "modern decks of original design." What she doesn't want is double decks of bridge cards, incomplete decks, or single decks of narrow (bridge size) cards without advertising on the Joker or Ace of spades. When contacting her, a Xerox™ of the Joker, Ace, any face card, and the back of the card is the best idea. If you can't do that, you'll need to tell her whether the deck is bridge or poker width, whether it has gilt edges or not, whether the corners are round or square, and the condition. She also wants advertising for cards, and will consider depictions of card playing on postcards, trade cards, and the like. She is secretary/treasurer of the 400 member 52 Plus Joker Collector's club.

> Rhonda Hawes
> 204 Gorham Avenue
> Hamden, CT 06514
>   (203) 288-6584

☆ **Playing cards**, pre-1945, from the U.S. and other countries, as well as advertising and other pieces with a card playing theme. "Packs should be complete, including Joker(s) and other extra cards, and preferably in their original box. I am especially looking for non-standard cards, unusual designs, advertising, pin-ups, comics, political, souvenir, etc., on the faces of the cards. I'll occasionally have interest in a more recent pack, if very unusual. I am not interested in standard cards or in foreign cards after 1900. I am also not interested in packs with damaged or missing cards, unless they are extremely unusual. No airline or gambling casino decks. Make a Xerox™ of the Ace of spades, Jokers, and any unusual cards as well as the back. It will help me to appreciate what you have."

> David Galt
> 302 West 78th Street
> New York, NY 10024
>   (212) 769-2514

☆ **Anything concerning playing cards and card games.** Unusual playing cards including transformation cards, non-standard decks, and decks with a different picture on the face of each card. Also single cards in quantity with colorful backs and unusual Jokers, Aces or court cards. Also **books, magazines**, and other items on the games of contract bridge, auction bridge, and whist. Will consider early or limited edition books on other card games as well as plates, figurines, and other artwork depicting card playing. Will pay $100 up for *Royal Beyreuth* china in the pattern called "Devil and the Cards." Photocopies almost essential. Include an SASE to get an answer.

    Bill Sachen
    927 Grand Ave.
    Waukegan, IL 60085
       (708) 662-7204

Collectors usually seek poker size cards rather than "bridge size." Poker decks are two and a half inches wide. Bridge cards are two and a quarter.

☆ **Punchboards** that are graphically interesting and unpunched. Give the condition and a photo or Xerox™ copy.

    Clark Phelps
    390 K Street
    Salt Lake City, UT 84103
       (801) 364-4747

☆ **Mechanical punchboards** and **other gambling equipment**, including pre-1940 **slot machines**. Mechanical punchboards are made of metal and reusable, loaded by the owner. A photo is required of all gambling items.

    Roger Snowden
    PO Box 527
    Vashon, WA 98070
       (800) 327-6437 or (206) 463-5656

☆ **Bridge tallies.** Please send a photocopy of bridge tallies and score cards dating from the 1920's through the 1950's.

    Fran Van Vynckt
    7412 Monroe Ave.
    Hammond, IN 46324

☆ **Bingo cages** and other interesting and early items or ephemera related to the game of Bingo. Primarily interested in professional items. When describing, include everything written on the item. For paper items, make a photocopy. No children's games are wanted.

    Roger Snowden
    PO Box 527
    Vashon, WA 98070
       (800) 327-6437   (206) 463-5656

☆ **Books on gambling.** "We can give anyone information as to whether their book or gambling paraphernalia has value if they write, call, or preferably fax us." Not a bad bet, since Howard has been described elsewhere as the man who "knows more about gambling literature than anyone else alive."

    Howard Schwartz
    Gambler's Book Club
    630 South 11th Street
    Las Vegas, NV 89101
       (702) 382-7555 (2 to 5pm)   Fax: (702) 382-7594

☆ **All types of lottery tickets** from the 1600's to the present, from any country. 18th and 19th century tickets are worth $3-$5 up depending on the country and age. Modern scratch off tickets newer than 1964 normally bring 5¢ each, but smaller less populated states and smaller games fetch more. Complete sets or series are desirable and also worth more. Non-negotiable "sample void" scratch off tickets issued to teach people how to play games are of particular interest. Condition is important; bends, tears or damage make 20th century tickets worthless. Photocopy preferred.

    Karen Lea Rose
    4420 Wisconsin Ave.
    Tampa, FL 33616
       (813) 839-6245

☆ **Scratch off type lottery tickets.** "I'll buy instant rub-off lottery tickets from the 1970's and 1980's."

    Bill Pasquino
    1824 Lyndon Ave.
    Lancaster, PA 17602

BEER COLLECTIBLES

☆ **Anything with the name of a beer on it.** It's called *breweriana*, and includes glasses, coasters, trays, calendars, label collections, signs, mugs, and anything else used to promote beer. Lynn particularly wants tin signs and other display advertising from the turn of the century. Lynn operates an auction service exclusively devoted to items associated with the golden brew. No *Billy Beer* or *J.R. Beer*.

> Lynn Geyer
> 300 Trail Ridge
> Silver City, NM 88061
> (505) 538-2341

☆ **Beer cans** from before 1950. This 18 year veteran beer collector also wants other beer advertising signs, trays, coasters, and bottles. He is particularly interested in cans for the seven brands of the Los Angeles *Monarch Brewing Company* (five of which will bring you over $1,000 each if you can find them). Make certain to describe condition carefully. No *Billy Beer, J.R. Beer*, or cans with pull tab tops.

> Mike Miller
> PO Box 1275
> La Canada, CA 91012

☆ **Glasses and beer mugs of all sorts,** including:
- **Beer glasses**, mugs, and steins from closed U.S. breweries and older items from present breweries;
- **Horse racing glasses** from important races such as the Kentucky Derby, Belmont, and Preakness;
- **Etched shot glasses** with names of whiskeys;
- **Whiskey pitchers**;
- **Soda glasses and root beer mugs**, but only early ones;
- **Cartoon and character glasses** issued by restaurants, fast food chains, TV shows, and others.

Peter buys outright, and also accepts items on consignment from pickers, dealers and private parties for his twice a year auctions of glasses, mugs, steins and related items. *Budweiser* mugs from the 1970's bring $100+, early 1900's beer glasses $40+, and some cartoon characters as much as $50. He does not want foreign beer glasses, glasses or mugs issued by current breweries in the last 10 years, or anything not in mint condition. He suggests you send a picture whenever possible. His 60+ page auction catalogs are $9 each and come with prices realized for nearly 2,000 auctioned items. Back issues are available.

> Peter Kroll
> Glasses, Mugs & Steins Auction
> PO Box 207
> Sun Prairie, WI 53590
> (608) 837-4818 days

☆ **Antique beer steins of all types,** from $10 to $10,000 as long as it was made before WWII. This active collector/dealer will buy one or a large collection. A photo is helpful, as are all markings, measurements, and a description of what is portrayed. Don't forget to note the condition of both the stein and lid. He offers free appraisals with no obligation and, if you telephone him with your stein in your hand, he can usually tell you its wholesale and retail value over the phone. He is available to give talks on steins.

    Les Paul
    568 Country Isle
    Alameda, CA 94501
        (510) 523-7480   Fax: (510) 523-8755

☆ **Beer mugs and steins** made in the 1970's and 80's by the *Ceramate Brazil Company.* "I'll buy both the lidded and unlidded varieties of such favorites as *Budman, Busch Gardens, Clydesdales, Olympics,* etc."

    Tony Steffens
    1115 Cedar Ave
    Elgin, IL 60120
        (708) 428-3150   Fax: (708) 742-5778

☆ **Beer and soda cans from small regional companies** before 1965. Prefers cone top cans but also buys flat top cans, brewery advertising, signs, trays, statues and glasses from the same period. Especially likes to find items from the *Manhattan Brewing Company* owned by Al Capone and the *Grace Bros. Brewing Company* in California. Prices on cans from these two companies tend to start at $500. No rusty cans are wanted by this 10 year veteran collector/dealer, but "some light spotting and aging is natural. I do require cans be sent before a final purchase offer is made because condition so greatly affects the value and I need to examine cans closely."

    Tony Steffens
    1115 Cedar Ave.
    Elgin, IL 60120
        (708) 428-3150   Fax: (708) 742-5778

☆ **Beer cans** from U.S. brands before 1950. "I'll buy all fine condition conetop and flattop cans with no pulltabs. Price is dependent upon the condition and rarity. Mint cone-tops are worth $20 and up. I do not want pull-tab beer cans." Give the brand name, type (beer, lager, bock, etc.), can style and condition.

    Steve Gordon
    3731 Gelderland Court
    Olney, MD 20832
        (301) 774-7651 eves

☆ **Beer bottles with painted labels.** American breweries only. Most of these are 6, 7 or 8 oz., but some older ones from the 1930's are 12 oz. There are a few, very desirable larger bottles with painted labels. He is particularly interested in finding New York bottles, especially from Buffalo, Rochester, Utica, Syracuse, Troy, Tonawanda, and New York City. Describe the condition of the paint and whether there are neck chips. No soft drink bottles, please, even if bottled in breweries.

    Jim O'Brien
    PO Box 885
    Sugar Grove, IL 60554
       (708) 466-4679

☆ *Hamm's* **brewery memorabilia** including advertising, packaging and bottles, souvenirs, foam scrapers, coasters, bottle caps, kegs, glasses, signs and so on, for all of *Hamm's* brands. These include *Buckhorn, Velvet Glove, Matterhorn, Burgie, Right Time, Old Bru*, and *Waldech*. When selling glasses or cans, it is important to include *all* writing that appears on the object. Pete wants everything he doesn't already have and says the areas around Houston, Los Angeles, San Francisco, Baltimore, and St. Paul "are particularly saturated with *Hamm's* breweriana."

    Peter Nowicki
    1531 39th Avenue
    San Francisco, CA 94122
       (415) 566-7506

☆ **New Jersey breweriana** from the 1930's or older including signs, calendars, trays, tap knobs and inserts, coasters, labels, cans and books. "I would buy some collections of general breweriana if they contained some NJ items I want." He warns amateurs not to guess at age of items, that it's better to ask and urges you not to "buy breweriana items with the thought of reselling them to make money, since the chances are you won't." This 17 year veteran collector requests that you make it clear whether you are seeking information or have the item for sale.

    Paul Brady
    32 Hamilton Street
    Newton, NJ 07860
       (201) 383-7204

☆ **Beer uniform sew-on patches from anywhere in the world.** Jim wants any sewn patch: arm, cap, shirt, all ages, all sizes, all breweries. He isn't interested in beer club patches. Please describe condition noting whether it is used or unused, clean or not, and indicate whether it is a "second" or has been cut from a larger patch. Photocopy helpful.

    Jim O'Brien
    PO Box 885
    Sugar Grove, IL 60554
       (708) 466-4679

☆ **Near beer advertising from the days of prohibition in Chicago** and items related to Chicago pre-prohibition beers and breweries like *Budweiser, Schlitz, Blatz, Old Milwaukee, Atlas, Keely, Schoenhoffen, Sieben's,* and *Manhattan.* Wants signs, beer barrels, bottles, etc.
Michael Graham, Roaring 20's
33133 O'Plaine Road
Gurnee, IL 60031
(708) 263-6285

☆ **Coasters with advertising, especially for beer.** "I buy U.S. coasters only. Ship any quantity for my fair offer by return check."
Art Landino
88 Centerbrook Road
Hamden, CT 06518

☆ **Pottery ginger beer bottles** and associated paper ephemera. Sven has an illustrated wants list of these bottles, some of which can be worth $150. Sven wrote *The Illustrated Stone Ginger Beer*, a limited edition available from him for $13.
Sven Stau
PO Box 437
Buffalo, NY 14212
(716) 825-5448 or (716) 822-3120

☆ **American and foreign miniature beer bottles** especially pre-prohibition 1880-1920. The earliest are about 5" tall, filled with beer, and have a cork stopper.   These are desirable only if the labels are complete or the bottles are embossed. Post-prohibition bottles are smaller and of interest only if all labels are complete and in good condition. Foreign bottles must be in mint condition to be of interest. Also bottle openers with handles in the shape of mini beer bottles, wood or metal. There is a small group of post-prohibition mini beers which can be worth to $100 each. They include *Old Glory, Royal Pilsen, Wagner, Spearman, Ambrosia, Nectar, Frederick's 4 Crown, Citizens, Manro, Atlantic, Pennsy* and others. Alex will pay top price for sets of mini bottles in their original box. Condition of the label is crucial so describe every scratch or discoloration. Measure exact height. Also buys bottle shaped bottle openers. No Taiwan bottles.
Alexander Mullin
331 North Lehigh Circle
Swarthmore, PA 19081
(610) 328-7381

☆ *Dixie* **beer and** *Lexington Brewery* **ephemera** including openers, trays, fobs, mirrors, letterheads, and what have you.
Thom Thompson
1389 Alexandra Drive, #5
Lexington, KY 40504

LIQUOR COLLECTIBLES

☆ **Everything associated with saloons and speakeasies** including **photos of interiors** and exteriors, advertising, saloon equipment catalogs, letterheads, etc. Also trade magazines such as *the National Police Gazette* pre-1919, *Fair Play, Brewers Gazette,* and others.

    Richard Bueschel
    414 North Prospect Manor Ave.
    Mt. Prospect, IL 60065
       (708) 253-0791 eves

☆ **Prohibition artifacts of all kinds,** 1919-1933, related to gangster activity in Chicago and environs. Seeks relics from famous speakeasies such as *Colosimo's Cafe, Four Deuces, Red Lantern, Pony Inn, Cotton Club*, and *The Green Mill*. Also pamphlets, posters, and the like from the **Anti-Saloon League, WCTU, the Prohibition Party** and other groups for or against prohibition.

    Michael Graham's Roaring 20's
    33133 O'Plaine Road
    Gurnee, IL 60031
       (708) 263-6285

☆ **Ceramic *Jim Beam* type figural liquor bottles** from all makers. Your description should include the brand name, the figure, all marks on the bottom, the dimensions, and all colors. Bottles *must* have their original stopper. Fred buys and sells ceramic decanter bottles and offers a price guide to 6,000 different figural bottles for only $5.

    Fred Runkewich
    PO Box 1423-T
    Cheyenne, WY 82003
       (307) 632-1462

☆ ***Dewar's* scotch figural liquor bottles made by *Royal Doulton*.** Called *KingsWare* by *Doulton* collectors, more than 100 different figural bottles were commissioned in the 1920's and 30's. These distinctive brown-glazed bottles feature various literary characters and English historical figures. He pays $300+ each, says this veteran *Royal Doulton* dealer, as long as the figure is not chipped or cracked. If you wish to sell yours, telephone with the item in front of you.

    Ed Pascoe
    Pascoe & Co.
    101 Almeria Avenue
    Coral Gables, FL 33134
       (305) 445-3229 Fax: (305) 445-3305

☆ **China whiskey jugs marked** KT&K on the bottom. Also **miniature whiskey and apple vinegar jugs** with mottoes, product names or names of liquor stores on them.

    Barry Friedman
    22725 Garzota Drive
    Valencia, CA 91355
    (805) 296-2318

☆ *Jack Daniels, Green River Whiskey,* **and** *Lem Motlow* memorabilia including crockery jugs, embossed bottles, cork screws, shot glasses, lighters, and old paper advertising. Only older items are wanted.

    Don Cauwels
    3947 Old South Road
    Murfreesboro, TN 37129
    (615) 896-3614

☆ *Green River Whiskey* **advertising** and that for J.W. McCulloch Distiller, Cliff Falls Distillers or the Oldetyme Distillers, Inc. "I want paper, cardboard diecut signs, display bottles, watch fobs, giveaways, counter displays, and company receipts, letterheads, etc. Will pay $250 for *Green River* shot glasses. Clear pencil rubbings of advertising coins and fobs is a must, as many types exist. No *Green River* soft drink or repro tin signs, please."

    Elijah Singley
    2301 Noble Ave.
    Springfield, IL 62704
    (217) 546-5143 eves   (217) 786-2251

☆ **Cocktail shakers** from before 1960 are wanted, especially unusual, chrome, etc. "I buy and sell so contact me with any fine condition, complete shakers and shaker sets you have."

    Stephen Visakay
    PO Box 1517
    West Caldwell, NJ 07007
    (914) 352-5640

☆ **Swizzle sticks made of hollow glass** with paper inserts advertising a specific bar, lounge, hotel, tavern, etc. Especially interested in those from Oldetyme Distillers of NYC advertising *Green River, Three Feathers,* or *Grand McNish.* No plastic. Also buys **Whiskey or spirits trade magazines** such as *Wine & Spirits Bulletin* from before 1920.

    Elijah Singley
    2301 Noble Ave.
    Springfield, IL 62704
    (217) 546-5143 eves   (217) 786-2251

☆ **Miniature liquor bottles**, especially American bourbon whiskey made in Kentucky from 1870 to 1970, in 1 or 2 ounce size or in the more popular 1/10th pint. He will consider anything in fine condition, but advises that in large quantities "there is so much junk included" that they may average only a dollar or two. Mike likes bottles from the 1930's best. Bottles are collected for their colorful labels, so those must be in fine condition (although caps may be missing). "Nothing made after 1970 is of interest," he says, pointing out that the date is often found embossed on the bottom of the bottle (often simplified to just two numbers). List the brand name and condition of the label. It's helpful to also give any dates, and the shape of the bottle ("most are flask shaped, he says). Indicate whether it is empty or full. He has no interest in figural ceramic whiskey bottles (*Jim Beam* type) or in wine bottles of any type from any period. A few of Mike's fellow collectors seek bottles of scotch, Canadian, vodka, and other booze although they are generally a lot less valuable. "I'll try to help you sell just about any good miniature liquor bottles, or **larger American whiskeys from Prohibition or before** if they are still sealed and full." More than 30,000 different mini liquor bottles range in value from 50¢ to $100, with half having no value at all.

    Michael Olson, MELO
    309 Knopp Valley Drive
    Winona, MN 55987
      (507) 454-1499

☆ **Wine bottles with embossed oval or circular seals on the shoulder** of the bottle marked with the name and vintage, especially fine wineries and vintages. "The more crude the bottle, the better." No beer, whiskey, or wine bottles that do not have shoulder ovals. Also **pre-WWII paper wine labels** especially 19th century European and pre-prohibition California companies. This expert wine dealer prefers loose labels but will buy important ones still on the bottle. Rene notes that "values are still relatively low for most labels, but they are appreciated as additions to my collection."

    Rene Rondeau
    120 Harbor Drive
    Corte Madera, CA 94925

☆ **Corkscrews and wine related items.** Collects hand held and bar mounted corkscrews that are unusual in some way. Also wants wine related items such as wine tasters, **pre-1930 bottles, silver or ceramic bottle labels**, bottle cradles and **buckets**, etc. "I have little interest in paper labels." Make a photocopy of smaller items if possible. Describe the others. "I will answer all letters," says Joe.

    Joe Young
    PO Box 587
    Elgin, IL 60123
      (708) 695-0108

TOBACCO ADVERTISING

☆ **All high grade tobacco related collectibles:** "We'll consider purchasing tobacco jars, tobacco tins, cigar labels, catalogs, books about tobacco, cigar boxes, posters, advertising, and other tobacco related ephemera. We prefer collections, but buy individual items if value or collectible interest is sufficiently high. We buy for resale. SASE required for an answer; we regret sometimes unavoidably long delays in response. We have no interest in poor condition items, drug store pipes, pipe racks, common tins, magazine ads, flat 50 cigarette tins, cigarette packages after WWII, things covered with cigar bands, or cigar boxes dating after 1940. *The Lucky Strike Story* from 1939 is also common."

> Tobacciana Resources
> 2141 Shoreline Drive #A
> Shell Beach, CA 93449

☆ **Cigarette, pipe tobacco, and chewing tobacco advertising and ephemera.** Specifically interested in early U.S. tobacco manufacturers such as Allan & Ginter, Kinney Bros., J.B. Duke, and Kimball. Wants trade cards, insert cards, pin back buttons, watch fobs, pocket mirrors, and all types of small items, but not common tins like *Prince Albert, Velvet, Edgeworth,* and *Dill's Best.* **Has particular interest in tin tobacco tags** which were inserted into plugs of tobacco to establish brand identification with a consumer. Values of tin tags run from $1 to $5, but those with Blacks or political and military figures command more. "Most items from around the turn-of-the-century are sought." Include a brief description, name of the manufacturer and an accurate statement of condition for this 10 year veteran.

> Chris Cooper
> Route 2 Box 55
> Pittsburg, TX 75686
>   (903) 856-7286

☆ **Tin tobacco tags** and tag collections are bought, sold, and traded by this very active collector, who offers a free "suggestion sheet for new collectors" that will teach you all about tin tobacco tags. He also has the remaining stock of Gary Schild's basic book on tobacco tags, and is happy to sell you one for only $10.

> Lee "Tagger Lee" Jacobs
> PO Box 3098
> Colorado Springs, CO 80934

☆ *Seal of North Carolina* smoking and chewing tobacco advertising. Does not want tin cans, only lithographed ads. Fine condition a must. Photos appreciated.

> Lisa Van Hook
> PO Box 13256
> El Cajon, CA 92022

☆ **Tin tobacco cans** from before 1940. Wants very fine condition smoking tobacco, chewing tobacco and cigar cans and signs only. Save time and effort by sending a photocopy of the top and front of your tin along with a description of the condition. SASE is a must. If you regularly pick or deal, he will send you an informative flyer listing some tins to look for. **Brands not wanted include** *Bond Street, Briggs, Buckingham, Bugle, Dial, Dills Best, Edgeworth, George Washington, Half & Half, Hickory, Holiday, John Middleton, Kentucky Club, Model, Philip Morris, Prince Albert, Red Jacket, Revelations, Sir Walter Raleigh, Stag, Target, Tuxedo, Twin Oaks, Union Leader, Velvet,* and *Willoughby Taylor.* "Flat fifty" cigarette tins such as *Lucky Strike* and *Chesterfield* have no value. "I apologize, but response is often slow except on very rare items."

> Tony Hyman
> PO Box 3028
> Pismo Beach, CA 93448
> (805) 773-6777   Fax: (805) 773-8436

To sell anything, you should provide the following information:

(1) What is advertised and what is pictured;
(2) Size, color, and material from which made;
(3) Names, dates, and numbers on the item;
(4) Statement of condition, noting chips, cracks,
*   and missing parts, pieces, or paint;*
(5) Make a Xerox© whenever possible.

CIGAR EPHEMERA

☆ **Cigar boxes, labels, advertising, photographs**, counter lighters, **cigar store figures**, and everything else related to cigar making, selling, and smoking before WWII. Especially wants trade directories 1865-1940 (these are books which list cigar and tobacco factories). Want all materials relevant to the **Cigar Maker's International Union** or to **Samuel Gompers**, former CMIU officer. Condition is important. Please photocopy the inside lid of boxes. Pays from $5 to $50+ for cigar boxes, with top boxes bringing approximately $300. Send a long SASE for an informative priced wants list (which includes a useful list of common boxes). Tony's hardcover *Handbook of Cigar Boxes* is available with *Price Guide* for $18. He warns, "I have little interest in bands or items covered with cigar bands and pay little for them."

> Tony Hyman
> PO Box 3028
> Pismo Beach, CA 93448
> (805) 773-6777   Fax: (805) 773-8436

☆ **Cigar bands** from before WWII, preferably sets of royalty, Presidents, playing cards, and other pictorials. No torn, damaged, or partial bands are wanted. Give the quantity, description, and an SASE. Myron heads the *International Label, Seal and Cigar Band Society* which you can join for only $6/year.
>   Myron Freedman
>   8915 East Bellevue Street
>   Tucson, AZ 85715
>   (602) 296-1048

☆ **Cigar bands.** Small or moderate collections of inexpensive bands are wanted by a relatively new collector. Your help in developing a collection is appreciated.
>   Margo Toth, c/o Up Down Tobacco Shop
>   1550 North Wells Street
>   Chicago, IL 60610
>   (312) 337-8505

☆ **Cigar band collections** especially U.S. bands prior to 1920. Only items in good or mint condition wanted by this long time collector.
>   Joseph Hruby
>   1511 Lyndhurst Road
>   Lyndhurst, OH 44124
>   (216) 449-0977

☆ **Cigar humidors** by *Tiffany, Dunhill, Davidoff, Benson & Hedges* and *Meridan*, preferably in silver or exotic woods. Has less interest in glass or ceramic humidors, "although I will consider them." Will buy table top, free-standing, and travel styles, paying up to $5,000 for exceptional humidors. Prefers humidors with sporting motif, such as hunting dogs. Not interested in plain or damaged humidors. Give the maker's name, dimensions, and type of material. Photo if possible.
>   Francis Lombardi II
>   PO Box 181-TH
>   Syracuse, NY 132089
>   (315) 422-3536

☆ **Cigar store Indians.** Wants full size wooden or metal figures, especially Punch, Captain Jinks, or Dandy. Take photos from more than one angle or phone with the item in front of you. Also wants items from **tobacco factories in Detroit:** signs, cans, advertisements, bills of sale, boxes, store figures, photos, cutters, lighters, match holders and trays. Especially wants *Hiawatha* by D. Scotten.
>   Gregory "Dr. Z" Zemenick
>   1350 Kirts #160
>   Troy, MI 48084
>   (810) 642-8129   (810) 244-9426

CIGARETTE PACKS, LIGHTERS & EPHEMERA

☆ **Cigarette packs, tins, and cardboard boxes** from obsolete U.S. brands of cigarettes. No cards, premiums, silks, flat 50's tins, or cigar or tobacco items. Give the series number found on the tax stamp. Dick is president of the Cigarette Pack Collector's Association and editor of *Brandstand*, a monthly newsletter for cigarette pack collectors.

> Richard Elliott
> 61 Searle Street
> Georgetown, MA 01833
> (508) 352-7377

☆ *Lucky Strike* **collectibles of any kind.** "I'll buy bridge hand cards, celebrity ads, pre-1930 magazine ads, and LS/MFT marked items."

> John Van Alstyne
> 466 South Goodman Street
> Rochester, NY 14607

☆ *Philip Morris* **ephemera** prior to 1955, including cigarette packs, tins, advertising, signs, stand-ups, matches, buttons, and what have you. This beginning collector does not want reprints, and expects you to price what you wish to sell.

> Stuart Morrell
> 8925 Laureate Lane
> Richmond, VA 23236

☆ **Cigarette holders.** Seeking older and more unusual holders in less common materials or shapes. Likes ivory and/or amber, especially those made for oval cigarettes. "No cheap Chinese carved junk," he pleads. Please Xerox™ what you have for his offer. Pre-turn-of-the-century cigarette rolling devices are also of interest, but no *Job, Tip Top, Bugler* or other common rollers please.

> Leonard Fox
> 2965 Marlin Road, Box 729
> Bryn Athyn, PA 19009
> (215) 938-1840

☆ **Ashtrays,** but *only* those shaped like people, animals or things, such as airplanes, frogs, etc., especially when combined with lighters or cigar cutters. No ordinary glass hotel or bar advertising ashtrays. Most are $5 to $15, but has paid $100+ for exceptional pieces. Send a clear photo or a good sketch. Tire ashtrays are fairly common. Ship yours (if it has the original glass) and we'll pay at least $5 each (more if it's one we need) plus reimburse your postage. Sorry, no SASE, no answer.

> Tobacciana Resources
> 2141 Shoreline Drive #A
> Shell Beach, CA 93449

☆ **Cigarette lighters.** This lighter historian buys old or new lighters, as well as books, catalogs, brochures, pictures, advertising, parts lists, instruction sheets, boxes, counter displays, etc. Will pay cash, trade for other lighters, or borrow for research. "All material is guaranteed safe return." Send a photocopy of what you have. Jack offers an interesting illustrated catalog of lighters for sale if you send $3.

>Jack Seiderman
>1631 NW 114th Ave.
>Pembroke Pines, FL 33026
>>(305) 438-0928   Fax: (305) 438-0932

☆ **Cigarette lighters and fire making devices.** Buys a wide range of items including:
- High quality *Dunhills, Ronsons,* and pre-1940 lighters, especially *Dunhills* with special features such as being built into a watch;
- Lighters with unusual mechanisms, burning lenses, etc.;
- Table lighters that are in the shape of people or things;
- Automatic lighters made before 1920 by *Thorens, Haway, RK*;
- Lighters consisting of cap, gear, and tinder cord;
- Flint and steel strikers and tinder pistols;
- Designer lighters made of 14K or 18K gold;
- Chemical lighters from 1790 to 1890.

Anything unusual. Has no interest in modern Japanese lighters, butane lighters, and most advertising lighters except those for political personages. Don't bother him with common or recent items. As a basic rule of thumb, he says, "If you've seen it before, I don't want it." Give a basic description including brand name, patent information, ornamentation, construction, and condition. This 20 year veteran collector says, "I'm happy to answer inquiries from beginners or advanced collectors."

>Tom O'Key
>124 South Alice Circle
>Anaheim, CA 92806
>>(714) 630-8919   Fax: (714) 632-8275

☆ *Zippo* **lighters,** especially with Navy and Marine Corps insignia, including ships, squadrons, submarines, etc. Will buy some imitation *Zippo* lighters from military units. Lighters with ZIPPO in block letters and "PAT.2032695" or PAT.2517191" are desirable as well as outside hinge or square cornered *Zippos* even if plain. Personalized lighters with names or dates or places or unusual decoration are sought, especially those decorated on both front and back. Please send a photocopy of your lighter. "We actively buy all quality lighters and lighter combinations. Our lighter museum is open to the public."

>Jeff Mogilner, Racine & Laramine, Ltd.
>2737 San Diego Ave.
>San Diego, CA 92110
>>(619) 291-7833   Fax: (619) 297-6653

MATCHCOVERS & BOXES

☆ **Matchcover collections,** match boxes, salesman's sample books, pamphlets, and other match industry ephemera. Send brief description and SASE to this head of the American Matchcover Collecting Club. Bill is author of the *Matchcover Collector's Price Guide,* available from him for $28 postpaid.

> Bill Retskin
> PO Box 18481
> Asheville, NC 28804
>   (704) 254-4487   Fax: (704) 254-1066

☆ **Paper matchcover collections.** Dave is a long time collector of matchcovers and past president of the Sierra Diablo Club. He collects many different types of matchcovers and buys accumulations and collections. Individual covers are not worth much, but collections of pre-WWII covers are worth your while. Dave is happy to hear from folks with questions or collections.

> David Hampton
> PO Box 1457
> Lower Lake, CA 95457
>   (707) 995-1411

☆ **Matchcovers and match boxes,** foreign or domestic. "I don't want damaged covers generally, but will consider those with *minor* damage if they're from the early 1930's or before." Wants to know approximately how many covers or boxes you have, whether they are U.S. or foreign, whether they are used or unused, whether the covers are in an album or loose, and whether the matches are present. John is secretary of the Rathkamp Matchcover Society.

> John Williams
> 1359 Surrey Road TH
> Vandalia, OH 45377
>   (513) 890-8684

☆ **Matchcovers and match boxes.** Wants interesting singles or entire estates. Hiller is a West Coast auctioneer who can handle large collections. The ideal condition for matchcovers is unused, open, with the staples carefully removed. No "grocery store" covers, "Thank You's," or covers not identified as to origin (like *Holiday Inn* covers that don't give a location). His favorite find would be a matchcover from the Lindbergh welcome home dinner, worth in excess of $100.

> Robert Hiller
> 2501 West Sunflower #H5
> Santa Ana, CA 92704
>   (714) 540-8220

Matchcovers are considered "damaged" if they are torn or dirty, or if their striker has been cut off. Collectors do not want matchcovers if they are glued, taped, or stapled into a book.

☆ **Match box dispensers** from days gone by are sought by this dealer in contemporary advertising match boxes. Please give a thorough description of the item and indicate whether it works or not. Photo is helpful. As a relatively new collector, he'd appreciate your setting the price, but will make offers if necessary.

> Ed Sabreen
> 907 Glenside Road
> Cleveland, OH 44121
>   (216) 381-0100   Fax: (216) 382 0969

☆ **Match box holders.** Send a photo or Xerox™ of what you have for sale. Dealers, price your goods, but offers will be made to amateurs.

> Charles Reuter
> 6 Joy Ave.
> Mount Joy, PA 17552

MATCH SAFES

☆ **Match safes.** "I'll buy figural, fancy, and unusual match safes and related items such as catalogs, advertisements, and ephemera prior to 1915. I'll take one or a collection, but interested in quality items only. I want a detailed description, including the type of material, size and condition. Asking price helpful. Photograph or photocopy." Nothing later than 1915.

> George Sparacio
> PO Box 791
> Malaga, NJ 08328
>   (609) 694-4167 eves

☆ **Match safes.** Buys small pocket match safes if they are in unusual shapes or if they advertise tobacco products or outlets. Xerox™ what you have, rather than take photos which show your safe as a small blur. Prefers you to price your safe(s), understanding that almost all are worth under $100 to him, and ordinary sterling match safes that are not figural will only bring $10 to $20 or so depending on the pattern.

> Tony Hyman
> PO Box 3028
> Pismo Beach, CA 93448

TOBACCO & OTHER INSERT CARDS

☆ **Cigarette cards and silks** for Canadian, British, and U.S. cigarettes. He wants complete sets or albums of cards, but buys silks in odd lots. Sorry, but he does not want to buy a handful of odd cards from you unless they are 19th century U.S. cards in near mint condition. He will buy large lots of odd cards. Give the title of the set or album. Dealers must price their goods. Amateurs may request an offer.

> W.T. Brown
> 230 Lake Avenue East
> Carleton Place, ON
> K7C-1J6 CANADA
> (613) 253-1790

☆ **Cigarette and other insert cards.**   Wants 19th century U.S. cigarette insert cards, especially the *State Seal* series from *August Beck Tobacco* and the *Wellstood Etchings* from *Wm. Kimball*. This 50 year veteran also wants cards from **Brooke-Bond Tea Company, Van Houten Cocoa,** and the **Liebig Meat Extract Company.** He will consider *Liebig* cards in any language, especially menu and calendar cards. Give quantities, and send a photocopy showing samples of the front and back of the cards you have for sale.

> Ron Stevenson
> 4920 Armoury Street
> Niagara Falls, ON
> L2E 1T1 CANADA
> (416) 358-5497

☆ **Cigarette and tobacco insert cards and other tobacco related paper.** Wants 19th and early 20th century U.S. tobacco and cigarette insert cards, tobacco advertising trade cards, counter stand-ups, hangers, posters, albums, giveaways, premiums, and cigarette slide packs. Will pay $25 each and up for many early American trade cards, and $700 for the Marquis of Lorne card issued in 1879. He does not want British or foreign cards,

"I buy only cards that contain one of the following words printed on the card: tobacco, cigarette, cigarros, smoking, cut plug, chewing, long cut, fine cut, scrap cut or navy cut."

cigar bands, cigar labels, tobacco caddy labels, reproductions or reprints, matchbooks or badly damaged items. Give the size (vertical then horizontal), the maker, and condition. A photocopy is a good idea. Items must be in at least very good condition.

> Peter Gilleeny
> 76 Rose Drive
> Fruitland Park, FL 34731
> (904) 728-4819

☆ **Cigarette cards, silks, leathers, flannels, and pins** in fine condition. Is particularly interested in the very early U.S. cards. Also buys some **gum, candy,** and other tobacco insert cards, primarily from pre-1920 U.S., but will buy some foreign cards and albums at a lesser price. No flags. Does not want silks or flannels that have been sewn together. Will not make offers to dealers.

> Charles Reuter
> 6 Joy Ave.
> Mount Joy, PA 17552
> (717) 653-8505

☆ **Cigarette and tobacco insert cards, silks, and leathers.** Wants 19th century U.S. items primarily, such as cards by *Allen & Ginter*, but buys many 20th century pieces. Also buys **tobacco advertising trade cards** and tobacco related **match covers.** "Please describe and price, or send on approval. I pay all postage expenses and respond within 48 hours of receipt of your cards. Condition is important as I do not collect trimmed cards, badly creased or otherwise battered items." Does not want flannel flags (often erroneously called "felts").

> William Nielsen
> PO Box 1379
> Brewster, MA 02631
> (508) 896-7389

☆ **Cigarette silks and flannels** and items such as **pillows and quilts made from them** are wanted by this prestigious quilt dealer. "No junk," she emphasizes, since everything is for sale in her shop. Please take a photograph or make a photocopy of your item. List how many flags and silks and their approximate size.

> Margaret Cavigga
> 8648 Melrose Ave.
> Los Angeles, CA 90069
> (310) 659-3020

ANTIQUE & BRIAR PIPES

☆ **Antique pipes** including carved meerschaums, opium pipes, water pipes, porcelain figural pipes, early bas-relief and high-relief wood pipes and selected clays. Ben is a specialist in the literature of tobacco, and buys **books, magazines and pamphlets** on all aspects of tobacco culture and use, in any language, from any period. If you are seeking literature on tobacco, he has the world's largest selection on that topic.

> Ben Rapaport, Antiquarian Tobacciana
> 11505 Turnbridge Lane
> Reston, VA 22094
> (703) 435-8133 eves

☆ **Antique smoking pipes and pipe parts.** Also buys **books and other publications** on pipes, tobacco, and related items. Primary interest is in **meerschaum,** but also buys other antique pipes, especially porcelains, and any historical or unusual items including pipes from any culture. Will purchase complete collections as well as individual pipes. Not interested in damaged pipes or reproductions. Give size (length and width), condition, and all other information you can provide.

> Frank Burla
> 23 West 311 Wedgwood
> Naperville, IL 60540
> (708) 961-0156

☆ **High quality pipes of all type** are wanted, including:
- Name brand "pre-smoked" **used briar pipes**, especially *Dunhill, Charatan, Barling, Castello, Radich, GBD, Kaywoodie* and "others too numerous to mention";
- **Meerschaum pipes** in good to excellent condition;
- **Carved briar pipes**;
- **Clay pipes** that are very large or that have been carved into faces, animals, and other figures;
- **Pipe tobacco advertising and books**;
- **Lighters** of many different sizes and shapes.

Larger sizes are particularly desirable. When describing a pipe, include the brand name, its dimensions, shape, finish and all stampings. If you are not familiar with standard pipe shapes, make a photocopy of the pipe and list everything written on the pipe's shank. He does not buy *Medico, Yellow Bole, Dr. Grabow* or other drugstore pipes.

> Gary Donachy
> 801 West Sunset
> Steeleville, IL 62288

☆ **High quality pipes of all types** are purchased by one of the nation's largest and oldest tobacconists. Both modern and antique pipes are bought for resale or for display, but don't bother them with junk. *Dunhill, Comoy, Petersen* and *Sasieni* are among briars purchased. "If they are part of a large collection, we'll buy any pipes, including inexpensive ones, as long as they are in fine condition." Highly carved meerschaum will also be considered. A photocopy is a good idea. Check your item carefully for damage and mention any defects you find. Also buys antique cigar cutters, cigar cases, and *Dunhill* **lighters**, as well as other old lighters made of gold or silver.

> Charles Levi
> Iwan Ries & Co.
> 19 South Wabash
> Chicago, IL 60603
> (312) 372-1306   Fax: (312) 372-1416

☆ **High grade briar pipes.** Brand names of interest include *Dunhill, Charatan, Barling, Comoy, Castello, Caminetto, Sasieni, Preben Holm,* and *Peterson*. "I'll buy them smoked or new, as long as they are in good looking condition, with no uneven surfaces on the rim, no tooth holes in the stem, etc." Wants collections of pipes, but will buy singles. He especially wants *Dunhills* with "ODA" or "ODB" and patent dates marked on the stem and *Peterson* pipes with IRISH FREE STATE or ERIE on the shank. Please, no "drug store pipes" like *Medico, Yellow Bole,* or *Dr. Grabow*. When offering pipes for sale, mention any writing on the pipe and its condition. There are dozens of standard pipe shapes, so if you don't know them, send a photocopy of your pipe.

> Marty Pulvers
> Sherlock's Haven
> 1 Embarcadero Center
> San Francisco, CA 94111
> (415) 362-1405

☆ **Pipes and tobacco items** including:
- **Antique meerschaum** pipes, carved or plain;
- Briar pipes, old or modern, especially fine European briars by *Charatan, Barling,* or *Frieborg & Treyer*;
- Books or catalogs about pipes or smoking;
- Advertising for pipes and smoking tobacco.

Please send photos or Xerox™ copies of what you have. Include an SASE for an offer.

> Lee Pattison
> 6 Christview Drive
> Cuba, NY 14727
> (716) 968-2458

☆ **Clay pipes and clay pipe ephemera.** Especially wants figurals, faces, or political clay pipes. Prefers American pipes, but buys others. This author-historian also buys **pipe molds, presses, or anything else involved in the making of clay pipes**. Also wants billheads, letterheads, checks, catalogs, and other advertising before 1950 for any clay pipe maker. Has a particular interest in William Kelman, a Baltimore pipe manufacturer. Generally not interested in plain white clay pipes with no markings or decoration. Please make a photocopy of your items, indicating any markings, and tell what you know about their origin or background. Paul has produced a giant limited edition book on 19th century pipe patents which he sells for $55, and a large reproduction of an 1892 tobacconists' wholesale catalog for $45.

S. Paul Jung, Jr.
PO Box 817
Bel Air, MD 21014
(410) 569-8194

☆ **Hookah (water) pipes.** "I'll buy one hose or multiple hose hookahs made of brass, ivory, or other materials. I'm seeking antique pipes, not head shop items, common glass bongs, and other drug paraphernalia. Please send a picture and information about the pipe's background. Dealers should price your goods but I will make offers for amateurs."

Mark Rivkind
363 Bailey Court
Palm Harbor, FL 34684
(813) 787-1169

IF YOU GO TO YARD SALES LOOKING FOR PROFIT...

You can resell good quality used briar pipes for $15 to $100 each, yet they are often found for under $5. As a general rule, only a handful of brands are resellable, with Dunhill the favorite.

ACCESSORIES, JARS & BOXES

☆ **Smoking accessories and other objects marked** *Dunhill* including **pipes**, cigarette holders, cigarette **lighters**, pens, etc. This disabled combat vet says, "I prefer items to be sent to me for my offer. I will refund shipping costs if my purchase price is rejected. But I would like to stress *that I do not need common items, junk, or damaged goods.* I buy only for my own collection and will pay fair prices."

> C. Ray Erler
> PO Box 36
> Pittsfield, PA 16340

☆ **Humidors** made of fine glass, china, or copper. Please send a photo or Xerox™ of what you have for his offer.

> Lee Pattison
> 6 Christview Drive
> Cuba, NY 14727
> (716) 968-2458

☆ **Tobacco jars.** "If you have old tobacco jars, I may be able to assist you to identify what you have and decide its relative rarity. If you would like to sell a tobacco jar, I can advise you how to go about it, and may be able to steer you to members who may be interested." Joe founded the international club for tobacco jar collectors and edits their newsletter. He has also written a book on jars which you can order through him.

> Joe Horowitz
> 3011 Falstaff Road #307
> Baltimore MD 21209
> (410) 358-1323

☆ **Snuff boxes** of all types, including early American, Civil War period, and Oriental.

> Eli Hecht
> 19 Evelyn Lane
> Syosset, NY 11791

EROTICA & GIRLIE MAGAZINES

☆ **Anything "racy"** from 1890 to 1969, with special interest in the 1950's. "I have been collecting this stuff for 20 years and have only scratched the surface. There's lots of stuff in all forms that I can use."
- *Esquire* and *True* magazines;
- Girlie **magazines of the "R" type**, including, but not limited to, *Playboy* and its early imitators, nudist, art and photography magazines, pulp magazines, risque humor and spicy stories;
- **Cheesecake photo magazines** like *See, Pix, Eye, Glance, Laff, Night 'n' Day,* etc.;
- **Tiajuana Bibles**, 8 pagers, and "dirty little comics";
- **Movies with risque content**, either "R" or "X";
- Photos of actresses, models, and strippers in **sexy poses**;
- **French postcards** of nudes and/or naughty ladies;
- **Petty and Vargas** centerfolds;
- Miscellany like matchbooks, lighters, ashtrays, ballpoint pens, blotters, playing cards, bar glasses, etc.

"Condition is not as important to me as it might be to someone else, especially where magazines are concerned. I have bought some which were missing pages, falling apart, smelled musty, and looked like junk, as long as the price was right. I would rather have something in my collection than see it thrown away."

Douglas Cowles
2966 West Talara Lane
Tucson, AZ 85741
(602) 297-9062

☆ **Erotic art in all forms and formats** including statues, paintings, prints, post cards, photography, and three dimensional objects of all kinds from the days of the Roman empire up to the present. Especially seeks Oriental and European erotic bisque or porcelain figures, revolving lamps from the 50's with pin-up shades, arcade "peep" machines, and photos of all types. Also **original art for pin-up calendars** or illustrations 1920-1970, especially work by **Alberto Vargas** and **George Petty**, but other artists are wanted including Earl Moran, Gil Elvgren, Zoe Mozert, Armstrong, Alk Buell, Al Moore and others. Also Vargas *Esquire* calendars and prints, other calendar pin-ups, and some homemade erotica, including obscene letters written by private parties. Describe condition. A photograph or photocopy is suggested. Include your phone number when you write.

Charles Martignette
PO Box 293
Hallandale, FL 33009
(305) 454-3474

☆ **Erotica of all types, all languages, all eras**, including hard and soft cover books, sex newspapers, typescripts and mimeos, sex comics, original erotic art, films, photos, statuary, and sexually explicit objects of all types. Not interested in most magazines.
> C.J. Scheiner
> 275 Linden Blvd. # B2
> Brooklyn, NY 11226
> (718) 469-1089

☆ **Erotica of all types,** including nude photos and photo books, original art and paintings, Oriental or European, and three dimensional materials of all sorts.
> Ivan Gilbert
> Miran Art & Books
> 2824 Elm Ave.
> Columbus, OH 43209
> (614) 421-3222   Fax: (614) 421-3223

☆ **Sexy books and magazines of all types,** old or new. "We will buy any quantities of all types of girlie magazines including newsstand titles, **nudist**, hardcore, softcore, and foreign. Will also buy boxes of real photos, picture pages from magazines and books, videos, calendars, and cards, most of which don't bring a great deal." Does not want regular monthly issues of *Playboy* after 1964, *Penthouse* after 1971, or any issues of *Playgirl*.   Condition has a lot to do with determining value. They pay freight, or will "travel for truckloads."
> The Antiquarian Bookstore
> 1070 Lafayette Road
> Portsmouth, NH 03801
> (603) 436-7250

☆ **Girlie magazines published by *Parliament*** from the 1950's, 60's, and 70's. Buys *Playboy* from the 1950's only. Buys related girlie material, calendars, and paperbacks, but nothing from the 1980's. Fine condition items only. For $3 Warren offers a catalog of girlie magazines he has for sale.
> Warren Nussbaum
> 29-10 137th Street
> Flushing, NY 11354
> (718) 886-0558

☆ **Girlie magazines published by** *Parliament, Nuance, Marquis* **or** *Briarwood* from 1969 to 1989. Will pay $1 each for magazines from these publishers and $2 each for a few of their "classic" issues. Will pay 25¢ to 50¢ for similar adult publications from the 1970's by other publishers. Pays $6 each for *Puritan* . Wants complete clean copies. "No need to write or call. No embarrassment. Ship one or a hundred for immediate cash. Ship via Post Office 'Special 4th Class Book Rate' and I'll reimburse. Every shipment evaluated individually." Does not want bondage, fatties, or biracial. Little interest in most xxx magazines with a cover price of $15+. No *Playboy, Penthouse, Oui, Hustler, Chic, Velvet, Club, Club International, Gallery* or other newsstand magazines. "If you're a *Parliament* collector write about trades."

>Hank Anthony
>PO Box 3001
>Shell Beach, CA 93448

☆ **Autographed** *Playboy* **playmate ephemera** including covers, gatefolds, and partial pages, but the photo must be from the magazine. Items may be dedicated ("To Bill," etc.) or not, but those without dedications are preferred, and bring from $20 to $50. Autographs of other women (actresses, models, celebrities) who have appeared in *Playboy* will be considered but only if they have signed the cover or photo spread in which they appear. Photocopy what you have. *Playboy* ephemera is wanted, but only a select list of items: *Playboy* jigsaw puzzles (preferably in their original unopened boxes), posters, playing cards, square yellow ashtrays, foreign issues of the magazine, and "unique novelties." No orange ashtrays, glasses, mugs, or calendars later than 1960. Wants #1, #2, and #3 of the U.S. edition of *Playboy*.

>David Kveragas, McTieg Books
>1943 Timberland
>Clarks Summit, PA 18411
>   (717) 587-3429

☆ **Alberto Vargas illustrations,** 1918-1960. "I'll buy magazine covers, Ziegfeld Follies posters, and other Vargas art depicting nudes, but only his work before he began drawing for *Playboy*." He does not want *Esquire* calendars unless they have their original jackets and is not interested in any of Vargas's *Playboy* art.

>David Kveragas
>McTieg Books
>1943 Timberland
>Clarks Summit, PA 18411
>   (717) 587-3429

☆ **Explicit hardcover sex novels published in France in the 1920's through 1950's.** "Usually inexpensively bound, 4" x 6" or so, in English, there are many titles. I pay $40 to $100 each for all good condition usable titles, $75 to $200 in dust jacket. I am not looking for romance novels, but very explicit xxx-rated novels. Please ship first class mail for inspection and check by return mail. I'll pay post both ways."

> Hank Anthony
> PO Box 3001
> Shell Beach, CA 93448

☆ **Burlesque, strippers, and sexy dances.** Buys photos, posters, signs and any unusual items related to these skinful arts. Likes to find 3-D picture books and unusual pictorial items, especially art originals.

> Charles Martignette
> PO Box 293
> Hallandale, FL 33009
>   (305) 454-3474

☆ **Betty Brosmer photos** and other items related to this 1950's pin-up queen, including magazine covers and stories, newspaper articles, film loops, and videos of her TV appearances. Xerox™ copies of paper items are helpful. Date them if you can.

> Harold Forsko
> PO Box 42
> Monmouth Junction, NJ 08852
>   (609) 936-1868 eves

☆ **Electric and pre-electric vibrators and hand held massagers.** "I especially like those with metal casings rather than plastic, those with hand-cranks, and vibrators with wooden bodies, handles or parts. Not interested in battery operated devices. You won't make a fortune selling to me, but your item could reside in the world's only vibrator museum and will be happier than in your attic." No *Oster* vibrators which are worn on the back of the hand. Describe, give numbers, and indicate whether the box and any attachments or instructional inserts are present. Will buy items which do not work but are not physically broken. Joani runs a specialty sex toy and book store, and offers two good sized catalogs of sexual self-help books and sexual aids.

> Joani Blank
> Good Vibrations
> 938 Howard Street #101
> San Francisco, CA 94103
>   (415) 974-8985   Fax: (415) 974-8989

☆ **Condom tins**, especially those with "nice colorful graphics" are wanted. The *Akron Tourist Tubes* tin which pictures a blimp is worth "about $250" but your old *Sheik, Ramses* and *Merry Widows* have no value nor do any tins in poor condition. Best if you make a Xerox™ of your tin to show its condition.

> Dennis and George Collectables
> 3407 Lake Montebello Drive
> Baltimore, MD 21218
> (410) 889-3964

☆ **Condom (prophylactic)** and **feminine hygiene** vending equipment, fine condition condom tins (the older and more colorful the better), and advertising relating to condoms or prophylactics, especially before 1960. Will buy single items or large lots.

> Mr. Condom
> 1635 Acorn Ano Road
> Somerset, KY 42501
> (606) 274-4848

☆ **Prostitution.** Buys a wide variety of ephemera from anywhere in the world, but is particularly interested in Nevada. What have you?

> Douglas McDonald
> Gypsyfoot Enterprises
> PO Box 350093
> Grantsdale, MT 59835
> (406) 363-3202 voice and fax

☆ **Bathing beauties and nudie photos,** pre-WWI.

> Steve DeGenaro
> PO Box 5662
> Youngstown, OH 44504

☆ **Provocative or obscene photographs** including nudes, semi-nudes, candids, home made pictures, outdoor frolicking, etc., from teasing to hard core pornography. Also pin-up photos of dancers, starlets, and sexy ladies of all ages and periods.

> Charles Martignette
> PO Box 293
> Hallandale, FL 33009
> (305) 454-3474

AMERICANA

In a book like this that tells you about millions of items, it is hard not to have a miscellaneous section. This is it.

The next fifty pages contain a wide array of things you can sell. A good many of the items are from the 19th century, but as you read the entries, you'll see many less than 100 years old.

If making money is your goal, learn about political buttons, scouting patches, and Christmas lights, three items likely to be found underpriced at yard sales and second hand stores. The most valuable items in the next 50 pages are Indian artifacts. Tens of thousands of dollars can be involved for rugs, and thousands for some pots.

I've worked hard to make it easy for you to make money. I want you to enjoy putting money in your pocket. Other readers claim they have had a lot of fun and met many wonderful people. I hope you do too.

Some of you are parting with things that are important to you. You want your treasure to get proper care. There's no better way than to put it in the hands of someone who cares. No one cares more than collectors.

Whether you want cash...preservation...or both, the dealers and collectors you meet in Trash or Treasure are ready to help. To find the right people, look in the index in the back of the book. It is your key to getting the most out of this book.

SCOUTING MEMORABILIA

☆ **Scouting items from Boy Scouts, Girl Scouts** and **Lone Scouts**, especially before 1940.
- **Uniforms, badges**, and **pins**. Patches with WWW from Order of the Arrow lodges, and badges from Senior Scout and Explorer groups particularly needed;
- **Rank and Honor medals**: lifesaving medals, medals for war service, Eagle and Golden Eaglet medals, Ranger, Silver, Ace and Quartermaster medals, and World Jamboree medals; he notes that some medals are worth $500+;
- **Girl and Boy Scout dolls,** soft or composition, in all sizes, if complete. *Kenner Steve Scout* dolls from 1975, if mint in box. All *Steve Scout* accessories, such as a summer uniform;
- **Scout toys and games**, including figures, boards, etc.;
- Scout table model *Bakelite* radios from the late 1930's;
- Official **books and other literature** including manuals and magazines before 1930, merit badge pamphlets and Cub Scout literature from before 1940, and "all Air Scout stuff".
- **Historical items** related to founders of Scouting, including Baden-Powell, Juliette Low, Seton, Beard, West, Boyce, and Robinson. Also wants books by or about these people.

When you are offering things to them for sale, they remind "a photocopy is worth 1,000 words."
> Fran and Cal Holden
> Box 264-H
> Doylestown, OH 44230
> (216) 658-2793

☆ **Boy Scout memorabilia and patches,** especially Order of the Arrow patches with WWW on them (for which he will pay from $2.50 to $1,000+). Items from National Order of the Arrow conferences from 1948 and earlier are especially sought, although *staff* items from *all* NOAC's are needed. Early Order of the Arrow National Committee items are needed such as the red felt sash which is worth $2,000. Pre-1960 National Jamboree *staff* items are wanted, as are pre-1955 World Jamboree items. As a general rule, the older the patch, the better. However, this does not apply to patches which have only local interest such as camporees, Scout-O-Ramas, Scout circus, and other local items. Ron says, "before you sell, compare what I pay to other offers."
> Ron Aldridge
> 250 Canyon Oaks Drive
> Argyle, TX 76226
> (214) 351 3490 days   (817) 455-2519 eves

☆ **Boy Scout items of all sorts** including toys, posters, photos, badges, Order of the Arrow, and magazines. Wanted books include the *Boy Scout Handbook* pre-1940, *Patrol Leader Handbook* pre-1945, and many other pre-1945 fiction and non-fiction Scouting books including *Every Boy's Library* with original dust jackets. Buys adult, Cub, and Air Scout uniforms pre-1940 and all pins and medals before 1960. Offers up to $750 for a 1924 World Jamboree patch. He is also interested in any items from the founders of Scouting.

> Doug Bearce
> PO Box 4742
> Salem, OR 97302
>   (503) 399-9872

☆ **Boy Scout items,** Eagle awards, and Order of the Arrow patches (marked O.A., Lodge, or W.W.W.). "I'll pay from $1 to $100 for most, though some very scarce items may bring $1,000 or more. I need a photocopy, although you may send what you have for sale to me and if we can't agree on a fair price, I will return it and pay shipping costs both ways." He does not want handbooks printed after 1915, first aid kits, neckerchief slides, belt buckles, knapsacks, tents, or camping gear.

> Greg Souchik
> PO Box 133
> Custer City, PA   16725
>   (814) 362 2642   Fax: (814) 362-7356

☆ **Girl Scout memorabilia.** "Try me for anything that says or means Girl Scout." She especially wants very old items, Mariner and Wing Scout items, Senior GS items, all pre-1938 items, World's Fair items, war time items, and pre-1945 items from Camp Edith Macy, Our Chalet, and Our Ark. Make certain to note condition and whether anything is missing. Asking price is appreciated. Since she will buy so many items, it is important to note she does not want the following: handbooks after 1918, 1940's green uniform, 1960's green cotton or Dacron Brownie and Intermediate uniforms, 1960's forest green two piece senior uniform, 1970's or 80's uniforms, any mess kits, canteens, back packs, sleeping bags, and other big camping gear after 1925.

> Phyllis Palm
> PO Box 5272
> Mt. Carmel, CT 06518

☆ **Girl Scout memorabilia.** Wants to buy pre-1960 catalogs, postcards, magazines, uniforms, equipment, and other items. Handbooks before 1921 only. Send Xerox™ or photo. Do not send items without prior arrangement.

> Jerry King
> 8429 Katy Freeway
> Houston, TX 77024
>   (713) 465-2500

POLITICS

☆ **Presidential, gubernatorial, and Congressional campaign memorabilia.** "I'll consider any and all items used in a political campaign for president, governor, U.S. Senate or the House of Representatives, including buttons, ribbons, banners, pennants, posters, and 3-D items like canes and hats." You are encouraged to inquire as " an item may look common but be very scarce." Send a Xerox™ copy. If this is not possible, this veteran of 21 years collecting and dealing asks you to give the size, color and condition of your item.

> David Quintin
> PO Box 800861
> Dallas, TX 75380
> (214) 934-1151   Fax: (214) 934-2660

☆ **Presidential campaign memorabilia made of paper or cloth,** from any campaign before 1976. *All* candidates are wanted including third party or those who lost in primaries, but **Lincoln** is a particular favorite. Small paper items from the 19th century are generally worth from $5-$15 and include pamphlets, posters, tickets, sample ballots, and cards of any kind. Cloth items such as bandanas, flags, ties, ribbons, and handkerchiefs are wanted, as long as they were used in a presidential campaign. He'll pay $75-$250 for bandanas picturing candidates. He does not buy buttons, bumper stickers, or daily newspapers. Prefers to buy piles of paper rather than single pieces, unless the items are early or unusual. When writing, indicate the candidate, the year (if you know), the size, any slogans or messages, and what's pictured.

> Charles Hatfield
> 1411 South State Street
> Springfield, IL 62704

☆ **Abraham Lincoln presidential campaign memorabilia** including items related to his various opponents: Douglas, Bell, Breckinridge, McClellan, and Jefferson Davis. Will buy flags, banners, posters, broadsides, tokens, ribbons, and photographic badges. A photographic Lincoln/Johnson badge would be worth "several thousand dollars" to this 30 year veteran collector/dealer. He does not want books, autographs, most photos, engravings, newspapers, magazines, memorial items created after his death, or commemoratives of any sort. "I'll only buy items issued during an election or for Lincoln's two inaugurations." He wants a photocopy or photo, or a sketch with dimensions and information about material, inscriptions, and all defects. "I require to see the item before I buy it."

> Donald Ackerman
> 33 Kossuth Street
> Wallington, NJ 07057
> (201) 779-8785   Fax: (201) 746-1533

☆ **Presidential memorabilia** including glass, china, campaign buttons and ribbons, posters, **White House gift items**, inauguration medals, invitations, Xmas cards, etc. Will pay $4,000 for a mint condition Theodore Roosevelt inaugural medal. Author of *Collectors Guide to Presidential Inaugural Medals and Memorabilia* available for $8.95.

> H. Joseph Levine
> 6550-I Little River Turnpike
> Alexandria, VA 22312
> (703) 354-5454

☆ **Political campaign items of all kinds.** Top priority given to better 19th century items, especially those associated with **Abraham Lincoln** and his contemporaries in the Civil War period. "I'll buy buttons, badges, ribbons, banners, tintypes, portrait flags, and three dimensional objects," says this 25 year veteran dealer /collector, but he is not interested in buttons later than 1960. Except for political quilts, he does not buy commemorative items not actually issued as part of a campaign. A photocopy or photo is of "great help."

> Cary Demont
> PO Box 19312
> Minneapolis, MN 55419
> (612) 922-1617

☆ **Presidential political items of all sorts.** Will buy buttons, banners, ribbons, and paper material, especially from candidates of the 1920's, Coolidge, Davis, Harding, LaFollette, Cox, Hoover, Smith, and Debs, with a strong interest in **Calvin Coolidge**. Please don't send him any *Kleenex* buttons, other reproductions, or anything in poor condition. This well known collector and dealer has been active for nearly 30 years. He requests a photocopy and thorough description. The price you'd like is appreciated but "will make offer if you have no idea of an item's value."

> Larry L. Krug, Americana Resources
> 18222 Flower Hill Way #299
> Gaithersburg, MD 20879
> (301) 926-8663

☆ **Political buttons, tokens, and ribbons from any election before 1925.** From before 1910, he will buy tokens, medals, ribbons, glass, china, paper, canes, figures, silks, etc. The only buttons after 1925 that he wants are those that catalog for more than $20 in Ted Hake's book on political buttons. Consignments to his auction are invited.

> Rich Hartzog, World Exonumia
> PO Box 4143 BFT
> Rockford, IL 61110
> (815) 226-0771

☆ **Election memorabilia of all types, 1780-1960**, for resale, especially higher quality items (not paper). Wants china, ribbons, mirrors, clocks, glass, paintings, textiles, etc., that are **political or patriotic** in content. "I'll pay from $500-$5,000 for small historical medallions with pewter rims and lithographed portraits of military and political figures." Rex does not do free appraisals. Please don't contact him unless you want to *sell*.

> Rex Stark, Auctioneer
> 49 Wethersfield Road
> Bellingham, MA 02019
> (508) 966-0994

☆ **Presidential campaign items**: buttons, badges, ribbons, tokens, canes, flags, china, posters, bandanas, banners, torches, lanterns, and novelty items. Does not want books. Has been buying and selling these items for 30+ years, and offers catalogs for $3 each.

> Historical Collections
> PO Box 42
> Waynesboro, PA 17268

☆ **Presidential campaign** buttons, ribbons, and posters. This active collector does not want common buttons like "I Like Ike" or "Nixon's the One." An SASE is a must for an answer.

> Peggy Dillard
> PO Box 210904
> Nashville, TN 37221
> (615) 646-1605

☆ **Victoria Woodhull memorabilia.** Anything in any condition is wanted about this spiritualist, feminist, and Presidential candidate, from 1865 to her leaving for England in 1877. Wants portraits, photos, programs, flyers, handbills, booklets, personal effects, and any newspaper or magazine stories by or about her that were written prior to 1900. Materials from **her 1872 Presidential campaign for the Equal Rights Party** are especially sought.

> Ronald Lowden, Jr.
> 314 Chestnut Ave.
> Narberth, PA 19072
> (610) 667-0257 anytime

☆ **Women's suffrage and political campaign** items, especially 19th century buttons, ribbons, posters, and pennants.

> Ken Florey
> 153 Haverford
> Hamden, CT 06517
> (203) 248-1233

☆ **William Jennings Bryan and Tom Dewey memorabilia.**
Rich Hartzog, World Exonumia
Box 4143 BFT
Rockford, IL 61110
(815) 226-0771

☆ **Teddy Roosevelt items** including books written by or about him before 1920, campaign buttons, newspapers or loose articles, photographs, recorded speeches, and what have you. Please photocopy.
Douglas Cowles
2966 West Talara Lane
Tucson, AZ 85741
(602) 297-9062

☆ **Personal and other memorabilia related to Harding, Coolidge, Hoover, FDR** and **Al Smith**. Documentation will be requested.
Michael Graham's Roaring 20's
33133 O'Plaine Road
Gurnee, IL 60031
(708) 263-6285

☆ **Richard M. Nixon collectibles.** "I'll buy campaign collectibles, anti-Nixon items, and Watergate related ephemera including, but not limited to, buttons, jewelry, textiles, glassware, medals, coins, games, novelties, pens and pencils, pocket knives, keychains, stamps, stickers, caricatures, matchbooks, postcards, puzzles, headgear...almost anything picturing or referring to Nixon." He does not want magazines, posters, bumper stickers, and newspapers. He is interested in Nixon's entire history as a public figure. Please send a "crisp photocopy or photo of the item along with a description of all flaws such as foxing, chips, scratches, fading, etc." Include the price you'd like (although he will make offers to amateurs) and SASE if you want photos returned. His book on Nixon collectibles may be ordered for $60 postpaid.
Eldon Almquist
975 Maunawili Circle
Kailua, HI 96734
(808) 262-9837 eves

☆ **Gubernatorial (governor) or U.S. Senate race political buttons** from any state. Pays $25-$50 each for those he can use. Photocopy. Describe condition if there are any problems not evident.
Dave Quintin
PO Box 800861
Dallas, TX 75380
(214) 934-1151   Fax: (214) 934-2660

☆ **Illinois and Chicago politicians of the 1920's.** Wants posters, pamphlets, photographs, and buttons from Chicago politicians of the prohibition era such as mayors William Thompson, William Dever, and Anton Cermak. Also Illinois Governor Len Small, US Senator Charles Deneen, and Cook County States Attorney Robert Crowe. Especially wants items related to prohibition and gangsters. If offering personal items, documentation will be requested.

>Michael Graham's Roaring 20's
>33133 O'Plaine Road
>Gurnee, IL 60031
>(708) 263-6285

☆ **Tennessee and other Southern political items.** Interested primarily in races for Senate, Congress and Governor in any Southern state. Pictorial buttons a favorite. Xerox© what you have.

>Peggy Dillard
>PO Box 210904
>Nashville, TN 37221
>(615) 646-1605

☆ **North and South Carolina political buttons and ephemera** with a special interest in locating items from Taft's 1909 visit to Charlotte. Asks that you photocopy and describe all defects.

>Lew Powell
>700 East Park Ave.
>Charlotte, NC 28203
>(704) 358-5229 or (704) 334-0902

☆ **Canadian election memorabilia,** pin back buttons and badges from Canadian political campaigns before 1965, especially material on John MacDonald and Wilfred Laurier. Small items may be sent on approval. If Mike does not buy them, he will reimburse your postage.

>Michael Rice
>PO Box 286
>Saanichton, BC
>V8M 2C5 CANADA

POLITICAL SYMBOLS

☆ **Flags.** Wants European, African, and all other obsolete foreign or domestic flags. Also buys some current U.S. state flags and all city flags. "I will consider just about any real flag, military, yachting, naval, or other, as long as it is priced appropriately, but I don't want 48 star flags or decorative banners and other tricolor bunting." Although rare flags exist, most flags bring $5 to $100. To sell your flag, provide dimensions, a guess at the material, any info about the flag's history, photo or sketch. As a point of interest, he notes, "Family oral history to the contrary, 13 star flags seldom date from the Revolution. Most were Centennial souvenirs dating from 1876, or they were Naval flags."

> Jon Radel
> PO Box 2276
> Reston, VA 22090

☆ **American flags.** "I'll buy cloth hand held size (smaller than 3') American flags with 47 stars, 43 stars, and all flags with less than 39 stars. I especially want unusual star patterns and flags with advertising printed on them. Large flags considered. Description should include the size, condition, and star pattern. No repros or pictures of flags."

> Mark Sutton
> 2035 St. Andrews Circle
> Carmel, IN 46032
> (317) 844-5648

☆ **Statue of Liberty.** Wants French bronzes of the statue, books from before 1890, advertising items depicting or satirizing the statue, tin signs or containers, bottles, thimbles, lamps, medals and tokens, and other 19th century items related to Liberty or sculptor **Auguste Bartholdi**. Wants U.S. Committee 6" or 12" pot metal models sold to raise money for the pedestal and will pay $300 to $1,000. Wants early ones only. Photo or photocopy requested. Not interested in postcards or centennial items.

> Mike Brooks
> 7335 Skyline
> Oakland, CA 94611
> (510) 339-1751

☆ **Statue of Liberty items.** What have you? Send a photo or photocopy of what you have to this well known stamp dealer.

> Harvey Dolin & Company
> 5 Beekman Street #406
> New York, NY 10038

SOCIALISM & UNIONISM

☆ **Socialism and Communism in the U.S. before 1940.** "I'll buy anything pre-1940: books, magazines, leaflets, brochures, buttons, postcards, pennants, etc., that were produced by radical groups such as the Communist Party, Socialist Party, I.W.W. (Industrial Workers of the World), Socialist Labor Party, etc. Would especially like to find the magazines *Masses, New Masses,* and *International Socialist Review."* Mike will purchase items written in Yiddish, Italian, and other foreign languages, but "I'm really not too interested in material not written in the U.S.A." What does Mike consider important? "Condition! Condition! Condition!"

> Michael Stephens
> 2310 Valley Street
> Berkeley, CA 94702
> (510) 843-2780

☆ **Labor union and Socialist material.** "I'll buy just about everything relating to organized labor, unions, and working people" including dues buttons and books, pins, convention and parade ribbons and badges, photographs of workers or unions, programs, contracts, labor trade cards, union magazines, books, and most any type of labor collectibles. "I'd like to find items about labor leaders, and the old and unusual from groups like the Knights of Labor, I.W.W., Railroad Brotherhood, AFL, and CIO. I'll consider anything but am most interested in learning about items before 1960."

> Scott Molloy
> 550 Usquepaugh Road
> West Kingston, RI 02892
> (401) 792-2239   (401) 782-3614

☆ **Cigar Maker's Union and Samuel Gompers.** "I'd like to know about anything from the Cigar Maker's Union or any of its top officers, including stamps, pamphlets, regulations, photographs, and letterhead." Does anyone have a letter by Samuel Gompers on CMIU stationery? Or a copy of the papers that dissolved the Union? Please include photocopies and price or ask for offer.

> Tony Hyman
> PO Box 3028
> Pismo Beach, CA 93448
> (805) 773-6777   Fax: (805) 773-8436

☆ **Atomic bombs, nuclear war, and the anti-nuclear movement** from the 1950's to mid-60's. Wants all information, official and anti-bomb, including stuff on CONELRAD, civil defense, government pamphlets on atomic survival, books, comic books, and anything else from that period on atomic bombs and survival, including postcards of the bomb tests. Would love to find a copy of the book *How to Build an Atomic Bomb in Your Kitchen* by Bob Bale. Also "funky" atomic bomb stuff from the 1950's and mid-60's.

> Edy Chandler
> PO Box 20664
> Houston, TX 77225
> (713) 531-9615 eves

☆ **Radical movements' paper ephemera** from Tories of the American Revolution, the social and political radicals of the 1800's, the labor unionists, women's suffrage, etc., right down to and including the Black activists, Peace movement, and other "hippies" of the 1960's. Wants letters, documents, posters, broadsides, books, and pamphlets.

> Ivan Gilbert
> Miran Arts & Books
> 2824 Elm Ave.
> Columbus, OH 43209
> (614) 421-3222

☆ **Civil rights movement.** Wants buttons and paper ephemera, flyers, handbills, and pamphlets related to the civil rights movement.

> Peggy Dillard
> PO Box 210904
> Nashville, TN 37221
> (615) 646-1605

☆ **Slave tags.** These were small metal tags worn by slaves to indicate their status or occupation. Pays $200-$600 and up for tags reading SERVANT, PORTER, MECHANIC, SEAMSTRESS, FISHERMAN, FRUITERER, etc. Some rare types, dates, styles, or occupations can bring $1,500 or more. Call collect or ship insured for his offer. *Do not* clean the tags.

> Rich Hartzog
> Box 4143 BFT
> Rockford, IL 61110
> (815) 226-0771 Fax: (815) 397-7662

MISC. HISTORIC EPHEMERA

☆ **British Royalty.** Buys souvenirs, tins, plates, mugs, medals, busts, postcards and programs from various ceremonies and events involving British royalty from Queen Victoria to Queen Elizabeth Reign. Also wants commemorative souvenirs from special events involving Prince Charles and Princess Diana. Wants pictorial items. Audrey is the author of *British Royal Commemoratives*, available from her for $25.

    Audrey Zeder
    6755 Coralite T
    Long Beach, CA 90808
       (310) 421-0881

☆ **British and European Royalty.** "Try me with whatever you have that's colorful, interesting, and in fine condition. No junk, no plastic, and nothing damaged."

    Pat Klein
    PO Box 262
    East Berlin, CT 06023
       (203) 828-3973 eves

☆ **All fraternal order** materials that are small and flat, such as coins, tokens, medals, badges and ribbons. Especially interested in Masonic chapter pennies and hand engraved badges of precious metal. Will consider larger BPOE items or unusual fraternal items. If what you have is pre-1930, ship it to him for an offer. Hartzog will send you a check for the lot. He claims to pay higher prices than anyone else.

    Rich Hartzog
    PO Box 4143 BFT
    Rockford, IL 61110

☆ **Odd Fellows items** including badges, medals, banners, posters, jewelry, furniture, arks, collars, signs, windows, lighting fixtures, rugs, and anything else with the three link emblem on it.

    Greg Spiess
    230 East Washington
    Joliet, IL 60433
       (815) 722-5639 days

☆ **Mafia or organized crime items** including books, **magazines**, photographs, autographs, videotapes, recordings, government reports, and any other memorabilia or artifacts. "I'd love to find a poster from the Italian American Civil Rights League meeting of June 28th, 1971." Wants nothing fictional.

    Ron Ridenour
    PO Box 357
    Moorpark, CA 93020
       (800) 457-7473 days

☆ **Spy material.** Will consider anything you have related to real spies, from any country, any period: documents, signatures, photos, etc.
> Keith Melton
> PO Box 5755
> Bossier City, LA 71171
> (318) 747-9616

☆ **Newsboy statues** around the U.S. including souvenir replicas, advertising for the figurines, and photos of any statue of a newsboy. Replicas of the statues bring $50 or more.
> Gary Leveille
> PO Box 562
> Great Barrington, MA 01239

☆ **3-D metal replicas of famous buildings and monuments.** Buys paperweights, banks, salt and pepper shakers, ashtrays...anything that is made of metal into a three dimensional representation of a famous place or structure. He does not want miniatures that you can buy today: Eiffel tower, US Capitol, Empire State building, Statue of Liberty, etc. Identify the building, give the dimensions, and report any names or marks on the piece.
> Dave Forman
> 1914 11th Street #3
> Santa Monica, CA 90404
> (310) 396-1272

☆ **Eastman Colleges.** "I'll buy anything you can find on Eastman Colleges, including postcards, books, paper ephemera, money, etc."
> Gus Meccarello
> 228 Vassar Road
> Poughkeepsie, NY 12603

IMMIGRATION EPHEMERA

☆ **Immigration memorabilia.** "I'll buy documents, photos, passports, pre-1920 naturalization certificates, books, postcards, and other material related to immigrants, Immigrant Aid Societies, Immigrant Social and Political Clubs, Ellis Island, Castle Garden, and ethnic festivals before 1950." Has particular interest in **Chinese immigration memorabilia,** and will consider purchase of anything having to do with movement of Chinese in the U.S. prior to 1950, including items related to Chinese laundries and Chinese social and political clubs. Also Immigration and Naturalization Service forms and documents from before 1930. Photocopy please.

K. Sheeran
PO Box 520251
Miami, FL 33152

☆ **Immigrant and ethnic stereotypes** of Jews, Orientals, Scandinavians, French, Poles, Russians, and other immigrants printed before 1920. They want stereotypes on prints, photos, valentines, postcards, magazines, posters, sheet music, trade cards, and what have you. They want Blacks only if shown with immigrant characters. Subject matter can include life in their country of origin, arrival, settlement, assimilation, etc. Not interested in reproductions, native costume, *Harper's Weekly* material, or general articles on immigration. They prefer photocopy of priced items. Don't send unsolicited material, please.

John and Selma Appel
219 Oakland Drive
East Lansing, MI 48823
(517) 337-1859

BLACK & NEGRO MEMORABILIA

☆ **Items depicting Blacks in an exaggerated, comic or derogatory manner** "I'll buy anything made before 1920 with Black Americans (not African natives) such as minstrel posters, spoons, toys, advertising, figurines, sheet music, postcards, trade cards, and the like." Emphasizes that he does not want reproductions. This authority on Black American items wants a careful description of condition.

> Sam Ginsberg
> PO Box 24944
> Ft. Lauderdale, FL 33307
> (305) 564-0147 voice and fax

☆ **Items depicting Blacks in an exaggerated, comic or stereotypical way** including cookie jars, older dolls, toys, kitchen items, prints, Black folk art, *Uncle Remus*, advertising items, *Aunt Jemima*, *Cream of Wheat*, *Amos 'n Andy*, and "all items relating to Blacks in America. Buys one piece or a collection."

> Judy Posner
> Rural Route 1   Box 273
> Effort, PA 18330
> (717) 629-6583 anytime

☆ **All items depicting Blacks** in a manner that is exaggerated, comic, or patronizing including dolls, folk art, sewing items, walking sticks, miniature bronzes, jewelry, paintings, valentines, playing cards, games, children's books, cookie jars, string holders, small advertising items, souvenir spoons, *Golliwogs*, linens, jigsaw puzzles, candy containers, Christmas ornaments, and items associated with the *Our Gang* comedy's Farina. No postcards, sheet music, trade cards, photos, outhouse figures, ads, large signs, damaged items, or reproductions. This active dealer/collector does not make offers.

> Jan Thalberg
> 23 Mountain View Drive
> Weston, CT 06883
> (203) 227-8175

☆ **Black memorabilia** that is comic or exaggerated including cookie jars, plates, lamps, clocks, salt and pepper shakers, table cloths, towels, plaster or ceramic items, and other household items depicting Blacks. "I also buy advertising pieces of all kinds that depict a Black person, including whiskey ads, *Aunt Jemima* items, *Cream of Wheat* packs, *Uncle Ben's Rice* memorabilia, etc."

> Diane Cauwels
> 3947 Old South Road
> Murfreesboro, TN 37129
> (615) 896-3614

☆ **Items depicting Blacks in an exaggerated, comic or derogatory manner** made between 1800 and 1960. Images of mammies, chefs, *Uncle Tom*, picaninnies, *Aunt Jemima*, butlers, *Topsy*, and other Pop Culture portrayals are wanted in almost any form:
- **Folk art** and primitives including rag dolls, whirligigs, etc.;
- **Figural kitchen items,** tea pots, pitchers, sugar bowls, etc., especially large faced items and Black cookie jars;
- **Mammy and chef salt shakers** with matching stove grease jars and mammy tea pots with wire handles;
- **Ceramic jugs** by *Weller*;
- **Plastic cookie jars**, sugar bowls, syrup jugs, etc., from *F&F Die Works* or marked LUZIANNE;
- **Humidors and bisque figurines** from Europe or Japan;
- **Papier-maché**, composition and glass **figurals** such as candy containers and Xmas ornaments depicting Blacks;
- **Advertising** on paper or tin, trade cards, die-cuts, packaging, and cereal boxes such as *Cream of Wheat* and *Korn Kinks,* and all *Aunt Jemima* products and ads;
- **Games of all types** which feature Blacks even if parts missing.

Needs a detailed description of colors, size, condition, place of origin and manufacturer's name. Clear close up photo or photocopy is strongly urged. Describe all damage, chips, stains, tears, faded spots, repairs, or missing pieces. Wants to know the color of skin (prefers black to brown) and expression on face. On pottery pieces, describe whether surface is shiny or matte (flat).

> Mary Anne Enriquez
> 1741 West Albion Street
> Chicago, IL 60626
> (312) 243-3425

☆ **Popular portrayals of Black dancers** on sheet music, figurines, postcards, etc. Wants dancers doing the cake walk, jitterbug, etc.

> William Sommer
> 9 West 10th Street
> New York, NY 10011
> (212) 260-0999

☆ **Malcolm X ephemera** such as letters, copies of speeches, autographs, and personal items. Photocopy what you have to offer.
Eric Mizrahi
11 Forest Ave.
Framingham, MA 01701

☆ **Racism and the civil rights movement.** "I'll buy buttons, posters, and other ephemeral items having to do with Martin Luther King, but no newspapers, magazines, or damaged items."
Peggy Dillard
PO Box 210904
Nashville, TN 37221
(615) 646-1605 after 4pm CST

KU KLUX KLAN EPHEMERA

☆ **K.K.K. items** of all type, including robes, swords, pamphlets, jewelry, knives, badges, medals, china, banners, books, letters, newspapers, magazines, figurines, rituals, etc. The buyer is a serious historian of this movement, not a Klan member. Please, no hate mail.
Historical Collections
PO Box 42
Waynesboro, PA 17268

☆ **Ku Klux Klan** paper, documents, photos, and small items.
Steve DeGenaro
PO Box 5662
Youngstown, OH 44504

☆ **Items related to Ku Klux Klan activity in the U.S.,** especially the Midwest, during the 1920's.
Michael Graham's Roaring 20's
33133 O'Plaine Road
Gurnee, IL 60031
(708) 263-6285

INDIAN ARTIFACTS

☆ **Antique American Indian and Eskimo items.** "I'll buy quality items made by Indians and Eskimos: baskets, bead work, quill work, pottery, clothing, weapons, old Navajo rugs, and blankets. If you've got a 16 foot long birch bark canoe I'll buy that too. I don't buy any Indian jewelry, books, or modern items purchased ten years ago at a trading post on the Interstate." A photo is a must, and please list dimensions and any flaws the piece has in your first letter. Dealers, price your goods, as he makes offers to amateur sellers only. Answers inquiries promptly. Veteran collector is advisor on Indian collectibles to several antiques publications.

> Barry Friedman
> 22725 Garzota Drive
> Valencia, CA 91355
> (805) 296-2318

☆ **Indian artifacts** including arrowheads, stone axes, celts, pipes, flints, ceremonial pieces, bannerstones, birdstones, baskets, beaded items, pottery, rugs, blankets, masks, wooden bowls, and any other Indian related items. He will pay high prices ($500-$1,000) for ancient birdstones he can use for his own collection. Please list what you have and make a drawing or photocopy, giving all measurements. Include your home and work phone. This 40 year veteran holds four to six auctions a year of Indian artifacts and is always ready to buy good items.

> Jan Sorgenfrei
> 10040 State Road 224 West
> Findlay, OH 45840
> (419) 422-8531 days

☆ **Indian arrow and spear heads** from Louisiana, Alabama, Mississippi, Florida, Georgia, South and North Carolina. He buys the following styles of "points" and especially likes those with "river varnish" brought up by Southern river divers: Simpson, Suwannee, Quad, Dalton, Wheeler, Bolen, Kirk, Pine Tree, Taylor, Hardaway, Palmer, Lost Lake, Decatur, Scottsbluff, and Pelican or San Patrice. He wants points from the Southeastern US, so other areas are not of interest, except he will buy Folsom points made anywhere in North America. "I do not collect rechipped points or points illegally collected from Federal or State property. You must be able to tell me how and where you obtained the points you have for sale, at least as to state of origin. Values range from $25 to $500. Photos helpful and will be returned."

> Charles Ray
> PO Box 881
> Winchester, KY 40392
> (606) 744-9789

*The value of an Indian artifact depends
on its size, age, condition, workmanship,
eye appeal and authenticity.
Because values can be quite high,
it's a good idea to check out all
Indian items which have been in your
family since before World War II.*

☆ **Museum quality American Indian relics.** "I'll buy fine baskets, pre-1900 Plains bead work, quill work, weapons, Southwestern pots, pre-1950 jewelry, Kachinas, Navajo blankets and rugs, Northwest Coast masks and carvings, Eskimo objects, old photos of Indians, and more. Some of these items can be worth $10,000 or more." Dan does not want anything modern, small pots, or reproductions of early work.

> Daniel Brown
> PO Box 149
> Davenport, CA 95017
>   (408) 426-0134

☆ **Hopi and Zuni Pueblo Kachina dolls.** "I especially want those made between 1900 and 1940. Other Indian items, dance wands, costume parts, pottery, baskets, and jewelry from Southwest Indians are also of interest." Kachina dolls can range in value from $100 to $5,000 or more, but there are many fake Kachinas. "An expert can tell the difference." He'll need a photo and all background information.

> John C. Hill
> 6962 East First Ave.
> Scottsdale, AZ 85251
>   (602) 946-2910

☆ **Indian baskets, pottery and other art** are wanted by this nationally known folk art expert.

> Louis Picek
> PO Box 340
> West Branch, IA 52358

☆ **North and South American Indian rugs** and weavings are sought by this major rug dealer. Color photo and dimensions, please.

> Renate Halpern
> Halpern Galleries
> 325 East 79th Street
> New York, NY 10021

☆ **American Indian and Eskimo art and artifacts,** including rugs, crafts, baskets, pottery, weapons, and clothing, especially old beaded buckskin moccasins. The museum does not buy modern Indian items. Prefers a color photo be sent with your inquiry. Prefers you price what you have to sell, but "our appraiser will suggest a value for your item, but only after examination of it in person."

> Lynn Munger
> Potawatomi Museum
> PO Box 631
> Fremont, IN 46737
> (219) 495-2340

☆ **Indian stone animal effigy pipes.** He has no interest in reproductions, but says he'll to pay from $100 to as much as $10,000 for well documented pipes. Photos are advisable.

> Mel Rosenthal
> 5 The Strand
> New Castle, DE 19720
> (302) 322-8944   (302) 322-3030

☆ **Indian totems and carvings** from before 1950, including good quality items made for the tourist trade. Please provide a physical description, noting all obvious signs of damage. If you know the history of the ownership of the item, please give that information as well. Photos are helpful.

> Edwin Snyder
> PO Box 156
> Lancaster, KY 40444
> (606) 792-4816 eves

COWBOY ARTIFACTS

☆ **Silver mounted parade saddles and spurs** by all makers, especially G. S. Garcia, Edward H. Bohlin or Visalia Stock Saddle Company. Always seeking quality cowboy items, such as fancy antique chaps and boots. Please send complete details along with a photo. This veteran collector is Indian/Western advisor to several antique publications.

> Barry Friedman
> 22725 Garzota Drive
> Valencia, CA 91355
> (805) 296-2318

☆ **Cowboy equipment and regalia** including:
- **Spurs** of all types except English and new military. Especially wants unusual spurs that are silver and maker marked;
- **Cuffs** made of leather, chaps, hats, scarves, and fancy boots;
- **Western saddles**, pre-1920, all types if maker marked, including black military McClellan saddles;
- **Saddle bags** with maker's marks;
- **Reatas, quirts,** and **bridles** that are marked, tooled, or carved;
- **Horse bits** more than 50 years old with silver mounts or inlay; some plain and/or foreign bought; inquire about any old bit;
- **Prison made spurs**, horse bits, quirts, belts, and lead ropes;
- **Catalogs for saddle makers** pre-1936;
- **Photographs** of old cowboy scenes;
- **Advertising related to the frontier**, especially watch fobs;
- **Movie posters** of cowboy movies;
- **Books by Will James**.

Especially wants marked spurs authenticated as having been made for some well known personality. Does not want anything made in the last 25 years or made in the Far East. In your description, make certain to describe all marks. Give dimensions and mention all damage or repairs. He prefers you to set the price, but will make offers to amateur sellers. No guns! Will buy single items or collections for resale.

> Lee Jacobs
> PO Box 3098
> Colorado Springs, CO 80934
>   (719) 473-7101

☆ **Cowboy gear** from before 1940 including Western guns, chaps, spurs, bits, brand books, law badges, saddles, reatas, quirts, cowboy hats, boots, vests, neckerchiefs, leather cuffs, early knives, beaded or embroidered gauntlets, and fine braided bridles or other items. Also wants old related catalogs, photos, documents, books, maps, and other items related to the life of the cowboy. He is most interested in spurs, holsters and cartridge belts which have maker's marks. Exceptional items can bring many thousands of dollars. Send a good photo and a description of your item, including a statement of condition. This 30 year veteran collector and museum curator, does not want horse collars, harnesses, and other farm related items. Bill's *Cowboy and Gunfighter Collectibles*, complete with price guide, is $22.

> Bill Mackin
> Museum of Northwest Colorado
> 1137 Washington Street
> Craig, CO 81625
>   (303) 824-6717

☆ **Cowboy clothing, gear, artifacts** and **ephemera.** Wants everything associated with both working cowboys and badmen and peace officers: clothing, trail maps and brand books, wanted posters, "historically important letters," photos of cowboys, badmen, and peace officers. Has strong interest in anything you have relevant to the lives of **Samuel Colt, Sam Houston** and **Benito Juarez.**

> Johnny Spellman
> 10806 North Lamar
> Austin, TX 78753
>   (512) 836-2889 days   (512) 258-6910 eves

☆ **Antique cowboy regalia** such as chaps, holsters, belts, badges, saddles, hats, boots, and lassos. Also buys *Colt* and *Winchester* guns and rifles pre-1900. No reproductions or fakes. Wants to know where you got your item(s). You must include photo and your asking price, and will be expected to ship for inspection. He does not make offers.

> Pierre Bovis
> The Az-Tex Cowboy Trading Co.
> PO Box 460
> Tombstone, AZ 85638
>   (602) 457-3359 voice and fax

☆ **Steer horns** from the 1930's or earlier. "Older horns are wrapped in various types of old cloth, buggy seat material, or natural hair. The wrapped center piece will usually be no more than 12" or 13" wide. Old horns will usually be various shades of yellow, brown, or dark green, frequently with black tips. Newer horns, **which I absolutely do not want**, are wrapped in tooled leather, vinyl or rope and are usually ivory or a mottled color. Newer ones also have wide, often 18" space between horns. The best old horns have heavy amounts of twist and curl, are mounted on a wood backboard, and are five to seven feet wide from tip to tip. The wrapping on most old horns is frequently in poor condition, so I am much more concerned with the condition of the horns themselves, with no cracks or serious bug damage. A photo is a must. Include the measurements from tip to tip and the measurements across the middle piece where the cow's skull would have been. If you can't send a color photo, make certain to describe the twist and the color of the horns, as well as the type of material." He also wants to buy **photographs of longhorn cattle.**

> Alan Rogers
> 1012 Shady Drive
> Kansas City, MO 64118
>   (816) 436-9008

EPHEMERA OF FAMOUS PEOPLE

☆ **Carrie Nation memorabilia** including vinegar bottles in her carica-ture, souvenir hatchet pins, photos, tickets to lectures, *The Hatchet*, newspaper articles about her, and *anything* else. You find it and you've got a buyer here if it's in any decent condition at all.

>Steve Chyrchel
>Route #2 Box 362
>Eureka Springs, AR 72632
>>(501) 253-9244 voice and fax

☆ **Stalin, Hitler, and Mussolini** items, especially those from the 1920's and 1930's, are bought. Wants documented personal effects, au-tographs, letters, photos and some magazine and newspaper accounts. Also **Al Capone** and **other Chicago prohibition era figures,** both good guys and bad guys, including gangsters, police chiefs, State attor-neys, FBI men, Elliott Ness, etc. Particularly interested in Capone and will pay from $50 to $1,000 depending on what you have, its condition, and its documentation. If offering personal items such as clothing, guns, jewelry or letters, you should phone and be prepared to discuss.

>Michael Graham
>33133 O'Plaine Road
>Gurnee, IL 60031
>>(708) 263-6285

☆ **John "Johnny Appleseed" Chapman memorabilia** including books and personal items. He's looking for artifacts from the real Johnny Appleseed, not the Disney cartoon character.

>Frederic Janson, Pomona Book Exchange
>Rockton PO, Ontario
>L0R 1X0 CANADA

☆ **Commodore Matthew Perry material** including autographs, letters, and manuscripts, especially any artifacts or documents related to his expedition to Japan.

>Jerrold Stanoff, Rare Oriental Book Co.
>PO Box 1599
>Aptos, CA 95001
>>(408) 724-4911   Fax: (408) 761-1350

☆ **L. Ron Hubbard collectibles** such as books, photos, documents, pulp magazines, and other ephemera. She does not want ratty condition pulp magazines or books reprinted after 1960 unless autographed. Pho-tocopy small items and send standard bibliographic information on books. Some autographed books are worth up to $5,000 each to her.

>Karen Jentzsch Barta
>1420 Colby Drive
>Glendale, CA 91205

☆ **Frank Lloyd Wright material** including drawings, furniture, letters, photographs, books, smaller publications, and other ephemera.
J.B. Muns' Fine Arts Books
1162 Shattuck Ave.
Berkeley, CA 94707
(510) 525-2420

☆ **Samuel Gompers ephemera** from before 1886 is sought, particularly items related to his career as a cigar maker or an NYC union officer, but please inquire about *any* Gompers item.
Tony Hyman
PO Box 3028
Pismo Beach, CA 93448

☆ **Lillie Langtry memorabilia** including photos, cigarette and trade cards, letters, programs, posters, tickets, costume or set sketches, and cosmetics issued under her name. Wants a wine label produced on Langtry Farms, 1889-1906, worth up to $500. Langtry was also known as Langtree, the Jersey Lily, Lady Lillie de Bathe, Mrs. Jersey, and Emilie Charlotte Le Breton. In addition to his interest in Mrs. Langtry, he also wants material on **Edward Langtry** and **Freddie Gebhard(t)**.
Orville Magoon
PO Box 279
Middletown, CA 95461
(707) 987-2385 days   Fax: (707) 987-9351

☆ **John Steinbeck** memorabilia, signed limited editions, first editions, first printings by subsequent publishers, appearances in anthologies, spoken word records and tapes, film and theater memorabilia, and things owned by him. Does not want book club editions, items in poor condition, or fakes. If a book originally had a dust jacket, slipcase, box or wrap-around, then it should still be present. Be specific about what you have, giving complete bibliographic information.
James Dourgarian, Bookman
1595-A Third Avenue
Walnut Creek, CA 94596
(510) 935-5033

☆ **Mark Twain memorabilia**, autographs, photos, stories about, books about, and especially first editions of his books, "but no books that are falling apart." Include the color of the cover when providing standard bibliographic information.
Duane and Eunice Bietz
6461 SE Thorburn
Portland, OR 97215
Fax: (503) 233-1602

☆ **Edgar Rice Burroughs and Tarzan.** Wants rare items related to stories and characters created by Edgar Rice Burroughs, including:
  • Hardback books, reprints with dust jackets or 1st editions with or w/out dust jackets (1st editions in dj's of *Tarzan of the Apes* and *Return of Tarzan* are worth $1,000+; others much less);
  • Pulp magazines, 1912 to 1919, featuring ERB stories;
  • Original *Tarzan* art by Ray Kuenkel, J. Allen St. John, Hogarth, Frank Schoonover, and Hal Foster;
  • Autographed items by ERB or by early movie Tarzans;
  • Toys, games and premiums before 1950;
  • Movie posters and lobby cards before 1945.
Does not want reprint hardbacks without dust jackets, paperbacks, recent comic books, or anything in poor condition. Make certain to include the publisher when describing a book. Give your phone number. Dealers must price your goods, but amateurs may request an offer.
> Jim Gerlach
> 2206 Greenbrier Drive
> Irving, TX 75060
>   (214) 790-0922

☆ **Jack London memorabilia, books** and **personal effects.**
> Winifred Kingman, Jack London Bookstore
> PO Box 337
> Glen Ellen, CA 95442
>   (707) 996-2888   (707) 996-4107

SHERLOCK HOLMES

☆ **Sherlock Holmes**, particularly rare and unusual. Wants pre-1930 books, early magazines, games, pamphlets, non-book three dimensional items, and "curious items." If items are very rare, they may date after 1930 and still be of interest. John is a Baker Street Irregular, owns 12,000 Holmes items, and is well known as a Holmes authority.
> John Bennett Shaw
> 1917 Fort Union Drive
> Santa Fe, NM 87501
>   (505) 982-2947

☆ **Sherlock Holmes.** Wants "anything related to Sherlock Holmes or **Sir Arthur Conan Doyle**" including figurines, drawings, autographs, posters, photos, etc. He wants books, but only first editions. Also wants ephemera from **actors who have played Holmes** including Nigel Bruce, Basil Rathbone and William Gillette.
> Robert Hess
> 559 Potter Blvd.
> Brightwaters, NY 11718
>   (516) 665-8365

WEIRD & MORBID THINGS

☆ **Anything odd, unusual** or **morbid,** especially:
- **Two headed calves** and other **freak animals,** natural or man-made, alive or mounted and preserved;
- **Mummies, skeletons** and **human skulls;**
- **Shrunken heads** and other **headhunter** and **cannibal items;**
- **Funeral equipment,** coffins, embalming kits, and **tombstones;**
- **Torture** and **execution devices** and photos of executions;
- **Mounted reptiles, trophy heads** and **uncommon animals;**
- **Man-made mermaids** (up to $300);
- **Medicine show** photos and literature;
- **Tattoo equipment,** tattoo photos, and tattooed skin;
- **Voodoo** and **black magic** ephemera;
- **Flea Circus** props and photos;
- **Human oddity** photos and artifacts.

For 50+ years, this wheelchair bound vet has been buying odd, unusual, and bizarre items for public exhibit in his traveling and stationary museums. He does not buy furniture, clothing, plates, or jewelry. If you have something you think he might want, send a photo, a description, a statement of condition, and your lowest price.

    Harvey Lee Boswell's Palace of Wonders
    PO Box 446
    Elm City, NC 27822
        (919) 291-7181

☆ **Giant people.** "I'll buy postcards, pictures and other information about American giants (not the sports team, but real giants) including giant rings, souvenirs sold by giants, books by or about giants, etc."

    Don Gorlick
    PO Box 24541
    Seattle, WA 98124
        (206) 824-0508

☆ **Skulls, skeletons, tusks, teeth, fossils, shrunken heads** and **mounted insects.** This relatively new dealer does not make offers.

    Ronald Cauble, The Bone Room
    1569 Solano Ave
    Berkeley, CA 94707
        (510) 526-5252

☆ **Animal trophies, skulls,** skins, fur rugs, teeth, claws, horns, antlers, and the like. Please give your phone number with your description.

    David Boone's Trading Company
    562 Coyote Road
    Brinnon, WA 98320
        (206) 796-4330   Fax: (206) 796-4511

☆ **Funeral ephemera.** "I'll buy things having to do with funerals such as funeral parlor advertising, mirrors, ribbons, trays, badges, and other items issued by funeral parlors. I am not interested in caskets, funeral or embalming equipment, or cemeteries."

> Rich Hartzog
> PO Box 4143 BFT
> Rockford, IL 61110
> (815) 226-0771 Fax: (815) 397-7662

☆ **Cemetery ephemera.** "I'll buy books, maps, magazines, photos, catalogs, deeds, etc., related to the cemetery business, especially:
- Cemetery advertising from before 1920;
- Maps and deeds of cemeteries, before 1900;
- Sales catalogs for mausoleums, before 1940;
- Photos and real photo postcards of mausoleums;
- Magazines like *The Cemetery Beautiful*;
- Burial society certificates, before 1940.

Since these are paper items, include a photocopy. "Do not confuse cemeteries with funerals. I am interested in land, monuments, and mausoleums, not funerals and embalming. The only funeral item I want is *The American Funeral Gazette* from the early 1880's." Not interested in colored photo postcards of famous tombs or cemeteries.

> Steve Spevak
> PO Box 3173
> Winchester, VA 22604

☆ **Human hair mourning pieces.** Human hair jewelry with black "beads" worked in, or human hair woven into wreaths, mounted in frames with photos worked in. Also buys **wicker or wooden caskets**. "Wicker ones were used for display of bodies at wakes and funerals. The bodies were removed and buried in plain pine boxes. Want wooden caskets that are dove-tailed, made of odd woods, tapered, or with face plates." Describe as well as you can, giving dimensions. Interested in buying **photos of caskets** with bodies on display.

> Steve DeGenaro
> PO Box 5662
> Youngstown, OH 44504

☆ **Human hair wreaths.** Wants wreaths made of human hair, either framed or unframed. Also patterns from old women's magazines for weaving human hair wreaths. If you have a family pattern for hair weaving, she'd like to learn it from you. Please send a photograph. Dealers must set their price. Amateurs may request help from this veteran fine arts appraiser and lecturer.

> Monica Murphy, Savannah's Antiques
> 9337 Lenel Place
> Dallas, TX 75220
> (214) 352-4137

MISCELLANEOUS

☆ **Hand bells.** Wants rare and unusual hand bells including:
- Figural bronze or brass;
- Oriental, especially with enamel;
- Historical, religious, and town crier's;
- Glass, especially colored glass;
- Silver, especially highly decorated, including rattles;
- Porcelain and china, such as *Royal Beyreuth*;
- Mechanical or tap bells that are unusual.

Does not want large bells, but will consider any unusual small hand bell except school bells, cow or other animal bells, sleigh bells, "collectible series" bells, and bells made in India. Give the size, weight, color, and markings. Photo a good idea. She offers five different books on bells priced from $11 to $14 postpaid.

> Dorothy Anthony
> World of Bells
> 802 South Eddy
> Fort Scott, KS 66701
> (316) 223-3404

☆ **Large bells,** especially cast bronze church, mission, train, boat, and school bells are bought, sold and installed. The country's largest broker in used bells buys and sells a wide range of bells, but is not interested in glass bells or "the little ting-a-ling type." Write or call if buying or selling larger bells. You will be expected to state the price you want for your bell as he does not give free appraisals or make offers.

> Charles Brosamer's Bells
> 207 Irwin Street
> Brooklyn, MI 49230
> (517) 592-9030 or (517) 592-6885

☆ **Items that look like something they're not.** "I am always looking for the odd, the unusual, and the curious, and don't hesitate to buy things that require an explanation. I like pens that look like mummies, dice cups that look like bullets, cigarette lighters that look like guns or pencils, compacts that look like 8-balls or watches, and what have you. Most of these things are not of great value, but the variety is endless, so describe what you have carefully, include a Xerox™ when you can, and I will make an offer. I like anything that isn't what it seems to be."

> Betty Bird
> Antiques, Etc.
> 107 Ida Street
> Mt. Shasta, CA 96067

☆ **Miniatures.** "I buy miniatures that will fit in a doll house (but not limited to dollhouse things). I also want children's size dishes, castor sets, hats in hatboxes, and almost anything else that is child size but not necessarily created for children." She cautions you to bear in mind that this takes in a vast area, and there are many reproductions (which she does not want). Mint condition is a must. "I love tiny things that are odd and unusual."

> Betty Bird
> Antiques, Etc.
> 107 Ida Street
> Mt. Shasta, CA 96067

☆ **Hear no evil, see no evil, speak no evil figurines** are sought by this collector. Although not particularly valuable, she would like to hear from you if you have one for sale, and will make a fair offer. Describe the size, material, any markings on the bottom, and information about where you got it, if possible. Lois also buys some single figurines of monkeys. Most aren't particularly valuable, "but they make me laugh."

> Lois Dwyer
> 2027 East Genesee #3
> Syracuse, NY 13201
> (315) 476-1014

☆ **Mermaids and mermen.** "I will consider any item, made of porcelain, china, metal, stone, or paper which has a mermaid, merman, or merbaby motif. The item must be old and unusual, but may be advertising, folk art, scrimshaw, jewelry, bottles, and what have you. I don't want Japanese bisque, anything new, or anything cracked or broken. Indicate the size, markings, and condition as part of your description.

> Stephanie Schnatz
> 17 Tallow Court
> Baltimore, MD 21244
> (410) 955-5910 days   (410) 944-0819 eves

☆ **Billikens.** Naked sitting pot-bellied figures with the bottoms of their feet facing you. Promoted as the god of things as they ought to be, or the god of happiness, luck, etc. Found in a variety of sizes and materials. Wants original 1908-1910 Billikens as featured on flatware, ice cream molds, charms, jewelry, dolls, games, banks, thimbles, toothpick holders, postcards, and all other items in the shape of Billikens. No jade or tusk Billikens, which are more modern items from Alaska.

> Judy Knauer
> 1224 Spring Valley Lane
> West Chester, PA 19380
> (610) 431-3477

☆ **Mannequins** from the Victorian era to the 1950's. "I'll buy heads or full body figures, in any size. I do not want plastic items, reproductions, or anything modern. Please send me a photo."
> Gwen Daniel
> 18 Belleau Lake Court
> O'Fallon, MO 63366
>> (314) 281-3190 anytime

☆ **Mannequin heads (department store dummies)** from before 1960. Female fashion window display torsos and full figures in full or miniature sizes. Older items especially desired, and molded hair "is a plus." He does not want items made after 1960 or items that are "damaged beyond repair." List the name of the manufacturer, the size, the condition, and the approximate date of manufacture.
> Art Dalessandro
> 523 Race Place
> Oakdale, NY 11769
>> (516) 563-3747

☆ **Hands.** "I'll buy wooden hands with fingers that move, generally used as glove stretchers, and **Palmistry hands** showing lines, zones, and mounds. I'm looking for wood or ceramic, not paper items."
> Don Gorlick
> PO Box 24541
> Seattle, WA 98124

☆ **Carved shells**, especially cowrie shells with the Lord's Prayer, personalized messages and/or dates, cities, foreign places with pictures (often sold as souvenirs), or events such as World's Fairs. "I buy any condition, any age, but do not want current souvenir shells made in the Philippines with zodiac signs and poor carvings of dolphins or fish done as souvenirs for coastal towns. I will buy modern items, but the quality of the carving must be exceptional." Values range from $5 to $50 or more.
> Vicki Tori
> 711 Oak Drive
> Capitola, CA 95010
>> (408) 479-7711

☆ **Pressed wood items.** Wants medals, plaques, political items, advertising tokens, illustrated checkers and other small items made of pressed wood. Does not want wooden nickels or flat wooden "paper money" used in promotions.
> Donald Tritt
> 4072 Goose Lane
> Granville, OH 43023
>> (614) 587-0213 eves

☆ **3-D items of all sorts** including:
- Any 3-D cameras, viewers, and projectors;
- *Viewmaster* views from before 1982;
- *Tru-Vue* filmstrips and viewers, but not *Tru-Vue* cards;
- 3-D color slides from the 40's;
- 3-D magazines and comic books from the 1950's;
- Stereoviews, especially of movie related subjects.

He would pay $300 for the stereoview card set from the 20's sold in Germany called "The Making of the Hunchback of Notre Dame" but has no interest in (1) stereoviews that are printed rather than actual photos, (2) stereoviews of scenery, (3) cartoon subjects, or (4) *Viewmaster* reels that are damaged or dirty. He needs to know the brand and model of equipment and the title, subject, and catalog number of reels and stereoviews. If you have original packet envelopes, boxes, instructions or other paper, make certain to note the fact. When offering views, you should understand that most of them are worth only $1-$5.

>Chris "Dr. 3-D" Perry
>306 Logenita Drive
>Palm Springs, CA 92264
>(619) 325-4530

☆ **Miniature pianos**. "I'm interested in child size real pianos as well as older miniature figurines of pianos, child-size player pianos and European jewelry boxes shaped like pianos. I'll even consider collector plates depicting pianos. I just started buying trade cards of piano manufacturers. I don't have any interest in the acrylic piano-shaped music boxes found in contemporary gift shops." When you write to her, a photo, along with any information you know about the item is helpful. "If I'm going to pass on the information to another club member, I need the seller's phone number to speed the process." Janice edits the quarterly newsletter for the Miniature Piano Enthusiasts Club ($10 a year).

>Janice Kelsh
>5815 North Sheridan Road #202
>Chicago, IL 60660
>(312) 271-2970

☆ **Puzzle bottles.** "I'll buy bottles that contain unusual items such as chairs, carved human figures, etc. I do not buy ships in bottles. Things in undamaged condition only, please. Photo suggested.

>Barry Friedman
>22725 Garzota Drive
>Valencia, CA 91355
>(805) 296-2318

RELIGIOUS ITEMS

☆ **Crucifixes, medals, Stars of David, and other symbols from any religion.** Wants a wide variety of items...interesting, unusual, precious, sentimental...anything you want preserved or displayed. Donated crosses and other items are preserved with your family name or other identification of your choice. "I can't afford to buy things as all my money is being set aside to build a religious museum. I'm hoping people will donate their items so they are preserved and cared for properly. I'm looking for an angel to subsidize a museum of religious artifacts and symbols." Send a stamped self-addressed envelope if you'd like an offer, response to a donation, an answer to a question regarding crosses, or simply more information about his goals.
>   Ernie Reda
>   3997 Latimer Ave.
>   San Jose, CA 95130

☆ **Catholic First Communion books.** "I'll buy small celluloid, mother-of-pearl, or ivory First Communion books and Catholic missals from the late 1800's to 1950, although the earlier ones are preferred. As long as the condition is near mint, will buy them in any language. Send photo and description with your asking price."
>   Monica Elliott Murphy
>   9337 Lenel Place
>   Dallas, TX 75220
>   (214) 352-4137

☆ **Catholic holy cards (religious cards) from pre-1940.** Holy cards are small decorated cards similar to trade cards, depicting various religious figures and events, usually beautifully printed. Prefers steel engravings and other quality pieces, "the older the better." Handmade ones particularly sought. "I do take donations of cards and do not resell them." Send your cards on approval, with the understanding that most cards are worth only 50¢ to $1 each, with a very few as high as $3, so keep expectations reasonable. Dealers, price your goods.

"People give cards to me because they know I'll preserve and take care of them, and give them the proper respect."

>   Mary Jo O'Neil
>   618 Riversedge Court
>   Mishawaka, IN 46544
>   (219) 259-0357

☆ **Catholic religious paper** such as **holy cards**, prayer cards, Infant of Prague materials, illustrated **prayer books**, religious school books, and visual aids, as long as they are before 1963. He does not want Bibles, postcards, items not made of paper, paper goods that are not illustrated, or items dating after 1963. Please, no Old Testament pictures or stories. Give the age, description, publisher, and condition. A photocopy is helpful. Sellers should note that these items are more spiritual than monetary in their value, but Joe does pledge to give your items a proper home.

 Joe Flynn
 PO Box 1473
 Greenwood Lake, NY 10925
  (914) 477-9373

☆ **Religious music, poetry and dance.** Wants hymnals, books, magazines, manuscripts, psalters, clippings, and original manuscripts (typed or handwritten, whether published or not) of religious music, poetry and dance notation or directions. May be in any language, but English is preferred. May be mixed collections of religious and secular music. Since these are "for use, not display, the appearance is unimportant" but items are preferred when complete. Values range from 25¢ to $300. He does not want Methodist hymnals after 1929, nor does he want reminisces or discussions about music, dance, poetry, values, ethics, social causes, or other religious topics. Give the exact title, edition or revision number, latest copyright date, editor or compiler, and indicate the total number of religious music or verse selections or number of pages. This non-profit group encourages donations.

 David Whitney
 The Pealing Chord
 8 Ellen Drive K.T.
 Wyoming, PA 18644
  (717) 696-2218

☆ **Methodist items** including histories, biographies, photos of preachers or churches, diaries, letters or manuscript material about Methodism, prints, placards, posters, sheet music, copies of the *Discipline* and *Hymnal* printed before 1850 as well as all Methodist publications such as *Christian Advocate* from any year any edition, especially Southern. Also wants identified personal items of preachers, bishops or prominent laity such as canes, hats, gloves, etc. "I do not want Sunday School material, Catholic holy cards, or general religious material like a postcard of the Holy Land."

 Rev. Kenneth Brown
 519 North Locust Street
 Hazleton, PA 18201
  (717) 454-0233

☆ **Protestant religious items** including old Bibles, hymnals, bronze statues, old pictures and prints, oil paintings, engravings, watercolors, books, autographs, and more. Gene asks you give a standard description, send Xerox™ copies or photos and estimate the age of what you have. Give standard bibliographic entries for any books.

> Gene Albert, Jr.
> 12324 Big Pool Road
> Clear Spring, MD 21722
> (301) 842-2401   Fax: (301) 733-5669

☆ **Pentecostal religious items** including histories, biographies of preachers or leaders, photos of churches or services, sermons and sermon notes, and anniversary items from holiness and Pentecostal churches such as mugs, plates, etc. Will buy oils, napkins, snake handling boxes, and identified hymnals, Bibles and disciplines of denominations. Also wants any and all books, periodicals, and tracts on the subject of sanctification, holiness, perfection, second blessing, speaking in tongues, faith healing and healers, or snake handling and will buy single issues or bound volumes of Pentecostal magazines. Does not want Sunday School items, pictures of the Virgin Mary, etc., but is looking for historical books, documents, photos and artifacts only.

> Rev. Kenneth Brown
> 519 North Locust Street
> Hazleton, PA 18201
> (717) 454-0233

☆ **Chautauqua and camp meeting revivalism.** "I'm seeking any and all materials related to Chautauqua and camp meeting revivalism including posters, stereoviews, postcards, photographs, letters, diaries, magazines, prints, souvenirs, etc. I'll even buy artifacts like lanterns, pulpits, signs and the like, but am primarily interested in items that are identified as to the preachers and/or dates involved. I *do not* buy average religious items like old Bibles, Sunday school postcards, photos of churches and the like, and do not buy Scouting items." Brown is editor of *Camp Meeting Challenge*, historian for the National Camp Meeting Association and author of *Holy Ground: A Study of the American Camp Meeting*, available for $42.

> Rev. Kenneth Brown
> 519 North Locust Street
> Hazleton, PA 18201
> (717) 454-0233

☆ **Missionary correspondence** from Protestant or Catholic missionaries in Asia, Africa, South Pacific and South America. The envelope must be intact as it is the stamps and cancellations (covers) that are of primary importance. Advisable to first phone or send a photocopy of the envelope by mail or fax. Pledges to repay your post on items you send on approval.

    Bruce Lewin
    Bridgewater Onvelopes Collectibles
    680 Route 206 North
    Bridgewater, NJ 08807
       (908) 725-0022   Fax: (908) 707-4647

☆ **Jewish ephemera** including business-related items such as signs, advertising, letterheads, and the like, but also photos, family documents, books, cookbooks, tins, bottles, postcards, Judaica, *chatchkelas*, and what have you. Also interested in **anti-Semetic material**. Please send a photocopy of what you have.

    Peter Schweitzer
    5 East 22nd Street Apt. 21-A
    New York, NY 10010
       (212) 677-6939

☆ **Judaica,** especially silver religious items and old books. Use standard bibliographic information for books. Send a photo of religious items, and include all markings found on the piece.

    Jay Brand
    PO Box 871
    Reynoldsburg, OH 43068
       (614) 868-8655

☆ **Israel, Palestine, and the Holocaust.** What have you? It could be worth your time to make an inquiry.

    Harvey Dolin
    5 Beekman Street #406
    New York, NY 10038

☆ **Sacred books, including Bibles before 1800, Books of Common Prayer, the Koran**, and other unusual, beautiful or early sacred book.

    Ron Lieberman, Family Album
    Route 1 Box 42
    Glen Rock, PA 17327
       (717) 235-2134   Fax: (717) 235-8042

☆ **Russian religious icons,** especially those with silver covers. Also **enameled bronze crosses** (wall size), icon lamps (*lampadki*) especially with "cut to clear" glass, and other pre-revolutionary religious items. Prices depend upon rarity, authenticity, and condition. Wants a full description but a good clean color photo is probably necessary. Phone to discuss your piece; he'll probably request that you ship for inspection and will tell you how to best ship. What you know of the item's history could be important.

David Speck
35 Franklin Street
Auburn, NY 13021
(315) 252-8566 eves

☆ **Shakers and other utopian groups.** "I buy and sell early and current (to 1970) books, hymnals, manuscripts, photos, and other ephemera by or about the Shakers and related utopian and communal groups. Particularly interested in 18th and 19th century items related to the American Shakers. An 1808 1st edition of *Testimony of Christ's Second Appearing* can bring $1,000, and other works can bring even more. Pamphlets for and against the Shakers printed in Ohio, Kentucky or surrounding states during the 1800-1840 period are of particular interest." Full bibliographic information on books is required, including full description of the condition. A photo or Xerox™ is suggested for other items. He produces periodic catalogs of items for sale. Cost: $4.

David Newell
39 Steady Lane
Ashfield, MA 01330
(413) 628-3240   Fax: (413) 628-3216

☆ **Shaker artifacts and ephemera.** "I specialize in Shaker books, pamphlets, photographs, and ephemera. I also buy and sell small Shaker artifacts such as bottles, sewing boxes, baskets, seed boxes, and the like. Four times a year, I publish a catalog of Shaker items for sale. If you have something to sell me, generally all I need is a photo or photocopy to come to a decision."

Scott DeWolfe
PO Box 425
Alfred, ME 04002
(207) 282-4773

☆ **Shaker furniture, books, diaries, and letters.** Will buy in any condition. Please write and describe what you have.

James Williams
HCR 01 Box 23
Warrensburg, NY 12885
(518) 623-2831

☆ **Mormonism.** Buys all types of books, photos, letters, and other paper ephemera related to Mormons.

Warren Anderson
America West Archives
PO Box 100
Cedar City, UT 84720
(801) 586-9497

☆ **Watchtower Society publications and ephemera** including *Golden Age, Consolation,* and *Awake* magazines, *Millennial Dawn* books, *Watchtower* books before 1927, items related to **Pastor Russell**, and any pre-1940 Jehovah's Witness literature.

Mike Castro
PO Box 72817
Providence, RI 02907

☆ **Mystical arts, crystal balls, tarot cards,** and ephemera related to astrology, spiritualism, pyramids, palmistry, Yoga, numerology, psychic research, Atlantis, Tibet, UFO's and the like.

Dennis Whelan
PO Box 170
Lakeview, AR 72642

☆ **Angels.** "I'll buy angels of any size and material except paper or plastic. I want wood, plaster, bisque, composition, etc., and will even buy them life size or larger. A photo, including dimensions, should be part of any description."

Gwen Daniel
18 Belleau Lake Court
O'Fallon, MO 63366
(314) 281-3190 anytime

CHRISTMAS DECORATIONS

☆ **Christmas decorations** from before 1920, and related items like:
- **Figural ornaments**, made of paper, tinsel, pressed cardboard, cotton batting, glass or other material;
- **Board games** with lithographed boxes depicting Santa;
- **Santa toys** and **other ephemera:** anything based on St. Nick, including advertising, banners, greeting cards, paintings, die-cuts, chromoliths, and prints;
- **Die cut children's books** 1880-1900 about Santa;
- **Litho on tin candle holders** for Christmas trees.

He does not want *anything* made of plastic or vinyl, nor anything made after 1920. There are many reproductions of Santa items, some of which are quite valuable and require an expert to authenticate. This 25 year veteran requests a photo or photocopy of what you'd like to sell.

    Dolph "Father Christmas" Gotelli
    PO Box 8009
    Sacramento, CA 95818
    (916) 456-9734

☆ **German glass Christmas ornaments,** shaped like animals, people, and cartoon characters, made before 1920. Also wants painted cotton ornaments, paper Dresdens, and old **candy containers** shaped like Santa. Also buys pre-1930 **postcards** and **photos of Christmas events** plus pre-1960 **department store Santas** with children.

    Jim Bohenstengel
    PO Box 623
    Oak Park, IL 60303
    (708) 524-8870

☆ **Early handmade folk art Christmas decorations.**
    Louis Picek, Main Street Antiques
    PO Box 340
    West Branch, IA 52358

☆ **Christmas tree ornaments.** Buys a variety of antique ornaments including *Kugel* ornaments; glass birds with spun glass wings, tails, or crests; Czech beaded ornaments with satin glass rings; birds perched in glass rings; unusual strings of glass beads; spun glass and paper decorations; chandelier or fantasy ornaments (where two or three small bells, pine cones, or other items hang from a larger ornament); and other delicate and unusual figural ornaments. Also buys catalogs and manufacturer's sales literature from manufacturers in any language.

    David Speck
    35 Franklin Street
    Auburn, NY 13021
    (315) 252-8566 eves

☆ **Electric Christmas decorations** including figural light bulbs, pre-1940 items only, please. Send photo.
> Cindy Chipps
> 4027 Brooks Hill Road
> Brooks, KY 40109
> (502) 955-9238   Fax: (502) 957-5027

☆ *Matchless Wonder Stars* **Christmas lights.** "I'll buy all stars, working, dead or broken. Boxed sets are desirable, but even empty boxes have value." This historian wants all factory wholesale literature and price sheets, as well as store display stands. He also buys other *Matchless* products plus **any old light sets that twinkle or bubble** by *Paramount, Sylvania, Alps, Royal, Peerless, Mazda, Majestic* and others. Especially interested in nice boxed light sets by *Propp* and *Clemco.* He wants a good description and if you still have the box, the information on it. "I generally avoid plastic items, and Christmas lights later than the mid 1950's. I don't need any more common *NOMA* or *Royal* bubble lights." Although he buys dead bulbs (except *Sylvania* fluorescents), he requests return privilege if things aren't as described.
> David Speck
> 35 Franklin Street
> Auburn, NY 13021
> (315) 253-8495 days

☆ *Hallmark* **figural ornaments** from 1973-1986. Excellent condition only. In original box preferred. No ball ornaments.
> Sharon Vohs-Mohammed
> PO Box 7233
> Villa Park, IL 60181
> (708) 268-0210

☆ **Christmas collector's plates and ornaments**, but only (1) *Royal Copenhagen* plates; (2) *Wedgwood Jasperware* plates; (3) *Bing & Grondahl* plates; (4) *Waterford* crystal "12 Days of Christmas" ornaments. Indicate the year and whether you have the original box.
> Old China Patterns Limited
> 1560 Brimley Road
> Scarborough, Ontario
> M1P 3G9 CANADA
> (416) 299-8880   Fax: (416) 299-4721

☆ **Christmas reindeer.** "I buy hard or soft plastic Christmas reindeer from the 1960's and 70's, and pay $2 to $5 apiece for these dimestore animals which originally sold for less than a buck. Must be in good condition. I'm not interested in metal, glass, ceramic, or plaster deer."
> Arnie Starkey, Starkey Art
> 11054 Otsego Street #5
> North Hollywood, CA 91601

EASTER

☆ **Russian Easter eggs** made of porcelain, solid glass, silvered hollow glass, and other materials. They are characterized by the letters "XB" or XHRISTOS VOSKRECE (Christ is risen) inscribed in paint, enamel, or other material. Value depends upon rarity, authenticity and condition.
> David Speck
> 35 Franklin Street
> Auburn, NY 13021
>   (315) 253-8495 days   252-8566 eves

☆ **Papier-maché or composition Easter rabbit candy containers** of rabbits wearing clothes.
> Dolph Gotelli
> PO Box 8009
> Sacramento, CA 95818
>   (916) 456-9734

VALENTINE'S DAY

☆ **Fine Valentines,** including handmade valentines from before 1940, interesting mechanical valentines, and any unusual ones. Evalene likes lacy 8" x 10" cards and large fan shaped cards from the 1800's, particularly if they say A TOKEN OF LOVE. Pays $25-$50 for folding ships, planes, and better fans. Please send a photocopy of what you wish to sell. She does not want children's penny valentines from any era. Evalene no longer has a shop, but runs an extensive mail auction of valentines. She is available for talks and displays of valentines.
> Evalene Pulati, Valentine Collector's Association
> PO Box 1404
> Santa Ana, CA 92702
>   (714) 547-1355

☆ **Valentines.** Wants early die-cut and elaborate valentines made before 1910, but buys others "if reasonable."
> Madalaine Selfridge
> 33710 Almond Street
> Lake Elsinore, CA 92530
>   (909) 674-9221

☆ **Valentines** dating from 1889 to about 1920, but only the three dimensional fold-out stand-up type.
> James Conley
> 2758 Coventry Lane NW
> Canton, OH 44708
>   (216) 477-7725

HALLOWEEN

☆ **Halloween.** "I'll buy older paper items, *Dennison Boogie Books*, Halloween pins, jewelry, decorations, etc., but only if they were made before 1945. Nothing new is wanted."
> Stuart Schneider
> PO Box 64
> Teaneck, NJ 07666
> (201) 261-1983

☆ **Candy containers in glass or plastic** especially scarce glass items and early 1950's figural headed plastic *PEZ* dispensers. Pays to $300 for pumpkin headed witches, goblins, or a pop-eyed jack-o'-lantern. No paper or tin items.
> Ross Hartsough
> 98 Bryn Mawr Road
> Winnipeg, MB R3T 3P5 CANADA

☆ **Halloween candy containers** in glass or papier-maché.
> Dolph Gotelli
> PO Box 8009
> Sacramento, CA 95818
> (916) 456-9734

4TH OF JULY MEMORABILIA

☆ **Anything with a fireworks company name** on it including:
- Fireworks, rockets, and Roman candles;
- Firecracker packs and labels;
- Fireworks boxes that held salutes, torpedoes, sparklers, etc.;
- Salesmen's display boards and samples;
- Fireworks catalogs from before 1969 (often $100 up);
- Paper ephemera: stock certificates, posters, banners, photos, letters, billheads, magazine articles, and other paper about American fireworks companies.

Would like to hear from former employees of U.S. fireworks companies. Please include your phone number when you write.
> Barry Zecker
> PO Box 217
> Martinsville, NJ 08836
> (908) 253-3400 from 8 to 8

☆ **Fireworks related items**, especially American and Chinese made. "I'll buy boxes, labels, advertising, catalogs, salesman's samples, display boards, company letters, patents, and posters." Colorful labels are worth from $5-$50 each. Hal does not want those marked DOT.

> Hal Kantrud
> Route 7
> Jamestown, ND 58401
>   (701) 252-5639 eves

☆ **Firecracker labels.** "I'll buy pre-1940 labels with aviation, space, atom bomb, animal, and Americana themes." Also fireworks catalogs. Send a photocopy of what you have. No modern labels.

> Stuart Schneider
> PO Box 64
> Teaneck, NJ 07666
>   (201) 261-1983

☆ **Fourth of July fireworks**, firecrackers, and firecracker labels. Wants "anything prior to the early 1970's, especially packs of *Golliwog, Picnic, Tank, Oh Boy, Typewriter, Evergreen, Lone Eagle, Spirit of 76, Minute Man, Columbia, Crab, Blue Dragon, Golden Bear, Green Jade, Santa Claus, Watermelon, Dwarf, China Clipper*, and many others." He wants most of these badly enough to pay $50 or more per pack! NOTE: if your package or label contains the letters DOT and/or "Contents do not exceed 60 mg," he's probably not interested. He eagerly buys catalogs of fireworks too. Photocopy when possible.

> William Scales
> 130 Fordham Circle
> Pueblo, CO 81005
>   (719) 561-0603

ALL HOLIDAYS

☆ **Cards from any holiday, 1880-1940.** Nothing later. Everything must be in suitable condition for resale.

> Madalaine Selfridge
> 33710 Almond Street
> Lake Elsinore, CA 92530

ANIMAL COLLECTIBLES

☆ *Royal Doulton* **flambe animal figurines.** Hundreds of different animals, both wild and domestic, are to be found in these attractive red pottery figures which range from 2" to 14" in size. They are still made today, so it's the older figures that are most sought after and bring the best prices. Have the figure(s) in front of you when you call this 20 year veteran collector. Or send a good description.

> Ed Pascoe
> 101 Almeria Avenue
> Coral Gables, FL 33134
> (800) 872-0195   Fax: (305) 445-3305

☆ *Royal Doulton* **animal figurines.** "I'll buy any, large or small, as long as they are marked ROYAL DOULTON and are in perfect condition. "Look for a number with the letters HN or K. Tell me the number and I'll make an immediate cash offer."

> Carol Payne
> Carol's Gallery
> 14455 Big Basin Way
> Saratoga, CA 95070
> (408) 867-7055

☆ **Miniature animal figures made of black amethyst glass** (purple glass that looks black until you hold to the light). Tell her what animal and how long or tall it is. These are a low value item, worth a buck or two, but they'll find a good home.

> Judy Polk Harding
> 2713 Friendship Street
> Iowa City, IA 52245
> (319) 354-2379

☆ **Books, prints, and paper ephemera about horses.** "I buy books, prints, and paper *only*, but I buy on all horse related topics: polo, horseback riding, carriage driving, sidesaddle, draft horses, horseshoeing, veterinary, etc." Buys horse farm catalogs, brochures, posters, prints of riding and recognized horse breeds, books (1st editions in dust jackets only), magazines, postcards (if horse is named), stud books, and breed registers. "I don't buy common books still in print, book club editions, *Diseases of the Horse*, books on racing or horse race betting, or books with highlighting or underlining in the text. Please, I am not in the market for figurines, bronzes, or anything other than books, prints and paper about horses. Your items must be in fine condition for resale."

> Barbara Cole's October Farm
> 2609 Branch Road
> Raleigh, NC 27610
> (919) 772-0482   Fax: (919) 779-6265

☆ **Dog related collectibles** "especially figurines, jewelry and post-cards, but everything doggy considered." Russian Wolfhounds and Greyhounds are favorite breeds, especially in porcelain. Size, material, and markings are key elements in description, along with the breed if you know dogs well enough to tell.

> Denise Hamilton
> 575 Latta Brook Road
> Elmira, NY 14901
> (607) 732-2550

☆ **Dog art and ephemera.** Wants many different quality items:
- Dog figurines by well known porcelain companies from England, Germany, Denmark, Austria and America as well as a few others, especially artist signed pieces;
- Ceramics representing purebred dogs in lifelike colors; these are usually of lesser quality than the above, but are often signed or labeled;
- Bronzes of dogs, especially signed;
- *Wedgwood* dog plates by Marguerite Kirmse;
- Woodcarvings by ANRI of Italy;
- Oil paintings or etchings of purebred dogs;
- Cigarette cards of purebred dogs;
- Kennel club, dog show, or dog club medallions pre-1920 which have a lifelike representation of a dog on them;
- Other interesting three dimensional items depicting dogs.

"I am not interested in chalkware, Staffordshire, toys, doorstops, cast metal souvenir items, plastic, celluloid, poor quality items, or books, nor do I buy paper items other than etchings and cigarette cards. Figures must be lifelike portrayals of purebred dogs." Photo is preferred, along with the size and manufacturer. The condition is very important. All scratches, chips, flakes, breaks and imperfections must be noted.

> Sharlene Beckwith
> Exclusively Dogs!
> PO Box 1858
> Upland, CA 91785
> (909) 946-1544   Fax: (909) 949-4796

☆ *Morton Studio* **figurines of dogs, wild animals or people.** These heavy ceramics are almost always marked on the bottom. Size, color, and shape are needed, along with condition.

> Denise Hamilton
> 575 Latta Brook Road
> Elmira, NY 14901
> (607) 732-2550

☆ **Bull terrier dog material** including books, manuscripts, photos and relevant ephemera.
> Frank Klein, Bookseller
> 521 West Exchange Street
> Akron, OH 44302
> (216) 762-3101 Fax: (216) 762-4413

☆ **Bull terriers and dog fighting.** Especially wants prints, paintings, and statuary. Books on dog fighting also wanted.
> Ron Lieberman
> RD #1 Box 42
> Glen Rock, PA 17327
> (717) 235-2134 Fax: (717) 235-8042

☆ **Cat items of any sort** including porcelain, carvings, prints, Orientalia, needlework, pottery, jade, ivory, jewelry, cookie jars, calendars, Art Deco, advertising, steins, medals, doorstops, bronzes, crystal, postcards, playing cards, prints and fine art, etc. Buys some cartoon cats (**Felix the Cat**, Sylvester, Kliban cats) but does not want any Garfield figures or reproductions in any form. Also she does not buy chalk figures, or anything broken or damaged.
> Marilyn Dipboye
> 33161 Wendy Drive
> Sterling Heights, MI 48310
> (313) 264-0285

☆ **Pet license tags, rabies tags, and all other metal tags related to animals.** Especially interested in Illinois tags. Especially wants tags pre-1900 for which he pays $15 and up.
> Rich Hartzog
> PO Box 4143 BFT
> Rockford, IL 61110

☆ **Dog license tags** including: (1) tags from any state if they are shaped like the date of issue; (2) tags from anywhere in the world pre-1910; (3) all NY tags issued before 1918; and (4) NY Conservation Dept. tags, 1917-35, which are worth from $10-$40. Dog tags from before the Civil War can bring up to $150, and pre-1900 tags start at $5.
> James Case
> Route 1 Box 68, Crane Road
> Lindley, NY 14858

☆ **Horse books and prints.** Buys books, magazines, posters, prints, stud books and breed registers for any recognized horse breed whether work or recreation: polo, horseback riding, carriage driving, sidesaddle, draft horses, **horseshoeing, veterinary,** etc. "I don't buy common books still in print, book club editions, *Diseases of the Horse,* or books on horse betting. I buy first edition books in their original jackets, only. If you want to sell to me, everything you have must be in fine condition, as I buy for resale."

    Barbara Cole, October Farm
    2609 Branch Road
    Route 2, Box 183-C
    Raleigh, NC 27610
        (919) 772-0482   Fax: (919) 779-6265

☆ **Zebras in many different forms,** including porcelain, carvings, paintings, folk art, etc. To be of interest, an item must be of a zebra, not just zebra striped. Please, no hides or parts of dead zebras.

    Dave Galt
    302 West 78th Street
    New York, NY 10024
        (212) 769-2514

☆ **Musk oxen figurines, prints, book plates, and other small ephemera,** 1750-1930. Especially wants postcards, cigarette silks, trading cards, pottery, stamps and other small paper items. Will pay up to $100 each for illustrations from *History of Quadrupeds* (1781) or *Arctic Zoology* (1784) both by Thomas Pennant.

    Ross Hartsough
    98 Bryn Mawr Road
    Winnipeg, MB R3T 3P5, CANADA

☆ **Wild boar ephemera.** "I'll buy paintings, bronzes, ceramics, advertising, anything featuring the wild European boar or its American counterparts, the peccary or javelina." Describe condition.

    Henry Winningham
    3205 South Morgan Street
    Chicago, IL 60608

☆ **Reptiles and amphibians** including frogs, snakes, turtles, crocodiles, lizards, etc. Wants figures, carvings, jewelry, pens, ceramics, postcards, stamps, and primitive art with reptile designs or parts. No modern items made of rattlesnake skins or ivory. Open access computer bulletin board about reptiles can be reached on (215) 698-1905.

    Mark Miller
    PO Box 52261
    Philadelphia, PA 19115
        (215) 464-3561 voice and fax

☆ **Whales and dolphins.** Interested in images of whales and dolphins that occur in books, photos, postcards, stereoviews, art of all types (paintings, prints, sculpture), advertising, posters, stamps, coins, money, toys and games. Also interested in film footage (including home movies) of whales and recordings of whale sounds. Will also buy whale bones, baleen, and other whale artifacts. "We already have most items made after 1975." Send "a detailed description, including a photo" asks this collector-dealer-nonprofit organization.

    Steve King
    Whales & Friends
    PO Box 2660
    Alameda, CA 94501
       (510) 769-8500   Fax: (510) 865-0851

☆ **Oyster memorabilia.** Got anything related to oysters? Cans, figurines, what have you?

    Sheldon Katz
    211 Roanoke Ave.
    Riverhead, NY 11901
       (516) 369-1100

☆ **Oyster related items** such as oyster cans, signs, posters, trade cards, labels, pinbacks, and what have you. Does not want oyster plates or reproduction signs. Describe the condition. Dealers, price your goods. Amateurs may ask for offers.

    John Baron
    2928 Marshall Avenue
    Cincinnati, OH 45220
       (513) 751-6631

☆ **Tropical fish tanks, equipment and ephemera.** Wants old books, magazines, catalogs directly related to tropical fish, as well as "pet shop" or turtle magazines and other paper relevant to the hobby. Photocopy what you have. Priced items preferred but will make offers.

    Gary Bagnall
    1615 East St. Gertrude
    Santa Ana, CA 92705

IF YOUR ITEM IS RELATED TO TRANSPORTATION, COMMERCE OR ONE OF THE PROFESSIONS, IT WILL PROBABLY SELL.

If it rolls, floats, flies or in any other way moves from one place to another... someone collects it.

If it has anything to do with business, manufacturing or commerce...someone collects it.

Most of these items aren't worth a great deal; but small sales add up to substantial sums of money.

__You shouldn't be the judge of what something is worth.__ Many of these items are obscure, so there isn't a great deal of competition for them, and prices stay relatively low. On the other hand, some items listed in these pages will sell for $10,000. You don't want to confuse the two, do you?

__If you aren't absolutely certain what you have and what its current market value is, you should turn to experts in Trash or Treasure to help you.__ I've tried to bring you the best in transportation and business buyers. Someone here will be just right for you.

__When sorting through old things, pay attention to paper items__, flyers and company brochures about any business or mode of travel. Letters about experiences aboard trains, planes, ships and automobiles are also wanted, as are photographs and records from manufacturers and retailers. Collectors gladly buy products, advertising signs, letters, bills, posters, store displays, and the like.

Collectors also buy tools, uniforms, instruments, badges, emblems, and other three-dimensional items characteristic of any industry. Packaging and advertising tend to bring the highest prices, especially for tobacco, coffee, alcohol, beer, and some foodstuffs.

Serious collectors want to learn about the manufacture and marketing of items which interest them today. In some industries, it can be difficult to find information about what took place 30 years ago. You can imagine how difficult it is to learn what was going on before the turn of the century! Colorful signs and informative catalogs bring the most money (from $100 up). Correspondence and the like may not be worth as much money, but the information it contains may be very useful. Take the time to sell even the less expensive items.

If you own old records or photos of transportation, business or the professions in the U.S. or Canada, please do not throw them away. Write the appropriate collector and offer to ship them in exchange for a fair price. Elsie in Florida listed a pile of paper expecting $10 and got $250. Give it away if you must, but don't let it get lost. Information lost is lost forever.

To sell your transportation, business, or profession related item, your description should include:

(1) What it is you wish to sell;
(2) What product or business it's associated with;
(3) What it depicts;
(4) What material(s) it is made from;
(5) Its size, shape, and color (especially colors of glass);
(6) Markings embossed (raised) or incised (stamped in);
(7) Information contained on an ID plate;
(8) Accurate information regarding condition.

The history and artifacts of some American industries is being preserved by fewer than a half dozen people, who can be difficult for you to find. **Trash or Treasure** sometimes puts you in touch with the only person in the country willing to buy what you have!

I've tried to bring you the best buyers I can find. Enjoy the experience of dealing with them.

BICYCLES & EPHEMERA

☆ **Bicycles and bicycle memorabilia,** generally before 1900, although some items are wanted to 1930. Wants all material about high wheelers and velocipedes ("bone shakers") including posters, advertising, trophies, photos, prints, toys and other representations or depictions, especially ephemera created by the *Pope Mfg. Company.* He does not want anything related to balloon tire bicycles.

> Pryor Dodge
> Box 71 Prince Street Station
> New York, NY 10012
>   (212) 966-1026

☆ **League of American Wheelmen memorabilia** is sought by this expert 20 year veteran collector who buys pins, medals, ribbons, magazines, etc., from 1880-1955. You might try him for general **early bicycle memorabilia** as well. Not interested in anything after 1955.

> Walley Francis
> PO Box 6941
> Syracuse, NY 13217
>   (315) 478-5671

☆ **Balloon tire bicycles** made between 1934-1960 in new or mint condition only, especially *Schwinn, Shelby, Monarch, Columbia,* or *Elgin* (Sears Roebuck). Please include a photo.

> Gus Garton, Garton's Auto
> 5th and Vine
> Millville, NJ 08332

☆ **Balloon tire bicycles** from the 1930's to 1960 are wanted. The most desired are boys' bikes with tanks, lights, horns, springs, and other accessories. "The more gaudy features, the better." Look for brands like *Schwinn, Road Master, Shelby, Evinrude, Elgin, Hiawatha* and *Western Flyer.*

"Collectible bikes usually have tires sized: 26"x1.125", 24"x2.125" or 28"x1.5" and are especially good if colored red or blue."

Will buy in any condition, but the value is determined by condition and accessories. Mike also buys parts, signs, shop fixtures, and literature relevant to this period of bicycles. No racing bikes, middleweights with 26 x 1.75 tires, or plain bikes. Photographs and a complete description are important to accurately estimate value.

> Michael Brown
> 2926 Pershing Boulevard
> Clinton, IA 52732
>   (800) 383-0049

☆ **Balloon tire bicycles** are wanted, especially gaudy style boy's bikes with tanks, lights, horns and springs. Especially wanted is the 1955 *Schwinn* "Black Phantom." A photo is a good idea, and your description should include information about where you got the bike.

    Kim Gutzke
    7134 15th Avenue S
    Minneapolis, MN 55423
        (612) 866-6183

☆ *Whizzers* **and balloon tire bicycles** are wanted. *Whizzers* are motor driven bicycles, some of which were factory built, others made from kits with a belt drive attached to the rear wheel. If you're selling a *Whizzer*, include the serial number as part of your description, which ideally should include a sharp photo of the vehicle. The bicycles he wants have tires sized 20", 24", or 26" x 2.125". Especially looking for a 1933 *Schwinn Aerocycle* or a 1938-39 *Shelby Speedline Airflow.* "The longer and weirder the bicycle's tanks are, the more I want them." Also buys **signs and shop fixtures**, including old brake parts cabinets, literature, and advertising. He does not want middleweight bikes with 1.75" tires or plain bikes with no tanks. Send a photo and complete description.

    Alan Kinsey
    1001 7 1/2 Avenue SW #8
    Independence, IA 50644
        (319) 334-2846   (515) 964-7046

☆ *Whizzer* **and** *Monarch Super-Twin* **motor driven cycles** are wanted. Indicate how complete it is and whether it runs or not. The model number should be part of your description, too. A photo is appreciated, as is information as to how you got it.

    Kim Gutzke
    7134 15th Avenue S
    Minneapolis, MN 55423
        (612) 866-6183

☆ **Bicycle license tags,** often called "sidepath licenses," from any state as long as they are from before 1930. Value ranges from $5-$40 depending on the age and place of issue.

    James Case
    Route #1   Box 68   Crane Road
    Lindley, NY 14858

AUTOMOBILES

☆ **American and European cars** of the 1920's through the 1960's in unrestored condition, as well as parts and accessories for those cars. "I prefer convertibles and two-door models, but occasionally will purchase unusual or limited production four-door models if very complete and original. **Pre-1940 race cars, sports cars and hot rods** are also very interesting to me." Wants large or small inventories of new or rebuilt obsolete mechanical parts and new or used aftermarket or original accessories for cars of the 1920's through the 1960's, including speed or high performance add-ons, **radios**, skirts, and sunvisors. Will also buy collections of older "automobilia" such as ornaments, mascots, literature, shop signs, etc. This 31 year veteran dealer says he'd like the year, make, model, body style, number of cylinders "as a good place to start." He warns that "scratched or faded original paint is far more desirable to a restorer than a cheap repaint, so sell your car as it sits, don't try to fix it up." Include your phone #.

>David "old car nut" Tomlinson
>Collectible Cars & Parts
>4739 Valley Boulevard
>Los Angeles, CA 90032
>(213) 222-4611 days   Fax: (213) 223-0752

☆ **Old and antique cars and car parts.** "I buy and sell all types of antique cars and parts, foreign and domestic, as well as all related materials such as parts, service manuals, advertisements and promotional toys." He specializes in **antique, classic, custom (hot rods), exotic and kit cars**, especially 1964 1/2 through 1968 *Mustangs* and *Shelbys*, and would particularly like to locate a good condition 1968 *Shelby KR500* convertible. Your description should include the type of item, and if a car, a description, including year, make, model, mileage, colors, and a brief history. Note its condition. "A color photo is helpful but doesn't replace seeing the actual item." Will make offers, but only if you intend to sell. Don't bother this busy 13 year veteran if you're only "price fishing." Operates a national computer database on which you can advertise autos and cycles for sale or wanted, complete with color photos! Call for info.

>Gregory Janaczek
>Janaczek Engineering
>Route 1 Box 1594
>Gouldsboro, PA 18424
>(717) 842-22??

☆ **Classic American and foreign automobiles.** One of the nation's largest auctioneers of high quality foreign and old domestic automobiles. If you have anything fast, sleek, limited production, or unusual, give Cole a call and discuss putting it up for sale in California's lucrative automobile market. Also *Corvettes, T-Birds*, older convertibles, and fine condition high quality American cars of the 1950's and 1960's. Don't sell your old car for too little.

> Rick Cole Auctions
> 10701 Riverside Drive
> North Hollywood, CA 91602
> (818) 506-6533

☆ **Race car "speed equipment"** to hop up automobiles from the 1930's, 40's, 50's, and 60's. Whether factory equipment or aftermarket, if it's designed to make a car go faster, and you want to sell it, give Dale a call. He'd especially like to find early *Ford* flathead engine cylinder heads, intake manifolds, and camshafts. 1955 to '58 *Chrysler* aftermarket intake manifolds or valve covers will bring top prices. He personally does not want complete cars, complete engines, or "any items that can't be shipped U.P.S." But, if you have these things for sale, you might inquire as he adds, "I do have quality buyers for this type item." Describe what you have, including manufacturer and date, when possible. Dale publishes *RPM*, a monthly catalog which includes 30 pages of classified ads for folks buying and selling speed parts. You can subscribe for $20 a year.

> Dale Wilch
> 2217 North 99th
> Kansas City, KS 66109
> (913) 788-3219   Fax: (913) 788-9682

☆ **Automobiles made between 1940 and 1969** if well maintained and low mileage, especially a *Cadillac* convertible from the 1950's or 60's. "I'd keep it as long as I live!" Also buys **automotive related signs**: auto sales and service, gasoline, motor oil, etc. Also **auto toys**.

> Gus Garton, Garton's Auto
> 5th and Vine
> Millville, NJ 08332

☆ *Dan Patch* **automobile** or parts and other ephemera from that brand. Call collect if you know of one of these cars for sale.

> Donald Sawyer
> 40 Bachelor Street
> West Newbury, MA 01985
> (508) 363-2983

AUTOMOBILE EPHEMERA

☆ **Paper ephemera, advertising, and promotional items associated with automobiles,** trucks, buses, campers, taxis, auto racing, police cars, ambulances, and hearses. Jay operates a large mail order business selling **transportation memorabilia of all sorts** and always needs clean old items such as catalogs, promotional items, emblems, promotional models given away by car dealers, auto company service pins, owner's manuals, and other small items associated with any form of vehicle. Will buy U.S. and foreign items, and multiples of some things. Will accept boxes sent on approval and "will make immediate offers to buy." Requests you include your phone number. Does not want shop manuals, parts lists, and magazine ads.

> Jay Ketelle
> 3721 Farwell
> Amarillo, TX 79109
>   (806) 355-3456   Fax: (806) 355-5743

☆ **Automobile related memorabilia** including promotional giveaways, **owner's manuals**, repair manuals, radiator emblems and caps, dial type tire gauges, fancy gear shift knobs, car clocks, **spark plugs**, horns, dash panels, brass speedometers, **DAV keychains**, automobile **magazines**, plant employee badges, canceled checks from auto companies, **stocks and bonds**, porcelain or leather license plates, driving awards and anything you can imagine having to do with automobiles except magazine ads.

> Joseph Russell
> 455 Ollie Street
> Cottage Grove, WI 53527
>   (608) 839-4736 eves

☆ **Automobile sales catalogs, brochures, owner's manuals** and **repair guides** printed by the auto company. Wants material for all cars and trucks, American or foreign, especially pre-1970. No magazines, clipped ads, *Motor's Manuals, Chilton's Manuals*, or books not printed by the auto company. Also buys **auto dealer promotional items** including signs, salesman's awards, and the like. "Please send me a list of each item by year and make. If a list is not practical, give me a count by decade, such as 'so many brochures from 1950 to 1959,' etc."

> Walter Miller
> 6710 Brooklawn Parkway
> Syracuse, NY 13211
>   (315) 432-8282   Fax: (315) 432-8256

☆ **Books, magazines, and factory literature about cars**, trucks, motorcycles, and bicycles. Also buys newsletters and magazines produced by automobile clubs devoted to one particular make of vehicle or another. Documents related to vehicle history 1895-1990 also purchased.

>Ralph Dunwoodie
>5935 Calico Drive
>Sun Valley, NV 89433
>(702) 673-3811

☆ **Books, catalogs, and owner's manuals**. Books may be on automobiles, auto history, racing, biography, auto travel, etc. Not interested in technical and repair manuals. Give standard bibliographic information, and note condition of cover, pages, spine, binding, and dust jacket. Also buys some photos of cars.

>David King's Automotive Books
>5 Brouwer Lane
>Rockville Center, NY 11570
>(516) 766-1561

☆ **Automobile dealership ephemera** including signs for any make of automobile, sales literature, and what have you from the period 1930 to 1970. Nothing newer. No reproductions. SASE a must.

>Gus Garton, Garton's Auto
>5th and Vine
>Millville, NJ 08332
>(609) 327-6090 days   (609) 825-3618 eves

☆ **1932 *Chevrolet* parts**, accessories and paper ephemera including ads, showroom literature, catalogs, repair manuals, and what have you. Will buy nearly any original parts, but especially needs dash clock, heater, various switches, tools, defroster, and many other items. If you regularly come across parts, send for his wants list.

>Reed Fitzpatrick
>PO Box 369
>Vashon, WA 98070
>(206) 463-3900 8am to 4pm PST

☆ ***Chevrolet* Corvette advertising** from 1953 on, including newspaper and magazine ads, sales brochures, direct mailings, race programs, sports programs, and auto show literature. Also "related Corvette memorabilia," including promotional giveaways. No reprints.

>David Facey, Auto-Ads
>7015 Klein Road
>Lakeland, FL 33813
>(813) 644-8369

☆ *Ford* **Motor Company memorabilia** from before 1955, including books, coins, badges, pins, postcards, and literature.

> Tim O'Callaghan
> 46878 Betty Hill
> Plymouth, MI 48170
> (313) 459-4636

☆ *Ford* **Motor Company memorabilia** and other items related to Ford automobiles: postcards, books, photos, Christmas cards, sheet music, records, pens, pins, china, silverware, menus, sales literature, joke books, and what have you. Also wants items related to Henry Ford. Has a special interest in sales literature from 1928 to 1936.

> Cliff Moebius
> 484 Winthrop Street
> Westbury, NY 11590
> (516) 333-3797

☆ *Ford* **parts**, 1932 to 1950, that are new and unused, including fenders, grill assemblies, radiators, etc. Does not want reproduction parts.

> Gus Garton, Garton's Auto
> 5th and Vine
> Millville, NJ 08332
> (609) 327-6090 days   (609) 825-3618 eves

☆ *Delorean* **items.** Wants "anything and everything related to John Z. Delorean and the *Delorean* car," including parts, newspaper clippings, magazine articles, posters, photos, commercials, certificates, and company greeting cards (worth $125 each!). Also items about the *Delorean* used in *Back to the Future* movies except bubble gum cards which are common. "The original Delorean sales brochure and John D's *On a Clear Day* are widely available; don't waste your time."

> Everen T. Brown
> PO Box 296
> Salt Lake City, UT 84110
> Fax: (801) 364-2646

☆ *Volkswagen* **related memorabilia**, literature, toys, etc. "My preference is for older bug related items, with spilt window bug and oval window bug toys and memorabilia the most desirable. However, any old VW items are of interest." Many foreign made toys are worth from $100 to $400 each, with some others, including some plastic ones, bringing even more! Does not want recent toys, *Avon*, or toys made in China. To sell toys, give the size, color, maker, and condition, noting whether you have the original box. Best to Xcrox™ other items.

> Mike Wilson
> 23490 SW 82nd Street
> Tualatin, OR 97062
> (503) 638-7074

☆ *Buick* **promotional items.**
Alvin Heckard
Route #1   Box 88
Lewistown, PA 17044
   (717) 248-7071

☆ *Mercedes* **and** *Rolls-Royce* radiator mascots and other parts, accessories, manuals, and literature made before 1960.
Joseph Weber
604 Centre Street
Ashland, PA 17921
   (717) 875-4401 from 3 to 5 p.m.

☆ *Rolls-Royce* **advertising,** pamphlets, cards, toys, and other information. Has particular interest in all models from the years 1957 through 1962, *Princess* through *Silver Cloud*.
Richard Melcher
PO Box 1812
Wenatchee, WA 98807
   (509) 662-0386

☆ **Parts and ephemera for** *Gardner* **and other autos made in St. Louis** such as *Moon, Diana, Ruxton*, and *Windsor*. Buys parts, hubcaps, mascots, owner's manuals, and the like. Will pay $75 for a single brochure on the front drive of a 1930 *Gardner*.
Robert Owen
PO Box 204
Fairborn, OH 45324

☆ **Radiator and hood ornaments** from autos before WWII, whether factory original or accessories. Does not want broken items or reproductions. Give a photo or detailed description.
Sy and Ronnie Margolis
17853 Santiago Boulevard #107-210
Villar Park, CA 92667
   (714) 974-5938   Fax: (714) 921-0731

☆ **Odd looking spark plugs.** "I'll buy as many as you have, the odder looking the better." He especially wants those with priming cups. No *AC* or *Champion* plugs.
Joseph Weber
604 Centre Street
Ashland, PA 17921
   (717) 875-4401 from 3 to 5 p.m.

☆ **Factory original automobile AM radios** 1926-1962. Only AM-FM from 1963-77. Wants brand and model number. Also **auto wheelcovers** (not hubcaps), 1950 to the present. Tell the make, model, condition, and quantity. Include your price, phone number and hours to call.

> John Sheldon
> 2718 Koper Drive
> Sterling Heights, MI 48310
> (313) 977-7979 days   Fax: (313) 977-0895

☆ *Firestone Tire Company* **promotional items** especially those shaped like tires including tire ashtrays, clocks, pen holders, cigarette cases. Also radios shaped like batteries, and other figural selling aids. List everything printed on the tire and on the insert. Does not want domestic ashtrays made after 1950. Pays $20-$35 for most items.

> Wayne Ray
> 10325 Willeo Creek Trace
> Roswell, GA 30075
> (404) 998-5325

☆ **Tire company promotional items** especially tire ashtrays, tire clocks, pen holders, radios, globes, *Tires* magazines, tire catalogs, and other literature and promotional items. "Will pay $50 for any original *Michelin* or *Overman* rubber tire ashtray." Also want foreign tires, tires with commemorative inserts, and other unusual promotional tires. Long priced wants list available.

> Jeff McVey
> 1810 West State Street #427
> Boise, ID 83702
> (208) 342-8447

☆ **Engine rebuilding equipment** and tools for working on antique auto, marine, truck, tractor, and stationary engines made by *KR Wilson, Kent Moore, Hempy-Cooper, Waterbury Simplicity, Van-Norman, Peterson* and others. Especially wants original equipment for Babbitt bearings including production equipment, smaller equipment for motorcycles and larger equipment for stationary engines. Please give the make, model, and power required. Indicate if it works or not, whether it has been modified, and what accessories are available. Not interested in home made equipment or items that have been "super modified."

> Shawn R. Aldrich
> Aldrich Engine Rebuilding
> 352 River Road
> Willington, CT 06279
> (203) 429-3111

BUSSES, TROLLEYS & TAXIS

☆ **Horsedrawn streetcars and pre-1920 electric railways.** "I'll buy **bells** marked with the name of a streetcar line, car gongs, car maker's plates, wall mounted and hand held fare registers, signs reading HAVE FARE READY or PAY AT REAR, hat badges, motorman's and conductor's certificates, fare tokens, and photos of early cars.
>   Jonathan Thomas, Trolley Fare
>   1208 Main Street North
>   Southbury, CT   06488
>   (203) 263-2233

☆ **Memorabilia from buses, taxis, hearses, ambulances, and any other public conveyance** before 1960 including emblems, badges, licenses, license plates, advertising, promotional giveaway trinkets, operator's manuals, sales literature, etc. May be foreign or U.S. as long as they are old and genuine. Will accept items sent on approval.
>   Jay Ketelle
>   3721 Farwell
>   Amarillo, TX 79109
>   (806) 355-3456   Fax: (806) 355-5743

☆ **Bus, trolley, and streetcar memorabilia** pre-1940 including photos, artifacts, driver's badges, caps, bus emblems, route maps, and advertising. Has particular interest in Florida companies but says "I will consider any item if the seller describes it well and attaches a price."
>   Sam LaRoue
>   5980 SW 35th Street
>   Miami, FL 33155
>   (305) 347-7466

☆ **Bus industry memorabilia** from 1935 to the present is wanted, including models, toys, banks, post cards of busses and terminals, time tables, bus manufacturer sales brochures, bus drivers' manuals, uniforms, driver's badges, promotional items, coach logos, bus industry trade magazines, and china, crystal, and flatware with bus company logos. This charter coach company owner will even consider actual **full size** *Greyhound* style buses. Please send a good description of the item and its condition for a fair offer. Regularly issues a catalog of bus related items for sale.
>   Charles Wotring
>   Royal Coach
>   911 Conley Drive
>   Mechanicsburg, PA 17055
>   (717) 691-1147

☆ *Greyhound* and *Trailways* **bus memorabilia.** Wants a wide range of items, such as cap badges, driver awards, etc., but mostly interested in toy *Greyhound* and *Trailways* busses, and *Greyvan Moving* truck toys. Prefers a picture or photocopy. No magazine ads, timetables, postcards or posters, but he does want internal company data like garage locations, driver assignments, and organizational directories.

    Eugene Farha
    PO Box 633
    Cedar Grove, WV 25039
       (304) 340-3201   (304) 595-4301

MOTORCYCLES & EPHEMERA

☆ **Motorcycles and motorcycle parts.** Wants *Harley-Davidson, BSA, Indian* and *Vincent* brands, not Japanese cycles. Your description should include the type of item, and if a cycle, a description, including year, make, model, mileage, and a brief history. Note its condition. "A color photo is helpful but doesn't replace seeing the actual item." Will make offers, but only if you intend to sell. Don't bother this busy 13 year veteran if you're only "price fishing." Runs a computer database on which you can advertise cycles for sale or wanted. Call for info.

    Gregory Janaczek
    Janaczek Engineering
    Route 1 Box 1594
    Gouldsboro, PA 18424
       (717) 842-2277

☆ **Motorcycles and motorcycle parts.** "I'm in the market for all American made parts for American motorcycles." Give marks and numbers when appropriate in your description. "I pay all shipping costs. I'm in the parts business and will travel to pick up large lots."

> Robert Fay
> Star Route Box AF
> Whitmore, CA 96096
>   (916) 472-3132

☆ **Motorcycle memorabilia** including advertising, giveaway trinkets, watch fobs, and other items, both foreign and domestic, pre-1960. "I will accept boxes sent to me on approval and will make immediate offers to buy." Pledges to repay your postage if his offer not accepted.

> Jay Ketelle
> 3721 Farwell
> Amarillo, TX 79109
>   (806) 355-3456   Fax: (806) 355-5743

☆ **Motorcycles and motorcycle ephemera** from before 1920. Wants advertising, factory sales catalogs, manuals, magazines, pins, fobs, trophies, medals, and related items.

> Herb Glass
> Route #1 Box 506-A
> Pine Bush, NY 12566
>   (914) 361-3657

☆ *Can-Am* **motorcycle parts and ephemera** including *Rotax* motors, brochures, decals, gloves, leathers, goggles, and anything else marked CAN-AM. This motorcycle is made by *Bombardier* of Canada.

> Don Schneider
> PO Box 1570
> Merritt, BC
> V0K 2B0 CANADA
>   (604) 378-6421

☆ *Cushman* **motor scooters** and related ephemera, especially signs and sales literature. Also **pre-1965 motorcycle** photos, postcards, sales literature, manuals, and magazines.

> Don Olson
> PO Box 245
> Humboldt, IA 50548

LICENSE PLATES

☆ **License plates before 1920,** especially undated plates made of leather, brass, or porcelain. Will buy old collections or accumulations. Describe condition carefully, including damage, chips, and crazing. He offers to answer questions about license plates and says, "If I don't want your plates, perhaps I can find someone who does." Gary is secretary of the Automobile License Plate Collector's Association and a valuable source of information.

> Gary Brent Kincade
> PO Box 77
> Horner, WV 26372
> (304) 269-7623 days   (304) 842-3773 eves

☆ **License plates.** Will buy any good condition pre-1935 plate plus collections or accumulations of plates:
- **Undated** or those made of porcelain, leather, or wood;
- Any U.S. pre-1915;
- Southern and South-western plates pre-1935;
- All Alaska, Hawaii or foreign plates before 1950;
- All motorcycle plates pre-1950;
- All plates issued on or for Indian reservations;
- Personalized plates "with cute names or phrases";
- Any pictorial plates;
- **Mini plates** from DAV, *Goodrich, Wheaties,* or *Post* cereals;
- **Car club emblems** such as AAA, especially foreign or pre-1925;
- **Chauffeur's badges** in good original condition, pre-1940;
- Ordinary plates in near new condition will bring 25¢ to $5 (for hard to find ones). "Ship up to 200 without inquiring first."

List the type of item, place of origin, date, number, condition, quantity, and price (if possible). Will make offer on any item if two loose stamps are sent. "If you don't like what I offer for your license plate, I'll let you run a free ad in my *License Plate Corner* magazine so you can try to sell it for more."

> George Chartrand
> PO Box 334
> Winnipeg, MB
> R3C 2H6 CANADA
> (204) 774-1186

☆ **Porcelain license plates** from U.S. and Canadian cars, trucks, and motorcycles before 1923. Also wants early **photos and photo post-cards of vehicles clearly showing readable plates.** Pays especially well for plates from Southern and unpopulated Western states. Does not buy painted metal plates. Photocopies suggested.

> Rodney Brunsell
> 55 Spring Street
> Hanson, MA 02341

☆ **License plates of all types** from anywhere especially early porcelain plates. "I am happy to receive inquiries even regarding common items. If I am not interested I will gladly refer readers to someone else or try to help out in other ways." Give the name of the issuing agency, type of plate, material from which it was made, the date, and its condition. Note any repainting or repair. Fluent in Spanish and French.

    Andy Bernstein
    43-60 Douglaston Parkway #524
    Douglaston, NY 11363
        (718) 279-1890

☆ **Expired obsolete license plates of all types and varieties** from anywhere. "I'll buy almost anything and everything ever used for registration or identification on a motor vehicle, front or back, domestic or foreign, from the earliest days of motoring up to and including current issues." Porcelain plates from before 1920, especially from less populous states. City and local issues and home-made plates bring the biggest premiums. Values depend on type of plate, numbers, rarity, condition, and degree of collector interest. He encourages you to write about *any* plate you think might be unusual, as long as you include a Xerox™ or clear color photo and a SASE. If a porcelain plate has a maker's name on the back, include that information. This long time collector/dealer asks that you also include your evening phone number.

    Dave Lincoln
    PO Box 331
    Yorklyn, DE 19736
        (610) 444-4144

☆ **License plates from Washington and Alaska**. Early leather and porcelain plates are wanted, but "I'll buy any Washington State plates 1915-1959 in most any condition. All Alaska plates are of interest. Unusual plates such as mobile home, taxi, trailer, state representative, etc., are particularly welcome." Also buys old **printed matter about vehicle licensing**, including titles, certificates, tonnage slips, etc. Also buys **license plate frames** with Washington and Alaskan car dealership names, and piggyback **plates that carry an advertising message** and fasten just above or below a license plate. Brass plaques, **auto club insignias**, and the like are of interest too. "When you contact me, I want to know the state, year, type of plate, whether you have a single plate or matched pair, condition (including rust, extra holes), and the material. I'll also consider **plates from other states** that are suitable for trading."

    Reed Fitzpatrick
    PO Box 369
    Vashon, WA 98070
        (206) 463-3900 8am to 4pm

☆ **License plates from Missouri, Kansas, and Colorado.** Also wants other states from the years 1936, 1976, and 1989. Also **miniature key chain license plates** produced by *B.F. Goodrich* or the DAV. Provide a list of the items you have and the price you'd like.

> George Van Trump, Jr.
> PO Box 260170
> Lakewood, CO 80226
>   (303) 985-3508

☆ **British Columbia license plates** before 1922 in any condition. Later BC plates will be considered if unusual, as will pre-1960 Yukon plates, Canadian **motorcycle** plates, and BC chauffeur's badges.

> Don Schneider
> PO Box 1570
> Merritt, BC
> V0K 2B0 CANADA
>   (604) 378-6421

☆ *B.F.Goodrich* **and DAV keychain license plate tags.** Pays 50¢ to $1 each, depending on age and state. The older the better.

> Dennis Schulte
> 8th Avenue NW
> Waukon, IA 52172

☆ **Aluminum license plate attachments.** "I'll buy unusual and attractive licence plate attachments which promote cities, states, turnpikes or special events. I don't need more Florida cities, but want other decorative aluminum brackets designed to fit above a license plate."

> Peter Capell
> 1838 West Grace Street
> Chicago, IL 60613
>   (312) 871-8735 eves

☆ **Chauffeur badges** and other badges that say DRIVER, OPERATOR, TAXI, HACK, or LIVERY. They may be issued by states or cities. He promises to pay $100 up for badges issued by the states of Alabama, Florida, Georgia, Montana, Utah and Nevada. He does not want badges after 1920 from the states of New York, Illinois, Ohio, or Michigan. Photocopy or tell him the issuing agency, the date (if dated), the serial number, and the condition.

> Albert Velocci
> 62 Cherrywood Drive
> New Hyde Park, NY 11040
>   (516) 437-6728 eves   Fax: (516) 358-0024

RAILROAD MEMORABILIA

☆ **Almost anything related to American railroads** especially dining car china, silverware, glass, marked lanterns, and marked brass locks. Pays $20-$85 for sugar tongs or spoons marked with railroad names. Make certain your description includes dimensions and all marks and logos. Rick does not want date nails, books, or model trains. This 25 year veteran (and railroad club president) says he'll answer questions from amateurs with or without things to sell. SASE appreciated.

> Richard Wright
> West Coast Rick's
> PO Box 8051
> Rowland Heights, CA 91748
>   (909) 681-4647

☆ **Railroad items** including dining car china, silverware, lanterns and lamps, stock certificates, engine builder's plates, ticket dating machines, depot signs, advertising, postcards of depots, brochures and timetables pre-1940, historical documents, hat and cap badges, wax seals, Express Company signs, annual passes from before 1920, and books, manuals, and guides. Nothing newer than 1959, no letters, receipts, or minor paper. This 30 year veteran requests your phone number.

> Fred Arone
> The Depot Attic
> 377 Ashford Ave.
> Dobbs Ferry, NY 10522
>   (914) 693-5858

☆ **Railroad and Express Company memorabilia** including dining car china, silverware, ashtrays, playing cards, paperweights, brass lamps and lanterns (including unmarked ones), locks, badges, switch keys, builder plates, steam whistles, caps pre-1960, uniforms pre-1920, railroad pocket watches if in perfect condition, pre-1916 timetables, posters, and calendars. Also *RR Cyclopedia*, dictionaries or other reference books published by *RY Gazette, Simmons-Boardman, Moody,* or *Poors* pre-1950. No large tools, large oil cans, spikes, low value paper, junky or damaged items, or material other than U.S. or Canadian. No "overly cleaned" or replated items. This 17 year veteran dealer always needs new merchandise.

> Scott Arden
> 20457 Highway 126
> Noti, OR 97461
>   (503) 935-1619 from 9 to 9 Pacific time

☆ **Canadian railroad memorabilia** from before 1950, especially *White Pass and Yukon Railway, Grand Trunk Railway,* and *Canadian Pacific,* among others.

> Michael Rice
> PO Box 286
> Saanichton, BC V8M 2C5 CANADA
> (604) 652-9047 eves

☆ **Railroad dining car memorabilia** including china, silver, glassware, menus, and anything else. Items without markings as to the railroad are "worthless" to him.

> Charles Goodman
> 636 West Grant Ave.
> Charleston, IL 61920
> (217) 345-6771

☆ **Railroad memorabilia** such as dishes, silver, lanterns, keys, locks, books, etc. "I'll pay at least $300 for the 10 1/2" china plates used on the trains." Especially interested in items from Southern roads. Also **pre-1930 postcards** showing exteriors of small town depots or trains, and cards of any era showing depot or train interiors. Does not make offers, but claims to be "willing to pay your price." Include your phone.

> Les Winn
> PO Box 80641
> Chamblee, GA 30366
> (404) 458-6194 eves

☆ **Chesapeake & Ohio Railroad memorabilia** of all sorts, as long as it features the two cats, "Chessie" and "Peake." A photocopy or photo is appreciated. No repros. SASE please.

> Charles Worman
> PO Box 33584 (AMC)
> Dayton, OH 45433
> (513) 429-1808 eves

☆ **Memorabilia from Arkansas railways** including *Eureka Springs Railway, St. Louis and North Arkansas Railroad, Missouri and Arkansas Railroad*, and the *Missouri and North Arkansas Railroad.* "I'll buy advertising, passes, china and silver, photos, switch locks and keys, lanterns, tickets, bills of lading, stock certificates, etc."

> Steve Chyrchel
> Route #2 Box 362
> Eureka Springs, AR 72632
> (501) 253-9244 voice and fax

☆ **Railroad date nails and other small railroad items** such as lanterns, locks, and keys. Will buy almost any date nails (nails about 4" long with a date on the head). If you describe the shape of the head, the number, and whether it is incised or raised, he says he's glad to tell you what you have. Dick is a collector with limited storage so is interested only in small fine items.

>   Dick Gartin
>   619 Adams Drive
>   Duncanville, TX 75137
>   (214) 296-8742 anytime

☆ **Date nails** used by railroads, telephone, telegraph, and power companies to record when their ties or poles were placed in service. Most, but not all, have either round or square heads and have numbers (or other symbols) either raised or indented on the head. Nails may be steel, copper, or aluminum. Although there are many common nails, there are also nails worth $50 up so describe what you have and Jerry will make an offer. Jerry is editor of *Nailer News* a brief bimonthly newsletter for nail collectors.

>   Jerry Waits
>   501 West Horton
>   Brenham, TX 77833
>   (409) 830-1495

☆ **Railroad books** of all types: fiction, biographies, histories, etc. Seeks *Poor's Manual of Railroads*, pre-1920. **Also other items, especially from Colorado and New Jersey,** such as pre-1920 annual passes, **uniform buttons,** pins, and brass padlocks with raised letters. Especially wants anything from Central RR of NJ (*The Blue Comet*).

>   Dan Allen
>   PO Box 917
>   Marlton, NJ 08053
>   (609) 953-1387 eves

☆ **Timetables and maps** for railroads, airlines, bus systems, trolleys, and ships. Also wants other paper, guides, passes, and railroad employee publications. Does not want any AMTRAK materials, or airline timetables after 1970. Give the line, date, and condition. Carl buys, sells, and produces a monthly catalog.

>   Carl Loucks
>   PO Box 484
>   North Haven, CT 06473
>   (203) 288-3765   Fax: (203) 288-6251

SHIPS & THE SEA EPHEMERA

☆ **Fine marine antiques of all types** including but not limited to:
- **Paintings** and **prints of boats**, ships and the sea, 1700-1900;
- **Navigational instruments** from the 19th century, sextants, **telescopes** on tripods, marine clocks, compasses, etc.;
- **Photographs** of **whaling**, yachting, ship launchings, and identified parts in the 19th or early 20th century;
- **Journals, logs** and **out-of-print books** about whaling, **yachting**, clippers, "but only in resellable condition";
- **Wood carvings** such as figureheads, pilot house eagles, name boards, and tail boards;
- **Scrimshaw** teeth and sailor's whimsies, inlaid boxes, **crimpers**, bone swifts, and tools, but only genuine quality old pieces;
- **Paper** and other ephemera including deck plans, broadsides, ship's china...anything rare, interesting and in fine condition;
- **Artifacts** related to **lighthouses** and the **Life Saving Service.**

Generally buys only 19th century items. He does not want fakes, altered items, modern scrimshaw, boxed compasses, or ship's telegraphs unless they are small, very early, or historically important. Description should include dimensions, note of repairs or restoration, history and price ("if you can"). He specializes in forming and liquidating collections and issues interesting catalogs of items for sale.

> Andrew Jacobson's Marine Antiques
> PO Box 2155
> South Hamilton, MA 01982
> (508) 468-6276

☆ **Model sailboats.**   "I'll buy wooden models that are at least 18" long, made of wood, with rigged canvas sails. May be up to 8' high. I prefer them to have stands. I'm looking for their decorative value so am not particularly looking for famous boats, ship builder's models, and other high ticket items. Send a picture of what you have, please." Should be in fine or readily restorable condition.

> Joan Brady
> 834 Central Ave.
> Pawtucket, RI 02861
> (401) 725-5753

☆ **Nautical instruments** by American and foreign makers including brass sextants, wood octants, spyglasses, pocket sundials, cased navigating devices, as well as map drawing tools. Must be made before 1890.

> Jonathan Thomas, Scientific Americana
> 1208 Main Street North
> Southbury, CT 06488
> (203) 263-2233

☆ **Ship models,** particularly identified 19th century American, English, or French vessels. "I also deal in 20th century high quality models of all types: sail, steam, liners, yachts, and **pond models.**" Also buys **builder's half models,** including 19th century American or British hulls, exceptional 20th century hulls, and all yacht models. Does not want reproductions, or items which have been heavily "restored" or otherwise altered. Please give the dimensions, age, condition, history, and price. "If you want an appraisal, I must examine the object personally, and there is a fee, although I will give 'ball park' verbal estimates on routine items, with the understanding there is no legal responsibility or liability."

> Andrew Jacobson's Marine Antiques
> PO Box 2155
> South Hamilton, MA 01982
> (508) 468-6276

☆ **Whaling industry artifacts.** "I'm looking for anything related to the American whaling industry, including scrimshaw, tools, and early copies of *Moby Dick*, especially the 1851 first edition."

> Greg "Dr. Z" Zemenick
> 13560 Kirts #160
> Troy, MI 48084
> (810) 642-8129   (810) 244-9426

☆ **Steamship memorabilia** including china, silver, ashtrays, whistles, locks, lanterns, badges, signs, uniforms and caps, calendars, posters, route maps, and numerous similar items. **Does not want** paper ephemera after 1910, low value paper goods, fake or altered items or big heavy tools. Nor does he buy items that are shabby or missing important parts.

> Scott Arden
> 20457 Highway 126
> Noti, OR 97461
> (503) 935-1619 from 9 to 9 Pacific time

☆ **Ocean liner memorabilia** from all companies, especially paper items such as deck plans, menus, booklets, and passenger lists from *Cunard, French, German, White Star, Italian, Canadian, Dutch,* and all others. "We do not buy reproductions or items that are strictly 'travel' interest, such as brochures describing Paris. You may send items on approval as we cannot make offers based only on your description."

> Alan Taksler, New Steamship Consultants
> PO Box 30088
> Mesa, AZ 85275

☆ **Ocean liner memorabilia,** deck plans, postcards, paintings, posters, and anything relating to passenger ship travel especially from "disaster ships" such as the *Titanic* or *Andrea Doria*. After 1945, only maiden voyage items wanted. Ken produces a large illustrated catalog for $15.

    Ken Schultz
    PO Box M-753
    Hoboken, NJ 07030
       (201) 656-0966

☆ **Canadian steamship ephemera** before 1950 such as deck plans, calendars, stock certificates, bonds, fancy letterheads, envelopes, etc. Seeks *Canadian Pacific* steamships, *BC Coast* steamships, and others.

    Michael Rice
    PO Box 286
    Saanichton, BC V8M 2C5 CANADA
       (604) 652-9047

☆ **Steamship ephemera collections** dating pre-1960, including menus, programs, deck plans, posters, etc., from either American or European lines. Promises a quick answer to all inquiries.

    George Theofilies
    The Miscellaneous Man
    PO Box 1776
    New Freedom, PA 17349
       (717) 235-4766 days   Fax: (717) 235-2853

☆ **Licenses for ship masters, mates, pilots, and engineers.** Wants those issued by the U.S. Coast Guard and the Steamboat Inspection Service. Please photocopy. Also wants boat license stickers and decals from any state or agency.

    Bill Smiley
    PO Box 361
    Portage, WI 53901
       (608) 742-3714 eves

☆ *Chris Craft* **material** such as factory catalogs, price lists, technical advisories, boat plans and other similar materials. "If the right thing came along, the club would also be interested in owning a model or full-size boat or *Chris Craft* outboard engine."

    Wilson Wright
    Antique Boat Club
    217 South Adams Street
    Tallahassee, FL 32301
       (904) 224-5169   Fax: (904) 224-1033

☆ **Wooden motor boat memorabilia** especially items related to Gar Wood, the man and his boats, 1923-47. Also *Chris Craft, Hacker, Old Town*, and others. Buys sales literature, catalogs, magazines, etc.

> Tony Mollica
> PO Box 6003
> Syracuse, NY 13217
> (315) 433-2643 days

☆ **Outboard motors.** "I'll buy outboard motors, boat and sales literature, and engine manuals from before 1940. Also **boating magazines**, nautical books, and other ephemera including information about marine engines, outboard motors, yachts, canoes, treasure hunting, Arctic voyages, and boat building." Nothing after 1940 please. When describing outboard motors, give serial number and tell whether the engine is frozen or turns over. Offers wants list and catalog of items for sale.

> Robert Glick, Columbia Trading Co.
> 504 Main Street
> West Barnstable, MA 02668
> Fax: (508) 362-3551

☆ **Outboard motors, 1940-1960.** "I'm especially interested in motors by *Flambeau, Neptune, Martin 200* and any racing outboards made in the United States, such as *Mercury* and *Champion*. If you send me a photo of your old outboard motor along with an SASE, I'll identify it for you, and if it's something I can use, I'll make an offer." Peter is the author of *The Old Outboard Book*.

> Peter Hunn
> c/o WZZZ Radio
> Lakeshore Road
> Fulton, NY 13069
> (315) 593-1313

☆ **Lighthouses, U.S. Coast Guard**, and **sea rescue services**, pre-1940. Wants all types of ephemera.

> Robert Glick, Columbia Trading Co.
> 504 Main Street
> West Barnstable, MA 02668
> Fax: (508) 362-3551

☆ **Hardhat diving gear** and old two hose SCUBA regulators.

> Thomas Szymanski
> 5 Stoneybrook Lane
> Exeter, NY 03833
> (603) 772-6372

AIRPLANE & AIRLINE ITEMS

☆ **Aviation history.** This active dealer in aviation equipment and history wants any authentic military and antique flying equipment, parts, props, engines, wheels, armaments, suits, helmets, goggles, overhaul manuals, jackets, survival gear, maps, photographs, histories, toys, artwork, jewelry, etc. If it's genuine, old, and aviation, they probably want it. They do not want reproductions or items that have been altered. Please supply data found on the manufacturer's ID tag, a condition statement, and what you know of the item's history. Photo suggested. Samples of their interesting catalog are $1 each.

>Lee and Diane Herron
>Aviators World
>1434 Flightline #13
>Mojave, CA 93501
>   (805) 824-2424   Fax: (805) 824-2723

☆ **Airplanes and old airplane parts**, early flight equipment, books, magazines, photos, etc., are sought by the 6,000 members of *The Antique Airplane Association*. Write what you have for sale in the way of early air memorabilia, and President Taylor will forward your letter to a member who is looking for what you have to sell. The Association is the parent organization of the Air-Power Museum and Bob is empowered to accept tax deductible donations of significant and interesting items from the history of air flight.

>Bob Taylor
>Antique Airplane Association
>Route 2 Box 172
>Ottumwa, IA 52501
>   (515) 938-2773 days

☆ **All early airplane memorabilia** including propellers, instruments, badges, flight awards, tools, manuals, emblems, accessories, china, checks, bonds, and virtually any good quality early item.

>Joseph Russell
>455 Ollie Street
>Cottage Grove, WI 53527
>   (608) 839-4736 eves

☆ *Pan Am's China Clipper* and all Chinese airline memorabilia, **1925-45,** including caps, uniforms, medals, photos, diaries, badges, posters, and what have you.

>Gene Christian
>3849 Bailey Ave.
>Bronx, NY 10463
>   (718) 548-0243

☆ **Pan-Am airlines and affiliates** ephemera wanted including toys, playsets, schedules, brochures, premiums, posters, photos, postcards, advertising, and other memorabilia. Other companies include **Panagra, Panair de Brasil, C.N.A.C., Pacific Alaska, Aeromarine, and N.Y.R.B.A.** Especially wants items from the Clipper ships of the 1930's. Does not want kiddie wings, pilot wings, swizzle sticks, uniforms, glasses, or china. Give a complete description including dimensions. Describe the logo or make a photocopy.

> Robert Horn
> 345 East 73rd Street
> New York, NY 10021
> (212) 371-1511   Fax: (212) 223-4911

☆ **Concorde and SST items.** "Everything related to the Concorde or SST is of interest, including newspaper reports, magazines articles, advertisements, autographs of people influential in building the planes, models larger than 24", jewelry, videotapes of commercials, china, silver, parts, old seats, gifts given away on flights and commemorative menus. No everyday menus, underarm portfolios, airline magazines, or duty free catalogs are wanted, nor is the video *How They Fly the Concorde.* Send a Xerox™ and "an honest description."

> Everen T. Brown
> PO Box 296
> Salt Lake City, UT 84110
> Fax: (801) 364-2646

☆ *Ford* **tri-motor airplane memorabilia.** "Will pay $100 for Ford Airplane Co. employee badge."

> Tim O'Callaghan
> 46878 Betty Hill
> Plymouth, MI 49170
> (313) 459-4636

☆ **Wooden airplane propellers.**

> Charles Martignette
> PO Box 293
> Hallandale, FL 33009
> (305) 454-3474

☆ **Helicopter, vertical flight, gyro-copter, jet-pack and experimental aircraft.** Buys everything: objects, photos, printed items, specs, blueprints, advertising for them or using them, paintings, prints, toys, and "anything else, military or civilian, in any age or condition" related to flight other than in standard fixed-wing aircraft.

> Rick Bohr
> 12865 NE 85th Street #239
> Kirkland, WA 98033
> (206) 828-9417

☆ **Commercial aviation memorabilia, American or foreign, 1919-50** including books, letters, magazines, photographs, and miscellaneous small artifacts. Especially interested in uncommon items. No books on how to fly, radio, or navigation. Book club editions or defective books are not wanted.

>Ron Mahoney, Air Age Book Co.
>PO Box 40
>Tollhouse, CA 93667
>(209) 855-8993

☆ **Commercial airline memorabilia** including pilot and stewardess wings, hat emblems, display models, anniversary pins, **playing cards, postcards**, buttons, flight schedules, kiddie wings, and almost anything else old and unusual from the airlines. Especially ephemera from *Northeast Airlines, Delta, Chicago and Southern* and *Western Airlines.*

>John Joiner
>52 Jefferson Parkway #D
>Newman, GA 30263
>(404) 487-3732

☆ **Airline models from travel agencies.** Buys all types of planes, from 1920 to 1990. Photo best.

>Charles Martignette
>PO Box 293
>Hallandale, FL 33009

☆ **Airline pilot and stewardess wings and hat badges** pre-1970. Also **stewardess uniforms** pre-1965 *if they are complete.* Looking for pilot and stewardess wings from the 1940's and 50's from airlines such as *Mohawk Airlines, Northeast Airlines, Inland Airlines, Pioneer Air Lines, Empire Airlines, Colonial Airlines, Chicago and Southern Airlines, Mid-Continent Airlines,* others. Also **metal desk models of airliners** (travel agent type) from 1940-70. No military items. Photocopies helpful.

>Charles Quarles
>204 Reservation Drive
>Spindale, NC 28160
>(704) 286-2962   (704) 245-7803 eves

☆ **Desk display models of aircraft, rockets and missiles** from various manufacturers such as *Convair, General Dynamics, Douglass, Lockheed,* and others. Models created by Topping are preferred but all will be considered. All models should have their original stands.

>Bob Keller, Starline Hobbies
>PO Box 38
>Stanton, CA 90680
>(714) 826-5218 days

☆ **Aviation models and toys** including desk models, travel agency and airline promotional display models, wind tunnel and manufacturer display models, ID and **recognition models**, and aviation toys of all types, including friction floor toys and battery operated toy airplanes. Seeks airplanes, **helicopters, missiles and rockets**, with civilian or military markings. He does not want plastic or wood kid's model kits or home-made items. Tell him the material from which it's made, the size, the type of stand and all markings. Indicate any and all missing or broken parts.

> Larry McLaughlin
> 17 Seventh Avenue
> Smithtown, NY 11787
> (516) 265-9224

☆ **China and silverplate** used by any airline.

> Les Winn
> PO Box 80641
> Chamblee, GA 30366
> (404) 458-6194 eves

☆ **Zeppelin, blimp** and **dirigible memorabilia** including anything shaped like, or about, the giant gas bags such as photos, paper ephemera, postcards, china marked "LZ," stereocards, timetables, books, souvenirs, stamps and covers, training films, toys, games, and Christmas ornaments. Especially wants pieces and parts of zeppelins. No repros, repainted or restored items, homemades, or fakes. "I am a historian not a dealer."

> Zeppelin
> PO Box 2502
> Cinnaminson, NJ 08077
> (609) 829-3959

☆ **Aviation magazines, pilot's handbooks**, and **overhaul manuals** dating from before 1940.

> Alan C. King
> PO Box 86
> Radnor, OH 43066

SPACE MEMORABILIA

☆ **Memorabilia of all early rocket research** including "newsletters, journals, books, magazines, reports, studies, correspondence, drawings, films, blueprints, photographs and any other documentation from France, Germany, UK, USSR or the US regarding speculation, research, development and implementation conducted by any amateur, military, or civilian group or any individual pertaining to rockets, missiles and space travel, 1900-1960." He especially wants "any material from WWII pertaining to work done at Peenemunde, Germany, by Wernher Von Braun, which led to the V-2 and rocket weapons. Also any material having to do with Robert H. Goddard and the experiments he conducted in Worcester, MA, and Roswell, NM, during the 1920's through the 1940's." He is not interested in science fiction or Pop Culture figures like *Buck Rogers* but does want speculative articles that are scholarly or serious.
    Randy Liebermann
    2874 South Abingdon Street #A-1
    Arlington, VA 22206
    (703) 824-9733

☆ **Space shot memorabilia** including souvenirs such as magazines, buttons, autographs, etc. Especially wants "internal" souvenirs such as special medallions, mission patches, models, etc., produced for people directly involved with some space "event" such as a launching or completion of construction. Also internal documents such as manuals, flight plans, charts, and so on. Also hardware, pieces of spacecraft, and other items discarded as part of mission preparation or completion. Also video tapes of launchings or reports from space. Does not want recent items which NASA still sells such as slide sets, T-shirts, etc.
    Mike Smithwick
    450 Navaro Way #109
    San Jose, CA 95134
    (408) 383-0627

☆ **Space memorabilia.** "Anything and everything, with special emphasis on the U.S. space program. I prefer items issued by NASA, larger items, autographs, models, spacesuits, and objects that have been in space and would like to find unopened box of *Pillsbury's* space food sticks. No newspapers. Please Xerox© and give accurate description."
    Everen T. Brown
    PO Box 296
    Salt Lake City, UT 84110
    Fax: (801) 364-2646

GOVERNMENT SERVICES

☆ **School, teacher, and student memorabilia** from before 1920, especially diaries, postcards, photographs, teaching certificates, teacher souvenirs, rewards of merit, report cards, letters, student assignments, and books having to do with teaching or operating schools. No student textbooks except those from before 1860. Has particular interest in ephemera associated with New England educator **Samuel Read Hall** (1795-1877), a prominent early textbook author.

    Tedd Levy
    PO Box 2217
    Norwalk, CT 06850
       (203) 852-9864

☆ **Civilian Conservation Corps (CCC)** memorabilia such as belt buckles, scarves, uniforms, sweetheart pillows, china, etc., which run $15 and up. Items marked with the unit camp number are the most desirable, especially the sleeve unit patches designed by the individual camps, worth $25 up. Honor awards will bring $150 each, more if found complete with original ribbon in good condition. Send photo, sketch or photocopy of what you have.

    Tom Pooler
    PO Box 1861
    Grass Valley, CA 95945
       (916) 268-1338

☆ **Civilian Conservation Corps (CCC)** memorabilia including uniforms, awards, footlockers, tools, photos, art, crafts, manuals, camp scrip, official records, diaries. "I'll buy just about anything you find at prices ranging from $10 to $5,000." Please, no WPA or other agencies.

    Ken Kipp
    PO Box 116
    Allenwood, PA 17810
       (717) 538-1440

☆ **U.S. Post Office memorabilia** including steel postmarking devices, locks and keys, uniform badges and buttons, scales, marked handguns, and postcards depicting post offices. Many other items are also wanted, but not postage stamps. If you have a postmarking device to sell, make an imprint. His large illustrated wants list can be had if you send first class postage on a large self addressed envelope. "Please, only offer me obsolete items no longer in use."

    Frank Scheer
    12 East Rosemont Ave.
    Alexandria, VA 22301
       (703) 549-4095 eves

FIRE FIGHTING EPHEMERA

☆ **Fire fighting and fire insurance ephemera** including, but not limited to, fire grenades, awards, helmets, buckets, axes, **badges, toys**, fire marks, fire insurance signs, advertising items, nozzles, apparatus parts, alarm equipment, **photos**, lanterns, **extinguishers**, **postcards**, books, salesmen's samples, models, etc., especially from pre-1900. Nothing made after 1940 is of interest.
>Ralph Jennings, Jr.
>301 Fort Washington Ave.
>Fort Washington, PA 19034
>(215) 646-7178 eves

☆ **Wood cased fire station gongs.** "I'll buy any wood cased fire station gong, working condition or not, made by *Gamewell Fire Alarm Telegraph Co., Star Co., Moses Crane Co.*, or other manufacturer. Gongs have wooden cases, glass doors, and key wind movements." Also wants literature describing gongs or photos of fire station watch desks showing a wall gong.
>Gary Carino
>805 West 3rd Street
>Duluth, MN 55806
>(218) 722-0964

☆ **Fire and casualty insurance company memorabilia,** especially reverse on glass signs and automobile bumper and grill tags that have an insurance company's name. Your description should include the name of the insurance company, size, material, and condition. "Best to send a photo, along with the dimensions." If he doesn't want your item, he will give you the name of another collector who might be interested in what you have, whenever possible. No life insurance items.
>Byron Gregerson
>PO Box 951
>Modesto, CA 95353
>(209) 523-3300

You'll find buyers for other insurance items on 334, 361 and 458.

☆ **Glass fire grenade bottles** in any color if embossed with a brand name and "fire grenade." He is particularly interested in finding those with the name of a railroad. He does not want glass bulb grenades from the 1940's that are filled with carbon tetrachloride. List the color, size, and all defects, especially chips, cracks, or damage to any labels.
>Larry Meyer
>4001 Elmwood Ave.
>Stickney, IL 60402
>(708) 749-1564

☆ **Fire fighting antiques and alarm equipment,** especially fire alarm boxes and **wood cased gongs** in any condition and quantity (would like to buy entire systems or collections). Will also buy extinguishers, nozzles, bells, lanterns, helmets, badges, **fire grenades**, **fire related toys**, and catalogs. Your description should give all markings, dimensions, and any history of the piece you know. Make sure you include your phone number and best time for him to call.

Stan Zukowski
1867 Ellard Place
Concord, CA 94521
(510) 687-6426

☆ **Fire fighting antiques** such as early leather fire helmets, leather fire buckets with paintings on them, speaking trumpets with fancy engraving, early fire nozzles from hand operated pumpers, fire department lanterns that burn kerosene or whale oil and have two color glass globes, gold or silver presentation badges, etc. **Anything from the Chicago Fire Department** from before 1940. Very old fire alarm boxes, wood cased fire gongs, fire alarm registers, and other old equipment marked *Gamewell, Star, Moses Crane, American,* or *U.S. Police & Fire* is wanted by this veteran fire fighter.

Larry Meyer
4001 Elmwood Ave.
Stickney, IL 60402
(708) 749-1564

☆ **Badges, lanterns, helmets** and other old fire department items. Have a special interest in fire items, including paper, from Cincinnati.

Stan Willis
6211 Stewart Road
Cincinnati, OH 45227
(513) 271-0454 days

☆ **Medals awarded to firefighters** for valor, service, longevity, participation in an event, or as a prize in a competition. They may be from any country and any period, especially pre-1920. He does not want fire convention medals from various states. A Xerox™ copy will describe the medal and accompanying paper.

David Cerull
PO Box 992
Milwaukee, WI 53201

LAW ENFORCEMENT MEMORABILIA

☆ **Law enforcement memorabilia** such as badges, patches, night-sticks, handcuffs, and restraints from all types of law enforcement officers including fish and game, railroad security, sheriffs, marshals, constables, Indian police, city police, and other. Also likes studio **portraits of law enforcement officers**. Make a photocopy of the front and rear of your badge or photo and give its history if you can. No security company, college police, or "gun show" brass badges. Include any wording or numbers you find on handcuffs or leg irons.

Gene Matzke
Gene's Badges
2345 South 28th Street
Milwaukee, WI 53215
(414) 383-8995   (414) 645-8288

☆ **Western peace officer's badges,** especially from Oklahoma and the Southwest. "I am especially interested in suspension badges (which hang from a bar by chains), stars, circles with cut out stars, shields, and others, depending on age and appearance. I buy some contemporary badges, depending on their hallmark and where they are from. Indian police badges from anywhere are also wanted, as is a genuine Arizona Ranger badge. Note there are a lot of fake badge #11's on the market; a genuine one is made of sheet silver and hand engraved. I am not interested in reproductions, phonies, fakes and cheap brass badges." This 30 year collector/author warns that it is important to have any badge authenticated by someone who really knows what he's doing. Gene wants to know the style of badge, the wording, who wore it and where, any hallmarks, and what you think the age of the badge is. "If you're in doubt, send the badge insured and I will inspect it, make an offer, or return it."

Ron Donoho
3600 Pama Lane
Las Vegas, NV 89120
(702) 451-1250

☆ **All items related to imprisonment, locking and restraint** including handcuffs, shackles, ball & chains, leather restraints, straight-jackets, prison uniforms and antique or unusual **padlocks**. Also wants magician's escape locks, lock picks and books about lock picking. Well known dealers in magic and escape devices offer their catalog for $2.

Joe and Pam Tanner
Tanner Escapes
3024 East 35th
Spokane, WA 99223
(509) 448-8457 voice and fax

☆ **Law enforcement badges, handcuffs, and leg irons** from anywhere in the U.S., the older the better. Also police department photos and histories, especially from Ohio. Mention whether your item works and has a key.

    Stan Willis
    6211 Stewart Road
    Cincinnati, OH 45227
       (513) 271-0454 days

☆ **Handcuffs, leg irons, torture and execution devices, and electric chairs,** both authentic and reproduction. Also wants photographs of these devices in use. Please photocopy any photographs you want to sell.

    Harvey Lee Boswell's Palace of Wonders
    PO Box 446
    Elm City, NC 27822
       (919) 291-7181

☆ **Northwest Mounted Police items** from before 1950. Also the Royal Northwest Mounted Police, the Royal Canadian Mounted Police, the BC Provincial Police, or the Alberta Provincial Police. Especially awards and medals, cap badges, collar badges, uniforms, and law enforcement items marked with the initials of one of these agencies.

    Michael Rice
    PO Box 286
    Saanichton, BC
    V8M 2C5 CANADA
       (604) 652-9047 eves only

☆ **Law enforcement memorabilia from prohibition era Chicago** including photos, police bulletins, warrants for arrests, court transcripts, police uniforms (1920's only), badges, and personal items from police chiefs Garrity, Fitzmorris, Collins, Hughs, and Russell. Only well documented personal effects, please, with value in part dependent upon the authenticity and story accompanying the item. If offering personal effects, tell how you obtained them and provide your phone number.

    Michael Graham's Roaring 20's
    33133 O'Plaine Road
    Gurnee, IL 60031
       (708) 263-6285

☆ **Paper related to law enforcement** before 1920 including wanted posters, warrants, subpoenas, letters, court documents, complaints, etc. Will consider anything signed by sheriffs, U.S. Marshals, or judges.

    Warren Anderson, America West Archives
    PO Box 100
    Cedar City, UT 84721

(801) 586-9497

☆ **Prison, jail, or penal colony related memorabilia** including items from juvenile detention centers and reform schools. Items include coins, tokens, uniforms, weapons, badges, letters about prison life, restraint devices, photos of prisons, items made by prisoners, postcards, and "just about anything at all." His prime interest is in **scrip**, the paper money used in institutions as a medium of exchange. If you have genuine prison material you may send it for his offer.

"Jailhouse Jerry" Zara
2414 Mark Place
Point Pleasant, NJ 08742
(908) 899-1016

☆ **Jail, prison, and law enforcement memorabilia,** with emphasis on all types of restraints, including U.S. or foreign military, third world, and Eastern European. Wants handcuffs, ball and chains, manacles, leg irons, thumb screws, nippers, iron claws, and comealongs. Also wants literature from manufacturers, copies of *Detective*, a peace officer trade magazine, and patent information on locks and restraints. Wants to find magician's key rings as well as restraint keys marked with the maker's name. He says now is a particularly good time to sell.

Larry Franklin
3238 Hutchison Ave.
Los Angeles, CA 90034
(310) 559-4461

☆ **San Quentin and Folsom prison and prisoner memorabilia,** 1890-1915 with special interest in prisoners Ed Morrell, Donald Lowrie, Jake Oppenheimer, Sir Harry Westwood Cooper, Jack Black, Christopher Evans, and George Sontag. Do you know or have anything about these people? If so, Jack wants to hear from you.

Jack Fleming
1825 Vine #2
Berkeley, CA 94703
(510) 526-4565

☆ **Fingerprinting equipment.** "I'll buy old police fingerprinting equipment including *Bertillon* equipment, fingerprint cameras, microscopes and especially books and magazines concerning fingerprinting." Also wants to buy **WANTED posters** and **police mug shots**.

Michael Carrick
1230 Hoyt Street SE
Salem, OR 97302
(800) 852-0300   Fax: (503) 588-0398

DOCTORS & DRUG STORES

☆ **Unusual medicines and things claiming to act like medicines.** "I'll buy pills, liquids, mixtures, devices and things promoted to cure ills or bring on better health. I'll consider items whether they work or not, whether scientific or crackpot, drab or colorful, sincere, absurd, or ridiculous. I'll even buy brand new items if they are odd or come with an interesting story."
  • **Bottles and containers**, empty or full of pills and powders;
  • **Bottling and filling materials**;
  • **Advertising flyers** and trade cards of all sorts for medicines;
  • **Medical catalogs**;
  • **Health devices, real or quack**, such as vaporizers, electric
      gadgets, etc., the more unusual the better;
  • **Any product that makes a health claim** such as tobacco,
      mineral water, etc.;
  • **Books and booklets**, serious or humorous, on medicines;
  • **Medical teaching devices**.
"I'd like as complete a description as possible, including the item's age, condition, price, and what you feel to be its unique characteristics."
   August Maymudes
   10564 Cheviot Drive
   Los Angeles, CA 90064
      (310) 839-4426 eves   Fax: (310) 481-8169

☆ **Medical and apothecary (drug store) equipment** from before 1900 including **doctor's instruments**, bleeding bowls, leech jars, apothecary tools, pontiled and embossed **patent medicine** bottles, especially with colored glass and all labels (will pay from $500 to $6,000 for fine ones), patent medicine tax stamps 1860-80, and all patent medicine advertising in *any* form especially signs, clocks, tins, and 3-dimensional papier-maché figures. A 26 year veteran collector/dealer, he'll pay from $150 to $3,000 for leech jars and to $1,500 for figures.
   Jerry Phelps
   6013 Innes Trace Road
   Louisville, KY 40222
   (502) 425-4765

☆ **Medical instruments such as monaural stethoscopes, ear trumpets and conversation tubes,** brass anesthesia masks from the drop ether days, all bleeders, especially mechanical, and old dental instruments if made from wood or ivory.
   Lucille Malitz, Lucid Antiques
   PO Box KH
   Scarsdale, NY 10583
      (914) 636-7825

☆ **Medicine, dentistry, apothecary and quackery** of all sorts:
- Surgical tools with wood or bone handles or in boxed sets;
- Bleeding instruments, leech jars and cupping sets;
- **Electric quackery**, including belts, boxes, helmets, etc.;
- Stethoscopes with woven tubes and hard rubber bells;
- Ear trumpets;
- Homeopathic medicine cases;
- Apothecary cases, pill rollers, **medicine bottles, mortars and pestles**, and bottles with gold painted labels;
- Tooth extractors;
- **Phrenology heads;**
- **Eyeglasses** with telescoping ear pieces or wide loops;
- Hanging signs for opticians;
- **Microscopes** and microscope lamps;
- X-Ray tubes and other oddly shaped vacuum tubes;
- **Medical books**, 1600 to 1900, the earlier the better;
- Planetarium models.

Send photos or photocopies of what you have for sale. Make a Xerox™ of eyeglasses as he does not want 20th century eyeglasses (they have nosepads). Give standard bibliographic information on all books. Always include your phone number so he can phone you if he needs to ask questions before purchase.

> Jon Lewin
> 622 Raleigh Avenue #3
> Norfolk, VA 23507
> (804) 625-6732

☆ **Microscopes and other medical or scientific instruments.** "I'll buy pre-1900 microscopes by the following makers: *Zentmayer, Grunow, Bullock, McAllister, Gundlock, Tolles, Queen, Pike* and *Charles Spencer*." Give the maker's name and serial number. Describe overall condition of the instrument, case, and accessories. "Don't clean or polish anything," he warns.

> Dr. Allan Wissner
> PO Box 102
> Ardsley, NY 10502
> (914) 693-4628

☆ **Enema equipment** and information about it. "I'll buy various sizes and styles of rubber bags, especially in different colors. I also want porcelain and glass irrigator containers." Also buys books and catalogs related to the subject, from any maker. "No new type fountain syringes with white plastic hoses." Items must not be made of plastic, and must have black, not white, fittings. Do you have the original box?

> Helen Roman
> 115 Baldwin Street
> Bloomfield, NJ 07003

☆ **Medical and drug store items** including trade cards, catalogs, advertising, journals, ledgers, photos, and other similar ephemera pre-1910. Also patent medicines, instruments and **quack devices.**
> Doug Johnston
> 529 West Encanto
> Phoenix, AZ 85003

☆ **Stethoscopes.** "I'll buy antique and unusual physician's stethoscopes, both monaural and binaural." Give all markings, patents, etc.
> Chris Papadopoulos
> 1107 Chatterleigh Circle
> Towson, MD 21286
> (410) 825-9157 eves

☆ **Embalming tools and bottles.** Embalming kits and tools are often in black bags and can be recognized by long aspiration needles. Many tools and bottles are marked with skull and crossbones. Look for *Dioxin* brand, and others. "I have enough embalming tables unless they're priced at $20 or less."
> Steve DeGenaro
> PO Box 5662
> Youngstown, OH 44504

☆ **Medically related advertising and memorabilia** especially tin containers, trays, signs, match holders, trade cards, advertising envelopes, calendars, old corked and labeled medicine bottles, pin back buttons, mirrors, **instruments**, and the like. Among tins, he wants medical, dental, veterinary, talcums, prophylactics, etc. Fine condition only.
> Eugene Cunningham, MD
> 152 Wood Acres Drive
> East Amherst, NY 14051
> (716) 688-9537

☆ **Old quack medical devices** which shock, spark, buzz, vibrate, or do nothing at all. Most devices were built into fancy boxes with dials, wires, hand electrodes, plated terminals, coils, and levers. Other devices consisted of therapeutic gloves, brushes, charms, and the like. There is an extensive list of brand names he seeks but he does not want common massage vibrators, violet rays, and *Electreat* devices. He also buys books, catalogs, pamphlets, and other paper ephemera promoting quack electrical items or other therapeutic gimmicks. Keller prefers you price your item but will make offers.
> Leland Keller
> 1205 Imperial Drive
> Pittsburg, KS 66762

☆ **Medical items and quackery.** Wants pre-1900 medical advertising, **patent medicine** ads and displays, and devices and ads related to medical quackery of any sort, except "I don't need any more violet ray machines." Send a good description; photocopy paper items.
>
> W.H. Marshall
> PO Box 1023
> Melrose, FL 32666

☆ **Phrenology items** including heads showing trait lines, or numbered zones on the head, posters, and wall hangings. No books.
>
> Donald Gorlick
> PO Box 24541
> Seattle, WA 98124
> (206) 824-0508

☆ **Medical books and ephemera.** Wants quality items including books from before 1840, medical broadsides, pamphlets, hand colored illustrations, stereo views, letters, documents, and catalogs. "I'll pay well for quality material," he states.
>
> Ivan Gilbert, Miran Arts & Books
> 2824 Elm Ave.
> Columbus, OH 43209
> (614) 421-3222   Fax: (614) 421-3223

☆ **Chiropractic equipment and books** especially electronic diagnostic gear or items from the Palmer College/School. Pre-1960 only, please.
>
> Mel Rosenthal
> 5 The Strand
> New Castle, DE 19720
> (302) 322-8944   (302) 322-3030

☆ **Optical supplies and equipment**: buys old, rare and unusual testing devices, trade signs, eyeglasses, eyeglass cases, quack devices, medicines for eye care, and "anything optical." Give the maker's name, serial number, and description of the piece.
>
> Tom Baltrusaitis
> Optical Museum
> 214 North Main
> Hannibal, MO 63401
> (314) 248-3937   Fax: (314) 221-2444

☆ **All human glass eyes** in any size or color, rights or lefts.
>
> Donald Gorlick
> PO Box 24541
> Seattle, WA 98124
> (206) 824-0508

☆ **Unusual eye cups.**
>   W.T. Atkinson
>   1217 Bayside Circle West
>   Wilmington, NC 28405

☆ **Dental cabinets, instruments, and catalogs,** but only before 1920.
>   Peter Chu, DDS
>   5470 Folkestone Drive
>   Dayton, OH 45459
>   (513) 435-6849

☆ **Twins, multiple births, and freak parasitic twin births.** This dedicated nurse archivist wants photos, newspaper clips, souvenirs, personal information, and *anything* statistical, scholarly, or informative. If you are one of a multiple birth, this is the lady who will preserve the experience. She always wants first hand information from multiples about their lives. *She does not want* undated clippings or items that have been damaged by pinning, pasting, or taping. When describing scrapbooks, make certain to note whether the clippings are dated. "My collection is not a hobby but a full time job in research, internationally recognized for its accuracy and extent, a source of factual information for physicians, researchers, and news media of all types." She has been at it since 1939, but Miss Helen always appreciates help, especially people sending clippings from local papers and obscure magazines about twins (as long as you tell where it came from and the date). Especially wants **photos and other Dionne quints** memorabilia.
>   Miss Helen Kirk's Multiple Birth Museum
>   PO Box 254
>   Galveston, TX 77553
>   (409) 762-4792

DRUG STORE ITEMS

☆ **Patent medicine advertising.** "I'll buy 19th century advertising, trade cards, almanacs, booklets, postcards, posters, sheet music, tokens, and giveaway items related to any patent medicine. I have a particular interest in *Hadacol* items, and will purchase them as late as 1950. In trade cards, I am looking for 'private' cards, made for one manufacturer, not stock cards with overprints. Please send a photocopy or send the item itself on approval." Walker has a new book forthcoming on the history of patent medicine advertising.
>   A. Walker Bingham
>   19 East 72nd Street
>   New York, NY 10021
>   (212) 628-5358 voice and fax

☆ **Almanacs published by patent medicine companies, between 1840-1920.** Many of these pay $20-$30. If you have many of them to sell it is advisable to have his detailed wants list. There were dozens of almanac companies that are wanted. He does not want any of the three most common almanacs: *Swamp Root, Nostetters*, or *Ayers*. No foreign language editions, either. The only almanacs he wants are printed before 1920. Please don't offer medical booklets, pamphlets, cookbooks, or paper items other than almanacs.

> Rodney Brunsell
> 55 Spring Street
> Hanson, MA 02341

☆ **Dark blue medicine and poison bottles.** Bottles must be cork tops, not screw tops. Particularly looking for bottles which held salts by *John Wyeth and Bro.* that have dose caps, contents, and paper labels. Also want *Warner's, Mulford's*, and other cobalt blue and green bottles complete with contents and labels. Pays $60+ for *Kickapoo* bottle with original stopper. No bottles marked TAIWAN or WHEATON or modern milk of magnesia. Give the color, size, and embossed letters or designs, and note existence of chips, cracks, labels, screw threads, etc.

> Adrienne Escoe
> PO Box 342
> Los Alamitos, CA 90720

☆ **Poison bottles**. Early poison bottles usually came in distinctive shapes and colors, so they could be readily identified, even in the dark. Many are marked with skull and crossbones, and others will say USE WITH CAUTION. Those with original labels and contents are of particular interest, and a blue bottle shaped like a skull with the word POISON on the forehead could bring you $1,000 or more. This veteran collector notes that there is a ceramic reproduction of the skull bottle which is of no interest. Condition is of "extreme importance" to bottle collectors. Chips, cracks, bruises, stains, weak or faint embossing can all affect the value of a bottle. Please give the height of your bottle after examining it carefully for any damage. Bottles with screw tops are not wanted.

> Tim Denton
> 113 St. James Street South
> Waterford, ON, Canada N0E 1Y0
> (519) 443-4162

BOTTLES

☆ **Bottles.** "I'll buy American bottles from *before* 1900 which have complete labels or interesting embossing. I prefer bitters, historical flasks, and barber bottles, but will consider cures, ink, patent medicine, figures, liquors, beer, soda, bar decanters, fruit jars, poisons, and miniatures. They may be clear, aqua, green, amber, blue, or milk glass in color." Bottles are *not* wanted if there is a side seam which goes from the base of the bottle to the top of the lip, or if they have screw tops (except canning jars, which all do). Bottles which do not have seams or which have seams that end before the neck of the bottle are usually old enough to be worth an inquiry. Age alone does not make value, though. Combinations of color, shape, embossing, and rarity are what makes a bottle worth money. Because color of bottles is so important in determining value, a clear accurate photo is essential when selling bottles. A rubbing of the embossing is advised. Dimensions should be included. Do not offer bottles which have cracks or chips. He will make offers to amateurs only. Dealers must set their price. Steve's one-page *Guide to Bottle Dating* is yours for only $1 and an SASE.
> Steve Ketcham
> PO Box 24114
> Minneapolis, MN 55424
> (612) 920-4205

☆ **Bottles.** "I buy antique bitters, figurals, historical flasks, poisons, cures, inks, sodas and mineral waters, fruit jars, whiskeys, free blown and pattern molded bottles, three mold bottles, decanters, and other forms. I'm looking for unusual colors and rarities, and will pay very well for them. I also want **advertising, trade cards, posters, boxes, display cases, tokens, tins, signs, etc., related to antique bottles,** or picturing old medicines and whiskey bottles." Nothing made after 1910 or marked WHEATON NJ. *Jim Beam* type collectible ceramics have no interest. Please send a sharp color photo. Note the size and all chips and cracks, no matter how tiny. If you know the item's history, please share it. Dealers price your goods. Amateurs may ask for an offer.
> Mike Waters
> 3947 Old Columbia Pike
> Ellicott City, MD 21043
> (410) 465-8095 eves   Fax: (301) 470-4148

☆ **Bottles and bottle company ephemera** of all types such as calendars, brochures, and signs. *Gayner Glass Co.* is of special interest, as are Salem squats, a type of New Jersey soda bottle.
> Charles McDonald's Bottle Museum
> 4 Friendship Drive
> Salem, NJ 08079
> (609) 935-5631

☆ **Early American bottles and historical flasks.** Wants hand blown figural bottles or those with embossed figures and portraits. Will pay $3,000 for *"The American System"* flask depicting a paddle wheeler. Also wants **figural bitters bottles** and hand-blown, pontil marked, **colored ink** and **medicine bottles.** Burt also buys **rare fruit (canning) jars** complete with lids, round and **colored milk bottles** and mineral water bottles. No cracks, chips, or bad stains are acceptable. Burt advises reading McKearin's *American Glass* to see bottles which attract top dollar. No machine made bottles or reproductions.

> Burton Spiller
> 49 Palmerston Road
> Rochester, NY 14618
> (716) 244-2229

☆ **Antique American medicine and beer bottles,** both glass and pottery, especially from the Buffalo area. Has a particular interest in the patent medicine bottles of *G. W. Merchant* of Lockport, NY. Also wants mineral waters, **poisons, and barber shop bottles**. Buys **trade cards, advertising, billheads,** and other items associated with makers or users of bottles in **Western New York state**. Sven publishes the newsletter of the Western New York Bottle Collectors Association.

> Sven Stau
> PO Box 437
> Buffalo, NY 14212
> (716) 825-5448 or (716) 822-3120

☆ **Early American bottles.** Buys a wide range of glass bottles, including bitters, campaign bottles, figurals, whiskey flasks and **glass jugs with handles.** Wants glass bottles with agricultural symbols, flags, sunbursts, portraits of national heroes, and the like, or bottles in the shape of log cabins, cannons, lighthouses, pigs, etc. Many of these items are worth in excess of $1,000. **Pottery pig bottles** are also wanted, but no *Jim Beam* type whiskey bottles.

> Robert Daly
> 10341 Jewell Lake Court
> Fenton, MI 48430
> (313) 629-4934

☆ **Bottles from California and the old West.** "I'll buy whiskey, medicine, food and other bottles from the days of miners, loggers, and cowboys in the West. I especially like bottles with the names of California towns and companies on them." He wants **whiskey bottles with pictures** embedded in the glass, which bring from $100 to as much as $2,500 for a *California Club* bottle. "Bottles without names or designs embossed in the glass are generally

"If your bottle says FEDERAL LAW FORBIDS THE RESALE... it isn't old enough to be of interest to collectors."

valueless to collectors as are most cracked or chipped ones." Tell him what it says on your bottle, what color it is and what condition it is in, particularly regarding neck chips.

> John Goetz
> PO Box 1570
> Cedar Ridge, CA 95924
> (916) 272-4644

☆ **Bottles from Artesian Mfg & Bottling Company**. This Waco, TX, company's bottles were marked as AM&B CO. He wants the early "blob top and bowling pin styles."

> Bob Thiele
> 620 Tinker Avenue
> Pawhuska, OK 74056
> (918) 287-3845 eves

☆ *Flaccus, Hunter and Exwaco* **bottles and jars** with colorful labels. All West Virginia food companies from before 1910 are wanted. Has special interest in food jars, bottles, and crocks from the above, but buys **any jars marked as made or used in Wheeling or Wellsburg, WV**. Give the color of the glass and its size. Report *exactly* what is written on the jar or crock, and note any cracks, chips, or unwashable stains. They will pay $200 for a *Flaccus* stoneware water cooler.

> Tom and Deena Caniff
> 1223 Oak Grove Ave.
> Steubenville, OH 43952
> (614) 282-8918

PACKAGING & ADVERTISING

☆ **Advertising signs and gaming machines.** Signs on paper, cardboard, and especially tin, advertising whiskey, beer, tobacco, and other home and personal products. Items must be old and in very fine condition to be of interest to the nation's largest auctioneer of this type item.
> James D. Julia Auctions
> PO Box 830
> Fairfield, ME 04937
> (207) 453-7904   Fax: (207) 453-2502

☆ **Advertising signs**, calendars, posters, display pieces, packaging, and small giveaway items. "We prefer food, soda, coffee, hunting and fishing, veterinary, medicines, sporting goods, gasoline and autos with nice color pictures, especially those featuring celebrities. Items related to *Planters* peanuts are especially sought, with some bringing $1,000+. Condition is vital in advertising items, so please don't offer items in only fair condition. We prefer to see photos of the items along with accurate description of size, flaws, blemishes, etc." This important regional auctioneer issues semi-annual catalogs for absentee auctions.
> William Morford, Wm. Morford Auctions
> Route 2
> Cazenovia, NY 13035
> (315) 662-7625   Fax: (315) 662-3570

☆ **Advertising signs, posters, trays, calendars** and other items including tip trays, die cut cardboard signs, trade cards, match holders, etched glasses, and tin or glass advertising display pieces. Things must be interesting, colorful, old, original, and in perfect or near perfect condition. "Although I will consider any products, I am particularly interested in beer, whiskey, soda, patent medicine, food, and tobacco items which feature colorful pictures of pretty girls, children, sporting scenes, animals, or products. I do not buy signs without interesting pictures nor do I buy reproductions." Send a good quality photo, dimensions, and a statement of condition. He will make offers to amateur sellers only. Dealers must set their price. Include an SASE.
> Steve Ketcham
> PO Box 24114
> Minneapolis, MN 55424
> (612) 920-4205

☆ **Trade signs from various businesses** including pawn shops, watch makers, jewelers, etc. "I'll pay large sums of money for American wooden carved trade signs."
> Greg "Dr. Z" Zemenick
> 13560 Kirts #160
> Troy, MI 48084
> (810) 642-8129   (810) 244-9426

☆ **Tin, porcelain, and cardboard advertising** from before 1920 including signs, posters, cans, trays, calendars, syrup dispensers, etc., for candy, gum, groceries, soft drinks, ammunition, tobacco, beer, and the like. No magazine or newspaper ads. "We pay the highest prices but do not make offers. Let us know what you have and what you want for it."
> Don Stuart
> 4751 NE Ocean Blvd.
> Jensen Beach, FL 34957

☆ **Three-dimensional advertising trademarked character displays from stores.** "I buy plaster, composition, plastic and wooden store figures depicting cartoonish advertising characters. Items wanted are store displays and statuettes, and promotional banks, figural ash trays, and bobbing head dolls. I'm particularly interested in items of the 1940's through the 1970's. Some character examples include *Speedy Alka Seltzer*, *Reddy Kilowatt*, *Elsie the Cow*, *Philip Morris*'s Johnny, the *Esquire* man, *Pep Boys* figures and other characters. Please provide a good description, paying close attention to damage. I prefer dealers to price goods, but will make offers to amateur sellers." Warren's *Advertising Character Collectibles: an Identification and Value Guide* is available at bookstores or from him for $21 postpaid.
> Warren Dotz
> 2999 Regent Street
> Berkeley, CA 94705
> (510) 652-1159

☆ **Motion display advertising,** especially by *Baranger*. These are small pieces, under 3' high, usually with animated people advertising watches from the 1930's and 40's, but other products are also found.
> Frank and Jay Novak
> 7366 Beverly Blvd.
> Los Angeles, CA 90036
> (213) 683-1963   Fax: (213) 683-1312

☆ **Neon advertising clocks and signs,** 1920-50. Buys those entirely of neon as well as those with "reverse painting on glass" that are lit by neon. Prefers smaller sizes that can be safely shipped via UPS. His favorite clocks and signs are "point of purchase" which sit on counter tops, although he buys wall models, too. He is particularly interested in signs with neon glow tubes made by AMGLO. Also buys **signs that bubble, create optical illusions, or are animated**. Value is based on visual appeal so a photo is essential. Does not want new neon beer signs, plastic signs of any sort, or signs lit by fluorescent tubes.
> Roark Vane
> 6839 Havenside Drive
> Sacramento, CA 95831
> (916) 392-3864   (407) 225-0900

☆ **Colorful tin cans, signs and trays** advertising beer, whiskey, soda pop, medicines, tobacco, and food such as peanuts, peanut butter, tea, coffee, and the like. Especially likes rare peanut butter pails and one-pound coffee cans from New York companies. Nothing rusty or damaged. Describe colors. Photocopy please.

> Burton Spiller
> 49 Palmerston Road
> Rochester, NY 14618
> (716) 244-2229

☆ **Tin cans which held any product,** but only those that are small, printed on the tin and in very fine condition. Typical products are aspirin, condoms, coffee (sample sizes only), cosmetics, needles, polish, typewriter ribbons and the like. He does not want any tins after 1940 or "anything common, including *Tums, Anacin, Bayer Aspirin* and kee-lox style typewriter tins." It is suggested that you send a Xerox™ of what you have. This 15 year veteran collector is among the few buyers found in this guidebook who insists you set the price wanted. However, he does offer to send you a 20 page list of over 2,000 items with the prices he will pay. This list is available to any picker who sends him an SASE with three stamps. David is co-author of *Encyclopedia of Advertising Tin Cans, Smalls, and Samples*, available from him for $34.

> David Zimmerman
> 6834 Newtonsville Road
> Pleasant Plain, OH 45162
> (513) 625-5188

☆ **Porcelain enamel signs,** 1880-1950, advertising any U.S. bicycles, automobiles, motorcycles, gasoline, oil, soda pop, food, soap, clothing, telephones, telegraph, money orders, etc. Likes all types of porcelain signs, including those with **neon trim, thermometers**, and the like, especially interesting figurals. Pays most for multiple color signs depicting animals, people, products, or fancy logos. Condition is very important. He is not interested in repros (look for brass grommets in the hanging holes). No signs bigger than 8 feet long or high. "I want a close up photo, dimensions, and any information the seller has on the item's background. Make certain to include your home phone."

> Robert Newman
> 10809 Charnock Road
> Los Angeles, CA 90034
> (310) 559-0539

☆ **Tin plates** from the turn of the century depicting women and/or advertising. Plates were usually printed by *Meek, Beech* or *Shonk*. Plates must be in fine condition. Photos are almost essential.

> Lisa Van Hook
> PO Box 13256
> El Cajon, CA 92022

☆ **Typewriter ribbon tins.** "I'm interested in any typewriter tin in good condition. I especially want tins made to hold ribbon wider than 1/2" and boxed sets of tins. Large quantities eagerly accepted, but no cardboard boxes of any type." Please send a photocopy.

> Darryl Rehr
> 2591 Military Ave.
> Los Angeles, CA 90064
> > (310) 477-5229 voice or fax

☆ **Damaged, bent, or rusty tin cans or signs** which are difficult to sell. They aren't worth much, but few people will buy them at all. Give him a try with those hard to sell items.

> Ron Knappen
> Route #2   Box 590
> 207 East Mill Road
> Galesville, WI 54630
> > (608) 582-4124   (608) 582-4593

☆ **Advertising featuring Indians, buffalo, or owls.** "I buy labels, cans, packages, hood ornaments, paperweights, bottles, and what have you, picturing Indians, buffalo, and owls. I do not buy anything made after 1960. The more colorful and unusual, the better."

> Charles Ray
> PO Box 881
> Winchester, KY 40392
> > (606) 744-9789

☆ **Salesmen's samples** and other well-made miniatures of real objects. "If your item is in miniature, all parts to scale, and complete, it can be well worth your while to contact me. A sample barber's chair, for example, is worth $10,000 to me. So is a *Wooten* desk sample. Other samples are worth from $300 to $5,000. I'm not interested in doll house miniatures, but want to hear about just about any other small well-crafted items. Since I am writing a book on salesmen's samples, I would like to hear from you even if your piece is not for sale." A photo is almost essential. Include dimensions. Note all repairs. Describe any marks or labels. Describe the case and its condition.

> John Everett
> PO Box 126
> Bodega, CA 94922
> > (707) 876-3513

☆ **Tin can and box making and labeling.** "I'll pay you cash for anything having to do with the history and processes of making cans, boxes, and labels of any kind before World War II. I want label collections, printer's proofs, artist's sketch books, and salesmen's samples of cans, boxes, and labels with special interest in items before 1910. Information, photos, and other ephemera from the people who created cans, boxes and labels, and those who made them, sold them, and used them. Xerox™ what you have whenever possible. Trade directories, instruction manuals, procedures books, job descriptions, and the like are sought. Unusual original historical photos always wanted."

> Tony Hyman
> PO Box 3028
> Pismo Beach, CA 93448

☆ **Canning machinery, catalogs and tools** of the *Ferracute Machine Company* of Bridgeton, NJ, are sought by this researcher who also wants anything related to company founder **Oberlin Smith**. The Oberlin Smith Society is particularly interested in advertising, catalogs, small presses, medals and tokens, but will consider anything related to FMCo or Smith himself. The OSS is a 501(c)(3) organization and seeks donations, too.

> James Gandy, Oberlin Smith Society
> Route #2   Box 109
> 192 River Road
> Bridgeton, NJ 08302
>   (609) 451-5586

☆ **Advertising paperweights made of cast iron.** Must advertise a product or service. "I am primarily interested in figural items, but will purchase some non-figurals. Must be in excellent condition, preferably will all original paint. I am also interested in **other cast iron items: shooting gallery targets, water sprinklers, and advertising.** I do not buy reproductions. Nor to I want damaged items, even if they have been repaired." Photo is important, along with dimensions. "All inquiries answered and photos returned."

> Richard Tucker
> PO Box 262
> Argyle, TX 76226
>   (817) 464-3752   Fax: (817) 464-7293

ADVERTISING FOR VARIOUS INDUSTRIES

☆ **Coffee cans with pictures printed onto the tin** are wanted, especially tall one pound cans with slip tops. No vacuum (key open) cans are wanted. $500 to $1,000 each will be paid for *Army & Navy, Blue Parrot, College Town, Convention Hall* (green or yellow only), *Festall Hall, Mayflower* or *Town Crier*. Most paper label cans are not as desirable and bring a substantially smaller selling price. Send the name of the tin, height and diameter, and state whether the condition is like new or scratched and worn. The *Luzianne* can is common, worth about $15.

> Tim Schweighart
> 1123 Santa Luisa Drive
> Solana Beach, CA 92075
> (619) 481-8315

☆ **Cigar advertising boxes, labels and tins,** especially boxes featuring nudes, sports, gambling, comic characters, and other colorful scenes. Also **gambling devices, trade figures, or signs related to cigars.** Also tin **tobacco cans** and boxes. Photocopy the inside lid of boxes you'd like to sell. Long SASE will bring you a priced illustrated wants list. Don't want items covered with cigar bands except as a gift. Nothing in poor condition. Will pay $400+ for *Asthma Cure, Cheez It* or any xxx rated box. *Handbook of American Cigar Boxes,* an illustrated limited edition, is available for $17.95 postpaid with price guide.

> Tony Hyman
> PO Box 3028
> Pismo Beach, CA 93448
> (805) 773-6777   Fax: (805) 773-8436

☆ **Gun and ammunition related advertising.** "I buy posters, calendars, envelopes with ads, cardboard shotshell boxes, gunpowder cans, pin back buttons, glass target balls, catalogs, etc., but I am only interested in items produced by a gun or ammunition maker (not secondary vendors) before 1940."

> Ron Willoughby
> 1072 Route 171
> Woodstock, CT 06281
> (203) 974-1226

☆ **Gun company advertising depicting cowboys, cowgirls or cattle.** Advertising from other products considered, but particular interest in items with Western orientation. Also wants all **original art for gun and ammunition company ads**. Please send color photo.

> Johnny Spellman
> 10806 North Lamar
> Austin, TX 78753
> (512) 836-2889 days   (512) 258-6910 eves

☆ **Stove company samples and toy stoves.** Wants salesmen's sample stoves, particularly made by *Majestic, Quick Meal, Engman-Matthews* and *Home Comfort.* Desirable toy stoves include *Dolly's Favorite* and all models of *Buck's Jr.* Also wants toy cooking utensils that accompany these stoves (skillets, Dutch ovens, and especially tea kettles up to 4" high) by such makers as *Wagner Ware* and *Griswold.* Dimensions and condition are helpful but a "picture is usually all I need."

> Ed Hullet
> 5200 North Lorraine
> Hutchinson, KS 67502
> (316) 662-9381

☆ **Monarch Stove Company sample.** "I'm looking for a 32" tall miniature *Monarch* kitchen stove finished in porcelain enamel. Will consider in any condition."

> Marilyn Wren
> 9073 Weidkamp
> Lynden, WA 98264
> (206) 354-1903

☆ **Round Oak Stove Company and Simmons Hardware Company** items, especially the *Keen Kutter* brand items put out by Simmons. "I will buy just about anything put out by these companies, such as calenders, tools, postcards, store displays, advertising and the like. Would love to find the Indian figure that stood atop the Round Oak stoves." He does not buy stoves, razors, or axe heads. SASE a must.

> Dennis Schulte
> 8th Avenue NW
> Waukon, IA 52172
> (319) 568-3628

☆ **Bread wrapper end labels.** These labels, mostly from the 1950's, came with many different pictorial themes, from cowboys to movie stars, space to baseball, James Bond to Howdy Doody and all are collectible. Prices for rare labels can reach as high as $150 for rare baseball labels, with most of them in the $5 to $30 each range. Also wants posters, label albums, and advertising referring to label issues and collecting. He does not buy labels from *Wonder Bread, Tip Top*, and other labels that are not part of a collectible series. Unless you have very large quantities of labels, your best bet is to Xerox™ them. Don wrote *Bread End Labels Illustrated Price Guide*, available for $18.

> Don Shelley
> PO Box 11
> Fitchville, CT 06334

☆ **Salmon cans and labels** from Alaska, Canada, or the lower 48. Also buys postcards, letterheads, and views of canneries, fish traps, etc. Only items dating from before 1960 are wanted. Send Xerox™ for offer. You have his authorization to send items on approval.

    W.E. "Nick" Nickell
    102 Peoples Wharf
    Juneau, AK 99801
       (907) 586-1733

☆ **Fruit crate labels and other advertising** from the packing, **canning and bottling trades** such as posters, tin signs, sales displays, letterheads, magazine ads, and other promotional items. He says he'll buy fruit and vegetable labels, American or foreign, but especially West Coast. Will consider singles, bulk quantities, and labels on crates. Especially interested in *Sunkist, Del Monte, Libby's*, etc. Pat's informative book on fruit labels comes with a price guide at $75 postpaid.

    T. Pat Jacobsen
    437 Minton Court
    Pleasant Hill, CA 94523
       (510) 930-8531

☆ **Florida citrus labels.** Also advertisements and other paper related to the Florida citrus industry.

    Jerry Chicone
    PO Box 547636
    Orlando, FL 32854
       (407) 298-555

☆ **Popcorn memorabilia** including boxes, cans, crates, brochures, catalogs, old machines, parts of machines, *Creator's* steam engines, and everything else related to popcorn.

    Jack Cory
    3395 West Pink Place
    Las Vegas, NV 89102
       (702) 367-2676   Fax: (702) 876-1099

☆ **Advertising for medicine and whiskey companies.**
    Robert Daly
    10341 Jewell Lake Court
    Fenton, MI 48430
       (313) 629-4934

ADVERTISING FOR SPECIFIC COMPANIES

☆ **Junk food character premiums** from 1950-1980 kid's junk food such as cookies, candy, cereal, ice cream, drink mixes, and snacks. "Characters I buy in include *Choo Choo Charlie, Quisp, Quake, Cap'n Crunch, Milton the Toaster, Mr. Bubble, Frankenberry, Count Chocula, Marky Maypo, Twinkles, Trix Rabbit, Mr. Wiggle, King Vitamin, Freakies, Farfel* and other cartoon ad trademarks. Products include *Jiffy Pop, Mr. Chips, Fizzies, Gunny Face, Cocoa Marsh, Bosco, Scooter Pies, Bugs Bunny Cookies, Nestle's Chiller, Kool Aid, Otter Pops, Kool Pops, Royal Pudding, Keds, P.F. Flyers, Big Shot Syrup* and especially discontinued oddball products. Will buy **watches**, toys, puppets, figures, banks, fan club kits, T-shirts, and especially store displays such as posters, stand-ups, animated displays and large 3-D figures. "I don't want fast food, generic products with no premium or character." Give condition, your phone number and best hours to call.

> Roland Coover, Jr.
> 1537 East Strasburg Road
> West Chester, PA 19380
> (610) 692-3112

☆ *Cracker Jack* **products,** packaging, prizes, point of sale advertising, etc., from before 1940. Not interested in plastic prizes from the late 1940's to the present, or anything marked "Borden Co." Also items associated with *Angelus* marshmallows, *Chums, Checkers, Reuckheim and Eckstein* and *Reliable* candies. Wes prefers you to Xerox™ what you have, or simply mail him your prizes for his offer. SASE required. Do not call at home.

> Wes Johnson, Sr.
> 106 Bauer Avenue
> Louisville, KY 40207
> (502) 899-3030 extension 228 days only

☆ *Cracker Jack* **prizes, advertising** and related items, including tins, jars, store advertising, point of sale, and dealer items from any of the following companies: *Checkers Confections, Angel Marshmallows, Shotwell Mfg. Co., Rueckheim Bros.* and *Eckstein Co.* He does not want plastic *Cracker Jack* toys and prizes. Note any obvious signs of wear. Price if you can.

> Edwin Snyder
> PO Box 156
> Lancaster, KY 40444
> (606) 792-4816

☆ *Planter's Peanut* **memorabilia.** "I'll buy all rare or unusual items" with particular interest in any and all figural, 3-D *Mr. Peanuts* such as:
- Wooden jointed doll;
- "Blinker" with lighted eyes;
- "Tapper" which taps on a window;
- Scale made of cast iron and aluminum, 4' high;
- Rubber squeeze toy about 8" tall;
- *Mr. Peanut* hand puppet;
- Fence sitter, cast iron, 42" high;
- Parade costume and anything papiermaché;
- Any tin displays and 5# and 10# peanut tins;
- Unopened key wind tins of peanuts;
- Cardboard display boxes peanuts came in;
- Wooden shipping boxes;
- Old jars with peanut finials.

Does not want reproductions or anything from the 1970's or 80's. Does not want plastic items, or tin nut dish sets except World's Fair set (worth about $20). No broken or incomplete items. Send a photo and complete description, including condition of the surface and paint. Enclose an SASE for picture return. Richard is author of *Planter's Peanut Advertising and Collectibles*.

> Richard and Barbara Reddock
> 914 Ilse Court
> North Bellmore, NY 11710
> (516) 826-2032 eves

☆ *Planter's Peanut* **memorabilia** from before 1970 including:
- Unopened key wind tins;
- Display items, statues, signs, and jars;
- Banks and other giveaways.

"I'm interested in anything rare or unusual. Send a description and the price wanted."

> Glenn Grush
> 5344 North Collingwood Circle
> Calabasas, CA 91302
> (818) 880-6200   Fax: (818) 880-6500

☆ *Elsie the Cow* **and other** *Borden's* **ephemera** including games, toys, cookbooks, comic books, cups, glasses, Xmas cards, employee magazines, neon signs, postcards showing the milk plants, magazine ads (especially from 30's medical magazines), milk bottles, trade cards and paper ephemera of all types. Also buys milk bottles and advertising from Du Page County, Illinois. Describe and price your items.

> Ronald Selcke
> PO Box 237
> Bloomingdale, IL 60108
> (708) 543-4848 eves

☆ **Arbuckle Coffee Company items** such as trade cards, advertising, receipts, coffee cans, and other ephemera. Send a Xerox™ if you'd like an offer. You have his permission to send items on approval.

W.E. "Nick" Nickell
102 Peoples Wharf
Juneau, AK 99801
(907) 586-1733

☆ *Sunshine Biscuits* **ephemera** including tins, boxes, signs, display racks, novelties, games, calendars, pin back buttons, trade cards, invoices, stationery and "things we have yet to imagine." Buys items from all brands produced by *Sunshine* or its predecessor, *Loose-Wiles Company*. These companies made potato chips, cookies, crackers, marshmallows, pretzels, candy, and several cereals. "We especially want uncut sheets of stuffed animal toys (worth $150 each), *Ann Hathaway* cookie tins ($250) and neckties advertising their products ($25 up)." Complete descriptions include size, shape, condition, what is pictured, and a photograph or photocopy of the best and worst side. "I will discuss an item with a seller on the phone but prefer a letter with pictures and SASE. I will not agree to purchase nor can I make an offer to buy or appraise an item without seeing it in person. I pay or reimburse for postage on anything I request be sent for inspection."

Liz and Dick Wilmes
38W 567 Brindlewood
Elgin, IL 60123
(708) 697-9679

☆ *Beech-Nut* **items** including any glass container with excellent paper labels, especially catsup, mustard, chili sauce, sliced beef, bacon, ginger ale, sarsaparilla, peanut butter, and jams. Also wants spaghetti cans, gum or candy store display racks, tin or cardboard advertising, biscuit or cookie containers, souvenirs, Christmas boxes, postcards of factories, and anything else. Describe the condition. Include photo when possible. Dealers, price your goods; amateurs may ask for an offer if they don't know an item's value.

Bruce Van Evera
94 Montgomery Street
Canajoharie, NY 13317
(518) 673-3522

☆ *Larkin Soap Company* **items.** "I'll buy items made by or relating to the *Larkin Company,* including products, trade cards, catalogs, advertising, calendars and other paper items. If the item says LARKIN, I'm interested. I want info about the *Larkin* administration building designed by Frank Lloyd Wright and would love to find dedication programs, etc." Please make sure you describe condition.

> Jerome Puma
> 78 Brinton Street
> Buffalo, NY 14214
> (716) 838-5674

☆ *Walgreens Drug Store* **products and ephemera.** "I'll buy a wide range of products marketed by this national chain between 1901 and 1960, including non-prescription drug and health aids, candy, tobacco, coffee, toys and what have you. Items were sold under many different brand names including: *Walgreens, Myers, Union Drug, Keller, Glide, Valentine, Carrel, Amoray, Ladonna, Olafsen, Orlis, Triomphe, Hill Rose, CRW,* and others. I'm especially interested in finding *Walgreens* tin cans for coffee and other products. I do not want any product marked with the words AGENCY or WALGREEN AGENCY, nor do I want heating pads, water bottles, or ice caps." To sell to this 10 year veteran collector, you need to tell him what you have, and its size, color, and condition. Indicate whether you have the original box or not, and give the original selling price, if it's marked on the container.

"There are only a few collectors of Walgreens so there isn't a lot of competition. But some items are quite rare and I'd love to hear from you if you have one."

> Gordon Addington
> 260 East Chestnut #2801
> Chicago, IL 60611
> (312) 943-4085

☆ **Blue bell paperweights** used as promotional items by the phone company. Values range from $30 to $1,500 so it's worth getting yours checked out. Also buys bell weights by the TPA (Telephone Pioneers of America). Give the color, embossing, and condition. She is author of *Blue Bell Paperweights* available from her for $12.

> Jacqueline Linscott
> 3557 Nicklaus Drive
> Titusville, FL 32780
> (407) 267-9170

☆ *Maytag* **items** including old gasoline engines, porcelain signs, pre-1940 literature, and other items. Give patent dates, model and serial number in your description. No washing machines made after 1915.

> Craig Donges
> 6724 Glenwood Avenue
> Youngstown, OH 44512
> (216) 726-1830 Fax: (216) 726-4740

☆ *Coleman* **products**, either U.S. or Canadian made, such as lamps, lanterns, irons, heaters, torches, parts, parts racks, tools, shipping boxes, advertising literature, salesmen's samples, hats and shirts with *Coleman* logo, repair manuals and what have you. He does not want clippings from old magazines or camping products other than *Coleman*. Pictures are helpful if you don't know the item's proper name or catalog number. Describe condition. Dealers price your goods. Amateurs may request offers.

> Ernest Hiatt, S.T.A. Shop
> 3404 West 450 North
> Rochester, IN 46975
> (219) 223-2276 Fax: (219) 223-2842

☆ *Big Jo Flour* and Wabasha Roller Mill items. "I'll buy anything *Big Jo*, and will consider any other advertising, large or small, related to Wabasha, MN." She does not want flour items other than that one brand and mill.

> Carla Schuth
> Route 2 Box 6
> Wabasha, MN 55981
> (612) 565-4251

INSURANCE COMPANY ITEMS

☆ *State Farm Insurance Company* **memorabilia,** 1922-52. He wants all items marked with their 3 oval emblem depicting a car, fire helmet, and cornucopia. Also selected items marked with either the home office or an old car. He buys ashtrays, pocket knives, pencils, tape measures, signs, stationery, and everything else. He does not want anything marked with the three ovals and the words AUTO, LIFE and FIRE.
> Ken Jones
> 100 Manor Drive
> Columbia, MO 65203
> (314) 445-7171

☆ *Prudential Insurance Company* ephemera, especially pre-1920 calendars. Also wants postcards, pens, key rings, paperweights, policies, advertising material, and other ephemera from other life and casualty companies. Make a Xerox™ of your item.
> Mike Sawrie
> PO Box 1228
> Sedalia, MO 65301
> (816) 584-6262 days   (816) 827-6399 eves

☆ *Prudential Insurance Company* **items.** "I want anything made before 1970, with the *Prudential* logo on it: clocks, banks, advertising, stock certificates, paperweights, pens, etc., especially unusual items. A Xerox™ or photo is helpful, along with your estimate of value."
> Jim Fernandez
> PO Box 5274
> Newark, NJ 07105

☆ **Fire service and fire insurance items** such as badges, histories of insurance companies, pre-1900 fire insurance policies, firemarks, signs, advertising, and postcards. Doesn't want anything except fire related items, and nothing modern. Please quote books that are fire related.
> Glenn Hartley
> 2859 Marlin Drive
> Chamblee, GA 30341
> (404) 451-2651

☆ **Anything relating to fire insurance companies** before 1940. Wants firemarks, illustrated policies, advertising, signs, and giveaways. Does not make offers, so price what you have.
> Ralph Jennings
> 301 Fort Washington Ave.
> Fort Washington, PA 19034

COCA-COLA

☆ *Coca-Cola* **memorabilia** from before 1945, including fancier *Coke* items with pretty girls and lots of color especially cardboard cutout signs and back bar decorations. He will pay up to $5,000 for pre-1900 calendars. Pays well for metal tins, trays, and signs. Magazine ads are wanted only if before 1932. No commemorative bottles, please.

    Randy Schaeffer, C-C Trayders
    611 North 5th Street
    Reading, PA 19601
       (610) 373-3333

☆ *Coca-Cola* **advertising** of all type before 1940. Buys cardboard cut-outs, festoons, and calendars, but has most interest in small items such as watch fobs, openers, pocket knives, and the like. "I pay premium prices for all advertising for *Coca-Cola* chewing gum." Thom says he "will be glad to help you evaluate the worth of your *Coca-Cola* items."

    Thom Thompson
    123 Shaw Ave.
    Versailles, KY 40383
       (606) 255-2727 days   (606) 873-8787 eves

☆ *Coca-Cola* **advertising.** "I'll buy pre-1969 calendars, trays, small signs, syrup bottles, clocks, thermometers, menu boards, ashtrays, playing cards, lighters, and just about anything else free of rust or wrinkles that says *Coca-Cola*." Loves to find salesman's sample coolers and dispensers. Describe condition carefully and include a photo. Also wants 5¢ and 10¢ front loading *Coke* machines with rounded corners, but has no interest in chest type coolers and dispensers. Does not want magazine ads, reproduction trays, or bottles of any sort including commemorative.

    Terry Buchheit
    204 South Jackson Street
    Perryville, MO 63775
       (314) 547-5628

☆ *Coca-Cola* **ephemera.** Wants pre-1960 signs, clocks, calendars, bottles and carriers, dispensers, machines, uniforms, etc. Will consider any item that reads "Drink *Coca-Cola*." Those that read *"Enjoy Coca-Cola"* are new. Please include your phone number.

    Marion Lathan
    Route 1 Box 430
    Chester, SC 29706
       (803) 377-8225

*If your item says
"Enjoy Coca-Cola"
it's too new.*

SOFT DRINKS

☆ *7-Up* **memorabilia.** "I'll buy almost any item that advertises *7-Up*, especially U.S. made items from the 1930's through the 1950's. I want historical items, company memos, photos of store displays and the like. The older the better. Watch for ads or items from Howdy Company's *Bib-Lable Lithiated Lemon-Lime Soda* which later became *7-Up.* Your description should include the shape of the *7-Up* logo (round, oval, square, or rectangular). Not interested in foreign items or most stuff after 1960. If you have good items, I'll try to find a buyer for you."
>
> Don Fiebiger
> 1970 Las Lomitas Drive
> Hacienda Heights, CA 91745
>   (310) 693-6484

☆ *Pepsi-Cola* **items** that are small, genuine, and in fine condition are wanted by this *Pepsi* VP who is primarily interested in ashtrays from the 1940's and 50's ($10-$20), cone top cans, bottle carriers from the 1930's and 40's made of paper, cigarette lighters from the 1950's and before ($5-$100), jewelry like pins and tie clasps from the early 1900's ($5-$200), bottle openers, celluloid pinback buttons, postcards, radios (worth up to $350), rulers, toys, vendor caps from the 1940's to 60's ($15-$75), trays from before 1910 ($200 to $1,000), and other small items. "I shy away from large signs and buy few paper items, although I don't mind answering any questions or trying to match people up with older items they may wish to sell. If I don't want something, I often know someone who does. I do not buy any reproductions or anything made after 1970." If you have items for sale, send a photo or Xerox™ and note all damage.
>
> John Minges
> PO Box 7247
> Greenville, NC 27835
>   (919) 756-4303 eves   Fax: (919) 758-5566

☆ *Dr. Pepper* **memorabilia** including signs, fountain items, pinback buttons, serving trays, calendars, jewelry, clocks, toys, clothing, games, and what have you. Especially wants very early bottles with "blob tops or bowling pin shapes. I don't buy new stuff such as found at flea markets, but if you're not sure, send an SASE and your description of the item." Give him the colors, dimensions, and condition. "No stupid shoot-the-moon prices."
>
> Bob Thiele
> 620 Tinker Avenue
> Pawhuska, OK 74056
>   (918) 287-3845 eves

☆ *Hires Root Beer* **memorabilia** pre-1930 in fine to mint condition. Wants trays, dispensers, and signs. No syrup extract bottles or reproductions of any *Hires* items.
>Steve Sourapas
>810 West Blaine Street
>Seattle, WA 98119
>>(206) 284-0580

☆ **Root Beer advertising** such as bottles, mugs, signs, caps, cans, syrup dispensers, and paper items. It *must* have the words "root beer" on the item. "If you don't recognize the brand name, or if it was sold only in a limited area, I'll probably be interested. I'd love to find a *Dr. Swett's* root beer mug in majolica with a false bottom half way up the mug and will pay $200 for a perfect one. For many of the 400 makers of root beer, only bottle caps survive. I pay $3 each for bottle caps I don't have." Doesn't want anything from brands sold on the market today or any *A&W* mugs except those that say 5¢. No photograph is needed if you give a good complete written description.
>Tom Morrison
>2930 Squaw Valley Drive
>Colorado Springs, CO 80918
>>(719) 598-1754

☆ *Moxie* **memorabilia.** Wants signs, fans, toys, advertising posters, metal trays, and other pre-1940 items associated with this old time soft drink. Will buy *Moxie* bottles only if the name of a town is part of the inscription. Bowers is the author of *The Moxie Encyclopedia*, a 760 page illustrated history available for $19.95.
>Q. David Bowers
>PO Box 1224
>Wolfeboro, NH 03894
>>(603) 569-5095

SODA BOTTLES & CANS

☆ **Soda pop cans** pre-1965, especially small local brands. Will buy quantities of rare cans, but no rusty cans are wanted by this 10 year veteran collector-dealer. "Some light spotting and aging is natural. I require cans be sent before a final purchase offer is made because condition so greatly affects the value and I need to examine cans closely."
Tony Steffens
615 Chester
Elgin, IL 60120
(708) 428-3150   Fax: (708) 742-5778

☆ **Soda pop bottles with painted labels from New England.** If you are offering one of these for sale, pay particular attention to describing all the colors that appear on the label, and accurately writing down what is printed on the bottle.
Steve Daniels
PO Box 218
Medfield, MA 02052

☆ **Soda pop bottles with painted labels** (called ACL's or applied color labels) are wanted, particularly minor bottling companies anywhere in North America. "I think I have West Virginia well covered, but I'm buying bottles from anywhere, including foreign soda pop bottles." **Ephemera related to local and regional bottlers** is also wanted, including factory or publicity photographs and soda pop advertising. Would love to find a three colored *Uncle Tom's Root Beer* from California. Please describe the color of the glass, all colors that are on the label and the exact wording "so I can make the best offer."
Gary Brent Kincade
PO Box 77
Horner, WV 26372
(304) 842-3773 eves   (304) 269-7623 days

☆ **Bottle caps** from soda pop. The world's largest collector of them still seeks early collections. Not interested in singles, unless you have something unusual like a prototype, error, etc.
Danny Ginzberg
26753 Basswood Ave.
Rancho Palos Verdes, CA 90274
(310) 378-1821

SODA FOUNTAIN MEMORABILIA

☆ **Soda Fountain memorabilia** especially historical ephemera related to soda fountain operations such as **photographs, trade catalogs,** bills and **letterheads,** recipe and formula books, **trade magazines** (like *Soda Dispenser* and *Soda Fountain*), and the like. Also wants **19th century soda fountain items** such as **hand crank milk shakers, crockery root beer mugs, straw dispensers** *with glass feet or tops,* **pink ice cream soda glasses,** and **colored banana split dishes with feet.** Especially interested in *True Fruit* and other advertising from the *J. Hungerford Smith Co.* of Rochester. The favorite find of this 20 year veteran collector would be an equipment and supplies catalog from before 1870. He does not want syrup well inserts for fountains, nor does he want match book covers, cup holders, trinkets, anything made of plastic, or anything related to the ice cream industry. "Please give as much reasonable detail as possible. A photo or photocopy is helpful." Dealers should price your goods. Amateurs may request an offer.

>Harold Screen
>2804 Munster Road
>Baltimore, MD 21234
>>(410) 661-6765

☆ **Ice cream and soda fountain memorabilia:**
- **Postcards** depicting ice cream or soda fountains, ice cream trucks, factories or any other ice cream topic (any year);
- **Photographs** of soda fountain interiors;
- Letterheads, envelopes and other **paper** with ice cream images;
- **Magazines** from soda fountain and ice cream trade, pre-1930;
- **Trade cards** with ice cream parlors, freezers, or soda fountains;
- **Catalogs** pre-1920 (except *Mills* #31);
- **Advertising giveaways**, fobs, buttons, tape measures, etc.

Allan buys a wide range of ice cream related items, but says his focus for the last few years has been on postcards with historical photos. He buys nothing damaged or made after 1945. He does not make offers, and requests you price what you have.

>Allan "Mr. Ice Cream" Mellis
>1115 West Montana
>Chicago, IL 60614
>>(312) 327-9123

☆ *Dixie* **ice cream cup picture lids** and other memorabilia 1930-54 including premium pictures and offers, albums, scrapbook covers, ads, and company literature. Also buys some non-*Dixie* pictorial ice cream cup lids such as *Tarzan* or American Historical Shrines series.

>Stephen Leone
>94 Pond Street
>Salem, NH 03079
>>(603) 898-4900

The collectibles of fast food chains are part of our "Pop Culture" and have become very sought after. Simple things you got free may find a buyer.

McDonald's is the most popular, but other restaurant collectibles are on the rise, especially Bob's.

Don't assume that what you have is common. Many fast food chain collectibles have very limited distribution, and may in fact have been given away in only a few restaurants. Rare doesn't always translate into great value, but it does sometimes!

RESTAURANT & FAST FOOD MEMORABILIA

☆ **McDonald's restaurant memorabilia** including Happy Meal toys, boxes, sacks, advertising pieces, postcards, paper items, uniforms, cups, glasses, mugs, pins, buttons, jewelry, foreign items, clocks, watches, displays, rings, retail items, games, clothes, shoes, special convention items, letters, newsletters, and other public and company items. Not interested in "common items which appear in Happy Meals nationwide." Your description should include what it is, the color, size, any trademarks, dates, and condition. Meredith is author of *Price Guide to McDonald's Happy Meal Collectibles*, available from the author for $27 postpaid. The McDonald's Collectors Club offers a 12 page monthly newsletter on collecting McDonald's items available for $22.

> Mr. Meredith Williams
> PO Box 633
> Joplin, MO 64802
>   (417) 781-3855   Fax: (417) 624-0090

☆ *McDonald's* **memorabilia** including:
* **Employee uniforms** with the M logo;
* **Paper goods** including boxes, place mats, napkins, flyers;
* **Displays and promotions** such as signs, decals, posters;
* **Anything in foreign languages**;
* **Not for public items** such as ID cards, newsletters, bulletins, sales and procedures manuals, and worksheets;
* **Fixtures, signs, and lights**.

Does not want items currently available in all restaurants. Take a photo of larger items please.

> Matt Welch
> PO Box 30444
> Tucson, AZ 85751
>   (602) 886-0505   Fax: (602) 722-3607

☆ *McDonald's* **happy meal counter displays.**
Mike Dyer
230 Eldon Drive NW
Warren, OH 44483

☆ **Fast food chain ephemera including kid's meal toys and boxes**
from before 1988. Also crew pins, displays, and other fast-food related
items that are odd or unusual. He's interested in chains like *Wendy's,*
Sonic Drive-In, Arby's, Burger King, Roy Rogers, Hardees, Carls Jr.,
What-a-Burger, and other similar.
Ken Clee
PO Box 11412
Philadelphia, PA 19111
(215) 722-1979

☆ *Bob's Big Boy* **restaurant memorabilia,** ceramic ashtrays and salt
and peppers, cups or dishes with logos, lunch boxes, game boards, toys,
comics, figurines, and other unusual pieces. Please write or fax with a
description, noting all repairs. Dealers must set the price they want;
amateurs may request offers. Vinyl plastic doll banks are not wanted.
Glenn Grush
5344 North Collingwood Circle
Calabasas, CA 91302
(818) 880-6200   Fax: (818) 880-6500

☆ *Bob's Big Boy* **items,** especially menus, lamps, matches, ashtrays,
salt and pepper shakers, and nodders. No plastic banks.
Steve Soelberg
29126 Laro Drive
Agoura Hills, CA 91301
(818) 889-9909

☆ *Coon Chicken Inn* **memorabilia** of all kinds that features Blacks.
Diane Cauwels
3947 Old South Road
Murfreesboro, TN 37129

☆ *Isaly's* **deli ephemera.** Wants advertising, paper ephemera and
souvenirs from this dairy/deli chain from Western Pennsylvania and
Ohio. Buys postcards, photos, guidebooks, roadside signs, etc.
Brian Butke
2640 Sunset Drive
West Mifflin, PA 15122

Glasses given away by restaurants are becoming
quite collectible, with a few of them at $50 each.
Look under "glasses" in the index for more buyers.

A reminder: the people in this book are often very busy professionals, working with no staff to help them answer letters. Many of them travel a great deal. One important buyer sets up at more than 50 antique shows a year. On the other hand, another top buyer told me, "I'm a lonely old man, and I love getting mail. So I always answer it the day it arrives."

Be patient. If you own something spectacular, you'll get quick response from everyone. My own mail is often months behind because there are so many demands upon my time.

HOTELS & MOTELS

☆ **Items from famous Chicago hotels** and their shops. Wants furniture, menus, stationery, fixtures, signs, etc., from places like the *Lexington, Metropole, Hawthorne Inn, Hawthorne Smoke Shop*, and *Scholfields Flower Shop*.
>   Michael Graham
>   33133 O'Plaine Road
>   Gurnee, IL 60031
>   (708) 263-6285

☆ **Swiss hotels paper ephemera,** pre-1930. Will buy illustrated bills, letterheads, wine lists, rate cards, envelopes, postcards and anything else pictorial showing Swiss hotels before 1930.
>   Ronald Lowden, Jr.
>   314 Chestnut Ave.
>   Narberth, PA 19072
>   (610) 667-0257 anytime

☆ **Tourist courts, tourist camps, and motel ephemera.** Wants *Tourist Court Journal* magazine and other pre-1950 ephemera related to motor travel lodging.
>   Kevin Regn
>   2127 15th Street NW
>   Washington, DC 20009

☆ **Youth hostel ephemera** such as handbooks, pins, magazines, etc.
>   Walley Francis
>   PO Box 6941
>   Syracuse, NY 13217
>   (315) 478-5671

BUSINESS CARDS, CATALOGS & OTHER PAPER

☆ **Business cards.** "I'll consider buying business cards that are unique, unusual, or have an interesting story. Cards from exotic or unlikely materials such as stainless steel, plastic, papyrus, tin, etc., and cards from celebrities. Looks for creativity, which is "timeless," so will consider anything imaginative in shape, color, message, or material. "I love cards that make you laugh." Photocopy what you have if possible, otherwise describe as best you can. Some **trade card collections** will be considered if they are suitable for resale or auction. Avery is president of the American Business Card Club.

> Avery N. Pitzak
> PO Box 460297
> Aurora, CO 80046
> (303) 690-6496

☆ **Business cards of all types.** "We buy business cards of all types with particular interest in cards 1700-1960. We even buy cards that are damaged or written upon if they are rare ones. We also buy paper items such as **photos, letters, and bill heads related to business cards**. We will pay postage both ways on items sent to us on approval." Few business cards have much value, but Jack will pay well for Mathew Brady and Benjamin Franklin. He emphasizes that chromolith (color printed) cards were stock items issued in large quantities. Photocopies are the best description. Jack edits *The Business Card Journal*.

> Jack Gurner
> 116 Dupuy Street
> Water Valley, MS 38965
> (601) 473-1154

☆ **Envelopes with color advertising for products** on the front or back, but only if they are from before 1940.

> Gordon McHenry
> PO Box 1117
> Osprey, FL 34229
> Fax: (813) 966-4568

☆ **Trade catalogs and piles of business letters,** pre-1920, from manufacturers, wholesalers, and retailers. "The earlier the better," says Jim. Most common catalogs bring from $5-$10, but "we have paid as high as $400 for some." Please check that all pages are present as you list the company name, the type of products, size and number of pages, and the type and number of illustrations. Photocopies are helpful. Mention *Trash or Treasure* for a free copy of Jim's catalog of catalogs.

> Jim Presgraves
> Bookworm & Silverfish
> PO Box 639
> Wytheville, VA 24382

☆ **Trade catalogs** for consumer products. "These are exciting peeks into their time, giving the unvarnished truth about their era. Prices vary from two figures (most catalogs are $10-$90) to over $10,000 for rare and desirable ones."
> Ivan Gilbert
> Miran Arts & Books
> 2824 Elm Ave.
> Columbus, OH 43209

☆ **Catalogs from Sears, Montgomery Wards** and other mail order companies. "The older the better," but will buy through the 1960's.
> Douglas Cowles
> 2966 West Talara Lane
> Tucson, AZ 85741
>   (602) 297-9062

☆ **Trade cards,** especially better quality and specialized collections. Especially interested in clipper ships, mechanical banks, *Currier & Ives*, metamorphic and mechanical, and other better items. Will pay $300 up for fine cards depicting mechanical banks, and $150+ for clipper ships. No interest in damaged, common cards, or stock cards with no company name. Must actually see an item in person before making offers. No phone appraisals or evaluations of items not for sale.
> Russell Mascieri
> 6 Florence Ave.
> Marlton, NJ 08053
>   (609) 985-7711   Fax: (609) 985-8513

☆ **Advertising trade cards** for chewing gum and **insert cards** issued by candy, gum, bakery, beverage, cereal or tobacco companies. "Photocopy your cards and tell me what you want for them, or I welcome approvals, pay all postage, and respond within 48 hours of receipt. Condition is important as I do not collect trimmed cards, badly creased or otherwise battered items."
> William Nielsen
> PO Box 1379
> Brewster, MA 02631
>   (508) 896-7389

☆ **Employee photo ID passes.** All photo ID badges are wanted, especially celluloid buttons with pin backs. Rich pays $3 each except for older ones. Don't bother to inquire, just drop your badge in the mail.
> Rich Hartzog
> PO Box 4143 BFT
> Rockford, IL 61110

OFFICE MACHINES

☆ **Unusual antique typewriters.** Wants items dating between 1870 and 1920. Look for typewriters with odd designs, curved keyboards, no keyboards, pointers, or more or less than the standard four rows of keys. The most desired machine is a *Sholes & Glidden,* worth as much as $5,000 in outstanding condition. Give the make and model number if it can be found on the machine, the serial number, and "an in-focus photo." Rehr will provide you with a free checklist to help you describe your typewriter to him. Also buys **ribbon tins** and **early literature and catalogs of typewriters.** Darryl also has an interest in small early hand-held **adding machines, calculators and calculating devices.** "I'll send you an evaluation of your typewriter if you send me a good sharp photo, or tell me the make, model, and serial number and include a long SASE." The Early Typewriter Collector's Association is $15 per year and includes an interesting illustrated newsletter. For more information about the Association, send a long SASE.

 Darryl Rehr
 Early Typewriter Collectors' Association
 2591 Military Ave.
 Los Angeles, CA 90064
  (310) 477-5229 voice or fax

If you recognize the brand name on your typewriter, collectors probably don't want it.
Remington, Smith-Corona, Oliver *and* Underwood *are common, not of interest to collectors.*
IBM *electrics are not wanted either.*

☆ **Typewriters** made before 1910, especially those with fancy or strange mechanisms, such as the *Sholes & Glidden* from the 1870's which strikes from below so the typist can't see her work. "I'm always willing to give you an opinion about a machine if you send a picture or good description."

 Joseph Weber
 604 Centre Street
 Ashland, PA 17921
  (717) 875-4401 from 3 to 5 p.m.

*When you look at a typewriter
ask yourself the following questions:*

*Does it have four rows of keys?
Does it have or take a ribbon?
Can I see the key hit the paper?
Are the keys English alphabet?*

*Did you answer yes to all?
If so, collectors don't want it.*

☆ **Check writers and protectors** pre-1910 in working condition. May be home, office, or hand held models. No machines by *Todd, F & E Lightning, Hedman, Paymaster,* or *Safeguard.* Also **antique staplers** and **paper fastening tools.** Not interested in anything that uses modern staples. "Older machines use wire or unusual staples or fasten paper without staples. Both kinds are wanted."
William Feigin
45 West 34th Street #811
New York, NY 10001
  (212) 736-3360

☆ **Telegraphones and other unusual magnetic recorders, especially wire.** Not interested in *Webster* or *Silvertone* machines.
Harold Layer, San Francisco State Univ-AV
1600 Holloway Ave.
San Francisco, CA 94132

☆ **Calculating devices before 1915** and associated ephemera including catalogs and advertising. Wants mechanical calculators such as arithmometers, generally in wooden cases. Brand names to look for include *Autarith, Baldwin, Calculmeter, Grant, Madas, Spalding, Thomas,* but interested in anything odd. Also rotary machine, heavy devices operated by a crank, and other types of calculators including **slide rules** (if they don't have patent numbers). He buys comptometers with wooden cases as well as **planimeters**, devices for measuring area on maps. Give a photo or sketch of what you have plus describe markings, serial numbers, etc. Weight and dimensions helpful. Photocopy your paper goods.

> Robert Otnes
> 2160 Middlefield Road
> Palo Alto, CA 94301
>   (415) 324-1821 eves

☆ **Cash registers made of brass or wood,** especially early wooden registers with inlaid cabinets, dial registers, or multiple drawers. Also registers that ring only to $1. He also buys brass or glass AMOUNT PURCHASED signs that were on top of registers, including electrified ones. Clocks marked "NCR" on the face are also of interest, as is literature about registers. Machines can be in any condition since he uses damaged machines for parts. Give both the brand name and model number of your machine and include the serial number. Provide your phone number so Ken can make arrangements to pick up your machine. Nothing after 1917, or with a serial number higher than 1,700,000.

> Ken Konet
> 4470 Westminster Place
> St. Louis, MO 63108
>   (314) 652-7505 eves   Fax: (314) 652-7842

☆ **Decorative resellable things found in the offices** of doctors, dentists, undertakers, blacksmiths, watchmakers, gunsmiths, locksmiths, opticians, jewelers, mines, hotels, brothels, police stations, prisons, firehouses, asylums, saloons, roadhouses, arcades, breweries, boat wrights, etc., including **furniture**, **cash registers**, display counters, **tools**, and the like. He requests a complete description indicating all wear or broken parts. If you know the item's history, it is helpful. Photos of larger items and photocopies of smaller ones are recommended. "I'd rather buy an entire store or business than a single item. No lot is too large. I will respond to any honest inquiry for help to evaluate an item that is actually for sale."

> Larry Franklin
> 3238 Hutchison Ave.
> Los Angeles, CA 90034
>   (310) 559-4461

☆ **Stock market tickers, books, and other memorabilia** having to do with speculation, panics, commodities, cycles, and other activities pre-1940. Also turn of the century prints depicting the stock market, and **stock market magazines** pre-1935.

    R.G. Klein
    PO Box 24A06
    Los Angeles, CA 90024

☆ **Banking relics, bank safes, money bags**, bullion and stage coach boxes, *Wells Fargo and Co.* or *Railway Express* locks, assay office items, scales, and **three fingered lock boxes** (which cut off your fingers if you put them in the wrong holes to open the box). Wants things before 1900. Not interested in paper.

    Larry Franklin
    3238 Hutchison Ave.
    Los Angeles, CA 90034
      (310) 559-4461

☆ **Safes.** "I'll buy small house type, pre-1910, black, cream or Burgundy colored safes, usually decorated with gold pinstriping and small painted vignettes. I also want early catalogs, photos, and other paper ephemera related to the use of safes, and would love to find a salesman's sample safe. I'll pay the cost of shipping safes via UPS."

    Greg "Dr. Z" Zemenick
    13560 Kirts #160
    Troy, MI 48084
      (810) 642-8129   (810) 244-9426

☆ **Bank bags** from banks which have changed names or are no longer in business. "I buy drawstring, locking and zipper types, and am particularly interested in leather bags, for which I pay $15 up. I do not want new bags or canvas vault bags." Give size, material, and condition.

    Larry Stults
    PO Box 313
    Wray, CO 80758
      (303) 332-5153   Fax: (303) 332-5212

☆ **Embossers and company seals** in interesting forms or made of less common material such as whalebone. Special interest in unusual companies and occupations. "I'll pay $25 to $250 for figural examples."

    Greg "Dr. Z" Zemenick
    13560 Kirts #160
    Troy, MI 48084
      (810) 642-8129   (810) 244-9426

☆ **Mimeograph memorabilia.** Advertising, instructions, service manuals, etc. If it's very *old* and about mimeos, he may be interested.
> Walley Francis
> PO Box 6941
> Syracuse, NY 13217
>> (315) 478-5671

☆ **Time clocks.** Give the brand name, model number and condition.
> Steve Chyrchel
> Route #2 Box 362
> Eureka Springs, AR 72632
>> (501) 253-9244 voice and fax

☆ **Telephones and phone company memorabilia** including:
- Pay phones with 3 coin slots;
- Candlestick and cradle phones;
- Bakelite phones, especially in colors;
- Wood wall phones;
- Character phones of the 70's;
- Parts for any of the above;
- Signs and advertising;
- Literature of all sorts before 1920;
- Magazines from before 1900 with phone ads.

No modern or electronic phones. They offer *History and Identification of Old Telephones* with 6,000 pictures of old phones for $58.
> Ron and Mary Knappen, Phoneco
> 207 East Mill Road
> Galesville, WI 54630
>> (608) 582-4124   Fax: (608) 582-4593

☆ **Telephones made before 1905,** porcelain signs featuring phones, telephone watch fobs, telephone pocket mirrors, and similar quality phone related items. **Also spring driven telegraph registers and fire station bells.** No interest in paper. "A photo is worth 1,000 words."
> Paul Engelke, Key Telephone Company
> 23399 Rio Del Mar Drive
> Boca Raton, FL 33486
>> (407) 338-3332

☆ **Telephones made before 1930.** His wants list and parts catalog's handy numbered illustrations will help you describe what you want to sell. Also buys **telephone directories** pre-1950, "the earlier the better."
> Gerry Billard, Old Telephones
> 21710 Regnart Road
> Cupertino, CA 95014
>> (408) 252-2104

☆ **Novelty telephones** shaped like products, food, drinks, household items, media stars, comic characters, etc. Tell whether it has its cord, its original box, and whether it works. Describe how much surface wear appears on the phone.

> Bob Roberts
> PO Box 152
> Guilderland, NY 12084

☆ **Rare glass insulators.** Describe the color, dimensions, embossing, whether it has threads, and its condition. Requests you describe insulators using numbers found in Milholland's *Most About Glass Insulators*, available for free at your public library or from Linscott, complete with price guide, for $39. No damaged insulators are wanted. Color of your insulators is particularly important.

> Len Linscott
> 3557 Nicklaus Drive
> Titusville, FL 32780
>   (407) 267-9170

☆ **Telegraph instruments** if old, complete, and professional quality, especially from railroads.

> Scott Arden
> 20457 Highway 126
> Noti, OR 97461

☆ **Telegraph instruments and ephemera** before 1900 including keys (worth $50-$100), sounders, relays, signs, catalogs, and stationery, and especially railroad instruments. Wants registers (clockwork driven devices to inscribe dots and dashes on paper tape) and pays $800-$1000 for them. Also seeking linemen's sets of very small portable keys in a hard rubber case. Items do not need to be in perfect condition. No *Boy Scout, Menominee, Western Electric,* or *Signal* equipment or post 1900 paper or telegrams, but he loves to find signs advertising telegraph companies before 1890. A photo or rough sketch is appreciated.

> Roger Reinke, Brasspounder
> 5301 Neville Court
> Alexandria, VA 22310
>   (703) 971-4095

☆ ***Western Union*** and ***Postal Telegraph*** instruments and ephemera. List all markings on items for sale. No cracked or damaged pieces.

> Charles Goodman
> 636 West Grant Ave.
> Charleston, IL 61920
>   (217) 345-6771

☆ **Scientific and technical devices** from before 1910 such as microscopes, surveying instruments, computing devices, stock tickers, planetariums, typewriters, precision clocks, mining and mineralogical instruments, medical and surgical instruments (before 1875), devices used in physics demonstrations and precision instruments related to telegraphy, navigation, and watch making. Items preferred when in their original cases. Does *not* want items made after 1910, items in poor condition or common items. Xerox™ all written information accompanying the device, tell anything you know of the item's history. Include a photo.

> Dale Beeks
> PO Box 2515
> Coeur d'Alene, AD 83814
> (208) 667-0830 voice and fax

☆ **Scientific instruments** by American and foreign makers including brass sextants, wood octants, spyglasses, telescopes, pocket sundials, surveying instruments, cased navigating devices, as well as map drawing tools and what have you. Must be made before 1890.

> Jonathan Thomas, Scientific Americana
> 1208 Main Street North
> Southbury, CT 06488
> (203) 263-2233

☆ **Antique surveying instruments** including compasses, transits, levels, wire link measuring chains, circumferentors, semi-circumferentors, railroad compasses, and solar compasses. Tools may be wood, brass, or wood and brass. "Also have interest in **mathematical and philosophical instruments** of the past." Give all names and numbers found on the body or lens.

> Michael Manier
> PO Box 100
> Houston, MO 65483
> (417) 967-2777 anytime

☆ **Slide rules.** Seeking early and unusual rules used for general calculation, carpentry, logging estimates, tax calculations on alcoholic beverages, chemical analysis, mechanical and electrical engineering, cement calculations, etc. Generally does not want simple slide rules with white painted surfaces and numbers printed over them although there are a *few* specialty ones such as musical scales that would be desirable. Please send manufacturer, model number, condition and whether it has a case or not. A Xerox™ would be very helpful. Dealers set your price, but genuine amateurs may request an offer. SASE.

> Dr. Wayne Feely
> 1172 Lindsay Lane
> Rydal, PA 19046
> (215) 884-5640

☆ **Portable electronic calculators** are wanted. Wants to buy items that are battery or nicad powered with "non-modern" LCD displays or with "displays that light up (LED, nixie tube, fluorescent digits) from about 1970 to 1978." He especially wants manufacturers like M.I.T.S., Busicom, Adler, Decimo, Sinclair, Melcor and Omron and calculators that were not marketed in the United States. He emphasizes that he seeks portable machines, not those that are powered exclusively by being plugged into the wall. Tell him the maker, model number, type of display if you can, some of the functions included, the power source and the condition. Most calculators from this period are worth from $5 to $20. Guy produces the newsletter for the International Association of Calculator Collectors, available from him for just $12 a year. You may request a sample for two 29¢ stamps.

> Guy "Mr. Calculator" Ball
> 14561 Livingston Street
> Tustin, CA 92680
>   Fax: (714) 730-6140

☆ **Portable electronic calculators** from the 1970's are wanted, as are earlier hand held devises for doing mathematical calculations, including some **slide rules**. They buy battery driven pocket calculators with LED (light emitting diode) displays which are usually covered with red or green plastic. These calculators typically are fairly thick, more than a half inch, and have a hole in the side for a wall adapter. They will consider calculators whether working or not." We do NOT want calculators made after 1980 with liquid crystal displays (LCD), most of which are solar powered. We also DO NOT want calculators of any type made by *Texas Instruments, Rockwell,* or *Unisonic*." Most electronic calculators from this period are worth from $5-$15, most mechanicals from $5 to $50 and most slide rules made of wood or metal from $5 to $15.

> Bruce and Jan Flamm
> 10445 Victoria Avenue
> Riverside, CA 92503
>   (909) 353-1326

☆ **Microcomputers and computer literature** including just about anything: machines, literature, catalogs, you name it, if it's from the pre-*Apple* pre-*Radio Shack* days (before 1977). Look for *Mark-8, Sphere, Scelbi, Intel* and other machines created for "do it yourselfers."

> Harold Layer
> SF State University AV
> 1600 Holloway Ave.
> San Francisco, CA 94132

ELECTRICAL DEVICES

☆ **Electrical devices pre-1900** manufactured by *Stanley Electric, Edison General Electric, Thompson-Houston, Weston, Westinghouse, Crocker Wheeler* and *Sprague.* "I want small open frame bipolar motors and generators, switchboard voltmeters and ammeters, carbon arc lamps, **electric fans with brass blades**, and watt-hour meters. I also want **catalogs**, photographs and paper related to these companies printed before 1905." Provide all nameplate data including patent dates and numbers. Prefers the seller to set the price, but will make offers.

    William F. Edwards
    932 State Road
    Richmond, MA 01254
    (413) 698-3458

As a rule, it's a good idea not to plug in any early electric device. Insulation breaks down over time and could cause a short, hurting you or damaging the equipment. Damage could make it worthless. Let the experts deal with it.

☆ **Electrical apparatus, tubes, test equipment, open frame motors, generators,** switch board meters, knife switches, **neon signs, fans,** Tesla coils, **quack medical devices** (Violet Ray, etc.), **unusual clocks,** etc., as well as books on radio and electrical theory and practice. Give info from the item's ID plate, and include a sketch or photo.

    Hank Andreoni
    504 West 6th Street
    Beaumont, CA 92223
    (909) 849-7539

☆ **Early electrical meters, gauges, and other apparatus** made by *Thompson-Houston,* or of the 133 cycle type. Also early direct current watthour meters, type CS, manufactured by *G.E.* Any very old unusual electrical items will be considered by this veteran collector and electrical museum owner. Give him the information found on the item's ID plate, measurements and weight. "I prefer the seller to set the price. I may need to see the item before buying."

    Tommy Bolack
    Electric Museum
    PO Box 2059
    Farminton, NM 87499
    (505) 325-7873

LOCKS & KEYS

☆ **Antique and unusual padlocks.** "We'll buy padlocks of all kinds and types, those that are oddly shaped, made of cast iron or brass, figural, *Wells Fargo, Winchester*, railroad, miniature, and many others." If you want so sell your lock, a photocopy will help them know what you have. Indicate whether your lock has a key with it.

> Joe and Pam Tanner
> Tanner Escapes
> 3024 East 35th Street
> Spokane, WA 99223
> (509) 448-8457 voice and fax

☆ **Padlocks and keys** are wanted, especially American locks marked with patent dates or the name of the maker. Some English and other European locks are of interest as well. Locks can be worth hundreds of dollars apiece, so it's worth your while to inquire, although he has no interest in modern locks made after 1930. A good rule of thumb is "the older and more unusual the better." A Xerox™ is a good idea. Note all dates, words, or symbols found on the lock, and indicate whether you have the key or not "as a lock without a key is acceptable, but definitely worth a lot less" for obvious reasons. Bob is editor of *West Coast Lock Collectors* newsletter, available for $10/year.

> Bob Heilmann
> Ace Lock & Key
> 1427 Lincoln Boulevard
> Santa Monica, CA 90401
> (310) 454 7295 eves

SCALES

☆ **Antique scales** of any type, in any condition and quantity, are sought by this 16 year veteran collector/dealer who also buys toy scales, signs, advertising scales, scale catalogs, postcards showing scales, scale parts, and "anything else" related to scales. Provide the brand name, model, serial number and condition. Note whether the scale is complete.

> Jan Berning
> PO Box 41414
> Chicago, IL 60641
> (708) 587-1839

ARCHITECTURE & BUILDING ITEMS

☆ **Architectural antiques,** including fireplace mantles, doors, stair railings and posts, large chandeliers, wall sconces, garden statuary, gargoyles, gates, large quantities of iron fencing, leaded and stained glass windows and doors, ecclesiastical items (benches, pulpits, etc.), bathroom fixtures, toilets and the like. Please send complete details and measurements along with a photo. They do not buy jewelry, china, small figurines, appliances, or reproductions. These folks have 17 years experience helping people find unusual items for remodeling.

> Architectural Antiques
> 801 Washington Avenue North
> Minneapolis, MN 55401
> (612) 332-8344

☆ **Architectural antiques.** If you have mantles, stained glass windows, chandeliers, iron fencing or gates, garden statuary, and other architectural relics, it may be profitable to give this giant dealer a call.

> United House Wrecking
> 535 Hope Street
> Stamford, CT 06906
> (203) 348-5371

☆ **Parts from buildings** such as cornices, gargoyles, arches, fireplaces, mantels, and anything unusual, as long as it dates before 1930. No material not related to building.

> Robert Des Marais
> 618 West Foster Ave.
> State College, PA 16801
> (814) 237-7141

☆ **Stained or beveled glass windows.** Send photos of the window, note all cracks or missing pieces, and include your phone number.

> Carl Heck
> PO Box 8416
> Aspen, CO 81612
> (303) 925-8011

☆ **Items related to building and architecture** pre-1930 including books about architecture, building, carpentry, and surveying. Also manuals and catalogs of cast iron, steel, plumbing, hardware, paint, and other building materials. Also **blueprints, architects renderings, drafting instruments** made of brass, early drafting or drawing machines, slide rules, and watercolor boxes.

> Robert Des Marais
> 618 West Foster Ave.
> State College, PA 16801
> (814) 237-7141

☆ **Architect's renderings** and other paintings of skyscrapers, houses, and other buildings.
> Charles Martignette
> PO Box 293
> Hallandale, FL 33009
> (305) 454-3474

☆ **Blueprints for buildings or machines** before 1920.
> Jim Presgraves, Bookworm & Silverfish
> PO Box 639
> Wytheville, VA 24382

☆ **Display cases and lighting fixtures,** especially from old drugstores. Wants early counter-top display cases with original glass, especially revolving cases, bow-front cases, and double tower cases. Also wrought iron or tin **lighting fixtures,** especially from commercial buildings. List all damage and give all data on maker's plate. Nothing after 1900.
> Jerry Phelps
> 6013 Innes Trace Road
> Louisville, KY 40222
> (502) 425-4765

☆ **Ornate doorknobs and other builder's hardware from 1870 to 1940.** Ornate lock sets, hinges, doorbells, knockers, door handles, bin pulls, **mail boxes,** mail slots, etc. May be brass, iron, wood, porcelain, glass, or other material, but must be ornately decorated. No plain porcelain or common octagonal glass knobs are wanted, but colored glass may bring a premium. "The decoration is the thing. I like state seals, railroads, Indians, and knobs that can be attributed to a particular building. Sets of knobs routinely bring $20-$30, but get my offer before you sell, as some can bring $300 each. Send SASE for my illustrated wants list. Photocopies speed offers. I must have a photo, Xerox™ or rubbing. Don't clean them. Paint and corrosion are not a problem for me."
> Charles Wardell
> PO Box 195
> Trinity, NC 27370
> (910) 434-1145

☆ **Antique doorknobs.** Loretta is editor of the club's newsletter and can put you in touch with collectors all over America who are interested in antique doorknobs and other door hardware. Send a good close up photo or a photocopy.
> Loretta Nemec
> Antique Doorknob Collectors of America
> PO Box 126
> Eola, IL 60519
> (708) 357-2381   Fax: (708) 357-2391

☆ **Sidewalk or paving bricks** marked with the name and/or address of a maker. "They're hard to mail, but fun to collect." No fire bricks.

> Ken Jones
> 100 Manor Drive
> Columbia, MO 65203
> (314) 445-7171

OLD TOOLS

☆ **Old tools of the trades and crafts** especially those used by woodworkers: wooden and metallic planes, folding rulers, chisels, levels, saws, plumb bobs, scribes, spokeshaves, hammers, squares, axes, trammel points, measuring devices, drills, bit braces, marking gauges, wrenches, fancy tool boxes, and hand or foot powered machinery. Also wants advertising items and hardware store displays, catalogs, and documents. "I'll pay $200+ for *Stanley* tool catalogs from before 1900. I especially want tools made in Ohio, although they're not worth as much as tools from New England." Does not want car mechanics' tools, electric tools, agricultural and farm tools, or any that have been "reconditioned." Give all markings. Keep your eyes open for an ivory plow plane made in Ohio, because "I'll pay $10,000 for one." John will accept select consignments at 10% commission for inclusion in his good looking quarterly newsletter on tools. John produced *Antique & Collectible Stanley Tools: A Guide to Identity and Value*, a detailed 455 page illustrated guide which you can obtain from him for $25. He also publishes *The Stanley Tool Collector News*.

> John Walter
> The Old Tool Shop
> 208 Front Street
> Marietta, OH 45750
> (614) 373-9973

☆ **Joiner's planes and other tools.** "I'll buy planes or any pre-1900 paper ephemera about them. I'll also buy, and pay retail prices for, fancy old woodworking hand tools."

> Richard Wood
> Alaska Heritage Books
> PO Box 22165
> Juneau, AK 99802
> (907) 789-8450 voice and fax

KNIVES

☆ **Pocket, hunting, and military knives.** A few of the good brands to look for: *New York, Canastota, Remington, Wabash, Winchester, Honk Falls, Napanoch, Henry Sears, Shapleigh, Union Cut, Keen Kutter, Bingham, American, Bridge, Capitol, Case, Cattaraugus, Phoenix, James Price, Platts, Press Button, Wallkill, Walden, Van Camp, Union Razon, Standard, Zenith, Northfield, Crandall*, and others. "I love large bone-handled knives made in the U.S." **If your knife is one of the following brands, it is not of interest:** *Ambassador, Atco, Camco, Colonial, Executive, Frontier, Hit, Ideal, Klien, Richards, U.S.A., Pakistan*, and *Sabre*. For an evaluation of your knife and an offer, photocopy knives with the blade(s) open, write down everything found on the blades and handles, identify the handle material and include an SASE.

> Charles Stapp
> 7037 Haynes Road
> Georgetown, IN 47122
> (812) 923-3483

☆ **Knives, tools and other items** by selected makers: *Keen Kutter, Winchester, Simmons, Shapleigh, Norvell-Shapleigh*, and various combinations thereof. "They made thousands of different things. Look at your tools carefully, as the names are often hard to read or find. I pay most for items in their original box. I don't want scissors or meat grinders that clamp on the table. I don't buy broken items, reproductions, heavily worn knives, or items that have been modified. If you call with an item made by one of these companies in front of you, I can usually evaluate it over the phone. Some items have been reproduced. When in doubt, call." He also buys catalogs, advertising, promotional items, signs, showcases, postcards, cookbooks, clocks, radios and other products marked with the name of one of those companies. Send photocopy or tracing, the exact wording of the mark and any other numbers or words. Include an SASE and your evening phone number.

> Tom Basore
> 715 West 20th Street
> Hutchinson, KS 67502
> (316) 665-3613 eves

☆ **Knives less than 1" long** are wanted, especially multi-bladed knives with mother-of-pearl, sterling, stag or horn handles. To sell your knife, give as much information as possible, including number of blades, maker, condition, etc. Old knives only. No new items or reproductions. Says he also "buys and trades swords and razors."

> Jim Kegebein
> 6831 Colton Blvd.
> Oakland, CA 94611
> (510) 339-1147

BARBERSHOP ITEMS

☆ **Decorated shaving mugs** depicting the owner's occupation, trade, or hobby above or below his name. Also hand painted personal occupational barber bottles. Since each was custom made, they must be evaluated individually. Also **salesman's sample barber chairs** made in porcelain or wood. No Japanese reproductions or "Sportsman's Series" mugs from the 1950's.

  Burton Handelsman
  18 Hotel Drive
  White Plains, NY 10605
   (914) 761-8880 Fax: (914) 428-2145

☆ **Shaving mugs depicting occupations**. Must have both a picture and a man's name. "I'll buy those with photo portraits for $500 and up and will pay $500-$1,500 for athletes (especially a high jumper), $400-$1,200 for automobile related professions, $500-$750 for an undertaker, and $500-$1,000 for a tugboat worker. Will also buy some mugs with emblems of fraternal organizations. Please give any maker's name on the bottom of the mug and indicate any damage, hairline cracks, or chips no matter how small."

  Robert Fortin
  Barber Shop
  459 South Main Street
  North Syracuse, NY 13212
   (315) 458-7465

☆ **Barbershop memorabilia** of all types including any good quality item associated with barber shops such as:
- Decorated **shaving mugs**;
- Fancy barber bowls, bottles, and waste jars;
- **Straight razors** with scenes or names engraved on the blades;
- Barber's emblem pins;
- Barbershop trade or business cards;
- **Catalogs** of barber supplies or equipment;
- **Salesmen's sample barber chairs,** and much more.

Powell both collects and deals so buys a wide range of fine items or accepts them on consignment. Names to look for include *Koken, Kochs, Kern, Archer, Buerger*, and others. Include a tracing or close up photo. New shaving mugs are not wanted. This well known historian is the only member of the Barber's Hall of Fame who isn't a barber.

  Robert Powell
  PO Box 833
  Hurst, TX 76053
   (817) 284-8145

FARMS, HORSES & TRACTORS

☆ **Farm machinery and tools** from before World War II (1940). Especially interested in catalogs and maintenance manuals about early farm equipment. Give make, model, serial number, patent dates, and description of condition. Photos are helpful. Cost of shipping or picking up old equipment is a factor in evaluation, but if your equipment is marketable, he may be able to put you in touch with a buyer who lives nearer to you.

> Craig Donges
> 6724 Glenwood Avenue
> Youngstown, OH 44512
> (216) 726-1830   Fax: (216) 726-4740

☆ **Antique farm equipment,** horse drawn vehicles, and "tools of all types" that are unusual, suitable for display in a museum of the odd and unusual. Send a photo and description of condition. "Farm equipment must be something out of the ordinary to find a buyer," he cautions.

> Harvey Lee Boswell's Palace of Wonders
> PO Box 446
> Elm City, NC 27822

☆ **Wagons, carriages, and commercial horse drawn vehicles,** in whole or in part. Buys carriage lamps, dashboard clocks, wagon tools, nameplates, wheel making machines, coachman's and groom's clothing, jacks, tack room fixtures, whip racks, wagon odometers, hitching post statuary, rein clips, wagon seats, wagon poles, **veterinary tools**, lap robes, life size harness maker's horses, **zinc animal heads**, and anything else related to carriages and wagons. Offers from $500 to $2,500 for lamps marked *Studebaker, Brewster,* or *Healey.* Also buys **goat and dog carts**. If your item is old, genuine, and in good condition you may ship it on approval. No harnesses, please. Don will send you a thick illustrated wants list if you send him a long SASE with four stamps on the envelope.

> Don Sawyer, West Newbury Wagon Works
> 40 Bachelor Street
> West Newbury, MA 01985
> (508) 346-4724 days   Fax: (508) 346-4841

☆ **Horse bits.** "I'll buy old iron, fancy, or strange horse bits as well as foreign, military, and medical bits. I also buy reference material about horse bits, including catalogs. I'd like to find Civil War bits and cowboy bits decorated with buffaloes. Draw a picture of what you have."

> Jean Gayle, Three Horses
> 7403 Blaine Road
> Aberdeen, WA 98520
> (206) 533-3490

☆ **Tractor memorabilia** including all sorts of paper ephemera and small trinkets given away as advertising promotion by tractor makers and dealers, such as watch fobs, pens, cigarette lighters, etc. You may ship on approval if it's old, original, and clean.

> Jay Ketelle
> 3721 Farwell
> Amarillo, TX 79109
> (806) 355-3456

☆ **Tractor, farm machinery, and gasoline engine paper ephemera** including pre-1940 manuals, catalogs, parts books, in-house publications, and sales literature. Also buys farm magazines such as *Implement Record, Farm Machinery & Hardware,* and *Farm Mech-anics*. Also buys "giveaways" such as signs, ashtrays, buttons, etc. associated with any farm machinery. No textbooks or reprints are wanted. Please indicate the color of the item and the price you'd like.

> Alan C. King
> PO Box 86
> Radnor, OH 43066

☆ *John Deere* **items** of all types made before 1960, including tractors, bulldozers, engines, corn shellers, signs, advertising and manuals. "If you have *anything* John Deere, contact me."

> Craig Donges
> 6724 Glenwood Avenue
> Youngstown, OH 44512
> (216) 726-1830   Fax: (216) 726-4740

☆ *J.I. Case Tractor Company* **memorabilia** including tractors and implements, toy tractors, advertising signs, catalogs, books, and anything else marked *J.I. Case*. If you want to sell an **old** *Case* **tractor** make certain to tell them where it is presently located.

> Ed and Carla Schuth
> Route 2 Box 6
> Wabasha, MN 55981
> (612) 565-4251

☆ **Windmill ephemera,** especially cast iron windmill weights, display model windmills and salesman's sample windmills. He does not want reproductions, damaged or repaired items, items with new paint, or "short tail horse" windmill weights. Please send a color photo, your phone number, and the price range you'd like to get.

> Richard Tucker, Argyle Antiques
> PO Box 262
> Argyle, TX 76226
> (817) 464-3752   Fax: (817) 464-7293

☆ **Windmill weights** in all shapes and forms. No damage or recent paint is acceptable. Photos are helpful.

    Craig Donges
    6724 Glenwood Avenue
    Youngstown, OH 44512
        (216) 726-1830   Fax: (216) 726-4740

☆ **Dempster Mill Mfg. Company memorabilia.** "I want anything from this long time maker of windmills and farm machinery especially salesmen's samples and photos of the factory, employees, or products. Contact me with anything."

    Craig Donges
    6724 Glenwood Avenue
    Youngstown, OH 44512
        (216) 726-1830   Fax: (216) 726-4740

☆ **Ice harvesting tools** are wanted, but "I have all the common ones." Buys crescent saws, house axes, and paper goods related to the history of ice. In general, most tongs, pikes, plows, and markers are not of interest, but some rare styles and makers *are* wanted, so you are encouraged to send a photo and maker's name. "Please, I don't need house signs which tell the ice man to stop." Phil lectures on ice harvesting and other 19th century practices, and heads the New England Tool Collectors Association, dues for which are $5/yr.

    Philip Whitney
    303 Fisher Road
    Fitchburg, MA 01420
        (508) 342-1350

☆ **Poultry industry items** including, but not limited to, egg cartons from before 1955, egg scales ($25-$60), stoneware chick waterers and feeders ($40-$80), books before 1940, and egg shipping containers and carriers. Does not want cracked or chipped stoneware or tops with no bottoms, nor does he want rusted scales, plastic egg cartons, or wooden folding egg carriers. Identify all labels or marks, patent numbers, etc. "A nice close up photo would be helpful."

    Roland Pautz
    371 Lincoln Street
    San Luis Obispo, CA 93405
        (805) 543-2049

☆ **Poultry raising.** Wants books, magazines and paper before 1930 about raising poultry (ducks, chickens, geese). Xerox™ helpful.

    W.L. Bill Zeigler
    12 North Bolton Street
    New Oxford, PA 17350
        (717) 624-2347

MILK & DAIRY EPHEMERA

☆ **Milk or dairy industry items marked with the name and address of a dairy** including old and unusual bottles, advertising, toys, and signs, especially from institutional bottlers such as prisons, colleges, railroads, hotels, and the like. Any bottles with character endorsements (sports, *Hopalong Cassidy*, etc.) are wanted with cartoon characters particularly desirable (Disney bottles bring $100+ each). Bottles and posters with WWII slogans are also sought. Unusually shaped bottles with faces or heads or those made of colored glass are always wanted, as are creamer size bottles marked with the name of a dairy, hotel, or restaurant. Bottles with glass lids, tin handles or lids and pour spouts can go as high as $300. Just about anything related to *Borden's* or their *Elsie the Cow* **trademark** is wanted, especially their ruby red bottles which bring from $700-$1,000 each. "I'll buy **catalogs of bottle makers** which show design variations offered." Large items like cream separators, churns, milk cans, and the like are not wanted. "If in doubt about the authenticity of what you own, feel free to call or send me a good photo. I will verify what you have and answer your questions about it, if you include a Self-Addressed Stamped Envelope."

"You can never give too much information when describing condition. List all flaws, chips, scratches, tears or cracks. I can give you a good appraisal only if you give me a good description."

   Ralph Riovo
   686 Franklin Street
   Alburtis, PA 18011
      (610) 966-2536

☆ **Round milk bottles with dairy names** embossed or printed on them. Square bottles are OK if amber colored or from any Western states. Nothing worn, cracked, or chipped is wanted.
   Leigh Giarde
   PO Box 366
   Bryn Mawr, CA 92318
      (909) 792-8681

☆ **Dairy creamers** made of glass with the names of dairies embossed or printed on are sought. He does not want ceramic creamers or those without names. Also **milk bottles** with cop tops, baby tops, or war slogans, but only in excellent condition.
   Ken Clee
   PO Box 11412
   Philadelphia, PA 19111
      (215) 722-1979

PLANTS, TREES & LUMBER

☆ **Everything about fruit and vegetable growing, packing and canning** is wanted, such as labels, photographs, postcards, magazines, buttons, ribbons and giveaway trinkets of all types. Wants all sorts of paper ephemera from various organizations and events promoting fruit and vegetable growing and packing. Buys **orange juicers, reamers and extractors** from major packers, if company name is impressed.

> T. Pat Jacobsen
> 437 Minton Court
> Pleasant Hill, CA 94523
> (510) 930-8531

☆ **Everything about fruit raising and varieties before 1900,** including illustrated books, magazine articles, ceramic tiles depicting fruit, postcards, prints, folders, and greeting cards depicting apples. Especially wants books and paper with color plates or descriptions of fruit varieties. May be in any language. No tropical fruit, or anything later than 1940. This veteran horticulture experimenter wants **cuttings from uncommon tree fruit varieties** you have on your farm. He wants temperate climate fruits, especially apples, but also pears, plums, quinces and medlars. Also buys **books on fruit propagation** which were printed before 1920.

> Fred Janson
> Pomona Book Exchange
> Rockton PO, Ontario
> L0R 1X0 CANADA

☆ **Canning machinery, catalogs and tools** of the *Ferracute Machine Company* of Bridgeton, NJ, are sought by this researcher who also wants anything related to company founder **Oberlin Smith**. The Oberlin Smith Society is particularly interested in advertising, catalogs, small presses, medals and tokens, but will consider anything related to FMCo or Smith himself. The OSS is a 501(c)(3) organization and seeks donations too.

> James Gandy, Oberlin Smith Society
> Route 2 Box 109, 192 River Road
> Bridgeton, NJ 08302
> (609) 451-5586

☆ **Lumber company and store tokens, scrip, stocks and bonds.** Please make a photocopy of your items.

> "Tip" Tippy
> 22 Cottonwood Lane
> Carterville, IL 62916

MINING

☆ **Mining and blasting items**, including carbide lamps, candlesticks, safety lamps, miner's bird cages, tools, lunch buckets, handbooks, tool catalogs, blasting cap tins, detonators, etc. He only wants items marked with a manufacturer's name, but warns "do not clean or wire brush your item, as I want them as is, not cleaned." Value depends on maker and condition, so give a good description including all names and marks. *Justrite* and *Autolite* lamps are not wanted, nor are any reproduction lamps or other items.

> Anthony Glab
> Sun Ray
> 4154 Falls Road
> Baltimore, MD 21211
> (410) 235-1777

☆ **Mining items** including safety lamps, oil wick cap lamps, carbide lamps, blasting cap tins and blasting machines, candle holders, and hundreds of other small tools, photos, souvenirs, and advertising items related to mining. Will even buy ore carts and buckets. Also wants ribbons, banners, and badges from the **United Mine Workers** (UMWA) and the Western Federation of Miners (WFM). Dave says he's willing to pay you in cash if you prefer.

> David Crawford
> 1308 Halsted Road
> Rockford, IL 61103
> (815) 637-6720

☆ **Coal company scrip, stocks and bonds,** and **cap lamps** worn by miners when underground.

> "Tip" Tippy
> 22 Cottonwood Lane
> Carterville, IL 62916

☆ **Colorado mining memorabilia 1859-1915** including photos, paper ephemera, stocks, maps, stereoviews, advertising, and small souvenirs, especially from towns of Cripple Creek, Victor, Central City, Leadville, Breckenridge, Idaho Springs, Telluride, etc. Also books about Colorado mining and any city directories pre-1915. No interest in "flatland cities" like Denver or Colorado Springs, nor in Colorado tourist attractions and parks. No photos unless a mine or mining town is featured.

> George Foott
> 6683 South Yukon Way
> Littleton, CO 80123
> (303) 979-8688

☆ **Mining company memorabilia,** primarily Pennsylvania and the Western U.S. Buys books, stocks and bonds, sheet music, photographs, and selected artifacts.

    Jeffrey Viola
    784 Eltone Road
    Jackson, NJ 08527
       (908) 928-0666   (908) 902-3313

☆ **Mining ephemera, especially paper goods from Arizona and Colorado mines.**   Interested in buying stock certificates and other paper pertaining to mining other than coal. Buys books on mining and gems, catalogs of mining equipment, photographs, etc.

    Russell Filer Mining
    13057 California Street
    Yucaipa, CA 92399
       (909) 797-1650

When you have tools to sell, don't even consider cleaning them. Collectors do not want things that have been scrubbed with a wire brush or rust removing solvent.

ROCKS, FOSSILS & CAVES

☆ **Meteorites.**   Many types exist, and he wants them all, rough or smooth, large or small. Look for rocks that are especially heavy, or with signs of melting or with rust. A freshly fallen meteorite often has a thin black skin, called "fusion crust." If you have a rock that attracts a magnet, you may have a meteorite. "A strong magnet on a string will swing towards all meteorites, which makes this one of the best preliminary tests. Other excellent field tests for meteorites include checking for rust, and filing off a tiny corner to look inside for bright metal or metal flakes. If you think you have found a meteorite, please send a small, dime-sized piece for me to examine along with a description and photo of the entire specimen. If you wish to have the sample returned to you, you must enclose return postage. All non-meteorite samples without return postage are discarded. If I suspect your sample is a meteorite, I will contact you, so be sure to enclose your name, address and phone number along with all samples." Rare forms of meteorites can be surprisingly valuable.

    Robert Haag
    PO Box 27527
    Tucson, AZ 85726
       (602) 882-8804   Fax: (602) 743-7225

☆ **Rock, mineral, and fossil collections** are wanted, as are samples of gold, silver, and copper, particularly samples associated with Western mining. Pays in any form you prefer.

> David Crawford
> 1308 Halsted Road
> Rockford, IL 61103
> (815) 637-6720

☆ **Cave or cavern memorabilia** before 1950, including books, magazine articles, pamphlets, prints, postcards, etc. "Any items that would make a contribution to the history of a particular cave or area such as journal entries, deeds, wills, maps, tickets, and advertising, are of interest." Common souvenirs and chrome postcards are not desired.

> Jack Speece
> 711 East Atlantic Ave.
> Altoona, PA 16602
> (814) 946-3155 eves

☆ **Caves or cavern memorabilia of all sorts.** "I'll buy anything old or unusual pertaining to caves or caverns worldwide" including photos, brochures, postcards, souvenirs, silver spoons, plates, etc. Does not want anything after 1940, and prefers items from before 1900.

> Gordon Smith
> PO Box 217
> Marengo, IN 47140
> (812) 945-5721

☆ **Cave-related items** from before 1944, including post cards, souvenir plates and paperweights, signs, etc., related to wild or show caves. Has a particular interest in items related to the Floyd Collins rescue in Sand Cave, KY, including souvenirs sold at the event, books on the topic, songs recorded about it, etc. A good description should include all markings. Photo suggested.

> Anthony Glab
> Sun Ray
> 4154 Falls Road
> Baltimore, MD 21211
> (410) 235-1777

OIL COMPANY MEMORABILIA

☆ **Oil company "everything" 1859-1939.** Wants "virtually anything" connected to specific companies, wells, or famous oil pioneers including pre-1900 books about oil and oil exploration, oil stocks (especially early with engraved views of oil fields), sheet music (from the 1860's), newspapers from early Pennsylvania oil towns, clippings, photos, deeds, and engravings.

> Jeffrey Viola
> 784 Eltone Road
> Jackson, NJ 08527
> (908) 928-0666 eves   (201) 902-3313

☆ **Oil company memorabilia from the 1920's** including advertising of all sorts, giveaways, stationary, point of purchase advertising, signs, pump globes, etc. Also seeks informative material such as early gas station **photos**, **trade publications**, and the like, from any company, as long as it's generally from the 1920's era. This 20+ year veteran collector does not want reproductions of any sort. Give him the name of the company, and a description of the item you have.

> Bill Allard
> 1801 Fernside
> Tacoma, WA 98465
> (206) 565-2545

☆ **Gas or oil company "everything" marked with a brand name:** gas pump globes and lenses, signs, oil cans, photos of gas stations, and paper items like road maps, credit cards, dealer publications, match-books, toys, trinkets, promotional items, and uniform patches. Especially likes to find items from smaller regional companies and discounters like *Spur, Dixie Vim, Erickson-Holiday, Crown Central, Ashland* and *Pan Am.* "We do not buy or sell reproductions or unbranded equipment type service station items, nor are we particularly interested in anything before 1925. We are a central clearing house for information about the gas/oil hobby and we will gladly refer people to other collectors if we can't use their item." Photos appreciated.

> Wayne and Debbie Henderson, Gasoline Specialty Company
> 20 Worley Road
> Marshall, NC 28753
> (704) 649-3399

☆ **Gasoline station items** including pumps, globes, signs, photos, and other things related to running a **pre-1940 filling station**. Photos helpful. Give serial and patent numbers if available.

> Craig Donges
> 6724 Glenwood Avenue
> Youngstown, OH 44512
> (216) 726-1830   Fax: (216) 726-4740

☆ **Gasoline and oil company advertising and promotional items from local, regional and independent oil companies** and dealers *only.* "I'll buy gas pump globes, banks shaped like oil cans or gas pumps, salt and pepper shaker sets, thermometers, transistor radios shaped like oil cans or gas pumps and small cans of oil. He is not interested in paper items, large signs, reproductions, or national brands like *Mobil, Shell, Esso, Phillips, Conoco, Amoco, Texaco, Flying A, Union 76,* etc. Describe the condition, and include a description of decals or labels.

    Peter Capell
    1838 West Grace Street
    Chicago, IL 60613
       (312) 871-8735

☆ **Gasoline and oil company signs** in porcelain or enamel. Also buys some other petroleum advertising.

    Gus Garton, Garton's Auto
    5th and Vine
    Millville, NJ 08332
       (609) 327-6090 days   (609) 825-3618 eves

☆ *Gulf Oil* **memorabilia** including signs, cans, maps, advertising junk mail, magazine ads, blotters, postcards, ashtrays, key chains, and anything else marked *Gulf*, especially older correspondence, paper items, and signs. This retired petroleum geologist also wants postcards which depict oil fields and wells. Prefers you to contact him first, then send your items on approval.

    Charles Roach
    3212 Tudor
    Oklahoma City, OK 73122
       (405) 942-4520

☆ *Mobil Oil* **memorabilia** including anything picturing the red horse. Also collecting service pins given to *Mobil* employees. Also buys porcelain signs from *Gargoyle, White Eagle*, and *Magnolia* gas and oil. No repros...and Billie says she has enough globes. She insists that the seller set the price wanted as she and Bob do not make offers for additions to their herd.

    Bob and Billie Butler
    1236 Helen Street
    Augusta, KS 67010
       (316) 775-6193

☆ **Oil cans in all sizes, all types, and all materials,** including brass, aluminum, glass, tin, graniteware or plastic. Wants everything from small sewing machine size up to and including railroad oil cans, advertising cans, and novelty cans.   Pays $10-$25 for a graniteware can especially with the name WHITE on it, $10-$15 for most others, more for railroad cans.   Not all desirable cans have names on them. Make a sketch. If it is a pump can, tell Robert whether the pump works.

    Robert Larson
    3517 Vernal Court
    Merced, CA 95340
       (209) 723-7828

☆ **Oil cans from Canada,** especially British Columbia oil in tin cans, and any quart oil cans related to motorcycles.

    Don Schneider
    PO Box 1570
    Merritt, BC V0K 2B0 CANADA
       (604) 378-6421

☆ **Oil company credit cards** and pocket **calendars** are purchased. You may send your items for his immediate offer and a return check.

    Noel Levy
    PO Box 32458
    Baltimore, MD 21208
       (410) 363-9040

☆ **Oil field stationary engines** with large flywheels, and other turn-of-the-century machines, **photos** of oil drilling and oil fields, **catalogs,** and paper ephemera related to operating oil drilling rigs and commercial oil fields.

    Craig Donges
    6724 Glenwood Avenue
    Youngstown, OH 44512
       (216) 726-1830   Fax: (216) 726-4740

Selling guns, weapons and military items is easy.

You're likely to own these items so I've supplied premium experts to help you dispose of them properly. If your item is is collectible, you'll find a buyer here.

To describe most military items, follow the basics: material(s) from which it is made, color(s), dimensions, serial numbers and other marks, what you know of its history, and the item's condition. If it's supposed to do something, does it do it? Are all parts and pieces there? Is it for sale or do you "just want a price"? It may be easier to photocopy small items.

When you offer a uniform for sale, you should describe all insignia and ribbons. They will decide the uniform's value. Your uniform should be in good condition. Buyers will forgive moth holes in a Revolutionary War outfit but not for most WWII uniforms.

When describing a sword, dagger, or bayonet measure from end to end and from the tip of the blade to the handle guard. Measure the width of the blade at the point it attaches to the handle guard. List every word or number found on the blade, hilt, or handle. Trace or photocopy any decoration on the blade or sheath. Describe the condition of the scabbard or sheath. Treat knives and swords as fragile objects. Mishandling can be costly.

To sell a gun make sure it is not loaded before anything else. Gun buyers want to know the make, model, serial number, caliber or gauge, barrel length, type and percent of finish, type of stock or grips, mechanical condition and condition of the bore. List all marks inside and out and note dings, defects and alterations.

The buyer will tell you how to ship your items. When rare or valuable weapons are involved, the buyer may prefer to pick them up personally or arrange for pick up.

Buyers prefer to obtain military items from the veteran who owned them, or from a direct heir. Counterfeits abound...especially of leather jackets and Nazi items.

GUNS

☆ **Antique and modern firearms.** "I'll buy a wide range of items, from Civil War carbines, Indian Wars guns, trap doors, rolling blocks, cap and ball, etc., to early *Winchester, Marlin, Savage* and *Remington.*" This 25 year dealer also buys some *Colt* **handguns**. If your gun or rifle is pre-1964 and all wood and metal surfaces are original and unrestored, it might be worth a call. Although he buys *Krag, Springfield* and others for parts, he does not want reworked guns or reproductions. Rudy offers a catalog of guns for sale.

> Rudy Dotzenrod
> 752 7th Street
> Wyndmere, ND 58081
>   (701) 439-2646

☆ **Guns and gun collections** of all types. "I'm always searching for **Gattling guns.**"

> Ed Kukowski
> Ed's Gun House
> Route 1
> Minnesota City, MN 55959
>   (507) 689-2925

☆ **Antique weapons of all types** including guns, swords, uniforms and other high grade military goods. Holds regular cataloged auctions of high grade guns.

> James D. Julia Auctioneers
> PO Box 830
> Fairfield, ME 04937
>   (207) 453-7904   Fax: (207) 453-2502

☆ **American percussion and early cartridge firearms,** both long guns and revolvers, 1840-1920. "I'll buy guns by any maker, but especially *Colt, Winchester, Remington, Marlin, Smith & Wesson, Manhattan, Sharps, Stevens,* and *Bacon.* I like to buy derringers of all types, especially those that are particularly small or short barreled, those that are very large caliber (.41 cal. up), or those which take metallic cartridges. I also like finding any pocket size pistols made by *Colt, Remington, Bacon, Marston, Moore, National, Reid, Terry, Warner,* and *Williamson,* among others." Pays $300 to $3,000 for these guns. Wants photos or photocopies of both sides of the weapon and all markings and numbers found anywhere on the gun.

> Steve Howard
> Past Tyme Pleasures
> 101 First Street #404
> Los Altos, CA 94022
>   (510) 484-4488 eves

☆ **Pinfire and other antique fire arms** are sought in any condition including cheap guns suitable only for parts. Provide a general description and all names, dates, and other numbers you find on the gun. If the parts of the gun have serial numbers, tell him whether the numbers match. This important 40 year veteran historian says, "I'll give free advice, but do not do free appraisals."

> Larry Compeau
> c/o Brinks
> PO Box 1225
> Darien, CT 06820

Any gun buyer wants to know the make, model, serial number, caliber or gauge, barrel length, type and percent of finish, type of stock or grips, mechanical condition and condition of the bore. Describe all marks inside and out, list alterations, and note dings and defects.

☆ **American guns** from before 1900, especially those with historic association. No interest in reproductions. If possible, send a clear photo of the item and write down all markings found anywhere on it. If it is a pistol, please make a photocopy, or draw a pencil outline. Mention any broken or missing wood, metal that is pitted, parts missing, etc. Does it work? Worman wrote a book on firearms of the American West and was firearms editor of *Hobbies* magazine for sixteen years. SASE please.

> Charles Worman
> PO Box 33584 (AMC)
> Dayton, OH 45433
>   (513) 429-1808 eves

☆ **High grade shotguns, double rifles, and big bore rifles**, whether English, Italian, or American made. Guns must be in original condition. "I do not want broken or damaged guns, paramilitary weapons, clunkers or guns you can buy at your local gun shop. I will pay up to $100,000 for rare sporting guns, but a personal physical inspection is essential before any purchase." Your first contact by mail or phone should include the brand name, serial number, caliber or gauge, length of the barrel, a description of any markings stamped on the metal or wood parts, and a statement of condition. The history of the gun is useful. If writing, include your phone number.

> Francis Lombardi II
> PO Box 181-TH
> Syracuse, NY 132089
>   (315) 422-3536

☆ **Black powder antique guns** made in Western New York State. Makers of interest include *Artis, Cutler, Ellis, Gardner, Lefever, Marsley, Miller, Plimpton, Southerland, Walker, Wood* and several others. Antique guns only.

    Alan Stone
    PO Box 500 5170 CR 33
    Honeoye, NY 14471
        (716) 229-2700

☆ **Revolvers (pistols).** "I'll consider any antique or collectible firearms to build my dealer's inventory or to enhance my personal collection, but my special interests are:

- Serial number one guns, antique or modern;
- Antique *Smith & Wesson* large frame top-break revolvers;
- Antique engraved revolvers;
- Unusual hammerless revolvers;
- Guns owned by famous individuals.

"I can travel if needed. Confidentiality assured. I try to be considerate and helpful in cases of divorce, bankruptcy, and estate liquidation. I can pay immediately or arrange auction or consignment sales. I'm interested in unusual or oddball older guns that many other collectors avoid. Honest wear and alterations from the period of use are OK, but do affect the value of the piece. I will consider heavily worn, broken, or refinished items only if they are rare or have documented historical connection. I am not interested in fakes, reproductions or modern guns. If offering an historic gun, quality of documentation is important. Send a copy of documentation and what you will swear to in a notarized affidavit. A personal inspection is required before final offer, especially on finely engraved guns. Please don't offer anything stolen or illegal. I won't buy it." Specific regulations govern shipment of firearms. Jim has the necessary licenses, but check for shipping instructions. If you don't want to sell your gun but want an informal appraisal, Jim charges only $1 each to appraise most handguns. Interesting catalog available.

    Jim Supica, Jr., Old Town Station
    PO Box 15351
    Lenexa, KS 66285
        (913) 492-3000   Fax: (913) 492-3064

Any gun buyer wants to know the make, model, serial number, caliber or gauge, barrel length, type and percent of finish, type of stock or grips, mechanical condition and condition of the bore. Describe all marks inside and out, list alterations, and note dings and defects.

☆ *Colt* **pistols with factory engraving.** "I'll buy single action *Colts* in 95% or better original condition, if they predate WWII and have factory engraving." Give the serial number when you write, and, if possible, a good close up photo of the artwork. Some newer single actions are also wanted. Also wants **guns from outlaws and lawmen** if they have proper documentation. All early **memorabilia from the** *Colt* **company,** including all advertising and literature are wanted, including *Coltrock* brand products and the boxes they came in.

> Johnny Spellman
> 10806 North Lamar
> Austin, TX 78753
> (512) 836-2889 days   (512) 258-6910 eves

☆ *Colt Firearms Mfg Co.* **ephemera** including all correspondence on factory letterhead, pamphlets and brochures by *Colt*, empty black and maroon boxes that *Colt* guns were packed in, instruction sheets and manuals, and "anything else pertaining to *Colt* products." John wants *Colt* factory catalogs, 1888-1910, for which he pays from $40-$500. 1910-1940 catalogs bring $20-$75. John also buys plastic and electrical items marked *Coltrock* as well as *The Book of Colt Firearms* by Sutherland and Wilson, 1971, for which he'll pay over $100.

> John Fischer
> 7831 Peachtree Ave.
> Panorama City, CA 91402

☆ *Newton Arms Co.* **guns and other memorabilia** from this progressive 1916-18 gunsmith. "I'll buy rifles, catalogs, **loading tools,** letters, stock, cartridges, and any other paper or memorabilia from the *Newton Arms Co.* or the *Chas. Newton Rifle Corp.* I will pay $5,000 for a .276 *Newton* rifle or a rifle in .280, .33 or .40 (.400) calibers if in mint condition, and will consider all other *Newton* guns at lesser prices. Also want these and **other unusual** *Newton* **cartridges.** I will gladly pay a finder's fee for *Newton* guns I buy. I'll take anything signed by Chas. Newton but nothing marked *Buffalo Newton Rifle Co.* Any items other than guns must be original condition."

> Bruce Jennings
> 70 Metz Road
> Sheridan, WY 82801
> (307) 674-6921

☆ **Junk guns and gun parts** in any condition. "I'm in the parts business and will travel to pick up large lots." Wants nothing having to do with current guns. Describe all markings and numbers. Bob is available for insurance appraisals of fire damaged gun collections.

> Robert Fay
> Star Route Box AF
> Whitmore, CA 96096
> (916) 472-3132

☆ *Iver Johnson* **products and memorabilia** including **guns, bicycles, catalogs,** etc. Special wants include engraved presentation guns and awards and any other unusual *Iver Johnson* item. This 30 year veteran collector does not want "common handguns in less than mint condition." Send a complete description, including a sketch or photo. Prefers seller to price, but will make offers.

> Charles Best
> 11523 Pinevalley Drive
> Franktown, CO 80116
> (303) 660-2318

☆ **Old double barrel shotguns** are wanted in any condition. "I will buy any kind of double barrel made before 1940 that is worth $300 or less. I especially want old side plate *Lefevers, L.C. Smith*, and most English or Belgian guns. Describe the condition, amount of bluing, rust, missing parts, engraving, butt plates, etc."

> Charles Black, The Gun Doctor
> Route 6 Box 237-D
> Athens, AL 35611
> (205) 729-1640

☆ **Brass military shell casings.** "I want to buy the casings for shells and projectiles in 37mm and larger sizes. Particularly wants an 8" Navy shell. I'll buy shell casings of all weapons, all nations."

> Charles Eberhart
> 3616 N.E. Seward
> Topeka, KS 66616
> (913) 235-1016

☆ **Ammunition and exploding devices** including grenades, mines, bombs, and fuses of all type, from the beginning of time to the present. "We buy everything from stone cannon balls to the **smart weapons** used in Operation Desert Storm. Also want books, films, reports, and videos about ordnance in any format or language." Schmitt's family has been making ammunition since 1849, so he particularly wants things marked with the *Crittenden* name. He is willing to pay $2,000 for a **.69 caliber** *Crittenden and Tibbals* **Rimfire cartridge**. He wants the measurements, condition, and all markings on what you have, preferring you also include a photo. He has no interest in store stock items. Schmitt is a contributing editor of two gun magazines and involved with cleaning up explosive ordnance from the Iraq/UN war.

> J. Randall Crittenden Schmitt
> Court House Station
> PO Box 4253
> Rockville, MD 20849
> (301) 946-2643

SWORDS & KNIVES

☆ **American swords from 1789-1902.** Especially wants swords with presentations or inscriptions to military persons with dates and rank, either etched or engraved on the blade or on the metal part of the scabbard. Inscribed Civil War swords are particularly desirable. The best makers marks are *Ames, Starr, Roby, Rose, Widman, Horstmann,* or *Glaze.* It is most important for sellers to send a very good drawing or photo of the hilt handle (guard and grip) of the sword. List all markings on the blade. Indicate the type of metal the guard is made from (brass, iron, aluminum), the type of grip or handle (ivory, bone, metal, wood, leather covered wood, or plastic). Note if the scabbard or sheath is included, and the condition of the sword and scabbard (rust? pitting?), and whether the scabbard is dented. Indicate the width of the blade at the handle, the length of the blade, and any engraving or etching. This 30+ year collector and dealer is interested in most swords, including early fakes and reproductions as long as the seller knows that the price will be considerably less than for an original. Common original swords are also purchased for resale. Ron is author of two books on swords and is active in gun and sword societies.

> Ron Hickox
> Antique Arms & Militaria
> PO Box 360006, Dept. T
> Tampa, FL 33673
> (813) 968-1571   Fax: (813) 744-5678

☆ **American swords and large knives** from before 1900. Please describe thoroughly, including any numbers or writing found on the weapon. Make a photocopy of the knife and of the sword handle if you can. Otherwise photograph it or make a good sketch. No fraternal, lodge or ceremonial swords, please. SASE requested.

> Charles Worman
> PO Box 33584 (AMC)
> Dayton, OH 45433
> (513) 429-1808 eves

☆ **British and American military knives** from WWI and WWII especially British Commando daggers, *Wilkinson Sword* fighting knives (marked FS FIGHTING KNIFE), and American special unit fighting knives. Value ranges from $50 to $1,500 depending on rarity, condition and its scabbard. It is very important for you to copy every word and symbol on the blade, handle, guard, and scabbard. John does not want bayonets that attach to the end of a rifle.

> John Fischer
> 7831 Peachtree Ave.
> Panorama City, CA 91402

☆ **U.S. and German bayonets and daggers,** either standard fighting issue or dress type. Other countries also purchased. He prefers to buy directly from the veteran or family, and wants information about your weapon's history. This 25 year expert appraiser offers free appraisals of **all military swords** and edged weapons to private parties.

    Hank McGonagle
    26 Broad Street
    Newburyport, MA 01950
        (508) 462-2354   (617) 594-1596

☆ **German swords and daggers** from the Nazi era (1933-1945). Will buy both common and rare variations, with etched or with plain blades. Especially wanted are swords and daggers with inscriptions giving name, date, and military unit etched on the scabbard or blade. Make a drawing or photocopy of the item, noting all rust, pitting, scabbard dents, blade dings, etc.

    Ron Hickox, Antique Arms & Militaria
    PO Box 360006, Dept. T
    Tampa, FL 33673
        (813) 968-1571   Fax: (813) 935-0190

☆ **German swords, knives, daggers, and bayonets** from WW I and WW II. Also buys selected other quality items of German war memorabilia. He is not interested in reproductions or in "lesser condition" items. Please send a photo, sketch, or photocopy. He requests you set the price you have in mind, but will make offers to amateurs who are selling. Send $5 if you'd like one of his catalogs of items for sale. For $20 you can subscribe to his quarterly newsletter on military collecting and collectibles around the world. Johnson is an internationally known appraiser, author of fourteen books on edged weapons, and can provide you a catalog of those still available.

    LTC (ret) Thomas Johnson, Johnson Reference Books
    312 Butler Road, Chatham Square Office Park #403
    Fredericksburg, VA 22405
        (703) 373-9150   Fax: (703) 373-0087

☆ **Japanese swords,** daggers, spears, armor and other Samurai items, especially fine swords and daggers, and sword and dagger parts. Ron will send you a checklist to help you describe a sword for sale. An SASE is appreciated. Please photograph your sword laying alongside its scabbard. Ron is an internationally known collector who has been studying Japanese swords for twenty years. He will be pleased to determine the quality of your sword and to make you an offer for it. No other guns, bayonets, or non-Japanese swords and daggers are wanted.

    Ron Hartmann
    5907 Deerwood Drive
    St. Louis, MO 63123
        (314) 832-3477

WAR & WEAPONS

☆ **Primitive weapons from around the world.** Also trade beads from various cultures.

> David Boone Trading Company
> 562 Coyote Road
> Brinnon, WA 98320
> (206) 796-4330

☆ **Anything military.** "My specialty is WWII paratrooper items from the U.S., Germany, and Japan, but **I will buy any military items from the Roman Empire to current issue Operation Desert Storm**. I buy small items like dog tags and big items like tanks, so look in the attic and give me a call." This 30 year veteran collector does not want reproductions or fakes but will consider anything you find in that trunk in your attic such as flags, uniforms, helmets, equipment, guns, daggers, hats, shoes, medals, jewelry, boats, jeeps, tanks. "I buy anything military." Take a photo if you can and tell him whatever history you know about the item(s) you have. "If you want to know what something is worth, but you can't take a photo, or find writing to be difficult," he says, "give me a call and I'll be happy to talk to you."

> Michael Burke
> Der Fallschirmjager
> 906 Chambers Ridge
> York, PA 17402
> (717) 840-4156

☆ **French and Indian War, Revolutionary War** and the **War of 1812** in northern New York, especially the Lake Champlain, Lake George, or Fort Ticonderoga area. All ephemera about the campaigns and the men involved especially Benedict Arnold and Rogers' Rangers.

> Breck Turner
> With Pipe and Book
> 91 Main Street
> Lake Placid, NY 12946

☆ **Boer war items**, with particular interest in carvings made of cedar wood. Describe thoroughly.

> Ernest Roberts
> 5 Corsa Street
> Dix Hills, NY 11746

☆ **Mexican War** (1846-48) photos and documents are sought.

> Johnny Spellman
> 10806 North Lamar
> Austin, TX 78753
> (512) 836-2889 days   (512) 258-6910 eves

☆ **Civil War artifacts, Union and Confederate** are wanted, including autographs of important military and civilian personalities, documents, photos, diaries, books, manuals, soldier's letters, personal items, campaign histories, regimental histories, G.A.R. or Confederate Veteran items. Has a particular interest in the battles of Gettysburg and Antietam. Provide a detailed description of items, especially condition.

 Stan Clark, Jr., Military Books
 915 Fairview Ave.
 Gettysburg, PA 17325
  (717) 337-1728

☆ **Civil War artifacts of all types** including guns, knives, canteens, uniforms, documents, swords, and **prisoner of war items**. No repros. It is important to indicate any markings. SASE requested.

 Charles Worman
 PO Box 33584 (AMC)
 Dayton, OH 45433
  (513) 429-1808 eves

☆ **Confederate Civil War letters,** envelopes, **paper money**, posters, pardons, passes, and other ephemera. Also, some other Civil War items, and **Lincoln photos** and manuscripts.

 Gordon McHenry
 PO Box 1117
 Osprey, FL 34229

☆ **Civil War items**, especially uniforms. Buys muskets, pistols, swords, photographs and sundry items including bottles and excavated artifacts related to the war. Also buys other military items up through World War II. Nothing later.

 Will Gorges Antiques
 308 Simmons Street
 New Bern, NC 28560
  (919) 636-3039 days (919) 514-5548 eves

☆ **G.A.R. china, mugs, and spoons.** Any pieces marked G.A.R. (Grand Army of the Republic).

 Don McMahon
 385 Thorpe Ave.
 Meriden, CT 06450
  (203)

☆ **United Confederate Reunion (UCV)** badges, buttons, and ribbons.

 Peggy Dillard
 PO Box 210904
 Nashville, TN 37221
  (615) 646-1605

☆ **Civil War regimental histories** and first person narratives.
Jim Presgraves, Bookworm & Silverfish
PO Box 639
Wytheville, VA 24382

☆ **Military items.** "I'll buy most military items, if original, especially
WWI, WWII Airborne (paratroopers), military aviation and glider op-
erations, and **Vietnam**. I do not want reproductions of WWII German
items." Give the origin of your piece. Photograph expensive items.
Robert Thomas, Jr.
Thomas Militaria
PO Box 1792
Santa Ana, CA 92702
(714) 448-0328   Fax: (714) 558-1536

☆ **Military unit histories** from any branch of the service, **American
or British**. Collects all eras, but especially needs Korean and **Vietnam**
wars. Guarantees "highest prices" for WWII fighter or bomber groups,
paratroopers, tank units or units of Black soldiers. "I am not interested
in reprints or later editions. I also collect **unit photos, military postcards, holiday menus, distinctive unit insignia, shoulder patches,
medals, guidons, scrapbooks and berets**. If you want an offer, send it
for my examination. I pay all postage, both ways."
Lt. Col. Wilfred Baumann
PO Box 319
Esperance, NY 12066
(518) 875-6753

☆ **Military books of World War I, World War II and Korean War**
on the air, land and sea. First editions in dust jackets preferred. Some
rare titles will be purchased in lesser condition. Provide standard bibliographic information, including printing data found on the title page
or reverse. No book club books and no paperbacks.
Edward Conroy
SUMAC Books
Route 1   Box 197
Troy, NY 12180
(518) 279-9638 voice and fax

☆ **Military books.** "I want all types of fine condition books on military history to resell, but my specialties are U.S. military and wars from
the Civil War to Vietnam." You may request his list of books for sale
by sending an SASE with two stamps.
Gaal Long
Route 1   Box 40
Sardis, MS 38666

☆ **Regimental and Battalion unit flags** from all nations and periods of history. "I'll also buy flag related items such as U.S. Army spear pole tops, color woven flag cords and tassels, engraved battle honor rings and battle streamers, canvas issue flag cover bags, and close up or **parade photos** showing unit flags." No national flags or reenactment group flags. Please make a sketch of the flag, noting size and material. Ben can provide info about unit flags if you send an SASE.

    Ben Weed
    PO Box 4643
    Stockton, CA 95204

☆ **Merchant Marine** photos, uniforms, and medals.

    Harvey Lee Boswell
    PO Box 446
    Elm City, NC 27822

☆ **Cloth shoulder insignia** of divisions, regiments, brigades, and units from the Civil War to Vietnam. WWI U.S. and German insignia are of special interest. Complete uniforms welcome. He prefers to buy directly from the veteran or family. Condition is important. This 25 year veteran does not want fakes or repros.

    Hank McGonagle
    26 Broad Street
    Newburyport, MA 01950
        (508) 462-2354   (617) 594-1596

☆ **Military medals and decorations** from all countries and periods. Also any documents or certificates related to military awards, medals and decorations. He prefers to buy directly from the vet or his family. Condition is important, and a photocopy is requested.

    Hank McGonagle
    26 Broad Street
    Newburyport, MA 01950
        (508) 462-2354   (617) 594-1596

☆ **Medals, Decorations, and Orders** for military gallantry and other campaign medals of the U.S. and British Empire, 1780 to the present. Especially wants U.S. Medals of Honor and **British Victoria Crosses** and U.S. Purple Hearts for WWII officially named to the Navy and Marines. Does not want reproductions. Photocopy both sides.

    Alan Harrow
    2292 Chelan Drive
    Los Angeles, CA 90068

☆ **Military newsreel and training films** from WWII on any military, naval, or aviation subject. British, American, Canadian, German, or Russian, but must be 16mm sound films shot 1939-45. Films may be training, propaganda or documentary. Buys military aviation films 1903-1985, especially WWI, Korean Conflict, and Vietnam. Give complete title, producer, length and defects. If possible, describe the contents. Nothing damaged. Also buys **military magazines**.

    Edward Topor
    4313 South Marshfield Ave.
    Chicago, IL 60609
      (312) 847-6392

☆ **General Douglas MacArthur memorabilia** of all types is wanted. "I'll buy books, scrapbooks, autographed items, pictures, documents, toys, dolls, medals, coins, any item with 'I shall return' or 'I have returned' on it, buttons, statues, and any item documented as having belonged to MacArthur." Please send a Xerox™ if you'd like an offer.

    Gaal Long
    Route 1 Box 40
    Sardis, MS 38666
      (601) 487-2457

☆ **Trench art brass vases and lamps** made from shell casings. "I am only interested if they are engraved or embossed." No plain casings are wanted. Also buys **helmets** and **anything on Benito Mussolini**. Make a sketch or take a photo and include dimensions, sizes, and decoration.

    Al Lanzetta
    PO Box 2464
    New York, NY 10185

NAVY & MARINES

☆ **U.S. Navy memorabilia** including postcards, ship or station postmarks and documents. Describe. Pricing appreciated.
> Frank Hoak III
> PO Box 668
> New Canaan, CT 06840

☆ **U.S. Marine Corps memorabilia** of all kinds including recruiting posters and materials, books, photos, belt buckles, cigarette lighters, steins, mugs, documents, autographs, postcards, **trench art**, bronzes, and **John Philip Sousa** ephemera. Also buys **toy soldiers, trucks, and planes** with Marine markings. Describe or make a photocopy.
> Dick Weisler
> 5307 213th Street
> Bayside, NY 11364
> (718) 626-7110 days   (718) 428-9829 eves

☆ **U.S. Marine Corps everything.** Anything used and/or worn by Marines from 1776 to 1946, such as **uniforms**, **medals**, helmets and weapons. Also buys unit histories, documents and **recruiting posters**. Wants photos of Marines at war, work, or play, especially amateur photos. Also wants trench art created by Marines and souvenirs of war brought home by Marines. Tell what you can of the item's history.
> Bruce Updegrove
> Route 5   Box 546
> Boyertown, PA 19512
> (610) 369-1798 eves

☆ **U.S. Marine Corps ephemera** including recruiting posters, other artwork, postcards, autographs, letters written by Marines, and "almost any" Marine related book, including signed books by or about Marines, personal memoirs, unit histories, campaign histories, biographies, fiction, juveniles, children's books and poetry. "I would especially like a set of monographs written by Marine Major Edwin McClellan in 1925, in book or mimeographed form." He is not interested in book club editions or in books "in questionable condition." To sell your Marine Corps books, give standard bibliographic information, including number of pages, size, and whether or not it has a dust jacket. This 10 year veteran distributes four catalogs a year of military books for sale. "If you are actually selling, give us a call. We don't have time for casual inquiries or information seekers. Sorry."
> Stan Clark, Jr.
> Stan Clark Military Books
> 915 Fairview Ave.
> Gettysburg, PA 17325
> (717) 337-1728

THE AIR WAR

☆ **Army Air Force A2 flight jackets,** AAF pocket insignia, sterling silver military aviation wings and WWI enlisted men's round collar discs. Nothing later than the Korean War.

> Jerry Keohane
> 16 Saint Margaret's Court
> Buffalo, NY 14216

If the seller did not get the jacket from the veteran or his family, it is probably not old.

☆ **WWII leather or cloth aviation jackets** with squadron patch and/ or painted artwork on the back, from any branch of the service, any branch of aviation. Needs information on jacket label, condition of the jacket and its patches or art, plus details about the art. Photo helpful. Does not want currently made flight jackets with antiqued paintings or patches. Clue: If the zipper isn't marked as being *Talon* brand, the jacket isn't old. Buys documented **Flying Tiger memorabilia, squadron patches and histories** and photos of **airplane nose art.**

> Gary Hullfish
> 16 Gordon Ave.
> Lawranceville, NJ 08648
>   (609) 896-0224   Fax: (609) 896-2040

☆ **Photos and bits and pieces of WWII aircraft**. It doesn't matter whether allied and axis, crashed or operational, Ken wants single snaps, albums, or negatives of photos of any aircraft used in WWII. Also wants instruments, gauges, fabric, fittings, data plates, unit or group insignia, and miscellaneous bits and pieces of the combat aircraft of any nation.

> Ken Francella
> PO Box 234
> Granite Springs, NY 10527
>   (914) 248-8138

☆ **Airplane identification models,** 1940-1970. Also promotional models, travel agency models, and **squadron and bomb group unit histories**. When writing, copy all info printed on the plane.

> John Pochobradsky
> 1991 East Schodack Road
> Castleton, NY 12033
>   (518) 477-9488

TANKS & HEAVY WEAPONS

☆ **Tanks, artillery, armored vehicles and machine guns and their parts and accessories.** "We are a Federally licensed machine gun manufacturer and dealer, and seek to buy registered operational machine guns and other military equipment, including **muzzle loading cannon** and **Gattling guns**. We buy machine gun parts and accessories including, but not limited to, barrels, buttstocks, magazines, clips, drums, bipods, tripods, mounts, loading machines, linkers, armorer's kits, etc. We are particularly interested in mounts for *Maxim* machine guns and will pay $150+ for them. We will buy **most anything made in the 19th or 20th centuries**. Parts and guns do not have to be in perfect condition. We will look at all items, but clear photos are a must. A VHS video is even better. Include dimensions and condition of accessories. Copies of any accompanying paperwork or manuals are helpful. If, after inspection, our offer is unacceptable, I will pay shipping both ways." Not interested in toys, miniatures, stolen firearms or U.S. Army manuals.

> Greg Souchik
> T.M.P. Company
> PO Box 133
> Custer City, PA 16725
> (814) 362-2642 Fax: (814) 362-7356

☆ **Half tracks, armored cars, tanks, Gattling guns,** howitzers, and cannons, especially a *FT-17 Renault* (M1917) tank in any condition. Larry will arrange for transporting what you have. Also wants:
- **U.S. women's uniforms** and accessories, WWI or WWII but only in fine condition;
- **Military diving** equipment and related items including catalogs;
- *Mercedes Benz 500K* or *540K* autos between 1930 and 1940;
- **German military staff cars**;
- **Military aircraft** from any country pre-1940.

Provide all the information printed on the machine's data plates. In most cases when you are trying to sell large equipment, a few photographs from different angles would be recommended.

> Larry Pitman
> Zanzibar War Museum
> 5424 Bryan Station Road
> Paris, KY 40361
> (606) 299-5022 (606) 299-4522

FOREIGN ARMIES

☆ **Napoleonic arms and armor.** This 30 year veteran collector/dealer in Western ephemera does not make offers. Requires you to send a photo and complete description including information about where you got it, and your asking price. No fakes or reproductions are wanted.

> Pierre Bovis
> The Az-Tex Cowboy Trading Co.
> PO Box 460
> Tombstone, AZ 85638
> (602) 457-3359 voice and fax

☆ **Canadian military medals and cap badges.** "I'll buy all cap badges with the initials CEF on them, or badges with a number and the words OVERSEAS BATTALION and CANADA or CANADIAN on them. I'll buy any war or period. Look for name, rank and military unit on the rims of medals as some are worth $1,000+." Answers all inquiries.

> Michael Rice
> PO Box 286
> Saanichton, BC V8M 2C5 CANADA
> (604) 652-9047

☆ **Military items of Great Britain or Commonwealth nations.** "I'll buy hat, collar or shoulder badges, headdresses, uniforms, field equipment (belts, packs, pouches) and **edged weapons**. Particularly seek Scottish bagpipers' headdress and badges, kilts and sporrans (leather kilt purses), dirks, and knives." 45 year collector will consider 1910-1945 items from other countries, especially cloth patches. No fakes or repros. Describe the material the item is made from, colors, etc. Note if anything seems to be missing and chips, dents, moth holes, stitch marks, corrosion, fading, stains and polish wear. Photocopy.

> Charles Edwards
> Pass in Review
> PO Box 622
> Grayslake, IL 60030
> (708) 223-2332

☆ **Military items from the Coldstream Guards.** The museum wants to buy uniforms, equipment, badges, and miscellaneous items used by the British Coldstream Guards before 1900. Other British Army ephemera from before 1900 may be of interest. A full description includes dimensions, materials, and age. Indicate anything you believe to be unique. Donations acknowledged. No U.S. items are wanted.

> Ernest Klapmeier
> Coldstream Guards Living History Museum
> PO Box 334
> Wayne, IL 60184
> (708) 584-1017 days

☆ **French or British military forces** overseas, British Indian Native States forces, Spanish or **French Foreign Legion**, Abraham Lincoln Brigade, Camel Corps, Free French and Vichy forces, French forces in China, Devil's Island, White Russian forces, Chinese Customs Service, Chinese bandits or pirates, China Navigation Company, international settlements in China, Chinese airlines, and similar topics. Wants badges, banners, **medals**, photos, certificates, souvenirs, etc. Material about American volunteers or **famous soldiers of fortune** of any nationality is particularly welcome. No repros of Devil's Island folk art or souvenirs produced by the Foreign Legion Veteran's Home.

> Gene Christian
> 3849 Bailey Ave.
> Bronx, NY 10463
> (718) 548-0243

✓☆ **Nazi notables** especially Heinrich Himmler, commander of the SS and Gestapo. Wants items given by or to Hitler, Goering, Goebbles, Hess, etc., including promotion and award documents, letters, trophies, **uniforms** or **medals**. "I am generally not interested in any item you or a member of your family did not personally bring back from overseas." He prefers you to call him with the item in hand. Otherwise write, describe what you have, make a photocopy, and include your phone number. Tom will pay $10,000 cash for some Nazi documents.

> Thomas Pooler
> PO Box 1861
> Grass Valley, CA 95945
> (916) 268-1338

✓☆ **German, Japanese, and Italian military** wanted, especially daggers and dagger parts, swords, medals, badges, spike helmets, flag-pole tops, etc. Pays $50 each for **German WWII helmets** complete with liner. "I will also buy flags, but the bigger the flag, the less they're worth. You may write, giving me your phone number. Take a photo or send insured for cash offer." This is a hobby for Dick, so he says that he's happy to help people if they send him an SASE. Makes offers only on items for sale. Also interested in U.S. military patches.

> Dick Pankowski
> PO Box 22
> Greendale, WI 53129
> (414) 421-7056 days   (414) 421-5212 eves

As a general rule, the bigger your Nazi flag, the less it is worth. Many are available and they are difficult to display.

THE HOME FRONT

☆ **Home Front and anti-fascist collectibles** from World War II especially related to important events or phenomena including the **Holocaust,** resistance, women during war, chaplaincy, soldier benevolent funds, etc. Anything related to **anti-Semitism** or the Allied war effort, from paper to pottery, considered if made 1939-1946. Items directly related to military occupation of Germany or Japan 1945-1955 considered. Interested in the rare or unusual. Does not want military uniforms, weapons, medals, or insignia, nor does he want souvenirs from Germany or Japan other than related to anti-Semitism. No magazines, newspapers, or damaged items. Requires some items be sent on approval. Reimburses postal costs.

> Richard Harrow
> 8523 210th Street
> Hollis Hills, NY 11427
> (718) 740-1088

☆ **Rationing material** worldwide. CSU owns most American items, buys only paper and "wants many foreign posters and other items." No U.S. ration books are needed.

> Ronald Mahoney, Head of Special Collections
> Madden Library
> California State University
> Fresno, CA 93740
> (209) 294-2595

☆ **Ration tokens.** Pays 2¢ each for red tokens, 3¢ each for blue. After the first 250, he pays 1¢ each. Pays "much more" for error tokens. Ship for his inspection and check.

> Rich Hartzog
> PO Box 4143 BFT
> Rockford, IL 61110

☆ **Patriotic embroidery.** "I want embroidered or hand stitched cotton or silk American or Confederate flags, patriotic or military themes, American eagles, and similar, especially turn of the century items with Marine Corps themes. Nothing made after 1960 is wanted, nor is anything with serious holes, tears, or insect damage." Photo is suggested.

> Stan Clark, Jr.
> Stan Clark Military Books
> 915 Fairview Ave.
> Gettysburg, PA 17325
> (717) 337-1728

COINS AND CURRENCY ARE SELDOM AS VALUABLE AS YOU HOPE.

Everyone seems to have old coins or bills tucked away in a drawer. Now's the time to find out. If you do have something good, cash in. I've got some fine folks from the world of collectible money standing by to help.

*Valuable coins and bills exist, and they are found on occasion, but **your bills and coins will probably not have collectors panting.** Since some unusual things do have value, including a few foreign bills, you should take the few minutes necessary to find out.*

***Photocopying makes it possible to check the value of your money easily and quickly.** If inquiring about modern currency, it is important to note the color of the Treasury seal to the right of the portrait on the face of each bill. Colors can be blue, green, red, brown, gold, or yellow. Value differs by color.*

***If you want an idea of your coins' value without anyone knowing what you have,** it's easy to do. Use A Guide Book of United States Coins by R.S. Yoeman. Called "The Red Book," it gives average selling prices of coins. Yoeman's Handbook of U.S. Coins ("The Blue Book") gives prices dealers pay for coins. These can be borrowed from most libraries. If you own anything that catalogs over $50, get expert advice. Coins valued under $10 will find few takers.*

***Amateur sellers overestimate condition.** Yoeman's books contain information you should read about coin grading, because amateurs over-estimate condition of coins and bills. Buyers will grade severely. A spot of wear at the tip of an eagle wing can cost 50% of a coin's value.*

*The coin world has attracted more than its share of shady characters. **Never sell coins, watches or jewelry to someone buying out of a motel room.** You get much less than you would from well-established dealers. Deal with folks in here instead.*

ANTIQUITIES & OLD COINS

☆ **Coins and antiquities, especially Biblical, Greek, and Roman.**
Ancient artifacts including Egyptian, Greek, Roman, and Biblical pottery, glass and relics. **Nothing made after 1000AD is wanted.** This 20 year veteran collector wrote *Guide to Ancient Jewish Coins* and other books, and issues periodic catalogs of relics for sale. He does not buy prints, rugs, weavings, or drawings of Biblical topics. He does not want reproductions, pictures, or drawings. Ancient artifacts *only.*
> David Hendin
> Amphora
> PO Box 805
> Nyack, NY 10960

☆ **European antiquities.** Wants relics and artifacts from Europe from prehistoric times through 1500 AD. Particularly interested in the British Isles, but all regions of Europe are wanted. Items may be of stone, bone, pottery, or metal, and include swords of bronze or iron, bone harpoon heads, pottery, blown glass, Celtic coins, Roman weaponry, Viking and Celt jewelry, Scottish Highlander items, etc. Especially wants flint arrowheads, axe heads of stone or bronze and pottery made before 600 AD. Does NOT want Roman, Greek or Etruscan pottery, figures, coins, or other art from these cultures, but will consider fine weaponry and jewelry. Tell where your item came from. Photos are helpful, "and at a minimum, I need a tracing, sketch or Xerox™ copy."
> Charles Ray
> The Keltoi
> PO Box 881
> Winchester, KY 40392
> (606) 744-9789

☆ **Spanish pieces of eight.** Wants *reales* minted in Spanish or South American mints. Seeks coins with globe and pillars known as "pillar dollars," "pieces of eight," or "pirate dollars."
> Sven Stau
> PO Box 437
> Buffalo, NY 14212
> (716) 825-5448   (716) 822-3120

COINS & PAPER MONEY

☆ **Coin collections of all types,** "from pennies to gold." Also individual gold coins, medals, and artifacts. Also pre-1930 U.S. banknotes and commemorative coins. No pennies after 1955, nickels after 1939, dimes, quarters, and halves after 1964, or silver dollars after 1936.
> Ron Aldridge
> 250 Canyon Oaks Drive
> Argyle, TX
> (214) 239-3574 eves

☆ **Silver and gold coins from any country** but especially wants perfect proof U.S. silver dollars. "No junk coins."
> Robert Hiett, Maple City Coin
> PO Box 47
> Monmouth, IL 61462
> (309) 734-3212   Fax: (309) 734-8083

☆ **Paper money.** "I buy all U.S. paper money issued before 1929, all **Confederate money** and all broken bank notes from any state. I especially want **items made of ground up paper money**, and will pay 60% of retail. I recommend making photocopies of bills you'd like to sell."
> William Skelton, Highland Coin
> PO Box 55118
> Birmingham, AL 35255
> (205) 939-3166 extension 3

☆ **Paper money.** "We'll buy any foreign and obsolete U.S. and **Confederate banknotes**. We will buy currency in any condition and quantity in order to supply fellow collectors in all parts of the world. We deal by mail only but telephone calls are welcomed. We will buy collections as well as single notes, but we do not want U.S. currency after 1928." A description should include the date, denomination, and the country of issue. A photocopy is the best way to describe currency. With his available research library, he is "able to identify and appraise any banknote ever issued."
> Josef Klaus, World Wide Notaphilic Service
> PO Box 5427
> Vallejo, CA 94591
> (707) 644-3146   (707) 643-8616 Fax: (707) 643-3806

☆ **U.S. currency with stars.** "I'll buy nice crisp U.S. bills with serial numbers that end in stars." Send a photocopy of what you have.
> Douglas Swisher
> PO Box 52701
> Jacksonville, FL 32201
> (904) 448-6214

☆ **All foreign paper money.** "I'll buy collections, accumulations, dealer's stock, hoards, rarities, **German inflation currency**, specimens, printer's proofs, banknote presentations, sample books and entire **numismatic libraries**." Will travel. Has been buying since 1964.

> AMCASE
> PO Box 5473
> Akron, OH 44334
>   (216) 867-6724

☆ **U.S. Coins and paper money.** Wants estates, collections and accumulations of early **U.S. silver and gold coins**, paper money, and all other U.S. coins from 1793-1900. This nationally known dealer has been around for 40 years, and will travel to see large lots and better collections. Send a list and description. Photocopy suggested.

> Littleton Coin Co., THCC
> 253 Union Street
> Littleton, NH 03561

☆ **Printed or manuscript items relating to coins, currency, medals, tokens, or counterfeiting.** Especially scholarly books on coins from any period or language. Also scholarly **numismatic periodicals** and catalogs of coin auctions pre-1940 in any language. Also **counterfeit detectors and bank note reporters** issued in the U.S., 1820 and 1900. No modern works or general surveys of numismatics. Makes offers on better items.

> George Frederick Kolbe
> PO Drawer 3100
> Crestline, CA 92325
>   (909) 338-6527   Fax: (909) 338-6980

☆ **Items made from macerated (ground up) currency** by the mint, including statues, plaques, postcards, shoes, hats, etc., which have a small tag reading, THIS ITEM MADE OF US GREENBACKS REDEEMED AND MACERATED BY THE US GOVERNMENT. Describe damage carefully.

> Donald Gorlick
> PO Box 24541
> Seattle, WA 98124
>   (206) 824-0508

☆ **Red coin books** printed before 1954.

> James Williams
> HCR 01 Box 23
> Warrensburg, NY 12885
>   (518) 623-2831

ERROR COINS & ELONGATES

☆ **Mis-strike and error coins created by the U.S. Mint.** Under most circumstances, it is best to send a good clear pencil rubbing or photocopy for evaluation if you wish an offer. Also **paper money of 1929 issued by banks.** Include photocopy and SASE for free appraisal.

>Neil Osina
>Best Variety Coin Center
>358 West Foothill Blvd.
>Glendora, CA 91741
>   (818) 914-6624

☆ **Elongated coins** dated before 1960. Also buys the machines and the dies to make them. "I'll pay well for scarce items I want."

>Gus Meccarello, Elongated Coin Museum
>228 Vassar Road
>Poughkeepsie, NY 12603
>   (914) 462-1693

☆ **Elongated coins.** If what you have is pre-1930, ship it for an offer, but *do not* ship COD. Hartzog pays $1-$5 and up for elongates before 1940. Large collections especially wanted.

>Rich Hartzog
>PO Box 4143 BFT
>Rockford, IL 61110

COUNTERFEITING DEVICES

☆ **Coin scales and anything used to detect counterfeit money,** coins or currency, including coin detectors, scanners, grids, magnifiers, Detectographs and other devices to check weight, thickness or diameter of coins. Also any scale with markings in amounts, such as "20 dol., 10 dol., 5 dol." Names to look for: *Ewing, Herpers, Fairbanks, McNalley, MBT, Rice, Statler, Meyers* among many others.

>Donald Gorlick
>PO Box 24541
>Seattle, WA 98124
>   (206) 824-0508

*Coin scales do not have pans
or weights like a gold scale.
They do have some method
of weighing a coin, and
another for testing thickness.*

☆ **Coin scales, coin detectors, and counterfeit detectors.** Will buy the devices and/or books about them and the processes of counterfeiting and counterfeit detecting. Buys items outright or may accept on consignment for auction.

> Rich Hartzog
> PO Box 4143 BFT
> Rockford, IL 61110
> (815) 226-0771   Fax: (815) 397-7662

CREDIT CARDS

☆ **Credit cards** from any source, paper or plastic, are desired. "Send items for immediate offer and check. I pay postage both ways."

> Noel Levy
> PO Box 32458
> Baltimore, MD 21208
> (410) 363-9040

☆ **Credit cards.** "I'll pay a flat $2 each for credit cards, charge plates, and charge coins made of celluloid, metal, paper or plastic, U.S. or foreign, as long as they are not abused. Ship what you have, for prompt payment." ATM and sample credit cards are only worth 25¢ each, if that.

> Lin Overholt
> PO Box 8481
> Madeira Beach, FL 33738

☆ **Credit cards.** "I've collected credit cards for over ten years and am seriously interested in buying both the older metal charge cards and modern plastic cards. Please ship any quantity of used or new cards. I pay $4 up for older metal charge cards and will pay *at least* $15 for any metal one I need for my own collection. Pre-1980 plastic cards bring $1 up, and those before 1970 average $2. More paid for local businesses, unusual types, etc. Post-1980 cards are worth 50¢ each, a few bring more. I will also reimburse your postage. Please ship for my check."

> Rich Hartzog
> PO Box 4143 BFT
> Rockford, IL 61110

THERE ARE TOKENS WORTH $1,000. TO YOU AND ME THEY LOOK JUST LIKE $1 TOKENS.

Collecting tokens is popular because they are inexpensive. Most retail for 25¢ to $3. You should have an expert dealer look at your tokens, however, as a few are worth $500. Tokens are difficult to evaluate on your own because more than 300 books are in print about tokens and tiny differences can mean a lot. The following definitions should help you describe "a little round thing" to a potential buyer.

__Coins__ are money issued by governments. Most modern coins contain the name of the issuing agency, the denomination, and the date of issue.

__Exonumia__ means all coin-like objects that aren't money. It refers primarily to tokens, but has come to include medals, orders, decorations, plaques, awards, ribbons, and the like. Dealers of exonumia often sell advertising mirrors (they were frequently trade tokens) and other small collectibles as well.

__Tokens__ are money substitutes, often marked with a value, such as "good for 5¢ in trade." Tokens were issued by local businesses usually for advertising. Sometimes they were issued because no legal coinage was available.

__Medals__ are "any piece of metal marked with a design or inscription, made to honor a person, place or event," according to one of our buyers. Medals vary in size and shape, although most are round. Medals larger than 3" in diameter are usually called __medallions__. Small rectangular medals are called __plaquettes__ and larger ones, meant to hang on the wall, are __plaques__.

__Orders__ and __decorations__ are an important separate category, generally related to diplomacy and the military. They are often worn around the neck or on sashes across the wearer's breast.

__Military medals__ are emblems of honor normally made with ribbons so they can be worn. __Badges__ have a top pin or device, with or without a ribbon, so they too can be worn. Both usually have a medallic device hanging from them (what amateurs think of when someone says "medals").

__Ribbons__ are commemorative items, printed with information about the event commemorated. They are usually associated with lodges, fraternal organizations, conventions, and the like.

Whichever one of these you have, make a pencil rubbing or a photocopy and let the buyers tell you exactly what you own and what they'll pay. Buyers of medals and tokens will be found throughout Trash or Treasure.

TOKENS & MEDALS

✩ **All types and quantities of tokens, medals, ribbons, badges, and related items.** Some old tokens are common, but others can be worth $1,500+ each if they picture a ship, trolley, horse car, ferry, or stage coach. Look for the words DEPOTEL, BAGGAGE, HOTEL, OMNIBUS, DRAYAGE, DEPOT TO HOTEL, and similar wordings. He buys trade tokens, medals of all sort, hard times tokens, Civil War tokens, **transportation and toll tokens** especially with pictures on them, amusement tokens, telephone tokens, sales tax tokens, **any token or medal made from another item, medals related to medicine or the arts** and humanities, **love tokens, World's Fair medals** and elongated coins, G.A.R. badges and tokens,

We sell bags of 2,500 modern tokens with cut-out letters for $99, so you can see they are not worth much."

Indian peace medals ($1,500 up), **slave tags, Canadian** tokens and medals, **military awards and medals,** counterstamped coins, and just about everything similar to the above including advertising mirrors and **Franklin Mint token sets.** There are millions of varieties, and condition plays an important role in value. If what you have is pre-1930, simply ship it to him for an offer, but do not ship COD. Hartzog will send you a check for the lot. "We cannot make individual offers on a long list of material. Our offers are for the entire lot as we want to purchase everything. We are not interested in pricing your material for you to sell to others, sorry!" He claims to pay higher prices than anyone else. If your collection is very early, very large, or very valuable, phone collect and Hartzog will make arrangements to see what you have. Hartzog can auction your materials for you if you prefer. A sample of his auction catalog is available for $3. Hartzog's lengthy wants list shows prices and is recommended. Also **Franklin Mint and other private mint issues.** "I will purchase all bronze, silver and gold singles, sets and other items such as plates, bronzes, etc., in any quantity. Many silver or gold pieces are worth substantially above issue price. Bronze tokens and medals are worth less than their issue price, most of them under 25¢ apiece. I pay reasonable prices for all modern mint items. Since I do not specialize in *Franklin Mint* items, do not ship them without inquiring first. State the price you want, or request my offer. If my offer is not accepted, I do not pay return postage on modern mint medals that have been shipped." There is little market for *Franklin Mint* items, so it's best to contact Rich first by phone or letter so you fully understand their value or lack of it.

Rich Hartzog
World Exonumia
PO Box 4143 (W7)
Rockford, IL 61110
(815) 226-0771

☆ **Transportation or toll tokens** for bridges, toll roads, ferries, horsecars, depot hacks, and early streetcars. Tokens *must* be made of metal or plastic. Cardboard tokens are wanted *only* if round, *not* square or rectangular. HOTEL TO DEPOT or TRANSFER LINE tokens are worth $25-$100, more if pictorial. A token reading I GIBBS BELLEVILLE & NEW YORK USM STAGE//GOOD FOR ONE RIDE TO THE BEARER would be worth $1,500 in nice condition.

> Rev. John Coffee
> PO Box 1204
> Boston, MA 02104
> (617) 277-8111

☆ **Medals and tokens of all sorts** are wanted by this 22 year veteran dealer. Identify what the token or medal is made from, and provide a photocopy or a good rubbing. "I buy them all," he says.

> William Williges
> PO Box 1245
> Wheatland, CA 95692
> (916) 633-2732

☆ **Medals and medallions from Canada, Britain, and other English speaking countries** issued for coronations, jubilees, town celebrations, victories, fraternal groups, achievement, athletics, and especially military valor medals awarded to Canadians. Also **love tokens** engraved with names, initials, dates, pledges, and the like from around the world especially pre-1900. Also merchant's **GOOD FOR trade tokens** from Canada, Britain and English speaking countries. Also buys **Canadian paper money** dating before 1937, singles or collections.

> Michael Rice
> PO Box 286
> Saanichton, BC V8M 2C5 CANADA
> (604) 652-9047 eves

☆ **U.S., British, and Soviet valor decorations** and war medals. **Foreign awards given to Americans** are of great interest, especially Soviet World War II orders and decorations. All items *must* have supporting documentation of the award to U.S. personnel. Hlinka also buys all letters, certificates, or documents pertaining to valor awards. He seeks a U.S. Medal of Honor awarded between 1917 and 1970. He encourages you to photocopy both sides of medals and supporting paperwork. Hlinka has been dealing in medals for 40 years and has been an officer in various collectors' societies.

> Peter Hlinka
> PO Box 310
> New York, NY 10028
> (718) 409-6407

☆ **Medals, decorations, and orders,** especially military gallantry awards from U.S. and England, but will consider **all governmental awards** from any Western nation. No Asian awards, please.

>   Alan Harrow
>   2292 Chelan Drive
>   Los Angeles, CA 90068

☆ **Indian War medals, badges and awards** issued by the U.S. government, states, or veteran's groups. An Indian scout's Medal of Honor can be worth $20,000. Other items from $100 to $10,000. "No offers based on phone calls or photos. Items must be seen. Ship insured with record of delivery. Your postage will be reimbursed."

>   Thomas Pooler
>   PO Box 1861
>   Grass Valley, CA 95949

☆ **Official presidential inaugural medals.** This 25 year veteran offers $4,000 for the Teddy Roosevelt inaugural medal.

>   H. Joseph Levine
>   6550-I Little River Turnpike
>   Alexandria, VA 22312

☆ **Medals commemorating or depicting Black Americans.** "I'll buy medals, medallions, badges, or tokens relating to, or depicting, Afro-Americans or including the words NEGRO, COLORED or BLACK-AMERICAN. Items may be positive or negative in tone. I'll pay $1,200 for the Franklin Mint set of 70 American Negro Commemorative Society medals." Tell him the material (silver, bronze, or aluminum), the size in millimeters, and inscriptions on both sides.

>   Elijah Singley
>   2301 Noble Ave.
>   Springfield, IL 62704

☆ **Tokens, medals, and exonumia (non-money coinage) from Georgia** including "good for" tokens issued by merchants, saloons and lumber companies, encased and **elongated coins**, advertising and commemorative medals and tokens, including those issued for the 1895 Atlanta Cotton States Exposition, and any agriculture awards and medals from Georgia state fairs, the earlier the better.

>   R.W. Colbert
>   4156 Livsey Road
>   Tucker, GA 30084

☆ **Animal rescue, school attendance, heroism or truant officer's** medals and badges.

>   Gene Christian
>   3849 Bailey Ave.
>   Bronx, NY 10463

*When people say they want "fiscal paper"
they mean documents having to do with
money, including stocks, bonds, checks,
mortgages, scrip, IOU's, revenue stamps,
and the like. Collectors buy fiscal paper
for the elaborate pictorial engravings
called vignettes. Fiscal paper is also
sought if signed by famous people or if it
is pre-1850. Values range from $1 to $500
with most selling under $30.*

STOCKS, BONDS & FISCAL PAPER

☆ **Stocks and bonds from around the world** issued before 1930, especially ornate 19th century transportation or mining certificates. Please send a Xerox© copy of what you wish to sell. This 30 year veteran stock expert cautions, "It is important that you not sell uncanceled certificates issued in your own name or in a family member's name without first having us check their value. These certificates could be worth much more if the company has changed names or left assets when it was liquidated. There are billions of dollars waiting to be claimed by people who believe their stocks are worthless."

    Micheline Masse
    Stock Search International
    10855 North Glen Abbey
    Tucson, AZ 85737
        (800) 537-4523   Fax: (602) 544-9395

☆ **Stocks, bonds, and other fiscal paper worldwide**. "I want to buy old bank checks, drafts, certificates of deposit, promissory notes, bills of exchange, U.S. postal money orders, postal notes, warrants, etc., just about every type of fiscal document which represents an order to pay from any country from 1500 to 1902 for bank instruments and up to 1933 for anything from Montana. Values vary widely, so all I can say is that I pay from $5 to $500 per piece. I do not buy plain checks without vignettes, nor do I buy receipts." Clear photocopies required. "I prefer sellers to place a price on their items, but I will make offers. I do not do appraisals except for a fee." His *Catalogue of Nevada Checks, 1860-1933* is available from him for $21 postpaid.

    Douglas McDonald
    PO Box 350093
    Grantsdale, MT 59835
        (406) 363-3202

☆ **Stocks and bonds,** especially decorative stocks from pre-1900 railroads and gold mines. "Although these are our main areas of interest, we would like to see photocopies of any and all stocks and bonds that you might have, and will promptly give you a free appraisal/offer." Generally, nothing after 1940 unless you have 5,000 or more of them.

> Richard Urmston
> Centennial Documents
> PO Box 5262
> Clinton, NJ　08809
>　　(908) 730-6009　　Fax:　(908) 730-9566

☆ **Fiscal paper** including **rare currency (U.S. and foreign)**, checks, stocks and bonds, certificates of deposits, books on money, other items. He is particularly expert in **California currency, national currency and Mexican currency.** Doesn't want items after 1935 or any kind of reproduction. A photocopy will often do, but "I'll usually request to see the item in person before making an offer."

> Lowell Horwedel
> PO Box 2395
> West Lafayette, IN　47906
>　　(317) 583-2784

☆ **Elaborately illustrated stocks and bonds.** All are wanted but have particular need for pre-1920 railroads, mining, telegraph, aviation, oil, and automobiles. Also stocks from unusual companies like a maker of life rafts. Items pre-1870 given special consideration. Especially want Western paper with autographs of important people like Rockefeller, Carnegie, Gould, James Hill, U.S. Presidents, and other recognizable people. "Send a photocopy and an SASE for fast payment."

> David Beach's Paper Americana
> PO Box 2026
> Goldenrod, FL　32733
>　　(407) 657-7403　　Fax:　(407) 657-6382

☆ **Stocks and bonds** issued in the United States before 1910, especially mining, railroads, or unusual companies. "I am not interested in stocks that were never issued and are unsigned. Stocks and bonds must have an original company seal."

> Phyllis Barrella
> Buttonwood Galleries
> PO Box 1006,　Throggs Neck Station
> New York, NY　10465

☆ **U.S. stocks and bonds,** issued before 1930, especially mining, railroads, energy and automobiles. Signed, illustrated, used documents are desired, with premium paid for Western items before the Civil War with interesting vignettes. Plain items are not of interest unless before 1850 or signed by someone famous. Send Xerox™ of what you have. His six sales catalogs a year cost $15.

> Warren Anderson
> America West Archives
> PO Box 100
> Cedar City, UT 84720
> (801) 586-9497

☆ **U.S. and Canadian stocks and bonds,** especially railroads, mining, oil, shipping, automotive, aviation, expositions, and others. Also stocks or bonds signed or owned by someone famous. Also seeks documents with a **printed revenue stamp**. This past president of the Bond & Share Society also wants all pre-1800 certificates from any company.

> Bob Kluge
> American Vignettes
> PO Box 155
> Roselle Park, NJ 07204
> (908) 241-4209

☆ **All paper items printed with fancy engraved illustrations by security printers,** including railroad passes, semi-postals (advertising stamps), souvenir cards, and annual reports. Security printers include the Bureau of Printing and Engraving, U.S.P.S, American Bank Note Co., Canadian Bank Note Co., and Homer Lee Bank Note Co. Wants to find *Annual Reports* of American Bank Note Co. and other security printers and engravers.

> Robin M. Ellis
> PO Box 8468
> San Antonio, TX 78208
> (210) 222-9882

☆ **Fiscal paper from South Carolina** before 1910, especially from the city of Charleston.

> Bob Karrer
> PO Box 6094
> Alexandria, VA 22306

LOTS OF PEOPLE THINK THEY HAVE VALUABLE STAMPS.

Only a few 20th century U.S. stamps have substantial value, but stamped and unstamped envelopes and letters dating before 1910 may be worth hundreds of dollars! Value is affected by the stamp, the cancellation, the carriers, and where it was mailed from and to.

Buyers of early letters are often interested in postmarks. Examine them with an eye toward historic places, vanished cities, and unusual cancellations as on board a riverboat, airplane, or military ship. Canadian buyer Mike Rice tells of a U.S. antique dealer who sent him two items and a bill for only $4. "If that dealer had taken your advice and asked me to make an offer, I'd have paid $300 for them. The postcard she sent me has the only known cancellation from a post office that was only open for a few months."

Empty envelopes sell, but an enclosed letter with interesting contents will add to the value. Decorated stamped envelopes sell too. Condition is crucial, although envelopes that have been opened messily can still find a buyer if the postmark and stamp are undamaged.

Letters about travel, Indians, mining, colorful people, disasters, famous events, business, military service, personal history, and the like, especially those which give details. are best. Someone looking for stamps paid $20 for a box of envelopes at a yard sale. Letters in those envelopes sold to experts for $500,000!

Don't be surprised if most foreign stamps turn out to have little value. Enough valuable ones do exist, however, to make it worth your while to check them, especially when they are on interesting envelopes. If you own a few foreign stamps you can look them up in Scott's Standard Postage Stamp Catalogue. U.S. stamps are in Scott's Specialized Catalogue of United States Stamps. Both are available at most public libraries. If you own many stamps, you are facing a tedious chore. Let **Trash or Treasure** *experts do it for you. They are faster and more efficient.* ·

STAMPS

☆ **U.S. and foreign stamp collections and accumulations** are wanted by this 35 year veteran dealer who buys:
- **Albums** from any country or from mixed countries;
- **Stockbooks** and **unsorted boxfuls** of duplicate stamps;
- **Old envelopes** with stamps from any country;
- Mint sheets and blocks;
- Old **revenue (tax) stamps** on documents of all kinds;
- **Duck hunting** and fishing permit stamps, mint or used, especially on licenses;
- Stamp-like labels and seals of all kinds;
- **Postal related souvenirs** including booklets, cards, and stamp announcements;
- **Philatelic reference books** from any period or country in any language;
- **Stamp magazines** pre-1945;
- **Worldwide stamp catalogs** pre-1925;
- **Philatelic (stamp) auction catalogs** pre-1945;
- **Photos or real photo postcards** of mail carriers, mail trucks, post offices, and mail delivery.

"If in doubt, include it! I must be one of the last people who collect EVERYTHING in stamps and stamp-related items." Doug says stamp collecting is a highly specialized hobby, and that even the most common looking items (especially envelopes with unusual markings) may have value. "Because of their nature and sheer numbers, stamps have to be sent for my personal inspection. Call first, because I can give you clear shipping instructions and help you eliminate heavy items that have no value, such as newer stamp catalogs, 3-ring notebooks, and empty albums. I can give you guidance on how to ship stamps to prevent damage and preserve value. Return postage must be included with your package if you want your items returned. Inquiries should include an SASE if you wish an answer."

"Three errors made by amateurs:
(1) Cutting stamps off envelopes and documents;
(2) Improperly storing and handling mint stamps;
(3) Forgetting that labor costs of preparing stamps for resale will affect how much money you are paid. It's very costly to make your piles into attractive packages."

Douglas Swisher
PO Box 52701
Jacksonville, FL 32201
(904) 448-6214 eves

☆ **Stamps from any country in any quantity.** "We'll buy everything you have," says Harvey, who has been dealing by the mail since 1934! He wants collections of singles, plate blocks, sheets, covers, and rarities. If you have a large or valuable collection, Harvey Dolin & Company will come to your home. Smaller collections may be shipped to them for their cash offer. "Your satisfaction is always guaranteed," say their ads. Dolin buys **stampless letters** (dating before the first U.S. stamps in 1843, or after), **Confederate stamps and envelopes, Wells Fargo envelopes**, and **Duck Hunting stamps.**

> Harvey Dolin & Company
> 5 Beekman Street #406
> New York, NY 10038
>   (212) 267-0216

☆ **Various stamps and envelopes.** McHenry has been in business for 30 years and provides a long list of covers (envelopes) he wants, including Presidential free franks, letters mailed without stamps, color advertising on envelopes, expositions, pioneer flights, and more. You should request his list if you have early or unusual envelopes for sale. In addition to covers, he buys **revenue stamps, Confederate stamps** and **letters, precancels**, and stamps from **U.S. possessions.**

> Gordon McHenry
> PO Box 1117
> Osprey, FL 34229
>   (813) 966-5563   Fax: (813) 966-4568

☆ **Stamp collections mounted in albums.** No interest in accumulations of loose stamps. Call for instructions.

> Myron Ross
> Heroes & Legends
> 5879 Kanan Road
> Agoura Hills, CA 91301
>   (818) 991-5979   Fax: (818) 889-8972

☆ **U.S. and foreign stamps and covers** (envelopes) have been purchased for resale for over 30 years by this veteran dealer.

> Bill Colby
> Kenrich Co.
> PO Box 248-T
> Temple City, CA 91780
>   (818) 286-3888

☆ **U.S. or foreign stamp collections** from before 1960.

> Ron Aldridge
> 250 Canyon Oaks Drive
> Argyle, TX 76226
>   (214) 351-3490 days   (817) 455-2519 eves

☆ **U.S. Internal Revenue special tax stamps,** licenses and permits for making and selling beer, liquor, wine, tobacco, cigars, margarine, firearms, opium and marijuana. Also for businesses such as brokers, pawnbrokers, dentists, lawyers, etc. No stamps from between 1873 and 1885 with punched holes are wanted. Also wants state stamps and licenses for any business, activity, or product including hunting and fishing. **USDA export stamps** and certificates for meat products are also sought. **Ration coupons for gas, fuel oil and sugar** are wanted, but no war books (1,2,3, or 4) or any red or blue tokens. "Photocopies are very helpful."

Bill Smiley
PO Box 361
Portage, WI 53901
(608) 742-6349   (608) 742-3714

☆ **Federal and state revenue and special tax stamps** including document stamps and all stamps used to show that taxes had been paid on a product. Special tax stamps are large and look like licenses to engage in various occupations, such as liquor dealer, cigar salesman, wine maker, etc. Some of these issues, notably 1875, 1877, 1879, 1883, and 1885, are available in large quantities and sell for very little. Photocopies are strongly urged by this 30 year veteran buyer.

Hermann Ivester
5 Leslie Circle
Little Rock, AR 72205
(501) 376-7788   (501) 225-8565 eves

☆ **Stamps, covers, postcards, and postal stationery from China, Hong Kong, Singapore and Macao.** Covers are decorated or embellished envelopes, and among philatelic items sought by this Hong Kong postcard/stamp dealer. Items should be before 1990, the older the better. Requests you photocopy. Dealers, price what you have.

Kin Leung Liu
PO Box 94056
Seattle, WA 98124
(206) 548-4900   Fax: (206) 767-3025

☆ **Envelopes with stamps mailed in the Orient.** Buys nearly all envelopes with stamps mailed in China, Tibet, Korea, Hong Kong, Nepal, Mongolia and Japan. Advisable to first phone or send a photocopy by mail or fax. Pledges to pay post on items sent on approval.

Bruce Lewin
Bridgewater Onvelopes Collectibles
680 Route 206 North
Bridgewater, NJ 08807
(908) 725-0022   Fax: (908) 707-4647

IF YOU ARE NOT TRAINED TO RECOGNIZE VALUABLE ART GET EXPERT ADVICE. MISTAKES CAN BE COSTLY.

Paintings and prints that look sloppy, amateurish or depressing to you may be snapped up for big dollars. Each year, a few turn up worth $10,000 or more and million dollar finds do happen. **If a painting has been passed down in your family for more than 50 years**, check the current value of that artist's work. Some painters whose work cost $50 in the 1930's are worth 100 times that today.

Researching art is work. So many paintings were created by unknowns, the vast majority of what you own will not be listed, cataloged or pictured. **Using experts to evaluate and sell your art is good strategy.**

To sell a print, give the dimensions of the entire sheet and of the printed area. List all signatures, dates, and other information. Photocopy whenever practical. Prints signed and numbered in pencil are more likely to have value. Some prints like Currier & Ives have developed cult status and sell for $30 to $2,000 up! Photocopy if possible.

To sell paintings, sculpture, or folk art, a good 35mm photo is essential, along with dimensions. Take a close-up of the signature if possible. **Folk art** includes items made by untrained amateurs, done with style, vigor, form and color. Anything hand-crafted in decorative ways may qualify. Quality pieces bring thousands of dollars.

Art from places other than the U.S. and Europe is doing well. Prices are rising fast for South Pacific masks, bowls and shields. Mexican and South American paintings and folk arts have hit record prices within the last year and Oriental items remain strong.

WARNING: If you have a painting you think valuable, showing it to many dealers and auctioneers in hopes of getting ever higher prices is likely to do the opposite. **Paintings often diminish in value in proportion to the number of people to whom they are offered.**

PAINTINGS & PRINTS

☆ **Paintings by listed artists of all types and periods,** including 20th century. This first rate auction house regularly handles works of art from $1,000 to $100,000 and may be the perfect outlet for your better quality paintings. Send a photo, give the dimensions, describe any damage and note any signature.

James D. Julia Auctions
PO Box 830
Fairfield, ME 04937
(207) 453-7904   Fax: (207) 453-2502

☆ **Paintings, prints, and photographs made by artists in** *Who Was Who in American Art.* Although he's primarily interested in American Impressionism, Peter will consider a wide range of works from 1800-1950, as long as the artist is listed. Among special interests are:
- **Art depicting competitive rowing** ($500-$1,500);
- **Color woodblock prints**, particularly the *White Line* prints of the Provincetown, MA, printmaker group ($500-$2,000);
- **Paintings and prints by American women artists** of any period ($500-$10,000+);
- **Photos of Abraham Lincoln** ($500-$10,000).

Does not want wood engravings from *Harper's, Leslie's*, and other periodicals Send photograph and the dimensions.

Peter Falk
170 Boston Post Road
Midison, CT 06443
(203) 245-2246   Fax: (203) 245-3589

☆ **Paintings and limited edition prints** by listed artists, particularly American and **Oriental**. Give the size and condition. Include photo.

Ivan Gilbert
Miran Arts & Books
2824 Elm Ave.
Columbus, OH 43209
(614) 421-3222   Fax: (614) 421-3223

☆ **Oil paintings** of any size, particularly American before 1940. Provide this veteran art dealer and appraiser with the name of the artist, the size, and a sharp photo of the painting, both front and back. He is not interested in newer paintings.

Robert Anderson
Aaron's Fine Antiques and Oriental Rug Gallery
1217 Broadway
Fort Wayne, IN 46802
(219) 422-5184

☆ **Charles M. Russell memorabilia.** "I'll buy just about anything illustrated by Russell: trays, posters, books, magazines, calendars, etc., as well as personal items, autographs, and other Russell memorabilia.
  Jim Combs
  417 27th Street NW
  Great Falls, MT 59404
  (406) 761-3320

☆ **Paintings by artists from Ohio, Kentucky, and Indiana** with a special interest in Cincinnati artists who worked between 1850 and 1950. Buys especially work by Blum, Twachtman, Hurley, Sawier, Weis, Vogt, Wessel, Selden, Casinelli, Duveneck, Sharp, Farney, Nourse, Potthast, Volkert, as well as selected other American and European artists. Please send a good clear photo of items for sale. If in doubt, telephone. Have your work in hand when you do.
  Riley Humler
  Cincinnati Art Galleries
  635 Main Street
  Cincinnati, OH 45202
    (513) 381-2128

☆ **Original illustration art for mystery, detective, horror, science fiction, adventure and fantasy magazines**, pulps, and paperbacks. "I want the original paintings created to illustrate these covers as well as black and white pen and ink illustrations for the stories inside." Seeks artists like Roy Kuenkel, J. Allen St. John, Paul, Frank Frazetta, Stromberg, Olson, and others, especially those that depict known characters like the Shadow, the Spider, Doc Savage, Tarzan, etc. Does not want covers, prints, or reproductions. Send a photo, including the dimensions, and the name of the artist if you can read the signature.
  Jim Gerlack
  2206 Greenbrier Drive
  Irving, TX 75060
    (214) 790-0922

☆ **Original art for comic books, comic strips, animated cartoons and pulp magazines.** Comic art is in pen and ink on drawing board and usually oversize. Animation art is in color on clear plastic cels. Send a Xerox™ of your art along with any info you have about its past. "Do not contact me with the actual newspapers or magazines. I only want the original drawing that was reproduced for publication."
  Tom Horvitz
  21520 Burbank Boulevard #315
  Woodland Hills, CA 91367
    (8180 716-8664   Fax: (818) 347-2357

☆ **Original paintings for American magazine covers and story illustrations,** 1900 to date. "I'll buy art for magazines and stories in the following genres: aviation, western, fantasy, science fiction, adventure, erotica, detective, mystery, and movie." Also buys **art for pin-up calendars, advertising campaigns, and paperback book covers with similar themes.** These covers were generally vividly painted on 24" x 30" canvas. Rough sketches for cover or story art can also have value. Sellers should send a photo of the art, the dimensions and an accurate description of the condition (any soil, holes, dents, scratches). Note the signature, in the unlikely event there is one. Check the back of the painting for exhibit or publishing history. Most pulp paintings are worth $500 to $2,000, depending upon the artist, subject and condition, although some *Tarzan* and movie covers bring up to $10,000. Jim is a popular artist and comic book illustrator who writes on Pop Culture and art and wrote two books on the history of comics.

"Don't ever guess what is and isn't worth something. Send us pictures and let us evaluate it for you."

    Jim Steranko, Supergraphics
    PO Box 974
    Reading, PA 19603
    (215) 374-7477

☆ **Original paintings by American illustrators for magazine covers,** magazine story illustrations, or advertising, 1910-1980, including artists such as **Norman Rockwell** and all his contemporaries. Also original art for magazine or calendar pin-ups. Has special interest in sexual or sentimental themes (children, dogs, families, patriotism, etc.).

    Charles Martignette
    455 Paradise Isle #306
    Hallandale, FL 33007
    (305) 454-3474

☆ **Printed illustrations by well known 20th century artists** such as Maxfield Parrish, the Leyendecker Bros., **Norman Rockwell**, Rolf Armstrong, Vargas, Petty, Rose O'Neill, Mucha, Erte, Grace Drayton, Will Bradley, and Coles Phillips. Wants **original art, prints, posters, advertising, calendars, magazines, and books**, 1895-1930. Especially Maxfield Parrish and pin-up calendars, 1920-1960. Give dimensions and condition of your print, and tell what book, magazine, calendar, etc., it came from. Denis does not want "free appraisals, pen pals, or time wasters." He is the author of price guides for print artists and edits *The Illustrator Collector's News*, available for $17 a year.

    Denis Jackson
    PO Box 1958
    Sequim, WA 98382
    (206) 683-2559

☆ **Maxfield Parrish paintings, watercolors, pen and ink sketches, letters, and 1st printings** including art prints, *Edison Mazda* calendars, *Brown & Biglow* prints and calendars, posters, books, playing cards, games, novelty items, and other advertising. She emphasizes she is not interested in "new prints" or reproductions of the first printings. This 18 year veteran dealer says she will pay $20,000 and up for paintings, $1,500 for a *Mother Goose in Prose* 1st edition from 1897, and from $800 to $3,500 for some posters and calendars, especially 1918, 1919, and 1920. "I need to know the size, color, and if there is any damage to the piece such as brown spots or water stains. It is helpful if you call with the piece in front of you."

> Michelle Ferretta, Maxfield Parrish Collectables
> 1314 Oak Street
> Alameda, CA 94501
> (510) 522-1823

☆ **Maxfield Parrish paintings,** calendars (all years), complete books, full decks of playing cards, original prints, autographs and unusual advertising items. Not interested in book fragments or modern reproductions. Describe condition. She offers "many thousands of dollars" for an original oil painting by Parrish.

> Debra Buonaguidi
> 540 Reeside Ave.
> Monterey, CA 93940
> (408) 375-7345

☆ **Original art and prints by F. Earl Christy** who specialized in beautiful society women. Wants his work on covers from movie and women's magazines, advertising, fans, blotters, calendars, postcards, and anything else illustrated by Christy.

> Audrey Buffington
> 2 Old Farm Road
> Wayland, MA 01778

☆ **Paintings and prints by R. Atkinson Fox, Maxfield Parrish, and Icart.** Claims she'll pay "top cash."

> Christine Daniels
> 135 East Shiloh Road
> Santa Rosa, CA 95403
> (707) 838-6083

☆ **R. Atkinson Fox prints wanted.** "I'll buy prints, calendars, postcards, or anything else with artwork by R. Atkinson Fox." Please telephone or send a photocopy.

> Pat Gibson
> 38280 Guava Drive
> Newark, CA 94560
> (510) 792-0586

☆ **Illustration art by Philip Goodwin** on trays, **calendars**, posters, and advertising. He can provide a detailed wants list of magazines, illustrations, books, and other items to dealers who send an SASE.
>Jim Combs
>417 27th Street NW
>Great Falls, MT 59404
>(406) 761-3320

☆ **Sketches, drawings, and paintings by Philip Boileau and Robert Robinson,** American 20th century illustrators. Boileau is known for his 1900-1917 paintings of attractive women done for private customers, magazine covers, and other commercial purposes. Robinson worked commercially from 1907-1952 also on magazine covers and other commercial work. Please provide Bowers with a good close up color photo and as much information about the work as you can. The value of paintings varies, and Bowers will work with you to determine value.
>Q. David Bowers
>PO Box 1224
>Wolfeboro, NH 03894
>(603) 569-5095

☆ **Commercial printed art by J.G. Scott** who specialized in cute round faced children. Most of his work is signed JG SCOTT and can be found on the covers of women's magazines, advertising blotters and calendars from the 1920's and 30's and on children's greeting cards printed by the *Gibson Co.*
>Robert Stauffer
>3235 Mudlick Road SW
>Roanoke, VA 24018
>(703) 774-4319

☆ **Paintings, drawings and original art for advertising** airlines, automobiles, gasoline, tires, soft drinks or whiskey. Especially likes paintings for ads for *Coke*, alcohol, movies, tobacco products, and other culturally significant items and events. If in doubt, call.
>Charles Martignette
>PO Box 293
>Hallandale, FL 33009
>(305) 454-3474

☆ **Damaged art of all kinds** is wanted. "If people send a good sharp photo I will make an offer on paintings, sculpture, and **Currier & Ives** prints that have been damaged but are still in restorable condition." Available on Internet.
>Alan Voorhees' Art Restoration
>492 Breesport Road
>Horseheads, NY 14845
>(607) 739-7898   Fax: (607) 733-8550

☆ **Paintings of 18th and 19th century American political figures** or historic events. Please send a photo along with a description of the painter's signature if there is one. Only original oils or watercolors in fine condition are wanted. No paper prints, engravings or illustrations torn from books.

> Rex Stark
> 49 Wethersfield Road
> Bellingham, MA 02019
> (508) 966-0994

☆ **Paintings and prints depicting smoking.** Buys a wide range of prints, paintings, and other items with a tobacco theme. Prefers smaller paintings but all sizes, all media, and all nationalities considered. Buys pre-1930 illustrations, prints, advertising, signs, posters, photographs and other items. Special interest in cigars, but anything related to tobacco considered. Buying for resale and for his personal collection.

> Tony Hyman
> PO Box 3028
> Pismo Beach, CA 93448
> (805) 773-6777   Fax: (805) 773-8436

☆ **Paintings depicting the industrial/machine age.** Wants paintings and signed prints depicting workers in industrial settings. He also buys **WPA paintings and prints**. Send photo.

> David Zdyb
> PO Box 146
> Dingmans Ferry, PA 18328
> (717) 828-2361

☆ **Paintings of cowboys, Indians or Eskimos.** Please send a photo for a prompt response. It's helpful if you can read the signature. Dealers, price your goods; amateur sellers may request an offer.

> Barry Friedman
> 22725 Garzota Drive
> Valencia, CA 91355
> (805) 296-2318

☆ **Paintings and prints depicting boats** including whaling, yachting, racing, working, etc., are sought by this well known dealer in marine antiques. Give the dimensions, history, and a careful account of any damage or restoration. Photo suggested. Will give "ball park" estimates of value on ordinary items, but appraisals are for a fee. Sporadically issues a pictorial catalog for refundable $5.

> Andrew Jacobson
> PO Box 2155
> South Hamilton, MA 01982
> (508) 468-6276

☆ **Prints, American and European.** Buys a wide range of prints. Generally prefers topical prints rather than scenics. Give a complete description, including size of image, size of sheet, colors, and any and all information printed or written at the bottom of the print.

    Kenneth Newman, The Old Print Shop
    150 Lexington Avenue at 30th Street
    New York, NY 10016
        (212) 683-3950

☆ **Chromoliths and hand colored prints** on topics of natural history (birds, bugs, fish and animals), military, medicine, old West, Indians, costumes and fashion, Negroes, sports, and Art Nouveau. Wants pre-1900 prints only, but does buy 19th and 20th century **advertising art and labels** on similar themes or with other attractive pictures. Describe fully for this major graphics dealer, known for paying high prices for quality items. Joe is author of two books on advertising labels.

    Joe Davidson
    5185 Windfall Road
    Medina, OH 44256
        (216) 723-7172

☆ **Prints, engravings, chromoliths, and woodcuts** before 1900 on many topics including city scenes of the U.S. and Canada, natural history (birds, bugs, fish, and animals), military uniforms, fashion, the old West, children, expositions and fairs, disasters, mining, Indians, and Oriental life in America. These are very difficult to buy by mail, and must be examined under high magnification. If your print is framed, he believes "it is wise to remove the print from the frame in order to find the publisher and date of publication." Indicate the size of the image, and the size of the overall print, including border. Include an SASE.

    John Rosenhoover
    100 Mandalay Road
    Chicopee, MA 01020
        (413) 536-5542

☆ **Prints and illustrations** of flowers, children and beautiful women including **calendars, yard-longs**, and books before 1919. **Also illustrations by** Harrison Fisher, Francis Brundage, Newton Wells, Catherine Klein, Maud Humphrey, and others. Also wants **magazines** with fashion prints and color pictures of women and children, such as *Ladies' Home Journal, Women's Home Companion, Butterick, Mc-Call's*, etc. Buys only color prints. Prefers unframed items. Must send photocopy. Note *all* defects. Will make approximate offers, but must see to determine condition before buying.

    Linda Gibbs, Heirloom Keepsakes
    10380 Miranda
    Buena Park, CA 90620
        (714) 827-6488

☆ **Woodblock prints by European, American and Canadian artists** (1895-1950) in color or black and white. He buys only pencil signed prints created and signed by the artist whose work they are. Particular interests include:

- **Landscapes and marinescapes by** the widely traveled artist **Arthur Wesley Dow** of Ipswitch MA. His prints are signed but unnumbered, usually 5x7 inches or smaller, and can be worth $1,000 and more.
- **Prints by Provincetown printers,** especially "white line prints" characterized by blocks of color separated by white lines. These run in size from 3x4 inches to 16x20, but are mostly from 5x7 to 8x10 inches. Values run from $1,000 to $15,000.
- **Prints with Oriental subjects,** but only those by Western, often British, artists. People to look for include Bartlett, Hyde, Keith and Lum.

"I do not want Oriental prints from Japan and the Far East or wood engravings from *Harper's Weekly* or other magazines and newspapers. Nor do I generally buy woodblock illustrations from books." If your print is loose and unframed, a photocopy is quick and accurate. If you feel you have one of these valuable prints, the expense of a color copy may be justified. If your print is framed, try to get a good photograph by shooting outdoors in open shade. Thomas makes offers *if your item is genuinely for sale*, but is not interested in doing free appraisals. In business for 10 years, Thomas issues annual catalogs of art for sale and will send you an illustrated wants list if you send a #10 (long) envelope.

"Woodblocks are rectangular with sharply defined borders. When printed in color, a slight registration problem is often apparent. They are usually signed in pencil outside the image area."

    Steven Thomas, Inc.
    PO Box 41
    Woodstock, VT 05091
      (802) 457-1764

☆ **Engraved portraits and photographs of famous people** in all walks of life. Will consider items loose or in books. Photocopies make the best descriptions.

    Kenneth Rendell
    PO Box 9001
    Wellesley, MA 02181
      (617) 431-1776   Fax: (617) 237-1492

☆ **Wallace Nutting pictures, books, furniture, and other memorabilia.** Among Nutting pictures, Mike particularly wants interiors, scenes with people, animals, and houses. He does not want single pictures of common exteriors of apple blossoms, country lanes, trees, lakes, and ponds, although he will take these as part of a large collection. Collections are preferred, but single pieces will be considered. No size is too large. Mike says he'll travel anywhere to view collections of considerable size and diversity. When describing pictures, give the title, frame size, and condition. When describing books give standard bibliographic information, including title, edition, color of the cover. Mike will either buy outright or consider accepting your items on consignment for one of his Nutting auctions. The 4th edition of Mike's *Price Guide to Wallace Nutting Pictures* is available from him for $17 postpaid.

> Michael Ivankovich
> PO Box 2458
> Doylestown, PA 18901
>   (215) 345-6094

☆ **Wallace Nutting pictures, books and other ephemera,** including furniture, lamps, wooden dishes, postcards, calendars, and greeting cards designed, built, or used by him. "Not interested in recent items, or things that are damaged, broken, or otherwise in less than very good condition," says this 7 year veteran Nutting dealer.

> James Buskirk
> Eleanor's Hand Tinted Photos
> 175 Cornell Street
> Windsor, CA 95492

High prices are being paid for good items in today's art world, even though the market is generally depressed. This is a very volatile time, and tastes are changing as a result of the movement of baby boomers into the market.

Personally, I believe their impact will be felt for a long time, so I'm selling any piece of art that I consider surplus that I don't feel has boomer-appeal.

If you get a good offer for something, remember, **prices do not always go up over time.** *Artists and styles fall in and out of favor.*

SCULPTURE & FIGURINES

☆ **Bronzes and porcelain figures** prior to 1935. Describe all marks and give dimensions and colors. A photo is highly recommended.
> Arnold Reamer
> PO Box 26416
> Baltimore, MD 21207
> (410) 944-6414   (410) 486-8412

☆ **Bathing beauties and "naughties" figurines.** Wants small bisque or porcelain figurines, 1900-1940, which are nude, in bathing suits, in their underwear, stockings, or dressed in lace. They are finely modeled and in coy poses. Some had actual mohair wigs. Naughties were hollow figurines, often of children or women, intended to be filled with water so they peed or squirted out of their breasts. Other naughties appeared to be innocent figurines until lifted up or turned over, displaying a risque (often explicit) side. "I am especially interested in finding Black naughties or bathers with a wig, but I am interested in *all* fine examples of bathing beauties and naughties. I am also looking for old catalogs, advertisements, and other information about them. A good wigged naughty is worth from $250-$450, depending upon the pose and execution." No Japanese figures or reproductions. Generally does not want damaged pieces, but will consider extraordinary figures with minor damage. Size and pose is important so accurate measurements and a sketch or photo is almost essential. Include your phone number. Will buy only if you grant right of refusal after inspection. If you too collect these figures, please call. She'd love to meet you. Sharon has written *Naughties, Nudies and Bathing Beauties,* available for $20.
> Sharon Hope Weintraub
> 3613-F Las Colinas Drive
> Austin, TX 78731
> (512) 323-9639

☆ **Female figurines, especially nudes** in bronze or porcelain in Art Deco or Art Nouveau styles. Wants work of fine makers without repairs. No figurines of children or from Limited Edition series. She does not make offers, expecting you to price what you have.
> Madeleine France, Past Pleasures
> 3 North Federal Highway
> Dania, FL 33004
> (305) 584-0009 days   Fax: (305) 584-0014

☆ **Nude figurines** in any material, made since 1900.
> Charles Martignette
> PO Box 293
> Hallandale, FL 33009
> (305) 454-3474

☆ *Royal Doulton* **figurines and character jugs** are purchased by this well known dealer who has been in business for 20 years. "No collection is too large or too small," he says, encouraging you to "call toll free as long as you have the name and HN number of the figurines and the name and size of the character jugs." Pascoe is especially interested in the rarest items, since they maintain a computer list of collectors worldwide who are looking for specific types of figure. Ed lectures frequently in the U.S. and England, and has edited price guides to these popular figures. He is not interested in buying dinnerware, and does not do pattern matching.

> Ed Pascoe
> Pascoe & Co.
> 101 Almeria Avenue
> Coral Gables, FL 33134
>   (800) 872-0195   (305) 445-3229

☆ **John Rogers statuary.** If you have a white or putty colored plaster grouping of figures, check for the signature JOHN ROGERS, often accompanied by NEW YORK and a date and patent number. These figural groups can be from 12" to 48" high, with most just under 2' tall. Themes are Civil War, Americana, theater, etc., with a few comic. A few are made of material other than plaster. Perfect condition is always best, but he will consider damaged pieces, as he is a restorer of Rogers' work. He needs to know the name of the piece (which is always found on the front of the base) and the condition of the putty colored paint. When describing paint, indicate how badly it is flaking from your statue. Prefers you to telephone him with your statue in front of you.

> Bruce Bleier
> 73 Riverdale Road
> Valley Stream, NY 11581
>   (516) 791-4353

☆ **Kewpie figurines of German bisque.** These 3"-5" figures are most interesting in action poses with cats, toys, brooms, ducks, etc. Look for German figures to be marked O'NEILL on the back. Doesn't want figures made in Japan or elsewhere. Must be mint: no damage or repairs.

> Linda Vines
> PO Box 721
> Upper Montclair, NJ 07043
>   (201) 746-5206

☆ *Noritake* **human and animal figures** are wanted by this well known glass auctioneer and porcelain collector.

> Tom Burns
> 109 East Steuben Street
> Bath, NY 14810
>   (607) 776-7942

FOLK ART

☆ **American folk art** such as:
- **Wood carvings, whirligigs,** and **decoys;**
- Old **weathervanes** of any and all materials;
- **Quilts** in fine, unworn condition;
- **Hooked rugs** with pictorials rather than patterns;
- **Handmade dolls** of wood and'or cloth;
- **Folk paintings of children** and animals;
- Figural 19th century **pottery;**
- **Fishing decoys** in fine condition and good provenance;
- **Architectural figurals** such as cherubs and gargoyles,
- **Game boards** in original finish;
- **Indian art,** rugs, baskets, pottery, pipes, and other artifacts.

No damaged or repaired pieces. Send a photo and SASE. Include complete description, dimensions, and condition.

> Louis Picek, Main Street Antiques
> PO Box 340
> West Branch, IA 52358
> (319) 643-2065

☆ **Folk art.** "We seek high quality American one-of-a-kind pieces in very good condition. We prefer old items, but also buy contemporary and outsider art, as well as a few old factory made items. We seek items which have good form, especially quirky, humorous, and colorful pieces, such as:
- **Tramp art chip carved pieces**, the bigger the better;
- Carvings that are whimsical, folky, interesting or unusual;
- **Quilts,** especially very old, funky, graphic patriotic, Amish,
  Black made, album, coarse;
- **Samplers;**
- Circus and **side show banners** and signs;
- Recycled **oddities made of found objects** like bottle caps,
  match sticks, ice cream sticks;
- Hand made items such as trade signs, barber poles, game boards,
  hitching posts, toys, and what have you.

Unusual depictions of people, places and animals are preferred. "We do not want 'cute' items like sunbonnet girls, most factory made items, damaged items, or things that are recently repaired or repainted (unusual or old repairs may be OK)." Description should include colors, size, materials, and history of the piece. "We want at least one good photo. Other photos of damage and details are helpful. Dealers should price their goods, but amateurs may request offers."

> Matt Lippa and Elizabeth Schaaf, Artisans
> 599 Cutler Avenue
> Mentone, AL 35984
> (205) 634-4037

☆ **Folk art** including painting, sculpture, weaving, wood, etc., including **American Indian, Oriental, African, or Eskimo** art. Provide the dimensions, condition, and photos. Condition critical. Special interest in current "outsider art." Contact Ivan only if your item is for sale.

Ivan Gilbert, Miran Arts & Books
2824 Elm Ave.
Columbus, OH 43209
(614) 421-3222   Fax: (614) 421-3223

☆ **Weathervanes** made of pressed tin in the shape of animals, whales, fish, carriages, etc. The quality of manufacture is the key to value. "Bullet holes and rust detract greatly from its worth." Photos are helpful, as some of these pieces can be quite valuable.

Craig Donges
6724 Glenwood Avenue
Youngstown, OH 44512
(216) 726-1830   Fax: (216) 726-4740

☆ **Tramp art** items made from cigar boxes or fruit crate wood which has been layered into edge-notched pyramids. Typical items include boxes, picture frames, doll furniture, banks, wall pockets and small furniture. Especially wants large items like chests of drawers, but will buy only those in fine condition. Original surface is important and information about its origin (such as signatures and dates) a plus. He does not want items made from ice cream sticks, clothespins or matches, nor does he buy recent repaints. "A photo is essential."

Michael Cornish
195 Boston Street
Dorchester, MA 02125

☆ **Carousel figures** from before 1930 only. Wooden figures from that period bring from $1,000 to $50,000 each. This 30 year veteran collector-dealer-auctioneer does not want reproductions or modern carvings. Send photographs of both sides of your animal. Also wants circus and side show banners.

Jon Abbott, Carousel Corner
PO Box 420
Clarkston, MI 48347
(810) 625-1244

☆ **Prisoner of war straw figures** woven or plaited by French prisoners during the early 1800's. Other documented prisoner art from the 19th century, including **ivory carvings**, are sought.

Lucille Malitz, Lucid Antiques
PO Box KH
Scarsdale, NY 10583
(914) 636-7825

☆ **Fraktur birth and baptismal certificates** dating before 1900. These certificates are usually, but not always, printed with hand done watercolor decoration. Some are totally freehand drawn manuscripts. Most are written in German, but some are in English. Prefers colorful watercolor birds and flowers that are "folky" rather than formal. These are wanted in any condition. Inquire by removing your fraktur from any frame and sending a photocopy, including the name of the printer. Do not make any repairs with tape or glue. Make sure the copy is clear and readable. These nationally known professional fraktur dealers send sales catalogs and have written numerous books on fraktur, including *Genealogist's Guide to Fraktur,* available for $17.

> Corinne Earnest
> Russell D. Earnest Associates
> PO Box 490
> Damascus, MD 20872

☆ **Mourning pictures** in watercolor or embroidery. These are characterized by willow trees, tombstones, birth and death dates, weeping women, etc. These are often for famous people, presidents, generals, etc. Those honoring "nobodies" are more rare and desirable. Will pay at least $100 and as much as $300-$400 for better ones.

> Steve DeGenaro
> PO Box 5662
> Youngstown, OH 44504

☆ **Samplers**, both U.S. and English, from before 1850, including mourning samplers and needlework pictures. Clear photo is essential, along with dimensions and the item's history as you understand it. Books on American and/or British needlework are also sought. Give standard bibliographic information.

> Donna Litwin
> PO Box 5865
> Trenton, NJ 08638
> (609) 275-0996

☆ **Folk art weavings worldwide,** including rugs, saddle blankets, tapestries, ponchos, and other old, fine, and rare pieces. Will consider Oriental, Middle Eastern, European, Indian, and South American fine quality rugs and other weavings. Also **Eskimo and American Indian weavings**. In addition to weavings, he buys **needlepoint, paisley shawls, and hooked rugs**. Nothing after 1920 or machine made.

> Renate Halpern Galleries
> 325 East 79th Street
> New York, NY 10021
> (212) 988-9316

*How do you tell ivory from bone
from plastic from celluloid?
Bone has fine brown specks. Plastic
sometimes has air bubbles or pits.
Ivory has grain like fine wood.
Celluloid is very smooth and can
be melted with a hot pin.*

☆ **Ivory items of all sorts,** including Eskimo and Oriental carvings, scrimshaw, ivory tusks (elephant, walrus, whale, hippo, etc.), dresser sets, poker chips, dice, and billiard balls. Dave does not want ivory jewelry, letter openers, or sewing and crochet tools, nor does he buy bone or synthetic objects. If you are selling tusks, give the length around the outside curve, and the diameter at the large end. He asks you to use a flashlight to carefully inspect for cracks in the hollow end. Follow standard description form. A sample catalog is $1. Please list your phone number and best time to call.

>David Boone
>Boone's Trading Company
>562 Coyote Road
>Brinnon, WA 98320
>>(206) 796 4330   (800) 423-1945   Fax: (206) 796-4511

☆ **Figures and native carvings made of ivory.** Ivory can be elephant, walrus, whale, hippo, wart hog, or narwhal, but he wants ivory art, not small useful items like pins, combs, spoons, brooches and toothpicks. Picture is a necessity, and he prefers you to set a price. Terry also buys **primitive and pre-Columbian artifacts.**

>Terry Cronin
>207 Silver Palm Ave.
>Melbourne, FL 30901

☆ **Micronesian, Polynesian, and New Guinea masks, ceremonial bowls,** and the like. Any art from that region that is interesting and in fine condition may find a buyer. They have some interest in scrimshaw if associated with that region of the world and whaling activities of the Pacific region.

>David and Cathy Lilburne
>Antipodean Books
>PO Box 189
>Cold Spring, NY 10516
>>(914) 424-3867

☆ **African or South Pacific tribal art** including masks, weapons, musical instruments, jewelry, household objects, bowls, furniture, feather work, textiles, and "almost anything else that was made for tribal use and not for the tourist trade." Especially old collections including artifacts with elaborate decoration and animal, human, or spirit figures. High quality tribal art can bring as much as $100,000 so is worth inquiry. Does not want items made after 1970, ebony carvings, tourist items, or figures of natives holding spears. A photograph is essential and Jones would like to know where the item was collected.

> Charles Jones
> African Art
> 6716 Barren Inlet Road
> Wilmington, NC 28405
> (910) 686-0717   Fax: (910) 686-1313

☆ **Pre-Columbian art** in all media: ceramic, stone, wood, textiles, and gold. Requests photos of the front and back of each piece, measurements, a description of condition, and information on where you got it. This collector-dealer has been in business for seven years.

> Jack Bond
> Kent Bond Gallery
> 9301 North 56th Street
> Tampa, FL 33617
> (813) 988-2132

☆ **Pre-Columbian pottery from Mexico or Peru** are sought, but *only* if documented and authenticated. Collections preferred. A photograph is essential and Jones would like to know where the item was collected or obtained, and any other history of the piece.

> Charles Jones
> 6716 Barren Inlet Road
> Wilmington, NC 28405
> (910) 686-0717   Fax: (910) 686-1313

Buyers generally do not want any art from Mexico or South America without good provenance (history). The markets of that region have been flooded with modern imitations for nearly a century. Skill of the local artisans remains high, so it is hard for anyone but an expert to attest to the age of a piece...and they get fooled too, especially evaluating items made of clay. Objects made of precious metals and stones are harder to fake and less likely to come to you. Many art dealers are concerned about grave robbing and disruption of ancient sites.

QUILTS

☆ **Quilts that are graphically artistic** made before 1940 especially made before 1900. Cotton, wool, and silk quilts all have value if made well but children's size quilts are best if they do not have children's subject matter. Solid color materials and small calico patterns are most desirable. Large patterns cut into small pieces usually make the quilt of no interest. All quilts should be in mint condition, with at least six stitches per inch, preferably more. No holes, tears, stains, thin spots when held to light, fading, soft from too much washing, and no patched repairs. A photo is very desirable. Herb says he will pay $5,000 for an album quilt made between 1840 and 1860, $15,000 for an album quilt from that same period made in Baltimore, and $600 up for navy blue and white quilts in excellent condition. Herb does not make offers.

> Herbert Wallerstein Jr., Calico Antiques
> 611 Alta Drive
> Beverly Hills, CA 90210
>   (310) 273-4192   Fax: (310) 273-1921

☆ **Patchwork quilts made by African-Americans,** especially unusual or improvisational quilts. Provide a full photo of the quilt, a statement of condition, and all information you can about its history. It is probably a good idea to discuss the value of the item with Eli before setting a price. "I'll also buy **fabric sample books,** especially of printed cottons."

> Eli Leon
> 5663 Dover Street
> Oakland, CA 94609

☆ **Patchwork quilts** of all types made before 1930, including ones that have some damage. Please send a photo which shows the colors and pattern, along with a description of condition. Also buys **ribbon pictures** (small, usually framed, 8"x10" or so, patchwork pictures made from dimestore ribbons in the 1920's and 30's).

> Bird In the Cage
> 110 King Street
> Alexandria, VA 22314
>   (703) 549-5114

Most desirable colors are blue/white, red/white, red/white/blue, red/green, and pre-1900 earth tones. Colors like yellow, orange, hot pink, and purple usually make a quilt less desirable.

ORIENTALIA

☆ **Antique Japanese netsuke, inro, and other art** including pouches, pipes and pipe cases, ivory and wooden statues, Japanese lacquer, metalwork, cloisonne, paintings, and ceramics. Will pay $10,000 up for ivory and wood 18th and 19th century netsuke and $1,000 for netsuke inlaid in various materials. No roughly carved pieces, manmade materials, or factory pieces bought in hotel lobbies, airports or gift shops. If you provide clear close-up photographs of your netsuke from all angles and an exact drawing of the signature, Denis will make an offer if interested. He has been president of the Netsuke Dealer's Association for 15 years, has written extensively on the topic, and is a member of the Appraisers Association of America. He does formal appraisals for a fee.

Denis Szeszler
Antique Oriental Art
PO Box 714
New York, NY 10028
(212) 427-4682 Fax: (212) 860-4426

☆ **Fine quality Oriental antiques** with special emphasis on Japanese netsuke, inro, lacquer, and fine Chinese porcelains. Marsha buys, sells, and collects all types of Oriental antiques from early ceramics to late 19th century items including furniture, Japanese swords, sword fittings, jade carvings, and jewelry. Many small ivory carvings are worth between $1,000 and $10,000. Modern or reproduction items are not wanted, nor is anything imported since 1960. Marsha is a senior member of the American Society of Appraisers, specializing in Oriental art, and will appraise for a fee. She will also help amateur sellers with fine items genuinely for sale if you make a good photo, give the measurements, and draw or photocopy all markings or signatures found on the bottom.

Marsha Vargas
The Oriental Corner
280 Main Street
Los Altos, CA 94022
(415) 941-3207 Fax: (415) 941-3297

No roughly carved pieces, manmade materials, or factory pieces bought in hotel lobbies, airports or gift shops. Modern or reproduction items are not wanted, nor is anything imported since 1960. Silk robes decorated with dragons brought back by WWII GI's are not of interest.

FIGURINES & LIMITED EDITION COLLECTIBLES

☆ *Heubach* **porcelain or bisque figurines and other items** including children's tea sets, trays, religious items, and anything else. Porcelain portraits of the Three Fates would be worth hundreds of dollars. Draw a picture of the mark, and give all colors. Frances is cataloging every *Heubach* product made and she'd like to hear from anyone who owns anything unusual by Gebruder Heubach, even if it is not for sale.
>Frances Sanda
>5624 Plymouth Road
>Baltimore, MD 21214

☆ *Hummel* **figurines** with full bee and crown markings preferred, though some later ones considered. Please give complete information concerning condition and an accurate drawing of all markings on the bottom. Price fishing is discouraged by this nationally known dealer who cautions that dealers can seldom use more common items, so can pay little if they buy them at all. "When you are ready to buy or sell *Hummels*, contact me, especially with rare items!" He is available to restore glass and porcelain, including your damaged *Hummels*.
>Donald Hardisty, Don's Collectibles
>3020 East Majestic Ridge
>Las Cruces, NM 88001
>   (505) 522-3721 for info   (800) 267-7667 to buy-sell

☆ *Hummel* **figurines** with the crown or full bee marks. Also wants *Goebel* vases, figurines, half dolls, wall plaques and monks in red robes. Also *Hummel* calendars from 1950 through 1975. Also *Precious Moments* **figurines** with the triangle or hourglass mark or with no mark at all. All *Hummels* must be marked. Please give all marks and numbers and note whether or not you have the original box. Please don't offer *Hummel* plates, bells, or anything that is chipped or cracked.
>Sharon Vohs-Mohammed
>PO Box 7233
>Villa Park, IL 60181
>   (708) 268-0210

☆ *Sebastian* **miniatures** by P.W. Baston including commercial issues, limited editions and private commissions. "Ask me about any *Sebastian* miniatures because some common ones have rare variations." Give the title of the piece, the color of the label (if any), and the condition. Jim buys and sells miniatures and can help you obtain custom made miniatures for promotions or fundraising purposes.
>Jim Waite, Blossom Shop Collectibles
>112 North Main
>Farmer City, IL 61842
>   (309) 928-3222   (800) 842-2593

☆ *Goebel* **figurines of cats.** "I don't want cats other than *Goebel* or *Goebels* other than cats." Include marks and numbers on the bottom.
>
> Linda Nothnagel
> Route 3 Box 30
> Shelbina, MO 63468

☆ *Osborne Ivorex* **plaques.** These 3-D plaster wall plaques were made between 1899 and 1968. In addition to plaques, the company made statuary of people and buildings, jewelry boxes, and other small items. Subject matter of the plaques includes individual characters to large cathedrals. Sizes range from a few inches to over a foot, with 3"x5" and 6.5"x9" being two popular sizes. Some premium items are factory framed in wood. Some poor quality repros exist. Most, but not all, *Ivorex* plaques are marked A/O (Arthur Osborne) on the lower right or left corner. In the 1930's they began marking them on the back with a three line ink stamp with the company name and copyright. Small vertical oval and rectangular plaques sometimes have markings on the lower rim. Values range from $30 up, with a few reaching $200. Andy wants to hear from other collectors for purposes of starting a club.
>
> Andy Jackson
> 823 Carlson Ave.
> West Chester, PA 19382
>   (215) 692-0269   Fax: (215) 272-7040

☆ *Erphila* German figurines, teapots and other ceramics, which are usually marked. Size, color and form are needed.
>
> Denise Hamilton
> 575 Latta Brook Road
> Elmira, NY 14901
>   (607) 732-2550

☆ **Wade figurines** including monks, Disney characters, circus animals and performers, animals, fairy tales, whimsies, and what have you.
>
> Ken Clee
> PO Box 11412
> Philadelphia, PA 19111
>   (215) 722-1979

☆ *Pen Delfin* **rabbits.** This mail order dealer in *Pen Delfin* is always looking for retired rabbits of all types, from the middle 1950's on. Will buy all, including the larger rabbits and houses, but wants quality undamaged items for resale. Note the figure's name on the bottom.
>
> George Sparacio
> PO Box 791
> Malaga, NJ 08328
>   (609) 694-4167 eves

☆ **Collector's plates.** The Ernst family is one of the nation's larger dealers in collector's plates. If you have plates to sell, they will help you in one of two ways, (1) by outright purchase of those they can sell promptly or (2) by selling your plates on consignment (in the more likely event you own plates in less demand). They charge 20% of the item's selling price for this valuable service. When you call or write, they will send you complete information plus specific instructions on how to pack and ship your plates safely. The Ernsts have been in business for 21 years and are listed in Dun & Bradstreet.

> Ross, Ruth and Ruth Ann Ernst, Collectors Plates
> 7308 Izard
> Omaha, NE 68114
>   (402) 391-3469

☆ **Child-like figures designed by Erich Stauffer.** Please give a detailed description of the kid's activity and props. Height is important, as is the style number and complete mark found on the base. These are usually marked either ARNART or ROYAL CROWN.

> Joan Oates
> 685 South Washington
> Constantine, MI 49042

☆ **Snow Babies.** "I'll buy all clean German 'Snow Babies' (china children in pebbly snow suits 1″-3″ high), especially jointed Snow Babies and 'action' Babies with animals or engaged in some activity." Also buys **small German bisque or papier mache Santas** dressed in felt with fur beards. Doesn't want items from Japan or Taiwan, nor does she want damaged or faded items or anything newer than 1940. Give the size and markings, if any, and note all damage, no matter how minor. No offers or free appraisals. She expects you to look them up in price guides and says she pays "50%-75% of book value."

> Linda Vines
> PO Box 721
> Upper Montclair, NJ 07043

☆ *Bossons* **artware** including heads, wall plaques and figures. These are made of plaster or *Stonite*, a vinyl/stone mix marketed as *Fraser-Art.* "We buy figures that are still available, but mostly seek discontinued figures, worth $85 up, with a few valued up to $15,000." There are *Bossons* look-alikes, but only figures marked BOSSONS CONGLETON ENGLAND COPYRIGHT are wanted. Slightly damaged figures will be considered by this authorized *Bossons* dealer and repairman. "If you truly want to buy or sell *Bossons*, contact me."

> Donald Hardisty, Don's Collectibles
> 3020 East Majestic Ridge
> Las Cruces, NM 88011
>   (505) 522-3721 for info   Fax: (505) 522-7909

READ THIS SECTION CAREFULLY.

*If you are handling an estate, closing a business, or have piles of family papers and photos, **read this section carefully.** Piles of papers can be piles of dollars.*

Paper is bought for one of two reasons:
(1) It is pretty, and collectible because it is, or
(2) it is historically interesting and informative.
Some paper is bought for both reasons.

Popular papers are postcards, photographs, catalogs, bills and letters, autographs, posters, and advertising. Minor types include menus, blueprints, scrapbooks, maps, labels, etc. Values of these range from a few cents to a few thousand dollars. Some photos bring even more. A box of letters found at a California yard sale for $20 resold for $500,000. "It was just old paper" said the 1st seller.

Historical data is not often worth a lot of money, but **Trash or Treasure** *buyers* will preserve what you have. Please, never to throw away paper with prices, formulas, processes, or descriptions of people or travels.*

Sports, movies, music, transportation, liquor, tobacco, business and Pop Culture paper is easiest to sell. You'll find buyers in the next few pages ready to buy a wide range of items. Don't give up if you don't find a buyer your first try.

***Condition is critical** for buyers of paper. Don't clean paper yourself. It is easy to do more harm than good. Let the buyer do it.*

***Describing paper is usually easy.** Photocopy it! If your item is too large to fit on a machine, take multiple copies and tape them together or go to a commercial copy center where larger machines are available.*

***Important tip:** unless you are certain your item is both rare and desirable, do not go to a great deal of effort to make photocopies of big piles of paper. Write to the buyer first, expressing a willingness to make copies if desired.*

POSTERS

☆ **Posters of all types**. This 30 year veteran dealer says, "I'll pay top prices for any printed poster done before 1960, especially WWI and WWII, film, travel, theater, circus, and transportation (ocean liner, railroad, and air). Also buys poster books, periodicals, postcards, and photos of posters being printed or posted. Include your phone number.
George Theofiles, Miscellaneous Man
PO Box 1776
New Freedom, PA 17349
(717) 235-4766 days

☆ **Posters of all types, 1880-1950**, all countries and subjects, especially U.S. posters from WWI and II and 1890-1910 American advertising. Army recruiting posters by Christy and Flagg from WWI bring $500 to $1,500. No reproduction posters are wanted. Poster Master offers an illustrated catalog for $3 which contains 800 posters for sale.
George Dembo, The Poster Master
215 Main Street #2
Chatham, NJ 07928
(201) 635-6505   (201) 655-0212

☆ **American posters of WWI.** No foreign, repros, or damaged items. Give the main slogan, the size, the artist if known, and the condition.
Ken Khuans
155 Harbor #4812
Chicago, IL 60601
(312) 642-0554

☆ **Rock and roll concert posters of all eras** and all types, especially 1960's posters by San Francisco artists (values range from a few dollars to a few thousand). Also buys handbills, postcards and tickets from rock and roll band concerts. To sell rock posters, you need to give the name of the lead band, the date, the location of the concert, and the condition. Note all creases, tears, and soil when you describe condition. "I'll buy the rarest posters in almost any condition." Leave a message on his machine. Please be patient, response time may be slow.
Bob Metzler, Flash Paradise
Moving as we went to press.
(310) 472-6668 voice and fax

☆ **Rock and roll concert posters** from the 1960's. Send a photo.
Bill and Linda Montgomery
12111 SE River Road
Milwaukee, OR 97222
(503) 652-2992

MISCELLANEOUS PAPER

☆ **All paper goods in good condition** are sought by one of the West's better known ephemerists. Kenrich Company buys **postcards, posters, sports cards, scorecards, playing cards, movie lobby cards, photos, stereoviews, panoramic photos, stamps and covers, philatelic items, letters, letterheads, trade cards, signs, insurance policies, timetables, slave documents, brochures, calendars, blotters, original artwork, bumper stickers, bookmarks, cookbooks, menus, napkins, coasters, matchbooks, seed packets, diaries, logs, autographs, scrapbooks, games, paper dolls, souvenirs, guidebooks, almanacs, directories** and more. If it's paper, collectible, and in fine condition, Bill will probably buy it. Closed Sunday and Monday.

> Bill Colby
> Kenrich Company
> 9418-T Las Tunas Drive
> Temple City, CA 91780
> (818) 286-3888   Fax: (818) 286-6035

☆ **Rare documents** from the time of papyrus to the present. Buys collections of letters, manuscript (hand written) material, land grants, photograph collections, diaries, hand colored maps, atlases, and "anything unusual in paper."

> Ivan Gilbert, Miran Arts & Books
> 2824 Elm Ave.
> Columbus, OH 43209
> (614) 236-3222   Fax: (614) 236-3223

☆ **Rare documents in all fields,** from autographs to stock certificates, from song sheets to pardons and passes, including handwritten documents, land grants, maps, and "most any other unusual paper items." Gordon buys lots of all sizes, from single items to entire estates.

> Gordon McHenry
> PO Box 1117
> Osprey, FL 34229
> (813) 966-5563   Fax: (813) 966-5563

☆ **Accumulations of paper items** from before 1920. Especially wants stocks and bonds, but also buys bills, checks, and letters with "pretty vignettes." Buys some **Western, circus,** and **magic posters** as well. Does not buy anything made after 1940. If you have a large collection, or just **boxes of old paper**, phone with your items in front of you.

> David Beach
> Paper Americana
> PO Box 2026
> Goldenrod, FL 32733
> (407) 657-7403   Fax: (407) 657-6382

☆ **Accumulations of paper items** related to business, finance, mining, or transportation before 1920. Buys stocks, bonds, billheads, advertising, land grants, maps, diaries, letters, photographs and other printed and manuscript items. Will consider all collections related to military, mining, railroads, energy, banking, express companies, law enforcement, and other topics generally associated with the old West.
> Warren Anderson
> America West Archives
> PO Box 100
> Cedar City, UT 84720
> (801) 586-9497

☆ **Manuscripts and printed documents with interesting content.** These need not be signed by anyone famous. "I particularly like colonial American documents from before the Revolutionary War, but will consider material from all periods. Please describe the contents and why you think the item is unusual." Photocopy advisable.
> Chris Wilson
> 8101 Revatom Court
> Dunn Loring, VA 22027
> (703) 698-7073

☆ **Paper items fringed in silk.** Buys Victorian greeting cards in any style from single sheets to little booklets, from any holiday or event, as long as they have silk fringe. Also wants sachets, menus, advertising, and similar trinkets that are silk fringed, made between 1875 and 1925.
> Ronald Lowden, Jr.
> 314 Chestnut Ave.
> Narberth, PA 19072
> (610) 667-0257 anytime

☆ **Prints, calendars, trade cards, advertising, and magazine covers** featuring the work of name artists such as Frances Brundage, Ida Waugh, Jessie Wilcox Smith, Maud Humphrey, Torres Bevins, Mabel L. Attwell, Henry Clive, Harrison Fisher, Coles Phillips, Rose O'Niell, Grace Drayton, Charlotte Becker, Maxfield Parrish, and others.
> Madalaine Selfridge, Hidden Magic Doll Museum
> 33710 Almond Street
> Lake Elsinore, CA 92530
> (909) 674-9221

☆ **Collections of labels, stickers** and **poster stamps** pre-1960. Wants collections of colorful, smaller graphics of all types, even if many are duplicates. Immediate answer if you include your phone number.
> George Theofiles
> PO Box 1776
> New Freedom, PA 17349

☆ **Paper puzzles in any printed format.** "I'll buy crosswords, mathematical puzzles, rebuses, tangrams, brain teasers, picture puzzles, etc. The format can be a book, magazine, pamphlet, broadside, trade card, or newspaper, but I do not want 'hidden image' puzzles or those that are too juvenile, intended for small children." In general, he is most interested in items from before 1950, the earlier the better, although value depends on the quality of the puzzle and the rarity of the material. He also wants material about the history of puzzles, directories of puzzles, and "anything with the byline 'Sam Loyd,' a famous turn of the century puzzlist." Give the date and condition, and describe the puzzle or state its objective. No jigsaw puzzles.
> Will Shortz
> 55 Great Oak Lane
> Pleasantville, NY 10570
> (914) 769-9128 voice and fax

☆ **Rebus puzzles.** Rebus puzzles are combinations of pictures, syllables, and letters which create a message when decoded. She only wants noncommercial hand drawn puzzles in letters or postcards, not printed ones. They can be from any period, if they're interesting. Preferably wants pencil or pen and ink rather than paintings, with less sophisticated drawings the most interesting to her. She doesn't care how difficult the puzzle is. No trade cards, greeting cards or puzzles printed in books.
> Linda Campbell Franklin
> 2716 Northfield Road
> Charlottesville, VA 22901

☆ **Scrapbooks compiled by children or adults before 1895.** A variety of contents may be of interest, *except* if primarily newspaper clippings. Any size considered. You must write detailed descriptions of contents, noting damaged or trimmed items. Your alternative is to photocopy pages from the book. He promises to return your materials promptly and unmarked if he invites you to ship them for inspection. Condition is an important factor in value for this 40 year vet.
> Ronald Lowden, Jr.
> 314 Chestnut Ave.
> Narberth, PA 19072
> (610) 667-0257 anytime

☆ **Scrapbooks** with diecut embossed scrap from the Victorian era, trade cards and prints. Also wants **collections of loose die-cut, embossed Victorian paper**, especially Santas, snow angels, and children. Also wants **cards from any holiday**, 1880 to 1940. Nothing later. Everything must be in suitable condition for resale.
> Madalaine Selfridge
> 33710 Almond Street
> Lake Elsinore, CA 92330

☆ **Scrapbooks of Victorian era trade cards.**
 Russell Mascieri
 6 Florence Ave.
 Marlton, NJ 08053
  (609) 985-7711 Fax: (609) 985-8513

☆ **Passports** and some other travel documents, pre-1940 American or foreign. Documents must be complete: nothing missing, removed or torn. Photocopy the page with the owner's description and inside pages that have been used. "No overpriced passports owned by celebrities."
 Dan Jacobson
 PO Box 277101
 Sacramento, CA 95827

☆ **Consular and foreign service stamps on documents** of any type, 1906-1955. Send photocopy.
 H. Ritter
 68 Heatherwood
 Norristown, PA 19403

☆ **Admission tickets of all types.** "I buy sports, political, theatrical, and social tickets. Must be complete. No stubs or foreign items. No transportation tickets for trolleys, railroads, etc. Please price what you have and ship it on approval."
 David Lamb
 48 Woodside Drive
 Rochester, NY 14624

☆ **"Dirty letters."** This long time erotica buyer wants sexy or risque letters 1800-1975, ideally with the original envelope if mailed. May be hand written or typed. "Even better if photos or other items mailed with the letters are still there."
 Charles Martignette
 PO Box 293
 Hallandale, FL 33009
  (305) 454-3474

MAPS & GLOBES

☆ **Maps**. Many different types of maps are wanted by this specialty dealer, especially U.S. areas pre-1920 and worldwide prior to 1900. Particular interests include:

- **Books with maps**: atlases, geographies, travel guides, gazetteers, land surveys and explorations prior to 1900;
- Wall maps before 1920;
- **Pocket maps** with folding covers, case maps which fit into cases, and other maps separately published (not as part of a book of maps) before 1920;
- **Hand drawn maps**, especially battlefields;
- City plat maps before 1900;
- Texas, the Southwest and Southeast maps before 1900;
- Decorative maps;
- Geologic maps;
- Railroad maps, especially of the entire world, USA or the US Southwest before 1920;
- **Bird's eye views of cities**;
- **Globes of the world** before WWII, especially those with unusual or decorative stands;
- **Games and puzzles** pre-1960, including jigsaw, based on maps.

Please do not offer atlases or geographies after 1900. Description should include the author or map maker, the title or area depicted, the latest date on the map, the size, whether or not it is colored, and the condition, especially noting anything missing.

> Murray Hudson
> Antiquarian Books & Maps
> 109 South Church Street
> Halls, TN 38040
> (800) 748-9946   Fax: (901) 836-9057

☆ **Maps and atlases** before 1890 wanted, particularly those showing the present day United States. Maps and books that are damaged, torn, moldy, or bug eaten are worth a small fraction of those in fine condition. Maps are worthless if laminated, dry mounted or glued to cardboard or Masonite. Best to send your map on approval but description will suffice if you include the title, date, mapmaker, size and condition. No reproductions wanted.

> Charles Neuschafer
> New World Maps
> 1123 South Broadway
> Lantana, FL 33462
> (407) 586-8723

☆ **U.S. maps and atlases before 1870**.
Joe Davidson
Antiquarian Graphic Society
5185 Windfall Road
Medina, OH 44256
(216) 723-7172

☆ **U.S. maps and atlases before 1870.**
Frank Klein
The Bookseller
521 West Exchange Street
Akron, OH 44302
(216) 762-3101   Fax: (216) 762-4413

☆ **Atlases with colored plates** before 1870 as long as they deal in whole or in part with the United States. It is important that double page plates should not have a white area separating the plate into two sections. Also interested in **commercial atlases prior to 1925** and **books of all types with foldout maps** in black and white or color, but they must be before 1870. Groups of loose color plate **maps** are also considered. Include dimensions with standard bibliographic information. Note tears, erasures, foxing, etc. If you have a book with many maps, give the number of maps in color and in b/w.
John Rosenhoover
100 Mandalay Road
Chicopee, MA 01020

☆ **Maps of any Asian country:** Japan, China, Korea, Vietnam, Siam, Tonkin, Cambodia, Laos, Malaya, Singapore, Indonesia, Philippines, Burma, Formosa, Taiwan, Tibet, Mongolia, Manchuria, New Guinea, or anywhere else in Southeast Asia and the Far East.   Maps before 1930 only, please. Photocopies are appreciated.
Jerry Stanoff
Rare Oriental Book Co.
PO Box 1599
Aptos, CA 95001
(408) 724-4911   Fax: (408) 761-1350

When describing an atlas or book of maps, use Standard Bibliographic Information consisting of: Title, author, publisher, city where published, and date when published.

☆ **Road maps** given away by gas stations, state highway departments, automobile clubs, and various tourist offices. Will consider all dates, but pre-1970 is preferred. Most maps are relatively low value, bringing $1 to $3 each if dated between 1930-1970, but a pile can add up, and some maps do bring more than those prices. Maps that are damaged, torn, moldy, or bug eaten are not wanted, although those with routes marked are "not a problem." He requests you send your maps on approval via 4th class book rate. Personal inspection is needed, since most maps are undated except for "secret codes" used by the printers.

> Charles Neuschafer
> New World Maps
> 1123 South Broadway
> Lantana, FL 33462
> (407) 586-8723

☆ **Road maps,** particularly from the 1920's and 30's. "I like city maps, state maps, and regional maps, foreign or domestic." Must be in good condition.   Also will buy old official State Highway Department maps, the earlier the better. Noel says you may send your items for his immediate offer and a return check. Will buy large quantities, too.

> Noel Levy
> PO Box 32458
> Baltimore, MD 21208
> (410) 363-9040

☆ **Globes of the world,** especially globes made of glass (not plastic) covered with paper with interior lights that shine through, globes with black oceans, globes with revolving planets, etc. Anything unusual or before 1940 (map will show Palestine) considered. Send photo, including stand. Give height and circumference. Condition critical.

> Frank and Jay Novak
> 7366 Beverly Blvd.
> Los Angeles, CA 90036
> (213) 933-0383   Fax: (213) 683-1312

☆ **Globes and models of the solar system** are wanted by this large but recent dealer in them. He espccially wants 19th century globes, both desk and floor models, and points out that some globes made in pairs between 1500 and 1850 can be worth $100,000 or more. He does not want globes made after WWII (look for Israel). Give the maker, diameter, material it's made from, and condition.

> Jonathan Blackman
> 511 North Robertson Blvd.
> Los Angeles, CA 90048
> (310) 274-3190   (310) 314-7307

PAPER DOLLS

☆ **Paper dolls of all types.** Wants to buy antique paper dolls and toys, 1910-1960 books, magazine dolls from adult or children's publications and newspaper comic strip dolls from the 1930's and 40's such as *Flash Gordon* and *Brenda Starr.* Celebrity or not. Will buy cut dolls if neatly done. Please give name, date if possible, book number and mention any writing on the front or back of the doll, the box, or the book.

> Madalaine Selfridge, Hidden Magic Doll Museum
> 33710 Almond Street
> Lake Elsinore, CA 92530

☆ **All types of paper dolls, cut or uncut,** one or a collection as long as they're pre-1960. Will buy commercial, magazine, or newspaper dolls. Sellers should list paper dolls by name, if possible, and indicate whether they are cut or not. Photocopies are helpful. Fran, a collector for 20 years, is available for slide shows about paper dolls.

> Fran Van Vynckt
> 7412 Monroe Avenue
> Hammond, IN 46324
> (219) 931-8081

☆ **Paper dolls and paper toys** of all kinds, cut or uncut, from boxed or book sets, newspapers, magazines, cereal boxes, etc. Especially wanted are paper dolls of real people. If you really want to sell your dolls, indicate names, dates, and quantity, and whether cut or not. Also indicate condition, mentioning bends, tears, missing parts, and tape. No need to photograph or photocopy any more than the doll (not the whole set). Will buy some rare sets even when damaged, and buys some current items, but no *Betsy McCall* sheets. For 23 years, Loraine has published *Celebrity Doll Journal,* a quarterly available for $7/year.

> *"Dolls that have been cut out are desirable as long as their arms and legs aren't bent. Do not mend with tape! Numbers on boxes or dolls are useful info."*

> Loraine Burdick, Quest-Eridon Books
> 5 Court Place
> Puyallup, WA 98372

☆ **Paper toys, figures, and buildings,** especially toys and models by *Builtrite,* but interested in any paper dolls and soldiers in good condition. In business for more than a decade, Paper Soldier publishes a large and informative catalog for $5.

> Jonathan Newman, Paper Soldier
> 8 McIntosh Lane
> Clifton Park, NY 12065
> (518) 371-5130

AUTOGRAPHS

☆ **Autographs in all fields** are purchased for resale by this collector and dealer. He buys old letters, envelopes, canceled checks, and various documents and photos signed by famous people.
> Bill Colby
> Kenrich Company
> 9418-T Las Tunas Drive
> Temple City, CA 91780
>> (818) 286-3888   Fax: (818) 286-6035

☆ **Letters, signed photos and signatures of famous people** in any category: Presidents, Hollywood, NASA, sports, Civil War, art, music, literary, scientific, historical, rock and roll, theater, aviation, old West. Also interested in old handwritten diaries, collections of letters from the not-so-famous, handwritten recipe books, and anything written while traveling across America. Wants California and New Orleans letters from 1800-1870. Offers $1,000 for signed Buddy Holly photo. Please photocopy what you have. No autopen or printed signatures.
> Michael Reese II
> PO Box 5704
> South San Francisco, CA 94083
>> (415) 641-5920

Politicians' signatures are worth little except Presidents. Movie and TV stars since 1960 are also of little value, with a few exceptions such as Marilyn Monroe and James Dean.

☆ **Autographs, signed books, and rare documents in all fields.** Particularly wants U.S. Presidents and first ladies and "investment quality items." Wants handwritten letters of Presidents while in office, particularly of William Henry Harrison and James A. Garfield, whose letters could be worth as much as $50,000! No facsimile or secretary signatures. "It is usually necessary to see the actual item, particularly in order to make a firm offer." Their monthly catalog is free. Larry and Mike are authors of *From the President's Pen: an illustrated Guide to Presidential Autographs,* available from them for $25.
> Michael Minor and Larry Vrzalik
> Lone Star Autographs
> PO Drawer 500
> Kaufman, TX 75142
>> (214) 932-6050 from 10 to 10 Central time daily

☆ **Autographed letters and documents** from ancient times to modern day in all fields. Significant medieval documents and manuscripts are always of interest. This 28 year veteran dealer does not want autographs obtained by writing celebrities, modern politicians, or movie stars. A photocopy is suggested.

> Kenneth Rendell
> PO Box 9001
> Wellesley, MA 02181
> (617) 431-1776 Fax: (617) 237-1492

☆ **Handwritten documents and letters of famous Americans.** "We particularly want Washington, Adams, Jefferson, Franklin, Hancock, and Lincoln, and specialize in U.S. Presidents." Famous scientists, inventors, authors and musicians also sought. Note all imperfections.

> Steve and Linda Alsberg
> 9850 Kedvale Ave.
> Skokie, IL 60076
> (708) 676-9850

☆ **Historical documents signed by U.S. Presidents.** "I'll buy land grants, military and civil commissions, ship's papers, passports, appointments of judges, postmasters, ambassadors, etc. I search for clean documents with no holes, stains, tape or trims. I'd love a George Washington land survey (to $10,000) or a Supreme Court appointment. Every mark, fade, crease or wrinkle *must* be described accurately."

> Richard Lechaux
> HC-60 Box 3712
> Fort Valley, VA 22652
> (703) 933-6305

☆ **Autographs in all fields** with a particular emphasis on Presidents and political, military, and historical figures. He does not want Hollywood or TV people after 1940. "The more information the better. Describe what it is written on, whether faded or bright, whether written in pen or pencil, and the wording of any inscription."

> Chris Wilson
> 8101 Revatom Court
> Dun Loring, VA 22027
> (703) 698-7073

☆ **American and foreign autographs in all fields throughout Western history,** including politicians, Presidents, signers of the Declaration of Independence, music and the arts, literature, the military, and scientists. Will buy one or collections. This 20+ year veteran is not interested in unsigned documents of any sort.

    Robert Batchelder
    1 West Butler Ave.
    Ambler, PA 19002
        (215) 643-1430   Fax: (215) 643-6613

☆ **Checks autographed by any famous person** are wanted, especially bounced checks. He'll pay from $750-$3,500 for checks he especially wants from Henry Ford, Harry Houdini, Greta Garbo, Buddy Holly, President Taylor, Gerald Ford, Lyndon Johnson, Al Capone, Richard Nixon, Charles Chaplin, President Tyler, and others. He also buys pay orders, certificates of deposit, and other small size **financial documents.** Send a fax or photocopy. "I want to know the condition, the date, whether the check is signed or endorsed, and the color of the check. If the seller has a price in mind, please quote it up front. If the seller has no idea of value, then I will make him a fair quote."

    Olan Chiles
    1892 Avenida Aragon
    Oceanside, CA 92056
        (619) 724-2339   Fax: (619) 726-4964

☆ **Famous people's signatures on manuscript documents, land grants, maps, photographs,** and other early paper. Has particular interest in Southern and Civil War figures and in letters signed by James McHenry, Washington's Secretary of War.

    Gordon McHenry
    PO Box 1117
    Osprey, FL 33559
        (813) 966-5563

☆ **Historic early American autographed documents,** books, letters, maps, prints, stock certificates, and bonds.

    Earl Moore
    PO Box 243
    Wynnewood, PA 19096
        (610) 649-1549 anytime

☆ **Composers, musicians and singers of classical music.** Buys signed photos, letters, musical notations, etc. No free appraisals.

    J.B. Muns, Books & Fine Art
    1162 Shattuck Ave.
    Berkeley, CA 94707
        (510) 525-1126

☆ **Composers, musicians, opera singers, and movie stars** from the late 1800's to the 1950's. Prefers to buy signed photos, letters with important content, or musical quotes. Among the many people they would like to find are Kathleen Ferrier, Conchita Supervia, Maria Galvany, Celestina Boninsegna, Fernando De Lucia, Guilio Grisi, and Marietti Alboni. "We are not interested in the autographs of current performers, but will pay very well for first class older items. Condition is important. We request photocopies and prefer to see the item in person, especially when large collections are involved." Will make offers for amateurs. Dealers, price your goods.

> Bill Safka and Arbe Bareis
> PO Box 886
> Forest Hills, NY 11375
> (718) 263-2276

☆ **Autographs of Hollywood stars** and other famous people. "If they were famous enough for you to recognize, I probably want their autograph." Tom urges you to get a quote from him, and points out that lots of stories in the popular press about autographs and their values are not accurate. Prefers autographed 8" x 10" b/w photos. Does not buy severely damaged items. "Since autographs and photos are subjective, please send me a Xerox™ of what you have for sale." Tom publishes address directories of famous people (mostly movie stars) and is interested in obtaining home addresses you might know. Tom prefers you to set the price wanted but will make offers. His autograph catalog costs $3, his star directory $25. SASE is essential if you want an answer, he advises.

> Tom Burford, Celebrity Access
> 20 Sunnyside Ave. #A241
> Mill Valley, CA 94941
> (415) 389-8133   (415) 381-2215

☆ **Autographs of celebrities and "newsworthy persons"** including photos, letters, checks, or other documents signed by mass murderers, assassins, spies, heads of state, royalty, rock stars, and other famous and infamous persons. Examples: Arafat, Jackie Kennedy, Madonna, Michael Jackson, David Berkowitz, John Hinkley, etc. Not interested in printed signatures or autopens. Photocopies are a must if you want an offer. "If I cannot tell from your copy whether the signature is authentic, it will be necessary to ship it for my inspection. Before I buy items, I expect the seller to sign a statement guaranteeing that they own the item in question and that there are no liens against it."

> Sheldon Kamerman, World Wide Auctioneering Group
> 466 11th Street #F
> Lakewood, NJ 08701
> (908) 363-6161 weekends

YOU SHOULD BE ABLE TO SELL ALL BUT THE MOST COMMON CARDS AS LONG AS THEY ARE IN GOOD CONDITION.

Postcards are collected for the photograph, message, artist, stamp, and the postmark. Real photo cards (black and white real photos of people, places or events) are among the most sought. If you have a card that pictures any business, occupation or vehicle, the folks interested in those topics will pay more for the card than will a postcard dealer or collector. **Scenics picturing rivers, trees, mountains, lakes and the like, are seldom wanted, and worth only a dime or so.**

If you want to sell postcards, you have two choices: (1) Send them on approval or (2) send photocopies. Because most of my readers have postcards, and many buyers want them (all through the book), I'm giving you guidelines on how to identify the various types of cards, and how to evaluate their condition.

TYPES OF POSTCARDS

EARLY "PIONEER ERA" CARDS: Cards from the mid 1870's to 1900. Until 1893 cards had no pictures other than advertising. These cards are wanted for the postmark as much as for the card.

POSTCARDS: In 1901, "real photo" cards were introduced. A black and white or sepia photo is on one side of the card and the address on the reverse. Messages were not allowed on the address side, so pictures were often defaced by messages.

DIVIDED BACK CARDS: Cards used between 1907 and 1914 are called "divided back" cards because the message was written on the left and address on the right, thus preserving the picture. Real photo cards often have divided backs. Very collectible.

WHITE BORDER CARDS: From around 1915 to 1930, most postcards had a white border around the picture. Desirable, but less so.

LINEN CARDS: During the Depression and WWII (1930-45), postcards had a textured surface, like linen. Inks from this period were usually bright. The colored printed photographs were usually of poor quality with little detail. Much less valuable.

CHROME CARDS: Modern brightly colored, slick surface postcards made since WWII. Their colors are vivid, the details are sharp, and the cards are of little interest to collectors.

Postcard buyers are fussy about condition. Poor condition cards seldom have a buyer, and prices drop dramatically for anything less than "excellent." That's why dealers and collectors want to see your cards before paying for them.

If you have a large quantity of cards, my advice is to ship them on approval after first contacting the potential *Trash or Treasure* buyer. A few postcard buyers like Bill Colby don't require you to contact them first.

HOW TO DESCRIBE CONDITION

MINT: A perfect card, as it comes from the press. No marks, bends or creases. No writing or postmarks. Rarely seen.

NEAR MINT: Like mint but very light aging or very slight discoloration from being in an album for many years. Not as fresh looking as mint.

EXCELLENT: Card looks like mint with sharply pointed corners (no blunt or rounded corners). It may not have any bends or creases. May be used or unused, but writing and postmark are only on address side, with clean fresh picture side.

VERY GOOD: Corners may be just a bit blunt or rounded, or it might have an almost undetectable crease or bend that does not detract from overall appearance of picture side. May have writing only on the address side.

GOOD: Corners may be noticeably blunt or rounded with noticeable but slight bends or creases. May be postally used or have writing, but only on the address side.

AVERAGE: Creases and bends more pronounced. Corners more rounded. Or it may have writing in margins on picture side, or the postmark may show through from address side but not on main portion of picture.

POOR: Card is intact, but has excess soil, stains, or heavy creases. Or it is written on the picture side, or has a cancel that affects the picture. Salable only if a very rare and desirable card.

SPACE FILLER: Poor condition, perhaps with torn or missing corners or breaks in the picture surface. Cards in this condition are neither desirable nor valuable.

POSTCARDS

☆ **Postcard albums and collections,** the older the better, in very good condition only. Interested in all topics, but does not want damaged cards. Joan conducts mail auctions and sells on approval. Wants to know the number of cards, condition, and types of subjects pictured. She's been a collector for nearly 50 years!

Jo Ann Van Scotter
208 East Lincoln Street
Mt. Morris, IL 61054
(815) 734-6971

☆ **All types of postcards,** old or modern, are purchased for resale. You may ship any quantity up to a shoebox full (about 600-700) together with your telephone number and he will make an offer. If the offer is unacceptable, postcards will be returned promptly.

Bill Colby, Kenrich Co.
9418-T Las Tunas Drive
Temple City, CA 91780
(818) 286-3888

☆ **Postcard collections, pre-1930,** especially American street views, disasters, railroad stations, fire departments, and diners. He also buys cards depicting foreign royalty, expositions, snowmen, full length Santas, and pre-jet commercial aircraft. Does not want foreign views, scenery, parks, woods, mountains, lakes, and flowers. Does not want damaged cards or those which have been pasted in albums. "If your cards are not for sale, or if my offer is not accepted, I will appraise your cards at a cost of only one postcard of my choice for each 100 cards I appraise." Cards must be shipped for inspection for purchase or appraisal. John runs auctions, postcard shows, and heads the Postcard History Society. He can supply you with many interesting free or low cost items regarding postcard collecting. For more information send a stamped return envelope for his "Postcard Opportunity" sheet.

John McClintock
PO Box 1765
Manassas, VA 22110
(703) 368-2757 eves

☆ **Postcards, American and foreign,** all subjects, used or unused, if before 1950. "I'll pay competitive prices for better single cards or will buy collections, box lots, accumulations, etc."

Sheldon Dobres
4 Calypso Court
Baltimore, MD 21209
(410) 486-6569

☆ **Picture postcards** before 1940 are sought by this paper dealer, who does not buy chrome cards of any type or subject matter.
>
> Mike Rasmussen
> PO Box 726
> Marina, CA 93933
> (408) 384-5460   Fax: (408) 883-1088

☆ **Postcards worldwide,** used or unused, before 1950, from any country, but especially from the U.S. and Canada. Wants street scenes, buildings, occupationals, sports, transportation, and people. Doesn't want water, forests, trees, mountains, deserts, etc. Also buys some pictorial "greetings." Pays 25¢ to $5 for most postcards, but a few European cards drawn or painted by famous illustrators can bring $100 up. No quantity too large. "Prompt payment if you send your cards on approval; unwanted cards are returned." Neil makes payment in the currency of the seller.
>
> Neil Hayne
> PO Box 220
> Bath, ON K0H 1G0 CANADA
> (613) 352-7456

☆ **Canadian and English postcards** from before 1930, used or unused. "I'm particularly interested in real photo views of small towns and interesting social history. I can not use damaged cards or boring mountain scenery. You may send cards on approval for my offer, and I'll pay the postage." Will pay in U.S. funds.
>
> Michael Rice
> PO Box 286
> Saanichton, BC V8M 2C5 CANADA
> (604) 652-9047 eves

☆ **Canadian postcards** especially from Ontario Province. Want small town views, events, railroad stations, and transportation. No scenics or items after 1950. "A photocopy of the item is almost essential."
>
> Peter Cox
> PO Box 1655
> Espanola, ON P0P 1C0 CANADA
> (705) 869-2441   (705) 859-2410

☆ **Views of China, Hong Kong, Singapore, and Macao before 1945.** Real photo cards only. Prices range from $5 to $100 depending on the stamp, cancellation, and subject matter. Dealers price what you have, but amateurs may request an offer. Send Xerox™ copy.
>
> Kin Leung Liu
> PO Box 94056
> Seattle, WA 98124
> (206) 548-4900   (206) 768-1389   Fax: (206) 767-3025

SOME PHOTOS ARE TREASURES.

Unidentified portraits typically have little value. But those same portraits will find buyers quickly if the sitters are in uniform or holding tools or weapons. Photos of officials, workers, events, outdoor city scenes, parades, stores, vehicles and uniforms will always find a buyer among collectors trying to learn more about an industry or era.

To sell a photo, Xerox© what you have. Condition of the photo and its mat are both important to a buyer. Note banged corners, stains, and the like. If the photo is faded, make certain you indicate that fact, as photocopies tend to make photos look better than they are.

TYPES OF PHOTOGRAPHS

DAGUERREOTYPES: 1839-1854, recognizable by a silvery image on glass. The leather and early plastic cases are often worth more than the photo. Outdoor and city views are rare. Large "Dags" can be valuable. Do not clean them and do not leave them exposed to sunlight.

AMBROTYPES: Photos on a glass negative backed with dark paper to make a positive image. Mid-19th century. Subject matter is the key to value. These often come in elaborate cases.

ALBUMEN PHOTOGRAPHS: Paper prints before 1890 usually used egg albumen in preparation of the image surface.

TINTYPES: Cheap popular portraits, 1858-1910, printed on sheets of black tin. Also called ferrotypes. Subject matter is the key to value. Pictures not taken in a studio are usually more valuable.

CARTES DE VISITE (CDV): Photos on card stock measuring 2.5" x 4" popular between 1860-1890, often found in albums.

CABINET CARDS: Photos on 4" x 7" cards, usually studio shots with the photographer's name at the bottom. These are found with pictures of celebrities, Presidents and generals.

STEREOVIEWS: Cards containing two shots of the same subject to give a 3-D effect seen through a viewer. Views before 1890 are larger, flat, have colored mounts (yellow, pink, etc.) and generally no printing on back. Later views have curved gray mounts (*Underwood* is common). Newest, and worthless, are colored printed stereoviews. Older views will often be curved, the result of being stored with newer cards.

SNAPSHOTS. Printed in b/w on thin paper, popular from 1920-1960, when color pictures and slides became the photo of choice.

PHOTOGRAPHS

☆ **Photographs** including tintypes, Daguerreotypes, ambrotypes, cartes de visite, cabinet photos, albumen prints, stereoviews, silver prints, platinum prints, cyanotypes, and photo albums. His list of "fine subjects" includes: banjo players, Russians, kids playing marbles, Brooklyn, photographers, auto racing, nudes, military, Civil War, autographed photos, funny photos, Lincoln, John Wilkes Booth, portraits taken in Philadelphia of identified people, unusual photos, Shakers, WWII, **mug shots**, writers, gunmen, artists, Philadelphia, famous people, Hawaii and Samoa in the 19th century, Puerto Rico, Indians, mining, Orientals, rockets, sports, aviation, people at work and similar topics dating before 1915. No ordinary studio portraits, and no photo equipment is wanted. Photocopy both sides of your photo and price what you have for sale.

> Richard Rosenthal
> 4718 Springfield Ave.
> Philadelphia, PA 19143
>   (215) 726-5493

☆ **Rare old photographs,** cased photos, stereoviews, etc., especially work by important Western photographers such as Jackson, Curtis, and others. Also buys books with actual photos tipped (pasted) in.

> Ivan Gilbert
> Miran Arts & Books
> 2824 Elm Ave.
> Columbus, OH 43209
>   (614) 421-3222   Fax: (614) 421-3223

If you have photographs of events, businesses,
industry, or sports, specialists in those subjects
are often your best buyers. It could put more $$$
in your pocket to read the chapter dealing with
the subject matter of your photo.

☆ **Photos and photographic literature.** Wants Daguerreotypes, ambrotypes, tintypes, stereoviews, round *Kodak* snapshots, and other interesting photos from any era. No portraits. Would love to find photos of photographers at work. Buys complete unpicked photo albums, specializing in Pittsburgh and Allegheny County, Pennsylvania. Also wants early **cameras, photographic accessories and literature.**

> Nicholas Graver
> 276 Brooklawn Drive
> Rochester, NY 14618
>   (716) 244-4818

☆ **Interesting photographs of all types** including Daguerreotypes, ambrotypes, tintypes, cabinet cards, albumen prints, real photo post-cards and stereoviews. Indicates a willingness to pay high prices for a wide range of photos including the following categories:

- Travel albums with mounted albumen photos, but not albums of black construction paper with mounted snapshots unless the subject matter is extraordinary (America, Egypt, Italy and the Far East are preferred);
- Extraordinary portraiture, strange people, people in costume, side show performers;
- Children or adults posed with unusual objects;
- Bizarre and unusual subject matter of all sorts;
- Death portraits;
- Political or holiday gatherings, or other events;
- Civil War soldiers and scenes;
- Presidents and famous 19th century persons, especially Lincoln;
- Street or riverfront scenes;
- American social life;
- Sports, circuses, and other amusements;
- Crime scene photographs and mug shots;
- Photographers in the studio or in the field;
- Artists and sculptors;
- Nudes, both artistic and erotic;
- Portraits of ordinary people in CDV or Daguerreotype form that are very sharp and in fine condition;
- Business cards with photographs attached.

He has a special interest in Michigan places and events and in early advertising by photographers anywhere. All photos must be undamaged and not faded. Do not inquire about printed or halftone reproductions. Make a Xerox™ copy of your photo for this relatively new collector/dealer who pledges prompt answers and competitive prices.

> Tom Harris
> 223 East 4th Street #14
> New York, NY 10009
> (212) 420-9121

☆ **Photos taken** in the United States before 1930 of special events, parades, sports, transportation, people with unusual clothing, people doing "something weird," twins, children with toys and "unusual photos." Is not interested in studio photos of men's and women's heads. Describe the photo's size, condition and content. Photocopy suggested, although this relatively new dealer may ask to see your photos before making final payment.

> Joe Burkart, Antique Photo Art
> 13015 West 104th Street
> Overland Park, KS 66215
> (913) 541-9243

☆ **Daguerreotypes** of famous people, Negroes, outdoor scenes, military, freaks, animals, people working or with tools, nudes, ships, fire engines, railroads, old West, balloons and disasters. premium for very large ones. Describe the picture, give the dimensions and describe the case and its condition.

    Russell Norton
    PO Box 1070
    New Haven, CT 06504
      (203) 562-7800

☆ **Stereoview cards** "in nearly all categories" are sought. He points out that there are two types of stereo cards, printed and photographic, and that he wants only photographic views of:
- Famous people;
- Ships, sailboats, riverboats, wharfs, etc.;
- Railroads, especially Western;
- Aviation, blimps, balloons, etc.;
- Automobiles, any early views;
- Fire fighting anything;
- Military, depicting equipment or arms;
- Western lore, cowboys, Indians, mining, etc.;
- Sports and games, from checkers to football;
- Music, bands, theatrical scenes, etc.;
- Street scenes from any city or town;
- Occupationals - people at work, especially photographers.

"I want any cards that capture a bygone era, people at leisure, at home, children playing, costumes, furniture, and the like. In addition to U.S. views, I will buy fine condition photos of Canada and Europe. Please describe your cards briefly, telling the subject matter and condition."

    Steve Jabloner
    7380 Adrian Drive #23
    Rohnert Park, CA 94928
      (707) 795-3081

☆ **Stereoview cards,** particularly older Western scenes, transportation, mining, Mt. Lowe, fires, high wheel bicycles, famous people, Civil War, and early California. "However, I buy most common stereos, too," presumably for a lot less. He particularly wants **stereos of Lincoln** published while Lincoln was alive. If you want to sell your cards, Chuck wants to know the subject of the card quite specifically, an accurate description of condition, and the publisher. If you have a price you want, say so. He does not want cards *printed* in color or in black and white.

    Chuck Reincke
    2141 Sweet Briar Road
    Tustin, CA 92680
      (714) 832-8563 eves

☆ **Stereoviews.** Buys most U.S. black and white views as well as other interesting pre-1920 photos. This large paper dealer buys for resale.

Bill Colby, Kenrich Co.
9418-T Las Tunas Drive
Temple City, CA 91780
(818) 286-3888

☆ **Stereoviews, U.S. and foreign,** that are real photos pasted on cards, not printed in color. Espccially wants the odd and unusual, old West, occupations, Indians, Civil War, freaks, the macabre, nudes, ships, railroads, animals, disasters, Negroes, whaling, stores, factories, harvesting, humorous, old mills, shoe shiners, street vendors, animals, circus, camping, ruins, and many more topics. Send an SASE for his informative handout and wants list which gives much greater detail. **Scenery** is of interest only from Western states or exotic foreign countries. All views must be in outstanding condition to be considered for purchase. Send a Xerox™ of both sides of the card if writing is on the back.

Russell Norton
PO Box 1070
New Haven, CT 06504
(203) 562-7800

☆ **Bizarre photos,** such as freaks, dwarfs, lynchings, slaves, public punishment, and what have you. Especially interested in photos of **death, especially post-mortem photos, but also mourning photos, executions, lynchings, and embalming and medical photos with doctors and cadavers.** Will take later photos if of someone famous. Likes to find old prints of the family gathered around the deceased. Worth from $5 to $75+ for the very early and unusual.

Steve DeGenaro
PO Box 5662
Youngstown, OH 44504

☆ **Stereoviews showing the development of the early West, 1860-1900:** expeditions, **railroad construction**, freighting in the Sierras, maritime scenes, **Indian portraits** and culture, **mining, logging,** and **early small town scenes** as well as **San Francisco.** Particular interest in Custer, Teddy Roosevelt, Mark Twain, Bret Harte, John Sutter, artist Albert Bierstadt, and all early **photographers and their equipment**. The latter will bring "hundreds of dollars" in excellent condition. Also wants paper advertising from early western photographers. Not interested in faded views or those with damaged mounts. No lithographed views, only real photos in excellent condition.

Jim Crain
131 Bennington Street
San Francisco, CA 94110
(415) 648-1092 eves

☆ **Photos of cowboys, Indians,** and related subjects, including cattle drives, early Texas towns, outlaws, lawmen, the Geronimo expedition (especially those taken by C.S. Fly), and the Mexican War. All types wanted, including stereo. Please send photocopies.

> Johnny Spellman
> 10806 North Lamar
> Austin, TX 78753
> (512) 258-6910 eves   (512) 836-2889 days

☆ **Original photos of Lincoln.** "I'll buy photos of Lincoln taken from life and printed before 1866. Will also purchase the Ayers photos of Lincoln printed in the 1880's and 1890's. I'll also buy photos of Lincoln look-alikes." No photos of prints, statues, or Abe's house. Send a photocopy of what you have. "Serious sellers only, please."

> Stuart Schneider
> PO Box 64
> Teaneck, NJ 07666
> (201) 261-1983

☆ **Photos of old Western personalities**, Wild West Show characters, armed cowboys and cowgirls, trappers and scouts dressed in buckskin, famous lawmen, armed Indian braves, and death views of outlaws. This 25 year veteran pays from $200 to $2,500 depending on the subject and type of photo. Excellent condition items before 1920 only. He does not want postcards, Indian women, children, cattle drives, or general Western views. Must send a clear Xerox™ of what you have. Dealers, price your goods. Amateurs may request an offer.

> Emory Cantey, Jr.
> Our Turn Antiques
> 1405 Ems Road East
> Fort Worth, TX 76116
> (817) 737-0430 voice and fax

☆ **Old photos of famous people, outdoor scenes and "the odd and the unusual."** Will buy Daguerreotypes, ambrotypes, tintypes and cartes de visite in fine condition. Send a photocopy.

> Chris Wilson
> 8101 Revatom Court
> Dunn Loring, VA 22027
> (703) 698-7073

☆ **Photographs and engravings of famous people** in all walks of life. Will consider items loose or in books. Please photocopy.

> Kenneth Rendell
> PO Box 9001
> Wellesley, MA 02181
> (617) 431-1776   Fax: (617) 237-1492

☆ **Photos of Indians and Eskimos,** especially the work of Edward S. Curtis. Also buys real photo postcards on the same theme. Please send photocopies for a prompt response. Dealers, price your goods, but amateur sellers may request an offer.

> Barry Friedman
> 22725 Garzota Drive
> Valencia, CA 91355
> (805) 296-2318

☆ **Photographs of people with guns.** Has a particular interest in Civil War and Western scenes but wants hunters, soldiers, sailors, Indians, and cowboys. All types of early images are considered, including cdv's, cabinet cards, tintypes, Daguerreotypes, etc. Send a photocopy of any image you want to sell, except those on Daguerreotypes, the cased photos with a mirror finish. SASE please.

> Charles Worman
> PO Box 33584 (AMC)
> Dayton, OH 45433
> (513) 429-1808 eves

☆ **Occupational photos,** especially baseball players, firefighters, Civil War soldiers, and other dramatic occupations. "I prefer cdv and cabinet card photos, and will pay particularly well for photos of doctors, nurses and other medical topics, especially related to embalming or medical school." Only items from before 1930 are wanted. Please photocopy.

> Steve DeGenaro
> PO Box 5662
> Youngstown, OH 44504

☆ **Photos in memorial matts** (ordinary portraits mounted in memorial matts after the person died). Memorial matts have printed or embossed angels, doves, Gates of Heaven, etc., and mottoes like "Free at Last."

> Steve DeGenaro
> PO Box 5662
> Youngstown, OH 44504

Watch for revenue stamps on the back of Civil War era cartes de visite and other photos. Most are common, but a few are quite valuable. Buyers of revenue stamps may be found on page 433.

CAMERA BUYERS WANT THE ODD, OLD AND UNUSUAL.

You may find it hard to recognize the earliest Daguerreotype cameras because they look like wooden boxes without a lens. They are quite valuable. So are hidden ("detective") cameras, popular in the late 1800's. Multi-lens cameras, panorama cameras, and other early oddities will also sell quickly.

If you want to sell a camera, provide the following information in your first letter:

(1) Brand name, and model name if you know it;
(2) All numbers on the body of the camera;
(3) The name of the brand of lens, and any numbers and other information printed around the front circumference of the lens;
(4) Whether or not the camera works;
(5) Whether or not the camera seems to be complete;
(6) Whether the case and camera are covered with wood, metal, leather or cloth...and its condition;
(7) Whether or not the camera has a folding cloth or leather bellows; if it does, the bellows' color;
(8) A list of accessories with the camera, such as lenses, boxes, instructions, etc.

Kodak cameras with built in flash are not collectible, but many brand-name German and Japanese 35mm cameras from the 1930's, 40's and 50's are. A few of them bring prices above $1,000. They are well worth your time.

Don't try to clean your camera or the lens. You're not helping...and you may cost yourself money. If there is old film in the camera, do not remove it. Whenever selling any equipment or mechanical devices, the less you do, the better off you are.

CAMERAS

☆ **Unusual and early cameras** including panorama cameras, wide angles, subminiatures, hidden cameras, and oddly shaped or novelty cameras such as those shaped like cartoon or advertising characters. When writing, include all names and numbers found on the lens. If the camera is unusual, make certain to take a picture of it or make a good sketch. Jim is author of *Collectors Guide to Kodak Cameras* and *Price Guide to Antique and Classic Cameras*.

      Jim McKeown, Centennial Photo
      11595 State Road 70
      Grantsburg, WI 54840
        (715) 689-2153

☆ **Cameras of brass, chrome, or wood** made before 1948. Anything interesting photographic, be it camera, book, or what have you, will be considered, including pre-1930 **photo magazines**, pre-1948 catalogs, and other ephemera. *No Polaroids.* Provide any numbers or names anywhere on the object. Describe condition of wood, leather, or metal. *Must* include an SASE. Available on Internet.

      Alan Voorhees, Cameras & Such
      492 Breesport Road
      Horseheads, NY 14845
        (607) 739-7898

☆ **Cameras.** "I'll buy complete camera collections and complete camera shops." Has a special interest in:
- **35mm cameras** by *Leica, Nixon, Canon, Voigtlander* and *Zeiss.*
- **Large format press** and view cameras, lenses, roll-backs, etc.
- **16mm movie cameras** by *Angenieux, Arriflex, Beaulieu, Bolex* and *Mitchell* only;
- *Polaroid* **passport** cameras with more than one lens;
- *Polaroid* models 180, 190, and 195 ONLY;
- **3-D** cameras and all accessories and advertising;
- **Subminiature cameras;**
- *Kodak* **"ladies'" cameras** in various colors (plus accessories);
- Art Deco styled cameras.

"An early *Canon* with a pop-up viewfinder is worth up to $5,000 to me, as are some *Nikon* and *Leica* cameras." *Kodak* Brownies, built-in flash cameras, anything made of plastic, and 16mm home movie cameras and projectors are all worthless to him.

      Harry Poster
      PO Box 1883
      South Hackensack, NJ 07606
        (201) 794-9606 weekdays before 7 pm

☆ *Kodak* **cameras, advertising, and memorabilia.** "I'll buy only pre-1930 cameras in near mint condition, especially those with original cardboard or wooden cartons. I'll also buy just the empty cartons!" Frank's list of cameras he seeks is too long to print here, but if you deal in cameras or if you have an old *Kodak*, it might be worth picking up his wants list. He also wants a *Kodiopticon* **slide projector**, and cameras made by companies absorbed by *Kodak* including *Poco, Columbus, Ludigraph, Kameret* and **Rochester Optical's** *Empire State View* camera. *Kodak* newspaper and magazine advertising before 1930 may also find a buyer, as will counter top advertising, posters, signs, wood framed pictures of people using *Kodaks*, and any of the hundreds of items with the *Kodak* logo. "If it says *'Kodak'* on it, I want to know about it. That includes books which use *Kodak* as part of the title, advertising in foreign languages, instruction books, stock certificates from any camera company, *Kodak* annual reports, and anything else that is old, in fine condition and related to *Kodak.*"

Frank Storey
324 School Lane
Linthicum, MD 21090
(410) 850-5728 eves

☆ **Cameras** are wanted, but only the rare, unusual, or very early (pre-1880), especially stereo, multiple lens, and panoramic. Cameras hidden inside other objects are of great interest, as are the very small cameras called subminiatures. Not interested in modern 35mm cameras or in *Kodak, Ansco,* or *Polaroid.* Give make, model, and names and numbers printed around the lens.

Russell Norton
PO Box 1070
New Haven, CT 06504
(203) 562-7800

☆ **Cameras, accessories, and photographic literature.** Wants early or unusual cameras and photo accessories, photography books, catalogs of photo equipment, advertising for cameras and film, and miscellaneous photographic ephemera such as lapel pins, buttons, *Kodak* items.

Nicholas Graver
276 Brooklawn Drive
Rochester, NY 14618
(716) 244-4818

Most Kodak *and* Polaroid *still cameras have little if any value, although commemorative, colored, and very early* Kodak *cameras are worth inquiry. 16mm home movie cameras and projectors have little value.*

VIEW-MASTER & 3-D EQUIPMENT

☆ *View-Master* **reels and equipment** made by *Sawyers* or *GAF*, the companies that owned *View-Master* before 1980. Will buy single reels, 3-pack reels, cameras and accessories, *Stereomatic 500* projectors, and the blue Model B viewer (worth $100 to him). Also buys some *Tru-Vue* and other 3-D items. Pays from 25¢ to $50 per reel, with top money going to 3-D movie preview reels and reels of commercial advertising for popular products. The more obscure 3-reel packets (such as those for *The Munsters* or *The Addams Family*) can bring good money. Does not want any cartoon reels or any damaged, broken, or worn items. Give numbers on the reels and state their condition. If you have anything from View-Master that was intended for in-house or factory use and not for the public, make certain you inquire as it might be valuable.

> Walter Sigg
> PO Box 208
> Swartswood, NJ 07877

☆ **3-D cameras, reels, and other** *View-Master* **equipment,** including flash, close up lenses, cases, film cutters, 3-D projectors, library boxes, adjustable viewers, and old order lists from *Sawyers* or *GAF*, the manufacturers of *View-Master*. Wants early views with blue backs, view reels that look like they're hand printed, Belgian made scenic views, pre-1970 U.S., and scenics of other continents. "I don't want children's cartoon reels made after 1950 or any scratched or damaged reels." The reel number and copyright date are more important info than the title.

> Robert Gill
> PO Box 1223
> Seaford, NY 11783
> (516) 781-8741

☆ **3-D stereoscopic cameras and accessories** including viewers, projectors, manuals, and books by *Airequipt, Realist, Kodak, TDC, Wollensak, Busch, Radex, Brumberger, View-Master* and other makers. Also wants books which discuss 3-D photography and dealer displays which show any 3-D image. "I will pay over $1,000 for some special 3-D items such as the *Macro Realist* outfit by David White." *View-Master* reels are worth $1 to $5 each in fine condition.

> Harry Poster
> PO Box 1883
> South Hackensack, NJ 07606
> (201) 794-9606 weekdays until 7 pm

DON'T THROW AWAY OLD SOUVENIRS!

Collectors of "places" want a wide range of items. Many of the buyers in the next 14 pages are historians of their region and focus on photos and old documents, while others are just having fun collecting colorful doodads.

Value will be determined by the content of the photos and documents, along with age, scarcity and desirability. The value of photos and documents generally ranges from $5 to $50. Particularly rare and important photos will bring more, sometimes in the many thousands of dollars. Few photos fall in this category.

Some collectors seek products made in or traditionally associated with the region of the country in which they live. Great Lakes shipping, Western mining, Florida citrus, and the like. A few collectors want it all, including art native to their area, guidebooks, minor paper ephemera, stocks, photos and trinkets.

I have arranged buyers into geographic regions of the country in an effort to make it easier for you to find them.

HIGHWAY SOUVENIRS

☆ **Roadside ephemera.** Wants ephemera from **diners**, tourist courts, **motels**, gas stations, **drive-in theaters**, and **other roadside businesses**, with particular interest in those designed to serve the Lincoln Highway traveler between 1920 and 1970. Buys postcards, photos, guidebooks, advertising, roadside signs, and books and magazines having to do with road travel. Especially interested in Pennsylvania items and seeking all ephemera from the S.S. Grand View Ship Hotel.
> Brian Butke
> 2640 Sunset Drive
> West Mifflin, PA 15122

☆ **Pennsylvania Turnpike memorabilia of all kinds.** What have you? Please photocopy or send a photo with your description.
> J.C. Keyser
> PO Box 937
> Powell, OH 43065

NORTHEASTERN EPHEMERA

☆ **New Hampshire ephemera** from before 1900. Please price and include a photocopy.
> Alf Jacobson
> PO Box 188
> New London, NH 03257
> (603) 526-6654

☆ **Great Barrington, Massachusetts, and Berkshire County souvenirs** including pictorial china, plates, pins, salt & pepper shakers, spoons, cups, postcards, photos and especially souvenir china from the years 1905-1916. Towns to look for are Housatonic, Van Deusenville, Risingdale, Egremont, North Egremont, Stockbridge and Sheffield.
> Gary Leveille
> PO Box 562
> Great Barrington, MA 01230

☆ **Ocean Grove, New Jersey memorabilia** including souvenirs, maps, photos, postcards, books, glass, porcelain, and anything else from this camp meeting seaside resort located south of Asbury Park. "I want everything, including beach, hotels, auditorium, etc."
> Norman Buckman
> PO Box 608
> Ocean Grove, NJ 07756
> (800) 533-6163

☆ **Hoboken, New Jersey memorabilia** including paper ephemera, books, photographs, postcards, prints, maps, articles, letterheads, labels, and any manufactured item with the word HOBOKEN molded or printed on the item. "We buy almost everything, no matter how trivial, including **personal reminiscences of early Hoboken residents** for inclusion in various local histories we are writing." You have the Hans's permission to ship any early Hoboken item on approval. They pay postage both ways.
> Jim and Beverly Hans
> Hoboken Historical Museum
> Box M-1220
> Hoboken, NJ 07030
> (201) 653-7392

☆ **New Castle, Delaware** items of historic value are sought, including books, photos, postcards, etc.
> Mel Rosenthal
> 5 The Strand
> New Castle, DE 19720
> (302) 322-8944   (302) 322-3030

☆ **Adirondack Mountains memorabilia** including all books, paper ephemera, photographs, stereoviews, hotel brochures and registers, transportation timetables, manuscripts, maps, guidebooks, diaries, postcards, sheet music and prints related to any mountain towns and lakes of the Adirondacks. Lake George, Lake Placid, Lake Luzerne, Old Forge, Keene Valley, Plattsburgh, and the counties of Clinton, Herkimer, Essex, Lewis, Warren, St. Lawrence, Franklin, and Saratoga are among the many places which interest him.

> Breck Turner
> With Pipe and Book
> 91 Main Street
> Lake Placid, NY 12946
> (518) 523-9096

☆ **Wooden Adirondack souvenirs.** "I'll buy the weird and the wonderful! I'm seeking items made in the Adirondacks and sold all over America, usually stamped with the name of the place where they were sold." The distinguishing feature of these rustic wood souvenirs is the maker always left some bark on the piece. He wants **lamps, mugs, tankards, picture frames, smoker's stands, clocks, plaques, inkwells, towel racks, wishing wells**, and just about anything else except nut bowls and salt and pepper shakers. Many of these items had decals of Indians on them and better pieces had carvings of big game animals like moose or bears. He will also buy **miniature canoes and canoe paddles** and other birch bark items of all types. All items must be completely undamaged. Price and describe fully in your first letter.

> Barry Friedman
> 22725 Garzota Drive
> Valencia, CA 91355
> (805) 296-2318

☆ **Souvenir china and glass from western New York state,** especially Rochester, LeRoy, and Batavia, but other cities as well.

> Burton Spiller
> 49 Palmerston Road
> Rochester, NY 14618
> (716) 244-2229

☆ **Coney Island souvenirs** including Dreamland, Luna Park, and Steeplechase. He particularly wants pitchers, glasses, dishes, and other cream colored diamond and peg pattern custard glass marked CONEY IS-LAND. SASE appreciated.

> John Belinsky
> 84 Day Street
> Seymour, CT 06483
> (203) 888-2225

☆ **Junction Canal between Elmira, NY, and Athens, PA** (1856-1872). Wants photos and all ephemera of any type about this canal. Also items depicting or related to any branch extensions of the canal, such as that along the Susquehanna River in Pennsylvania.

> F.C. Petrillo
> 95 Miner Street
> Wilkes-Barre, PA 18702

SOUTHERN EPHEMERA

☆ **Tennessee small town souvenirs.** Buys a wide range of items including bottles, stoneware jugs of all sizes, real photo postcards of street scenes, merchant tokens, phone books, business letterheads (especially general merchandise stores), small size flour sacks, calendar plates, manufacturers' catalogs, miscellaneous souvenirs marked *Wheelock* or *JonRoth, Germany* on the reverse. No *Coca-Cola* bottles or current *Jack Daniels* reproductions, please. A typical complete description will be enough: size, material, colors, marks, and condition. Make certain to mention any cracks or chips, no matter how small.

> Paul Jarrett
> 111 West End Drive
> Waverly, TN 37185
> (615) 296-3151

☆ **Tennessee ephemera** wanted, including trade tokens, medals, pins, badges, real photo postcards of small towns, city business directories and phone books printed before 1950, Civil War tokens, city and county histories, and items from **the Tennessee Centennial Expo of 1897.** This major token collector asks that you describe your item well, including its condition. He is not interested in modern reproductions.

> Joe Copeland
> PO Box 4221
> Oak Ridge, TN 37831
> (615) 482-4215

☆ **Dawson Springs, Kentucky souvenirs from their Mineral Well Springs** including jugs, mugs, pottery, glass, pitchers, and plates. These souvenirs usually have a decal showing a hotel or the Mineral Well. "I will pay $150 for a wire handled white crockery jug which says SALOON on it." He is not interested in anything made after 1930, including reproductions made by *Jack Daniels*. Make certain to mention any cracks or chips, no matter how small.

> Paul Jarrett
> 111 West End Drive
> Waverly, TN 37185
> (615) 296-3151

☆ **Southern souvenirs, especially pictorial** china from before 1920, but also glass, postcards, sterling, and pottery decorated with names of Southern cities and places. Send long SASE for list of other souvenirs.
    Abbie Bush
    PO Box 503
    Elkader, IA 52043
       (319) 245-2128

☆ **Panoramic group photos** taken in North or South Carolina.
    Lew Powell
    700 East Park Ave.
    Charlotte, NC 28203

☆ **Charleston, South Carolina memorabilia** including letters and envelopes, maps, tokens and medals, books, pamphlets, postcards, stock certificates and other fiscal paper. Also any South Carolina item related to the Confederacy.
    Bob Karrer
    PO Box 6094
    Alexandria, VA 22306
       (703) 360-5105 eves

☆ **Great Smoky Mountains National Park** in NC and TN, before 1970. "I'll buy guidebooks, maps, photos, brochures, pamphlets, and similar paper ephemera including b/w real photo cards. Also souvenirs, especially plates and glassware associated with the Park. Also interested in similar items for the towns of **Gatlinburg and Townsend, TN, and the Cherokee Indian Reservation, in NC.** Not interested in any color postcards or in any materials from Chattanooga or Lookout Mountain," Photocopies appreciated.
    Doug Redding
    16532 Baederwood Lane
    Rockville, MD 20855
       (301) 926-6158

☆ **Georgia, South Carolina, and Florida paper pre-1870** that is related to **slavery, the Civil War,** indentures, King's grants, state grants, wills, or historically interesting topics. Georgia is of particular interest and documents can bring $100-$500 depending upon contents.
    John Parks
    203 Tanglewood Road
    Savannah, GA 31419
       (912) 925-6075

☆ **Eureka Springs, Arkansas souvenirs and paper ephemera.** Wants informative or colorful paper, plates, cups, spoons, etc., from this resort capitol of the Ozarks. Only pre-1930 items in fine condition.

    Janis Watson, Bank of Eureka Springs
    PO Box 309
    Eureka Springs, AR 72632
        (501) 253-8241

☆ **Eureka Springs, Arkansas, before 1920.** "Anything wanted from souvenirs to advertising, photographs to books, but I'll especially buy any information, maps, lawsuits, newspaper reports, etc., on the early land disputes in Eureka Springs. Also the Eureka Springs railroad. Also have strong interest in **Dr. Norman Baker's Cancer Hospital** in the Springs in the 1930's and will buy all ephemera related to it."

    Steve Chyrchel
    Route #2 Box 362
    Eureka Springs, AR 72632
        (501) 253-9244 voice and fax

☆ **Florida historical paper and memorabilia,** especially items from Fort Jefferson, Florida.

    Gordon McHenry
    PO Box 1117
    Osprey, FL 34229
        (813) 966-5563 Fax: (813) 966-5563

☆ **Orlando, Florida memorabilia.**

    Jerry Chicone
    PO Box 547636
    Orlando, FL 32854
        (407) 298-5550

☆ **Coral Gables, Florida souvenirs and advertising,** especially related to land sales.

    Sam LaRoue
    5980 SW 35th Street
    Miami, FL 33155
        (305) 347-7466

☆ **Puerto Rico.** Wants pre-1930 books, postcards, and other memorabilia of Puerto Rico. Please price and describe in your first letter.

    Frank Garcia
    13701 SW 66th Street #B-301
    Miami, FL 33183

MIDWESTERN EPHEMERA

☆ **Ohio memorabilia,** especially books, manuscripts, maps and photographs, from before 1900. Particularly interested in local history prior to the Civil War, especially in the Akron area.
>   Frank Klein
>   The Bookseller
>   521 West Exchange Street
>   Akron, OH 44302
>   (216) 762-3101   Fax: (216) 762-4413

☆ **Waukesha, Wisconsin memorabilia.** Waukesha was noted for its spring waters and a number of food products, so keep your eyes open for all sorts of things marked as being from Waukesha.
>   W.E. Schwanz
>   S. 45 W22339 Quinn Road
>   Waukesha, WI 53186
>   (414) 542-8586   (414) 333-9127

☆ **Michigan and the Great Lakes** ephemera and historically inter-esting paper goods of all types from that region.
>   Jay Platt, West Side Book Shop
>   113 West Liberty
>   Ann Arbor, MI 48104
>   (313) 995-1891

☆ **Midwestern souvenir china** from before 1920, especially from Iowa. "All good items from all Iowa towns, especially Colfax, Clayton and Elkader are sought." Send a long SASE for her wants list.
>   Abbie Bush
>   PO Box 503
>   Elkader, IA 52043
>   (319) 245-2128

☆ **Iowa souvenirs.** "Always interested in all Iowa souvenirs, especially china. Towns of Colfax, Ackley and Sibley are particularly wanted, but all nice Iowa pieces will be considered."
>   Mary Yohe
>   6827 South Juniper
>   Tempe, AZ 85283
>   (602) 820-7442

☆ **Humboldt or Rutland, Iowa** pictorial postcards and advertising from those two towns.
>   Don Olson
>   PO Box 245
>   Humboldt, IA 50548

☆ **Trade tokens and dog licenses from Iowa.**
  Dennis Schulte
  8th Avenue NW
  Waukon, IA 52172
    (319) 568-3628 before 10 p.m.

☆ **Rockford, Freeport, and Belvidere Illinois tokens, medals,** buttons, badges, ribbons, and other small flat collectibles. Also banks, early signs, coffee tins, bottles, etc. Loves to find larger items marked as being from Rockford. No paper or cardboard items.
  Rich Hartzog
  PO Box 4143 BFT
  Rockford, IL 61110
    (815) 226-0771

☆ **Dakota Territory, South Dakota, North Dakota, Minnesota, Wyoming, and Montana photographs and small ephemera** from before 1930 in any format, including real photo postcards. Wants all historically or pictorially interesting paper ephemera, advertising, letters, books, bottles, and small objects. Especially wants items marked DT, DAKOTA TERRITORY, DAK or SOUTH DAKOTA. Buys single items or collections. Is often as interested in the photographers as the subject matter of the photo. Photocopies are recommended. If your items are in fine condition, you may ship them on approval.
  Robert Kolbe
  1301 South Duluth
  Sioux Falls, SD 57105
    (605) 332-9662

When writing about these generally inexpensive items, include an envelope addressed to yourself with the appropriate postage. If you are sending pictures and it takes two stamps, it will take two stamps to return them. Always indicate whether you want pictures returned.

I called these "generally inexpensive," but there are valuable photos, catalogs, bottles, and china out there...items worth more than $100 each. That's why I always advise getting advice from people you find in **Trash or Treasure**.

WESTERN EPHEMERA

☆ **Western U.S. paper ephemera** (1840-1920) related to the military, early forts, ghost towns, Mormons, railroads, mining, banking, cowboys, Indians, lawmen, cattle, courts, and financial matters. Buys letters about the West, autographs of famous Westerners, and most illustrated pre-1920 Western documents such as checks, stocks, and the like. Subscription to his 6 annual sales catalogs is $15.

> Warren Anderson
> America West Archives
> PO Box 100
> Cedar City, UT 84720
> (801) 586-9497

☆ **Dallas ephemera** pre-1915, including pamphlets, letters, documents, postcards, photos, and items related to **the Texas State Fair.** *The Artwork of Dallas* folio will bring $300 or more.

> Ron Pearson
> 10620 Creekmere Drive
> Dallas, TX 75218
> (214) 321-9717

☆ **Maps of Texas** from before 1900. Also trail driving maps.

> Johnny Spellman
> 10806 North Lamar
> Austin, TX 78753
>   (512) 836-2889 days   (512) 258-6910 eves

☆ **Colorado mining memorabilia,** 1859-1915, especially Cripple Creek and all other mining towns and camps and the railroads that served them. Wants photos, stereoviews, advertising, letterheads, billheads, brochures, pamphlets, mining papers, stock certificates, maps, badges, candlesticks, souvenirs, and other small items marked with the name of one of these towns. Photos should be of mining, railroad, or downtown activities, not people or scenery. Albums with numerous photos eagerly sought, as are business or mining directories and books on Colorado mining. Does not want *anything* from the flatland Colorado towns like Denver, Pueblo or Colorado Springs, nor anything from state or national parks. Give whatever info is printed or written on the backs of photos.

> George Foott
> 6683 South Yukon Way
> Littleton, CO 80123
>   (303) 979-8688

☆ **Colorado and Wyoming memorabilia** from 1860 to 1930. Wants real photo and advertising postcards, souvenirs, "good for" trade tokens, stereoviews, envelopes and letterheads, fancy whiskey bottles, posters, calendars, trade cards, political buttons, ephemera from the Leadville Ice Palace, *any* item from the 1908 Democratic National Convention held in Denver, items from military forts, and items from fairs, rodeos, and Cheyenne Frontier Days. All items *must* be from Wyoming or Colorado within the 1860-1930 time frame. "I do not want items from National Parks, items after 1930, newspapers, or magazines. Please give a complete description." He emphasizes, "Please do not send unsolicited items."

> Edward Marriott
> 9191 East Oxford Drive
> Denver, CO 80237
> (303) 779-5237

☆ **Nevada and Death Valley ephemera** including books, newspapers, magazines, diaries, letters, maps, promotional brochures, "and anything else printed or written on paper." Also stereoviews, merchant tokens, dog tags, hunting licenses, photos, postcards and what have you. He requests prices but will make offers.

> Gil Schmidtmann
> Route #1   Box 371
> Mentone, CA 92359
> (909) 794-1211

☆ **Las Vegas, Nevada souvenirs and memorabilia** from before 1970. Buys gambling tokens and chips, casino playing cards, match covers, postcards, stationery, plates, ashtrays, buttons, charms, menus, business directories, showroom programs, magazines with stories about Las Vegas history, paintings, prints, photos, and all sorts of other minor trinkets and souvenirs. Also interested in photos of Las Vegas celebrities. Will consider other ephemera from this desert playground.

> Marc Weiser
> PO Box 28730
> Las Vegas, NV 89126
> (702) 871-8686

☆ **All Montana memorabilia** from before 1950 is wanted, including maps, photos, postcards, stationery, tokens, and other ephemera but especially items related to banks and finance including bank bags, letterheads, documents, stocks, checks and scrip.

> Douglas McDonald
> PO Box 350093
> Grantsdale, MT 59835
> (406) 363-3202

☆ **Montana memorabilia of all types**, with a particular interest in Great Falls, and its breweries and famous saloons like *The Mint* and the *Silver Dollar*. Among Montana items he wants are:
- Photos of saloons, cowboys, Indians, etc.;
- Tokens;
- Advertising from Montana companies, especially saloons and breweries;
- Books about Montana;
- Paper ephemera from Montana Territory.

This 25 year veteran prefers you to set the price you want, but you may ask for offers if you provide a good description.

> Jim Combs
> 417 27th Street NW
> Great Falls, MT 59404
> (406) 761-3320

☆ **Montana, New Mexico, Nevada, Utah and Wyoming** souvenirs are wanted including china, glass, sterling silver, postcards, pottery, and other small items originating in those states. SASE for wants list.

> Abbie Bush
> PO Box 503
> Elkader, IA 52043
> (319) 245-2128

☆ **Idaho, Montana, and Washington items** including trade tokens, postcards, letterheads, calendars, buttons, ribbons, wooden nickels, stocks, match holders, calendar plates and other advertising china. Pays $1-$3 for postcards with postmarks from obscure post offices. Pays $2-$10 for cards of small towns he can use. Nothing after 1930.

> Mike Fritz
> 1542 Stevens Street
> Rathdrum, ID 83858
> (208) 687-0159

☆ **Yakima County, Washington, items.** "I buy pre-1950 photos, phone books, newspapers, directories, souvenirs, promotional booklets, and postcards, but no chrome faced postcards." Yakima HS yearbooks from pre-1910, 1933-34, and 1953-54 are also wanted. If in doubt, send for his wants list of 28 towns he seeks.

> Ron Ott
> 10 North 45th Ave.
> Yakima, WA 98908
> (509) 965-3385

☆ **San Francisco Bay area ephemera** pre-1910, especially related to the 1906 quake. Photos, diaries, letters, family mementos, and the like are wanted with emphasis on unusual. Ron has particular interest in items associated with schools and education before 1906 and in meal tickets and other items related to life in relief camps immediately after the disaster. No newspapers, postcards, or checks. Ron heads the S.F. History Ass'n and can accept tax deductible gifts from any period.

> Ron Ross
> 1982-A Fulton Street
> San Francisco, CA 94117
> (415) 752-9704

☆ **Central California beach towns** of Pismo Beach (also spelled Pizmo/Pizmu), Shell Beach, Oceano, Avila Beach, Port San Luis, Cambria, Los Osos, and Morro Bay. Especially photos and stereoviews, but will consider anything interesting. Please Xerox™ what you have.

> Tony Hyman
> Box 3028
> Pismo Beach, CA 93448

☆ **San Bernardino, California items** from buildings, fairs, and resorts. Wants ceramic souvenirs including cups, plates, sterling silver spoons, badges, ribbons, pins, etc. Particularly interested in items associated with the 1903 Street Fair, 1908 Festival of the Arrowhead, 1910 Centennial, and the National Orange Show, from 1911 to 1920.

> Gary Crabtree
> PO Box 3843
> San Bernardino, CA 92413
> (909) 862-8534

☆ **San Gabriel Valley, California items.** Wants pre-1930 items from any San Gabriel Valley towns: Arcadia, Temple City, El Monte, San Gabriel, Baldwin Park, Rosemead, Pasadena, Covina, San Marino, Monrovia, Duarte and Azusa. Also wants anything related to **Emperor Norton** and **Lucky Baldwin**. He suggests you ship your items to him via UPS at 650 West Duarte, #309, to get his offer.

> SC Coin & Stamp Co.
> PO Drawer 3069
> Arcadia, CA 91006
> (800) 367-0779

☆ **San Diego, California,memorabilia** including postcards, pamphlets and photographs.

> Ralph Bowman's Paper Gallery
> 5349 Wheaton Street
> La Mesa, CA 91942
> (619) 462-6268

☆ **Alaska and Yukon memorabilia.** Wants real photo postcards, salmon cans and labels, advertising mirrors, matchbook covers, trade tokens, ashtrays, cards, maps, dishes and brochures about Alaska, Alaskan industry and Alaskan steamshipping. "You name it and I want it." Will be happy to answer any questions about Alaska collectibles. Send a Xerox™ copy if you'd like an offer. You have his permission to send pre-1940 Alaska and Yukon items on approval.
> W.E. "Nick" Nickell
> 102 Peoples Wharf
> Juneau, AK 99801
>> (907) 586-1733

☆ **Alaskan memorabilia.** "I'll buy nearly anything old about Alaska, the Yukon, or the Polar Region including postcards books, maps, photographs, letters, souvenirs, china, spoons, and miscellaneous ephemera. I buy for resale, and seldom buy items newer than 1945."
> Richard Wood, Alaska Heritage Books
> PO Box 22165
> Juneau, AK 99802
>> (907) 789-8450 voice and fax

☆ **Alaskan memorabilia.** Wants license plates, postcards (not scenery), Klondike novelty material, brochures from the Alaskan & Canadian Railroad & Steamship lines, and "all very early newspapers, photographs, and printed matter." Does not want Alaska-Yukon Exposition material. Give description, condition, date of origin, and indicate what cities, towns, or regions are featured. Do not send items unsolicited. Will send a wants list for SASE.
> Reed Fitzpatrick
> PO Box 369
> Vashon, WA 98070
>> (206) 463-3900 8am to 4pm

☆ **Hawaiian items** that can be resold in a shop specializing in Hawaiian souvenirs, photos, menus, lithographs, paintings, fiction and non-fiction books, magazines devoted to Hawaii (especially *Holiday*), postcards, souvenirs, salt and pepper shakers, hula lamps, hula dolls and nodders, bolts of material and Hawaiian ukeleles. The more colorful the better. Does not want other islands, items after 1970, Hawaiian shirts, vinyl hula dolls, C&H dolls, damaged postcards, or paper with parts or pages missing. Items must be in condition for resale. Your description should include dimensions and a brief history. Not interested in hearing about anything that you are not willing to sell now. Some items, especially art, will have to be examined before final payment,
> Susan Mast
> 849 Almar Avenue #C-270
> Santa Cruz, CA 95060
>> (408) 423-7001 voice and fax   (408) 423-9786 eves

☆ **Hawaii, South Seas and Samoa ephemera.** Wants:
- Books before 1920 about Hawaii, written by Hawaiians,
   or printed in Hawaii;
- Magazines from 1940 or earlier with stories of Hawaii;
- Paintings and prints of Hawaii, the South Pacific, or Asia;
- Printed ephemera of any type before 1920 about these areas;
- Oriental block prints, tapa cloth, ethnographic carvings from the
   South Pacific, and any other art of this region of the world;
- Photographs of Hawaii, South Pacific or Asia before 1940;
- Postcards mailed from, or depicting, this region;
- Diaries or manuscripts about this area;
- Whaling souvenirs;
- Jewelry, pottery, and jade from these areas.

And other memorabilia from Hawaii or the South Pacific, as long as it's
pre-1920. Send insured. No Hula dolls or Hawaiian shirts.

> Bernie Berman
> 755 Isenberg Street #305
> Honolulu, HI 96826
> (808) 941-8639

FOREIGN EPHEMERA

☆ **Canadian items:** calendars, stock certificates, bank notes, old letters in original envelopes, fancy letterheads, all Canadian railway, merchants' tokens from Western Canada, Canadian military or law enforcement, and postcards of BC, Yukon, NWT, AB, SK, and
Newfoundland. Nothing after 1950, please. No road maps, tourist
brochures, and postcards of tourist attractions or scenery. Prefers items
be sent on approval or a photocopy made and included in your letter.

> Michael Rice
> PO Box 286
> Saanichton, BC V8M 2C5 CANADA
> (604) 652-9047 eves

☆ **Panama Canal Zone and the Isthmus of Panama memorabilia**
including postcards, letters, stamped envelopes, scrapbooks, tokens,
medals, maps, coins, stamps, and everything else including souvenirs.
Especially likes pre-1915 picture postcards with cancellations from obscure Panama post offices. "I usually offer to buy anything Isthmus."
Bob is the long time editor of a newsletter for Isthmus collectors.

> Bob Karrer
> PO Box 6094
> Alexandria, VA 22306
> (703) 360-5105

☆ **Bermuda ephemera** including photographs, stereoviews, real photo postcards (worth up to $100), travel brochures, hotel stationery, luggage labels, guide books, maps, posters, phone directories, china plates with scenes of Bermuda, sterling silver souvenir spoons, and books. Does not want items after 1950. Describe "well enough for me to know exactly what I am buying." Dealers, price your goods.

> Ernest Roberts
> 5 Corsa Street
> Dix Hills, NY 11746

☆ **Cuban memorabilia** before Castro including coins, stamps, money, historical documents, postcards, souvenir spoons, maps, stocks and bonds, lottery tickets, cigar bands, military decorations and insignia, "or any other collectible items including those related to the Spanish domination of the Island." He'll pay from $80-$400 for the 10, 20 and 50 peso bank notes of 1869. There is a 1916 coin and a 1944 banknote each worth more than $50,000, so it could pay you to look.

> Manuel Alvarez
> 1735 SW 8th Street
> Miami, FL 33135
> (305) 649-1176

☆ **Brazil.** Books, photos, and paper ephemera from the colonial period through 1945. Especially interested in travel and exploration books with early information about Rio de Janeiro and/or the Amazon. Also wants letters and diaries of military personnel who served in Brazil during WWII or in the Joint Brazil-U.S. Military Commission. Material may be in any language. Please include your phone number.

> Lee Harrer
> 1908 Seagull Drive
> Clearwater, FL 34624
> (813) 536-4029 evenings

☆ **Philippine Islands.** "I'll buy postcards, photos, books, magazines, maps, and other paper items, especially real photo postcards from Manila or elsewhere in the Philippines. I don't want coins, stamps, paper money, or books on the Spanish American War."

> Michael G. Price
> PO Box 7071
> Ann Arbor, MI 48107
> (517) 764-4517

☆ **Australia and Antarctica items from before 1920,** including prints, maps, photographs, ship's logs, scholarly ethnographic studies, novels, travel books, children's books, postcards and paper ephemera.

> David and Cathy Lilburne, Antipodean Books
> PO Box 189
> Cold Spring, NY 10516

☆ **Antarctic and Arctic ephemera** especially books but also diaries, posters, photographs, letters, pamphlets and *Aurora Austrailis*, the Antarctic newspaper 1907-09. Will buy any clean copies of the latter.
> Jay Platt, West Side Book Shop
> 113 West Liberty
> Ann Arbor, MI 48104
> (313) 995-1891 days

☆ **Arctic and Antarctic exploration items:** diaries, journals, articles, newspaper accounts, and memorabilia from expeditions. Send Xerox.
> Everen T. Brown
> PO Box 296
> Salt Lake City, UT 84110
> Fax: (801) 364-2646

☆ **Greenland, Pitcairn Island, Hudson's Bay, Canada, Mexico, and other countries' ephemera** especially tokens and medals, but other small items, especially before 1930 are likely to be of interest. Your best bet is to photocopy what you have.
> Rich Hartzog
> World Exonumia
> PO Box 4143 BFT
> Rockford, IL 61110
> (815) 226-0771

☆ **Micronesia, Polynesia, and New Guinea ethnographic materials,** masks, ceremonial bowls, and the like. Also maps, mariner's charts, voyage books, and ship's logs from vessels traveling in that region, in any language. Some interest in scrimshaw associated with the Pacific.
> David and Cathy Lilburne
> Antipodean Books
> PO Box 189
> Cold Spring, NY 10516
> (914) 424-3867   Fax: (914) 424-3617

☆ **Switzerland ephemera** including books, medals, badges, emblems, postcards from before 1930, travel brochures, luggage labels, boxed stereoviews, trade cards, maps, prints posters and other collectibles.
> Donald Tritt
> 4072 Goose Lane
> Granville, OH 43023
> (614) 587-0213 eves

☆ **Russian and Slavic antiquarian items** including books, art, sculpture, paintings, silver, swords, Cossack militaria and photos, with a special interest in items from early Siberia. Note that only items from pre-Soviet Russia are wanted, not items after 1917. Give a good description. No ordinary samovars, Soviet items, or items in poor condition. Only high grade pieces are wanted.

> Igor G. Kozak
> East-West Features Service
> PO Box 15067
> Washington, DC 20003
> (301) 236-5966

☆ **Imperial Russian antiques** and memorabilia whether civil, military, or religious. Buys pre-1917 Russian:
- Orders, decorations, badges, buttons, medals, and other militaria;
- Porcelains, bronzes, icons, prints, paintings and graphic arts;
- Coronation and other commemorative memorabilia.

Items are bought for cash or brokered. "Please send a clear photo or photocopy and details, including price wanted." Mail order catalog and appraisal services available. No Soviet items are wanted.

> ART Co.
> PO Box 278183
> Sacramento, CA 95826
> (916) 366-8850

☆ **Hong Kong, Macao, China and Singapore** postcards, stamps, envelopes, mass transit railway tickets, and phone cards. He does not want stamps after 1990 or modern postcards. Xerox™ both sides and give your phone. Stamps and postcards range from $5-$100, commemorative railway tickets bring $10 to $100, regular tickets $10 or less. Dealers should price their goods.

> Kin Leung Liu
> PO Box 94056
> Seattle, WA 98124
> (206) 768-1389   Fax: (206) 767-3025

☆ **Asian books and paper ephemera:** books, maps, photos, prints and paintings on Japan, China, Korea, Vietnam, Tonking, Siam, Cambodia, Laos, Burma, Malaya, Singapore, Indonesia, Philippines, Formosa, Taiwan, Tibet, Mongolia, Manchuria, New Guinea, South-East Asia and the Far East.

> Jerry Stanoff
> Rare Oriental Book Co.
> PO Box 1599
> Aptos, CA 95001
> (408) 724-4911   Fax: (408) 761-1350

MAGAZINES CAN BE MINOR TREASURE

People are attracted to magazines for many reasons. Some buy for the covers and illustrations. Others look for early articles or advertising relevant to their hobby. Some folks just collect magazines!

To describe items for sale, give the name and date of the magazines and note all tears, creases, address stickers, writing, or anything else affecting the cover or contents. If you have many issues, list them, counting only those with covers and pictures intact, no water damage, and no mildew smell. Describe the condition of a typical issue.

If you offer a magazine to someone because of an article contained in it, give the name and date of the magazine, the author of the article, and the number of illustrations. It's a good idea to photocopy the cover.

Collectors who buy books, magazines, photos, maps, postcards and other paper items tend to be fussy about condition. Don't overestimate the condition of a magazine. What you think of as "normal wear" can be "serious damage" to any paper collector. If you you find a magazine with pictures cut out, it's likely that others in the pile will also be cut.

DESCRIBING CONDITION OF MAGAZINES

VF (very fine) = fresh, bright copy without flaws except for minor aging of paper;

F (fine) = bright copy with very minor wear and only minute cover tears or creases;

VG (very good) = cover and spine wear, tiny tears and creases, minor chipping , browning of paper;

G (good) = obvious cover and spine wear, discoloration, water stains, pieces missing, tears up to 1" long;

FA (fair) = tight and complete, but longer creases, tears, rubbing, fading, and/or store stamps or dates;

P (poor) = many defects, serious damage, well worn; referred to as a "reading copy," not us a collectiblo.

MAGAZINES

☆ **Volume 1, Number 1 (first issue) magazines,** newspapers, comic books, or miscellaneous publications including newsletters, catalogs, fan publications, etc. Also buys pre-publication issues, dummies, proofs and premier issues. "When I don't buy, I will try to help the seller find someone else who might."

> Stan Gold
> 7042 Dartbrook
> Dallas, TX 75240
> (214) 239-8621

☆ **Most magazines in quantity** if before 1950 and most newer **movie, fashion** and quality **photography** magazines. Has a particular interest in erotica, nudity, and spicier men's publications except *Playboy* and similar general newsstand magazines. Give quantity of each title and a description. They don't want *National Geographic* after 1910, *Reader's Digest* after 1930, *Life* after 1936, *Arizona Highways* after 1940, or *American Heritage* hardcovers. One of the largest magazine dealers, they will pick them up if you have a truckload.

> The Antiquarian Bookstore
> 1070 Lafayette Road
> Portsmouth, NH 03801
> (603) 436-7250

☆ **Women's, children's, theater, motorcycle, farm, and many other illustrated magazines, including pulps, 1895 to 1930.** Titles such as *Collier's, Esquire, Vogue, Saturday Evening Post, Vanity Fair, American* and others are wanted. Buys **movie and men's adventure** magazines up to 1960. Does not want magazines from 1970's or 80's. Give the date, condition, and price you'd like. Most of these magazines do not have extreme value. Denis publishes *The Illustrator Collector News* ($17/year), offers a large catalog of magazines for sale, and produces many reasonably priced price guides to magazines and magazine illustrators. Send SASE for info. Denis makes his information available in many different publications. He does not give free appraisals. "I'm happy to talk to you if you're seriously buying or selling, but I don't have time for pen pals or time wasters."

> Denis Jackson
> PO Box 1958
> Sequim, WA 98382
> (206) 683-2559 voice and fax

☆ **Movie magazines** before 1960. Xerox© the covers.

> Claude Held
> PO Box 515
> Buffalo, NY 14225

☆ **Bound volumes of illustrated fashion and other magazines** including *Graham's, Godey's Ladies Magazine,* and others published before 1880. Wants *Craftsman* (1900-1915), *Ladies Home Journal, Delineator, Woman's Home Companion, Vogue* and *Saturday Evening Post* from 1910-1922. Condition is important. Note cracks, tears, foxing. Include SASE for answer.

> John Rosenhoover
> 100 Mandalay Road
> Chicopee, MA 01020

☆ **Fashion magazines** from 1890 to 1910, including *Harper's Bazaar, Delineator,* and others. Also buys pictures, postcards, and catalogs showing women's fashions of that period.

> Cheryl Abel
> 103 Jacqueline Ave.
> Delran, NJ 08075

☆ **Men's outdoor magazines.** "We are active and good buyers in need of magazines on hunting, fishing, archery, hunting dogs, and guns. We buy *Stoeger Shooter's Bibles* (1924-1949), *Gun Digests* (1944-1962) and gun and fishing tackle catalogs (1850-1949). We will currently purchase all fine copies, including current years, of *Guns, Man at Arms, Gun Report, Gun World, Arms and the Man, World & Recreation, Rifle, Shooting and Fishing, Shooting Times, American Angler, Handloader, Guns and Ammo* and certain issues of other similar magazines. Special wants include *Chicago Field* (1876-1880), *Forest & Stream* before 1930, *Sports Afield* before 1932, *Field and Stream* before 1920, *Outdoor Life* before 1920 and others. We need magazines in fine condition, both covers as originally attached, with no bad musty smell, and nothing cut out. Sometimes in the case of very old and scarce magazines we can use them in less than fine condition. Don't ship anything in advance as our wants change over time."

> Lewis Razek
> PO Box 1246
> Traverse City, MI 49684
> (616) 271-3898

☆ **Men's outdoor magazines** including *Field & Stream, Outdoor Life* pre-1920, and *Sports Afield* before 1932.

> Thomas McKinnon
> PO Box 86
> Wagram, NC 28396
> (910) 369-2367

☆ *Sports Illustrated* and other sports magazines from before 1970.
Gary Alderman
PO Box 9164
Madison, WI 53715
(608) 274-3527   Fax: (608) 277-1999

☆ **Magazines about diving and underwater activities.** Buys foreign and domestic magazines such as *Skin Diver, Aquarius, Diver,
Scuba Times, Sport Diver, Ocean Realm,* etc. No books, hardcover or
soft. Also interested in old Mike Nelson *Sea Hunt* comic books and
Primus comic books.
Thomas Szymanski
5 Stoneybrook Lane
Exeter, NH 03833
(603) 772-6372

☆ **Scandal and exploitation magazines** from 1952-1973 including
but not limited to *Behind the Scenes, Bunk!, Celebrity, Exposed,
Hollywood Tattler, Hush-Hush, Inside Story, The Lowdown, Naked
Truth, Sensation, Top Secret, TV Scandals, Untold Secrets,* and
Whisper. "I'll pay $35 each for complete issues of *Inside Stuff* from the
1930's." Also wants *Police Gazette* in good condition, especially
bound. Nothing current, soiled, damaged or with pages clipped. Give
title, date, and volume.
Gordon Hasse
Box 1543 Grand Central Station
New York, NY 10163-1543

☆ *Esquire* **magazine,** 1933-1959. Also buys *Playboy* **pre-1960** only,
True, and complete years of *Cosmopolitan, McCalls, Vogue, Ladies
Home Journal, Woman's Home Companion, Redbook,* **Saturday
Evening Post***, Country Gentlemen* and *Collier's*. List the years and the
condition of the covers and magazines. Do they smell musty?
Charles Martignette
PO Box 293
Hallandale, FL 33009

☆ *TV Guide* and other TV log magazines, 1948-1970. Selected U.S. issues from 1971-1994 and Canadian issues 1977-1994 are also purchased. Also wants early local editions, and all weekly newspaper TV supplement magazines from any period. Issues of NY City's *Television Guide* from 1948 are worth $25-$50 each. Note if there is a mailing label on the cover, and if it affects the picture.

    Jeffrey Kadet
    PO Box 20
    Macomb, IL 61455
    (309) 833-1809

☆ *TV Guide* **magazine** from before 1970, and Fall Preview issues up to 1985. Also wants other TV and movie magazines, and publicity photographs from TV shows. Will buy, sell, or trade **videotape of TV shows** no longer on air.

    Douglas Cowles
    2966 West Talara Lane
    Tucson, AZ 85741
    (602) 297-9062

☆ *Humorama* **magazine.** Pays $1 and up. Give dates and condition.

    Jeff Patton
    3621 Carolina Street NW
    Massillon, OH 44646

☆ **National Geographic Society publications of all types.** Buys magazines, books, maps, article reprints, atlases, pictorials, school bulletins, advertising, invitations, slides, videos, postcards, and calendars produced by the NGS. Also buys materials published by other companies with articles about the NGS, which spoof the NGS, are funded by the NGS, or in any way refer to the NGS. He particularly wants magazines before 1913, technical books such as that on Machu Picchu (he'll pay $1,000) and the complete advertising brochure sent to prospective members in 1888. He'll pay you $5,000 for a Vol. 1, No. 1 magazine. **No magazines after 1959.** Nick buys outright or accepts items on consignment. He encourages correspondence from buyers and sellers.

    Nick Koopman, Collectors Exchange
    10600 Lowery Drive
    Raleigh, NC 27615

☆ **Crossword and other puzzle magazines** before 1970. "It doesn't matter if they're filled in." Give the name, date and condition. The first 18 issues of *The Eastern Enigma* are worth $1,000.

    Will Shortz
    55 Great Oak Lane
    Pleasantville, NY 10570
    (914) 769-9128 voice and fax

PULP MAGAZINES

☆ **Pulp magazines.** Buys many types, especially hero, superhero and character pulps such as *The Shadow, The Spider, Doc Savage, Captain Hazard, Captain Zero, The Wizard, Wu Fang,* etc. Also aviation pulps like *G-8, Dusty Ayres, Battle Aces* and similar titles. Other collectible pulp categories are detective, spicy, terror, and odd like *Gun Molls* and *Speakeasy Stories.* Not interested in romance or Westerns. Give the title, date, and overall condition. Include your phone number. Please don't ask about comic books or family magazines like *Post, Life* or *Readers Digest.* Also buys **items related to pulp magazines and characters** including pins, badges, rings, membership cards, art, displays, and autographs of writers and artists.

     Jack Deveny
     6805 Cheyenne Trail
     Edina, MN 55439

☆ **Pulp magazines.** Buys nearly 1,000 titles: **adventure, aviation, crime and detective, hero, mystery and menace, Western, science fiction and fantasy, romance, spicy, sports, confession**, and others. Give the title, date, and condition of each magazine, with emphasis on the condition and graphic appearance of the cover.

     Jim Steranko
     PO Box 974
     Reading, PA 19603

☆ **Pulp magazines.** Buys mystery, detective, spicy, adventure, superhero and character pulps such as *The Shadow, The Spider, Gun Molls, Dime Detective, Doc Savage, Black Mask,* and similar. Not interested in romance or Westerns. Give the title, date, and overall condition. Include your phone number. Offers $1,000 for the October 1912 *All Story* in very good condition.

     Claude Held
     PO Box 515
     Buffalo, NY 14225

Pulp magazines are lurid fiction magazines popular in the teens, twenties, thirties, and forties. As you can tell from reading about these three buyers, they came in many titles. They were usually approximately 6 1/2" x 10", printed on newsprint, and had colorful covers. The paper and covers are often very fragile today because they used such poor paper stock. Handle them with care, as some can be quite valuable. I found two magazines in an old barn, sent them off, and got the easiest $30 I ever made.

NEWSPAPERS ARE SELDOM WORTH MUCH.

Newspapers seldom sell for much money, even if they're over 100 years old. A whole year of the London Gazette from 1800 is only worth about $300. Some 19th and early 20thcentury publications are important, however, because they contain the first printing of stories by famous writers. In some cases, it is artwork found in the papers which has itself become collectible. The newspapers that are always welcome are illustrated weeklies like Harper's and Leslie's from 1855-1900.

To describe a paper you wish to sell give the name, city, date, number and size of pages, and mention any significant stories. If bound, indicate the type and condition of the binding (leather or boards, loose, split, leather crumbling, etc.). If it is a small town 18th or 19th century paper, a photocopy of the masthead is suggested.

When offering 19th century illustrated papers, make certain they are complete as the value drops significantly if important pictures are missing. Tell the buyer about tears, rips, stains, cut outs, and foxing (brown spots). If the paper is dry, brown, orbrittle, it is seldom of value unless it's before 1750 or the only known copy of a title.

Both newspapers and magazines can be shipped "Special Fourth Class Book Rate," which is inexpensive. Ask for the latest rates at your post office.

NEWSPAPERS

☆ **Confederate newspapers.** Any paper printed in the South during the War. Give the name, place and date on the masthead.
> Peggy Dillard
> PO Box 210904
> Nashville, TN 37221
> (615) 646-1605

☆ **Newspapers covering any important event before 1945.** Also all half year bound runs of pre-1870 papers, especially from Southern U.S., Confederate states, early West, or anywhere in the U.S. pre-1800. Wants specialty papers covering the women's movement, labor, railroads, abolitionism, temperance, or the Civil War. Also **illustrated newspapers** like *Harper's, Leslie's, Ballou's, Southern Illustrated News, London Illustrated News,* etc. Also bound volumes of British newspapers and magazines pre-1700 (although he will buy later issues if historically significant). Also issues of any American magazine before 1800. Pays $100 each for newspapers before 1730 but notes that many reprints exist so they need be authenticated. No 20th century items except mint condition reports of important events. No severely defective papers.

> Phil Barber
> PO Box 8694
> Boston, MA 02114
>   (617) 492-4653   Fax: (617) 868-1534

☆ **Newspapers of historical significance** especially relative to Lincoln's speeches or death, George Washington, the Revolution, the Civil War, colonial America, early Illinois and the Chicago fire. Buys individual issues of historical significance or bound volumes. Buys all *Harper's Weekly* and *Frank Leslie's Illustrated,* 1855-1916.

> Steve and Linda Alsberg
> 9850 Kedvale Ave.
> Skokie, IL 60076
>   (708) 676-9850

☆ **Bound volumes of American and European illustrated newspapers dated 1850-1910** including *Harper's Weekly, Leslie's, Illustrated London News, Judge, Vanity Fair, Das Plachate, Puck,* and the like. Prefers to buy in large quantities. Prepared to buy entire libraries.

> Joe Davidson
> 5185 Windfall Road
> Medina, OH 44256
>   (216) 723-7172

☆ **Bound volumes of illustrated weekly newspapers** such as *Puck, Harper's, Scientific American* and others, but before 1890 only. Loose stacks considered but single copies are not wanted. Fine condition only.

> John Rosenhoover
> 100 Mandalay Road
> Chicopee, MA 01020
>   (413) 536-5542

WHAT'S AN OLD BOOK WORTH?

Chances are, not much. Books have been printed in the hundreds of millions. Valuable ones exist, but most are destined for yard sales and thrift shops. There are some surprises, though.

Buyers look for books on specific topics, by specific authors, published by certain publishers, illustrated in a particular manner, from a particular period or country, and of a specific type, such as leatherbound or first edition.

When writing to potential buyers about a book, provide what we call "Standard Bibliographic Information."
* Title as on the title page, not as on the spine;
* Author, publisher, and place of publication;
* All printing and copyright dates;
* Number of pages;
* Type and approximate number of illustrations.

A Xerox© machine can capture that in seconds; copy the title page, back of the title page and dust jacket.

Remember, a book has parts. Describe the condition of each part: (1) cover, (2) spine, (3) binding, (4) pages and (5) dust jacket. Tell the buyer about bookplates, writing, and all damage. **Don't offer books that are damaged or not the buyer's specialty as listed in Trash or Treasure.** Books with missing pages, covers off, bindings collapsing, water stains simply aren't wanted unless they're before 1800.

The amount a dealer will pay for books depends upon his customers and present stock, the rarity of your offering, current market, and his cash flow at that moment. Read the next fifteen pages and try selling on your own. Many people report being pleasantly surprised by selling books local dealers told them were worthless.

Books can be shipped Special 4th Class Book Rate which permits three pounds for around two dollars. However, books are fragile and may be damaged in transit. It only costs $1 or so more to send a book first class. Since the buyer is paying for shipping, use the faster, safer method. **Books are fragile objects.**

BOOKS

☆ **Large collections of good books,** especially:
  • Collections of books on a single topic, such as Michigan history,
     the Civil War, theology, golf, Indians, art, architecture, etc.;
  • **Books with color plates;**
  • **Leatherbound books;**
  • **Autographed books** by famous authors.
Catalogs are issued periodically. If you want to sell, give standard bibliographic information. One of the nation's largest used and rare booksellers, John does not buy *Reader's Digest* books, *National Geographic* magazines, book club editions, textbooks of any kind, encyclopedia sets, or anything in poor condition.

> John K. King Books
> 901 West Lafayette Blvd.
> Detroit, MI 48226
>   (313) 961-0622   Fax: (313) 963-9138

☆ **Various fine and early books,** including:
  • **Incunabula,** hand written books before 1501;
  • **European books** before 1600;
  • **English books** and manuscripts from before 1700;
  • **American books before 1800;**
  • **Books published in Pennsylvania** before 1810 in English or
     1830 in German. Especially seeks items printed by Benjamin
     Franklin in Philadelphia, the Brotherhood in Ephrata, or the
     Saurs (Sower) in Germantown;
  • **Fine leatherbound books** in sets;
  • **Books with fore edge paintings**; "Let us hear about all fore
edge   paintings, no matter what era;"
  • **Books illustrated in color**, especially chromoliths before 1900;
  • **Books on China or Japan** if scholarly and illustrated;
  • **African exploration and development** and materials devoted to
     problems faced by less developed countries today;
  • **Arabic studies** including material relating the spheres of Mos-
lem   influence, both ancient and modern. Buys important books in
     Arabic and related languages;
  • **Urban studies** including all aspects about any cities anywhere
     and in all eras;
  • **City view books of buildings and streets of cities worldwide.**
Make certain to include count of pages and photos in your description.
Photocopy the title page. In business for 20 years, Ron offers a series
of fine catalogs.

> Ron Lieberman, Family Album
> Route #1   Box 42
> Glen Rock, PA 17327
>   (717) 235-2134   Fax: (717) 235-8042

☆ **Any book, pamphlet, almanac, magazine, or tract printed in English speaking America before 1800.** "Books need not be complete nor necessarily in good condition. We will purchase damaged books or even fragments." If you own a book without a title page that you believe to be very old you may send them the book for identification. It's always best to write first, though, and if possible send them a photocopy. The Haydn Foundation for the Cultural Arts is a non- profit public institution.

> Michael Zinman, Haydn Foundation
> 495 Ashford Avenue
> Ardsley, NY 10502

☆ **Fine and antiquarian books,** pamphlets, and original manuscripts, especially dealing with **medicine**, Old West travel and photography. Also **children's books** that are "old, rare and colorfully illustrated."

> Ivan Gilbert, Miran Arts & Books
> 2824 Elm Ave.
> Columbus, OH 43209

☆ **Any type of book from art and archery to Zen and zoology.** This important Florida dealer prefers rare books but is interested in a wide variety of topics and subject matter, especially **limited edition books by fine presses** such as Derrydale, Kelmscott Press, Black Sun Press, Grolier Club, Grabhorne Press and the like. He does not buy school books, encyclopedias, medical texts, Book of the Month Club editions, or reprints of famous novels. "Only tentative evaluations are possible without seeing your book." Give all bibliographic information.

> Steven Eisenstein, Book-A-Brack
> 6760 Collins Ave.
> Miami, FL 33141
> (305) 865-0092

☆ **Books.** A selection of books is sought, including:
- **Books signed** by U.S. Presidents, or by movie and TV stars;
- **Etiquette book**s before 1920;
- **Cookbooks** before 1920;
- **Children's books** *(see page 520 for more detail);*

Books must be in fine condition and complete with dust jackets if originally issued with them. Torn or missing pages, writing, water damage, missing covers or other damage is not acceptable as this specialty dealer buys these for resale to collectors. Give standard bibliographic information, including edition number.

> Barbara Rupert
> 711 Studewood
> Houston, TX 77007
> (713) 774-2202 voice before 6pm, fax eves

☆ **Historical non-fiction.** Will consider just about any subject matter. Has a particular interest in **medical texts** pre-1900, outdated lectures on marriage and sex instruction, and how-to books on glamour and nude photography. Give standard bibliographic date, and description of condition of cover, pages, and binding.

> Douglas Cowles
> 2966 West Talara Lane
> Tucson, AZ 85741
> (602) 297-9062

☆ **Fine quality books from all periods** are wanted. "My book buying is guided by the belief that the quality of a book comes from both the content and from the physical book itself. The books I seek are generally first or early printings or are examples of high quality hand made private press bookmaking. I am particularly interested in buying books in the fields of **art, architecture, Americana and the West, science and medicine, literature and literary criticism, travel and exploration, philosophy and religion, and world history**, but will consider any high quality book. I am always looking for examples of **fine binding, printing and illustration**, especially books signed by Zachnsdorf, Sangurski and Sutcliffe, Riviere, and other fine binders. Some fine private press books to look for include Kelmscott Press, Ashendone Press, Doves Press, Cranach Press, Nonesuch Press, Arion Press, and Golden Cockerel Press, among others. **Books signed by the author or illustrator** are also of particular interest to me as are Chagall's *Illustrations for the Bible* and *Drawings for the Bible*, Harold Bell Wright's *To My Sons,* pre-1800 copies of *The Book of Common Prayer*, pre-1935 *Alcoholics Anonymous* books, and the Limited Editions Club books, especially *Lysistrata* and *Ulysses*. I do not want book club editions, *Reader's Digest* books, dictionaries or encyclopedia sets after 1850, Bibles after 1750, and incomplete sets of books. I generally prefer the seller to set the price, but if you want an offer, you should provide all information on the title page and copyright page. Make a photocopy of these two pages if you can do so without damaging the book. Describe the binding and format, and the condition of the cover, binding and pages." Don't forget your SASE.

> Paul Melzer, Fine & Rare Books
> 12 East Vine Street
> Redlands, CA 92373
> (909) 792-7299

"Standard Bibliographic Information" consists of: Title, Author, Publisher, City where published, Date when published, and Printing number when possible. Not hard to do.

☆ **Books published by the Limited Editions Club.** "I'll buy all years, all titles, as long as they are in fine condition in a fine box. I'll also buy Club ephemera including monthly letters, prospectus, etc." Only *Lysistrata* and *Ulysses* are acceptable without original box. Also buys *Heritage Press* books, *Encyclopedia Britannica* published after 1980, and *Encyclopedia Judaica* (any edition). Please describe fully.

> Lee and Mike Temares
> 50 Heights Road
> Plandome, NY 11030
> (516) 627-8688   Fax: (516) 627-7822

☆ **Roycroft and other high quality small press books,** especially editions of less than 500 with hand tooled binding and/or hand painted illumination or illustration. Buys the books of 60 small hand presses of the 1890-1920 era (dealers are encouraged to send an SASE for his list). He does NOT want "Little Journeys to...," *Scrapbooks* or *Notebooks* published by Roycroft. Give the title, date, material of binding, unusual characteristics, and the condition if you want an offer. A Xerox™ is a good idea.

> Richard Blacher
> 209 Plymouth Colony/Alps Road
> Branford, CT 06405

☆ **Leatherbound books.** "I'll buy decorator leatherbound books in quantity for $3 to $5 each. Not interested in fine first editions, just old books with little other value. Must have good spines and covers, but can be in any language from any period, as I want them only for their decorator potential. Call if you've got a bunch of them."

> Joan Brady
> 834 Central Ave.
> Pawtucket, RI 02861
> (401) 725-5753

☆ **Sporting books.** "We are always interested in purchasing sporting books on hunting, fishing, bird dogs, archery, guns and gun collecting, game animals and birds, books by the Derrydale Press, and many more. We purchase for stock, so there is no delay. We do ask that if you quote a book to us, you wait until you hear from us. We answer all quotes even if we do not buy them. We are good active buyers and ask that you keep our wants in mind. Among many authors we seek are Frank Forester, Havilah Babcock, Robert Ruark, Archibald Rutledge, Robert Traver and Corey Ford." Provide standard bibliographic info.

> Lewis Razek, Highwood Bookshop
> PO Box 1246
> Traverse City, MI 49685
> (616) 271-3898

☆ **Technical books and paper ephemera,** pre-1910. He wants books on trades, machines, manufacturing and technical processes.

    Jim Presgraves
    Bookworm & Silverfish
    PO Box 639
    Wytheville, VA 24382

You are more likely to have valuable books when you own a private library of hundreds on a single topic. Never break up a private library on a particular topic without help. All fiction, even if fairly recent, should be checked out if it is by a famous author and has its original dust jacket.

☆ **Asian books, maps, photos, and prints** on Japan, China, Korea, Vietnam, Tonkin, Siam, Cambodia, Laos, Burma, Malaya, Singapore, Indonesia, Philippines, Formosa, Taiwan, Tibet, Mongolia, Manchuria, New Guinea, South-East Asia and the Far East. Has a special interest in **books illustrated by Japanese woodblocks**.

    Jerry Stanoff
    Rare Oriental Book Co.
    PO Box 1599
    Aptos, CA 95001
        (408) 724-4911   Fax: (408) 761-1350

☆ **Books on the following subjects:**
  • **Russian and East European Royalty**, especially Romanovs**;**
  • **Russian Revolution;**
  • **World Wars I and II** in Europe and in Asia;
  • **Aviation** and air wars;
  • **Korean War;**
  • **Tibet and environs;**
  • **Soviet Union, Eastern Europe, Communism, Socialism.**
First editions in dust jackets preferred. Some rare titles purchased in lesser condition. Provide standard bibliographic information, including printing data found on the title page or reverse. No book club books and no paperbacks.

    Edward Conroy
    SUMAC Books
    Route 1   Box 197
    Troy, NY 12180
        (518) 279-9638 voice and fax

☆ **Hollywood biographies** of all types in hardcover with dust jacket.
Edward Conroy , SUMAC Books
Route 1 Box 197
Troy, NY 12180
   (518) 279-9638 voice and fax

☆ **Books about reptiles and amphibians** including snakes, turtles, crocodiles, lizards, frogs, etc. Prefers older, illustrated volumes as well as scientific monographs. Would pay $1,000 for Holbrook's *North American Herpetology*. Not interested in books still in print, biology textbooks, children's and juvenile titles published after 1960 (but will consider early ones) or Ditmar titles less than $5. Please send a photo of unusual items and give complete bibliographic info. A computer bulletin board about reptiles can be reached on (215) 698-1905.
Mark Miller
Herp-Net
PO Box 52261
Philadelphia, PA 19115
   (215) 464-3561 voice or fax

Publishers have many different ways of making their first editions. Some do it in code. Many make it easy buy listing the printing near the bottom on the front or back of the title page. Look for a string of numbers which usually start around 10 and count backwards. Whatever the lowest number is...that's the number of the printing you have.

☆ **Social etiquette (manners) books** for adults, children, or teens, especially first editions. Excellent condition preferred, but scarce titles will be considered in lesser condition. Only books published before 1950 are wanted. Please do not inquire about cookbooks, party books, or health books. Give this 20 year veteran collector standard bibliographic information, including the number of pages.
LuAnn Gavula
Route 2 Box 112
Barrington Hills, IL 60010
   (708) 658-1500

☆ **Genealogy books.**
James Williams
HCR 01 Box 23
Warrensburg, NY 12885
   (518) 623-2831

☆ **Alcoholics Anonymous books** earlier than 1975. Nothing later. Will pay $50 to $100 each for 1939 to 1954 first editions. Does not want 3rd editions, plain books or those in poor condition. Describe the dust jacket, date, and printing number.

> Clark Phelps
> 390 K Street
> Salt Lake City, UT 84103
> (801) 364-4747

☆ **Occult and mystic science,** astrology, magic, numerology, alchemy, palmistry, spiritualism, pyramids, tarot, Yoga, Atlantis, UFO's, ESP, and anything else metaphysical. "I'll also buy art, posters, cards, games, antique crystal balls, and other mystical and occult ephemera. I'll buy one or one thousand, if in fine condition."

> Dennis Whelan
> PO Box 170
> Lakeview, AR 72642

☆ **Crossword puzzle books.** It doesn't matter if the puzzles are filled in, as long as the books are hardcover and before 1955. Give standard bibliographic information.

> Will Shortz
> 55 Great Oak Lane
> Pleasantville, NY 10570
> (914) 769-9128 voice and fax

☆ **Pre-1970 crossword and other word puzzle books,** hard or soft cover, even if written in. Especially wants Simon and Schuster hardcover puzzle books 1924-60. Give the complete title, date, and series number, and how much of the book has been filled in. No crossword dictionaries, but does buy **crossword magazines**. Wants list sent for large SASE.

> Stanley Newman
> American Crossword
> PO Box 69
> Massapequa Park, NY 11762

"Standard Bibliographic Information" consists of: Title, Author, Publisher, City where published, Date when published, and printing number when possible. Not hard to do.

BOOKS WITH MAPS & ILLUSTRATIONS

☆   **Books illustrated with color pictures before 1890** depicting plants, animals, birds, fish, Indians, sports, cowboys, medicine, military, buildings, costumes, fashion, or advertising. Standard bibliographic data is requested.

> Joe Davidson
> 5185 Windfall Road
> Medina, OH 44256
> (216) 723-7172

☆   **Books illustrated with full page b/w illustrations,** including steel engravings, etchings, copper plates, and woodblocks. Wants views of the U.S. and Canada, North American Indians, explorations and Western America, animals, art, railway surveys, pre-1880 fairs and Centennials, architecture, Civil War, and pre-1860 Hawaii (Sandwich Islands). Indicate size along with standard bibliographic information. Note tears, foxing, etc. Count the number of illustrations.

> John Rosenhoover
> 100 Mandalay Road
> Chicopee, MA 01020
> (413) 536-5542

☆   **Books illustrated with color plates before 1899,** especially German before 1895, American natural history (plants and animals) before 1870, and Indians. Especially wants **books illustrated by** Kate Greenaway, Arthur Rackham, Jessie Smith, K. Nielson, Wyeth, W. Crane, Maxfield Parrish, Pogany, Dulac, Newell, Maud Humphrey, Remington, Erte, or Harrison Fisher. Books must date between 1890 and 1926. Give standard bibliographic information, noting tears, erasures, foxing, etc. Count and indicate the number of illustrations in color and in b/w.

> John Rosenhoover
> 100 Mandalay Road
> Chicopee, MA 01020

☆   **Used and rare books, manuscripts** and **maps.** "We specialize in **U.S. maps and atlases before 1870,** books on the military, aviation, lighter-than-air craft and Ohio subjects. We also have interest in obtaining old **bookbinding tools** and equipment."

> Frank Klein, The Bookseller
> 521 West Exchange Street
> Akron, OH 44302
> (216) 762-3101   Fax: (216) 762-4413

FICTION

☆ **Detective and mystery 1st editions** in hardcover or paperback. Also biography, reference, and bibliography related to the detective/mystery genre. Wants Dashiell Hammett and Raymond Chandler and other classics, and authors like Tony Hillerman, Sue Grafton, Robert Block, and other popular contemporary writers in 1st editions with dust jackets. Computerized for modem access.

Richard West's Booking Agency
PO Box 406
Elm Grove, WI 53122
   (414) 786-8420

☆ **Large 20th century fiction collections.** If you have many hundreds of hardback fiction books with their original dust jackets, give him a call. Has strong interest in **John Steinbeck** including signed limited editions, first editions, first printings by subsequent publishers, appearances in anthologies, spoken word records, tapes, film and theater memorabilia, and things owned by him. Does not want book club editions or items in poor condition. If a book had a dust jacket, slipcase, box, or wrap-around as originally issued, these items should still be present. Be specific about what you have for sale, giving complete bibliographic information and a full description. No interest in paperbacks or contemporary remainders.

James Dourgarian, Bookman
1595-A Third Avenue
Walnut Creek, CA 94596
   (415) 935-5033

☆ **Books by Jules Verne** are wanted, but only British and American editions. Most interested in buying first or other early editions, or editions of lesser known titles such as *Clovis Dardentor, Mathias Sandorf* and *Foundling Mick,* but will also buy many of the G. Monro *Seaside Library* paperbacks. "If you find an old edition of any work in good shape, you might send a quote." Give full title, copyright date(s), publisher, and the type and number of illustrations. It's best to Xerox™ the cover, as they are generally highly decorated. Give complete statement of condition of the cover, binding, and pages. Include your phone number. Eales cautions, "Don't bother me with comic books or little books or books in poor condition."

Dana Eales
2447 Delta Drive
Uniontown, OH 44685
   (216) 699-5341

☆ **Books by Harlan Ellison,** U.S. or foreign. Will consider mint condition paperbacks or fine hardcovers with dust jackets. Especially wants U.S. first editions, numbered editions, and autographed copies. Wants to find *Sex Gang*, written under his Paul Merchant pseudonym.

> Edy Chandler
> PO Box 20664
> Houston, TX 77225
>   (713) 531-9615

☆ **Books by Steven King or Larry McMurtry.** Want first editions, foreign editions, and uncorrected proofs. Books must be in fine condition and complete with dust jackets. Torn or missing pages, writing, water damage, missing covers or other damage is not acceptable as this specialty dealer buys these for resale to collectors. Give standard bibliographic information, including edition number.

> Barbara Rupert
> 711 Studewood
> Houston, TX 77007
>   (713) 774-2202 voice before 6pm, fax eves

☆ **Science fiction hardcover 1st editions** only. Autographed books are of particular interest. Also interested in trade paperbacks issued at the same time as the hardcover editions. "Please, no book club editions (these are usually marked on the dust jacket). No ex-library books and nothing in poor condition. Please note I am not interested in fantasy. Only science fiction. Fantasy involves witches, warlocks, wizards, dragons, magic and is usually set in a Pre-Industrial Revolution technology." When describing your book remember to give complete bibliographic information.

> David Kveragas
> 1943 Timberlane
> Clarks Summit, PA 18411
>   (717) 587-3429 eves

☆ **Dime novels and serial story papers.** These were issued between 1860 and 1919, reprinted through 1933, and star such heroes as Frank Merriwell, Nick Carter, Buffalo Bill, Deadwood Dick, and many others. There are many he seeks, but especially **Merriwell sports stories** marked "Merriwell Football Stories" or "Merriwell Baseball Stories." Make a photocopy of the cover. Ed publishes a newsletter for dime novel collectors.

> Edward LeBlanc
> Dime Novel Round Up
> 87 School Street
> Fall River, MA 02720

☆ **Paperback books from the 1940's, 50's and early 60's.** "If it had an original cover price of 25¢ or 35¢ and it's in nice condition, we want to buy it. We are very competitive for any books, and will travel worldwide to buy complete libraries of these books. We specialize in science fiction, mystery, Western, and 'sleaze' but will consider other fiction from this period as well. We will also consider **digest size books and pulp magazines** in these same fields. Please don't send us badly creased, soiled, water damaged, or destroyed copies, as we buy for resale. We cannot use reprints either." Give standard bibliographic information and include what the original cover price was. Describe condition of cover and binding. Gorgon Books issues monthly catalogs of books for sale, sponsors the annual paperback expo, and was a founder of the Paperback Collector's Club.

    Joe Crifo and John Gargiso
    Gorgon Books
    102 JoAnne Drive
    Holbrook, NY 11741
        (516) 472-3504   Fax: (516) 472-4235

☆ **Paperback books** from before 1960, but only in mint or near mint condition. Give title, publisher, catalog number (usually on the spine), cover price, and edition or printing number.

    James Williams
    HCR 01 Box 23
    Warrensburg, NY 12885
        (518) 623-2831

Book buyers want to know standard bibliographic information: title, author, publisher and place of publication, all dates of printing or copyright, number of pages, the illustrator, and approximate number of illustrations. Describe condition of the cover, spine, binding, pages and dust jacket. Note bookplates, writing, and all other damage.

CHILDREN'S BOOKS

☆ **Children's books** including:
- *Dick and Jane* readers in all their forms;
- Boys' and girls' series books like *Nancy Drew, Hardy Boys, Tom Swift*, and many others as long as they are in fine condition and have original dust jackets;
- **Judy Bolton and other modern children's** books in fine condition with dust jackets;
- *Little Black Sambo, Nicodemus, Little Brown Kokos* and other stories about black/negro children;
- *Oz* books by Baum and others;
- *Uncle Wiggly;*
- *Uncle Remus;*
- Books with high quality illustrations, especially by Parrish, N.C. Wyeth, J.W. Smith, T. Tudor, Pogany, Rackham, Pyle, Potter, Lenski, Gruelle, Nielson, Dulac, Crane, Ward, and other prominent illustrators;
- Books that have won the Newberry or Caldecott Award;
- Children's pop-up books from before 1940;
- Old Mother Goose and Father Goose stories.

Books must be in fine condition and complete with dust jackets if originally issued with them. Torn pages, writing or crayoning, water damage, missing covers or other damage is not acceptable as this specialty dealer buys these for resale to collectors. Give standard bibliographic information, including edition number.

> Barbara Rupert
> 711 Studewood
> Houston, TX 77007
> (713) 774-2202 voice before 6pm, fax eves

☆ **First editions of children's books** in very good condition. Wants books illustrated by Mabel Lucie Atwell, Jessie Wilcox Smith, Charles Robinson, Maxfield Parrish, Charles Folkard, Maurice Sendak, Edward Gorey, and Ralph Steadman, among others. Can send you a wants list.

> Joel Birenbaum
> 2486 Brunswick Circle #A1
> Woodridge, IL 60517

☆ **Children's books,** American or English, from the 1400's to 1925, including **educational books** such as McGuffey's readers.

> Ron Graham
> 8167 Park Ave.
> Forestville, CA 95436

☆ **First editions of the** *Bobbsey Twins* series published by Mershon or Chatterton-Peck. No Grosset & Dunlap editions. Also wants **Frank Merriwell items**, especially *Frank Merriwell's Book of Athletic Development*, Merriwell postcards, and the Tip Top League badge.

> Audrey Buffington
> 2 Old Farm Road
> Wayland, MA 01778

☆ **Children's series books.** Must be in dust jacket if issued that way. Especially seeking the last 3 or 4 titles in any series. Describe condition of dust jacket. Better if you Xerox™ both sides.

> Lee and Mike Temares
> 50 Heights Road
> Plandome, NY 11030
> (516) 627-7822 voice and fax

☆ **Children's school books** from before 1910. Please give standard bibliographic information and make a Xerox™ of the cover if possible.

> Douglas Cowles
> 2966 West Talara Lane
> Tucson, AZ 85741
> (602) 297-9062

☆ **Children's early readers** and other colorful children's books in fine condition for resale. Wants primers and pre-primers like the Dick and Jane series: *Look and See, Come and Go, Work and Play, Good Times with our Friends, Happy Days,* and *Fun with Dick and Jane.* Also wants *Our Big Book,* a flip chart version of the readers which stood in the front of a classroom. He'll buy foreign editions, teacher's editions, and Catholic school editions (with John, Jean, and Judy). Other early readers, "dating back as far as you can go," are also wanted. "We'll buy school books other than readers, if fine condition and well illustrated." He also buys *Tom Swift* **and other children's series** books in fine condition, with original dust jackets.

> Joe Perry Collectibles
> PO Box 5967
> Garden Grove, CA 92645

Book buyers want to know standard bibliographic information: title, author, publisher and place of publication, all dates of printing or copyright, number of pages, the illustrator, and approximate number of illustrations. Describe condition of the cover, spine, binding, pages and dust jacket. Note bookplates, writing, and all other damage.

☆ **Children's coloring books** from 1930's and 40's if all uncolored.
Fran Van Vynckt
6931 Monroe Ave.
Hammond, IN 46324
(219) 931-8081

☆ **Thornton W. Burgess and Harrison Cady books** and ephemera.
Does not want any of their books published by *Grosset & Dunlap*.
Stephen Kruskall
PO Box 418
Dover, MA 02030

☆ **Little Golden Books and other children's literature.** "I buy and
sell mass produced children's literature of the 1940's through 1960's.
Primarily want *Little Golden Books, Wonder Books, Elf Books, Bonnie
Books, Cozy Corner, Friendly* and *Tell-A-Tale*. These were mass production items, so I'm looking for fine condition ones only. Please give
the title, catalog number (it it has one), cover price, and condition. If
you know what edition you have, please tell me. I don't buy *Little
Golden Books* with a 5 digit catalog number (eg., 124-33) as these are
too new." Steve wrote the comprehensive *Collecting Little Golden
Books,* available from him for $25. Fans of children's books can sub-
scribe to his *The Poky Gazette,* an $18 newsletter about *Little Golden
Books* and other children's literature.
Steve Santi
19626 Ricardo Avenue
Hayward, CA 94541
(510) 481-2586

*Book buyers want to know standard
bibliographic information: title, author,
publisher and place of publication,
all dates of printing or copyright,
number of pages, the illustrator, and
approximate number of Illustrations.*

*Describe condition of the cover, spine, binding, pages and dust
jacket. Note bookplates, writing, and all other damage.*

Index of people who buy

Index of things people will buy

CHANGES AS OF SEPTEMBER 1, 1995

To obtain a more recent change sheet
send a long Stamped Self-addressed Envelope
and a dollar bill to cover handling to:
Trash or Treasure, Box 3028, Pismo, CA 93448

Altman, Vi & Si	181	no longer wish to buy piano rolls. Other activities continue.
ART Co.	501	12410 Wethersfield, San Antonio, TX 78216 (210) 545-2176
Birenbaum, Joel	142+	2765 Shellingham Drive, Lisle, IL 60532
Black, Charles	403	512 Coman St., Athens, AL 35611 (205) 230-3773
Cornish, Michael	447	92 Florence St., Roslindale MA 02131 (617) 323-6029
Daly, Robert	8+	area code changed to (810)
Daniel, Gwen	293	wants only church-type angels made of plaster or chalk.
Dement, Cary	261	PO Box 16013, Minneapolis, MN 55416
Donges, Craig	61+	8389 S. Pricetown Rd, Berlin Center, OH 44401 (216) 547-6300
Dunlop, Paul	26	asks that within North Carolina you use (704) 871-2626.
Friedman, Barry	6+	has a new phone number: (805) 255-2365
Gill, Robert	484	PO Box 485, Allendale, NJ 07401 (201) 934-7754
Gutzke, Kim	200+	no longer wishes to buy *Coke* machines or bicycles.
Hartzog, Rich	76+	has a fax machine (815) 397-7662
Jacobsen, Pat	107+	PO Box 791, Weimar, CA 95736 (916) 637-5923
Jarrett, Paul	164+	611 West Main, Waverly, TV 37185
Jones, David	177	3206 32nd Street, San Diego, CA 92104, same phone.
Knappen, Ron	351	no longer wishes to purchase old tin cans.
Kveragas, David	254+	is buying only a few very rare items these days.
Marshall, W.H.	64+	is no longer buying.
McDonald, Doug	256+	PO Box 5833, Helena, MT 59604 voice/fax: (406) 449-8076
Metzler, Bob	457	is temporarily unavailable. **To sell Rock & Roll memorabilia:** Danny Perkins, 17927 River Court, Pierrefonds, Quebec, Canada H9J 1A2 (800) 607-ROCK Fax: (514) 624-8942
McNece, Judalene	118	Route 5 Box 885, Poplar Bluff, MO 63901 Dial (800) 735-2466 and ask for (614) 686-0938
Murphy, Monica	48+	3619 State Street Dr., New Orleans, LA 70125 (504) 866-4261
Pankow, Nadine	28	PO Box 207, Willow Springs, IL 60480 (708) 839-5231
Perry, Chris	156+	7470 Church St, #A, Yucca Valley, CA 92284 (619) 365-0475
Price, Michael	499	PO Box 1384, Jackson, MI 49204 (517) 764-4517
Rosenthal, Mel	167+	has sold his collections and is no longer buying.
Singer, Leslie	130	phone should be: (501) 375-1860
Speezak, Judy	86	425 Fifth Avenue, Brooklyn, NY 11215
Stolz, Connie	39	72 Longacre, Rochester, NY 14621 Same phone
Svacina, Larry	98	7812 NW Hampton Road, Kansas City, MO 64152 (816) 587-1203 Fax: (816) 587-8687
Van Hook, Lisa	239+	PO Box 2666, Spring Valley, CA 91979
Wallerstein, Herb	451	address is 611 *North* Alta Drive